D1605175

CRITICAL COMPANION TO

Tim O'Brien

A Literary Reference to His Life and Work

SUSAN FARRELL

Facts On File
An Infobase Learning Company

Critical Companion to Tim O'Brien:
A Literary Reference to His Life and Work

Facts On File, Inc.
An imprint of Infobase Learning
132 West 31st Street
New York NY 10001

Library of Congress Cataloging-in-Publication Data

Farrell, Susan Elizabeth, 1963–
Critical companion to Tim O'Brien / Susan Farrell.
p. cm.
Includes bibliographical references and index.
ISBN 978-0-8160-7870-7 (alk. paper)
1. O'Brien, Tim, 1946—Handbooks, manuals, etc. I. Title.
PS3565.B75Z65 2011
813'.54—dc22
2010038664

Facts On File books are available at special discounts when purchased in bulk
quantities for businesses, associations, institutions, or sales promotions.
Please call our Special Sales Department in New York at (212) 967-8800
or (800) 322-8755.

You can find Facts On File on the World Wide Web at http://www.infobaselearning.com

Text design by Joan M. Toro
Composition by Hermitage Publishing Services
Cover printed by Yurchak Printing, Inc., Landisville, Pa.
Book printed and bound by Yurchak Printing, Inc., Landisville, Pa.
Date printed: July 2011

Printed in the United States of America

10 9 8 7 6 5 4 3 2 1

This book is printed on acid-free paper.

CONTENTS

INTRODUCTION

Tim O'Brien is one of the most widely read and admired contemporary authors in the United States. Many of his novels and short stories are rooted in his experiences as an infantry soldier in the Vietnam War, but, as he repeatedly reminds readers in lectures and interviews, his body of work is not necessarily about war itself—about bullets and foxholes and military maneuvers—but rather the feelings, experiences, and moral decisions made by human beings who are often under unbearable duress and in untenable circumstances. Even though O'Brien frequently uses sophisticated postmodern techniques, such as including metafictive commentary on the stories he tells as he tells them, utilizing multiple narrators and complicated perspectives, as well as questioning the reliability of historical truth, nevertheless his fiction is always accessible to readers. He does not allow technical accomplishments or dazzling word games to get in the way of his own dictum that, above all, a writer must tell an interesting story. Readers find meaning in O'Brien's work because his stories "make the stomach believe" (*TTTC* 78), as he says that all true war stories must do. His work involves readers emotionally, making them feel what his characters feel and asking them to question their own values and beliefs. In a lecture delivered at the Bread Loaf Writer's Conference, O'Brien argued that good literature involves the practice of "moral philosophy," that is, the devotion of careful and rigorous thought to the problem of what human beings should value and what happens when values of equal merit come into conflict with one another.

This notion of moral philosophy gives rise to the significant recurring themes in O'Brien's work: the futility and cruelty of war; the terrible things human beings are willing to do for love; the power of storytelling to shape and explain reality; and the persistence of faith and a belief in miracles even in the most dire circumstances.

O'Brien's characters often share his midwestern, small-town background. In his early works especially, these characters tend to be dreamers and philosophers who desire, above all else, to be loved by those around them and to behave honorably and morally, even in terrible conditions. In his memoir, *If I Die in a Combat Zone, Box Me Up and Ship Me Home*, readers watch a young O'Brien contemplate the line separating courage from cowardice as he tries to sort out what he owes his country from what he owes himself, much like the young narrator of the later story "On the Rainy River" will do as well. Both narrators ultimately fear losing the love of family and friends and the respect of the small-town communities they have grown up in so much that they agree to go to a war that they feel is morally wrong. In O'Brien's first novel, *Northern Lights*, Paul Perry is torn between his desire to live a peaceful, domestic life with his wife, Grace, and his competing longing to fit the mold of traditional masculine courage embodied in his brother, Harvey, and expected of him by his stern Lutheran father. Paul Berlin in *Going After Cacciato*, who hates the war but is afraid of being thought a coward, tries to imagine a way out but is tormented by the reality of his war memories, which keep intruding into his vision of escape. And in *The Things They Carried,* war-hardened soldiers not only grieve for lost comrades but accept blame and responsibility for the deaths they witness. While Paul Berlin experiences a "failure of the imagination" in *Cacciato,* imaginative storytelling is given transformative power in *Things*—in the final story of the collection, O'Brien imagines the dead brought back to life through the stories he tells.

Several of O'Brien's works, however, take on a darker, more menacing tone as they explore characters whose desire to be loved becomes so intense that it leads to madness and obsession. William Cowling in *The Nuclear Age* so fears losing his wife, Bobbi, and daughter, Melinda, that he imprisons them in his backyard bomb shelter and threatens to blow them up rather than allow them to leave him. Similarly, John Wade, from *In the Lake of the Woods,* is so obsessed with Kathy, his college girlfriend and later his wife, that he secretly spies on her, desiring to know everything about her. When his involvement in the My Lai massacre is exposed many years later, Wade very possibly murders Kathy to prevent her leaving him. Thomas H. Chippering from *Tomcat in Love,* while more a comic figure than a truly menacing one like Cowling or Wade, nevertheless shares their obsessions in many ways. Fixated on Lorna Sue Zylstra nearly his whole life, he cannot bear that she divorces him, and he plots an elaborate revenge. Likewise, Billy McMann in *July, July* broods about his former college girlfriend, Dorothy Stier, and her perceived betrayal of him; he cannot forgive her even 30 years later, despite his having lived a full life, with a wife and daughter of his own.

All of O'Brien's works, both those centered on good-hearted dreamers overwhelmed by moral quandaries and those centered on needy, frightened men obsessed by the desire to be loved, are concerned with the malleability of truth—the difficulty of getting at the full truth of events and the difficulty of knowing the full truth about another human being. One of the reasons that Paul Berlin concocts his elaborate story about the pursuit of an AWOL soldier in *Going After Cacciato* is to provide order to his tangled, chaotic war memories.

Berlin's months at the war, the real experiences he lived during that time, are difficult for him to acknowledge and remember—the chronology is confusing, the villages and deaths blend into one another, and some memories are simply too painful for Berlin to admit. Historical facts, O'Brien shows, are often inaccessible or hopelessly contradictory. What we are left with is story, and, as he explains in *The Things They Carried,* he wants readers to understand how "story-truth is truer sometimes than happening-truth" (179). Absolute occurrence, he claims, may be "irrelevant" (83) in understanding an event. One might have to "make up a few things" (77) to get at truth. Nowhere does O'Brien make this suspicion of absolute truth more evident than with *In the Lake of the Woods,* a novel that refuses to provide a solution to the mystery it raises. For O'Brien human character can be just as mysterious and unknowable as historical truth. In his 1991 essay "The Magic Show," he writes that interesting, compelling characters are not achieved by a process of "pinning down" (182) what a person is like, but through deepening and enlarging the riddle of human character. "What intrigues us, ultimately," O'Brien writes, "is not what we know but what we do not know and yearn to discover" (182). The biographer/historian of *Lake of the Woods,* despite his years of effort, can never fully know what made John Wade the man he was, or what sins he was ultimately capable of committing. Characters such as William Cowling, Jimmy Cross, and Thomas H. Chippering long to fully know and even possess the women they love, but they are doomed to remain unsatisfied in this desire.

Yet, despite the overwhelming odds that often work against O'Brien's characters, many of them persist in their faith in the future or in themselves; they hold onto a belief in miracles in the most unlikely circumstances. Thus, Paul Perry in *Northern Lights* manages to bring his brother, Harvey, home safely after being lost in the woods in a blizzard without food for many days. In *Going After Cacciato,* Paul Berlin refuses to give up on his imagined journey to Paris, even when he is returned abruptly to the war in the novel's final chapter. As Berlin and Lieutenant Corson keep guard together during the night, they speculate that Cacciato "might make it," that he "might do all right" despite the "miserable odds" against him (336). The narrator of *The Things They Carried* retains his faith in the ability of stories to save us, despite repeatedly depicting characters who either cannot or will not listen to the true war stories they are told. And David Todd in *July, July* listens on a transistor radio to the *Apollo 11* Moon landing and thinks about the Miracle Mets in the summer of 1969 as he lies alone and severely injured alongside a river in Vietnam. The "bounce of joy" (34) David feels when the *Eagle* finally touches down on the Sea of Tranquility motivates his choice to survive in the jungle.

O'Brien even ends several of his works with symbolic baptism rituals that suggest a cleansing of sins, the promise of a new life, and new possibilities in the future. While Norman Bowker's walking into the lake at the center of his small hometown at the end of "Speaking of Courage" might be a failed attempt at a cleansing ritual, and John Wade's possible murder of Kathy with a teakettle of boiling water seems a perverse reversal of a baptism ritual, other baptisms in O'Brien's works are more hopeful. At the end of *Northern Lights*, Paul Perry swims in Pliney's Pond in what "seemed almost a ritual" (347). Emerging from the water, Paul sees the beautiful Northern Lights and is able to accept the grace and domestic warmth offered by his long-suffering wife. Likewise, Thomas Chippering at the end of *Tomcat in Love* bathes his face in the birdbath in Mrs. Robert Kooshoff's backyard, literally washing charcoal dust off his face but symbolically washing away the past—his obsession with Lorna Sue—and recommitting himself to Mrs. Kooshoff. While happy endings do not exist for all of O'Brien's characters—miracles seem parceled out more by luck than by merit or worth—nevertheless in his fiction O'Brien explores the human desire to behave morally in immoral situations, to forge some kind of domestic harmony in a culture that celebrates a warrior mentality, and to hope for miracles in the midst of great suffering.

Critical Companion to Tim O'Brien is meant for the casual reader or student who would like to learn more about O'Brien's life and work as well as for the more serious scholar looking for a convenient O'Brien reference tool. Most of the literary criticism written about Tim O'Brien focuses on his trio of Vietnam War novels—*Going After Cacciato, The Things They Carried*, and *In the Lake of the Woods*. This book is the first to offer a comprehensive look at O'Brien's entire literary output—including his war memoir, seven novels, several essays, and dozens of short stories, which are examined both in their original magazine format and in the context of the novels they often appeared in after being revised. Furthermore, it explains how O'Brien's work fits into the genre of Vietnam War literature as well as into the more general context of contemporary American fiction, and examines O'Brien's influences, his connections to other writers and artists, and his dominant themes, ideas, characters, and settings.

How to Use This Book

Part I of this volume offers an overview of O'Brien's life and his major publications. Part II provides detailed synopses and analyses of O'Brien's literary works, including all of his books and short fiction, as well as three key essays. The entries for the memoir, novels, and stories each contain subentries identifying all of the individual characters in the work. Part III provides a short encyclopedia of all things O'Brien. It includes alphabetized entries on people, places, events, and topics that are important to his work. These entries cover biographical background; military acronyms and references; and historic, literary, and artistic influences and allusions. Throughout the text terms that are listed as entries in Part III are displayed in SMALL CAPITAL LETTERS, indicating a cross-reference. Part IV contains a chronology of O'Brien's life, a bibliography of his works, and a bibliography of secondary sources about O'Brien's fiction.

A Note on Editions

All page numbers for O'Brien works cited in this book are from the following editions:

Going After Cacciato, 1978. Reprint, New York: Broadway Books, 1999.

If I Die in a Combat Zone, Box Me Up and Ship Me Home, 1973. Reprint, New York: Broadway Books, 1999.

In the Lake of the Woods, 1994. Reprint, New York: Penguin Books, 1995.

July, July. New York: Houghton Mifflin Company, 2002.

Northern Lights, 1975. Reprint, New York: Broadway Books, 1999.

The Nuclear Age, 1985. Reprint, New York: Penguin Books, 1996.

The Things They Carried, 1990. Reprint, New York: Broadway Books, 1998.

Tomcat in Love, 1998. Reprint, New York: Broadway Books, 1999.

PART I

Biography

Tim O'Brien

(1946–)

Best known for his wrenching accounts of American soldiers who fought in the Vietnam War, particularly the National Book Award–winning novel *Going After Cacciato* (1978), the collection of interrelated short stories, *The Things They Carried* (1990), and the mystery-thriller *In the Lake of the Woods* (1994), Tim O'Brien is considered by many critics to be one of the finest American writers of his generation. His work is frequently taught in high school and college English classes, making him an extremely popular writer among young people, but his books resonate as well with a diverse group of readers ranging from Vietnam combat veterans to people who do not ordinarily like war literature. The author of a war memoir, seven novels, more than 35 short stories, and numerous essays and reviews, O'Brien is admired for his emotionally honest and heartbreaking examinations of human beings who face moral and philosophical crises in their lives. O'Brien's characters typically share his own midwestern background. They range from decent men who try their best to behave honorably in untenable situations to morally complicated, damaged people who are willing to do anything for love. He frequently uses the techniques of METAFICTION in his work, sometimes commenting on the stories he is telling as he tells them, as well as blending elements of fact and fiction. Despite these experimental techniques, O'Brien's work always remains accessible to the ordinary reader. Above all, he is interested in the process of narrative itself—how telling stories can be a way at arriving at truth, often a more meaningful and emotionally charged truth than can be achieved through factual history.

Born in AUSTIN, MINNESOTA, on October 1, 1946, William Timothy O'Brien is the son of WILLIAM T. O'BRIEN and AVA ELEANOR SCHULTZ O'BRIEN. As O'Brien explains in his memoir, his parents were both World War II veterans who met and married while in the service. "I grew out of one war and into another," he writes. "My father came from leaden ships of sea, from the Pacific theater;

my mother was a WAVE [Women Accepted for Volunteer Emergency Service]" (*If I Die* 11). O'Brien's father, William ("Bill"), was originally from Brooklyn, New York, where he studied commercial law, bookkeeping, and accounting at night school before joining the Naval Reserve in 1942 at the age of 27. As a chief yeoman who saw duty in the Pacific, Bill O'Brien sent home accounts of his military experiences, several of which were published in the *Norfolk Seabag,* the newsletter of the U.S. Naval Station at Norfolk, Virginia, where he had undergone training. Ava Shultz, O'Brien's mother, who was born in Fillmore County, Minnesota, worked as an elementary school teacher before joining the WAVES (Women Accepted for Volunteer Emergency Service) in October 1943, a division of the U.S. Navy during World War II made up entirely of women volunteers. She and Bill were married in October 1944 at the Naval Operating Base in Norfolk. Both Ava and Bill were officially discharged from the service in the fall of 1945. The couple first settled in Austin, Minnesota, before moving in 1954 to WORTHINGTON, where Bill worked as an insurance salesman and Ava raised their three children: Tim, who was seven when his family moved, and his younger siblings Kathy [KATHY O'BRIEN ADJEMIAN] and Greg [GREG O'BRIEN].

Worthington, Minnesota, was a typical midwestern small town when Tim O'Brien was growing up. Dubbing itself the "TURKEY CAPITAL OF

Ava and Bill O'Brien in the navy during World War II
(Harry Ransom Humanities Research Center, The University of Texas at Austin)

O'Brien as a child, dressed as a cowboy, undated (*Harry Ransom Humanities Research Center, The University of Texas at Austin*)

this period include several stories about World War II soldiers, a few romantic tales of teenagers in love, and a piece of historical fiction set in 1770 in the woods of northern Minnesota that depicts the travails of three young boys who try to make it rain. Although O'Brien characterizes these junior high school efforts as "awful," they nevertheless lay out several of the themes that he would explore over and over again in his adult fiction: the struggle to adapt to a harsh natural world, the behavior of men at war, and the nature of obsessive love. As a boy O'Brien also loved magic and illusion. In an essay called "The Magic Show," published in 1991, he describes practicing magic tricks for hours at a time in front of a stand-up mirror in the basement of his family home. He stuffed neighbors' mailboxes with flyers advertising his magic shows, and he would frequently perform at birthday parties, club meetings, and similar events. These details from his

Adolescent O'Brien practicing magic, undated (*Harry Ransom Humanities Research Center, The University of Texas at Austin*)

THE WORLD," because of its preponderance of turkey farmers, Worthington in many ways offered the young O'Brien the idyllic life of a small-town American boy in the prosperous postwar years of the 1950s. As a child, O'Brien played war games with his friends and golf with his father. Tim loved baseball, playing catcher and shortstop on various Little League teams. Perhaps inspired by his father's published accounts of his experiences in the Pacific, O'Brien was an aspiring writer from an early age, at one point publishing his own handwritten newspaper, and attempting his first novel—*Timmy of the Little League*—when he was still in elementary school. By junior high O'Brien was already a dedicated short story writer. Pieces from

High school debate team, 1963 (O'Brien on far right)
*(Harry Ransom Humanities Research Center, The
University of Texas at Austin)*

childhood would later work their way into his novel
In the Lake of the Woods, in which John Wade is
also an amateur magician as a child.

But also like John Wade from *In the Lake of the
Woods,* O'Brien's childhood was not necessarily as
idyllic as it appeared on the surface. Bill O'Brien,
by all accounts a charming, gregarious, well-liked
man, was also an alcoholic who left the family for
extended periods in the early 1960s as a patient
in rehabilitation facilities. During one of these
stays, Ava began divorce proceedings against her
husband, although the couple ended up staying
together. His father's alcoholism had a traumatic
effect on the young O'Brien, who has written that
he craved to be loved above else but who often
felt he could not please his father. While he was a
successful and ambitious high school student—he
won several awards as a member of the debate
team; he belonged to the National Honor Society; he acted in a school play; and he secured a
part-time job writing for the local newspaper, the
WORTHINGTON DAILY GLOBE—O'Brien has also
written about the simmering anger he felt as a
young man growing up amid the complacency of
the American Midwest. He writes that he took
up an interest in politics in high school, but that
he had trouble distinguishing between members
of the Democratic Party and RICHARD NIXON sup-

porters—the values of both groups seemed blandly
similar to him. In a 1991 interview with Daniel
Bourne, O'Brien rails against the "Middle American ignorance" of places like Worthington, and he
blames people in his community for sending him
to a war they did not know anything about. When
he decided to attend MACALESTER COLLEGE in St.
Paul, Minnesota, after having graduated in the top
10 percent of his class at Worthington Senior High
School, O'Brien was eager to leave Worthington,
and as he writes in his memoir, "the town did not
miss me much" (*If I Die* 15).

At Macalester College, where he enrolled in
the fall of 1964, O'Brien continued his interest in
politics and debate. He was elected president of the
student body in both his junior and senior years,
and, as protest against the war in Vietnam began
to mobilize students across the country, O'Brien

O'Brien as a college student at Macalester *(Harry
Ransom Humanities Research Center, The University of
Texas at Austin)*

acted as a volunteer for the EUGENE MCCARTHY campaign, knocking on doors and handing out literature describing the candidate's antiwar platform. He also expressed his political views in a regular column—called "Soapbox"—that he wrote for the college newspaper. In the summer of 1967, following his junior year, O'Brien traveled to PRAGUE, CZECHOSLOVAKIA, as part of the SPAN (Student Project for Amity Among Nations) Program. Injured in a serious motorcycle accident in HERSBRUCK, GERMANY, O'Brien spent a week in the hospital recovering. Nevertheless, as part of his SPAN project during the summer in Prague, he still managed to draft more than 200 pages of an early novel, tentatively titled *A Man of Melancholy Disposition.* (He would eventually publish a short story by that name in *Ploughshares* magazine in 1974.) Back at Macalester in fall of 1967, O'Brien began to think about life after graduation. One option was to return to Worthington, where he had been offered a job upon completion of his degree as a reporter for the Worthington Daily Globe, the newspaper where he had worked as a sports and feature writer beginning in high school and continuing through college holidays and vacations.

Macalester College graduation *(Harry Ransom Humanities Research Center, The University of Texas at Austin)*

The Vietnam War DRAFT also loomed large, and at one point O'Brien wrote to his father explaining that he was considering joining the navy as an alternative to being drafted into the army. But the path O'Brien ultimately decided to pursue was graduate school. He received a four-year fellowship to study for his doctorate at HARVARD UNIVERSITY's School of Government. However, the U.S. Army had other plans for O'Brien.

Shortly after graduating from Macalester in May 1968, summa cum laude, he received his draft notice. The summer of 1968 was a difficult one for O'Brien, as he weighed his options—should he honor his draft notice or flee to Canada? He writes in his memoir that he was persuaded at the time, and remains persuaded, that the war was wrong, that people were dying for ethically murky reasons. Yet, he also felt that "he owed the prairie something" (*If I Die* 18). Like SOCRATES in the *CRITO*, O'Brien in his memoir reasons that he had lived under the laws of the land for 21 years, accepted the education it offered, eaten its food, "wallowed in its luxuries" (*If I Die* 18). O'Brien would later memorialize in fiction the confusion he felt during the summer of 1968 in the story "On the Rainy River," which appears in his 1990 collection, *The Things They Carried.* While O'Brien did not actually work at an ARMOUR meatpacking plant or spend six days at the nearly deserted TIP TOP LODGE along the RAINY RIVER as the O'Brien character in the story does, nevertheless he felt the same type of moral paralysis and indecision. And like the character in the story, O'Brien decided to go to war, although, in the end, he writes, "it was less reason and more gravity that was the final influence" (*If I Die* 18).

O'Brien was inducted into the army on August 14, 1968. He underwent basic training at FORT LEWIS, WASHINGTON, an experience he despised from beginning to end, despite the close friendship he developed with another literary-minded soldier, ERIK HANSEN. While Erik avoided a combat assignment by signing up for an extra year in the army at the beginning of basic training, O'Brien decided not to follow suit, gambling that he would be assigned a rear job. Much to his dismay, however, when the trainees received their assignments, he was classified as an infantry soldier and ordered

O'Brien in full army uniform *(Harry Ransom Humanities Research Center, The University of Texas at Austin)*

Assigned to ALPHA COMPANY of the 5th Battalion of the 46th Infantry, which was part of the 198th Infantry Brigade, O'Brien served as a rifleman, radio-telephone operator (*see* RTO), and squad leader from February 1969 through the summer of that same year. In spring of 1969 he patrolled the same areas of QUANG NGAI PROVINCE—nicknamed PINKVILLE by American soldiers—where LIEUTENANT WILLIAM CALLEY and the men of CHARLIE COMPANY had committed the atrocities of the MY LAI MASSACRE a year earlier, although the tragedy would not be revealed to an incredulous American public until November 1969. Wounded during combat in May 1969, O'Brien was relieved from field duty and assigned a position as battalion clerk in the fall of that same year. During his 13-month stint as a combat soldier, O'Brien, like his father before him, wrote accounts of some of his wartime experiences, several of which were published in the Minneapolis *Tribune and Star* and the Worthington *Daily Globe*. Many of these articles would later work their way into his 1973 memoir. During his months in Vietnam, O'Brien also served as editor for *The Professional*—a publication of the 5th Battalion, 46th Infantry. In addition, he met men he would remember his whole life and whom he

to undergo Advanced Infantry Training (*see* AIT), also at Fort Lewis. It was during AIT that the reality of being drafted began to sink in for O'Brien, as he was training alongside a group of men who fully expected in a few brief weeks to be fighting on the ground in Vietnam. In his memoir O'Brien writes that he seriously considered desertion at this point in his army career, researching the logistics of draft evasion at the TACOMA LIBRARY and even going so far as to take the bus to SEATTLE one weekend shortly before Christmas 1968, a city he had planned as the launching point for his flight to Canada and eventual journey to Sweden. Yet, O'Brien could not bring himself to carry out his plans. He returned to Fort Lewis sick and depressed at the end of the weekend and was shipped out to Vietnam a little more than a month later, in the winter of 1969.

O'Brien in the army *(Harry Ransom Humanities Research Center, The University of Texas at Austin)*

O'Brien's last day in the bush in Vietnam, along the coast of the South China Sea, Vietnam, 1969 *(Harry Ransom Humanities Research Center, The University of Texas at Austin)*

would fictionalize in his later work, including the much-admired CAPTAIN BEN ANDERSON, who served as the model for Captain Johansen in his memoir, as well as an African-American soldier named CHIP MERRICKS, who died on May 9, 1969, and who influenced the portrait of Curt Lemon in *The Things They Carried*. O'Brien returned home in March 1970, having attained the rank of sergeant and having earned a COMBAT INFANTRYMAN BADGE, a Purple Heart, and a BRONZE STAR, among other decorations.

Soon after his return to the United States, O'Brien enrolled in graduate school at Harvard University, which had guaranteed him readmittance and deferred his scholarship when he was drafted. During his graduate school years, he continued to write both fiction and nonfiction, publishing a piece about his war experiences called "Step Lightly" in *Playboy* magazine in July 1970, and working for two summers, 1971 and 1972, as an intern reporter at the WASHINGTON POST. Hoping to work for the *Post* full time when he finished his Ph.D., O'Brien took a leave of absence from graduate school during the 1973–74 academic year to work as a national affairs reporter at the Wash-

ington paper, where he covered general politics, Senate hearings, and other events of national interest. But this was to be a period of important life changes for O'Brien as well. In 1972 the memoir he had put together of his war experiences, which drew on some of the newspaper accounts he had published previously, was accepted for publication by SEYMOUR LAWRENCE. Originally titled *Pop Smoke*, then *Fire in the Hole: War Stories of a Young Liberal*, the book was released by Delacorte Press in 1973 under the title *If I Die in a Combat Zone, Box Me Up and Ship me Home*. The memoir was well received, with Annie Gottlieb of the *New York Times* writing that "O'Brien brilliantly and quietly evokes the footsoldier's daily life in the paddies and foxholes," and ending her review with the comment that "Tim O'Brien writes . . . with the care and eloquence of someone for whom communication is still a vital and serious possibility. . . . It is a beautiful, painful book, arousing pity and fear for the daily realities of a modern disaster" (10). Also in 1973 his first short story, "Claudia Mae's Wedding Day," about a Vietnam veteran who gets married shortly after he returns from the war, was published by *Redbook* magazine. The story was a finalist for a National Magazine Award in fiction. O'Brien's personal life was changing as well during the early '70s. He married Ann Weller [ANN WELLER O'BRIEN], an editorial assistant at Little, Brown, the same year that his memoir and short story appeared.

Following the publication of *If I Die*, O'Brien turned his attention back to fiction, beginning to work seriously on what would become his first published novel, *Northern Lights* (1975), a story of two brothers raised by a stern Lutheran minister in northern Minnesota who choose very different paths in life. Harvey Perry is a recently returned Vietnam War veteran, whose older brother, Paul, stayed in his small hometown to work as an agent for the U.S. Department of Agriculture. The first half of the novel describes the readjustment of Paul and his wife, Grace, to Harvey's return home. The second half shifts direction, focusing mostly on a long-distance ski trip undertaken by the two brothers. Lost in a blizzard, Paul and Harvey wander for days in the deep wilderness, without food or shelter. While Rosellen Brown in the *New Republic* wrote that *Northern Lights* was a "surprisingly beautiful book" (27) and other critics agreed that, in spots, the writing itself was strong and affecting, the *New York Review of Books* set a more critical tone, opening with the line, "Is it possible to read *The Sun Also Rises Too Often?*" (Sale 31). The review goes on to criticize the novel for being too derivative of HEMINGWAY. Despite lukewarm reviews for *Northern Lights,* O'Brien made the decision to withdraw from Harvard graduate school in 1976 and devote himself full time to his writing. By this point he had published several more short stories in outlets ranging from the women's magazine *Redbook* to more prestigious literary publications such as *Ploughshares* and the *Massachusetts Review.* Many of these early stories would work their way into the novel that O'Brien began working on in the mid-1970s: *Going After Cacciato.*

True literary success first arrived for O'Brien in the late 1970s. Two of his short stories—"Night March" (originally published as "Where Have You Gone, Charming Billy?") and "Speaking of Courage"—were chosen as O. Henry Prize Stories, the most prestigious award granted American short fiction. "Night March" appeared in the 1976 O. Henry Prize collection and "Speaking of Courage" in the 1978 edition. But the event that propelled O'Brien into the literary limelight more than any other was winning the 1979 National Book Award for his novel *Going After Cacciato,* published the previous year. A surprise victory for a still largely unknown writer who was teaching at EMERSON COLLEGE in Boston as a visiting writer-in-residence when the award was announced, *Cacciato* was chosen over two strong favorites—*The Stories of John Cheever* and John Irving's best-selling *The World According to Garp.* Groundbreaking in its ability to describe the horror and atrocity of life as experienced by everyday soldiers at the same time that it refuses to be bound by literal or realistic narrative, *Cacciato* tells the story of a young soldier who simply walks away from his platoon one day, planning to march all the way from the jungles and paddies of Vietnam to PARIS. Cacciato's platoon members follow him, hoping to retrieve the AWOL (Absent Without Leave) soldier, but fantastic events that

occur along the way soon make readers question just how much of the journey after Cacciato is supposed to be "real" and how much of it exists only in the mind and imagination of Paul Berlin, a fellow soldier torn between his own desire to flee the war and his sense of obligation to his friends, family, and country. Many reviewers praised the novel as the best piece of fiction to come out of the Vietnam War, with several commenting that the book was about much more than the war. Thomas R. Edwards of the *New York Review of Books* wrote that *Cacciato* was "about the imagination itself" (41), and Richard Freedman famously commented in his *New York Times* review that "to call *Going After Cacciato* a novel about war is like calling *Moby-Dick* a novel about whales" (1).

While *Cacciato* probes the experiences of a soldier who reluctantly enters the war, O'Brien's next novel, *The Nuclear Age,* released in 1985, examines the life of a young college graduate who evades the draft, choosing to join a radical antiwar protest organization rather than allow himself to be sent to Vietnam. The novel is narrated in the first person by William Cowling, who grows up in the small town of FORT DERRY, MONTANA, a place not unlike O'Brien's own hometown of Worthington, Minnesota. The product of two loving parents and a safe little all-American town, William is nevertheless terrified from an early age of the possibility of nuclear war, and he cannot believe that the people who surround him can live their lives in an ordinary way, undaunted by the very real nature of the threat. The novel follows William from childhood to college, where he starts an antiwar protest group, to his life as an underground radical after he evades the draft. Eventually breaking ties with the radicals, William returns to Montana, discovers uranium in the mountains bordering Fort Derry, and eventually marries Bobbi Haymore, a former flight attendant he had been obsessed with for years. A wealthy man now, William settles down with Bobbi in a beautiful house in the SWEETHEART MOUNTAINS of Montana. In 1995, the novel's present time—the events from the past having been narrated in flashback—readers watch Cowling becoming increasingly mentally unhinged as his marriage to Bobbi begins to dissolve. Still terrified by the threat of nuclear destruction, he obsessively digs a bomb shelter in his yard, eventually imprisoning his beautiful blonde wife and young daughter in the hole he has dug. William Cowling, then, is the first of a series of protagonists, including John Wade from *In the Lake of the Woods* and Thomas H. Chippering in *Tomcat in Love,* whose desire to retain love drives them to violent and/or ludicrous behavior.

The novel, like O'Brien's earlier *The Nuclear Age,* received mixed reviews at best. Richard Lipez of the *Washington Post* called it an "imperfect but very lively" book (9), while Marcus James of the *Nation* criticized the main character, William Cowling, as being too "passive and disconnected" (450) from the events around him to reveal much truth. Grace Paley, writing in the *New York Times,* admired the premise of a clear-sighted young man who sees the threat others close to their eyes to. Nevertheless, she critiqued the book for its "clichéd" women characters, for the middle road it takes between the real and surreal, and for not fully exploring "the powerful places from which the real madness radiates" (7), in other words, for not presenting a strong enough political critique of the policies that led to the arms race. Michiko Kakutani in a separate *New York Times* review was more negative, arguing that William Cowling's account of his life "grow[s] increasingly vague and full of clichés" as he moves away from his childhood, and that his women characters were "ridiculous in the extreme" (12).

Over the next five years, O'Brien would direct his attention more fully to the art of short story writing. During this period he published in *Esquire* magazine stand-alone versions of several of the short stories that would later appear as part of the collection *The Things They Carried.* The stories were well received by critics and fellow writers, the stand-alone version of "The Things They Carried" winning the National Magazine Award for fiction in 1987, and "The Sweetheart of the Song Tra Bong" named a finalist for the same award in 1990. But it was when the interrelated stories were set alongside one another, interwoven with new material not previously published, that critics and readers really took notice. The book version of *The*

Things They Carried was published by Houghton Mifflin in 1990. Part short story collection, part meditation on the art of fiction writing, the book also functions as a pseudo-memoir. It is narrated in the first person by a 43-year-old writer named Tim O'Brien from Worthington, Minnesota, who attended Macalaster College, served as an infantryman during the Vietnam War, and published an earlier novel called *Going After Cacciato.* Yet, despite these biographical similarities to the real Tim O'Brien, the book's narrator is a fictional character who relates stories about a group of soldiers from Alpha Company who together experience the boredom, horror, and guilt of the war in Vietnam. This narrator also includes metafictional commentary on the difficulty of writing stories and meditates on the power of narrative itself. The book was a great critical and popular success. Robert Harris, writing in the *New York Times,* hailed it as being "high up on the list of best fiction about any war" (8) and Rosellen Brown in the *Massachusetts Review* wrote that *The Things They Carried* was "stunningly original in concept and daring in execution" and that "it ought to become a classic" (144). In addition, the book was chosen as one of the 10 best works of fiction of the year by the *New York Times,* named as a finalist for the Pulitzer Prize, and awarded the *Chicago Tribune's* Heartland Prize as well as the French Prix du Meilleur Livre Ètranger. *The Things They Carried* has become one of the most-taught books by a living author in high school and college classrooms, and it is the book that thrust O'Brien onto the lecture circuit. As a result of the book's popularity, Tim O'Brien frequently visits schools and universities around the country, often serving as the featured author at convocation and graduation ceremonies, writers' series and luncheons, and all kinds of similar events.

Yet, despite his literary success, the early 1990s were not easy years for O'Brien. Having been separated from his wife, Ann, for many years, O'Brien experienced a second devastating breakup when his girlfriend KATE PHILLIPS, a Harvard University graduate student, left him a few months after the couple returned from a trip to Vietnam they had taken together in February 1994, O'Brien's first time back in Vietnam since the war. O'Brien describes the trip, the breakup, and his near-suicidal depression in an anguished essay called "The Vietnam in Me" that was published in the *New York Times Magazine* on October 2, 1994. Despite having a seemingly smooth transition back into civilian life in the early 1970s, the essay suggests that the horror and guilt of his Vietnam War experiences were finally beginning to catch up with O'Brien. He writes that after speaking with villagers who survived the My Lai Massacre he experiences the "guilt chills" (53), remembering the "black, fierce, hurting anger" (53) he himself felt while stationed in Quang Ngai Province. In the summer of 1994, after his return from the visit to Vietnam with Kate, O'Brien describes sitting up in the wee hours of one June night, staring at a bottle of sleeping pills that were not working and contemplating suicide: "not whether, but how" (50). In the essay he writes that during that summer he was living on "war time," which, he informs readers, "is the time we're all on at one point or another: when fathers die, when husbands ask for divorce, when women you love are fast asleep beside men you wish were you" (55). The essay was controversial when published, its intimacy and confessional nature startling to many readers. In an interview with Bruce Weber several years later, O'Brien speaks about "The Vietnam in Me," claiming that writing the piece literally saved his life, even though he later regretted actually publishing it:

> I'm glad I wrote it, but I wish I hadn't published it. . . . It's a perceptive piece, about the inner penetration of love and war, and eerie, uncanny similarities between the two. But it hurt people I love, and probably me too, a little. Though it saved my life, in one way. It was written moment by moment. Should I jump off the balcony or not? I'd literally leave the typewriter and go to the balcony, and think about jumping off and go back and type another sentence. (Weber E1)

O'Brien's painful depression during the early years of the '90's worked its way into the novel he was writing at that time: *In the Lake of the Woods*, which was published by Houghton Mifflin in 1994.

The book is a dark meditation on love and war and on the secrets human beings keep from others and even from themselves, as well as a philosophical examination of the elusive nature of truth. *Lake* tells the story of John Wade, a successful Minnesota politician running for the U.S. Senate, whose life unravels when news of his past involvement in the My Lai Massacre, a history that Wade had worked to suppress for nearly 20 years, appears in the press. After a crushing and humiliating election defeat, John and his wife, Kathy, retreat to an isolated cabin in the remote Minnesota wilderness to recover. But after only a few days at the cabin Kathy mysteriously disappears, never to be seen again. The novel offers a number of different hypotheses concerning Kathy's disappearance. Did she simply leave her husband, disgusted at the revelations about his past? Or is her disappearance more sinister? Did John murder his wife, terrified that she might leave him? Or perhaps the two planned the disappearance together, the first step in the couple starting a new life under new identities? The novel, a suspenseful page-turner that stubbornly refuses to supply neat solutions to the mystery it explores, both adopts and explodes the genre of the mystery-thriller. Like *The Things They Carried*, it was a critical and commercial success, winning the James Fenimore Cooper Prize for Historical Fiction, an editor's choice award from the *New York Times Book Review*, and named the best work of American fiction in 1994 by *Time* magazine. Reviewers praised the book as well. Verlyn Klinkenborg of the *New York Times* wrote, "In his new novel, [O'Brien] turns . . . matters of truth, time and responsibility inward, letting them weigh on an individual character in a manner he has never done before" (1). Phoebe-Lou Adams of the *Atlantic* commented that *Lake* "is a fine and intelligent novel" (146), and Pico Iyer in *Time* magazine praised O'Brien's "clean, incantatory prose" (74).

Over the next several years, O'Brien changed directions in both his writing and his personal life: His divorce from Ann Weller O'Brien was finalized in 1995; he began dating a drama teacher named Meredith Baker [MEREDITH BAKER O'BRIEN] the following year; and in 1999 he moved from Cambridge, Massachusetts, where he had lived since

1970, to AUSTIN, TEXAS, having accepted the Mitte Chair in Creative Writing at TEXAS STATE UNIVERSITY in San Marcos, a small town neighboring Austin. In the 1998 interview with Bruce Weber, O'Brien comments, "I'm a happy person now. . . . Maybe the world isn't the horrid place it seemed to me four years ago" (E1). The late '90s saw O'Brien take a new tack in his fiction as well, trying his hand for the first time at a comic novel. *Tomcat in Love*, the story of a pompous, woman-chasing, self-deluded linguistics professor, was published by Random House's Broadway Books in 1998. The novel is narrated in the first person by Thomas H. Chippering, a middle-aged professor distraught over his recent divorce from his childhood sweetheart, Lorna Sue Zylstra. As Chippering attempts to win back Lorna Sue and punish the two men he holds responsible for her desertion—her brother, Herbie, and her new husband, a Florida businessman—he manages to get himself into a series of awkward, embarrassing predicaments, often the result of the romantic overtures he makes to nearly every woman he meets. While Chippering is a Vietnam veteran, and small portions of the novel detail his experiences during the war, the Vietnam setting definitely retreats to the background in this novel.

Critical reaction to the book was mixed. The novelist Jane Smiley, reviewing *Tomcat* for the *New York Times Book Review*, perhaps best expressed the ambiguous response felt by many of the novel's readers. Smiley wrote that O'Brien makes his main character, Chippering, "almost too insufferable to bear" (11). She remains unsure, at the end of the review, whether O'Brien pulled off his comic novel or not, but she does praise him for the new direction he takes, arguing that "*Tomcat in Love* is a complex affair that invites a complex response and offers a complex reward" (11). Other reviewers' reactions were not so ambiguous. Some, including Michiko Kakutani of the *New York Times* and Jody Bottum of the *Washington Times,* hated it. Kakutani wrote that "the reader can only wonder at the disparity between the power of those earlier books by Mr. O'Brien—distinguished by their inventive storytelling and their evocative depiction of the visceral and emotional realities of war—and the

mangled mess that is *Tomcat in Love*" (E7), while Bottum referred to the novel as "a train-wreck of a failure" (B8). Yet, there were also reviewers such as David Nicholson of the *Washington Post* who loved the book. Nicholson calls it "a wonderful novel, laugh-out-loud funny" and "one of the best books" he has come across in years (B1). In the review he admonishes readers to put down the paper they are holding and rush out to buy the book immediately. O'Brien at least partially anticipated such mixed reaction to *Tomcat in Love*, acknowledging his fear that "some people are going to say that Chippering is such a sexist pig that O'Brien must be one" too (Weber E1). Nevertheless, he also insists, as he often found himself doing with his previous novels, that a book's narrator should not be mistaken for the living, breathing, author—that Thomas Chippering, just like the Tim O'Brien who narrates *The Things They Carried,* is a fictional character. O'Brien sympathizes with Chippering, but he also laughs at the bumbling professor, mocking him throughout the novel.

Following the publication of *Tomcat,* O'Brien again turned his attention to short fiction, publishing nine stories between 1998 and 2002 in *Esquire* and the *New Yorker* magazines. These nine stories would later become the core of *July, July,* a novel published by Houghton Mifflin in 1992. *July, July* tells the story of a group of old friends who graduated from DARTON HALL COLLEGE in the St. Paul/Minneapolis area in 1969. The gang has gathered in July 2000 to celebrate their 30th college reunion, one year late. The novel alternates between present-day scenes that take place during the long reunion weekend and flashbacks that explain how the large cast of characters arrived at their present circumstances. Among the close friends are a Vietnam War veteran, a draft dodger, a Republican housewife suffering from breast cancer, a Presbyterian minister, a mop and broom entrepreneur, and a woman married to two men at the same time, as well as several others. The novel depicts the compromises and failed dreams these former idealists and campus radicals have fallen into over the years. Again, as with *Tomcat in Love,* reviews of the novel were mixed, though largely negative. Several critics, including Jonathan Yardley in the *Washing-*

ton Post and David Gates in the *New York Times Book Review,* found the novel's entire premise to be clichéd; they argued that the book offered only a trite rehashing of sixties idealism turned sour—a story they believed all Americans had heard before in works such as the 1983 film *The Big Chill.* Nevertheless, some other reviewers noted that several of the individual stories in the book were strong and memorable, and certain critics, such as Sara Lawrence, a reviewer for the London *Times,* argued that the novel worked well as a whole: "*July, July* is sharp, perceptive, and affectionate, and will linger in the mind long after the pages are turned" (Lawrence 16).

Not long after the 2002 publication of *July, July,* O'Brien married his longtime girlfriend, Meredith Baker. He became a first-time father at the age of 56, when his oldest son, Timmy [TIMMY O'BRIEN], was born in June 2003. A second son, Tad [TAD O'BRIEN], joined the family two years later, in late June 2005. But since *July, July* appeared, O'Brien has been fairly quiet as a writer. He has continued to teach at Texas State University, to deliver lectures around the country, and to edit fiction collections, but his published works have consisted of a few essays, most notably two pieces in *Life* magazine—a moving letter to his young son Timmy, published in 2004, and a reflective piece about fatherhood published in 2006—as well as an essay about what constitutes good storytelling that appeared in the 2009 fiction edition of the *Atlantic.* Much of O'Brien's time in the later part of the decade has been devoted to a newly revised and edited edition of *The Things They Carried,* published in 2010 to coincide with the book's 20th anniversary. Speaking about the rerelease in a National Public Radio interview in March 2010, O'Brien summed up his views about the art of writing fiction: "The goal, I suppose, any fiction writer has, no matter what your subject, is to hit the human heart and the tear ducts and the nape of the neck and to make a person feel something about [what] the characters are going through and to experience the moral paradoxes and struggles of being human" (Conan). It is just this emotional involvement that has made Tim O'Brien's work, particularly his trio of Vietnam War novels, so memorable to readers.

Americans continue to be moved by Tim O'Brien's visceral, heartrending accounts of events in Vietnam nearly 40 years after the war ended.

FURTHER READING

Adams, Phoebe-Lou. Review of *In the Lake of the Woods,* by Tim O'Brien. *Atlantic* 274, no. 5 (November, 1994), 146.

Bottum, Jody. "A Chronicler of the Vietnam Experience Takes a Comedic Turn." Review of *Tomcat in Love,* by Tim O'Brien. *Washington Times,* 27 September 1998, B8.

Bourne, Daniel, and Debra Shostak. "A Conversation with Tim O'Brien." *Artful Dodge* 17 (1991): 74–90.

Brown, Rosellen. Review of *Northern Lights,* by Tim O'Brien. *New Republic* 7 (February 1976), 27.

———. Review of *The Things They Carried,* by Tim O'Brien. *Massachusetts Review* 32, no. 1 (Spring 1991), 144–146.

Edwards, Thomas. Review of *Going After Cacciato,* by Tim O'Brien. *New York Review of Books,* 19 July 1979, 41–42.

Freedman, Richard. "A Separate Peace." Review of *Going After Cacciato,* by Tim O'Brien. *New York Times Book Review,* 12 February 1978, 1.

Gates, David. "Everybody Must Get Sloshed." Review of *July, July,* by Tim O'Brien. *New York Times Book Review,* 13 October 2002, 6.

Gottlieb, Annie. "Two Sides of a Modern Disaster." Review of *If I Die in a Combat Zone, Box Me up and Ship me Home,* by Tim O'Brien. *New York Times Book Review,* 1 July 1973, 10.

Harris, Robert. "Too Embarrassed Not to Kill." Review of *The Things They Carried,* by Tim O'Brien. *New York Times Book Review,* 11 March 1990, 8.

Iyer, Pico. "Missing in Contemplation." Review of *In the Lake of the Woods,* by Tim O'Brien. *Time,* 24 October 1994, 74.

James, Marcus. Review of *The Nuclear Age,* by Tim O'Brien. *Nation,* 2 November 1985, 450+.

Kakutani, Michiko. "Books of the Times; Prophet of Doom." Review of *The Nuclear Age,* by Tim O'Brien. *New York Times,* 28 September 1985, Sec. 1, 12.

———. "Shell Shock on the Battlefields of a Messy Love Life." Review of *Tomcat in Love,* by Tim O'Brien. *New York Times,* 15 September 1998, E7.

Klinkenborg, Verlyn. "A Self-Made Man." Review of *In the Lake of the Woods,* by Tim O'Brien. *New York Times,* 9 October 1994, Sec. 7, 1.

Lawrence, Sara. Review of *July, July,* by Tim O'Brien. *The Times* (London), 19 July 2003, Features, 16.

Lipez, Richard. "In the Shadow of the Bomb." Review of *The Nuclear Age,* by Tim O'Brien. *Washington Post,* 13 October 1985, Book World, 9.

Nicholson, David. "Laughs of the Red-Hot Lover." Review of *Tomcat in Love,* by Tim O'Brien. *Washington Post,* 1 September 1998: B1.

O'Brien, Tim. "*The Things They Carried,* Twenty Years On: Interview with Tim O'Brien." By Neal Conan, National Public Radio, March 24, 2010. Available online. URL: www.npr.org/templates/story/story.php?storyId=125128156&ft=1&f=1035. Accessed April 26, 2011.

Paley, Grace. "Digging a Shelter and a Grave." Review of *The Nuclear Age,* by Tim O'Brien. *New York Times,* 17 November 1985, Sec. 7, 7.

Sale, Roger. Review of *Northern Lights,* by Tim O'Brien. *New York Review of Books,* 13 November 1975, 31.

Smiley, Jane. "Catting Around." Review of *Tomcat in Love,* by Tim O'Brien. *New York Times Book Review,* 20 September 1998, 11.

Weber, Bruce. "Wrestling with War and Love; Raw Pain, Relived Tim O'Brien's Way." *New York Times,* 2 September 1998, E1.

Yardley, Jonathan. "Tim O'Brien Forsakes the Jungles of Vietnam for Dispatches from the Domestic Front." Review of *July, July,* by Tim O'Brien. *Washington Post,* 13 October 2002, T2.

PART II

Works A to Z

"Calling Home" (1977)

The short story "Calling Home" was first published in *Redbook* magazine in December 1977 before being reprinted in the 1978 novel *Going After Cacciato*. The story depicts a small group of soldiers on stand-down in Vietnam who make phone calls to family members back home using newly developed long-distance satellite technology.

SYNOPSIS

The story is set in August 1968, when Paul Berlin's platoon is on stand-down at the CHU LAI base camp after spending two months in the bush. On their final day at the camp, four soldiers—Oscar Johnson, Eddie Lazzutti, Doc Peret, and Paul Berlin—hike to the camp of a nearby army outfit that has installed a radio-telephone hookup with the United States. First Eddie, then Doc, then Oscar enter a small, soundproof booth, where they place phone calls and speak to family members back home. Each man is somewhat giddy when he emerges from the booth, awed at the experience of speaking with their relatives who are so far away. When it is Paul Berlin's turn, he enters the booth and thinks about the black telephone in his kitchen back home as the call is placed. He imagines his mother vacuuming the carpets on Saturday afternoons and his father putzing about the house on Sundays. The connection is finally made, and Paul Berlin listens to the phone ring, recognizing the familiar sound from his youth. The phone, however, continues to ring and ring. Apparently no one is at home to pick up the line. Berlin leaves the small booth disappointed as the other men clap him on the back and tell him that his parents were probably out somewhere and that the world does not stop because he is away.

COMMENTARY

"Calling Home" is a story that emphasizes the distance between soldiers fighting in the Vietnam War and "the world" back home in the United States. While brand-new technology is able to make communication between these opposite ends of the Earth possible, it is not enough to span the emotional and psychological distance between sol-diers and their loved ones back home, any more than shiny new technological advances can easily win the war for the Americans and their South Vietnamese allies. When Eddie Lazzutti and Oscar Johnson leave the small soundproof booth after placing their phone calls, each man seems partially elated, partially bewildered by the experience. It is as if they have participated in a miracle and are unsure exactly how to behave afterward. In the story O'Brien highlights the disconnect between those back home and the soldiers in Vietnam. Eddie's mother does not recognize her own son's voice immediately, and even when he identifies himself by name, she replies "Eddie who?" (75). Oscar's father does not seem to know how to speak with his son in any meaningful way, falling back on talk about the weather and overutilizing military lingo. As Oscar reports, "My old man, all he could say was 'Over'" (76). While the men laugh about these quirks, amazed by the "wizardry" that allowed for the phone calls, readers sense a slightly sadder aspect to the experience. Eddie's younger brother, Petie, for instance, can talk only about the Pittsburgh Pirates baseball team and cannot begin to understand his older brother's experiences in Vietnam. Petie, a high school student who should know better, "Thinks we're over here fightin' the Russians" (76), according to Eddie. The boy's ignorance represents the inability of those back home to fully understand or appreciate the experience of the soldier in Vietnam.

When Paul Berlin's turn to phone home finally arrives, he feels great nostalgia for the commonplace, small-town life he lived before the war. Small details, probably unimportant to him previously, such as his mother vacuuming the carpets on Saturday afternoons, suddenly gain great significance as such ordinary housekeeping duties now suggest to him "An uncluttered house. Things in their places" (76). What Paul Berlin misses is a general orderliness and sense of ease that is absent in the chaos and brutality of war. When Paul Berlin remembers that his father enjoyed "putzing" on Sundays, "tinkering and dreaming and touching things with his hands, fixing them or building them or tearing them down, studying things" (76), he hopes that it is Sunday. The building and tinkering that his father did while putzing around are also missing from Berlin's wartime experiences, where destruction rather than creation is the order of the day. The disconnect between soldiers and those back home is emphasized as well when Berlin plans what he will say to his parents. He feels that he must protect them from the truth of the war, that he must keep things light and humorous so that they will not worry about him. He determines not to let them know about the deaths he has witnessed or how afraid he truly is.

But in many ways the outcome of Paul Berlin's phone call—the fact that no one even answers the line—is even more devastating to him than having to hide his real feelings would have been. While the other men clap him on the back and try to comfort him, Oscar's admonition that "The world, it don't stop turning" (76) may be difficult for Berlin to accept. Although he is quiet after the failed phone call and never expresses his disappointment except to voice a resigned "Yeah" (76) in response to Oscar's observation that the world goes on, readers are meant to understand that the idea that people back home are continuing with their ordinary, day-to-day activities, that they can go about buying groceries or taking a drive while their sons and brothers are risking their lives in Vietnam, is a hard lesson for Paul Berlin. It is something that he most likely recognized in an intellectual way, but the continually ringing phone forces Berlin to face the emotional gulf separating him from those back home, a gap that all the technological wizardry in the world cannot span.

Differences in Versions
"Calling Home" is reprinted in *Going After Cacciato* with almost no changes at all—only a few words are altered here and there. The one significant revision involves a removed line at the end of the story. While Oscar in the original *Redbook* version twice repeats to Berlin that "The world don't stop" (76), he makes the statement only once in the revised, novel version. Perhaps this is because, as the final line of the story, O'Brien does not want to dilute the phrase's impact by having Oscar already have made the observation a few lines earlier.

CHARACTERS

Berlin, Mr. As he places his phone call home, Paul Berlin remembers that his father likes to "putz" around the house on Sundays, "tinkering and dreaming and touching things with his hands" (76). In the longer novel, readers will discover that Mr. Berlin, a veteran of WORLD WAR II, is now a home builder in Dodge City, Iowa. Berlin's imaginings of his father's happy, peacetime life spent building things contrasts with the chaos, death, and destruction of Berlin's current wartime existence.

Berlin, Mrs. During his phone call home, Paul Berlin imagines his mother vacuuming his childhood home on Saturday afternoons. This small, seemingly insignificant chore takes on a deep significance when Berlin thinks about "an uncluttered house" and "things in their places" (76). The world he comes from seems unfathomably far away from the world Paul Berlin finds himself in as a soldier in Vietnam, where his life is chaotic and disorderly. However, in the novel *Going After Cacciato*, readers will also discover that Berlin's mother is an alcoholic who goes to great lengths to hide her drinking from her family. The idyllic small-town life Berlin leaves behind him is perhaps not as neat or orderly as he nostalgically remembers it to be.

Berlin, Paul Paul Berlin, the protagonist of *Going After Cacciato* and of most of the stories from *Cacciato* published individually, is also the focus of "Calling Home." While three other soldiers also place satellite telephone calls back to the States, O'Brien spends the most time on Berlin's call, and he is the only character whose mind readers can see into. The story depicts Berlin's nostalgia for home and his disappointment when no one is at home to answer the phone.

Johnson, Mr. Oscar Johnson's father, himself a veteran who had served as a radio-telephone operator in Italy during World War II, seems awkward in the conversation he holds with his son over satellite hookup. Mr. Johnson repeats "Over" and "Roger that" throughout the conversation, a quirk that Oscar laughs about when the call has ended.

Johnson, Oscar Oscar Johnson is one of the four soldiers who hike to a neighboring army outfit to place telephone calls back to the United States. Oscar talks to his father over the satellite connection and is strangely happy afterward, even though his father speaks mostly about the weather and awkwardly overuses military lingo during the conversation.

Lazzutti, Eddie Eddie Lazzutti is the first of the four soldiers to place a telephone call home over the highly sophisticated satellite-radio system at a neighboring army encampment. When he reaches his mother, she initially does not recognize his voice. Eddie is also amazed at how much his younger brother, Petie, seems to have grown up while Eddie has been in Vietnam. Like Oscar, Eddie is giddy after the phone call, repeating bits of his conversation to the other men and shaking his head at the miracle of technology.

Lazzutti, Petie Petie Lazzutti is the soldier Eddie Lazzutti's younger brother. Petie has just started high school and knows nothing about the war. Eddie, in fact, reports to the other men that Petie thinks American soldiers are fighting the Russians overseas. All the young man cares about is the Pittsburgh Pirates baseball team.

Lazzutti, Mrs. Eddie Lazzutti's mother does not recognize her son's voice when she answers the phone, most likely because the call, coming all the way from Vietnam, is so unexpected. Even when he identifies himself, she responds, "Eddie who?" (75) and seems to fear that her son is calling from "Graves Registration, or something . . ." (75).

Lynn, Bernie Bernie Lynn is one of the members of Paul Berlin's platoon who has died in Vietnam. In other O'Brien works, readers discover that Bernie Lynn died in an underground tunnel. Berlin, as he places his phone call home, determines that he will not tell his parents about Bernie Lynn's death or about any other deaths he has witnessed as a soldier. He decides to talk about cheerful things so that his parents will not suspect how afraid he really is.

Peret, Doc Doc Peret makes his phone call home after Eddie and before Oscar. Readers, however, are not provided any information about what occurs during this call, although Doc, like the two others, seems alternately giddy and pensive after speaking with his family members back home.

PFC An unnamed private first class, who is young, redheaded, and who wears gold watches on each wrist, explains the MARS satellite telephone technology to the men and oversees the placing of each phone call. When no one answers at Paul Berlin's home, the young PFC shrugs and tells Berlin that it happens sometimes.

Stone, Mrs. Mrs. Stone is a neighbor of the Berlin family back home. As a young PFC sets up Paul Berlin's phone call, Berlin plans what he will talk about with his parents. Desiring to keep things light and not let on how afraid he truly is, Berlin imagines that he and his father can discuss Mrs. Stone, an eccentric woman who frantically sweeps her lawn in all kinds of weather.

Tucker, Frenchie As Paul Berlin plans out what he will discuss with his parents during his long-distance phone call home, he decides specifically not to mention his fear or the recent deaths he has witnessed, including that of Frenchie Tucker.

Watkins, Billy Boy Berlin determines not to mention to his parents during the satellite phone call he is placing the death of Billy Boy Watkins, one of his more disturbing Vietnam experiences. Berlin wants to keep things light and funny so that his parents will not worry about him. In other O'Brien stories, as well as in the novel *Going After Cacciato*, readers learn that Billy Boy died of fright on the field of battle, a death particularly alarming for Berlin, who himself is terribly afraid in Vietnam.

"Civil Defense" (1980)

The story "Civil Defense," about a young boy growing up in the late 1950s who is terrified by atomic weaponry and the specter of nuclear devastation, was first published in *Esquire* magazine in August 1980. The story was later included as the second chapter in the 1985 novel *The Nuclear Age*.

SYNOPSIS

"Civil Defense" depicts a young boy named William, maybe 11 or 12 years old, growing up in the small town of FORT DERRY, MONTANA, in 1958. Despite having a loving family and a normal home life, William is so terrified by the prospect of the atomic bomb that he turns his basement Ping-Pong table into a fallout shelter, covering the table's surface with lead pencils, charcoal briquettes and lumber. William's parents, worried about his psychological state, bring in the town's doctor, an old man named Crenshaw, to examine the boy. But Dr. Crenshaw believes William is simply faking his fear in order to avoid going to school. After the doctor's visit, William rides his bike to the town library, where he researches real fallout shelters. When a kindly librarian speaks to him, however, he begins sobbing uncontrollably and has to be picked up and driven home by his parents. That night, William has terrible dreams in which he imagines the world ending. He runs to take shelter in his basement, crouching underneath his makeshift bomb shelter, where his father finds him. After comforting his son, William's father challenges the boy to a Ping-Pong game. In order to play, they must first clear off all of the items that William has used to transform the table into a shelter. After several fierce games of Ping-Pong, his father tucks William into bed, and the boy sleeps well, his dreams "clean and flashless" (88) for the next decade.

COMMENTARY

"Civil Defense" depicts how growing up in the all-American, conformist decade of the 1950s, in the midst of postwar prosperity, is anything but normal for a young boy who takes world events seriously. Despite popular perceptions of the 1950s advanced by nostalgic television shows such as the 1970s ABC series *Happy Days* or the 1978 movie *Grease*, in which teenagers' biggest worries involve dates gone awry and fitting in at high school, William, the young narrator of "Civil Defense" writes, "The

year was 1958, and I was scared" (82). It is the height of the COLD WAR, the Russians seem to be winning the space race, having launched the first Sputnik satellite in 1957, and atomic war is a very real possibility. William practices duck-and-cover drills at home, listens to tests of the Emergency Broadcast System on the radio, and sees pictures of H-bombs in *Life* magazine. Yet, O'Brien is quick to emphasize that, in most ways, William's life is routine. He grows up in a "typical small town" with "all the ordinary small-town values" (82). He is a "regular kid" (82) who plays war games and baseball, rides his bike, feeds the dog, even runs a lemonade stand—usual activities for a 12-year-old in 1958. "Normal, normal" (82) the older William writes, thinking back on his childhood.

While William lives a normal life in most ways, what he has difficulty comprehending is why his overwhelming fear is not considered normal as well. Throughout the story, he repeats phrases such as "I wasn't a lunatic" (84) and "I wasn't wacko" (84), suggesting that the people who surround him—his parents, his teachers, the local doctor and librarian—feel that he is psychologically unbalanced when he goes to extremes such as turning his basement Ping-Pong table into a makeshift fallout shelter or sobbing uncontrollably at the library. The pressing question, both in the story and in the longer novel it will eventually become part of, is the question of who is actually crazy in a world that has the capacity to destroy itself many times over: the boy who recognizes the facts as they exist, or the people around him who go on with their ordinary lives as if the cold war were not happening, as if atomic destruction were not a very real and frightening possibility.

The adults in William's life initially refuse to take him seriously. William's mother, who notices her son behaving differently, first speculates that he has ordinary problems—"girl problems, school problems" (85). When he manufactures a story about seeing flashes, she worries that there is something physically wrong with her son: "There were all kinds of diseases around, polio and mumps and measles" (85), she tells him. Thus, she calls in Dr. Crenshaw to examine the boy. The doctor is even more skeptical about William's story. Failing to comprehend that the boy's tale of seeing flashes is a metaphor for his very real fear of atomic war, he says that he "never heard of such crap" (85). Dr. Crenshaw seems more intent on gaining revenge for William's having kicked him hard as a seven-year-old, when he was being treated for an injured penis, than in truly understanding what is wrong with the boy. In fact, William writes that his penis looks like it had "been sewn up by a blind man" (85). The doctor is certainly blind to William's very real fears. Even William's father, who clearly loves his son and tries to be sympathetic to him, laughs heartily with the doctor about William's attempts to protect himself by using pencils to line the top of his bomb shelter. Even the kind librarian does not fully understand when she sees William looking at real fallout shelters in old magazines—she merely thinks he is interested in politics, and she praises him for paying attention to the world around him.

In many ways, this story continues and carries forward the existential angst of modernist literature, the way writers reacted to World War I. When William relates his nightmare of May 1957, in which it seemed to him "that the universe had died in its sleep," emitting "not a whisper" (84), and when he "whimper[s]" (86) in the library, readers might be reminded of the famous ending lines of T. S. Eliot's well-known 1925 poem, "The Hollow Men":

This is the way the world ends
Not with a bang but a whimper.

As in the Eliot poem, the adults in William's world seem spiritually empty and blind. The natural world is polluted by looming atomic devastation, but no one, except William himself, seems to notice. No one is making a fuss; only the whimper of a young boy expresses the anxiety that the world at large *should* be feeling in the midst of cold war, facing weaponry even more devastating and the threat of destruction on a much larger scale than the atomic bombs of World War II.

The story ends by associating the politics of nuclear deterrence with William's own psychological state. After dismantling his bomb shelter in order to play several Ping-Pong games with his father, William is able to quell his fears, as all the adults surrounding him do, at least for the next decade or so. He sleeps well that night, and his dreams "were clean and flashless" (88). "The balance of power held" (88), he writes, referring to his own ability to balance his fears with the necessary psychological repression that allows him to live his life. But the phrase has political overtones as well, suggesting the strategy of mutually assured destruction (MAD) that developed between the Soviet Union and the United States during the cold war. The idea was that nuclear deterrence would occur because the use of nuclear weapons by either side would provoke an equally destructive counterattack. Thus, the theory goes, each side would avoid launching a nuclear strike in order to avoid the worst possible outcome—total nuclear annihilation. In order to avoid the annihilation of his personality, a complete psychological meltdown, William must suppress his fear.

Differences in Versions

The story remains mostly intact when it is revised for inclusion in *The Nuclear Age*. The changes, however, though small, are significant. First, readers learn more about the town of Fort Derry and about William's father in the novel version of "Civil Defense" than they do in the story. The novel includes several paragraphs describing Fort Derry's annual CUSTER DAYS event and the role that Mr. Cowling plays in the festival—that of GEORGE ARMSTRONG CUSTER himself. Rather than calling his son by the nickname "Tiger" as he does in the story, in the novel Mr. Cowling calls William "Partner." Thus, the novel makes a stronger connection to Fort Derry's western frontier heritage, specifically to the Indian Wars of the past and to the near-genocide of a previous culture. The older William, looking back on the annual reenactment of the BATTLE OF LITTLE BIGHORN, writes that he "craved the miracle of a happy ending" (TNA 11). The fact that his father dies year after year as Custer, however, drives home to William the idea that happy endings are not possible—that death and destruction are inevitable.

In the novel as well, William seems like a slightly more ominous character than he does in the original story. For instance, when Dr. Crenshaw cackles and limps away after asking William how his penis is, O'Brien has William comment: "Murder, that's all I could think" (21). Other indications of William's anger are added in the novel version as well. He cannot stop saying "Piss" after he hears his parents laughing with Dr. Crenshaw about his fallout shelter, and when his father tells him about the graphite in pencils, William not only says, "Graphite, *Piss* on it," but he is also said to feel a "killing rage" (*TNA* 28), while in the original version he had simply felt a "raw jolt of rage" (87). William's entire relationship with his father is presented as more intense in the novel, with him at times telling readers he "worshipped the man" (*TNA* 10) and at other times that he "hated him" (*TNA* 28). Surely, these additions are meant to make William appear even more psychologically damaged and more threatening than he seems in the original *Esquire* story, someone whom readers could believe capable of imprisoning his wife and daughter later in the novel and coming dangerously close to blowing them up.

CHARACTERS

Crenshaw, Doctor Doctor Crenshaw is FORT DERRY's decrepit old doctor, whom William dislikes intensely, mostly because the old man had treated him several years ago for an injury to his penis, leaving noticeable scars on the organ from a careless stitching job. The doctor is called in to examine William when the boy tells his mother that he had been seeing colored flashes. Cynical and abrupt, Dr. Crenshaw calls William's story "crap" (85) and believes the boy made up his symptoms simply to get out of going to school the next day. He seems incapable of understanding the serious psychological trauma that the boy is experiencing.

Librarian After the visit from Dr. Crenshaw, William rides his bike to the FORT DERRY Library, where he looks at pictures of real bomb shelters in back issues of *Time* and *US News*. An attractive female librarian praises William for his interest in politics. The young boy, however, soon begins sobbing uncontrollably. The kind librarian brings William into her office and calls his parents on the phone to come pick the boy up. This incident lets

William's father and mother see the seriousness of his growing atomic anxiety.

Stewardess The story ends with William as a grown-up, recounting how his childhood fears returned after college on a late-night plane ride from Miami to Boston. He pushes the call button on the plane, and a stewardess brings him a martini, wipes his brow, and holds his hand for a while.

William William, whose last name readers never learn, is an 11- or 12-year-old boy growing up in FORT DERRY, MONTANA, in the late 1950s. While he lives in an ordinary small town and has a loving family, William is psychologically damaged because he is so completely terrified of atomic weaponry. Because of the COLD WAR, indications of the possibility of atomic war surround him: He sees pictures of H-bombs in *Life* magazine, practices duck-and-cover drills in school, and hears tests of the Emergency Broadcast System on the radio. In an attempt to combat his fears, William turns the Ping-Pong table in his family's basement into a makeshift fallout shelter. At the end of the story, William's father is able to comfort him, at least temporarily, by turning William's handmade bomb shelter back into a Ping-Pong table and playing several fiercely competitive games with his son.

William's Father William's father is a real-estate salesman in FORT DERRY, MONTANA. Although he is kind to his young son, he does not understand the extent of William's fear of atomic weaponry. He inadvertently insults his son when he laughs with the town doctor about the makeshift bomb shelter that William has crafted out of the family Ping-Pong table in the basement. Although the doctor finds nothing physically wrong with William, the boy's parents begin to understand the seriousness of his fear when a local librarian calls them to pick up their son, who has sobbed uncontrollably in the library. William's father cleverly comforts his son at the end of the story by turning the bomb shelter back into a Ping-Pong table.

William's Mother Well-intentioned and kind, William's mother becomes worried about her son's health when he begins to display a high level of anxiety about the possibility of atomic war. She questions him so intently about his feelings one night that William makes up a story about seeing colored flashes. William's mother calls in the town doctor, but the unsavory old man believes that William's story is simply a "crock of you-know-what" (85).

"Class of '68" (1998)

"Class of '68" is a very short story, published as a one-page piece in *Esquire* magazine in March 1998 under the heading of "snap fiction." The story involves a middle-aged man and woman trading barbs and drinking heavily at a table on the edge of a dance floor at what seems to be a high school or college reunion. The story was later revised and included as chapter 8 of the 2002 novel *July, July.*

SYNOPSIS

The story opens with an unnamed woman announcing to a man whom readers later learn is named Billy, that she has breast cancer and is 51 years old. The two are facing each other, standing up on the edge of a dance floor. While the occasion for the dance is never clearly defined, Billy at one point sits down at a table and watches "the jolly old faces bob above their name tags" (160), suggesting that this is some kind of reunion gathering. What is clear is that the woman and Billy have a past together, a past in which the woman with cancer hurt Billy deeply. Billy resents the woman for leaving him many years ago in order to marry a man named Ron, with whom she subsequently had two blue-eyed sons, now grown up. Apparently, the woman had promised to fly with Billy to WINNIPEG, but had broken her promise. Billy, in his anger, is cruel to the woman and tries to hurt her with his words. In response, she drinks heavily, draining half-empty glasses on their table. The woman also threatens to take off her shirt and dance alone, to show off her cancer-ridden breasts to others at the gathering. The pair abruptly break off their conversation at this point. Later, Billy

sees the woman dancing alone, although she has kept her shirt on.

COMMENTARY

This very short story works like a puzzle. Readers are never told explicitly why this man and woman are so angry at each other, where exactly they are, or why they have gotten together again after so many years. O'Brien supplies clues, however, that help readers piece together for themselves the background to the story. We first realize the couple were acquainted in the past but have not seen each other for many years when Billy asks the woman about her husband and children, and the woman reminds Billy that her children are now grown. We find out that Billy and the woman were close in the past because she seems to know him well when she comments that he used to adore dancing. It also soon becomes clear that the woman's marriage is what so angers Billy; he betrays his resentment about Ron several times in the story, suggesting that he and the woman once had a romantic relationship. The setting of a school reunion is implied by the title of the story and confirmed when readers discover that people at the dance are wearing name tags and have "jolly old faces" (160), suggesting that these are old friends from the past. The woman apparently left Billy for political and religious reasons since she twice reminds him that she was Catholic and Republican.

Readers also discover that Billy went somewhere in the past, an act that was at least partially responsible for the breakup. The woman says that Ron wanted to marry her and that Billy was "gone." While we cannot be exactly sure where Billy went, he does hint that it was someplace not too far away or exotic: "It's not Siberia," he tells the woman, adding that the place had "indoor malls. Places to get your nails done" (160). Perhaps, readers might conjecture, the place Billy went was Canada, since he had suggested earlier that he and the woman should have their picture taken, drop it off at the hotel, then "catch that famous flight up to Winnipeg," implying perhaps that in the long-ago past the two had plans to do just that. The year that this school class graduated—1968—is another clue. Why would a young man suddenly depart for Winnipeg in 1968? Perhaps Billy was fleeing the Vietnam War DRAFT and the cancer-stricken woman had agreed to go with him, but, as a Catholic and Republican, she backed out at the last minute, staying at home and marrying a man named Ron instead.

Such a scenario explains the extent of Billy's anger, which seems out of proportion for a breakup that occurred 30 or more years ago. Billy's anger is larger than simply an anger at an old girlfriend who left him. He is angry, perhaps, about the war itself, about a country that forced him into exile, at friends who forgot about or abandoned him. He is angry about the life he missed out on. Once readers untangle the background to the story, the woman's cancer becomes even more ominous as well. Billy seems unsympathetic to her suffering, perhaps even viewing the cancer as proper payback for what he perceives as her cowardly betrayal of him so many years ago. When the woman says that she has been given three to five years to live—adding that her cancer is like "a manslaughter sentence"—it confirms the perception of the cancer as punishment for her behavior in the past. Her threat to take her shirt off and dance alone is an attempt to appease Billy by humiliating herself, much as he, perhaps, was humiliated by his draft evader status and the woman's abandonment of him in the past. However, just as the woman cannot bring herself to board the flight to Winnipeg, she cannot bring herself to remove her shirt either. Although Billy does see her dancing alone later in the story, she remains a "sensible woman" and keeps her shirt on, as afraid, perhaps, of making an extravagant gesture now as she was 30 years ago.

Differences in Versions
When O'Brien revised the story for the novel, he changed the date of the class reunion from 1968 to 1969, and he aged the woman in the story, making her 52, a week away from her 53rd birthday, rather than 51 as she is in the original short *Esquire* piece. He also added some more background detail. In the novel version, the characters are named right away as Billy McMann and Dorothy Stier. In the revised version readers are told as well that it is 4 A.M., and that the couple are among the few reunion attend-

ees still talking and drinking in a school gymnasium that has been decorated for a dance. In the novel Dorothy also makes a more explicit reference to the past when she says to Billy, "Nobody cares what happened a whole lifetime ago" (*July* 105), then has to quickly apologize for her thoughtless words. The allusion to a flight to Winnipeg has been removed from the novel version as well, since Dorothy's failure to meet Billy at the airport as planned is depicted elsewhere in the book. But the most important difference in the original *Esquire* story version of "Class of '68" and the version that appears in *July, July* has to do with the air of mystery that surrounds the arguing couple in the story version. The novel's context provides the background information that readers of the very short stand-alone story have to work to puzzle out for themselves. Readers of the novel clearly know who Billy and Dorothy are and are already acquainted with much of the story of their past relationship when they come to this scene.

CHARACTERS

Billy   Billy is the man in the story who speaks angrily at a school reunion with a former girlfriend, who is now 51 years old and stricken with breast cancer. Although readers are never fully informed about what happened in the past, the story implies that the woman left Billy for a man named Ron, that she had promised to accompany Billy on an airline flight to WINNIPEG, but had backed out. Billy is clearly still seething about the long-ago injury and wants to hurt the woman as badly as she had hurt him.

Ron   Ron is the husband of the unnamed woman with breast cancer and the father of the woman's two blue-eyed boys, who are now grown up. Apparently, the woman in the story left an old boyfriend named Billy in order to marry Ron, and Billy is still angry about the betrayal. Ron seems to be a wealthy man. When Billy first asks the woman how Ron is, she replies that he is "Fine. Rich" (160). In addition, Billy tells the woman at one point that she married well and also comments cruelly that Ron can afford the funeral should she die of her cancer.

Unnamed Woman The story opens with a woman whose name is never supplied, announcing to a man named Billy that she is 51 years old and has breast cancer. As the story unfolds, readers infer that the pair are at a school reunion and that they once had a romantic relationship. Billy is still angry about their long-ago breakup, and the woman with cancer repeatedly tries to justify herself to him, explaining that she was Catholic and a Republican, thus suggesting that political and religious reasons may have been behind their breakup. When Billy continues to treat the woman cruelly, she begins to drink heavily and threatens to take off her shirt in the midst of the crowd. The two part, and Billy later sees the woman dancing alone. She is sensible enough, however, to have kept her shirt on.

"Claudia Mae's Wedding Day" (1973)

Tim O'Brien's first published short story, "Claudia Mae's Wedding Day," appeared in *Redbook* magazine in October 1973. The story depicts a young man just returned from service in Vietnam whose fiancée back home has planned a June wedding at her family's Maine cottage.

SYNOPSIS

The story opens by informing readers that a young American soldier in Vietnam, Robert, has just proposed to his girlfriend, Claudia Mae, from a foxhole south of CHU LAI. Back home, Claudia Mae sets about planning a "simple and elegant" (103) outdoor wedding for the last day of June, to be held under the pine trees at her family's summer cottage in Maine. Robert, who is happy to leave Vietnam and who seems not to have suffered unduly from his wartime service, soon arrives back in the United States and joins Claudia Mae's family in Maine, where it has been raining steadily since the middle of June. As he eats dinner with Claudia Mae's family and plays Scrabble with her father, his future wife and in-laws assume that Robert is

scarred from his stint in Vietnam and that it would be painful for him to speak about his wartime experience, despite Robert's repeated protests that he is happy to talk about the war and to answer any questions they might have. When the wedding day arrives, it is still raining. Guests carry umbrellas and dash into the house, where Claudia Mae is locked in her room, still wishing for an outdoor wedding. Her father pours drinks for the guests, and Robert speaks with various friends and relatives of the bride's family, several of whom also make assumptions about Robert's time in the service and who would rather speak about World War I or WORLD WAR II rather than Vietnam. Eventually, Robert leaves the house, going to stand under the grove of pines where the wedding was supposed to take place, in the midst of a torrential downpour. Although puzzled by his behavior, Claudia Mae soon runs out to join him, holding an umbrella and wearing rain boots over her elegant bridal slippers. The other guests follow suit, and the ceremony takes place quickly. When the guests have finally departed, Claudia Mae's father puts his old VICTORY AT SEA record on the stereo and the story draws to a close.

COMMENTARY

"Claudia Mae's Wedding Day" explores the assumptions that people back home make about Vietnam veterans. While O'Brien writes that Robert "soared out of Cam Ranh Bay, joyful and grateful and unscarred" (142), Claudia Mae and her family fall prey to prevalent stereotypes about veterans, stereotypes that come in two versions: first, that veterans are dashing war heroes who performed gallant acts in battle, and conversely, that they are psychologically damaged, rebellious dopefiends who spent much of the war high. In either case, the people waiting at home believe that the veterans' time in Vietnam is far too painful to talk about, and they refuse to really listen to an actual soldier who participated in the war, preferring to hold onto their misconceptions.

The women in the story are the ones who cling to heroic stereotypes. When Robert first steps off the plane in Boston and kisses Claudia Mae in the terminal, she coos, "You look so . . . gallant. Tell me what all those medals are for?" (142). After a six-hour drive through the rain, as the young couple finally arrives at the cottage in Maine, Claudia Mae's mother greets Robert using language nearly identical to that used by her daughter: "You look so gallant!" she cries, "What are all those pretty medals for—goodness?" (142). Later in the story, a guest at the wedding named Hazel Stein will fawn over Robert as well, also asking him what his medals are for. But none of these women are truly interested in hearing Robert's war stories or the tales behind his medals. After commenting on his supposed gallantry, they move quickly on to other subjects. Like many women characters in later O'Brien works, especially *The Things They Carried,* these women do not want to listen. Truly listening to Robert's stories might upset their preconceived notions about heroism and war. Robert seems painfully aware of this fact as his answers to each woman in succession grow increasingly more preposterous. While he tells Claudia Mae that he won the medals for simply surviving—"They give them to all the live guys" (142), he says—he tells Claudia Mae's mother that the medals were earned for "killing time" (142), and he informs Hazel Stein that he won the medals for being the beer-drinking champion of his infantry brigade.

While the women in the story cling to stereotypes of gallant warrior heroes, the men back home, often war veterans themselves, are not much better. Claudia Mae's father immediately begins to interpret Robert's experience in Vietnam in terms of his own wartime experiences, as a navy ensign in World War II. He simply assumes that Robert has readjustment problems coming home, never bothering to listen to Robert's own views. O'Brien drives home the irony of the father's position in the following exchange:

". . . Those first months, back in civvies, back on the block. It wasn't easy. Not something you want to talk about. Forgetting is the tough part, I remember."

"You remember forgetting?"

"You betcha. I'll never forget it." (142)

On the one hand, Claudia Mae's father suggests that the only proper way for Robert to deal with his wartime experience is to completely forget it. But at the same time, he cherishes and holds onto his own war memories, believing that Robert must have the same experiences as he did.

Later in the story, however, as the two men are playing Scrabble together after dinner, Claudia Mae's father betrays the fact that he, too, holds stereotypes of Vietnam veterans. Evoking what he presents as insider knowledge in a man-to-man way, and using the old-fashioned term for marijuana, "Mary Jane," Claudia Mae's father tells Robert confidently that he knows all about the drug use that goes on among soldiers in Vietnam. Somewhat bewildered by the terminology employed by his fiancée's father, Robert is at first confused. But he soon comprehends: "Grass? You mean grass?" (143). Robert explains that there may have been some marijuana use going on among the soldiers, but not "out in the boonies. . . . Out there everybody's too busy staying alive" (143) he adds. Claudia Mae's father, however, looks unconvinced and immediately changes the subject. Like his daughter and his wife, he is not interested in listening to true war stories. He continues to insist that Robert must be at least "a little messed up" (143) from the war, that he must suffer from bad dreams or blank moments.

The older generation of men in the story, in fact, revel in their own war experiences. A common thread in American literature of the Vietnam War is the difference between World War II in particular—for many writers, their father's war—and the Vietnam War. World War II evoked widespread and patriotic support from those back home, while American involvement in Vietnam, a much more morally ambiguous war, spurred massive protest and divided the country. Despite Robert's assertion that to the common soldier one war looks like any other war, Claudia Mae's father and his friend Mr. Stein persist in romanticizing previous wars. When the two men put a recording of EDWARD R. MURROW describing the LONDON BLITZ on the stereo, Claudia Mae's father remarks nostalgically, "Wow. That was a war" (149). Mr. Stein tells Robert that he has read extensively about World War I, and he chastises the young soldier for not knowing the meaning of the word *caissons* from the old war song. The two old veterans prefer to wallow in nostalgia than talk in a meaningful way with the young soldier.

Those back home who protested the war do not seem capable of understanding Robert's experiences either. The preacher in the story, whom Claudia Mae chooses because he is "enlightened" (103)— young and liberal-minded rather than traditional— seems foolishly naïve and optimistic as he enters the house, beaming and declaring that it is a beautiful day despite the pouring rain. He confides proudly to Robert that as a seminary student he marched against the war. Like the young woman protester in *Going After Cacciato* who gives the soldiers in Paul Berlin's platoon a lift in her Volkswagen van, this young preacher goes so far as to equate his war protest experience with the soldiers' experience on the battlefield. He offers Robert his counseling services, divulging that he considers these services, "in GI lingo," to be like "mopping up" on the battlefield, adding, "That's my job, mopping up after the war" (148). The rawness of the young preacher is revealed when readers discover that this is his very first wedding, despite his seeming confidence. And when it comes time to perform the service, he cannot find the copy of the prayer book he brought with him, opening instead a book called *Winning the War Against War*. The preacher, though well-intentioned, is incompetent and too smug about his own war protest experiences, however trivial these might actually have been, to really listen to or understand Robert any more than Claudia Mae's friends and family members can.

At the end of the story, when Robert, exasperated by all of the assumptions being made about him, goes out to stand in the rain, Claudia Mae's father dismisses his actions as more of his Vietnam craziness, simply shaking his head and muttering "Vietnam . . . Vietnam" to himself. Claudia Mae's mother is concerned only about Robert's ruining his handsome uniform and thus spoiling the picture of the gallant soldier that he otherwise presents. The story does offer some hope for the marriage, however, when Claudia Mae puts on rain boots and picks up an umbrella to join Robert under the pines. Although she does not fully understand her husband-to-be, and although the rain signifies that

this is not going to be the fairy-tale wedding or marriage she had hoped for, she is willing to accommodate herself at least partially to the weather and to Robert, and the wedding is performed outdoors after all, in the midst of the pouring rain. Perhaps the young couple will have a chance to make their marriage work, despite the reactions of all those around them—the preacher who still wants to treat Robert's "troubled mind," Hazel Stein who kisses Robert passionately, attracted to the glamour of the soldier in his uniform, the two old ladies who cry at the end about the "splendid" wedding they just witnessed, and Claudia Mae's father who retreats inside to put a VICTORY AT SEA record on the stereo, settling comfortably back into his World War II nostalgia.

CHARACTERS

Claudia Mae Claudia Mae is the girlfriend to whom Vietnam soldier Robert proposes by writing her a letter from a foxhole south of CHU LAI. Back home in Maine, Claudia Mae eagerly begins planning her wedding for the last day in June, not deterred by the heavy rains that begin falling in the middle of the month. Insisting that she wants a simple yet elegant outdoor wedding, Claudia Mae travels to BANGOR to find an "enlightened" (103) preacher—one who believes that the outdoors is "God's church" (142). While Claudia Mae does seem to love Robert, or at least the idea of being married, she does not want to hear about the war, asking her future husband only about the medals he won. Nevertheless, despite her dismay that the rain continues right up until the time of the planned marriage ceremony, Claudia Mae resolutely dons rubber rain boots and joins Robert under the pine trees outside her family's cottage, where she is married in the midst of a downpour.

Claudia Mae's Father (Jonathan) Claudia Mae's father is rather cynical about his daughter's planned wedding to Robert, mocking the idea that a preacher could be "enlightened" (103) and telling his daughter and wife that it *always* rains in June in Maine. A WORLD WAR II navy veteran himself, Claudia Mae's father, whose first name is Jonathan, believes that Robert's Vietnam War experiences must have psychologically damaged him—that the young man will have readjustment problems, bad dreams, and experience moments of blankness. He seems to think of himself as something of an expert on the war, accepting the popular stereotype that most Vietnam veterans are drug users and suggesting that Robert spent the war doped up on "Mary Jane." The story ends by highlighting Jonathan's nostalgia for previous wars. With his friend Mr. Stein he listens to a recording of EDWARD R. MURROW describing the LONDON BLITZ, and when the wedding ends, he retreats back into his house to put a VICTORY AT SEA record on his stereo. This is presumably a recording of the music for the popular 1952 documentary on World War II.

Claudia Mae's Mother Like her daughter, Claudia Mae's mother is in love with the very idea of weddings. She enters into Claudia Mae's wedding plans wholeheartedly, sending out invitations and helping Claudia Mae find the perfect gown. When Robert, Claudia Mae's fiancé, arrives at the cottage in Maine, Claudia Mae's mother asks him about the medals he has won. Like her daughter, she seems entranced by her vision of a gallant soldier. Also like her daughter, she does not bother to listen to anything Robert has to say about the real world, preferring to cling to her romantic ideal of heroism.

Preacher Claudia Mae goes all the way to BANGOR in her quest to find what she calls an "enlightened" (103) preacher to perform her wedding ceremony. The preacher she engages is young and naive, just out of seminary. He tends to speak in clichés, opining that the outdoors is "God's church," a statement Claudia Mae's father cynically guesses he will make. Waiting for the rain to stop, the preacher confides to Robert that he marched in protests against the war during his time in seminary. He, like Claudia Mae's more jaded father, assumes that Robert is psychologically damaged by his experiences in Vietnam. He even likens the counseling services he provides to a soldier's "mopping up" in the aftermath of battle. The preacher, proud of his own actions during the war, does not listen to or understand Robert anymore than Claudia Mae's friends and family members do.

Stein, Hazel Hazel Stein is a family friend invited to Claudia Mae's wedding. Although she is the age of Claudia Mae's parents, she gushes and fawns over Robert, the groom, when she meets him, asking him about his medals and even kissing him on the mouth twice. Like the other women in the story, Hazel Stein seems entranced by a handsome soldier in uniform.

Stein, Mr. Mr. Stein is the husband of Hazel Stein. Like Claudia Mae's father, Mr. Stein is something of a war buff, reading everything he can about World War I and listening to recordings of EDWARD R. MURROW reporting on the LONDON BLITZ with Claudia Mae's father. Mr. Stein comments somewhat lewdly on Claudia Mae's "great legs" (148) and seems to have scorn for Robert, deriding him for not knowing what World War I caissons are.

Two Old Ladies Two old ladies who attend the wedding of Claudia Mae and Robert sit on the couch inside the Maine cottage, waiting for the rain to stop, and drinking martinis. At the end of the story, the two old ladies have to be carried to their car by Claudia Mae's father. They are weeping with joy and declaring what a "splendid" (150) wedding they just witnessed.

"Enemies and Friends"

"Enemies and Friends" tells the story of a vicious fistfight between two American soldiers at the Vietnam War—Dave Jensen and Lee Strunk. Although the two Americans later make peace with each other, their relationship remains uneasy. The story was first published in *Harper's* magazine in March 1990. It appeared later that same year as part of the collection *The Things They Carried*.

SYNOPSIS

The story begins by depicting a brutal fistfight between the American soldiers Dave Jensen and Lee Strunk over a missing jackknife. Jensen, the larger man, holds Strunk down and hits him repeatedly in the face, eventually breaking the other man's nose. Strunk is helicoptered to the rear but soon returns to his unit, wearing a metal splint and gauze on his injured nose. After Strunk's return, Jensen becomes increasingly nervous, expecting the smaller man to gain his revenge. Jensen eventually becomes so paranoid and tense that he loses control one afternoon, wildly firing off his weapon and shouting Strunk's name. Later that night, Jensen uses his pistol to hit himself in the face, breaking his own nose. He shows his injury to Strunk and asks if everything is even now between them. Strunk agrees, but he later tells the other soldiers in his unit that he actually *had* stolen Jensen's jackknife. The second half of the story begins a month later. Strunk and Jensen have learned to trust each other to the extent that they enter into a signed pact, each agreeing that if one of them suffers a terrible injury the other man will "find a way to end it" for him (31). But when Lee Strunk steps on a rigged mortar round that causes him to lose his right leg at the knee, he becomes deathly afraid that Jensen will actually carry out the pact. Slipping in and out of consciousness, Strunk makes Jensen promise not to kill him. The story ends with the information that Strunk died in an evacuation helicopter somewhere over CHU LAI. When Dave Jensen hears the news, he feels that an enormous weight has been lifted from him.

COMMENTARY

"Enemies and Friends" highlights the specific tensions and unease of fighting a guerrilla war. While a normal fistfight between two young men might have ended the same day it began, the atmosphere of paranoia and nervous tension in Vietnam is so great that the enmity between Strunk and Jensen continues for days afterward. When Strunk returns from the rear with his bandaged nose, O'Brien writes, "In any other circumstances, it might've ended there. But this was Vietnam, where guys carried guns, and Dave Jensen started to worry" (30). The fear that Dave Jensen feels in relation to Strunk, however, is described in terms that could just as well explain the situation of most American soldiers in Vietnam:

Jensen couldn't relax. Like fighting two different wars, he said. No safe ground: enemies everywhere. No front or rear. At night he had trouble sleeping—a skittish feeling—always on guard, hearing strange noises in the dark, imagining a grenade rolling into his foxhole or the tickle of a knife against his ear. The distinction between good guys and bad guys had disappeared for him. (30)

Because the American war in Vietnam was fought largely against the guerrilla units of the VIET CONG, many American soldiers felt the way Jensen does in the story. Unlike a war with set battles and a clearly defined rear area, there was no safe ground in Vietnam. The Viet Cong could attack anywhere. Many American soldiers in Vietnam died as a result of sniper fire or by setting off booby-trapped explosives, so there was indeed the sense that one was never entirely safe. And also like Dave Jensen, American soldiers had difficulty in distinguishing the good guys from the bad guys. It was nearly impossible to tell who among the Vietnamese villagers was a Viet Cong guerrilla and who was a South Vietnam loyalist. But the problem went even deeper than that. This was a war in which American soldiers' own perceptions of themselves as the "good guys" was subject to serious doubt, especially with media exposure of American atrocities such as the MY LAI MASSACRE. The fight between Jensen and Strunk, rather than being an anomaly, simply magnifies the effects that the war had on most American soldiers. The tension becomes so unbearable for Jensen, in fact, that he gives himself a self-inflicted wound, an escape mechanism taken by other soldiers depicted in O'Brien's work, such as Rat Kiley, who shoots himself in the foot in the story "Night Life" from *The Things They Carried,* or Ben Nystrom in *Going After Cacciato,* who deliberately shoots himself in the foot to escape the war as well.

In its depiction of American soldiers fighting one another rather than the enemy, this story also employs what has been identified by critics such as Katherine Kinney as one of the main tropes of Vietnam War literature—that of "friendly fire." Kinney argues that American literature about the

Vietnam War depicts numerous instances of Americans fighting other Americans—she points to the frequent scenes of conflict between enlisted men and officers, often resulting in fragging, (see FRAG), as well as to literary depictions of disagreement between doves and hawks and tensions between Americans on the home front and the soldiers at war. Kinney and several other commentators criticize Vietnam War literature for this tendency, since in their view it is a type of literary narcissism that tends to erase the Vietnamese from the war, depicting the country simply as a staging ground where Americans went to fight out their own internal ideological disagreements.

Nevertheless, despite such criticisms, O'Brien's story is interesting for the way it captures the psychological edginess of men at war, the feeling of never being safe or in control, even among supposed "friends." What is perhaps most intriguing about the story is the second half, in which Jensen and Strunk arrive at their uneasy truce, their mutual horror of the specter of a "wheelchair wound" (31) bringing them together. But the new friendship and trust between the two men is shown to be fragile and illusory. Strunk at the end of the story, after he has lost his leg to the rigged mortar round, fears Jensen more than he fears the wound that will eventually kill him. He begs his fellow soldier not to carry out the pact they had both signed. The story ends fairly ambiguously as well. When Jensen learns of Strunk's death, he feels relieved, as if an "enormous weight" (31) had lifted off him. But readers remain unsure whether Jensen's relief is the result of his no longer having to fear Strunk's revenge for the nose-breaking incident at the opening of the story, or whether he feels relieved of his guilt for not carrying out the pact he and Strunk had made in the second half of the story, for not killing Strunk as he had promised. Either way, the story ends on a cynical note that raises questions about the notion of soldiers as close comrades or "brothers in arms" that has become nearly a cliché of so much war literature. War does not bring these two Americans closer together. Their shared battle experiences do not cause Lee Strunk and Dave Jensen to forge a bond of brotherhood between them. Instead, war rips the two men apart, causing each to suspect and fear the other.

Differences in Versions

The original *Harper's* story was divided into two separate stories when it appeared in *The Things They Carried*, the first titled "Enemies" and the second titled "Friends." Other than that, the story as published in the later collection is nearly identical to its original version.

CHARACTERS

Jensen, Dave   Dave Jensen is an American soldier in Vietnam who gets into a fistfight with fellow soldier Lee Strunk. Jensen suspects Strunk of having stolen his jackknife, and he pummels the smaller man mercilessly, eventually breaking his nose. After Strunk's return to the unit, Jensen becomes increasingly paranoid, worried that Strunk is planning vengeance for the injury. Jensen becomes so nervous and jumpy after a week of worry that he loses control, shooting his rifle in the air and shouting Strunk's name. That night Jensen picks up his pistol and hits himself in the face with it, eventually breaking his own nose in order to make things "square" between himself and Strunk. In the second half of the story, the two warring soldiers have learned to trust each other. They enter into a pact, each agreeing to kill the other should that soldier suffer a "wheelchair wound" (31). When Lee Strunk steps on a rigged mortar round and loses his right leg below the knee, he is terrified that Dave Jensen will actually carry out the pact and shoot him. Dave Jensen swears not to kill Strunk, but he feels relieved at the end of the story when he learns that the injured soldier had died in the helicopter on the way to CHU LAI.

Kiley, Rat   Rat Kiley is the company medic who ties a tourniquet around the stump of Lee Strunk's leg after the soldier steps on a rigged mortar round. Kiley administers morphine to the injured man and runs plasma into him, but there is not much else he can do except wait for the helicopter to arrive and evacuate the injured man. Despite Kiley's ministrations, Strunk will die in the helicopter on the way to Chu Lai.

Strunk, Lee Lee Strunk is an American soldier in Vietnam who gets into a vicious fistfight with another soldier named Dave Jensen. Jensen breaks Strunk's nose and then so fears Strunk's possible retaliation that he uses a pistol to break his own nose. After this incident, Strunk laughingly tells the other men in the unit that he had indeed stolen Jensen's jackknife, the cause of the fight in the first place. The second half of the story depicts an uneasy alliance between Jensen and Strunk. Both men are so frightened by the possibility of a debilitating wound that they enter into an agreement that should one of them suffer such an injury, the other will kill him. When Lee Strunk steps on a rigged mortar round and loses the lower portion of his right leg, he is terrified that Jensen will shoot him. As Strunk drifts in and out of consciousness, he begs his fellow soldier not to carry out the pact. Strunk later dies from his injury, as the evacuation helicopter is transporting him to the American base at CHU LAI.

"Faith" (1996)

"Faith," the story of a seven-year-old boy growing up in small-town Minnesota in the early 1950s, whose father promises him an engine for his homemade plywood airplane and delivers a turtle instead, was initially published in the *New Yorker* magazine in February 1996. It was subsequently revised to become the opening chapter of the 1998 novel *Tomcat in Love*.

SYNOPSIS

On a Minnesota summer morning in 1952, seven-year-old Tommy and his friend, eight-year-old Herbie Zylstra, nail two plywood boards together and call it an airplane. When Tommy tells his father he will need an engine for his airplane, his father readily complies: "One airplane engine, coming up" (62). The boys wait all summer for the promised engine, building homemade bombs out of Mason jars filled with gasoline, and practicing pretend bombing runs on neighbors' homes, the Methodist church down the street, and even on Her-

bie's own large, dilapidated yellow house. When autumn arrives, Tommy's father presents the boys with a turtle named Toby rather than the promised engine. Herbie is particularly outraged, telling Tommy that his father is a liar. The hyperactive eight-year-old boy then sets the airplane tail down against Tommy's garage and proclaims that it is no longer a plane, but a cross instead. The boys persuade Herbie's younger sister, Mary Jean, to let herself play Jesus and be nailed to the cross. But Tommy's mother, coming out of the house to hang laundry on the clothesline, catches the boys carrying their hammer and nails and stops them just in time. Yet, a few weeks later, Herbie, without Tommy's help, will try again to nail Mary Jean to the cross, this time succeeding in driving a nail partly through the little girl's hand. As a result, Herbie is sent away to a Jesuit boys' school in the Twin Cities, and Tommy does not see his friend for a year.

The story, which is narrated in the first person by an older Tommy looking back on his childhood experiences, then jumps forward nine years. Tommy is now 16, in high school, and dating Mary Jean Zylstra. He remembers how he and Mary Jean first made love on the hood of his father's Pontiac in the middle of a cornfield in rural Minnesota. Herbie, though, who has changed from the somewhat wild but charming boy he once was into a quiet, self-absorbed loner, disapproves of the relationship. One night, when Tommy drives Mary Jean home and the two are petting and kissing in her driveway, Mary Jean suddenly pulls away, informing Tommy that her family is watching. The boy looks up to see the entire Zylstra clan crowded into the large bay window overlooking the driveway, their faces pressed up against the glass. Following this incident, Tommy provides glimpses into his adult life. Readers discover that he grew up to marry Mary Jean. But after 20 years the marriage goes sour when Mary Jean meets a man on the beach and falls in love while on a trip to TAMPA, FLORIDA, with Tommy. Mary Jean seems to blame the dissolution of the marriage on Tommy's jealousy and paranoia, and she demands that he "seek help" for his problems. Tommy, however, blames the breakup on Herbie, who reveals to Mary Jean a secret that he discovers about his former boyhood friend—under his mattress Tommy has stashed numerous checks made out to a phony psychiatrist. He had simply pretended to comply with Mary Jean's insistence that he receive counseling. The story ends with a bitter Tommy musing about how certain words are forever polluted for him: *turtle* and *TAMPA* chief among them.

COMMENTARY

While the story is called "Faith," it is really about the way that faith is constantly betrayed. Tommy and Herbie, as young imaginative boys, believe they can make an airplane out of two pieces of plywood board, and they happily occupy their entire summer playing with their creation. As a child, Tommy also believes his father's promise to deliver an engine for the plane, even though he does not entirely understand what an engine is. "I did not envision machinery," the older narrator writes, "I envisioned thrust: a force pressing upward and outward, even beyond. . . . My engine would somehow *contain* flight. Like a box, I imagined, which when opened would release the magical qualities of levitation" (62). Tommy has full faith in his father initially, believing that the older man has the power to magically procure for him this intangible quality of flight. When his father delivers an ordinary turtle rather than the promised engine, the disappointment is palpable. Even in middle age, the narrator says that the twin syllables of the word *turtle* still claw at him, that he cannot "encounter that word without a gate creaking open inside" of him (62). This gate is the chink in Tommy's image of his father, his first knowledge that his father is not superhuman, larger-than-life, able to fulfill extravagant promises, but only a human father who did the best that he could.

While Tommy's faith in his own father is damaged by this incident, the turtle seems to confirm for Herbie an even larger disappointment and loss of faith. He raises suspicions about fathers in general when he says to Tommy, "Your dad's a liar. They all are. They just lie and lie—they can't stop. They're made for it. Fathers. They lie" (63). Herbie is probably talking at least partly about his own father here—his house, unlike Tommy's, is frightening and decrepit, the lawn unmowed, the screen windows patched with tape and newspapers, the hallways filled with clutter, too many children. Tommy writes that even as a kid he "knew that things were not happy inside" (65). But Herbie's family is also Catholic, and the young boy's diatribe against fathers suggests his burgeoning lack of faith in God the Father himself. In fact, Herbie's attempted nailing of Mary Jean to the cross can be read as a testing of his religious faith. If it is true that Jesus could be nailed to a cross, die, and be resurrected, what real harm will come from nailing Mary Jean to a cross? And Mary Jean's own faith as a seven-year-old girl in her brother and her brother's friend is charmingly naïve as well. When the boys suggest she play Jesus, she says simply, "I guess so," and demands only that the game be fun, completely unconcerned about the harm that will come to her. But childhood faith is betrayed once again. Herbie, when he eventually succeeds in driving a nail into Mary Jean's hand, is not rewarded for being a devout Catholic; he is punished by being sent away to a Jesuit "hospital school" (64). Mary Jean, bearing on her hand the mark of the stigmata, or of Christ's suffering, loses faith in her older brother, telling the 16-year-old Tommy to ignore Herbie because "it'll drive him crazy" (65), and holding up her hand and claiming that she "owns" her brother because of what he did to her as a child.

The love affair between Tommy and Mary Jean Zylstra is marked by a loss of faith and multiple betrayals as well. Although Tommy first knows that he loves Mary Jean when she gives him a "gorgeous, breathtaking smile" (63) when playing with her dolls in the family attic when she is seven years old, Tommy's willingness to nail her to the cross sets in motion a lifetime of betrayal. Tommy, only seven, senses something wrong in what the boys are about to do: He feels a frothiness in his stomach, as if he is sick, but he goes along with Herbie's plan anyway, because he is curious. "You think this'll hurt?" he asks Herbie, but Herbie merely shrugs in response, never contradicting Tommy's apprehension. At dinner that night, when Tommy's parents confront him with the reality of the hammer and the nails, and of what the boys were planning to do to Mary Jean, Tommy is forced to concede that the tools are "real." Yet, he also asks his father whether

Toby the turtle is a real engine. As a seven-year-old, Tommy feels "wronged and defenseless" (64), and links his own bad behavior to an earlier betrayal he himself had experienced—his father's lies about the airplane engine. In this story betrayal begets further betrayal.

This childhood incident marks what will become a pattern in Tommy's life, a tendency to self-pity, to blaming others when things go wrong, to feeling constantly wronged and betrayed. When Herbie actually drives a real nail part-way through Mary Jean's hand, Tommy feels cheated that he was not there to witness it, as if he had "been robbed of fair due or denied access to something rare and mysterious" (64). After all, he points out, he deserved to be there—it was his plywood and his green paint. As a 12-year-old, he kisses a girl named Francie Graff, betraying his love for Mary Jean. When Mary Jean confronts him, he accuses her of betraying him first—by kissing a series of boys named Bill, Dennis, and Eddie. Twenty years after he marries Mary Jean, Tommy lies to her about seeking psychiatric help, but again he sees this deception as stemming out of a wrong done to him—Mary Jean's infatuation with Kersten, the business tycoon she meets in Florida.

But perhaps the most profound betrayal of all in the story revolves around what Tommy perceives to be the deceptions performed by language itself. Initially, the young boy loves what seem to him the powerful, nearly magical qualities of language. Lying in bed at night, he murmurs the word *engine* over and over, not quite understanding what the word means, but loving its very sound. When the longed-for engine transforms into an ordinary mud-turtle, however, named Toby as every other turtle in the world is, the magical qualities of language that Tommy believed in are diminished. Language, he learns, is duplicitous; words and the objects they signify do not have a one-to-one correlation. Remembering the turtle incident, Tommy writes, "The words 'turtle' and 'engine' seemed to do loops in the back-yard sunlight. There had to be some sort of meaningful connection, a turtleness inside engineness, but right then I couldn't find the logic" (62). Even more, in the backyard that afternoon, Tommy feels a sort of helplessness as a window opens into the adult world of ambiguity and half-truths. "In a dark, pre-knowledge way," he writes, "I understood that language was involved, its frailties, its mutabilities, its potential for betrayal. My airplane, after all, was not an airplane. No engine on earth would make it fly. By renaming things, reinventing things, Herbie and I had willfully deceived ourselves—as children do" (62–63). Tommy's boyhood belief that words themselves have a kind of magical, incantatory quality is crushed here—he realizes that simply naming his nailed pieces of plywood an airplane is not enough to make it so.

This original betrayal will follow Tommy throughout his life. As an adult, he continues to dwell on the deceptive nature of language itself. He wonders specifically about the word *love*. What is love? If love can die, was it ever love in the first place? Doesn't or shouldn't love imply an "absolute and abiding and indestructible" quality (66), a sense of permanence? What Tommy longs for are the absolutes of his childhood, a feeling of security and permanence. Above all, he longs for faith itself—the kind of faith that he initially had in his father as a young boy and in the mysterious word *engine*. But he recognizes that such innocent faith is not available in the adult world. Tommy imagines that the unnamed reader whom he addresses several times in the story—a kind of everyman or everywoman in love relationships—has been betrayed by love in the same way that he has, that the ex-lover of this unnamed reader has gone to FIJI to live with a new love. Betrayal and deception, then, are finally hallmarks of the human condition. Although the Christian Bible professes that all creation springs from the word of God, Tommy in this story recognizes that we live in a fallen world, one in which language is used for deception. The story comes full circle by the end. Tommy once again recognizes the powerful qualities of language, as he did with the word *engine* in the beginning, but now he sees this power as a dark, violent force:

> Does language contain history the way plywood contains flight? Are we bruised each day of our lives by syllabic collisions, our spirits slashed by combinations of vowel and consonant? Do verbs destroy us? Do proper nouns kill and maim?

As in many of his other works, O'Brien elevates language and storytelling, understanding full well how language shapes our perceptions of reality. But while in a story like "The Lives of the Dead," he argues for the redemptive quality of language, suggesting that "stories can save us," that in stories, "miracles can happen," the dead can sit up and come back to life again, here he recognizes the dark ancillary of this proposition. If language can save us, is it not powerful enough to kill us as well? "Can a word stop your heart as surely as arsenic?" (67), Tommy muses at the very end of the story. *Turtle* and *Tampa*, with all the dark history of betrayal each carries with it, are just such words for him.

Differences in Versions

O'Brien made numerous small changes when he revised the short story version of "Faith" for inclusion in *Tomcat in Love*. For instance, the name of the main female character is changed from Mary Jean to Lorna Sue. He also cuts out the four or five sisters that Herbie is said to have in the original story. In the novel Lorna Sue seems to be Herbie's only sibling. In addition, in the novel version the narrator, Thomas H. Chippering, is clearly raised Catholic himself, while in the story, the Catholicism of the Zylstras seems frightening and foreign to Tommy. Perhaps more important, the unnamed reader, the "you" whom the narrator frequently addresses has been made unequivocally female in the novel version. In the original story the first reference to this unnamed reader seems to posit him as male. Tommy asks, "Have you ever loved a woman, then lost her, then learned she lives on Fiji with a new lover?" (62). In the novel O'Brien changes gender references, so that the new question reads, "Have you ever loved a man, then lost him, then learned he lives on Fiji with a new lover?" (*TL* 4). This change was perhaps made for the sake of consistency, since elsewhere in the story the unnamed reader does seem to be female. But it is also likely that Thomas H. Chippering in the novel, avowed sexist that he is, wants to cajole and placate female readers by suggesting that their experiences are not all that much different from his own.

The novel version also includes some changes that suggest Thomas Chippering's tendency else-

where in the novel to exaggeration and humorous self-aggrandizement. The child Herbie, for instance, seem more threatening in the novel than he appears in the story. The statement that "Herbie could be impatient at times" in the original story is changed to "Herbie could be vicious at times" (*TL* 3) in the novel version. And in the novel Herbie's eyes are said to be "like the eyes of certain trained assassins" (*TL* 6) that Thomas Chippering would later encounter in the mountains of Vietnam. Readers also see evidence of Chippering's tendency to melodrama in the stronger hints in the novel than in the story that the love between Herbie and Lorna Sue is a sexualized one. Chippering in the novel says that Herbie not just loved, but "coveted" his own sister (*TL* 11), and later he says that Herbie worshipped Lorna Sue "in the biblical sense" (TL 16), phrases that do not appear in the original story version. Chippering also includes self-serving descriptions of himself that are not spoken by Tommy in the original story. "By any estimate," the novel's narrator opines, "I am a man of some majesty, tall and eye-catching, no paunch, no deficits worth the spill of ink . . ." (*TL* 11). In addition, the list of girls that the young Thomas supposedly kissed when he was 12 is much longer in the novel version, and readers are also told that Chippering wrote these names down on a list, which Lorna Sue found. Most of these changes are intended to make the story's narrator fit better with the somewhat ludicrous character of the narrator of *Tomcat in Love*. Tommy in the original story version of "Faith" seems like a more grounded character than the pompous, preening professor of the novel version, Thomas H. Chippering.

CHARACTERS

Bill, Dennis, and Eddie Bill, Dennis, and Eddie are young boys whom the story's narrator, Tommy, accuses Mary Jean Zylstra of kissing when they are 12 years old. Tommy's accusation comes in response to Mary Jean's anger over his kissing of a girl named Francie Graff. In her defense Mary Jean replies that the boys love her, to which Tommy counters that Dennis does not. This childhood flirting will lead to the later marriage of Tommy and Mary Jean, which will also be marred by accusations of infidelity when Mary Jean meets a rich businessman in TAMPA, FLORIDA.

Catchitt, Mrs. Mrs. Catchitt is a neighbor who lives close by Tommy and his friend Herbie Zylstra when they are young boys. The summer that they build a makeshift airplane out of two plywood boards, the boys pretend to bomb the house of Mrs. Catchitt and other people they "despised" (62).

Constantine, Dr. Ralph Late in the story, the middle-aged Herbie Zylstra finds 14 uncashed checks made out to Dr. Ralph Constantine under the mattress of his sister, Mary Jean, and her husband, Tommy, Herbie's old boyhood friend. Tommy admits to readers that Dr. Constantine is a phony psychiatrist whom he invented in order to appease Mary Jean's demand that he "seek help" (66) for his jealous and paranoid behavior. The psychiatrist's name represents Tommy's longing that the love between him and Mary Jean remain constant.

Graff, Francie Francie Graff is a girl whom Tommy kisses when he is 12 years old. Mary Jean Zylstra becomes angry when she finds out about the kiss and informs Tommy that Francie "puked mice" (67) afterward. When Mary Jean asks Tommy whether he loves Francie, he replies "probably" (67), even though he still claims that the girl forced him into the kiss. Tommy then says that he'll stop loving Francie and love Mary Jean instead. The girl laughs in reply and tells Tommy that her brother, Herbie, will kill him.

Kersten When Tommy has been married to Mary Jean Zylstra for 20 years, the two take a vacation together to TAMPA, FLORIDA, where she meets a businessman named Kersten on the beach. Mary Jean will eventually leave Tommy for this man, whose name Tommy has vowed never to utter (although he breaks his promise by telling readers the tycoon's name). A wealthy man who makes his living in real estate, Kersten has been able to provide well for Mary Jean. When the narrator spies on them in Tampa, he sees that his former

wife is "well dressed" with "expensive jewelry" and "tanned skin" (67).

Powell, Jerry and Ernest Jerry Powell and his cousin Ernest are neighbors of Tommy, the story's narrator, when he is a seven-year-old boy growing up in Minnesota. They are among the people that Tommy and his friend Herbie "despised" (62) as children. The boys use their plywood airplane to pretend to bomb the Powell house in the summer of 1952.

Tommy Tommy is the first-person narrator of "Faith." He begins the story when he is a seven-year-old boy, disappointed by his father's reneging on a promise to provide him and his friend Herbie with an engine for his homemade plywood airplane in the summer of 1952. But readers soon discover that Tommy will suffer numerous other disappointments in life as well, most important the dissolution of his marriage to Mary Jean Zylstra, Herbie's younger sister. While the tone at the beginning of the story seems almost wistful—a humorous, nearly nostalgic looking-back at his past, Tommy's adult bitterness increasingly shows through as the story progresses, as he describes his 16-year-old self first dating Mary Jean, and then later Mary Jean's relationship with the tycoon from TAMPA.

Tommy's Father When the story's narrator is seven, his father cheerfully promises to get him an engine for his plywood airplane, expecting, perhaps, that his young son will soon forget the request and move on to other interests. But Tommy spends the entire summer dreaming of flight. When his father finally brings him a turtle rather than the promised engine, the young boy experiences his first loss of faith, and the first of many disappointments that will plague his life.

Tommy's Mother The mother of seven-year-old Tommy initially prevents her son and a neighbor boy, Herbie Zylstra, from nailing Herbie's little sister to a plywood cross. She catches the boys with hammer and nails when she goes out into the yard to hang up laundry. That evening, the hammer will occupy a place at the center of Tommy's family's dining room table, his father attempting to explain to him the difference between playing games and actually driving a nail through someone's hand.

Unnamed Reader Several times in the story, the narrator, Tommy, directly addresses an unnamed reader. Initially, he asks this unnamed reader if he has ever loved a woman only to have lost her to a new lover in FIJI. Later, Tommy imagines this reader as a woman whose ex-husband now lives on Fiji. He speculates about whether the ex-husband ever truly loved the woman, since he was willing to leave her. The story ends with Tommy again making an appeal to this unnamed reader, asking her if her husband is still in the Tropics, if she contemplates revenge, if her life has been a lie. O'Brien seems to use the device of this unnamed "you" to illustrate Tommy's belief that heartbreak and betrayal, loss and sorrow in love, are universal human emotions that almost anyone has probably experienced. As Tommy relates his story, he assumes that his readers can understand his emotions because they most likely have had similar experiences of their own.

Zylstra, Herbie Herbie Zylstra is the childhood friend and neighbor of Tommy, the story's narrator. A hyperactive eight-year-old boy when the story begins, Herbie is even more disappointed than Tommy when his friend's father gives the boys a turtle rather than the airplane engine he had promised them. Herbie retaliates by telling Tommy his father is a liar, and by turning the plywood airplane they had constructed together onto its end and claiming that it is now a cross. Although the boys are foiled by Tommy's mother in their first attempt to nail Herbie's sister, Mary Jean, to the cross, a few weeks later, Herbie will actually drive a nail into his younger sister's hand. As a result, he is sent to a Jesuit school for boys up in the Twin Cities. Herbie comes home a changed person—more secretive and more of a loner than he had been before. His relationship with Tommy is destroyed as well. When the boys become teenagers and Tommy starts to date Mary Jean, Herbie will attempt to break the couple up. He will not succeed, however,

until he is a middle-aged man and Tommy and Mary Jean have been married for 20 years. Herbie reveals to his sister that Tommy has been lying to her about seeing a psychiatrist, showing her the pile of phony checks that Tommy has stored under his mattress.

Zylstra, Mary Jean Mary Jean Zylstra is the younger sister of Herbie. A beautiful little seven-year-old girl when the story begins, Mary Jean unquestioningly allows her brother to attempt to nail her to a cross, believing simply that she is playing Jesus in a recreation of a Bible scene. The injury she receives on her hand, however, will shape the rest of her life. She tells Tommy when she starts to date him as a teenager that she "owns" Herbie (65) because of what he did to her as a child. Although Mary Jean ends up marrying Tommy, she leaves him 20 years later for a business tycoon named Kersten, whom she meets on a beach in TAMPA, claiming that Tommy's own jealousy and paranoia are what destroyed their marriage.

"Field Trip" (1990)

A story that details an American veteran's trip back to Vietnam 20 years after the war ended, "Field Trip" was first published in *McCall's* magazine in August 1990. A slightly revised version of the story appeared the same year in the collection *The Things They Carried.*

SYNOPSIS

"Field Trip" depicts an unnamed narrator, presumably Tim O'Brien—the same narrator of several other stories that would later be collected into *The Things They Carried*—who takes his young daughter, Kathleen, on a trip with him back to Vietnam 20 years after he served there as an American soldier. After showing his daughter the usual tourist sites—HO CHI MINH's mausoleum, the tunnels at Cu Chi, and the like—the narrator arranges a side trip to QUANG NGAI PROVINCE, where he searches out the field that his best friend, Kiowa, had died in during the war. While he is able to find the spot, the field does not resemble the menacing terrain of the narrator's memory. Twenty years later, the small, sunny field is unremarkable, and the narrator has a hard time calling up the emotions he had expected to feel. Ten-year-old Kathleen does not understand her father's interest in this particular spot and mostly stays in the jeep with a government interpreter who performs magic tricks for her. The story ends with the narrator wading into the murky, chest-deep water of the small river that runs through the field and burying an old hunting hatchet of Kiowa's in the soft bottom. An old Vietnamese farmer watching the narrator raises a shovel in salute before the narrator emerges from the water. When Kathleen asks if the man is mad at him, the narrator replies simply, "No . . . All that's finished" (79).

COMMENTARY

Starting with its title, which suggests a school outing organized for young children, the story "Field Trip" works by contrasting the naïve innocence of 10-year-old Kathleen with the world-weary experience of her father. While Kathleen is presented as a good-natured child who had "held up well" (78) during the long trip to a foreign country, she nevertheless has difficulty understanding the war, the motives behind it, or the deep emotional effect it had on her father. She prefers to stay in the jeep, laughing at the magic tricks performed by the government interpreter to wandering the field with her father, and she declares that he is "weird" for being unable to forget "some dumb thing" (78) that happened a long time ago. Yet part of the problem lies with the narrator's own inability to communicate to his daughter what the war meant or how it shaped his life. Kathleen is smart and interested and asks questions, but the narrator cannot explain to her why he was in Vietnam 20 years ago or what he is doing in the remote field in Quang Ngai now. Although Kathleen is certainly old enough to understand the DRAFT, the narrator, in response to her query about why he was even in Vietnam in the first place, responds simply, "I don't know," explaining that his presence there as an American soldier is a "mystery" (78). Rather than explain to Kathleen about Kiowa's death, the narrator merely

states that he is going for "a quick swim" (79) when he wades out into the mucky river. Receiving such responses to her questions, it is no wonder that Kathleen has difficulty understanding the war and its effects.

The narrator's difficulties in communicating the experience to his daughter, despite his initial desire that the trip offer Kathleen "a small piece of her father's history" (78), stem at least partly from his own emotional uncertainty upon revisiting the field. He is surprised at how different the place looks from the images locked in his memory—the field is smaller and much less menacing than it seemed 20 years ago. It is bone dry and filled with sunlight, birds, and butterflies rather than ghosts of the past. Here, as in much of his fiction, O'Brien is concerned with the difficulty of getting at historical truth. Memories, he points out, are unreliable. As he writes in "How to Tell a True War Story," events as they actually unfold "get jumbled; you tend to miss a lot" (TTTC 71). And when someone tries to explain what happened to them during a war, the events are surrounded by a "surreal seemingness, which makes the story seem untrue" (TTTC 71). So, in returning to the field where Kiowa died, the narrator has to struggle with the disjuncture between his memories of that night and the appearance of the field 20 years later. Along with the unreliability of memory is also the simple fact that things have changed. Vietnam has become a tourist destination; the Vietnamese government interpreter, a Communist official who would have been an enemy of the narrator 20 years ago, has become "fast friends" (78) with Kathleen, performing magic tricks in the jeep to entertain her. The Vietnamese farmer raises a shovel rather than a gun to the narrator, a foreigner in his country.

The narrator has changed emotionally as well. As he stands in the midst of the grass on a hot day in August, he thinks about how the little field "had swallowed so much"—not just his best friend but also his "belief in [him]self as a man of some small dignity and courage" (78). The narrator remembers that he had seemed to grow cold inside the night of Kiowa's death, a coldness that has never quite left him over the years: "There were times in my life when I couldn't feel much, not sadness or pity or passion, and somehow I blamed this place for what I had become, and I blamed it for taking away the person I had once been" (78). "Field Trip," like many war narratives, marks a move from innocence to experience. The narrator feels that he lost his own childhood self, the innocence that his daughter still retains, in the Vietnamese field. All the waste and carnage associated with Vietnam are made concrete in this simple image of the field, which, readers find out in other stories, was the location where villagers relieved themselves, where they deposited their bodily waste. Literally, this spot was the village "shitfield"; metaphorically, as the narrator writes, it represents "all the waste that was Vietnam, all the vulgarity and horror" (78). These are things too big and, perhaps the narrator feels, too dangerous to communicate to his daughter. Even when all alone he tries to find the right words to say after burying Kiowa's hunting hatchet, the narrator can only muster the phrase, "There it is" (79). Like Norman Bowker in the story "Speaking of Courage," the narrator is unable to express his deepest feelings. He is unable to tell Kiowa what a good friend he had been; he is unable to explain to Kathleen his experiences in the war or his reasons for returning to Vietnam.

It is perhaps appropriate, then, that the old Vietnamese farmer communicates only silently with the narrator at the end of the story. O'Brien sees one of the old men watching him from the dike, and as the two stare solemnly at each other, the American veteran feels something "go shut in [his] heart while something else swung open" (79). While these lines are difficult to interpret, perhaps the narrator feels some closure concerning the death of Kiowa and an opening to new possibilities, to some of the changes that he has observed in the country he revisits so many years later. Although the narrator briefly wonders if the old man will come speak to him, exchange a few war stories, the farmer, like the narrator himself, remains silent. He does, though, seem to acknowledge a connection with the narrator—a shared loss—as he raises his shovel silently and grimly "like a flag" (79) that marks the new, uneasy truce between the two men. Kath-

leen, also witnessing the raised shovel, speculates that the old farmer is mad at her father, but the narrator replies that that is not the case. "No . . . All that's finished" (79), he responds, suggesting that the two former enemies communicated with each other despite the silence and that perhaps the narrator has at least partially found "the signs of forgiveness or personal grace" (78) that he went to Vietnam to seek.

Differences in Versions
The only significant difference between the *McCall's* magazine version of the story and the version that appears in *The Things They Carried* is the object that the narrator buries in the river bottom. In the story version the narrator buries Kiowa's old hunting hatchet, but in the novel he buries Kiowa's moccasins. The change is an interesting one—both items are tokens of Kiowa's Native American heritage. O'Brien in many of his works thematically touches on America's frontier past, particularly the subjection of the Plains Indians. William Cowling's small hometown of FORT DERRY, MONTANA, for instance, in *The Nuclear Age* celebrates an annual festival called CUSTER DAYS, while the narrator of *In the Lake of the Woods,* as he explores the My Lai atrocity, cites earlier massacres as well, including the butchering of Indians at Sandy Creek and the annihilation of CUSTER's 7th Cavalry at the BATTLE OF LITTLE BIGHORN. Perhaps O'Brien wanted to retain the allusion to Kiowa's Indian heritage while deemphasizing the violence that might be associated with the hunting hatchet. Kiowa, after all, is presented elsewhere in *The Things They Carried* as a gentle person, a devout Baptist who praises the narrator for refusing to mock the dead. The moccasins rather than the hunting hatchet might have seemed to O'Brien, upon revision, to be a more appropriate emblem of Kiowa's personality.

CHARACTERS

Cross, Jimmy Lieutenant Jimmy Cross is mentioned only briefly in the story when the narrator recognizes a small rise in the Vietnamese field where the officer had set up his command post the night that Kiowa died.

Government Interpreter   The narrator and his daughter, Kathleen, are accompanied on their trip to rural QUANG NGAI by a Vietnamese government interpreter who remains in the jeep as the narrator wades out into the murky water in the field where Kiowa had died. The interpreter becomes fast friends with Kathleen and entertains her with magic tricks while her father explores the field and river.

Kiowa   Kiowa was the narrator's best friend, who died in Vietnam 20 years previously. Readers do not find out much about Kiowa's death in the story, discovering only that his fellow soldiers had found his rucksack in the muddy water and had been forced to dig their dead friend out. In other stories that appear in *The Things They Carried,* however, such as "Speaking of Courage" and "In the Field" readers are given more information about how Kiowa died. Apparently, he drowned in a muddy field filled with human waste during a night attack. Several men feel responsible for Kiowa's death—Lieutenant Jimmy Cross for camping in the "shit field" in the first place, and Norman Bowker and the young Tim O'Brien, who both claim to have let go of Kiowa's boot as he was pulled under the mucky water. In "Field Trip" the story's narrator describes searching out the spot where Kiowa had drowned 20 years ago and marking the death by burying the dead soldier's old hunting hatchet in the soft river bottom where the men had dug his body out.

O'Brien, Kathleen   Kathleen O'Brien is the 10-year-old daughter of the story's narrator. Hoping to show his daughter an important piece of his life, the narrator brings her with him to Vietnam 20 years after he fought there as an American soldier. After visiting all of the usual tourist sites, the narrator hires a jeep to take him to a remote spot in QUANG NGAI PROVINCE where his best friend during the war, Kiowa, had drowned in a muddy river in the middle of a field. Kathleen, not fully understanding her father's past or the reasons for the war, tells her father that he is "weird" because "some dumb thing happened a long time ago" (78) and he cannot forget it. When the old Vietnamese farmer raises his shovel at the end of the story, Kathleen thinks that he is mad at her father, not understanding the connection that exists between the two men because of their shared past.

O'Brien, Tim   "Field Trip" is told in the first person by a former American soldier in Vietnam who, 20 years after the war has ended, revisits the site where his best friend, a soldier named Kiowa, died. Accompanied by his 10-year-old daughter Kathleen and a government interpreter, the veteran wades out into the water of a muddy river to bury his old friend's hunting hatchet in the spot where he drowned. Although the story's narrator is never named, he seems to be the same Tim O'Brien character who appears in numerous stories published in the late 1980s. When the story was revised and included in *The Things They Carried,* the narrator is clearly identifiable as the Tim O'Brien who narrates the rest of the collection. But this Tim O'Brien should not be confused with the real-life Tim O'Brien, who wrote the story. As author O'Brien pointed out in interviews, he has no daughter, and the character bearing his name is a fictional construct.

Sanders, Mitchell   Mitchell Sanders was a fellow soldier of the narrator 20 years ago during the Vietnam War. The narrator remembers that it was Sanders who found Kiowa's rucksack in the muddy river and who had helped dig out the dead soldier's body.

Vietnamese Farmers   Two old Vietnamese farmers work to repair a dike near the spot where the story's narrator wades into the water to bury Kiowa's hunting hatchet. Although the farmers watch the narrator carefully, they never say a word. At the end of the story, however, one of the old men raises a shovel above his head, "grimly, like a flag" (79) and holds it there for a short while. Although the narrator's daughter, Kathleen, fears that the man is angry at her father, the narrator explains that "All that's finished" (79). The man seems to be acknowledging an unspoken connection with the American veteran—their shared past of loss and violence.

"The Fisherman" (1977)

The short story "The Fisherman," which depicts a squad of American soldiers in Vietnam planning to murder their commanding officer with a fragmentation grenade, was first published in *Esquire* magazine in October 1977. The story was later revised and divided into two chapters that appear in the novel *Going After Cacciato*: Chapter 34, "Lake Country" and chapter 35, "World's Greatest Lake Country."

SYNOPSIS

"The Fisherman" begins with Lieutenant Sidney Martin ordering a soldier named Oscar Johnson down a Viet Cong tunnel in order to search it. Oscar insists that the lieutenant simply blow up the tunnel without searching it first and refuses to go down. Martin carefully writes Oscar's name down in a notebook after his refusal. He then orders each of the men in the squad in turn to go down the tunnel, noting their name in his notebook after each refuses. One soldier, however—Cacciato—is not ordered down the tunnel since he is not present. One of the men tells Martin that the boy is off fishing. Lieutenant Martin eventually removes his equipment and enters the tunnel to search it himself. When the lieutenant is out of sight, Oscar Johnson produces a hand grenade and asks every man to touch it, all the while talking about self-preservation. It is clear that the men intend to blow up Sidney Martin with the grenade while he is in the tunnel. The men face a dilemma, though, when they realize that Cacciato is not present to join in the pact. Despite Stink Harris's urging that Johnson throw the grenade down the tunnel anyway, Oscar slips the pin back into the weapon, hands it to a soldier named Paul Berlin, and orders him to go talk with Cacciato. Before he can do so, Sidney Martin emerges from the tunnel unscathed. Later that afternoon, Berlin, armed with the grenade that all the other men have touched, finds Cacciato fishing in a burned-out bomb crater. Berlin urges the simpleminded soldier to touch the grenade, but Cacciato hedges, until Berlin finally picks up the boy's hand and forces it to the grenade himself. He

then returns to the camp. In response to the men's queries about whether Cacciato had touched the weapon, Berlin replies that, like all fishermen, Cacciato's mind was "a million miles away" (134). The story ends here, readers never discovering whether the fragging (*see* FRAG) is carried out or not.

COMMENTARY

On one level the story "The Fisherman" depicts the very real turmoil that existed between officers and enlisted men during the Vietnam War, particularly in its later stages. Officers were college-educated and trained in military strategy and standard operating procedures, or SOPs, as Sidney Martin is in the story, while ordinary foot soldiers were young, often uneducated—many were even high school drop-outs—and largely drafted (*see* DRAFT) into a war that they often did not understand or support. While Oscar Johnson's proposed solution to the problem of Sidney Martin might seem extreme to readers, combat refusals—men refusing to carry out direct orders—and even the murder of overzealous or incompetent officers were real problems in the later years of American involvement in Vietnam. While exact statistics are difficult to determine, hundreds of possible fragging incidents were investigated over the course of the war, climaxing in the years 1969–72, when the morale of American soldiers was at its lowest and when it was clear that the tide has turned against South Vietnam and its American allies. Searching tunnels was a particularly dangerous mission and figures prominently in much imaginative literature written by Vietnam War veterans. In "The Fisherman," it is the fear of going down into the tunnels that prompts the murder conspiracy. In the story O'Brien emphasizes the ease with which Oscar Johnson makes his decision to initiate the fragging—the grenade he lifts from his belt is "the new kind, shaped like a baseball, seamless, easy to handle and easy to throw" (92). Readers are intended to see the dark irony in this description. Young men, even 17-year-olds like Cacciato, who should more properly be living their carefree teenage years back home playing baseball and engaging in other wholesome activities, are fighting this war. The all-American symbol of a baseball morphs into a fragmentation grenade.

The story also details the devastation that the war has wreaked upon the Vietnamese landscape. Often it seemed to American soldiers in Vietnam that their real enemy was the land itself. As Major Li Van Hgoc tells the men of Third Squad in *Going After Cacciato*, the novel that a revised version of "The Fisherman" would later appear in, "The soldier is but the representative of the land. The land is your true enemy" (86). The brutal heat and monsoons, the harsh jungle and mountain terrain, the booby-trapped paths and trails, the underground tunnel complexes at Cu Chi and elsewhere all afforded danger to the American soldier. Napalm and Agent Orange, perhaps the most notorious weapons used by the Americans, were intended to burn, destroy, and defoliate the lush Vietnamese vegetation, to provide the enemy fewer places to hide troops and weapons. In "The Fisherman" readers see the results of a bombing attack on the landscape:

> Things were wet and still. No birds: that was one of the odd things—no birds and no trees. Once there had been plenty of them, a green forest, but now the trees were stumps burned to the color of coal. No underbrush, no hedges, no grass. Everywhere the earth was scorched and mangled, bombed out into bowl-shaped craters full from a week of rain. (92)

When Doc Peret nicknames this devastated landscape "LAKE COUNTRY," all of the men except Cacciato are aware of the irony Doc intends. As O'Brien points out elsewhere in his fiction, "words make a difference" (*TTTC* 238). The soldiers make jokes about the death and destruction they see, often renaming things—dying is called "kicking the bucket"; a VIET CONG nurse, burned by napalm, becomes a "crispy critter"—in order to control their fear, to pretend that death "was not the terrible thing it was" (*TTTC* 238). The ironic nickname even helps Paul Berlin to pretend that he is no longer in Vietnam but back home, camping in the lakes and woods of Wisconsin, safe from the war.

Cacciato, however, literal-minded and simple, seems to take Doc's nickname seriously. He fishes in the dead water of the rain-filled bomb craters, clinging to the belief that there might actually be fish in "Lake Country." But it is this very hopefulness that sets Cacciato apart from the other men. He still seems like an innocent boy rather than a hardened soldier like the others in the platoon. He appears to be more concerned about the sugar being gone from his chewing gum than he is about the danger presented by searching the tunnels that so unnerves the other American soldiers. Cacciato retains a certain purity about him as well in that he does not refuse a direct order as the other men do. Because he is away fishing when Lieutenant Martin orders the tunnels searched, Cacciato's name is not written down in Martin's notebook. But more important, Cacciato never joins the conspiracy to murder Martin. While Berlin takes the boy's hand and forces him to touch the grenade, Cacciato is the only platoon member who does not touch the weapon by his own volition. The title of the story, with its Christian overtones—in the Gospels Christ promised to make his disciples "fishers of men"— suggests that Cacciato is Christlike in that he has not fallen into sin like the other men. Not only that, he retains faith in the face of overwhelming odds, continuing to believe in the miraculous possibility of catching a fish in the bomb craters, despite being repeatedly told that there are no fish. Cacciato in the larger novel becomes a symbol for the lost innocence of the other men in the platoon, particularly for Paul Berlin, who wrestles with his own guilt over the death of Sidney Martin. Berlin imagines the men chasing or hunting Cacciato as they attempt to regain their own innocence. The ending line of the story suggests the separation between the simpleminded fisherman and the rest of the men in the platoon. Cacciato's mind is "a million miles away" from the war, while the other men are trapped within the deadly and dangerous environment of Vietnam, struggling to preserve themselves as best they can.

Differences in Versions

"The Fisherman" remained largely intact when it was revised for inclusion in *Going After Cacciato*. The most significant change may be in the story's title. When O'Brien divides the story into two chapters and renames them "Lake Country" and "World's Greatest Lake Country," he deemphasizes the Christian references in the original version, focusing instead on the ironic name given the burnt-out landscape by Doc Peret. This move makes sense considering that in the novel this memory becomes one of many that arises in Paul Berlin's mind during his night on the observation tower. O'Brien seems to want to shift focus away from Cacciato as a potential Christ figure and toward Paul Berlin himself and his troubled conscience over the part he played in the murder conspiracy. It might also be that O'Brien felt the religious overtones associated with Cacciato had already been made sufficiently clear elsewhere in the novel, for instance when the simpleminded young soldier dresses as a monk in MANDALAY. Perhaps O'Brien felt that retaining the original title would make the Christian references in the novel too heavy-handed.

The majority of changes in the revised story, however, are surface revisions that seem intended to make the story mesh more seamlessly with the larger novel. For instance, in the original story Paul Berlin's rank is Spec Four, while in the novel he is referred to as Private First Class. This is because in the novel the incident in Lake Country most likely occurs in August 1968, *before* readers see Paul Berlin undergo his promotion interview in September. In addition, Frenchie Tucker and Bernie Lynn, whose deaths are mentioned only once in the story, are referred to more often in the novel version. Oscar Johnson, when first ordered down the tunnel by Sidney Martin in the novel, immediately reminds the lieutenant of the two men who died previously while searching tunnels. And later, when Jim Pederson suggests the men try to talk to Martin before taking more drastic action, Oscar again mentions Frenchie Tucker. These repeated references remind readers of the earlier deaths they have already read about in the novel and set up more clearly the reasons behind the conspiracy against Martin. The novel also emphasizes more fully what O'Brien refers to as the "bobbing secret in Lake Country"—literally, the aerosol can of Secret deodorant that Cacciato is using as a fishing bobber, but more significant, the secret of Sidney Martin's death, which will haunt Paul Berlin during the long night he

spends thinking and pretending on the observation post. While the original story only mentions this "secret" once, it is referred to at least three times in the novel version, perhaps because in the original *Esquire* story it is never clear whether the men actually carry out their murder plan, since the story ends with Sidney Martin still alive. The novel, however, very strongly hints that Lieutenant Martin has died in the tunnels as the result of a fragging—thus the "bobbing secret" takes on even more importance.

Other changes include a slightly longer conversation between Paul Berlin and Cacciato near the end of the novel version of the story, with Berlin telling the young soldier that the other men are worried about him and that touching the grenade is for his own good. Also in the novel version, Cacciato asks Berlin about his own motives, to which Berlin replies, "I'm a messenger" (GAC 240), a line that does not appear in the original story. The addition of this line suggests to readers Berlin's attempts to justify and excuse his own involvement in the conspiracy, a pretense he tries to cling to throughout his night on the observation post when he imagines telling his father that he held himself separate, that he did not become one of the group. The revised version also adds a short paragraph at the very end of the story, in which Oscar picks up the grenade, hooks it to his belt, and proclaims, "That's everyone" (241). This change suggests to readers more emphatically that the men will indeed continue with their fragging plot. Thus, the revised version of the story ends somewhat less open-endedly than the *Esquire* version.

CHARACTERS

Berlin, Paul While Paul Berlin tries his best to pretend that he is not at war, that he is back in Wisconsin, camping in lake country, he nevertheless joins the conspiracy against Lieutenant Sidney Martin, first when he refuses to go down the Viet Cong tunnel, and more important when he touches the fragmentation grenade held out to him by Oscar Johnson. Berlin is also the man elected to talk Cacciato into touching the grenade as well. When Cacciato demurs, Berlin reaches out for the boy's hand and forces him to touch the weapon.

Buff   A soldier named Buff is said to be one of the men who touches a fragmentation grenade proffered by Oscar Johnson. Buff, like the other men in the unit, understands that this action signals his willingness to join in the murder plot against Lieutenant Sidney Martin.

Cacciato   Cacciato is a simpleminded soldier who leaves his unit to go fishing in a burned-out bomb crater, apparently not comprehending that the dead water cannot possibly contain any fish. Because he is absent when Lieutenant Martin orders the men down a Vietnamese tunnel, Cacciato cannot refuse the assignment as the other men do. The boy also declines to touch the fragmentation grenade that the men plan to murder Martin with, signifying his refusal to join in the plot. While Paul Berlin reaches out to take Cacciato's hand and bring it to the grenade, the touching is not willed on Cacciato's part. Thus, the boy retains a sort of innocence and hopefulness that the other soldiers have lost. His refusal to participate in the sinful fragging (see FRAG), along with his designation as "The Fisherman" of the story's title, set Cacciato up as a possible Christ figure.

Harris, Stink   Stink Harris is the first member of the platoon to touch the fragmentation grenade after Oscar Johnson orders the men to do so. Stink is eager to commit the murder of Sidney Martin, urging Oscar to throw the grenade down the tunnel that Martin has entered, even before Cacciato has been found and told about the plan.

Johnson, Oscar   Oscar Johnson initiates the plot to kill Lieutenant Sidney Martin, arguing that it is a matter of self-preservation since two men have already died in the tunnels and Martin insists on following the standard operating procedure (see SOP) of searching the tunnels before blowing them up.

Lazzutti, Eddie   Eddie Lazzutti is a soldier who touches Oscar Johnson's grenade immediately after Stink Harris does. Like the other soldiers in his unit, Eddie joins the conspiracy to use the grenade to murder Lieutenant Sidney Martin.

Lynn, Bernie   Bernie Lynn was one of the members of the platoon who had previously died in Viet Cong tunnels after Lieutenant Sidney Martin ordered that the tunnels be searched. Lynn's death contributes to the men's anger at Martin and their ultimate decision to murder him with a fragmentation grenade.

Martin, Lieutenant Sidney   Lieutenant Sidney Martin in a no-nonsense officer who carefully follows procedures when he demands that his men undertake the extremely dangerous operation of searching Viet Cong tunnels before blowing them up. When each man in the platoon refuses to enter a tunnel, Martin, no coward, searches the tunnel himself. While the lieutenant is underground, the men in his command plot to murder him with a fragmentation grenade. The lieutenant emerges unscathed from the tunnel in the story, but the fragging plot has been set into motion. In the novel *Going After Cacciato*, Sidney Martin will indeed be killed by the men in his platoon.

Murphy, Harold   Harold Murphy is one of the men in the platoon of American soldiers who refuses a direct order to search a Viet Cong tunnel and who later touches a fragmentation grenade, signaling his willing participation in a plot to murder Lieutenant Sidney Martin.

Nystrom, Ben   Ben Nystrom is mentioned only briefly in the story—he, along with the other men in the platoon, touches a fragmentation grenade as he joins the plot against Lieutenant Sidney Martin. In other O'Brien works, Nystrom will shoot himself purposefully in the foot in order to be sent home from the war.

Pederson, Jim   Jim Pederson is the only one of the soldiers present to object when Oscar Johnson initially unveils his plan to murder Lieutenant Sidney Martin with a fragmentation grenade. Pederson suggests the men try reasoning with Martin, but he is overruled by Oscar, who claims that "the man don' *grasp* facts. All he grasps is S.O.P.'s" (92). Oscar's reasoning persuades Pederson, who nods, looks away, and finally touches the grenade along with the rest of the men in the platoon, except for Cacciato.

Peret, Doc   Doc Peret is one of the soldiers in the platoon who touches the fragmentation grenade held out by Oscar Johnson, thus joining the conspiracy against Lieutenant Sidney Martin. Doc Peret is also the one who invents the nickname "LAKE COUNTRY" for the mountainous, bombed-out area where the men are on patrol. The aerial bombardment has created huge craters amid the burnt trees and vegetation, craters that have filled up with water from the never-ending rain. Cacciato, who seems to take Doc's cynical nickname seriously, insists on fishing in the bomb craters.

Tucker, Frenchie   Like Bernie Lynn, Frenchie Tucker is a member of the platoon who died in the complex of underground tunnels carved out by the Viet Cong. Because searching the tunnels is so dangerous, the remaining soldiers refuse orders when Lieutenant Sidney Martin insists that they go down. The deaths of Frenchie Tucker and Bernie Lynn contribute to their decision to FRAG Lieutenant Martin.

Vaught   Vaught is the soldier who first informs Lieutenant Sidney Martin that Cacciato is fishing. Thus, Martin cannot order Cacciato to search the Viet Cong tunnel as he does the other men. Vaught, like the other members of the platoon, touches a fragmentation grenade proffered by Oscar Johnson, signaling his complicity in the murder plot.

"The Ghost Soldiers" (1981)

"The Ghost Soldiers" was initially published in *Esquire* magazine in March 1981, nearly 10 years before it was revised and included as a chapter in *The Thing They Carried*. The story is about an injured Vietnam War soldier named Herbie who plans revenge on the young, inexperienced medic who fumbled his treatment in the field, nearly causing Herbie to die of shock.

SYNOPSIS

The story is told in the first person by a soldier named Herbie, who is shot twice while serving in Vietnam. The first time he is injured, Teddy Thatcher, the company medic, risks his own life to patch Herbie up and to crawl back to the injured man repeatedly during an intense firefight to check on him, cracking jokes all the while. But Teddy Thatcher is killed in the war, and Delta Company gets a new medic, a skinny young man named Jorgenson. When Herbie is shot a second time, his wound is much more serious. Jorgenson, scared and inexperienced, takes 10 full minutes to work up his courage to move over to Herbie and tend to him. He also neglects to treat for shock, a condition the wounded soldier nearly dies from. During his recovery at the hospital and back at the base in CHU LAI afterward, Herbie is filled with rage at the young medic—the wound in his buttocks is embarrassing and painful, and Herbie serves as the punch line for many jokes. When Delta Company arrives at the base for a stand-down, Herbie plans revenge on Jorgenson, enlisting the help of a gung ho soldier named Azar. The two use noise-makers and a rigged-up sandbag covered with a sheet to terrify the medic when he is on guard duty one night. As their plan unfolds, however, Herbie becomes increasingly sympathetic to Jorgenson and begs Azar to halt their plans. The fierce and wild Azar, though, refuses. The story ends with Jorgenson bandaging up Herbie's knee, which had been injured during the night's activities. Herbie awkwardly and half-jokingly suggests to the medic that they work together to kill Azar.

COMMENTARY

"The Ghost Soldiers" exposes the Hollywood-induced fantasies that young American men have about fighting and the way that the realities of the war do not match up to these fantasies. The first time that Herbie is shot, he immediately thinks of his traumatic experience in terms of the movies that he has grown up with: "*I've been shot. I've been shot. Winged, grazed, creased: all those Gene Autry movies I'd seen as a kid*" (90). Yet, his initial euphoria—he writes that he even laughed on first being wounded—soon gives way to fear. Herbie begins to worry that he might bleed to death, and he experiences a sinking sensation as if he were going underwater. But Teddy Thatcher's quick attention and the jokes he makes help pull Herbie together. When the injured soldier is loaded onto the DUSTOFF helicopter, Teddy Thatcher bucks him up with a media allusion to western heroes, saying, "Happy trails to you" in his best Mexican accent as if he were the CISCO KID from movies and television. The two soldiers then play out their assigned roles. Herbie, even though he barely feels up to it, says, "Oh Cisco," and Teddy kisses his neck and replies, "Oh Pancho" (90), performing the shtick that the popular 1950s television series *The Cisco Kid* always ended with. Because Herbie's wound does not hurt very much and turns out not to be too serious, he is able to get through the experience by pretending to be a character from the movies and television shows he grew up watching.

When Herbie is wounded the second time, however, the movie allusions fail. While PANCHO and Cisco always survived their adventures on television, Teddy Thatcher has been killed and is no longer around to aid his loyal sidekick. The new medic, Jorgenson, does not make a good substitute Cisco Kid since he is frightened, inexperienced, and incompetent. Any illusions Herbie once had about the glory of being wounded in battle are crushed as well. "Getting shot," he writes, "should be an experience from which you can draw a little pride" (92). But his own experience is simply painful and humiliating. He is shot in the buttocks and has to endure the nurses at the hospital joking that he has "diaper rash" and treating him like a child. His recovery is slow; he is unable to sleep at night or sit comfortably during the day; and the ointment he must use three times a day leaks through his pants in a humiliating way. Herbie's real experience of being wounded turns out to be not at all like the sanitized versions of war presented in Hollywood movies or on television.

But distinguishing between reality and fantasy turns out to be difficult for the American soldiers in the story in other ways as well. The story's title derives from what the soldiers perceive to be the mysterious nature of the enemy they are fighting:

We called the enemy "ghosts." "Bad night," we'd murmur. "Ghosts are out." To get spooked, in the lingo, meant not only to get scared but to get killed. "Don't get spooked," we'd say. "Stay cool, stay alive." The countryside was spooky: snipers, tunnels, ancestor worship, ancient papa-sans, incense. The land was haunted. We were fighting forces that didn't obey the law of twentieth-century science. (95)

The guerrilla nature of the war in Vietnam meant that the enemy was often hard to distinguish. The VIET CONG did not wear uniforms, did not often engage in set battles with the Americans, and were able to hide among villagers who looked like them. Their tactics were those of guerrilla fighters: They attacked the Americans through bombs attached to trip wires, PUNJI PITS dug into the ground, sniper shootings, and ambushes. The extensive underground tunnel system used by these guerrilla fighters also led to their ghostlike reputation. While there was nothing supernatural about the Viet Cong, the American soldiers, reacting to a different culture, unfamiliar military tactics, and even stereotypes of the mysterious, enigmatic Asian often interpreted their enemy in fantastical terms. Azar expresses the otherworldly feel of the war to many American soldiers when, in response to Herbie's reminder that their scaring of Jorgenson "isn't for real," he says, "What's real . . . Eight months in Fantasyland, it tends to blur the line. Honest to God, I sometimes can't remember what real *is*" (95). Confused by romantic expectations of war set up by the movies as well as by the unfamiliar culture they find themselves in, these soldiers have difficulty distinguishing between reality and fantasy.

Herbie's plan to gain revenge on Jorgenson takes advantage of the very difficulty Azar describes. Particularly on night watch, when men's imaginations begin to get the better of them, it is hard for soldiers to tell what is real and what is not. Despite not going to college and not being "a whiz in high school either" (95), Herbie understands the psychology of fear, how the "stories . . . about Charlie's magic" (95) seem more plausible when one is alone in the dark. And the line between reality and fantasy becomes even more blurred as Herbie prepares his trap for Jorgenson. "Unreal, unreal" (96), he thinks to himself as he waits to pull the strings of his noisemakers and ghostlike sandbags. While the ambush he and Azar are setting up is not real—it is a phony ambush—Herbie's musings here also suggest the larger, otherworldly feel of the war itself. Waiting to spring his trap, Herbie once again begins to feel like he is in the movies:

> It's like you're in a movie. There's a camera on you, so you begin acting, following the script: "Oh Cisco!" You think of all the films you've seen, Audie Murphy and Gary Cooper and Van Johnson and Roy Rogers, all of them . . . old lines old movies. It all swirls together; clichés mixing with your own emotions, and in the end you can't distinguish . . . (95).

Fantasy and reality become jumbled in many ways in this story. Just as Herbie's remembrance of the movies mingles with his actual wartime experience, and wild stories of supernatural enemy soldiers mix with facts about Viet Cong tactics, the tormenting of Jorgenson occupies a hazy border between the real and the unreal. While Herbie insists that the tricks played on the medic are only a "game" (98), Azar will not quit when Herbie begs him to. He takes their plan as seriously as if it were a real-life ambush. Yet, at the same time he says that the war sometimes make him "feel like a little kid again. Playing war" (98). For Azar, who "*love[s] this shit*" (98), the war itself is unreal; Vietnam is a fantasyland where he can be as violent and brutal as he pleases.

Another romantic, Hollywood view of war that the story plays with is the idea of soldiers as brothers-in-arms who come to love one another and are willing to lay down their lives for their comrades. Like much Vietnam War literature, the story debunks such notions by depicting Americans fighting *themselves* more than it shows them fighting the actual enemy. Herbie, who had felt like one of the group when out on patrol and was ambushed with the other men in Delta Company, feels separate from his former comrades when the company stands down in CHU LAI. He has not witnessed the same events that the other

members of Delta Company have, such as Morty Becker wasting all his luck by going swimming, and he no longer has the same stories to tell. His buddy Lemon, in fact, reprimands Herbie for his desire to gain revenge on the medic, telling the angry soldier, "look, you're not *out* there anymore, and Jorgenson is" (93). "Comrade-in-arms. Such crap" (95), Herbie thinks to himself at one point when Lemon refuses to participate in his scheme. Yet, ironically, it is in many ways his love for Lemon and the other soldiers that motivates Herbie's revenge. When he sees Lemon in the mess hall one day, sitting next to Jorgenson and "having this chummy-chummy conversation," he acknowledges, "That's probably what cinched" (95) his plans. Herbie acts as much out of jealousy over losing the close friendship of Lemon and the others as he does out of anger at Jorgenson's fumbling of his medical treatment. While Hollywood and television depict the love of brothers-in-arm as noble and self-sacrificing, O'Brien depicts it as fickle and subject to the same jealousies and selfishness that all love is susceptible to.

The end of the story does show some reconciliation between Jorgenson and Herbie, partly because the punishment meted out to the medic seems out of proportion to his crime, and partly because Herbie understands Jorgenson's fear so well. When he and Azar first begin circling around behind Bunker Six, where Jorgenson is keeping watch, Herbie at first cannot move. His boots feel heavy, and it is as if he is paralyzed. Interestingly, Jorgenson had earlier described to Herbie that his lack of prompt action after the shooting was due to the fact that he could not make himself move: "After you got hit, I kept telling myself to move, move, but I couldn't *do* it. Like I was full of Novocaine or something. You ever feel like that? Like you can't even move" (93). While Herbie did not answer Jorgenson at the time, he does feel like he cannot move later in the story, a feeling that perhaps prompts some of the empathy he begins to feel for the medic as the night wears on.

The story returns to the movie theme again at the end, Jorgenson telling Herbie that he has a real sense of drama and that he "should go into the movies or something" (100). When the two half-jokingly discuss killing Azar, the line between movie fantasy and reality blurs again. Jorgenson exclaims, "What a movie!" after he suggests they should scare the brutal soldier to death. But Herbie merely shrugs in response and says, 'Sure. Or just kill him'" (100), indicating perhaps a more serious intent to his initial suggestion than Jorgenson comprehends. Despite the fact that American soldiers fall back on media images in order to make sense of their experiences, Vietnam, O'Brien suggests, does not offer the glamour of Hollywood versions of war. Men are afraid and sometimes act badly during battle; it is not glorious to be wounded; soldiers' love for one another is not as noble and altruistic as we might like to imagine. Above all, the horror of war is real, not glorious like that depicted in John Wayne movies.

Differences in Versions

In order to fit the story into the collection *The Things They Carried*, O'Brien had to make several changes on the surface level. Most noticeable, the characters in the original story morph into characters that have already appeared in the novel. Herbie becomes the young Tim O'Brien, the writer/narrator of *Things*, and the competent medic who treats O'Brien the first time he is shot becomes Rat Kiley. Delta Company in the story is transformed into ALPHA COMPANY in the book and is commanded by Lieutenant Jimmy Cross rather than an unnamed captain. Norman Bowker and Mitchell Sanders take on roles assigned to soldiers named Lemon and Curtis Young in the original story, and the company's stand-down is switched from July to March in order to better fit the novel's time line.

But in addition to these changes, O'Brien makes some larger, thematic alterations as well. He tones down a bit the allusions to movies that occur in the original story, removing the "Oh, Cisco," "Oh, Pancho" exchange between Herbie and Teddy Thatcher when he revises, and also removing a later reference to Herbie's attempt to grin wryly, "like Bogie or Gable" (98). He chooses to emphasize instead in the novel version the theme of the brotherhood that develops among soldiers in the field and the way that a soldier removed to a rear area feels separate from his former comrades. The novel version contains additional language about soldiers becoming "close friends . . . part of a tribe" that shares "the same blood" (*TTTC* 192). Later, the narrator O'Brien in the novel version writes that a soldier in the rear "forfeit[s] membership in the family, the blood fraternity" (*TTTC* 194), and Azar even tells O'Brien that he no longer fits in, that he is a "has-been . . . one of those American Legion types, guys who like to dress up in a nifty uniform and go out and play at it" (*TTTC* 212)—lines that do not appear in the original story. The additional focus on the brothers-in-arm theme ties "The Ghost Soldiers" more fully to earlier stories in the novel, for instance "How to Tell a True War Story," in which the narrator tells a kindly older woman that she was not listening, that the story of Rat Kiley shooting a water buffalo after Curt Lemon's death was a *love* story, not a *war* story.

But perhaps the most significant alteration in "The Ghost Soldiers" is an emphasis in the revised version on how the war has changed the narrator, made him turn mean and dark inside. Tim O'Brien, unlike Herbie, the original story's narrator, is a summa cum laude college graduate who possesses all the "high, civilized trappings" (200) of a young, well-educated American in the late 20th century. Yet, he writes that he had somehow been crushed by his seven months in the bush: "I'd turned mean inside. Even a little cruel at times. For all my education, all my fine liberal values, I now felt a deep coldness inside me, something dark and beyond reason" (*TTTC* 200). Later, when O'Brien talks about sitting on guard duty in the night, he says there is nothing to do "but stare into the big black hole at the center of your own sorry soul" (*TTTC* 205). While Herbie in the original story had also contemplated staring out into a big black hole, only in the revised version is this hole placed into the narrator's own soul. Finally, a paragraph is added in the novel version that concludes with narrator O'Brien again contemplating the darkness within himself: "I was Nam—the horror, the war" (209). These additions place the novel more firmly in the direct line of descent from Joseph Conrad's classic 1902 novel about European imperialism, *The Heart of Darkness*, in which a sense of primitive evil that the Westerners first perceive as being part of the landscape of Africa is finally acknowledged to reside within their own hearts. While much Vietnam War literature takes up a similar theme, it is perhaps nowhere so readily apparent as in Francis Ford Coppola's 1979 film *Apocalypse Now,* which retells Conrad's novel, but sets it in the jungles of Vietnam.

CHARACTERS

Azar   Azar is a violent and gung ho young soldier who served in Delta Company with Herbie before Herbie's injury removed him from his original unit. When Herbie's friend Lemon refuses to participate in a revenge scheme against the medic Jorgenson, Herbie is forced to enlist the aid of Azar. The brutal soldier, however, takes things further than even Herbie would like. Stating, "I *love* this shit" (98), Azar proclaims his pleasure at being in Vietnam in general and in planning the phony ambush of Jorgenson in particular. Azar refuses to stop tormenting Jorgenson during the night even when Herbie begs him to. The story ends with Herbie visiting the medic in his tent and suggesting that the two work together to kill Azar.

Becker, Morty   When the members of Delta Company arrive in CHU LAI for a stand-down, they tell Herbie a story about a soldier named Morty Becker who "wasted his luck" (92). Becker had gone swimming unaccompanied one afternoon in a Vietnamese river and returned unharmed, much to the amazement of his fellow soldiers. But a few days later, he comes down with a high temperature and fever and eventually dies from a virus he had contracted from the water. Lemon, who tells Herbie the story of Becker, draws this conclusion from it: "Don't throw away luck on little stuff. Save it up" (93).

Captain of Delta Company   Delta Company's captain figures into the story that Lemon tells Herbie about the death of Morty Becker. When Becker goes missing in Vietnam one afternoon, Lemon reports, "Captain's about ready to have a fit" (92). Although Becker reappears unharmed, having foolishly gone swimming by himself in a Vietnamese river, he will die soon after from a virus.

Herbie   The story is narrated in the first person by a soldier in Delta Company named Herbie who is shot twice in Vietnam. The first injury is fairly minor, and Herbie is quickly patched up by Teddy Thatcher, a medic who risks being shot several times to crawl over and check on the wounded soldier. The second time Herbie is injured, however, he nearly dies of shock. A new medic named Jorgenson, who has replaced Teddy Thatcher, bungles Herbie's treatment, mostly out of fear and inexperience. Angry and humiliated by a severe wound in his buttocks, Herbie plots revenge against Jorgenson during his recovery and eventual assignment to a rear job. He enlists the aid of a fellow soldier named Azar, and the two terrify Jorgenson one night while the medic is on guard duty. Herbie begins to regret his scheme as the night wears on, however, and the story concludes with his half-joking suggestion to the young medic that they work together to kill Azar.

Ingo, Ron   Ron Ingo is a soldier in Delta Company who steps on a booby trap in April. Herbie tells readers that the soldiers, to comfort themselves, make jokes about Ingo's death, saying the man has been made into a "deviled egg—no arms, no legs, just a poor deviled egg" (95).

Jorgenson   Jorgenson is the new medic who replaces Teddy Thatcher in Delta Company. Inexperienced, Jorgenson is paralyzed with fear when Herbie is shot the second time. He not only takes 10 full minutes to work up the courage to crawl over to the wounded man but Jorgenson's fear causes him to administer to Herbie incompetently as well. He neglects to treat for shock, and he bungles the job of patching up the bullet hole. The pain and humiliation that Herbie suffers as a result of this injury soon boils over into a hatred of Jorgenson. When Delta Company stands down at CHU LAI, Herbie plots with another soldier named Azar to frighten Jorgenson while he is on guard duty one night. Jorgenson, however, has changed since his first encounter with Herbie. He has learned to control his fear, and he has become a much more competent medic. He seems dignified and mature in his dealings with Herbie at Chu Lai.

Lemon Lemon is a soldier in Delta Company who was a good friend of Herbie's when the two were in the field together. When Delta Company arrives back at CHU LAI in July for a stand-down, Herbie is pleased to see his old friend again, but Lemon is not sympathetic to Herbie's plans to gain revenge on Jorgenson, the young medic who bungled his treatment when Herbie was shot the second time. Lemon defends Jorgenson, telling Herbie the medic has learned a lot and that he has become one of the group. It is at least partly jealousy over Lemon's new friendship with Jorgenson that seems to cement Herbie's plan for revenge.

Olson Herbie, in explaining to readers why American soldiers call the enemy "ghosts," thinks about a soldier named Olson who was killed in February. When Olson died, Herbie reports, "everybody started saying, 'The Holy Ghost took him'" (95).

Pinko Pinko is a member of Delta Company who stepped on a mine sometime after Herbie had been injured and taken to the hospital. Lemon uses the example of Pinko to try to persuade Herbie that the incompetent medic, Jorgenson, has changed: "[W]hen Pinko hit the mine—I mean, the kid did some good work" (93), he tells Herbie, referring to the medic and his increasing skill in the field.

Thatcher, Teddy Teddy Thatcher is the original medic of Delta Company who tends to the story's narrator, Herbie, when he is shot the first time. Thatcher is not only brave, but his jokes calm Herbie down and distract him from his fear. When Herbie returns to Delta Company 26 days after being shot, however, he tells readers flatly that "Teddy Thatcher was dead, and a new medic named Jorgenson had replaced him" (90). Readers never discover how Teddy Thatcher died.

Young, Curtis Curtis Young is one of the soldiers in Delta Company. He is mentioned briefly when Herbie reports that the company arrives at CHU LAI for a stand-down in July. Curtis and a few other soldiers slap hands with Herbie and tell jokes as a sign of their affection for their former comrade

Going After Cacciato (1978)

Tim O'Brien's second novel, *Going After Cacciato*, was published by Delacorte Press in 1978. The story of a squad of soldiers in Vietnam who pursue a simpleminded member of their platoon after he walks away from the war, planning to march all the way to PARIS, *Cacciato* received glowing reviews upon its publication and was awarded the prestigious National Book Award in 1979. The novel depicts both the boredom and brutality of everyday life for American soldiers during the war but at the same time asks large questions about courage and cowardice, about the morality of war, and above all, about the stories we tell about war. While offering a realistic glimpse into the psyches of men trapped by violence, the novel also serves as a metafictive (*see* METAFICTION) and poetic meditation on the power of the human imagination to find a way out of war, to overcome atrocity.

SYNOPSIS

A structurally complex novel, *Going After Cacciato* alternates between three main time frames. The present time of the novel takes place on a late November night in 1968 while Paul Berlin, a young, frightened draftee from FORT DODGE, IOWA, serves guard duty in an observation post overlooking the SOUTH CHINA SEA along the BATANGAN PENINSULA in South Vietnam. During his night in the tower above the sea, Berlin's mind works continuously, revolving back and forth between his disturbing war memories and an imagined story he invents about the pursuit of the deserting soldier Cacciato across Vietnam, into LAOS, Burma, India, Afghanistan, Turkey, Iran, Greece, and finally into PARIS. He ends up staying awake the entire night, not rousing his fellow soldiers to relieve him when his two-hour watch shift ends, or even when the next two-hour stint has expired. This present time is narrated in chapters titled "The Observation Post," brief vignettes that link the other two types of chapters that make up the bulk of the novel: the war memory chapters and the chapters that detail the imagined pursuit of Cacciato. The structure is initially quite challenging for readers to follow. Paul

Berlin's war memories are tangled and chaotic. They do not come to him in chronological order, but rather as his mind conjures them up. Thus, it can be difficult for readers (as it is for Berlin himself), to sort out what happened and when events occurred in these war memory chapters. In addition, the chapters that treat the imagined pursuit of Cacciato are so fully imagined with realistic details that it might take even alert readers some time to realize that these events are occurring only in Paul Berlin's imagination.

FRAMING STORY:

Chapters 1 and 46

The novel opens in October 1968 with what turns out to be Berlin's final war memory before his night on the observation post. A member of Berlin's platoon in ALPHA COMPANY, a large, round-faced boy named Cacciato, has deserted, telling fellow soldiers about his plan to walk all the way from Vietnam to Paris. The platoon commander, Lieutenant Corson, orders the members of Third Squad to set out after Cacciato, who leaves puzzling clues for the men to follow, including abandoned equipment, candy wrappers, and even maps marked with his proposed route out of Vietnam. When squad member Stink Harris trips the wire of a smoke grenade, rigged by Cacciato in order to terrify his pursuers, the men's moods begin to change from curiosity to anger. After unsuccessfully sending Sergeant Oscar Johnson to negotiate a surrender from Cacciato, the squad makes plans to ambush him. Several men are sent ahead through the jungle to cut Cacciato off. When the men are in position, they fire flares. Paul Berlin sends up an answering flare, then shouts "Go," and the chapter ends abruptly.

The very end of the novel, chapter 46, which is titled "Going After Cacciato," just as the first chapter is, will return to this opening scene, offering a fuller explanation of what happened. Readers learn, in this final chapter, that Paul Berlin had panicked during the ambush, shooting his rifle off wildly, and thus possibly warning Cacciato of his impending capture and allowing him time to escape. Berlin was so consumed by fear during the operation that his whole body shook uncontrollably, he urinated on himself, and he lost track of

what was happening around him. He comes back to his senses to find himself on his knees, rocking and swaying with his eyes closed, unsure of what had just occurred. Lieutenant Corson and Doc Peret, the squad's medic, comfort Berlin, telling him that he had experienced an outpouring of the fear biles and that "sometimes it happens" (332), but other members of the squad are not so forgiving. Oscar Johnson mutters "stupid" under his breath while Stink Harris laughs. In any case, the mission fails, and Cacciato is not captured.

Chapters 2–12

While the events described in the opening and closing chapter are war memories that occurred about a month before Paul Berlin's night on the observation post, the rest of the chapters that detail Third Squad's pursuit of Cacciato are part of a long, complex story Berlin imagines during the course of his night watch. He begins by pretending that the squad members had followed Cacciato through the jungle and into the mountains for several more days, before arriving at a river signaling the Laotian border with Vietnam. The men animatedly discuss whether to cross the border or not, debating whether such an act would constitute desertion or simply an extension of their mission to retrieve the fleeing Cacciato. They end up crossing the river and marching through the jungles of Laos for six more days before ultimately taking a vote about whether to turn back. Paul Berlin metaphorically casts the deciding ballot when he votes to move on. But the squad loses its first member at this point when Harold Murphy, who had argued heatedly that the group should turn back, disappears during the night, taking his big gun with him.

Nevertheless, the squad continues its march, eventually moving out of the jungle and into country consisting of broad meadows and plains where deer, antelope, and gazelle graze. When the men spot a swirl of smoke coming from over a line of hills in the distance, they believe they have caught up to Cacciato. They advance cautiously, soon hearing a high squeal. Stink Harris, still smarting from when he tripped the smoke grenade earlier, begins firing his automatic rifle wildly. The smoke, however, turns out to have come not from Cacciato's cooking fire but from a fire lit by two old Vietnamese women who are accompanied by a young refugee and two water buffalo. Stink's shots, unaimed and chaotic, hit both water buffalo, mangling and killing one and injuring the second. The two old Vietnamese women mourn inconsolably at the loss of their beloved pet, and the men are forced to take the remaining members of the small party along with them as they continue their march. Berlin is especially interested in the young refugee girl, Sarkin Aung Wan, who is fleeing CHOLON with her ancient aunts. However, after several days' journey, Lieutenant Corson informs Berlin that the women can no longer accompany the soldiers, that they must be dropped off at the next village. Berlin tries to convince the lieutenant that Sarkin Aung Wan, at least, should stay with the squad, to guide them in their search for Cacciato. When the lieutenant refuses, Berlin desperately tries to concoct a reason for her to stay but can think of nothing plausible. Finally, in what the narrator describes as a "lapse of imagination" (75), Paul Berlin pretends that a giant hole opens in the road and that the squad members, the ancient Vietnamese aunts, the water buffalo, Sarkin Aung Wan, and himself all fall and fall down it in slow motion. It is at this point in the story that most readers realize that the pursuit of Cacciato is no longer taking place in the real world but within Paul Berlin's imagination.

Periodically interrupting the invented pursuit story, as happens throughout the novel, are Berlin's war memories. In chapter 4, "How They Were Organized," Berlin remembers his initial arrival in Vietnam, at the CHU LAI COMBAT CENTER, on June 3, 1968. Bewildered by military protocol and feeling lost, Berlin writes home to his father, asking him to look up Chu Lai in a world atlas. Berlin remembers as well getting lost in the woods of Wisconsin as a child, having gone there with his father to camp as a member of the INDIAN GUIDES organization. War memories arise again in chapter 9, which details the death of Bernie Lynn, a soldier sent down into a VIET CONG tunnel to retrieve a fallen comrade, Frenchie Tucker, who himself had been shot in the same tunnel a few minutes earlier. In chapter 11, "Fire in the Hole," Berlin recalls a DUSTOFF helicopter arriving to pick up the remains

of another fellow soldier, Jim Pederson, who "was a mess" (77). Following the helicopter's departure, the men call in an air strike on the village of HOI AN, completing destroying it, and reducing it, in the narrator's words to "a hole" (79).

Chapters 13–20

Specific details of these war memories will work their way into Berlin's imagined story as he picks it up again. When the men finally land after their surreal fall through the hole that opens in the road, they find themselves in a complex system of underground tunnels built by the Viet Cong, the old Vietnamese women and the remaining water buffalo having vanished, but Sarkin Aung Wan remaining. While the "hole in the road to Paris" (71) in Berlin's imagined story evokes what has become of the village of Hoi An, the underground tunnel system is conjured out of Berlin's memories of the deaths of Frenchie Tucker and Bernie Lynn. Paul Berlin continues his story by imagining that the squad members follow the tunnel's tangled passageways until they finally come upon a large, lighted chamber, where they meet a small man wearing a green uniform, sandals, and a pith hat. The man, whose name is Li Van Hgoc, turns out to be a major from the 48th VIET CONG BATTALION, sentenced to live underground for the crime of desertion 10 years previously. When Li is unable to tell the squad members how to escape the tunnel maze, they overpower him and tie him up, hoping to force an answer from him. But Li Van Hgoc does not know the way out; like the American soldiers, he, too, is a prisoner of the tunnels. To the surprise of the men, Sarkin Aung Wan claims to be able to lead them from the tunnels, stating simply that, "The way in is the way out" (97). She takes the old lieutenant's hand, and the men follow as she guides them single file through the circuitous underground, finally working her way upward until the whole group emerges from a manhole cover onto the streets of MANDALAY in Burma. In Mandalay, the squad enjoys the comforts of civilization; the men sleep in a hotel and eat meals at restaurants while spending their days out on the streets searching for Cacciato. When Paul Berlin finally spots the AWOL (absent without leave) soldier, dressed in a long brown robe and attending evening prayers with a group of monks, he pushes into the crowd, attempting to close in on Cacciato. But Berlin ends up getting crushed in the throng, knocked down and unable to breathe, in a scene that evokes the failed ambush of Cacciato that had occurred in October. When the crowd disperses, Sarkin Aung Wan points out that Cacciato has fled toward the railway station: "The way to Paris" (123).

The war memories that punctuate this segment of Berlin's story include the death of Frenchie Tucker in the tunnels, recounted in chapter 14. While Frenchie's death actually takes place a few minutes before Bernie Lynn is shot in the same tunnels, Paul Berlin's memories come to him in a chaotic fashion. Thus, he recalls the second tunnel death before the first. Readers also learn in this section of a quiet but tense time in July and August 1968 spent playing pick-up basketball games as Alpha Company moves along a series of villages bordering the SONG TRA BONG River. As the games grow increasingly violent, the tension the men feel is broken only when Rudy Chassler steps on a mine on August 13 and is killed. In chapter 20, Berlin remembers more details about the death of Jim Pederson, a loss initially referred to in chapter 11, which recounts the burning of the village of Hoi An. Chapter 20 reveals that Pederson was apparently killed by friendly fire during a combat assault (*see* CA) mission, in which the men were helicoptered into a rice paddy along the Song Tra Bong.

Chapters 21–26
Berlin's imagined journey next places the squad on a train called the DELHI EXPRESS, which slowly makes its way out of Burma and toward India. Believing that Cacciato is aboard, the men carefully and methodically search the train, angering the locals, and reminding Berlin of the shameful memory of frisking villagers back in Vietnam. When the train finally arrives in DELHI, the squad stations itself at the HOTEL PHOENIX, where Lieutenant Corson soon falls "madly in love" (147) with the Indian proprietor, a woman named Hamijolli Chand, who had spent two years studying in Baltimore and subsequently loves all things American. The men stay in Delhi for quite a while, Paul Berlin

and Sarkin Aung Wan spending their days walking, shopping, and eating. The search for Cacciato continues only in a very desultory and halfhearted way until one day when Doc Peret sees in the Delhi newspaper what he believes to be a picture of Cacciato at the local train station. The discovery reenergizes the men of Third Squad, who determine to follow Cacciato to KABUL, AFGHANISTAN, where they believe he is headed. When Lieutenant Corson informs his men that he plans to stay behind with Jolly Chand, they wait until evening, when he has passed out after drinking a whole bottle of Cognac, carry him into a waiting taxi, and load him aboard the train.

Following the brief chapter 22, "Who They Were, or Claimed to Be," which provides background information about several of the men in Third Squad—information not connected to a particular time or place—the remaining war memory chapters in this section of the novel focus on Alpha Company's experiences in August 1968. Berlin first remembers a stand-down at the Chu Lai Combat Center in mid-August when he, Oscar Johnson, and Eddie Lazutti hiked down to the 82nd Commo Detachment to make phone calls home using a newly installed radio-telephone hookup with the United States. While Eddie and Oscar both become emotional after speaking with relatives back home, no one answers the phone at Paul Berlin's home in Fort Dodge, Iowa. In late August, following the stand-down, the men of Alpha Company hike into the mountains between the QUANG NGAI PROVINCE and the border of Laos, a march detailed in chapter 25. Not precisely a memory, this chapter, while written in the third person like the rest of the book, takes on the viewpoint of Lieutenant Sidney Martin, the young West Point–educated officer who initially commands Berlin's platoon. Martin watches the weary soldiers slog up the trail in single file, all the while thinking about the relationship between men and mission.

Chapters 27–37
Back in Paul Berlin's imagined story, the train out of India makes a brief stop in OVISSIL, AFGHANISTAN, where Berlin and the rest of the men stay overnight in the stone house of the town mayor and his wife,

who feeds them biscuits, milk, and mutton stew. Eventually arriving in TEHRAN, IRAN, the men take rooms in a boardinghouse and celebrate Christmas. One day in January in the streets of Tehran the men stumble upon a public execution, a grotesque, disturbing scene, in which a young man of about 20 initially faces death with dignity, but panics when a fly lands on his nose right before the axe falls on his neck. Shortly after witnessing the beheading, the members of Third Squad themselves are arrested and taken to police headquarters, where they are questioned by a sympathetic captain in His Majesty's Royal Fusiliers named Fahyi Rhallon, who wonders why they are traveling through his country so heavily armed and without papers. Although Doc Peret initially satisfies Rhallon and wins the men's release by claiming that the squad is traveling under an invented treaty of 1965, the men are soon rearrested. This time they are not treated so kindly. They must answer to a cruel colonel in the SAVAK, the Iranian secret police, who accuses them of desertion, and they are eventually condemned to death. Again desperate to find a way out of his own imagined story, Paul Berlin, as he did in the earlier tunnel scene, invents an unlikely escape. Cacciato himself appears at the prison window, sets off an explosion, then leads the men through the streets to a waiting getaway car before vanishing into the night. In a chase scene that seems to come straight out of a Hollywood movie but that also evokes the earlier combat assault scene in which Jim Pederson had been killed, the men drive wildly, bullets denting the metal of the car frame. The members of Third Squad eventually outrun their pursuers, making it to IZMIR, TURKEY, where they board a ship bound for ATHENS.

Berlin's imagined story in this Tehran segment has become increasingly more wild, dangerous, and frantic, partly because dawn is approaching and he is in a hurry to find an ending, but also because his most troubling war memories begin to intrude into his mind as the night on the observation post progresses, including memories of the disturbing death of Billy Boy Watkins, who dies of a heart attack after stepping on a mine that blows off his foot. Billy Boy, said to have "died of fright on the field of battle" (208), serves as a potent symbol to Paul Berlin of

what could happen to him if he is unable to control his own fear. But perhaps even more troubling to Berlin are his memories of what happened in an area called "LAKE COUNTRY." The men, led by Oscar Johnson and angry that Lieutenant Sidney Martin has repeatedly risked their lives by forcing them to search Viet Cong tunnels before blowing them up, conspire to murder Martin with a fragmentation grenade. Cacciato is the only member of the squad who does not willingly touch the grenade, a gesture that signals complicity in the plan. This memory, and his own sense of culpability for his role in the murder, remain so painful to Berlin that he never confronts them directly. Readers see the men planning the murder, and they are told that Lieutenant Martin is replaced by Lieutenant Corson, but the fragging (*see* FRAG) itself takes place offstage.

Chapters 38–45
Back in Berlin's imagined pursuit narrative, the freighter that the men have booked for Athens arrives at a dock in PIRAEUS, GREECE. Much to the squad's dismay, the wharf is swarming with customs agents, seemingly making escape impossible. Stink Harris, enraged that the men do not try harder to save themselves, jumps off the ship's deck into the water, not to be seen again. But after Stink's disappearance, the men simply walk through the crowd of police and customs agents with their eyes down and are waved through without incident. After spending a week resting up in Athens, they take a bus to ZAGREB, CROATIA, where they spend the night. Hitchhiking out of town the next morning, they are picked up by a disaffected American college student driving a Volkswagen van, a naïve girl from the counterculture who offers to connect the men with a network of DRAFT dodger supporters, who can help them desert to Sweden. The men end up leaving the girl by the side of the road and driving her van through Austria and Germany. When the stolen van breaks down, they march to a railroad depot and catch yet another train, this time bound for LUXEMBOURG and finally, Paris.

Meanwhile, Berlin's last few war memories involve another stand-down at Chu Lai, this time in September, where he is interviewed for a promotion from Private First Class to the rank of SPEC 4.

He also recalls the death of a fellow soldier nicknamed Buff—short for Water Buffalo—who was found hunched in a ditch with part of his face blown off into his own helmet. But Berlin quickly suppresses these memories and returns to his story, eager to finish it before dawn arrives. Astonished to have finally reached his destination as the train pulls into Paris, in the following days Paul Berlin spends his time as a tourist, visiting VERSAILLES and the EIFFEL TOWER and other famous sights with Sarkin Aung Wan. When the young girl begs Berlin to move out of the hotel where the squad is stationed and rent an apartment with her in the hopes of making their stay in Paris more permanent, Berlin at first hesitates, afraid of abandoning his fellow soldiers, but he eventually gives in. Berlin's dreams of a lasting peace are interrupted, though, when Oscar Johnson and the other squad members arrive at the rented apartment one evening, reporting that they have been picked up by Paris gendarmes and questioned about their military gear and lack of passports. Oscar insists that the men's only chance of avoiding prosecution as deserters is to find Cacciato, who will serve as evidence that the squad members were actually performing a mission, not simply running away from the war. Again, it is Paul Berlin who spots Cacciato after the search begins anew. Berlin follows the runaway to a hotel room in a poor part of town and later reports back to the squad members where Cacciato is to be found.

At this point, Berlin temporarily suspends his pursuit story to insert an imagined scene between himself and Sarkin Aung Wan that mimics the 1968 Paris peace talks (PARIS PEACE ACCORDS) held between the United States and North Vietnam. Berlin sets the scene in a large, ornate conference room. He and Sarkin Aung Wan, wearing headphones and speaking into microphones, debate across a large circular table. The Vietnamese refugee speaks first, arguing that it takes imagination to build a lasting peace and urging Paul Berlin to be brave and to "march proudly into [his] own dream" (318). When it is Berlin's turn to speak, he talks movingly about his obligations to family, town, country, and his fellow soldiers, concluding that "even in imagination, obligation cannot be outrun. Imagination, like reality, has its limits" (321). The

debate over, with Berlin having had the final word, the imagined story reverts back to Paris. The squad members plan an ambush on Cacciato's hotel room, with Oscar insisting that Paul Berlin take a rifle and enter the room first. As Oscar shoulders the door open and someone shouts "Go," Berlin, as he charges through the door into the empty hotel room, is immediately thrust back into the war and into reality: to the actual ambush on Cacciato that took place in late October. Paul Berlin's imagined story has ended. Rather than pursuing Cacciato to Paris, Berlin had shot his rifle uncontrollably, warning Cacciato and allowing him to escape. The men radio in a missing-in-action report for Cacciato the next day, and the novel closes with Berlin and Lieutenant Corson speculating about the odds of Cacciato's making it all the way to Paris.

COMMENTARY

Going After Cacciato is a novel about the Vietnam War, but perhaps more important, it is a novel that explores how the human psyche attempts to deal with atrocity. Paul Berlin's imagined pursuit of the deserting Cacciato during his night on the observation post serves several functions. First, the story is Berlin's attempt to control what Doc Peret calls the "fear biles." Berlin's fear has overwhelmed him on at least two separate occasions in the novel: during the battle in LAKE COUNTRY after the long march into the mountains, when he hid, twitching and shaking, in a small depression in the landscape (177); and during the ambush of Cacciato, when he discharged his rifle wildly, fell shaking to his knees, and urinated on himself. Berlin must attempt to overcome his fear not only because he does not wish to be thought of as a coward by his fellow soldiers but also because extreme fear can be dangerous. One of Berlin's most harrowing memories, after all, involves the death of Billy Boy Watkins, who "died of fright on the field of battle" (208). Doc Peret advises Berlin that the best way for him to overcome his fear is to concentrate: "When he felt the symptoms, the solution was to concentrate. Concentrate, Doc had said, until you see it's just the biles fogging things over, just a trick of the glands" (28). Berlin's imagined story, then, with its exacting, realistic details about the places the men

Two U.S. Marines rest in the rain during a search-and-destroy mission on the Batangan Peninsula. *(Courtesy of the National Archives)*

visit, is just that—an attempt to concentrate, to focus his mind on possibilities outside the war and thus to conquer his fear, at least temporarily.

A second function of the imagined story is to provide order in the chaos of war. Berlin's memories are jumbled and unclear and chaotic. He is not always certain of when men died or even of the exact date during his night on the observation post. "The order of things—chronologies," he thinks to himself, "that was the hard part" (47). For Berlin the war consisted of "stories that began and ended without transition. No developing drama or tension or direction. No order" (287). Unlike the war memory chapters, which appear in the novel out of chronological order, Berlin's imagined story follows an orderly, linear model. The pursuit chapters are told chronologically, and they describe a clear journey from one place to another. These chapters can be read as Berlin's attempt to control his experiences, to impose order—drama, tension, direction—on the confusing and chaotic events he

has experienced during his six months in Vietnam. Readers see other attempts in the novel to provide control and structure in the midst of unsettling war experiences as well. The pickup basketball games that the soldiers of ALPHA COMPANY play during the end of July and beginning of August as they patrol villages along the SONG TRA BONG River are just such attempts. Berlin enjoys the games because "you knew the score, you knew what it would take to win, to come from behind, you knew exactly. The odds could be figured" (109). Unlike the war, where men die unexpectedly and undeservedly, the basketball games operate according to agreed-upon rules, and merit—playing the game well—is rewarded. The critic Tobey Herzog, writing about war literature in general, identifies this need to impose order and control as one of the defining characteristics of the genre: "Within modern war literature, a soldier's pursuit of order and control in his life and in his environment becomes one of the most common responses to . . . war initiation and loss of innocence" (*Vietnam War Stories* 33). Herzog goes on to argue that feelings of helplessness and loss of control can have different outcomes in war literature, especially in the literature of the Vietnam War. Soldiers may either become numb and desensitized to wartime atrocity, they may try to escape their feelings of entrapment through drug use or daydreaming, or they may focus nearly obsessively on the surface details of daily life, the details which they *do* have control over. In *Cacciato* O'Brien portrays Paul Berlin as a dreamer who invents an intensely detailed story in order to overcome his feelings of helplessness and the loss of control he associates with his war memories.

In addition to the practical desires to control his fear and to impose order on chaotic and confusing experiences, Berlin's imagined pursuit story also functions as a metafictive (*see* METAFICTION) meditation on the power of the human imagination. As Berlin begins thinking about the "splendid idea" (26) of Cacciato's leaving the war, he looks at the night all around him on the observation post and wonders, "not for the first time, about the immense powers of his own imagination" (26). His musings are described not as a dream that comes to him passively but as an active idea: "an idea to develop, to tinker with and build and sustain, to draw out as an artist draws out his visions" (27). In order to create a way out of war, the human mind must imagine new possibilities. It is no accident that Paul Berlin thinks of his imagined story in terms of tinkering and building—pursuits that are associated with his father, who builds houses for a living and who tinkers around on Sunday mornings. "His father liked to putz on Sundays. Putzing, he called it, which meant tinkering and dreaming and touching things with his hands, fixing them or building them or tearing them down, studying things. Putzing . . ." (157). As in his previous novel, *Northern Lights*, in which Paul Perry is torn between domesticity and a more traditionally masculine adventurous life, Paul Berlin's imagined story of chasing after Cacciato allows him to explore the pull between the desire to build a domestic life away from the war and the traditional obligations that tie him to the war. Berlin is desperate to find an honorable way out of the war (just as the United States under RICHARD NIXON

strove to achieve peace with honor), and his story constantly returns to the theme of desertion versus mission. It will take a powerful imagination to envision a world in which one can leave war behind, and the novel asks whether the artistic imagination is strong enough to do so.

The novel opens with the scene that will fire up Paul Berlin's imagination during his night on the observation post—the departure of a young soldier named Cacciato from the war. Although readers do not actually witness Cacciato's desertion, the book begins with other members of Third Squad informing the aged and ailing Lieutenant Corson that Cacciato is AWOL and further, that he plans to walk the "eight thousand six hundred statute miles" (5) to PARIS. This scene is set amid the destruction of war. The lieutenant is propped up in a destroyed pagoda that had served as a Buddhist temple in happier days, but that is now "junk," suggesting the ravages that the war has brought to the small country: "Sandbags blocked the windows. Bits of broken pottery lay under chipped pedestals. The Buddha's right arm was missing but the smile was intact" (4). And the Americans have suffered as well, as indicated by the list of the dead members of Alpha Company that is recited in the book's first paragraph. Other images of death and decay abound in these opening pages, from the fungus that is described as growing in the men's boots and socks, to the mention of skin so rotten that it can be scraped off with a fingernail, to the DYSENTERY that has ravaged the lieutenant's intestines. It truly is a "bad time" (1), as the novel's opening sentence informs readers.

Cacciato's departure, then, coming as it does amid such descriptions of death, rot, and waste, offers a startling contrast to the suffering the men have endured. The deserting soldier's destination is "Gay Paree" (3), the City of Light, a place that looms in the Western imagination as the civilized antithesis to the jungles and rice paddies of Vietnam. The romance and historical significance of Paris ignite Berlin's imagination, providing him with a spark of hope in the midst of the horrors of war. Not only is Paris a symbol of the worldly, decadent pleasures that contrast so strongly with the deprivations of life in the war, but historically

Paris suggests the possibility for peace on several different levels. Paris is associated with the beginning of the end of WORLD WAR II, often called "the good war," in which the Allies arrived in the city to triumphantly liberate it from Nazi control. In addition, Paris suggests escape from involvement in Southeast Asia. The French had recently disentangled themselves from their own costly and disastrous war in Vietnam, following the Battle of Dien Bien Phu in 1954. Even more important, as Berlin well knows, Paris was the site of staged peace talks between the Americans and North Vietnamese beginning in the spring of 1968—talks that continued covertly under the Nixon administration in 1969 and into the early 1970s. In fact, it was at the MAJESTIC HOTEL in Paris where the PARIS PEACE ACCORDS that allowed the United States to withdraw its troops from Vietnam were actually signed in 1973. Symbolically, Paris also looms large in the American literary past, in stories that have been told about war—it is the place where ERNEST HEMINGWAY and other members of the Lost Generation lived after World War I, and it is the setting in which Jake Barnes in Hemingway's *THE SUN ALSO RISES* tries to rejuvenate himself after his devastating war injury. The men's march west to Paris evokes as well the frontier and western mythology that permeates much of American literature. Cacciato can be seen as a latter-day HUCK FINN "lighting out for the territories," a young man who runs away to the West to escape the American institutions that have curtailed his freedom. Paris serves as a shining beacon to Paul Berlin, offering him all that the war does not: the pleasures of civilization, the possibility of peace and domestic tranquility, and freedom from the coercive institutions to which he is bound.

Cacciato himself is a figure who ignites Berlin's imagination as well. The young soldier is so simple-minded and childlike that Doc Peret speculates he may be mentally deficient, that he borders on having Down syndrome: "'I mean, hey, just take a close look at him. See how the eyes slant? Pigeon toes, domed head? My theory is that the guy missed Mongolian idiocy by the breadth of a genetic hair. Could've gone either way'" (8). The narrator adds that, "there was something curiously unfinished about Cacciato. Open-faced and naïve and plump, Cacciato lacked the fine detail, the refinements and final touches, that maturity ordinarily marks on a boy of seventeen years. The result was blurred and uncolored and bland" (8). The permanently childlike quality of Cacciato, who remains cheerful and upbeat in the worst of conditions, suggests an innocence, a naivety, that the other members of Third Squad, including Paul Berlin himself, have lost during their time at the war. It makes sense, then, that Cacciato, whose name in Italian means "caught" or "hunted," is the object of pursuit in Berlin's imagined story. Symbolically, Berlin is attempting to recapture his own lost innocence, particularly in light of the fragging death of Lieutenant Sidney Martin. Cacciato's blurry, unfinished nature makes him a ripe subject for imaginative speculation, allowing Berlin to finish out Cacciato's character in any way he chooses. Cacciato, then, becomes the repository for Berlin's uneasiness about his own desire to flee the war. Berlin uses Cacciato to work out his own questions about courage and cowardice, a pressing thematic concern not only in *Going After Cacciato*, but in many of Tim O'Brien's novels and stories.

During the actual pursuit of Cacciato, before Berlin spins the story out in his imagination, the members of Third Squad get close enough to the deserter to observe him through binoculars. As Berlin watches Cacciato through the glasses, he notices that the boy is spreading his arms out, opening them up and dropping them down again. It soon dawns on Berlin that Cacciato is pretending his arms are wings: "flying, Paul Berlin suddenly realized. Awkward, unpracticed, but still flying" (12). While the thought of flight, of escaping the war, appeals to Berlin, Stink Harris immediately squeals the word *chicken* in response to Cacciato's gesture: "A squawking chicken, you see that? A chicken" (12). Stink, then, reads Cacciato's desertion as an example of cowardice. Later, Berlin will contemplate this view of the boy, arguing to Doc Peret that Cacciato did some "dumb things" while at the war, but that he did "brave things" as well (15). "He did some pretty brave stuff," Berlin muses, adding that "You can't call him a coward. You can't say he ran out because he was scared"

(15). What intrigues Berlin most about Cacciato is the possibility he raises that one can desert the war, simply walk away, and yet not be a coward in the usual sense. Berlin tells himself that despite the fact that the "odds were poison" (23), Cacciato still might make it all the way to Paris. He tries hard to imagine a happy end to Cacciato's journey, speculating that he might even have tried such an exploit himself: "With courage, he thought, he might even have joined in, and that was the one sorry thing about it, the sad thing: He might have" (23). Reversing usual notions of cowardice and courage here, as O'Brien does at the end of his story "On the Rainy River," when he writes, "I was a coward. I went to the war," Paul Berlin sees leaving the war as the courageous choice. He eventually does join Cacciato in his journey, but only through his imaginative speculation during his long night on the observation post.

These observation post chapters, inserted periodically throughout the novel, and containing what most critics agree to be the novel's present time, serve largely as metafictional reflections on the powers of narrative as well as on the interplay between reality and fiction. While Berlin is quite literally stationed on an observation post while serving guard duty, metaphorically the post allows him a position outside of his war experiences and his invented pursuit story to observe the workings of his own mind, to "search out the place where fact ended and imagination took over" (27). Berlin realizes that answers to his questions about courage and cowardice, about peace and war, about obligations to himself and others, could "come only from hard observation" (206). Further, Berlin recognizes that observation "requires inward-looking, a study of the very machinery of observation—the mirrors and filters and wiring and circuits of the observing instrument . . . a fierce concentration on the process itself" (206). So, while Berlin examines his own mental processes during his night on the observation post, trying to figure out how his memories shape his imagined story, *Going After Cacciato* also examines its fictive process. A novel that is not only about the Vietnam War, *Cacciato* also explores how we imagine the war, how we tell stories about the war. It asks whether fiction itself,

telling stories, can lead us out of the tangled web of war. "The issue was courage," Paul Berlin muses in his observation tower. "The real issue was the power of will to defeat fear. A matter of figuring a way to do it. Somehow working his way into that secret chamber of the human heart, where, in tangles, lay the circuitry for all that was possible, the full range of what a man might be" (81). Echoing Socrates in the *Laches,* Berlin determines that courage is a matter of knowing "how to act wisely in spite of fear" (80). Yet, the human psyche is described here as a labyrinth that must be unraveled, sorted out, in order to determine what wise action consists of within the bewildering entanglements of war.

The novel's dominant image, in fact, might be that of the labyrinth or maze. *Cacciato*'s complex structure is itself labyrinthine, alternating as it does between the past in the war memory chapters, the present on the observation post, and the imagined future as Berlin invents his fanciful pursuit story. Paul Berlin's experiences in Vietnam are tangled and mazelike as well. From his earliest days in country, Berlin feels lost amid the unfamiliar geography and a bewildering array of military organization and protocol. Sent initially to a large base at Chu Lai, Berlin writes home to ask his father to look up his new location in the world atlas. "Right now," he confesses, "I'm a little lost" (38). Similarly, Berlin must untangle the differences between divisions, brigades, battalions, companies, platoons, and squads, and he must meet and sort out the personalities of his new companions in Alpha Company. Nor does the training provided the young draftee offer him much help in untangling his new position and responsibilities. He attends a lecture on surviving the war in which a "small, sad-faced corporal" (37) gazes out to sea for an hour, never speaking—a scene that suggests war experience cannot be taught but must be lived. No one can lead Berlin out of the maze or untangle it for him. In addition, he endures a training drill that consists of a make-believe minefield—an obstacle course with no physical objects to avoid, merely an NCO (noncommissioned officer) "hollering *Boom*o when the urge struck him" (38). When Berlin complains that the drill is unfair and that there was nothing in the sand to indicate a mine, "no wires or prongs or covered pits to detect and then evade," the NCO replies that of course there is nothing there: "You just fucking *exploded* it" (38). Berlin finds himself trapped in a new, bewildering world in Vietnam, and just as in a maze, there is no clear way out.

But O'Brien pushes the labyrinth imagery even further when he has Paul Berlin imagine Third Squad falling into the complex system of underground VIET CONG tunnels beginning in chapter 10, "A Hole in the Road to Paris." Critics such as Dean McWilliams have briefly noted that the imagery in this section of the novel evokes the Greek myth of Theseus and Ariadne. In the myth the Cretan king, Minos, victorious in a war against ATHENS, demands that every seven years, 14 Athenian youth be sacrificed to the Minotaur, a half-man, half-bull monster who is imprisoned at the center of a maze built by the Greek master craftsman, Daedalus. When Theseus volunteers as one of the 14 youth, the king's daughter, Ariadne, falls in love with him and gives him a ball of string so that Theseus can find his way back out of the maze after slaying the monster. The tunnel episode in *Cacciato*, where this imagery is evoked, is absolutely central to the book and will echo throughout the rest of the story. As Berlin attempts to discover the way out of the underground maze, which suggests not only the bewildering complexities of U.S. involvement in Vietnam but also Berlin's own troubled, tangled memories from which he is trying to flee, he tries on the role of the classic Greek hero Theseus as a possible model for courageous behavior. Berlin uses this well-known myth of heroism to discover whether classical notions of courage and cowardice can help him resolve his fears in a very new and different kind of war. If Berlin can imagine himself into the role of the hero Theseus, it is possible that he can change from passive victim, from the quaking, fearful boy who wildly discharges his rifle and urinates on himself in terror in the novel's opening scene, to the competent, courageous, masculine hero he longs to be.

The underground tunnels first creep into Berlin's imagined story as a way to keep the beautiful young refugee Sarkin Aung Wan with the men of Third Squad: "Paul Berlin could not stop toying with the idea: a mix of new possibilities. A whole new range of options. He wanted Sarkin Aung Wan to join the expedition. He wanted it badly . . ." (59). Paul Berlin's fantasy journey is described as a puzzle, a working out of possibilities; yet, at times, Berlin's imagination fails him. He cannot "imagine a happy ending" (75) to the puzzle of Sarkin Aung Wan's continued presence as the platoon pursues Cacciato out of Vietnam, into LAOS, Burma, and farther west, especially after Lieutenant Corson has informed him that Sarkin and her ancient aunts must be dropped off at the next village. When solving the imaginative puzzle becomes too difficult, too complex, Berlin conjures up the image of a real, physical labyrinth, the underground tunnel system constructed by the Viet Cong. O'Brien writes, "No solutions. A lapse of imagination, so it simply happened" (75). What happens is the tearing open of the earth and the falling of the entire platoon, along with water buffaloes, cart, Sarkin Aung Wan, and her ancient aunts, into a "hole in the road to Paris." Readers know that they've left the realistic world behind when the falling continues in slow motion for several paragraphs, like Alice falling down the hole of the white rabbit in Wonderland.

Paul Berlin's lapses in imagination, the places in the novel where his imagined pursuit of Cacciato becomes unrealistic or even surreal, are directly connected to his most disturbing memories of war, memories that Berlin tries very hard to suppress during his night in the observation tower. It is when these very troubling memories start to intrude into Berlin's mind that his carefully ordered, logical pursuit narrative begins to implode. The "Hole in the Road to Paris" chapter is immediately followed by a war memory chapter called "Fire in the Hole," in which Berlin's platoon calls in an air raid on a village after the death of Jim Pederson. As the village burns, the men line up and fire into it until they are exhausted. "The village was a hole," O'Brien writes at the end of the chapter. The "falling" imagery, repeated over and over when Berlin imagines the hole opening in the road to Paris, evokes the men's actual retaliation against the village—the platoon has "fallen" into the sin and evil of the war. And the tunnel system that Berlin imagines the platoon landing in after their fall is linked to Berlin's

U.S. infantryman in Quang Ngai Province being lowered into a tunnel by members of his reconnaissance patrol, 1967. *(Courtesy of the National Archives)*

most unsettling war memories of all: the deaths of Frenchie Tucker and Bernie Lynn after being ordered to search Viet Cong tunnels as well as the eventual fragging death of Lieutenant Sydney Martin, the officer who orders the men down the tunnels.

After his "lapse" of imagination, when the hole opens up in the road, Berlin imagines his platoon, now in the heart of the tunnel system, encountering the enemy in the form of Li Van Hgoc, a major in the 48th Viet Cong Battalion. Like the Cretan minotaur, Li can be seen at first as a mon-

ster of nearly supernatural proportions. The 48th Vietcong Battalion had a particularly dangerous and almost ghostlike reputation among American soldiers—it was, in fact, the unit being pursued by CHARLIE COMPANY in Quang Nai Province during the weeks leading up to the MY LAI MASSACRE. Li's appearance in the tunnels seems otherworldly as well—he sits in his sandals and pith helmet "peering into a giant chrome periscope mounted on a console equipped with meters and dials and blinking lights" (84). The marriage of nature and technology in this scene—the primitive underground tunnels with sophisticated modern machinery—suggest the chimeralike nature of the minotaur, a creature with the body of a man and the head of a bull. Yet, the platoon members soon discover that, like the minotaur, Li is also a captive of the maze; he explains that he has been banished to the labyrinthine underground by his superiors for desertion. He, then, is the enemy of both the Viet Cong and the Americans, as the minotaur is the enemy of the Cretian king, Minos, a symbol of his unfaithful wife who gave birth to the creature after coupling with a bull, and of the Athenians who must send their youth to be devoured.

Li's particular crime, though—desertion—is especially resonant for Paul Berlin. Throughout his imagined journey, Berlin tries to untangle the problem of desertion. Is the platoon on a "mission" to retake the AWOL Cacciato, or are they themselves deserters? Paul Berlin is trying to find a way out of this puzzle—how to credibly leave the war—yet his mind keeps conjuring up images of what happens to deserters. Li has been prisoner of the labyrinth himself for 10 years. Telling his story to the American soldiers, he describes his years underground as a "terrifying," "insane" experience in "a prison with no exit. A maze, tunnels leading to more tunnels, passages emptying in passages, dead ends and byways and forks and twists and turns, darkness everywhere" (96). Later in the novel, Berlin's mind will conjure up even more terrifying images of the fate of war deserters: a boy beheaded for desertion in TEHRAN, the platoon members themselves held prisoner, their necks shaved closely every morning, possibly in preparation for the same fate. These images signify Paul Berlin's guilt for the real "monster" at the heart of his labyrinthine memories: the platoon's murder of Lieutenant Martin in the underground tunnels. Despite his best attempts to imagine a plausible, orderly exit from the war, his troubling memories keep surfacing to disrupt his imagined story.

To avoid this most painful of all his memories, Berlin returns to the classic Greek story of heroism as he tries to imagine a different ending to the horror of the tunnels. The American soldiers' first instinct is to overpower Li Van Hgoc, to use force to find a way out, as Theseus simply overpowered the Minotaur. Lieutenant Corson tells the Vietnamese major that he is "outmanned, outgunned, and outtechnologized" by the Americans (93). Yet, just as American military power and technological superiority failed in Vietnam, force does not help Berlin's platoon find an exit from the tunnels. Li does not know the way out—"the puzzle," he tells the Americans, "is not yours alone" (95). Despite Li's years of crawling through the tunnels looking for light, and despite the Johnson administration's assurance to the American public that there was "light at the end of the tunnel in Vietnam," the North Vietnamese and Americans are trapped together in war. Like Theseus in the Greek story, Paul Berlin finally imagines himself led out of the underground tunnel system by a young foreign woman, a native of the locale his own country is fighting against. Just as Ariadne, Minos's daughter, had provided Theseus a ball of string to find his way back out of the Greek labyrinth, the refugee Sarkin Aung Wan tells Berlin that "the way in is the way out" (97). Sarkin's motivation is similar to Ariadne's as well. While Ariadne tells Theseus the secret of the maze in exchange for his promise that he will take her back to Athens with him and marry her, Sarkin hopes that Paul Berlin will take her to Paris with him where they can set up house together and escape from war into domestic harmony. Sarkin Aung Wan exists only as a figment of Berlin's imagination, yet she is nevertheless a very significant character. First, as a Vietnamese refugee herself, she suggests that perhaps the best exit from the tangled mess of the war is a Vietnamese-authored solution—national self-determination. O'Brien proposes that perhaps Americans should not be taking the lead in determining Vietnam's future—that role should be played by Vietnamese natives themselves. Second, as a woman, Sarkin Aung Wan represents Paul Berlin's desire to find a way out of the patriarchal mythology of war: the long-standing cultural expectations of manhood and heroism that he cannot fulfill.

A reluctant soldier who dreams of building houses with his father and of settling in a Paris apartment with Sarkin Aung Wan, Paul Berlin, like Paul Perry in *Northern Lights* and like the young Tim O'Brien in "On the Rainy River" from

The Things They Carried, is torn apart by conflicting emotions about his warrior role. Even his name— Berlin—alludes to a city divided into communist East Berlin and democratic West Berlin following World War II. On the one hand, Paul Berlin wants to be a strong, courageous soldier who wins medals for valor, as his culture expects of men. He dreams of being awarded the SILVER STAR and even persuades himself at times that he almost did win it. On the other hand, he hates the violence and sin the war has forced him into, and he longs for the domestic tranquility that his culture labels feminine. Sarkin Aung Wan seems to represent for Berlin a new, imaginative way of thinking about war, a way of thinking beyond traditional gender expectations. And when he listens to Sarkin Aung Wan, Paul Berlin *is* able to imagine a way out of war. "We have fallen into a hole," Sarkin tells him. "Now we must fall out." To "fall out," of course, as the critic Edward Palm argues, is military lingo for leaving orderly ranks, for disbanding or breaking from formation. Sarkin advocates that the men abandon the military mindset and institutions that inevitably lead to war. After the men "fall out," Sarkin leads them through increasingly narrow tunnels, through which they are forced to crawl, until they finally emerge through an iron manhole cover onto the streets of MANDALAY: "Civilization," Paul Berlin says. O'Brien's imagery here is radically revisionist. Via their underground journey, Paul Berlin imagines himself and his platoon reborn from war into peace, with Sarkin Aung Wan as midwife.

Yet, as Berlin will be forced to acknowledge later in his made-up story, civilization itself is not necessarily as peaceful and free of violence as he would like to imagine. When the men of Third Squad stumble upon the public beheading in Tehran, Doc Peret is the first to suspect what is taking place. He suggests to his fellow soldiers that they are about to witness a "spectacle . . . It's one of those true spectacles of civilization" (184). He somewhat cryptically adds, "Can't get away from it. . . . You try, you run like hell, but you just can't get away" (184), suggesting that atrocity exists not only in war but outside of the war experience as well. Doc particularly addresses his comments toward Paul Berlin, whose story this is, after all, directing Berlin to

"*watch* this shit," and hinting that Berlin's predilection to look for the "pretty details" along the road to Paris is dangerously naïve, as it causes him to ignore the political and historical realities that lead to the atrocities of war (186). Berlin's own feelings of shame enter into this imagined story when a fly settles on the nose of the boy facing death. While previously dignified and brave, the boy begins to cry as he cannot get the fly off, and Berlin himself experiences "a wet leaking feeling that smothered fear in shame" (188). Certainly harking back to his own experiences during the ambush of Cacciato, when Paul Berlin shakes uncontrollably and urinates on himself, the experience in Tehran evokes Berlin's fears of being condemned as a coward if he himself should desert. That evening, when the members of Third Squad are drinking in a bar with Fahyi Rhallon of the Iranian secret police, the captain tells them that the executed boy "had merely gone AWOL," adding that, "For true deserters the punishment is not so kind" (201). It is fitting that Paul Berlin images Cacciato saving the men of Third Squad after they themselves have been arrested in Tehran and slated for execution. In Berlin's imagination, Cacciato achieves a seemingly impossible paradox—he is both brave and a deserter. Moreover, as we have seen already, Cacciato retains his innocence in the murder of Lieutenant Sidney Martin and thus does not carry the secret burden of guilt that Berlin does.

This "secret" is specifically referred to in one of Berlin's war memories, detailed in chapter 35, "World's Greatest Lake Country." Cacciato in typical simpleminded fashion attempts to fish in the water-filled craters left behind in a mountainous area of Vietnam after an American bombing attack. Fashioning fishing gear out of a paper clip tied to a length of string, Cacciato makes his bobber from an empty aerosol can of Secret deodorant. In this war memory chapter, the "bobbing secret in Lake Country" (240) is referred to several times and clearly suggests something much larger than the aerosol spray can. The real secret, one that Paul Berlin has trouble facing up to, is the fragging death of Lieutenant Sidney Martin. Berlin, while imagining looking his father in the eye and telling him, "I never joined them—not them—

but I learned their names and I got along" (210), nevertheless *does* join in the conspiracy initiated by Oscar Johnson, willingly touching the grenade to signal his complicity in the scheme, and even trying to talk Cacciato into touching the grenade as well. In fact, several critics have pointed out that the cruel, unnamed SAVAK colonel in Tehran who refuses to listen to the men's excuses and jokes, might be Berlin's imagined version of Sidney Martin. While Lieutenant Corson allows the men to disobey military regulations and blow the Viet Cong tunnels without searching them first, Martin is a stickler for standard operating procedures. He is a no-nonsense officer who values mission over men and who realizes that hard sacrifices must be made during battle. In his imagination, Paul Berlin resurrects a cruel and angry Martin in the guise of the Savak colonel, who sees through the men's machinations and will punish them severely for their transgressions.

Torn by his guilt over Martin's death but still wishing to profess his innocence, Paul Berlin, in chapter 39, "The Things They Didn't Know," imagines justifying his actions to the Vietnamese villagers whom he and his fellow soldiers find so mysterious and unknowable: "Who were these skinny, blank-eyed people," Berlin wonders. "What did they want?" (262). He particularly focuses on "a little girl with gold hoops in her ears and ugly scabs on her brow" (262), inventing a conversation with her in which Berlin makes the little girl realize that he is innocent of any atrocities, that he is, in fact, "just a scared-silly boy from Iowa" (263). He imagines telling her that the two of them are "in it together, trapped, you and me, all of us" (263), just as the American soldiers, the Vietnamese refugee, and the Viet Cong soldier were all trapped together underground in Berlin's imagined story. And again, a figure from Berlin's war memories is transformed into a character in his made-up story. While Sidney Martin is reborn as the cruel Savak colonel in Berlin's imagined pursuit story, this little Vietnamese girl seems to be the impetus for the character of Sarkin Aung Wan. Sarkin, while altered into a beauty in Berlin's imagined story, retains the gold hoop earrings, the youth, and the foreignness of the little girl. Yet, in his imagination Berlin is able

to make Sarkin his ally, someone who understands his predicament, who sees that she and the men in Third Squad are literally all trapped together in the insoluble maze of American involvement in Vietnam.

After Berlin imagines himself actually finding Cacciato in Paris, he must decide what to do next. His mind conjures up a scene suggestive of the American/North Vietnamese peace talks held in Paris. Sarkin Aung Wan and Paul Berlin himself are depicted as diplomats, representative of either of the warring sides. Sarkin is the first to speak, and she pleads for peace:

> "Spec Four Paul Berlin, I urge you to act. Having dreamed a marvelous dream, I urge you to step boldly into it, to join your dream and to live it. Do not be deceived by false obligation. . . . Do not let fear stop you. . . . [N]ow it is time for a final act of courage. I urge you: March proudly into your own dream." (318)

Paul Berlin replies by speaking of obligation. Like Socrates in the CRITO, he acknowledges that one owes certain debts to one's family, friends, town, and country: "Obligation is more than a claim imposed on us," Berlin imagines himself arguing. "It is a feeling, an acknowledgment, that through many prior acts of consent we have agreed to perform certain future acts" (319). While Sarkin argues for the possibilities of a limitless imagination, for the view that we can and must imagine new endings to war stories, invent ways out of war, Paul Berlin ends his rebuttal by stating that "even in imagination, obligation cannot be outrun. Imagination, like reality, has its limits" (321). Berlin thus resigns himself to returning to the war, to accepting the status quo, and to acknowledging the limited ability of the mind to overcome war.

Critics of the novel disagree strongly about how readers are to view this ending. Some argue that Berlin makes a brave decision, others that he is cowardly, still others that he does the best he can in unbelievably difficult circumstances. However, if we read the ending in light of the heroic Theseus myth that runs so strongly throughout the novel, it seems plausible that Berlin's fear of letting go of the cultural mythology he has been raised with is what ultimately traps him in the end. After all, that is what happens to the young Tim O'Brien in "On the Rainy River." He imagines his entire hometown, as well as fictional and historical people from both his real-life past and his Western cultural heritage, amassing on the other side of the river to cheer him on to war. In most versions of the Greek labyrinth story, Theseus abandons Ariadne on the island of NAXOS, whether deliberately or inadvertently. By the end of *Cacciato* as well, Paul Berlin will abandon Sarkin Aung Wan and all that she represents. After trying on the role of Theseus in his mind, Berlin cannot break out of the traditional masculine model of courage represented by the Greek hero. Despite his lofty talk of moral obligations in the imagined Paris peace talks scene, Paul Berlin admits his real motivation for returning to the war: "But please, I don't want to overemphasize all this," he says. "More than any positive sense of obligation, I confess that what dominates is the dread of abandoning all that I hold dear. I am afraid of running away. I am afraid of exile . . . I fear being thought of as a coward. I fear that even more than cowardice itself" (320). Thus, like Theseus who leaves Ariadne behind, Paul Berlin abandons Sarkin Aung Wan. And in abandoning her, he gives up on a new creative solution out of the mess of the war; he gives up on the ability of the imagination to overcome wartime horror and undo patriarchal, heroic tradition.

The Greek myth of the labyrinth then plays itself out in Berlin's mind. In most versions of the Theseus story, Ariadne is comforted by Dionysus after Theseus's departure. When Berlin figuratively abandons Sarkin Aung Wan, she turns to the dissipated Lt. Corson, a Dionysian figure who drank heavily in the past and who has been busted from captain twice. Together, the older man and the young refugee leave the war, determined to march east, "Back to where it started" (325). While the suggestion here is that Sarkin and the lieutenant will try to work their way out of the maze, Paul Berlin, in rejecting the Ariadne figure and the alternatives she suggests, is returned to the labyrinth. The description of the hotel in Paris where Cacciato is holed up echoes the earlier underground tunnel scene. Located in a "dead end alley," the hotel's long dark hallways are like the corriders of the underground maze. The squad leader Oscar Johnson forces Berlin to enter Cacciato's room ahead of him, saying, "Heroes first." The actual moment of breaking into the room suggests Theseus's confrontation with the minotaur. Although the room is empty, Berlin feels great fear and "a monstrous sound hit him. It jerked him back" (330). Berlin's imagined journey suddenly comes to an end, and he is immediately returned to the scene of his greatest shame, when panic-stricken, shaking and whimpering uncontrollably, he wildly shoots off a dozen rounds of his rifle. Berlin is back in the labyrinth of the war, facing it in all its monstrousness.

Finally, the labyrinth Paul Berlin is trapped within is a Western cultural heritage that glorifies war and warrior heroes. The heroic myth of Theseus, which Berlin thought was a way *out* of the labyrinth, is itself a trap. Paul Berlin's failing is that he cannot escape *this* labyrinth. Theseus abandons Ariadne again, and the cycle of war and violence continues. Like the young protagonist of "On the Rainy River," who finishes his story with the line: "I was a coward. I went to the war," Berlin simply cannot break free from received notions of heroism, from the cultural perceptions he knows he will be judged by. "The issue was courage," O'Brien writes, "and courage was will power, and this was [Berlin's] failing. . . . With courage it might have been done" (322–23). The night after the failed ambush on Cacciato, Paul Berlin sleeps deeply, and O'Brien writes that, "There were no dreams" (336). Berlin's dreams of leaving the war, of peace, domestic tranquility, and the pleasures of civilization have faded away. Still, despite Berlin's having to accept the limits of his own imagination, the novel does not completely close off the possibility that a way out of war can be found. The failure of the ambush, after all, allows Cacciato to continue his journey. The book ends with Berlin and the Lieutenant Corson musing about Cacciato's chances of making it to Paris; they acknowledge that the odds are "miserable" (336), but the book ends with the words "Maybe so" (336). Maybe, with courage, luck, and willpower, the suggestion seems to be, human beings will one day be able not only to imagine a world without war, but to make such a world real.

CHARACTERS

Alpha Company Mail Clerk When Paul Berlin joins ALPHA COMPANY at LANDING ZONE GATOR, after having spent six days at the CHU LAI COMBAT CENTER immediately upon his arrival in Vietnam, an unnamed mail clerk asks him how long he has been at the war. Berlin replies that he has been at the war for seven days. The mail clerks laughs and tells Berlin that he is wrong: "Tomorrow, man," the clerk tells Berlin, "that's your first day at the war" (44). The mail clerk is referring to the fact that the next day will be Paul Berlin's first combat mission. The next morning, when a wiry soldier with ringworm in his hair—most likely Stink Harris— asks Paul Berlin the same question, Berlin, a fast learner, replies that today is his first day at the war.

Berlin, Paul Paul Berlin, the novel's protagonist, is a young soldier from FORT DODGE, IOWA, who was drafted (*see* DRAFT) into the war after he dropped out of community college. His father is a WORLD WAR II veteran who now builds houses in Fort Dodge. His mother is an alcoholic who hides her habit by burying liquor bottles in her garden. Berlin arrives in Vietnam on June 3, 1968. In late November of that same year, he spends a night awake on an observation post overlooking the SOUTH CHINA SEA, where he both mulls over his war memories from the previous six months and spins out a fantastical tale about the members of his squad chasing a deserting soldier named Cacciato from Vietnam all the way to PARIS. While Cacciato was a real soldier in Third Squad who went AWOL, telling the men of his plans to walk to Paris, Berlin and his fellow soldiers only pursued the deserter for a brief time, staying within the borders of Vietnam. But in his imagined story, Berlin pretends that the men followed Cacciato into LAOS, Burma, Turkey, Afghanistan, Iran, Greece, and finally into Paris. As the night wears on, Berlin's war memories, which he often tries to suppress because of their frightening and chaotic nature, rise up in his mind to influence and shape the Cacciato story that he is inventing. Readers discover that Berlin himself had

not been a brave soldier but had been overcome by fear in several instances. He has witnessed numerous deaths during his short time in Vietnam, and most disturbing of all, has participated in a fragging (*see* FRAG) conspiracy against his commanding officer. Berlin's Cacciato story is an attempt to control his fear and to provide order to his chaotic war experiences. He also uses the story to work out his feelings about desertion. Just as his surname refers to a divided city, Paul Berlin himself is a deeply divided character, torn between his desire to be brave and fight honorably and his desire for peace and domestic tranquility, his longing to flee the war. Although Berlin tries hard to imagine a happy ending, to invent a way to leave the war without suffering disgrace or shame, he finally has to give up his story, acknowledging that, even imagination, "like reality, has its limits" (321). The novel's final chapter returns readers to the real pursuit of Cacciato, which ends with Paul Berlin in an attempted ambush of the deserter giving in to his fear and firing his rifle wildly, thus allowing Cacciato a chance to escape. The men report Cacciato as missing in action, and the book closes as Paul Berlin and Lieutenant Corson muse about Cacciato's chances of actually completing his journey all the way to Paris.

Berlin's Father Although never given a first name in the novel, Paul Berlin's father is an important character who appears frequently in Berlin's memories of his past before the war. Currently a house builder in FORT DODGE, IOWA, Berlin's father is also a WORLD WAR II veteran who advises his son to look out for the good things that will happen amid the carnage of war. Berlin especially remembers boyhood outings with his father, some as members of the INDIAN GUIDES organization when he and his father donned the nicknames Little Bear and Big Bear, but also camping along the DES MOINES RIVER shortly before Berlin leaves for Vietnam. In Berlin's memories, his father is a kind, understanding man who takes him out for hamburgers and root beer after Little Bear gets lost in the woods and who explains to his son how the houses he built "would be strong and lasting, how it took good materials and good craftsmanship and care to build houses that would be strong and lasting" (48). While remaining largely unspoken, part of Berlin's disgust at his own cowardly behavior seems to be motivated by a desire to impress his father. He imagines himself winning medals in the war, then coming home to tell his father, "I did okay . . . I won some medals" (47), and his father nodding in approval.

Berlin's Mother Paul Berlin's mother, whose first name readers never learn, lives with Paul's father in DODGE CITY, IOWA, where she runs her Hoover vacuum cleaner on Sundays and loves to work in her garden. But underneath these conventional small-town trappings, Mrs. Berlin is also an alcoholic who "buried strong drink" (180) in the garden she loves to work and who "hide[s] booze" (211) in the perfume and lotion bottles that line her dresser. One night, as the members of Third Squad are on patrol outside a sleeping village, they move through a graveyard where the incense-laden air reminds Berlin of the perfumy smell of his own backyard in Dodge City on an earlier evening. His father had discovered his wife's alcohol-laden bottles and carried them outside to burn in a hastily built fire, where they "made sharp exploding sounds like gunfire" (211) and released a sweet odor into the air.

Big Fox Big Fox is the nickname of one of the adult men who participates in the INDIAN GUIDES organization during Paul Berlin's boyhood. In real life, a "gray-haired father from Oshebo, Illinois" (40) who owns a paper mill, Big Fox plays the role of wise Indian chief during the Guides' campout in Wisconsin, telling stories around the campfire during mock Powwows.

Buff Buff is a soldier in ALPHA COMPANY whose nickname is a shortened form of "Water Buffalo," a moniker he won in the war because of his "proven strength and patience and endurance" (146). The shooting of Buff is the final traumatic war death that Paul Berlin remembers during his long night spent on the observation post, the details of which are related in chapter 41, "Getting Shot." Following a gun battle outside of two Vietnamese villages, in which the men never actu-

ally see the enemy, Buff's body is found lying in a ditch, facedown in his helmet. The men drag him from the ditch, and afterward Cacciato is sent to clean out the helmet, which contains the remains of Buff's face, the shots apparently striking him in the head. Paul Berlin remembers feeling not sadness after Buff's death, but relief that he was not the one shot, a sort of relief "you couldn't pretend away" (282).

Cacciato Cacciato is a simpleminded 17-year-old boy in ALPHA COMPANY who simply walks away from the war in October 1968, telling his fellow soldiers that he plans to march all the way to PARIS. A naïve and round-faced young man who loves to chew gum and who remains unfazed by the deaths he has witnessed, Cacciato seems an unlikely candidate for desertion. Doc Peret, Third Squad's medic, speculates that the boy might be mentally deficient, arguing that he missed "Mongolian idiocy by the breadth of a genetic hair" (8). Cacciato, whose name means "hunted" or "caught" in Italian, captures the imagination of Paul Berlin, the novel's protagonist, partly because his daring attempt to make it to Paris seems courageous to Berlin and partly because Cacciato also seems to represent a sort of uncorrupted innocence. During the fragging (*see* FRAG) conspiracy aimed at Lieutenant Sidney Martin, Cacciato was the only member of Third Squad who did not willingly touch the hand grenade that signified complicity in the scheme. Thus, Paul Berlin in his fanciful pursuit story imagines that the men are chasing their own lost innocence as they pursue Cacciato. Although Cacciato keeps appearing in foreign cities, teasing his pursuers forward—he is spotted dressed as a monk in MANDALAY, waiting on a train platform in a newspaper photo in DELHI, shopping at a crowded market in Paris, and even breaking the men out of prison in TEHRAN—he proves difficult to apprehend. When Berlin finally bursts into Cacciato's hotel room in Paris, hoping to capture the deserter in order to prove that the members of Third Squad are not deserters themselves but on a military mission, he is thrust immediately back into the war, and the fate of Cacciato remains a mystery.

Cacciato's Family Paul Berlin remembers that Cacciato used to carry a tattered photo album in his rucksack, with the phrase VUES OF VIETNAM written across the cover. A picture identified as "my family" depicts Cacciato standing with four solemn people in front of an aluminum Christmas tree. Cacciato's father is said to be a "grey-faced" and "worried" man who works as a salesman or actuary. His mother is pretty, "slim and hipless and well-dressed" (119). Rounding out the family are Cacciato's twins sisters, who are both pretty as well.

Chand, Hamijolli Paul Berlin imagines that, when the members of Third Squad arrive at the HOTEL PHOENIX in DELHI, India, Lieutenant Corson falls in love with the Indian woman proprietor, Hamijolli Chand. First spotted behind the registration desk "riding an Exer-Bike" (147), Jolly (as she tells the Americans to call her) is dressed in blue jeans and a gauze muslin blouse. With her plucked eyebrows, "bright carmine lipstick," and "streaks of auburn deftly folded into black hair" (147), she immediately reminds Berlin of his own mother back home in DODGE CITY. The men soon learn that Jolly Chand had spent two years in Baltimore, studying hostelry at Johns Hopkins University, a time she considers "the loveliest period of her entire life" (148). Since then, Jolly has become obsessed with all things American, and she is delighted when the soldiers enter her hotel. Despite having a shadowy husband, Jolly soon takes up with Lieutenant Corson, and the pair is seen laughing and drinking together most nights. When the men become impatient to return to the pursuit of Cacciato, Berlin imagines that they have to drag a drunken and unconscious Corson onto the train departing from Delhi, the old man having become so enamored of his new love that he refuses to leave of his own accord.

Chand, Haques Haques Chand is the tiny, shadowy husband of DELHI hotel proprietor Hamijolli Chand. He silently serves the members of Third Squad a dinner of blood-rare roast beef their first night in Delhi, which Jolly Chand jokingly calls "the sacred cow" (149), a direct insult to her husband's Hindu religion that forbids the consumption

of beef. The next morning, when neither the lieutenant nor Jolly Chand comes down to breakfast, the men are embarrassed as Haques serves them tea, and they speculate about whether it is safe to drink, suspicious that the wronged husband might have poisoned it.

Chassler, Rudy Paul Berlin remembers that the death of Rudy Chassler occurred after a long quiet period in July and August along the SONG TRA BONG River. The men of ALPHA COMPANY had spent their time patrolling the area, searching villages, and playing pickup basketball games to pass the time. The games grow increasingly competitive, several fights breaking out as the days grow hotter and the tension among the men increases. On the morning of August 13, 1968, the platoon moves out to search the village of TRINH SON 2. Rudy Chassler breaks the tense, nearly unbearable quiet of the preceding weeks when he steps on a mine and is killed, a death described in a single sentence at the very end of chapter 16, "Pickup Games." O'Brien writes, "When Rudy Chassler hit the mine, the noise was muffled, almost fragile, but it was a relief for all of them" (110).

Concierge's Son in Paris In PARIS, when Paul Berlin imagines that he and Sarkin Aung Wan are searching for an apartment to rent, the son of a concierge for a building behind LES INVALIDES (a famous complex of museums and monuments in the city) shows them a sixth-floor apartment that overlooks the belfry of a nearby church. The boy tells Paul and Sarkin that the apartment costs only 300 francs a month, with the bugs paying only half that amount, and that the apartment has not been occupied since 1946. Sarkin falls in love with the place, and the two make arrangements to lease it.

Corson, Lieutenant Lieutenant Corson, whose first name readers never learn, is the officer sent to replace Lieutenant Sidney Martin, Paul Berlin's original commander in ALPHA COMPANY, who dies in LAKE COUNTRY. Unlike Sidney Martin, who is fresh out of West Point, Lieutenant Corson has worked his way up through the ranks, has been busted down from captain twice, and is a KOREAN

WAR veteran who loves the U.S. Army, but who does not understand the mess that is the Vietnam War. He understands mission in terms of concrete situations and, again unlike Martin, does not make the men search tunnels before destroying them, which the men love him for. Although he is weak and sick with DYSENTERY throughout much of the novel and said to be "much too old" for this war (43), Corson is included in Paul Berlin's fantasy pursuit of Cacciato, even falling temporarily in love with an Indian hotel owner in DELHI. When the squad finally reaches PARIS, Berlin imagines that the lieutenant, increasingly disenchanted with the war and refusing to pretend that the men are still on a mission, disappears with Sarkin Aung Wan, the two planning to walk the 8,600 miles back to Vietnam.

Crew Chief on Chinook Helicopter In chapter 20, "Landing Zone Bravo," Paul Berlin remembers a combat assault (CA) undertaken by ALPHA COMPANY in which the men are helicoptered into a hot landing zone where Jim Pederson dies from friendly fire. The crew chief of the CHINOOK, described as a "fat man in sunglasses" (128), shouts out the minutes until landing. When the helicopter comes under fire, he screams and pushes the men toward the ramp to unload them as quickly as possible. Pederson, who is frightened both of heights and machines, has to be dragged down the landing ramp and thrown out into the rice paddy by the fat, angry crew chief.

Daniels, Jack On the train on the way to DELHI in Paul Berlin's imagined story, Lieutenant Corson tells Berlin about an experience he had in SEOUL during the KOREAN WAR when he had met a giant SEABEE (a member of the Construction Battalions in the U.S. Navy) named Jack Daniels who took him out drinking one night. When Daniels gets into a drunken brawl in a nightclub, he and Corson are both picked up by the MPs (Military Police), and Corson loses his officer rank as a result. As he tells Berlin, this is the incident in which the lieutenant is "busted" (134) from captain the first time.

Desk Clerk at Hotel Minneapolis When the men of Third Squad arrive in MANDALAY, Burma,

after being led out of the underground tunnels by Sarkin Aung Wan in Paul Berlin's imagined pursuit story, they are directed to the HOTEL MINNEAPOLIS. There, a woman in leather sandals, a greasy brown robe, a mustache, and "a face bubbly with carbuncles" (113) checks them in and leads them to their rooms through the squalor of a dozen naked children sitting on the floors, the desk, and on the stairs. One brave little boy touches Oscar Johnson's hand. Oscar kneels down, allows the boy to touch his face, and says "Nigger," which the child repeats happily.

Door-gunner along the Song Tra Bong On July 8, while the men of ALPHA COMPANY are patrolling along the muddy banks of the SONG TRA BONG River, a resupply chopper arrives. Paul Berlin hands the helicopter's starboard door-gunner a packet of letters he had written to his parents, and the door-gunner tosses back a Spalding Wear-Ever basketball in return. The men will use this gift all through the coming weeks as they play increasingly intense and violent pickup basketball games to pass the time.

Door-gunners on Chinook Helicopter As the members of ALPHA COMPANY are flown in to a hot landing zone during a combat assault (CA) on a Vietnamese village, the door gunners of the CHINOOK helicopter transporting them fire and fire their weapons "in long brilliant arcs like blown rain" (131). Jim Pederson, frightened of both machines and heights but otherwise a good soldier, cannot bring himself to exit the helicopter, so the crew chief throws him off. Once in the rice paddy, Pederson is shot repeatedly by friendly fire from the door gunners. He fires back several times at the Chinook as it is departing, before succumbing to his injuries.

E-8 When Paul Berlin first arrives at LZ Gator to join ALPHA COMPANY, after a six-day orientation period at the CHU LAI COMBAT CENTER in Vietnam, a soldier described only as an E-8, his military rank designation, takes Berlin aside and offers him a rear job painting fences. Although Berlin understands that the man is toying with him, he plays along, smiling at the E-8's question of whether he would like a "nice comfy painting job . . . No paddy humpin', no dinks" (41). The E-8 then delivers his punch line: "Well, then . . . I fear you come to the wrong . . . fuckin . . . place" (41).

Girl from California   When the members of Third Squad leave ZAGREB, CROATIA, in Paul Berlin's imagined story, they hitch a ride north with a girl from California who is driving "a battered VW van that smelled of grease and orange peels" (274). The girl, who considers herself a revolutionary, lectures the men on the happenings back home during the turbulent year of 1968: "assassinations, cities on fire, students swarming through Washington, universities under siege" (274). She believes that the men are deserting the war because they have seen its evil firsthand and naively compares her own situation as a drop-out from SAN DIEGO STATE UNIVERSITY to their perceived status as war deserters. She informs the men, as well, that she has connections with people who can get the soldiers tickets to Sweden, money, jobs, and housing. The soldiers, very ambivalent about their relationship to the war and continuing to insist to themselves that they are on a mission, not deserting, dump the girl by the side of the road and drive her van on through Austria.

Harris, Carla   Carla Harris is the favorite sister of Stink Harris, one of Paul Berlin's fellow soldiers in Third Squad. When Bernie Lynn befriends Stink during training, Stink introduces his new friend by letter to his youngest sister, Carla. Soon, Bernie and Carla are exchanging a daily correspondence. On June 30 Stink finds a naked photograph of Carla performing a jumping jack in Bernie's wallet, and the friendship comes to an end. "Stink Harris was made to be betrayed," O'Brien writes (144).

Harris, Stink   Stink Harris is the point man for Third Squad in their march after Cacciato. A small, rabid youth with ringworm circling through his crewcut, who is said to be "stewing with passions and depressions and petty angers" (143), and who is "made to be betrayed" (144), Stink Harris is the member of Third Squad most eager to

capture the runaway soldier. Stink, after all, is the one who tripped the wire Cacciato had rigged to a smoke grenade, terrifying the men when it went off. Overly emotional and trigger-happy, Stink is also the squad member who, in Paul Berlin's invented pursuit story, opens fire on the pair of water buffalo belonging to Sarkin Aung Wan and her old Vietnamese aunts. Berlin imagines that Stink leaves the squad shortly after their escape from execution in TEHRAN, when the ship the men have booked to Greece docks at PIRAEUS, and they discover that the wharf is swarming with police and customs agents. Stink, furious that his fellow soldiers seem to concede defeat at this point, jumps from the ship into the harbor waters below and is never seen again.

Johnson, Oscar   Oscar Johnson is the African-American buck (lowest rank) sergeant for Third Squad who takes control of the men during the pursuit of Cacciato and who also organizes the conspiracy to FRAG Lieutenant Sidney Martin, arguing that taking such an action amounts only to self-defense on the part of the men. Johnson holds the rank of sergeant because he has survived the war for nearly nine months. Although Paul Berlin realizes that "Oscar Johnson knew very little about surviving" (43), the men look up to him because nine is considered a lucky number, and ALPHA COMPANY is organized largely around luck and superstition. Johnson's background is somewhat enigmatic. Although he claims to be from DETROIT, and although he talks the tough language of the inner city, he can only name Detroit sports heroes from long ago, and his mail goes to BANGOR, MAINE. Thus, the men of Third Squad refer to him as "the nigga from Ba-Haba," as "the Down-east Brother," and as "the dude with lobster on his breath" (142). While Berlin suspects that Oscar's "ghetto undercurrent of pending violence" (142–43) is somewhat too deliberate, Oscar never explains the discrepancy and thus cultivates an aura of mystery and even power about himself. In his invented pursuit story, Paul Berlin imagines that Oscar is the one who insists that Cacciato be captured in PARIS and who shames Berlin into abandoning Sarkin Aung Wan and joining the mission, much as he has persuaded Berlin to touch the grenade that would be used to murder Sidney Martin in LAKE COUNTRY during the war. At the very end of the novel, when readers return to the scene of the late October ambush of Cacciato, Oscar Johnson is disgusted by Paul Berlin's raw display of fear.

Johnson, Mr. During one of ALPHA COMPANY's stand-downs at CHU LAI, Oscar Johnson makes a phone call home. He speaks to his father, a former RTO (Radio Transmission Operator), who had served in Italy during the WORLD WAR II. The usually staid Oscar chuckles over his father's tendency to use military lingo during the conversation; he reports to Eddie Lazzuti and Paul Berlin that his father had said "Over" and "Roger that" repeatedly throughout their conversation.

Korean Stripper Watching students dance in a nightclub in TEHRAN during his imagined pursuit story, Paul Berlin is reminded of a Korean stripper he saw once during a stand-down in CHU LAI. The girl took off her clothes to the same slow and sad song that the students dance to, and Berlin remembers the men singing along and watching her strip, feeling sad and happy at the same time.

Lazzuti, Eddie One of the soldiers in Third Squad who participates in Paul Berlin's imagined pursuit of Cacciato, Eddie Lazzuti has a beautiful singing voice and often sings marching songs and nursery ballads as the men move from village to village. After Billy Boy Watkins dies of fright on the field of battle, it is Eddie who remembers the song whose lyrics go, *"where have you gone, Billy Boy, Billy Boy, oh, where have you gone, charming Billy."* Although Eddie pretends to hate classical music, he tunes in every Saturday night at 6:00 to a program called THE MASTER'S MASTERS, a classical music show broadcast from Danang. After Ben Nystrom shoots himself and leaves the war, Eddie is given the trust of carrying the unit's radio, a position he appreciates because "he prided himself on his voice" (43). While readers do not find out much about Eddie's family background, he seems to come from a large Italian-American clan, possibly living in the Pittsburgh area, since his younger

brother, Petie, is a fanatical follower of the Pirates baseball team.

Lazutti, Mrs. When Eddie Lazutti makes a phone call during one of ALPHA COMPANY's stand-downs in CHU LAI, his mother does not initially recognize his voice, asking "Eddie who?" (155). Eddie tells the other men that when his mother figures out who it is, she "almost passes out" (155), figuring that a phone call from Vietnam must mean that Eddie has been shot or injured.

Lazutti, Petie Petie is the younger brother of Third Squad member Eddie Lazutti. During his phone call home while on a stand-down in CHU LAI, Eddie talks to his brother on the phone. Eddie is amazed that Petie is already in high school and that he now insists on being called "Pete, not Petie" (156). Petie, who is obsessed with the Pittsburgh Pirates baseball team, informs his older brother that the Pirates are out of the pennant race. Eddie good-naturedly tells Oscar and Paul Berlin after the phone call that Petie knows nothing about the war—"Thinks we're over here fightin' the Russians" (157)—and that the Pirates are *all* that Petie knows.

Li Van Hgoc Paul Berlin imagines that the men of Third Squad meet a major in the 48th Vietcong Battalion named Li Van Hgoc in a complex underground tunnel system after falling through a hole in the road to Paris. Dressed in a green uniform and sandals, wearing a pith helmet, and peering into a giant chrome periscope when the men first see him, Li has been sentenced to live in the underground maze for desertion, a crime particularly resonant to Paul Berlin, who struggles with his own longing to desert the war. Li tells the Americans that he is only 28 years old, although he looks 50. He had come from a good family and been a brilliant student when he was drafted (*see* DRAFT). Despite the best efforts of his family to save him from military service, he was inducted into the army, trained as a soldier, and given orders to head south, which he disobeyed. "I . . . well, I ran," he tells the Americans. When he was captured, the trial lasted eight minutes, and he was condemned to live in the tunnels for 10 years. Although the Americans try to overpower Li and force him to tell them the way out of the maze, he replies that he does not know it: "The puzzle," he informs the American soldiers, "is not yours alone" (95). The larger implication here is that the Americans and Vietnamese are trapped together in the war, neither side able to disentangle itself from the complicated political and historical ties that have consigned them to the struggle. When Sarkin Aung Wan offers to lead the Americans out of the tunnel, suggesting that "the way in is the way out" (97), Li Van Hgoc scoffs, calls Sarkin crazy, and tells the Americans to simply accept the fact that they are all prisoners together. He chooses to stay behind when the Americans leave, deathly frightened of returning to the "beastly hell" (98) of the war.

Little Elk   Little Elk is the nickname of one of the boys who participates in the INDIAN GUIDES group that Paul Berlin is a member of during his boyhood years. On one memorable camping trip in Wisconsin, Berlin, also known as Little Bear, gets lost in the woods, prefiguring his later geographical uncertainty when in Vietnam. Little Elk uses his flashlight to find Berlin, who is discovered "bawling under a giant spruce" (41).

Lynn, Bernie   Bernie Lynn is one of the soldiers in ALPHA COMPANY whose death haunts Paul Berlin during his night on the observation post. Bernie, whose death is related in chapters 9 and 14, is shot when he enters a VIET CONG tunnel in order to retrieve Frenchie Tucker, a fellow soldier who had been shot after being sent down to search the tunnels a few minutes earlier. Although Bernie is no friend to Frenchie—he had once poured insecticide into Frenchie's canteen—he becomes angry when none of the men will act after hearing a shot while Frenchie is underground. Swearing, he strips off his gear and enters the tunnel headfirst. Bernie is shot in the throat while his feet are still sticking out of the tunnel entrance. The other men pull him out, and Doc Peret does the best he can for the injured man, as Bernie talks obsessively about hearing the shot that got him. When Doc begins to feed Bernie M & MS, the other soldiers move away,

recognizing this as a sign that nothing can be done to help him. Readers do not find out a great deal of background information about Bernie Lynn, except that he had struck up a friendship with Stink Harris back in June, who had encouraged Bernie to exchange a correspondence with Stink's youngest sister, Carla. Stink is betrayed when he discovers in Bernie's wallet a snapshot of a naked Carla performing a jumping jack. During his night on the observation post, Paul Berlin's memories of the tunnel deaths of Bernie Lynn and Frenchie Tucker prompt his invention of the underground tunnel system that the members of Third Squad fall into when the hole opens up in the road to PARIS.

MARS Attendant   When Paul Berlin, Eddie Lazutti, and Oscar Johnson hike down to the 82nd Commo Detachment outside Chu Lai to make phone calls home, the MARS (*see* Military Affiliate Radio System) equipment is explained to them by a young, friendly private with red hair and freckles who wears a gold wristwatch on each wrist, which he nervously glances at "as if to correlate time" (154). The PFC seems impressed by the fact that Berlin, Eddie, and Oscar are real GRUNTS as he explains the wizardry of how the radio relays work. While Eddie and Oscar become emotional after speaking with family members, no one is home at Paul Berlin's house in DODGE CITY, IOWA.

Martin, Lieutenant Sidney   Lieutenant Sidney Martin is the original commander of Paul Berlin's platoon in ALPHA COMPANY when Berlin first arrives in Vietnam. Martin is a young, by-the-books lieutenant fresh out of West Point who has thought hard about men and mission and who believes that mission must come first in war. Therefore, he follows SOP (standard operating procedures), such as calling in coded coordinates for helicopter DUSTOFFS after men have been injured, even though working out the codes takes precious time, and ordering the men to search VIET CONG tunnels before blowing them up, even though this is an extremely dangerous assignment. Such diligence to duty makes the men of Alpha Company hate Martin. They believe that he risks their lives needlessly and that he is too green to understand the war as it is being fought in Vietnam. When Martin informs the men that they will search tunnels in LAKE COUNTRY, even after two members of the platoon—Frenchie Tucker and Bernie Lynn—had previously been killed in the tunnels along the SONG TRA BONG River, Buck Sergeant Oscar Johnson organizes a plan to murder Martin with a fragmentation grenade. Insisting that his plan is simply a matter of self-defense, Oscar requires all members of his squad to touch the grenade, signaling their compliance in the conspiracy. Although readers never actually see the murder take place—these memories are so painful to Paul Berlin that he cannot face them directly during his night on the observation post—nevertheless, the novel provides numerous hints that the plan was actually carried out. A new lieutenant, Corson, is sent to lead Alpha Company; the men repeatedly mention the "sad thing" that happened to Martin; and there is reference to a bobbing secret in Lake Country that suggests something much greater than the fact that Cacciato is fishing in a bomb crater using an old can of Secret deodorant to weight his line.

Mayor of Ovissil   The men of Third Squad make a brief stop in OVISSIL, Afghanistan on their way to Iran in Paul Berlin's imagined story. There, the town's mayor allows them to spend the night in his stone house. The mayor, described as "a big man with moustaches drooping to his chin" (179), tells Berlin and his fellow soldiers that he is a history-teller, since "fortune-telling is for lunatics and old women" (179). When Berlin asks the mayor to tell his history, the man responds that Berlin is too young and suggests that he come back in 10 years when he has made a real history for himself. This passage can be read as ironic in light of the fact that Paul Berlin does have a deep and traumatic history involving his war experiences—a history that he often tries to repress during his long night on the observation post. While Berlin *is* still young, as the mayor points out, he is no longer an innocent boy.

Mayor's Wife   In OVISSIL, Afghanistan, the wife of the town's mayor, "a sturdy woman on wide hips" (178–79), feeds the men of Third Squad mutton stew and biscuits and cups of milk.

Monks in Mandalay   In Paul Berlin's invented pursuit story, he imagines spotting Cacciato in a crowd of monks heading toward evening worship in MANDALAY. Cacciato, dressed in a "long brown robe" looks like FRIAR TUCK to Berlin and blends in well with the other monks, who are all bald and "smiling Cacciato's vacuous smile" (120). When Berlin pushes into the crowd in an attempt to apprehend the deserter, he falls to the ground, feeling himself to be smothered and crushed by the monks. He comes to consciousness as Sarkin Aung Wan licks his forehead, the monks gone, and Cacciato nowhere in sight either.

Murphy, Harold   Harold Murphy is a soldier in Third Squad who participates briefly in Paul Berlin's imagined pursuit of Cacciato. A big man, Harold Murphy is entrusted with carrying the unit's largest weapon: the "big gun" (35). But Murphy is skeptical about the squad's decision to follow Cacciato across the Vietnamese border and into LAOS. When the men take a vote whether to keep going or turn back after they have spent six days marching through the Laotian jungle, Murphy argues for turning back, pointing out that what the men are doing amounts to desertion: "Desertion . . . that's the word. Running off like this, it's plain desertion. I say we get our butts back to the war before things get worse" (35). Paul Berlin, however, casts the deciding vote, determining that the men will continue their pursuit. The next morning, Harold Murphy and his big gun are gone, and the men continue on their westward trek without him.

NCO 1 at Chu Lai   When Berlin first arrives at the CHU LAI COMBAT CENTER in June 1968, he undergoes a peculiar training drill, in which an unnamed Non-Commissioned Officer (NCO), "a huge black man" randomly yells "Boomo" as the men navigate their way through an obstacle course. When Berlin complains that the drill is unfair, that there was nothing in the sand to indicate a mine, the NCO simply smiles and replies, "Course not, you dumb twerp. You just fucking *exploded* it" (38). This scene indicates the illogic and random nature of how death and injury come to the members of

ALPHA COMPANY. Survival for Berlin and his fellow soldiers seems more a matter of luck than skill.

NCO 2 at Chu Lai Berlin recalls a second non-commissioned officer (NCO) at the CHU LAI COMBAT CENTER, the youngest of all the NCOs, who is described as "a sallow kid without color in his eyes" (39). This NCO tells a cautionary tale to the young, green soldiers about a man named Uhlander, who died because "he made the mistake of thinking [the war] wasn't so bad" (39). The young NCO concludes his lecture by insisting that the war is indeed bad, that it is evil in fact, and that the men he is speaking to "are gonna *die*" (39).

Nguyen Nguyen is the name of the water buffalo that is shot to death by Stink Harris in Paul Berlin's invented pursuit story. Nguyen had been the beloved pet of the two old Vietnamese aunts of Sarkin Aung Wan. The girl tells Paul Berlin, in fact, that the aunts had raised Nguyen from a tiny baby, suckling him at their own breasts. The old women mourn their lost pet every night they travel with Third Squad, howling and wailing for hours. A scene similar to the death of Nguyen occurs in O'Brien's later novel *The Things They Carried* when Rat Kiley and others shoot to death a baby water buffalo in anger and frustration following the death of their comrade, Curt Lemon.

Nystrom, Ben Ben Nystrom is a radio operator in ALPHA COMPANY who cries uncontrollably when Bernie Lynn is shot in the Vietnamese underground tunnel after being sent down to retrieve the body of Frenchie Tucker. In early August, during the bad times along the SONG TRA BONG River, Nystrom has another collapse, in which he lies faceup on the trail, cradling his head and unable to stop crying. Soon after, Nystrom will deliberately shoot himself in the foot in order to get sent home from the war. He writes no letters to the men after he has left.

Officers at the Battalion Promotion Board In September 1968, after he has been in the war for several months, Paul Berlin is called before the battalion promotion board to be considered for a promotion to the rank of Specialist Four. The board is made up of a three-officer panel. A "plump, puffy-faced major with spotted skin" and sunglasses (265) asks Berlin about his name, commenting that it does not sound American. A captain dressed in tiger fatigues participates in the questioning as well, playing straight man as the major asks Berlin if he is a "Jewboy," and dishes out other insults. The third officer sits silently during most of the review, speaking only to supply an answer to the question of why the Americans are fighting this war: "To win it," he says (268). When the major asks Paul Berlin what effect the death of HO CHI MINH would have on the population of North Vietnam, Berlin realizes that he will win the promotion. He replies, "Reduce it by one, sir" (269) and is promoted to the rank of SPEC 4.

Old Vietnamese Man Paul Berlin in his invented pursuit story imagines that he and the other members of Third Squad search the DELHI EXPRESS train as they hunt for Cacciato. As the soldiers frisk the Indian peasants, Berlin is reminded of the shameful searching of villagers that he and his fellow soldiers were forced to undertake in Vietnam. He particularly recalls frisking a patient but scrawny old man "dressed in white shorts, nothing else, wisps of thin hair on his chin like Ho Chi Minh" (138). The old man has a caved-in chest and sores in his mouth, and Berlin is ashamed and inwardly apologetic as he searches the man. He imagines justifying himself to the old villager—"*I don't like it either, nobody likes it, but we do what we do*" (138)—and the man responding with a smile as if he understands the situation and forgives Berlin.

Pederson, Jim Jim Pederson is another one of the soldiers in ALPHA COMPANY whose death Paul Berlin remembers while serving guard duty on the observation post in late November 1968. Pederson, a deeply religious man who carries picture postcards of Christ to hand out to any Vietnamese he sees wearing a crucifix or carrying rosary beads, is also said to be the most trusted member of Third Squad. Because of this, he is given the responsibility of triggering ambushes when out on patrol. Pederson is perhaps the most moral of the men Berlin meets in the war as well, one time giving first aid to a dying VIET CONG woman and writing a letter to Billy Boy Watkins's parents after their son dies. Because Paul Berlin's memories are so jumbled and chaotic, readers first experience the aftermath of Pederson's death, described in chapter 11, "Fire in the Hole," before they are given a description of the death itself. Chapter 11 begins, "Pederson was a mess" (77). The men wrap Pederson in his poncho, slip his broken dog tags into his mouth and wait for the DUSTOFF. Later, and seemingly in revenge for the death, the lieutenant orders an air strike on the nearby village of HOI AN. The men watch as the village burns, eventually lining up and firing their weapons into the smoke-filled, destroyed hamlet. O'Brien at the end of this chapter writes, "The village was a hole" (79), linking Paul Berlin's imagined story of the squad falling and falling through a hole in the road on the way to PARIS into an underground tunnel complex with this memory of what happened after Pederson's death.

The death itself is not described until chapter 20, "Landing Zone Bravo," which details Berlin's memory of a combat assault (*see* CA) mission along the SONG TRA BONG River, near the village of Hoi An. When the helicopter carrying the members of Third Squad attempts to make a landing, they come under heavy fire. Jim Pederson, afraid of flying and of machines to begin with, has to be pushed out of the helicopter and into the rice paddy at the last minute. As he wades into the muddy water, he is accidentally shot several times by the door gunners of the U.S. helicopter that choppered the men in. The chapter ends with Pederson calmly lying down in the paddy and firing back at the helicopter. The memory of Pederson's death will later work its way into Berlin's imagined pursuit story of Cacciato when the men make their escape from a prison in TEHRAN. The getaway car is cold and windy and strafed by whizzing bullets that sink into its metal, just as the helicopter had been in this earlier scene.

Peret, Doc Third Squad's medic and resident philosopher, Doc Peret feeds the men M&Ms when they are mortally injured, diagnoses Paul Berlin as having a case of the "fear biles," and minis-

ters to the ailing Lieutenant Corson. Described as having grey eyes behind wire-rimmed spectacles, a straight nose, thin lips, and a tall frame, Doc Peret is a chain smoker who believes deeply in science but who is also a pragmatist unafraid to diagnose Billy Boy Watkins as having died of fright on the field of battle. In many ways Doc motivates Paul Berlin's imagined story about Cacciato by advising the young draftee that he can control his fear by concentrating, telling Berlin to "look for motives, search out the place where fact ended and imagination took over. Ask the important questions" (27). If Oscar Johnson is the shadow leader of Third Squad, Doc Peret is the brains of the outfit. He is the one who makes up a fictional "Mutual Military Travel Pact of 1965" that initially gets the men out of trouble after they are arrested in TEHRAN. He is also the one who stays up late into the night debating Captain Fahyi Rhallon about whether wars have separate identities or whether they all feel alike to soldiers on the ground. In the final chapter, when readers realize that Paul Berlin had been overcome by fear and shot off his rifle uncontrollably during the ambush of Cacciato, Doc Peret is sympathetic, soothing the frightened young man and offering him Kool-Aid from his canteen, joking that it is a vintage Chablis.

Prisoner in Tehran In his invented story about the pursuit of Cacciato, Paul Berlin imagines the members of Third Squad stumbling upon a public execution in TEHRAN. A young soldier of about 20 years old, with his hands bound behind him, is brought to a platform crowded with flags and banners and army officials. The boy maintains his dignity during the proceedings, keeping his eyes level, his spine erect, acceding courteously to having his neck shaved and listening politely as several speeches are made by officers. However, at the moment before the execution, as the boy's head is being pushed down onto the execution block, a fly alights on the tip of his nose. The boy twists his head in a panic, flicks out his tongue, and tries vigorously to dislodge the fly, but unsuccessfully. As Paul Berlin watches in horror, he realizes that the tears in the boys eyes signify not fear but shame at the indignity he is being forced to undergo. The beheading is carried out with the fly still perched on the boy's nose. Later, the men are informed that the boy had been executed for being AWOL from the army, a crime that speaks to Paul Berlin's own tormented struggle over the issue of desertion. This incident also suggests that atrocities are not limited to wartime; Doc Peret angrily orders Paul Berlin to watch the spectacle closely, suggesting that the "Civilization" (186) Berlin has longed for is tainted and corrupt as well.

Radio Voice   In the opening chapter, while the members of Third Squad are actually pursuing Cacciato before the story gets spun out in Paul Berlin's imagination, Lieutenant Corson radios back to headquarters that the squad is in pursuit of the enemy. An unnamed voice responds over the radio, asking if gunships are needed. When the lieutenant replies in the negative, the radio voice, like a pushy salesman, tries to interest him in some artillery or ordnance, or even illumination rounds. The lieutenant finally extracts himself from the conversation, calling the radio voice a "monster" (13).

Ready Mix   Ready Mix is a soldier who is with ALPHA COMPANY only 12 days before being shot in LAKE COUNTRY as the men advance into what Paul Berlin remembers as "the one big battle of the war" (177) after a long, exhausting march into the mountains. Described as an "Instant NCO, a pimpled kid with sergeant's stripes earned in three months of statewide schooling" (146), Ready Mix is not mourned by the men because it was expected he would die quickly, and he did. His fellow soldiers in Alpha Company never even bothered to learn his full name.

Rhallon, Fahyi   When the members of Third Squad are first arrested in Tehran in Paul Berlin's imagined pursuit story, they are questioned by a "tall, gaunt man with a neat moustache and deeply tanned skin" (189) named Fahyi Rhallon, a captain in His Majesty's Royal Fusiliers recently transferred to temporary duty with the SAVAK or Iranian secret police. Unfailingly polite, helpful, and self-deprecating, captain Rhallon listens intently to Doc Peret's lies about the soldiers traveling under

a mutual treaty ratified in Geneva in 1956. Promising to study the rules more carefully in the future, the Captain insists that he buy the American soldiers drinks to compensate for the inconvenience they have suffered. He escorts them to a nightclub, where students dance long after curfew. There, he and Doc Peret engage in a thoughtful argument about the nature of war, Peret arguing that all wars feel alike to the men fighting them, and Fahyi Rhallon maintaining that each war has "an identity separate from perception" (196). Later, when the men are rearrested, Captain Rhallon, despite his best efforts, is unable to help them.

Sarkin Aung Wan   Sarkin Aung Wan is a young, beautiful, half-Chinese, half-Vietnamese refugee whom Paul Berlin imagines meeting in his invented pursuit story of Cacciato. Fleeing from the town of CHOLON, which had become a combat zone during the war, her own father having been executed by VIET CONG cadres, Sarkin is traveling west with her two ancient Vietnamese aunts in a cart pulled by a pair of water buffalo. After Stink Harris accidentally shoots one of their water buffalo to death, the men allow the three women to accompany the squad for a short time. The aunts disappear when Paul Berlin imagines a huge hole opening in the road to PARIS. Sarkin Aung Wan, however, stays in Berlin's story, even leading the members of Third Squad out of the complex system of underground tunnels that they have fallen into, much like Ariadne guiding Theseus out of the labyrinth in the well-known Greek myth. Since she exists only as a figment of Paul Berlin's imagination, it is not surprising that Sarkin Aung Wan has some of the qualities of the stereotypical Asian geisha girl. She attends to her looks assiduously, rubbing her body with creams and oils, and she ministers to Paul Berlin by clipping his toenails, massaging him, and performing other small services. There is a sense, however, that this relationship is fragile and innocent in Berlin's mind—thus, he never actually pictures himself making love to Sarkin, as if afraid of tipping his story into mere sexual fantasy. Sarkin also seems to represent a part of Berlin's own torn psyche, especially in the scene of the mock Paris peace talks, in which the two formally debate about whether Paul Berlin should leave the war or not. Sarkin urges Berlin to step into his imagination and make it real, to create a happy ending, but Berlin responds that he has too many obligations to family, to community, and to his fellow soldiers. Following this scene, Sarkin departs with the older Lieutenant Corson, the two claiming that they plan to reverse their route and walk all the way back from Paris to Vietnam.

Sarkin's Father   Paul Berlin in his invented pursuit story imagines the young refugee Sarkin Aung Wan telling him that her father "died in childbirth" (53). Sarkin's father had owned a restaurant in CHOLON, Vietnam, where many Chinese people lived. However, he was shot to death by a VIET CONG cadre for supposedly pilfering chickens from the cadre's slaughterhouse. Sarkin's father is captured in a hospital waiting room as his wife is giving birth to twin babies. He is led out of the waiting room and executed against a hospital wall. When Sarkin's mother dies of grief two years later, the family disperses, and Sarkin heads west with two ancient aunts to become a war refugee.

Sarkin's Mother   Sarkin Aung Wan's mother dies of grief two years after her husband is executed for allegedly pilfering chickens from the slaughterhouse of a VIET CONG cadre. She had been in the hospital giving birth to twin babies when her husband was captured and shot. Following her mother's death, Sarkin's large, extended family breaks apart and scatters all over the country. CHOLON has become a combat zone, and Sarkin, along with her numerous brothers and sisters, has no choice but to leave the city.

Sarkin's Uncle   An uncle of Sarkin Aung Wan takes over the family's restaurant in CHOLON after Sarkin's father is executed by a VIET CONG cadre.

Savak Colonel   Paul Berlin imagines that the members of Third Squad are rearrested in TEHRAN after having been released by the friendly Captain Fahyi Rhallon upon their initial arrest. This time they are interrogated by a cruel colonel in the SAVAK, the Iranian Internal Security force, who

"could have been Rahyi Rhallon's twin: dark skin, a moustache, creased trousers" (229). This man's resemblance to Captain Rhallon is only skin deep, however. The Savak colonel refuses to listen to the American soldiers' jokes and excuses, crushing Oscar's sunglasses when he does not immediately remove them, breaking Oscar's nose with his elbow, and brutally smashing Paul Berlin in the face when Berlin cannot stop smiling. The colonel forces the men to confess that they "ran like pigs" and that they are "clowns" (231), notions that Paul Berlin has been trying to deny in his invented story. Several critics read the Savak colonel as a transformed version of the real-life Lieutenant Sidney Martin. While Martin was never cruel to the members of ALPHA COMPANY, he was a no-nonsense commander who insisted on following Standard Operating Procedures (SOP) and who did not allow the men to evade dangerous duties such as searching the VIET CONG tunnels. Berlin's guilt over the fragging (*see* FRAG) death of Sidney Martin perhaps works its way into his imagined story in the form of the Savak colonel who refuses to let the men off the hook for their crimes.

Stone, Mrs.   When Paul Berlin unsuccessfully tries to call home during a stand-down in CHU LAI, he decides that he will get his father to talk about their crazy neighbor, Mrs. Stone—a topic Berlin deems to be "fun and cheerful" (158), something that will allow him to avoid having to talk about the war. Berlin remembers that Mrs. Stone's backyard was always immaculate. The old woman would use her broom to sweep it in all kinds of weather, even sweeping snow away during blizzards.

Trainmaster of the Delhi Express   When the men of Third Squad search the DELHI EXPRESS train, frisking passengers, going though luggage, and creating a general uproar, Paul Berlin imagines that the trainmaster approaches them wielding a huge wrench and screaming "*Shame!*" (139). Described as "bearded," with his "head wrapped in an oily linen turban" and a face that shines "like varnish," the trainmaster becomes increasingly agitated by the American soldiers, screaming "*Evil! Wicked! . . . Illegal!*" at them and waving his wrench around like a sword (139). When the trainmaster incites a mob that begins to approach Berlin and his fellow soldiers, the Americans barely escape by stepping into the neighboring first-class compartment and locking the door. Berlin mutters "*Savages*" after this experience, forgetting his own previous shame at the role he was forced to play in the humiliating search.

Tucker, Frenchie Frenchie Tucker is a soldier in ALPHA COMPANY who dies after being ordered to search a VIET CONG tunnel, most likely sometime in August while the men are conducting operations along the SONG TRA BONG River. The details of Frenchie's death are first mentioned in chapter 9, "How Bernie Lynn Died After Frenchie Tucker," and explained in more detail in chapter 14, "Upon Almost Winning the Silver Star." A passionate man who becomes enraged when his fellow soldiers refuse to consider larger political questions, Frenchie is also a "big hairy guy who was scheduled to take the next chopper to the rear to have his blood pressure checked" (89) and thus an unlikely candidate to serve as a tunnel rat. But when Lieutenant Sidney Martin tells Frenchie that "it was a matter of going down or getting himself court-martialed" (89), the big man strips off his pack and boots and socks and helmet, barely wiggling his whole body into the enclosed space and disappearing from sight before the men hear a shot. Hoping desperately that Frenchie is all right, the men at first wait, until it becomes clear that someone will have to go down after him. A soldier named Bernie Lynn, swearing in anger at the other men's inaction, eventually drops his gear and enters the tunnel headfirst. He, too, is shot, although he is still alive when first pulled out of the tunnel by his feet. Frenchie's body is eventually pulled out as well, his T-shirt crumpled up around his arm pits, his fat white belly exposed and his head turned to the side. Bernie Lynn will die soon after.

Uhlander Uhlander is a soldier who supposedly died in Vietnam after making the mistake of believing that the war was not that bad. Paul Berlin is told the story of Uhlander by a young Non-Com-

missioned Officer (NCO) at the CHU LAI COMBAT CENTER, who is trying to scare the green recruits.

Ulam, Sergeant Sergeant Ulam is the arresting officer who apprehends the members of Third Squad in TEHRAN in Paul Berlin's imagined pursuit story. Ulam believes the men are American soldiers traveling without passports. Captain Fahyi Rhallon, the interrogating officer, however, seems to believe Doc Peret's lies about a mutual treaty and tells the men of Third Squad that he will inform Sergeant Ulam that he is "loco" (190), that his accusations are mistaken.

Vaught Vaught is a soldier in ALPHA COMPANY who had been a friend of Cacciato's. In September 1968, however, before Cacciato's desertion in late October, Vaught had contracted an infection from scraping a layer of mushy skin off his forearm with his bayonet. He is sent to a hospital in Japan to recover and writes a letter back to his buddies in Alpha Company, enclosing a snapshot of himself with two pretty nurses. The men are shocked to learn later that Vaught's infected arm had been amputated.

VietCong Boy Shot by Cacciato Several times during his night on the observation tower, Paul Berlin remembers a VietCong boy who was shot by Cacciato. When he first learns that Cacciato has walked away from the war, Berlin remembers some of the unexpected things the young soldier had done, "like winning the Bronze Star for shooting out a dink's front teeth" (8). Later, talking to Doc Peret, Berlin argues that Cacciato is not a coward, that he, in fact, did "some pretty brave stuff" like "the time he shot that kid. All those teeth" (15). Musing that he had never seen the living enemy, Berlin recalls that he "had seen Cacciato's shot-dead VC boy" (85). The dead VC boy appears again when Paul Berlin remembers Cacciato's tattered photo album, entitled *VUES OF VIETNAM*. Included inside is a photograph of Cacciato squatting beside the corpse of the dead VC boy, who is clad in green pajamas. In the picture Cacciato is holding up the dead boy's head by his hair and smiling (120).

Vietnamese Aunties During Berlin's imagined pursuit of Cacciato, the members of Third Squad come upon the smoke of a cooking fire. Believing this to be an indication of the missing Cacciato and startled by a loud squealing noise, Stink Harris shoots his gun wildly. It turns out that the men have stumbled not upon their missing comrade but upon two very old Vietnamese women refugees traveling with their young, beautiful niece, Sarkin Aung Wan. Stink has killed a water buffalo that the two old women raised from infancy, and the ancient aunts cry and wail inconsolably for their lost Nguyen. The men have no choice but to bring the women along with them. Every evening the two old women continue their wailing and moaning for the lost water buffalo. When Lieutenant Corson tells Paul Berlin that the Vietnamese women will have to be dropped off at the next village, Berlin, wanting to keep Sarkin Aung Wan along but unsure how to imagine a coherent reason for this, has what the narrator calls a "lapse of imagination" (75), and he pretends that a giant hole opens up in the road to PARIS swallowing up the men, the cart, the remaining water buffalo, the Vietnamese aunts, and Sarkin Aung Wan, who all fall down through the hole as if in slow motion. When the squad finally hits the ground, the Vietnamese aunts and their remaining water buffalo have mysteriously disappeared, leaving Sarkin Aung Wan behind.

Vietnamese Girl with Gold Hoop Earrings In chapter 39, "The Things They Didn't Know," Paul Berlin remembers meeting a little girl "with gold hoops in her ears and ugly scabs on her brow" (262) in one of the nameless Vietnamese villages that the men search. Berlin, as he desperately wonders about the villagers—"Who were these skinny, blank-eyed people? What did they want" (262)—imagines justifying his motives to this little girl. He would like to tell her that he is "just a scared silly boy from Iowa" and that the two of them are in the war together, "trapped, you and me, all of us" (263). This little girl seems to be the impetus for the character of Sarkin Aung Wan in Berlin's imagined pursuit story, who is trapped in the underground tunnels with the men of Third Squad in the first part of the book. Sarkin is described as young,

anywhere from age 12 to 21, and she retains the gold hoop earrings of the real village girl, although she is transformed into a beauty in Berlin's imagination. And in his made-up story, Berlin befriends Sarkin, even falls in love with her, so that the rift between the Vietnamese and the Americans is at least partially healed. Yet, at the end of the novel, Berlin imagines Sarkin leaving PARIS and himself returning to the war, finally unable to escape and create a new life for himself or to overcome the immensity of the "The Things They Didn't Know" about the Vietnamese and the war.

Vietnamese Scout In chapter 25, "The Way It Mostly Was," Paul Berlin remembers a platoon of soldiers from ALPHA COMPANY making a long, arduous march into the mountains to join a battle, while Lieutenant Sidney Martin watches them and thinks about mission and the duties of soldiers during wartime. The 38 American soldiers are led by a young Vietnamese scout who is a mere boy of 13. The boy's apparent fearlessness in leading the column contrasts with Paul Berlin's knowledge that he will not fight well. Although Berlin mentally decides to simply stop marching and fall down beside the road, his legs continue to carry him up the mountain against his will, and he eventually joins the battle, along with the other members of his platoon.

Waiter in Mandalay When the members of Third Squad arrive in MANDALAY, Burma, Paul Berlin imagines that they eat dinner at a rooftop restaurant, where a waiter serves them fried fish and later brings them wine and "seven thimble-sized glasses of orange liquid" (118). The men toast their lieutenant, Sarkin Aung Wan, Oscar Johnson, and several dead members of ALPHA COMPANY before ending the evening by drinking a toast to Cacciato.

Watkins, Billy Boy Billy Boy Watkins was a fellow soldier of Paul Berlin's in ALPHA COMPANY who was said to have "died of fright on the field of battle" (208). Although somewhat confused about chronology, Berlin remembers that Billy Boy died in June, on what Berlin thinks of as his first day at the war—the first day that he actually sees action. Berlin had arrived in Vietnam on June 3, 1968 and joined Alpha Company on June 11. Alpha Company's mail clerk tells Berlin that the next day, June 12, will be Berlin's first day in the war, and Berlin, learning quickly, tells Stink Harris the next morning that it is his first day in the war. This puts Billy Boy's death on June 12, 1968. But the story of how Billy Boy died is one of Berlin's worst war memories and one that he represses for as long as he can during the long night he spends on the observation post, spinning out his tale about the pursuit of Cacciato. Nevertheless, despite Berlin's best efforts not to think about what happened to Billy Boy, the memories come back to him. In Berlin's invented pursuit story, the men of Third Squad are in TEHRAN, drinking at a bar with Captain Fahyi Rhallon when they begin to tell war stories. Doc Peret is urged by the other men to tell the captain "the ultimate war story" (203)—the death of Billy Boy Watkins. Although Paul Berlin imagines that he feels sick and has to leave the bar as Doc begins to speak, the details of Billy Boy's death are related in the following war memory chapter, "Night March." Berlin remembers a hot afternoon, the men taking target practice at a brightly colored row of Coke cans, then setting out on a march. Soon after, Billy Boy trips a mine, which blows his foot, still laced into his boot, right off his leg. Although Doc Peret reassures Billy Boy, explaining that he's got a "million-dollar wound" (216) that is sure to get him sent home from the war, Billy Boy panics, trying clumsily to put the boot, with his foot still in it, back on his leg. The panic increases until Billy Boy suffers a heart attack and dies. This story is particularly frightening to Paul Berlin because he, too, has what Doc refers to as an "excess of fear biles" (28). Berlin worries that if he is unable to control his fear, a similar fate could befall him.

Wiertsma, Louise   During his night on the observation post, Paul Berlin, sounding like Lieutenant Jimmy Cross from the story "The Things They Carried," with his memories of Martha, remembers a girl from high school named Louise Wiertsma, who "had almost been his girlfriend" (180). Ber-

lin had taken Louise to the movies, and the two had talked meaningfully afterward. Berlin had even "pretended to kiss her" (180). Later, drinking in a nightclub in TEHRAN in his imagined story and watching couples slow-dance, Berlin feels himself "sliding away" (201), back to his high school gym when he was at a dance with Louise Wiertsma. Berlin remembers the girl's "blond hair and curious smile; the way she hummed as she danced" (201), and is filled with longing, an ache that makes him both sad and happy at the same time.

FURTHER READING

Calloway, Catherine. "Pluralities of Vision: *Going After Cacciato* and Tim O'Brien's Short Fiction." In *America Rediscovered: Critical Essays on Literature and Film of the Vietnam War*, edited by Owen W. Gilman Jr. and Lorrie Smith, 213–224. New York: Garland, 1990.

Herzog, Toby. "*Going After Cacciato*: The Soldier-Author-Character Seeking Control," *Critique: Studies in Contemporary Fiction* 24 (1983): 88–96.

———. *Vietnam War Stories: Innocence Lost*. New York: Routledge, 1992.

Kinney, Katherine. "American Exceptionalism and Empire in Tim O'Brien's *Going After Cacciato*," *American Literary History* 7, no. 4 (1995): 633–653.

McWilliams, Dean. "Time in Tim O'Brien's *Going After Cacciato*," *Critique: Studies in Contemporary Fiction* 29, no. 4 (Summer 1988): 245–255.

Palm, Edward F. "Falling In and Out: Military Idiom as Metaphoric Motif in *Going After Cacciato*," *Notes on Contemporary Literature* 22 (1992): 8.

Raymond, Michael W. "Imagined Responses to Vietnam: Tim O'Brien's *Going After Cacciato*," *Critique: Studies in Contemporary Fiction* 24 (1983): 97–104.

Slabey, Robert. "*Going After Cacciato*: Tim O'Brien's 'Separate Peace.'" In *America Rediscovered: Critical Essays on Literature and Film of the Vietnam War*, edited by Owen Gilman and Lorrie Smith, 205–212. New York: Garland, 1990.

Slay, Jack Jr. "A Rumor of War: Another Look at the Observation Post in Tim O'Brien's *Going After Cacciato*," *Critique* 41, no. 1 (1999): 79–85.

Vannatta, Dennis. "Theme and Structure in Tim O'Brien's *Going After Cacciato*," *Modern Fiction Studies* 28 (1982): 242–246.

"Going After Cacciato" (1976)

The short story version of the novel *Going After Cacciato* was first published in *Ploughshares* magazine in 1976 before appearing, with only slight modifications, as the opening chapter of O'Brien's 1978 novel. The story concerns a small group of American soldiers in Vietnam during the monsoon season in October 1968. When one of the squad members deserts, planning to walk all the way to PARIS, the rest of the squad go after him.

SYNOPSIS

The story opens with a small group of soldiers encamped in a damaged Buddhist pagoda in Vietnam in October 1968. It is the rainy season, and the platoon members are suffering from skin infections, DYSENTERY, and general low spirits following the deaths of several men over the past few months. Toward the end of the month, a soldier named Cacciato leaves the war, announcing to his fellow platoon members that he plans to walk all the way to Paris. When Doc Peret brings the news to Lieutenant Corson, the platoon's commanding officer, the older and ailing lieutenant stares and splutters in disbelief. But he eventually rounds up the members of Third Squad, Cacciato's unit, and follows the deserting soldier through the jungles and mountains of Vietnam all the way to the border of LAOS. Cacciato leaves behind equipment and trash along the way—discarded ammunition belts, chocolate wrappers, cans of burnt-out Sterno—that allow the men to follow his trail. The squad is so close behind Cacciato, in fact, that they spot him several times. Once, Cacciato sets up a rigged smoke grenade, tripped by Stink Harris, that sends the squad members scrambling and diving for cover and frightens them badly, especially Paul Berlin. At the Laotian border, the men set an ambush for Cacciato, some of them circling around to surround the AWOL soldier. Paul Berlin fires a flare, signaling the advance, but the story ends inconclusively, with Berlin shouting "Go!" Readers never discover whether Cacciato is captured or not.

COMMENTARY

From the beginning, the story "Going After Cacciato" reflects the unheroic nature of the American war in Vietnam. It opens with a list of the soldiers in Paul Berlin's platoon who have recently died. The first man named, Billy Boy Watkins, died ignominiously of fright on the field of battle, two men died in tunnels, and Frenchie Tucker was shot through the neck. The deaths of the other men are not described in any detail—they are simply, flatly, said to be dead, their individuality lost along with their lives. In fact, Lieutenant Corson cannot even tell them apart and mistakes Paul Berlin for a soldier named Vaught at one point. The men who remain alive suffer the physical indignities of a difficult climate. The constant rains have rotted the skin on the feet and arms of some; a leech makes itself at home on the tongue of a soldier named Stink Harris; and the lieutenant is racked by dysentery. Men injure themselves in shameful ways: Vaught by scraping a layer of mushy skin off his arm with the blade of his own bayonet, and Ben Nystrom by purposefully shooting himself in the foot. Oscar Johnson likens the feeling of the war in October 1968 to DETROIT in the month of May when dark and gloom provide a perfect cover for criminal behavior, hinting at the unsavory nature of the American mission in Vietnam. As the ailing Lieutenant Corson suggests throughout the story, with his repeated query, "What's *wrong* with you people?" (46), something is wrong with this war. It is not just a "bad time" as the opening sentence of the story asserts, but a bad war, a rotten war.

What is so astonishing to the men when they receive the news of Cacciato's departure is the contrast between the deserting soldier's goal of reaching "Gay Paree" and the life they lead encamped in Vietnam. As much Vietnam War literature shows, the disconnect between the wartime experiences of American soldiers in Vietnam and their lives back home was so great that soldiers often referred to home as "the world," implying that they were in a different place entirely, a completely alien environment impossible for those back home to imagine or understand. Doc Peret makes this disconnect clear when he insists that "none of the roads go to Paris" (55). Literally, no road goes to Paris from Vietnam—there are oceans and seas in the way, as Lieutenant Corson points out, but symbolically, everything that Paris stands for—the ease and comfort of civilian life; the art, literature, and music of the "city of lights"; and the possibility of peace itself—seems completely unattainable to men mired in the war environment.

Yet, despite the seeming impossibility of Cacciato reaching his goal, despite the fact that "the odds were like poison" (63), Paul Berlin repeatedly reassures himself that "it could be done" (63). Berlin is hoping for a miracle, as O'Brien characters frequently do. At one point, during a long and rainy night in the midst of the pursuit after Cacciato, Berlin is "suddenly struck between the eyes by a vision of murder" (55). He imagines seeing Cacciato's right temple caving inward, followed by an explosion of "outward-going brains" (55). This vision seems to Berlin the natural conclusion to Cacciato's desertion. The boy is stupid, and Berlin muses that "Nobody can get away with stupidity forever, and in war the final price for it is always paid in purely biological currency, hunks of toe or pieces of femur or bits of exploded brain" (56). While the war has accustomed Berlin to expect violent death, specifically called "murder" in the story, Paul Berlin wishes hard for a different ending. He not only wants Cacciato to make it to Paris, but Berlin insists as well, in speaking with Doc Peret, that the boy is brave, not a coward, as a deserter would usually be called. When the story is revised as part of the longer novel, the focus will shift even more firmly to Berlin's contemplations of bravery and cowardice. He himself considers leaving the war, but he understands that desertion is traditionally the coward's way out. His long, invented story of Cacciato's trek to Paris is Berlin's way of leaving the war honorably, without the shame of being thought a coward. Thus, at the end of the story, when Berlin shoots the flare that signals Third Squad's ambush of the deserting soldier and shouts "Go," it is unclear exactly whom Berlin is shouting to. While the other soldiers in the squad most likely assume that Berlin is encouraging them to advance as planned, readers understand that the shout is more likely intended for Cacciato

himself. Berlin is urging Cacciato to continue his improbable quest to leave the war behind and hoping desperately for a miracle that will allow the boy to succeed.

Differences in Versions

The story version and novel version of *Going After Cacciato* are quite similar. O'Brien makes mostly small, stylistic changes in dialogue and description as well as minor changes to certain surface details so that this opening chapter will mesh better with the rest of the novel. Most of the small cosmetic changes involve the cast of characters. For instance, Walter Gleason, a soldier said to have died in the tunnels in the original story, is omitted in the novel's version, while Rudy Chassler and Ready Mix are added to the list of the dead when the story is revised, to better reflect events detailed elsewhere in the novel. Bernie Lynn, who is simply said to be dead in the story, is identified more specifically as dying in the tunnels in the novel, in order to better set up the later fragging (*see* FRAG) death of Lieutenant Sidney Martin. And some soldiers are given slightly larger roles in the revised story that are intended to match their depictions elsewhere in the novel. For instance, Harold Murphy, who is mentioned only briefly in the original story, actively petitions Lieutenant Corson to turn back and give up the chase after Cacciato in the novel's version, a change that anticipates Murphy's desertion of the squad at the Laotian border later in the book. Eddie Lazzutti, also mentioned very briefly in the story, uses his rich singing voice in the novel as the men march along a trail in their pursuit of Cacciato. Also in the novel, Oscar Johnson, not Harold Murphy, is the one who lights up a joint and passes it around to the men, and Stink Harris rather than the lieutenant serves as point man for the squad.

In addition to these minor alterations, in the novel's version O'Brien emphasizes a bit more fully the workings of Paul Berlin's imagination; Berlin more clearly enjoys "the pleasure of pretending" that the march after Cacciato "might go on forever: step by step, a mile, ten miles, two hundred, eight thousand" (GAC 16). O'Brien adds a paragraph as well in which Berlin speculates that "he might even have tried himself" to walk to Paris, that "with courage," he might have joined Cacciato in his desertion (23). These additions help prepare readers for Berlin's own imagined journey after Cacciato that will take place later in the novel, his long mental debate about whether to flee or to stay in the war. O'Brien also revises the smoke grenade scene somewhat, to emphasize more fully Berlin's fear and humiliation. Berlin feels a "warm wet feeling on his thighs" (20) as he urinates on himself in the revised version, and he seems to remain immobilized with fear longer than in the original story. In addition, he is more "keenly aware" (20) of being watched by the other men of Third Squad in the novel, and he is more harsh on himself in his own thoughts as well, calling himself an "asshole" and a "ridiculous little yo-yo" (21). This self-deprecation paves the way for Berlin's desperate attempts later in the novel to control his fear and to bring order to his chaotic memories through his carefully detailed and constructed story of the continued pursuit of Cacciato.

CHARACTERS

Berlin, Paul While both the story and novel versions of "Going After Cacciato" are told in the third person, the events are filtered through the consciousness of Paul Berlin. This is less readily apparent in the original story, since readers are not aware that the tale of Cacciato's disappearance is an incident that Berlin remembers during his long night on the watch tower above the SOUTH CHINA SEA. Nevertheless, the Berlin of the story very much matches the Berlin of the novel: Both are overcome with fear when Stink Harris trips the smoke grenade set by Cacciato, and both first whisper and then shout "Go" when the men attempt their ambush of the deserting soldier.

Buff Buff is one of the dead soldiers mentioned at the very beginning of the story. Later, the narrator will tell readers that Cacciato remained smiling "in the most lethal of moments," even when "Buff's helmet overflowed with an excess of red and gray fluids" (49). This description matches the depiction of Buff's death in the novel's version of *Going After Cacciato*, when the large soldier is shot in the

face and found kneeling in the grass, facedown in his own helmet.

Cacciato Cacciato is the soldier who deserts the platoon in late October 1968, planning to walk all the way to PARIS. The other men claim that Cacciato is simply "dumb," Doc Peret even suggesting that he missed "Mongolian idiocy by the breadth of a single, wispy genetic hair" (48), but Paul Berlin insists that the boy is nevertheless brave, that he cannot be considered a coward. Cacciato seems to almost taunt his followers, carelessly leaving indicators of his trail behind and even rigging a trip wire to a smoke grenade at one point. Whether or not Cacciato escapes the ambush set by Third Squad at the end of the story is not clear, as the piece ends with Paul Berlin shouting "Go!" Cacciato is presented very similarly in both the *Ploughshares* version of the story and the later novel.

Corson, Lieutenant Lieutenant Corson is the officer sent to replace Lieutenant Sidney Martin after Martin dies in a Vietnamese tunnel. Described as "too old to be a lieutenant" (43), Corson is a KOREAN WAR veteran who feels bewildered in Vietnam. The veins in Corson's nose and cheeks are "shattered by booze" (43) and he is suffering from DYSENTERY. Despite his age and illness, the officer determines to follow the deserting soldier Cacciato, and he leads his men in the hunt all the way to the border of LAOS. The description of Corson in the *Ploughshares* story matches his character in the novel's version of *Going After Cacciato*.

Gleason, Walter At the beginning of the story, the narrator informs readers that a soldier named Walter Gleason had died in the Viet Cong tunnels before the October disappearance of Cacciato. Walter Gleason, however, does not appear as a character in the novel's version of *Going After Cacciato*.

Harris, Stink Stink Harris is one of the members of Third Squad who follows Cacciato after he deserts. Stink is the point man of the squad, and thus he is the soldier who trips the wire rigged to the smoke grenade set by Cacciato. Angry after this incident, Stink is intent on catching Cacciato in the ambush that ends the story. He is "excited and happy" (64) as he releases the bolt on his rifle and slams it into place.

Johnson, Oscar   Oscar Johnson is a black soldier in the platoon who likes to talk about the "rape and looting" he did back home in DETROIT. The other men do not believe Oscar's stories, commenting that he "had a pretty decent imagination for a nigger" (43). In the novel version of *Going After Cacciato*, the men suspect that Oscar is actually from BANGOR, MAINE, since that is where his mail gets sent. Oscar plays an important role in the novel, leading the mutiny against Lieutenant Sidney Martin and serving as informal commander when Lieutenant Corson is too sick to do his job.

Lazzutti, Eddie   Eddie Lazzutti is mentioned only briefly in the original short story version of "Going After Cacciato," when Paul Berlin informs Lieutenant Corson that Lazzutti is a member of Third Squad. As such, Lazzutti participates in the search for the AWOL soldier.

Lynn, Bernie   Readers are bluntly informed that Bernie Lynn is one of the dead members of the platoon at the beginning of the story. No mention is made of how or when he died. In the novel version of *Going After Cacciato*, however, Bernie Lynn is shot in the throat in the Vietnamese tunnels when he goes down to retrieve the wounded Frenchie Tucker.

Martin, Lieutenant Sidney   Lieutenant Sidney Martin is said to have died in a tunnel in the *Ploughshares* short story. Lieutenant Corson has come to replace him. While this is the only mention of the officer in the story, he will play an important role in the novel version of *Going After Cacciato*, where readers learn that Sidney Martin dies of a fragging (*see* FRAG) committed by the men of Third Squad.

Murphy, Harold   Harold Murphy is one of the members of Third Squad who follows Cacciato after the soldier deserts. At one point, Murphy claims that the 17-year-old soldier is dumb as "an oyster fart" (43). Later, he is depicted rolling a marijuana cigarette and passing it along for the other men of Third Squad to enjoy. In the novel *Going After Cacciato*, Murphy argues against following Cacciato over the Laotian border. The big soldier deserts the squad when they vote to continue the chase, apparently choosing instead to return to the American base in Vietnam.

Nystrom, Ben   Just as in the novel version of *Going After Cacciato*, Ben Nystrom in the story version is said to have shot himself in the foot on purpose. He is sent home and does not write back to the platoon members he has left behind.

Pederson   Only two mentions of Pederson occur in the *Ploughshares* story: first, when the narrator informs readers at the beginning of the story that he is dead, and second, when readers are informed that Cacciato kept smiling even when "Pederson floated face-up in a summer day's paddy" (49). Jim Pederson, however, plays an important role in short stories such as "Keeping Watch by Night" and "Landing Zone Bravo," and in the novel version of *Going After Cacciato*. His death as briefly described in the *Ploughshares* story matches his death by friendly fire in a rice paddy in the novel version.

Peret, Doc   Doc Peret is the member of Third Squad who brings the news of Cacciato's departure to the jaded and sick Lieutenant Corson. Doc also serves in the story as a sounding board for Paul Berlin's musings about Cacciato's bravery. While the doctor diagnoses the AWOL soldier as semi-retarded, he does not refute Berlin's assertion that the boy is brave.

Radio Voice   When Lieutenant Corson radios in to headquarters that he and Third Squad are "in pursuit of the enemy," a voice comes back over the radio offering to supply a whole arsenal of artillery fire to the unit. Corson refuses, but the radio voice continues to urge the firepower on the officer, until the lieutenant finally ends the radio call by calling the faceless voice a "monster" (54).

Tucker, Frenchie The only information readers find out about Frenchie Tucker in the short story version of "Going After Cacciato" is that he died before Cacciato left by being shot through the neck. In the novel, Frenchie dies in a VIET CONG tunnel after being ordered to search it by Lieutenant Sidney Martin.

Vaught Vaught is a soldier who was friends with Cacciato. He leaves Vietnam before Cacciato's desertion, however, after scraping his arm with the sharp edge of his bayonet in an attempt to remove a layer of mushy skin. When the wound becomes infected, he is choppered to Japan to recover. He sends back a picture of himself with two pretty nurses, but his fellow soldiers are shocked to learn that he has lost the arm.

Watkins, Billy Boy As evidence that "it was a bad time" (42) in the war, readers are informed that Billy Boy Watkins is dead, having been scared to death on the field of battle. While this is the only mention of Billy Boy in the *Ploughshares* short story, he will have a chapter devoted to him in the novel, describing his death in more detail.

"Half Gone" (2002)

The story "Half Gone," about a middle-aged woman named Dorothy Stier who goes out into her front yard topless one July afternoon after losing her left breast to cancer, was first published in the *New Yorker* magazine in July 2002. The story, with slight revisions, was later published as chapter 15 of the novel *July, July.*

SYNOPSIS
Set on the afternoon of July 19, 1997, "Half Gone" opens with Dorothy Stier removing her shirt and bra and marching out into the driveway of her upper-class suburban home, where her husband, Ron, is lovingly washing his two prized Volvos. Dorothy has drunk a number of vodka lemonades and is determined to force her husband to look closely at her, something he has apparently

refused to do since she lost her left breast to cancer several months ago. When Ron tries to persuade Dorothy to return inside, the tipsy woman refuses, choosing instead to walk over to her neighbor Fred Engelmann's back yard and chat with the retired Marine colonel, who is watering his flowers. Good friends for the past 10 years, Fred and Dorothy are both staunch Republicans who share a hatred for liberal politics. As Dorothy confesses her desire to leave Ron, Fred reveals that he knows a great deal about Dorothy's life and her past—items that even a close friend would not be privy to. Principal among these details is Dorothy's past relationship with a college boyfriend named Billy McMann, a DRAFT dodger who had hoped that Dorothy would flee to Canada with him. Fred also seems to understand that Dorothy is now second-guessing this long-ago choice, wondering if she made the wrong decision in choosing the safe, conservative Ron over Billy. Suspicious of Fred's knowledge about her life, Dorothy asks if he is God or an angel. Fred responds "not exactly" (71), but he does seem to display omniscience of the future at the end of the story when he informs Dorothy that her cancer will eventually kill her, that she has only five years, two months, and a handful of days to live.

COMMENTARY
The story's title, "Half Gone," references Dorothy Stier's mastectomy—the fact that her breasts are half gone and she feels deformed and unloved as a result—but it also has multiple other meanings in the story as well. The Stiers' marriage, for instance, is half gone as well, neither partner seeming to be fully committed after the unsettling changes that have occurred in their lives. Dorothy is seriously considering leaving Ron, having contemplated taking off for some exotic locale such as PARIS or Hong Kong, or even simply escaping to Duluth. And Ron, while rock solid during Dorothy's diagnosis and treatment, seems unsure of how to behave around his wife after the surgery. When she refuses to go back inside the house after walking outside tipsy and topless that July afternoon, Ron himself threatens to leave. Although he only plans to go back into the house, not leave the marriage, his statement that he has "had it," that

he is "Gone. Out of here" (68) is certainly meant to echo the "Half Gone" of the story's title. Ron has withdrawn emotionally from the marriage after Dorothy's surgery, unwilling to touch her or even look at her full on.

Readers might suspect that this marriage has been troubled from some time long before Dorothy's cancer diagnosis, perhaps even going back to its very beginnings. Dorothy, after all, married Ron "for his looks" (68) shortly after she dumped his best friend, her college boyfriend, Billy McMann, a man she had loved with her "whole heart" (70). Although she has come to "appreciate [Ron], even love him, for more substantial reasons" (68) than his handsome appearance, readers are left to wonder how well she even knows her husband. Dorothy is surprised when she hears Wagner playing on the radio of one of Ron's Volvos: "She hadn't realized Ron liked Wagner." "She hadn't realized, in fact, that he cared much for music" (67). While Dorothy appreciates the comfortable lifestyle that Ron has provided her, it seems as if she does not truly know Ron as well as a wife usually knows her husband. Readers are left to wonder whether in their life of social climbing with their fancy cars and their memberships in two ritzy country clubs the Stiers have been too distracted by material comforts to fully know and love each other.

The title of the story refers as well to Dorothy's past. Fred Engelmann suggests that Dorothy had gone so far as to plan to flee to Canada with Billy McMann back in 1969 before she broke off the relationship. "Figure it had to eat at you, too," he tells Dorothy, "the way you changed horses in midstream. Missed that flight to Canada" (69). So, three decades ago, Dorothy "half went" with Billy to Canada before changing her mind and missing the planned flight. Dorothy now wonders if she had made a terrible mistake so long ago. Although at the time she justified her decision by reminding herself that she "was no flower child," that she "was a Goldwater babe, and proud of it" (70), she now wonders whether the "sensible" (70) choice she made was the correct one. After being diagnosed with cancer, Dorothy cannot help but realize that there are no truly safe choices in life. As she contemplates leaving Ron, she even considers depart-

ing for the "frigid streets of Winnipeg" (66) and perhaps attempting to rekindle her earlier romance with Billy.

When Dorothy goes out topless into her yard, she is exposing herself in more ways than one. While she literally bares her mangled breasts in an attempt to force Ron to look at her, she also exposes her innermost fears and regrets—not only to Ron but also to her neighbor Fred. Dorothy is tired of hiding behind the stereotype of the well-behaved and good-looking wife—she is described as "a vintage Bentley amid a fleet of utilitarian S.U.V. housewives" (66)—or of the brave cancer patient. She wants the neighborhood and the world to see her as she really is—a scared, regretful, and angry woman who feels betrayed that the safe choice she made in the past has turned out to be not so safe after all. Fred Engelmann seems to fulfill Dorothy's desire to be truly seen. Throughout their 10-year friendship, Fred has been able to "understand Dorothy exactly as she most wanted to be understood. . . . it was as if the man had unlocked the code of her personal history, developed a dossier on her dreams, certain regrets and longings" (69). Perhaps this is why Fred does not act with more surprise when he actually sees Dorothy physically naked. Metaphorically, he has seen her naked, unprotected self for years. But Dorothy needs to be careful what she wishes for. Fred's ability to see her as she truly is also leads to his devastating prediction that Dorothy will be dead in slightly more than five years.

In the story version, it is possible to read Fred Engelmann as perhaps a slightly cruel man who wants to punish Dorothy for her strange behavior with his prediction of her imminent but not exactly imminent death. When the story is included in the novel *July, July*, however, Fred seems less ambiguously a supernatural figure. This is largely because of the other seemingly omniscient characters who appear throughout the novel: Master Sergeant Johnny Ever, who speaks to Second Lieutenant David Todd over a transistor radio as he lies wounded in Vietnam; the young policeman who drives Ellie Abbott to the station after the drowning death of her lover; and the misshapen young man who snaps erotic photographs of Jan Huebner and later threatens to blackmail her, among others. In the context of these other characters—all of whom have privileged knowledge about the DARTON HALL graduates of 1969—Fred's foreknowledge of Dorothy's impending death seems real and certain rather than simply the cruel speculations of a neighbor who, after all, had been a trained assassin in Vietnam. Nevertheless, Dorothy continues to insist at the end of the story that she can shape her own future, that she is not destined to die as Fred predicts. "Stick around, Freddie," she says. "I'll make it. Wait and see" (71). Though Dorothy might already be "half gone" from the cancer eating away at her body, she remains feisty, refusing to accept Fred's death sentence. Readers are left to wonder whether Dorothy's newfound determination, her will to live, will be enough to overcome her predicted fate.

Differences in Versions
While O'Brien made some very minor changes in the first part of the story, the most significant differences between the story version and the version in *July, July* occur near the end. A few of these changes seem intended to make Dorothy's feelings for her former college boyfriend, Billy McMann, more ambiguous in the novel than they are in the original story. For instance, appearing in the original story but removed from the novel version is a line about Dorothy experiencing a "quick, frightened tingle go through her thoughts" (69) when Fred Engelmann first mentions Billy's name, a line that suggests Dorothy still has strong feelings for Billy. In addition, the stand-alone story includes a whole paragraph of background information about Dorothy's college relationship with Billy that is omitted in the novel, perhaps because readers gain this knowledge elsewhere in the book. Significantly, however, this omitted paragraph includes the detail that back in college Dorothy had loved Billy "with her whole heart" (70). When this phrase is omitted in the novel version, readers remain unsure about how Dorothy actually felt about Billy back in 1969. The novel never makes as clear a statement about Dorothy's past feelings for Billy. The other main alteration from story to novel version is the removal of Dorothy's query to

Fred about whether he is God or an angel. O'Brien possibly chose to remove this line because of its similarity to a question that David Todd asks deejay Johnny Ever in chapter 2 of the novel: "Are you God?" (*July* 32).

CHARACTERS

Engelmann, Alice Alice Engelmann is the wife of Fred Engelmann. Although readers never actually see Alice in the story, she seems to be a conventional housewife. Fred tells Dorothy Stier that Alice has probably taken to bed after peeking out the window at her topless next-door neighbor standing in her side yard at two in the afternoon in full sight of anyone who cared to look.

Engelmann, Fred Fred Engelmann is Dorothy Stier's next-door neighbor. The retired Marine colonel is in his back yard, watering his sunflower patch with a garden hose, when Dorothy emerges from her house topless. When Dorothy's husband, Ron, retreats angrily indoors, the tipsy woman joins Fred in his flower garden, and the two begin to talk about Dorothy's life—her cancer, her feelings for Ron, and her past boyfriend whom she abandoned in favor of Ron. It soon becomes clear that Fred Engelmann has privileged knowledge about Dorothy. At first, she believes that he has been spying on her. As a Marine colonel in Vietnam, after all, he had been involved in covert counterinsurgency operations. He certainly knows how to build a dossier on someone. But by the end of the story, Dorothy suspects that Fred is something more than what he appears. She asks if he is God or an angel. Although Fred replies, "not exactly" (71), he proceeds to predict the exact length of time Dorothy has left to live before her cancer kills her. Either the man is playing a cruel joke on Dorothy, or he has access to some kind of supernatural, omniscient knowledge about his neighbor.

Jimmy Jimmy is the Stiers' gardener. When Dorothy Stier emerges topless from her house on the afternoon of July 19, 1997, Jimmy looks at her with a "bewildered gaze" (66), then glances down at his hedge clippers, not quite sure how to react.

McMann, Billy   Billy McMann is the name of Dorothy Stier's college boyfriend. He was a pony-tailed, blue-eyed young man who fled to Canada in 1969 to escape the DRAFT. Dorothy had initially planned to fly to WINNIPEG with him but had instead stayed behind and married his best friend, Ron Stier. Now that she is middle-aged and stricken with cancer, Dorothy looks back at the past and wonders if she made a mistake in choosing the safe, conservative Ron over Billy, whom she had loved "with her whole heart" (70).

Stier, Dorothy   The protagonist of the story, Dorothy Stier, is a 49-year-old woman with a wealthy husband, two terrific sons, and a fancy suburban home. Dorothy, however, is also suffering from breast cancer and nine months ago had a mastectomy of her left breast. Since the surgery, her husband, Ron, has been unwilling to look at or touch her mangled body, and Dorothy is starting to rethink her entire life. On the afternoon of July 19, 1997, she drinks several vodka lemonades, then goes out into her driveway topless in a desperate attempt to gain Ron's attention. Her actions, however, end up simply embarrassing her husband, who soon retreats inside. Dorothy then stumbles over to the yard of her next-door-neighbor, Fred Engelmann, an old friend and retired Marine colonel who treats Dorothy courteously and speaks with her about her desire to leave Ron. Fred, who has an uncanny knowledge of Dorothy's most hidden feelings as well as secrets from her past, eventually predicts to the tipsy woman that her cancer will kill her in slightly more than five years. The feisty Dorothy, however, refuses to accept this death sentence, insisting to her neighbor at the very end of the story that she will beat the cancer.

Stier, Ron   Ron Stier is the husband of Dorothy Stier. A solid, dependable man who has been a good husband and father, Ron nevertheless seems more interested in the trappings of his wealthy lifestyle than he does in his cancer-stricken wife. Although he had supported her through her diagnosis and surgery, remaining cheerful and upbeat, Ron has refused to touch Dorothy's body since the mastectomy, or even to look at her fully. In fact, Dorothy feels that Ron's "relentless, can-do solicitude" during the breast-cancer nightmare "had almost killed her" (68). Late in the story, readers discover that Dorothy initially married Ron for his looks, that she had truly been in love with Ron's best friend in college, Billy McMann. But when Billy fled to Canada to evade the DRAFT, Dorothy stayed behind and married Ron instead. Although Dorothy talks with her neighbor Fred Engelmann about her desire to leave her husband, Fred predicts that she will do no such thing, that she will be unable to give up the comfortable lifestyle she had chosen so many years previously.

"How to Tell a True War Story" (1987)

"How to Tell a True War Story" depicts the death of Curt Lemon, an American soldier in Vietnam, as well as the reaction of Rat Kiley, Curt's best friend, to the devastating loss of his buddy. The story was first published in *Esquire* magazine in October 1987, then revised and included in the 1990 collection, *The Things They Carried.*

SYNOPSIS

Curt Lemon has already died when the story begins. Curt's friend Rat Kiley is writing a letter to the dead man's sister, explaining what a great guy Curt was and how everyone misses him. Rat is enraged, however, when the sister never writes back. As the story unfolds, readers learn more about how Curt died. He and Rat had been goofing around one day, playing a game of chicken with smoke grenades when Curt stepped onto a booby-trapped 105 explosive. His body was torn apart and thrown up into a nearby tree. The story's narrator, Tim O'Brien, and a fellow soldier named Norman Bowker are ordered to climb the tree and throw down the body parts. Soon after Curt dies, Rat Kiley slowly and methodically shoots to death a baby water buffalo. The American soldiers then dump the carcass down the well of a Vietnamese village.

Intermingled with the story of Curt's death and Rat's revenge is a story that a soldier named Mitchell Sanders tells O'Brien about a six-man patrol that is ordered up into the remote Vietnamese mountains to man a listening post. The men begin to hear strange, spooky noises in the night, including, eventually, a cocktail party, a glee club, a barbershop quartet, and chamber music. The noises seem to be coming from the landscape itself, as if the rocks and trees are talking to the men. They end up calling in an enormous air strike that completely incinerates the area where they had been stationed. When the men return to their camp, a colonel demands to know what they heard, why they called for all the fire power. The six men just stare at him, realizing that he will never understand. The day after he tells O'Brien this story, Mitchell Sanders confesses to making up certain details in order to convince his friend of the truth of the story.

"How to Tell a True War Story" concludes long after the war. O'Brien is now a writer who sometimes tells the story of Curt and Rat at various speaking engagements. Often, when he finishes the story, a woman will come up to him and explain that, although she usually hates war stories, she liked this one. But she also urges O'Brien to put the war behind him, not to wallow in all the blood and gore. O'Brien tells readers that after the woman leaves he thinks to himself that she is a "dumb cooze" (215), the same expression Rat had used to describe Curt Lemon's sister who never answered his letter. The woman, O'Brien writes, was not listening—he was telling a love story, not a war story.

COMMENTARY

"How to Tell a True War Story" is a strange, hybrid piece of writing. Part fiction, part autobiography, part essay, the story includes metafictional (see METAFICTION) commentary on how to tell a war story as it unfolds a war story of its own. The narrator is named Tim O'Brien, as is the author, but the two Tim O'Briens are not the same. The story opens with the line, "This is true" (210), then goes on to confess that most of the details are made up. The story is clearly set during the Vietnam War, and it describes the death of an American soldier, but the narrator at the end claims that it is *not* a war story but a love story. How are readers to make sense of all these confusions and contradictions within the story? Perhaps we can begin with the title. The key word in the title might very well be *true*. The story probes definitions of truth, dismantling readers' usual associations with the notion to substitute others in their place. Generally, we tend to think of history as "true"—as a recounting of actual, real events that took place in the past. Conversely, we think of fiction as "not true"—as stories that are made up or invented and not to be taken as historically accurate. It is these definitions that O'Brien will play with in "How to Tell a True War Story." He will not only question the possibility of recording history accurately, but he will also propose that fiction may be a way to explore a deeper sort of truth than merely recounting what happened in a given place at a given time. For O'Brien fiction gets at emotional truth, a truth that communicates the feeling of a particular experience, that "makes the stomach believe" (213). Truth, as the story illustrates, is subjective, difficult to pin down, and elusive. Getting at truth involves the hard work of careful storytelling and careful listening.

From the beginning, O'Brien depicts the subjectivity of "true" experience. Rat Kiley's letter to Curt Lemon's sister is a good example of this. While Rat interprets Lemon's sister as a "dumb cooze" for never responding to his letter, and while narrator Tim O'Brien seems to concur with this assessment, never contradicting or questioning Rat's judgment, author Tim O'Brien subtly crafts the letter so that readers can see beyond the grieving young soldier. When Rat writes about what a great guy Curt was, he glorifies the dead soldier's racist language and violent behavior, telling the sister about her brother's propensity to burn down villages, blow up "gook" fish (208), and go out into the night stark naked, his body painted in lurid colors. He then tells the sister that he is just like Curt, that the two are "like twins or something" (208). Finally, he promises to look the sister up when the war is over. Careful readers should not be surprised when this description is followed immediately by the information that Curt's sister never writes back. The sister lives in a very different world than Rat Kiley does; she is not inured to the daily violence and atrocity that have hardened these men at war. The letter most likely frightens her. While she might have a difficult time understanding the experiences the men have undergone, author O'Brien shows that this misunderstanding works two ways. Rat cannot comprehend the effect that his letter will have on Curt's sister, and he is shocked and hurt when the young woman does not respond. The truth of a given situation, then, depends on where one is situated, on the experiences he or she has undergone.

But the difficulty comes in communicating these experiences. How can someone who has never been at war possibly begin to understand what the war was like for American soldiers in Vietnam? The answer, O'Brien suggests, lies in careful story-telling and empathetic listening. The story-within-a-story told by Mitchell Sanders emphasizes this point. It is a story about listening and about silence. The six-man patrol that Sanders describes is sent up into the mountains on a simple mission: "The idea's to spend a week up there, just lie low and listen for enemy movement. . . . They keep strict field discipline. Absolute silence. They just listen" (210). As the men begin to hear strange, spooky sounds in the night, part of their problem is that they cannot resort to soldiers' usual methods of controlling their fright. Sanders explains, "And what makes it extra bad, see, is the poor dudes can't horse around like normal. Can't joke it away. Can't even talk to each other except maybe in whispers, all hush-hush, and that just revs up the willies" (212). As O'Brien shows in other short stories set in Vietnam, the soldiers use hard, ironic language to try to diminish death, to change it into something less frightening. For instance, in "The Lives of the Dead," O'Brien writes, "In Vietnam, we had ways of making the dead seem not quite so dead. . . . By slighting death, by acting, we pretended it was not the terrible thing it was. By our language, which was both hard and wistful, we transformed the bodies into piles of waste" (*TTTC* 238). These usual methods of joking away their fear are unavailable to the six-man patrol in Mitchell Sanders's story, who must maintain a rigid silence. Thus, their fears escalate, and they begin to hear

voices in the landscape. The trees and fog begin to talk to them, as if the land itself is throwing an immense cocktail party, with choirs and operas and glee clubs singing in the background. And when the men return to their base after calling in a massive air strike in the mountains, they are unable to tell the colonel in charge of their unit the story of what happened: "They head down the mountain, back to base camp and when they get there they don't say diddly. They don't talk. Not a word, like they're deaf and dumb" (212). They just stare at the officer, believing that he has wax in his ears, that he does not even want to hear what happened to them.

Mitchell Sanders, however, is able to communicate the experience of this six-man patrol by telling the story to narrator O'Brien, who listens carefully. For Sanders the specific details of what actually happened to the men up in the mountains are less important than communicating to O'Brien the *feel* of the event, the emotions of the men involved. Therefore, the day after telling the story, he confesses to O'Brien that he had to invent some of the details—there was no opera, no glee club. O'Brien, an empathetic listener, responds that he understands, and he allows Sanders to tell the moral of the story—"Hear that quiet, man?" Sanders asks, "There's your moral" (213). So, the point is, as O'Brien will explain in the following paragraphs, that "true" war stories do not necessarily have neat morals that one can extract. When Sanders gets to the moral of the story, he can evoke only silence. The experience of war cannot be generalized into a tidy package. It must be felt, it must trigger an emotion, it must turn something inside the guts or the stomach. If O'Brien as he listens to the story can at least begin to imagine how the men must have felt when they were up in the mountains, Sanders's story has been successful, regardless of how accurately he portrayed the historical facts of what actually happened to the men.

When at the end of "How to Tell a True War Story" the kindly older woman of humane politics comes up to talk to O'Brien, he becomes angry because he believes the woman was not listening carefully to the story he told about Curt and Rat and the baby water buffalo. He thinks to himself that the woman is a *"dumb cooze,"* the same phrase that Rat had used to describe Curt's sister when she did not respond to his letter. "It wasn't a war story," narrator O'Brien thinks to himself. "It was a love story. It was a ghost story" (215). This is an interesting moment because readers are implicated right along with the kindly older woman. The vast majority of readers, in all probability, have initially read the story as a war story. After all, it is set in Vietnam and involves the death of one soldier and the tragic reaction of his friend. O'Brien emphasizes here the difficulties inherent in both listening to and telling stories. These are not easy things to do. As the teller of the story, O'Brien says that all he can do "is tell it one more time, patiently, adding and subtracting, making up a few things to get at the real truth. No Mitchell Sanders. . . . No Lemon, no Rat Kiley. And it didn't happen in the mountains, it happened in this little village on the Batangan Peninsula. . . ." (215). Like Mitchell Sanders earlier, O'Brien confesses that in order to get at the emotional truth of the war, he has to make up some details. And he might have to tell the story again and again, in different ways. As he commented earlier, "You can tell a true war story by the way it never seems to end" (212). But listening to war stories is also difficult and entails patience and care. While the story is certainly set in the war, it is also a story about one soldier's love for a fellow soldier and the sorrow he feels after his buddy's death. While it may be impossible for a person to fully understand the traumatic experiences of another human being, careful listening and reading and imagining, and even rereading and relistening as stories are told and retold, can jump-start the process. As O'Brien points out at the very end of the piece, all of his stories, whether set in the war or not, are "never about war"—they are about love and joy and loss and sorrow, emotions that all human beings experience.

Differences in Versions

When the story was revised and published as part of *The Things They Carried,* perhaps the most important change was the difference that the larger context makes in the story. O'Brien's imagined response to the kindly older woman at the end of

"How to Tell a True War Story"—that it was a love story, *not* a war story she had been listening to—seems even more meaningful when the story is placed into a book that opens and closes with two love stories: the tale of Jimmy Cross's love for Martha and of Timmy's love for Linda. In addition, several of the axioms that O'Brien provides about telling true war stories are illustrated in the stories that both precede and follow "How to Tell a True War Story" in the larger collection. Readers actually witness O'Brien patiently telling and retelling stories, adding and subtracting details when he tells about the death of Kiowa or about the man he killed. Readers see how true war stories never seem to end when the war follows Norman Bowker home to a small town in the Midwest, where he kills himself. Readers observe how a true war story can be embarrassing when narrator O'Brien describes the revenge he takes on the medic Bobby Jorgenson. And when readers finish the collection and wonder if there was a real Kiowa or Norman or Linda, if we ask ourselves when we finish reading if all this is true, then, as O'Brien writes, we've got our answer. If we care deeply enough about the truth of a story, the story must have the feel of truth about it.

As far as specific changes go, the original *Esquire* story is quite similar to the revised version that appears in *The Things They Carried.* The only changes involve a few added phrases and lines and a few minor substitutions. Some of these small changes seem designed to fit the story more smoothly into the context of the other stories in the collection. For instance, when Mitchell Sanders concludes his story about the six-man patrol that goes up the mountains, he adds to the list of people who do not listen: "Your girlfriend. My girlfriend. Everybody's sweet little virgin girlfriend" (*TTTC* 76). This addition underlines the gender politics that will be explored more fully in stories such as "Sweetheart of the Song Tra Bong" in the larger collection. In addition, in the revised version it is Dave Jensen, not Norman Bowker, who sings the song "LEMON TREE" as he throws down parts of Curt Lemon's body. This change was most likely made to fit the nature of these characters as described elsewhere in the collection. Bowker is said to be a gentle person, but Jensen seems fairly callous, particularly in the final story, when he tries to force O'Brien to shake the hand of the dead old Vietnamese man.

Other slight rewordings and additions work to emphasize even more strongly the importance of listening as well as the powerful nature of fictive truth—what O'Brien will call later in the collection "story-truth" as distinguished from "happening-truth." In the original *Esquire* version, for example, Mitchell Sanders has this to say about the moral to his story about the listening post in the mountains: "Hear that quiet, man? . . . There's your moral" (213). In the revised version, however, Sanders says, "Hear that quiet, man? . . . That quiet—just listen. There's your moral" (*TTTC* 77). Although a small addition, this change emphasizes the efficacy of careful listening. In the revised version, O'Brien also adds another sentence about Mitchell Sanders, which is inserted after Sanders confesses that he made up some of the details in his tale of what the men hear in the mountains: "He wanted me to feel the truth, to believe by the raw force of feeling" (*TTTC* 74). This addition stresses the importance of a story's ability to communicate the emotional truth of an event, to "make the stomach believe" (*TTTC* 78) as O'Brien writes a few pages later.

At times O'Brien adds small phrases that heighten the truth claims made in the story. For instance, in the revised version he writes in an early paragraph describing Curt Lemon's death: "It happened, to *me*, nearly twenty years ago" (*TTTC* 70), while the original story merely reads, "It happened nearly twenty years ago" (210). The addition of the phrase "to *me*," with its italicized emphasis on the word *me*, makes the story seem even more factual, more the tale of an actual eyewitness than the original version. Ironically, at the same time that O'Brien occasionally revs up the truth claims, he also more thoroughly dismantles these claims by the end of the story. The most significant changes occur in the final paragraphs of the revised version, when O'Brien adds several sentences that more thoroughly debunk the story he has just told about Curt and Rat and the baby water buffalo. When talking to the kindly older woman at the end, he adds the following sentences: "No trail junction. No baby buffalo. No vines or moss or white blos-

soms. Beginning to end, you tell her, it's all made up. Every goddamn detail—the mountains and the river and especially that poor dumb baby buffalo. None of it happened. *None* of it" (85). The added sentences here draw more attention to the narrator's anger as he responds to the woman—he curses at her and speaks disparagingly of the animal that had moved the woman to tears. But they also more fully stress the fictive nature of the story as he insists that *none* of what he has just told actually happened.

CHARACTERS

Bowker, Norman   Norman Bowker is one of the American soldiers in the platoon depicted in the story. He is present when Curt Lemon steps on a booby-trapped explosive device and is blown up into a nearby tree. Bowker, along with the story's narrator, Tim O'Brien, is ordered to climb up into the tree and throw down the party parts. Bowker whistles the tune "LEMON TREE" as he complies with this order.

Colonel   In the story about the listening patrol told by Mitchell Sanders, the six men who call in an air strike in the mountains must face an angry colonel upon their return to base camp. They had, after all, used up a great deal of expensive fire power and weaponry. Although the "fatass colonel" (212) wants an explanation and splutters at the men, all they can do is stare at him, as if to say, "man you got *wax* in your ears . . . poor bastard, you'll never know—wrong frequency—you don't *even* want to hear this" (212). The men then walk away from the colonel, giving no explanation for their behavior.

Harris, Stink   At the end of the story, after O'Brien becomes angry with the kindly older woman whom he feels was not properly listening to his tale of Curt Lemon and Rat Kiley and the baby water buffalo, he says that all he can do is patiently retell the story, adding and subtracting details and "making up a few things to get at the real truth" (215). There was no Rat Kiley, he confesses, no Lemon, no Mitchell Sanders. The story is actually about a guy named Stink Harris, who woke up screaming one night with a leech on his tongue. Stink appears as a character in O'Brien's earlier novel *Going After Cacciato,* where the first time readers see him he does wake up with a leech on his tongue.

Jensen, Dave   Dave Jensen is one of the American soldiers who witness the death of Curt Lemon. Later, when Rat Kiley shoots to death a baby water buffalo in revenge, Jensen will be astonished by the cruelty, exclaiming, "Amazing . . . My whole life, I never seen anything like it" (213).

Kiley, Rat   Rat Kiley was the best friend of Curt Lemon, a soldier who is killed in Vietnam when he steps on a rigged explosive devise. Rat is devastated by the death and writes a long letter home to Curt's sister, explaining what a great guy Curt was and how much he meant to Rat and the other men. Enraged when Curt's sister never writes back, Rat dismisses her as a "dumb cooze" (208). Later, Rat seeks his revenge for Curt's death by torturing a baby water buffalo. He slowly shoots the buffalo, aiming to cause as much pain as possible. The American soldiers then dump the buffalo's corpse down a village well.

Kindly Older Woman   The Tim O'Brien narrator at the end of the story tells readers that at various speaking engagements he often relates the tale of Curt Lemon and Rat Kiley and the baby water buffalo. He says that from time to time someone will come up to him to talk afterward. This person is always a woman, usually "an older woman of kindly temperament and human politics" (215). This woman will tell the writer that as a rule she hates war stories but that she liked this one. Nevertheless, she will urge O'Brien to move on, to stop wallowing in all the blood and gore of his wartime experiences. O'Brien writes that after the woman speaks he will think to himself, "you dumb cooze," because she was not listening. "It wasn't a war story. It was a love story. It was a ghost story" (215).

Kiowa   Another member of the American platoon in Vietnam depicted in the story, Kiowa is dozing with a few other soldiers when Curt Lemon

trips a rigged explosive device and dies, his body blown into a nearby tree. Later, Kiowa will help Mitchell Sanders dump a dead baby water buffalo into a village well, seemingly in revenge for Lemon's death.

Lemon, Curt   Curt Lemon is an American soldier who dies unexpectedly in Vietnam while playing a silly game involving smoke grenades with his best friend, Rat Kiley. As the two men toss the harmless grenades back and forth, Curt steps on a rigged 105 explosive device that blows his body apart and up into a tree. When Tim O'Brien and Norman Bowker are ordered to climb up and retrieve the body parts, Bowker, in a gruesome detail, whistles the song "LEMON TREE" as the men throw down what remains of their buddy. Later, Rat Kiley will write a long, heartfelt letter home to Curt's sister, who never responds.

Lemon, Curt's Sister   When Rat Kiley writes an, emotion-filled letter home to the sister of his dead best friend, Curt Lemon, she never responds, which angers the men greatly. Rat calls her a "dumb cooze" (210), and the story's narrator, a character named Tim O'Brien, accepts this judgment. However, readers are supposed to understand that Rat's violent letter, along with his promise to look the sister up after the war, might have frightened the woman.

O'Brien, Tim   The story is narrated by a character named Tim O'Brien, who becomes a writer after the war has ended. This character, however, should not be confused with the real, author Tim O'Brien. While both served in Vietnam and both become writers, the story quite purposely mixes fact and fiction, and in numerous interviews O'Brien warns against reading the narrator of this and other stories as representing his true self. O'Brien is the listener for Mitchell Sanders's story about the six-man patrol that calls an air strike in the mountains, and he describes his own telling of stories after the war has ended.

Sanders, Mitchell   Mitchell Sanders is one of the soldiers in Curt Lemon and Rat Kiley's platoon in

Vietnam. Sanders, who is depicted playing with a yo-yo throughout the story, is also a teller of stories himself. He tells narrator Tim O'Brien about a six-man patrol sent up into the mountains to man a listening post. When they begin to hear eerie, inexplicable noises, including a glee club, a cocktail party, and an opera with a soprano, the men call in an air strike that destroys the landscape for miles around. Later, Sanders admits to his friend O'Brien that he had to make up some of the details of the story in order to communicate the truth of how the men in the patrol felt. Mitchell Sanders will later help Kiowa dump the baby buffalo shot to death by Rat Kiley into a village well.

Six-Man Patrol   In a story within the larger story, Mitchell Sanders tells of a six-man patrol sent on a listening mission into the mountains of Vietnam for a week. The men, required to remain quiet and listen intently, gradually begin to hear stranger and stranger noises; they feel as if the rocks and trees themselves are talking. Scared and confused, the men call in a massive air strike that completely burns the mountainous area where they had been stationed. Later, back at camp, all the men can do is stare uncomprehendingly at a colonel who demands to know what they heard out there.

FURTHER READING

Calloway, Catherine. "'How to Tell a True War Story': Metafiction in *The Things They Carried*," *Critique: Studies in Contemporary Fiction* 36 (1995): 249–257.
King, Rosemary. "O'Brien's 'How to Tell a True War Story.'" *Explicator* 57, no. 3 (Spring 1999): 57–59.

"How Unhappy They Were" (1994)

"How Unhappy They Were" depicts John and Kathy Wade lying on the front porch of their rented cabin at the LAKE OF THE WOODS in remote northern Minnesota one night following John's landslide loss in an election for the U.S. Senate. The two

try to put the crushing defeat behind them as they make halfhearted, unrealistic plans for the future. The story was first published in *Esquire* magazine in October 1994 and also appeared as the opening chapter of the novel *In the Lake of the Woods* that same year.

SYNOPSIS

The story opens in September immediately after a primary election for the U.S. Senate. John Wade has suffered a crushing defeat, although in the short story readers never discover why. He and his wife, Kathy, have rented a remote cabin on the shores of the Lake of the Woods in northern Minnesota to gain some solitude and to try to escape the humiliation of John's recent election loss. At night the couple spread blankets on the porch of the small cabin and lie together watching the fog creep up over the lake. They try their best to pretend that everything is all right, even making plans to save money, pay off their campaign debt, and buy a handsome Victorian house in Minneapolis. They also dream about traveling to VERONA, ITALY, to start over, as well as about having a baby. But despite their plans, and despite Kathy's insistence that she loves her husband and does not care about elections or newspapers, it is clear that everything is not all right for John Wade, who cannot forget his humiliation and who feels an overwhelming rage, sparking his desire to scream the phrase, *"Kill Jesus!"* which echoes inside his head. Although the story ends with Kathy insisting that she and her husband will be happy, the narrator hints to readers that something traumatic is going to happen instead when he writes, "In less than thirty-six hours, [Kathy] would be gone" (136). While readers never find out what happens to Kathy, there is an ominous feel to the ending, with the narrator predicting that John Wade would remember the aliveness of Kathy's touch after she is gone.

COMMENTARY

While nothing much happens in the story on the plot level, "How Unhappy They Were" succeeds largely because the moody atmosphere surrounding the cabin on the lake so nicely reflects the characters' own moral quandaries. The lake seems a reservoir of secrets, with its many thousand square miles of unexplored wilderness, its "secret channels and portages," and its "tangled forest and islands without names" (136). The surface is even described as being "like a great, curving mirror" (136) as it reflects the hidden disappointments and tangled emotions lurking within John and Kathy Wade. Although this couple is desperate to rebuild their lives, they hide their true feelings from each other and even from themselves, repeatedly "pretend[ing] things were not so bad" (136), that the election loss "was not the absolute and crushing thing it truly was" (136). Readers never find out the facts behind John's election defeat in the story, but the references to disgrace, humiliation, and John's loss of honor and reputation certainly suggest that the couple is reacting to more than a simple election loss, that some scandal that helped create the landslide defeat was involved. But like so many things in this short story, the facts are kept hidden.

What readers do have to go on are all the signs of impending tragedy that surround the Wades at their remote cabin in the woods. It is no accident that the romantic place Kathy dreams of visiting is Verona, the setting for perhaps the most famous story of doomed love of all time—Shakespeare's *Romeo and Juliet*. The repeated image of trapdoors in the story suggests as well an incipient fall that it is certain to take place in this marriage. As John and Kathy try to convince themselves that the election defeat was not that terrible, they experience "sudden trapdoor feeling[s] in their stomachs" (136); as they lie on the porch and listen to the night noises around them, "they would feel the trapdoor go open, and they'd be falling into that emptiness where all the dreams used to be" (136). The fog that they watch creep up over the lake has ominous overtones as well, as it slowly envelops the boathouse and dock, pausing "as if to digest those objects" before it continues to move "heavily up the slope toward their porch" (137), as it threatens to consume John and Kathy themselves.

The fog, which covers up objects in the night, has its metaphorical equivalence in the rage that consumes John Wade's inner being. Having lost his faith in himself and in the future after his election loss, John suffers the "emptiness of disbelief" (137).

As the rage eats him up inside, he screams *"Kill Jesus!"* in his mind, the "most terrible thing" (137) he can think of, but a phrase also indicative of his loss of faith and fall into sin and spiritual emptiness. John is like Lucifer in this scene, the fallen angel who had rebelled against God. He feels crazy, "real depravity . . . a tight, pumped-up killing rage" that makes him want to "hurt things," to "grab a knife and start cutting and slashing and never stop" (137). John's feelings of rage seem so disproportionate to the loss of an election and to the happy plans he pretends to make with Kathy that readers are left wondering what secrets remain unspoken, what back story could possibly have engendered these feelings in the former candidate. The repeated forecasts of Kathy's disappearance, scattered throughout the story, prevent readers from imagining a happy ending to this tale as well. While it is possible that Kathy simply leaves her husband, the reference to the feel of her hand on John's forehead as "purely alive" may suggest that Kathy's being "gone" involves more than her walking away from the marriage.

Differences in Versions

The short story as published in *Esquire* magazine in October 1994 is nearly identical to the opening chapter of *In the Lake of the Woods*, published later that year. In addition to minor changes in a very few phrases, the characters' ages are slightly altered in the novel version. While John is 42 years old and Kathy is 39 in the original story, both characters are one year younger in the novel.

CHARACTERS

Wade, John John Wade, readers discover, is a Minnesota politician who had been elected lieutenant governor at 38 and become a candidate for the U.S. Senate at 41. Now, in September of an undetermined year, Wade, 42-years old, has suffered a crushing defeat in the Senate primary elections. He, along with his wife, Kathy, has escaped to a remote cabin at the LAKE OF THE WOODS in northern Minnesota to try to put the humiliation of his landslide loss behind him. But unlike Kathy, who genuinely seems to want a new future, John cannot forget his loss. And the memory of it fills him with an overpowering rage, making him "want to scream the most terrible thing he could scream—*Kill Jesus!*" (137). While John goes along with his wife's big dreams for the future, making unrealistic plans with her to buy a house or to travel to VERONA, ITALY, it is clear that he is simply pretending that everything is all right.

Wade, Kathy   Kathy Wade, wife of losing U.S. Senate primary candidate John Wade, tries her best to comfort her husband and retain her optimism as the pair lie on blankets on the porch of their rented cabin in remote northern Minnesota. Desperately wanting to be happy, Kathy makes plans to have babies and travel to VERONA, ITALY, with John, telling him that the election loss is "not really so terrible . . . I mean it's bad, but we can make it better" (136). Readers, however, are given several hints that despite Kathy's desperate attempts to make things better something is soon about to go horribly wrong. Only a few paragraphs into the story, the narrator writes that it is the couples' sixth night at LAKE OF THE WOODS, adding, "In less than thirty-six hours, [Kathy] would be gone" (136). As the evening wears on, Kathy pushes back the blankets and moves toward the railing at the far end of the porch, where she claims not to be crying. At the end of the story, the narrator again reminds readers of the fact that Kathy will soon be gone, writing, "In the days afterward, when she was gone, [John] would remember . . . the feel of her hand against his forehead, its warmth, how purely alive it was" (138). While readers never discover what happens to Kathy, the future that the narrator hints at seems an ominous one.

If I Die in a Combat Zone, Box Me Up and Ship Me Home (1973)

Published by Delacorte in 1973, *If I Die in a Combat Zone, Box Me Up and Ship Me Home* is Tim O'Brien's memoir of his Vietnam War experiences. It covers the period from when he is first drafted

(*see* DRAFT) in the summer of 1968, follows him to basic training at FORT LEWIS, WASHINGTON, and describes his actual tour of duty as an infantry soldier in Vietnam from his arrival in January 1969 until his return home in March 1970. *If I Die* sets out the basic themes and questions that O'Brien will return to over and over again in his later fiction: the futility and cruelty of war, the debts one owes to one's country and to one's self, the relationship between courage and cowardice, and perhaps above all, how a person can behave honorably in the most dreadful circumstances.

SYNOPSIS

Chapter 1

The memoir opens with a chapter that describes a typical day for O'Brien while a soldier in Vietnam. He and a buddy named Barney talk about the futility of the war and the sameness of the days as they lie next to each other on the ground, trapped by sniper fire. When the barrage of bullets ends, ALPHA COMPANY moves out to search a village near the BATANGAN PENINSULA, where the unit has been seeing action for several weeks. The men discover tunnels in the village, but several soldiers throw hand grenades down to blow them up before the officers can make up their minds about whether to search the tunnels or not. The company takes mortar fire as they leave the village, but nobody is hurt. When night falls, the men dig new foxholes, take turns at guard, and expect the worst. Only a few mortar rounds fall that night, and the soldiers of Alpha Company consider themselves lucky. The chapter ends with the men cooking C RATIONS early in the morning, then breaking camp and moving out to start the whole routine over again with the new day.

Chapters 2–3

The stage set, O'Brien moves back in time in the next two chapters to discuss his family background, his small hometown of WORTHINGTON, MINNESOTA, and his experience of being drafted into the war. At the beginning of chapter 2, "Pro Patria," he writes, "I grew out of one war and into another" (11). O'Brien explains that his father and mother were both WORLD WAR II veterans, his father having seen action in the Pacific theater, and his mother serving as a WAVE (Women Accepted for Volunteer Emergency Service), a U.S. Navy division. Like other young men of his generation, O'Brien grew up playing war games, pretending to "tak[e] on the Japs and Krauts along the shores of Lake Okabena" (12). He reminisces as well about boyhood baseball games, Fourth of July celebrations, and the voluminous reading he did as a child—devouring everything from the HARDY BOYS to PLATO to ERICH FROMM and subsequently asking hard questions about God and existence, about moral obligations, and about the difference between right and wrong. These questions, O'Brien writes, became especially pressing for him in the summer of 1968, when, after having graduated from college, he received his induction notice into the U.S. Army. Convinced that the war was wrong, yet feeling that he owed a moral obligation to the place where he was raised, O'Brien tells readers that his decision to honor his draft notice "was no decision," that it was "a sort of sleepwalking default" that led him to war (22). Chapter 3 ends with O'Brien speculating that the moral uncertainly he felt that summer remains present with him even as he is writing the book. While he wishes the memoir could be "a plea for everlasting peace," or at least "confirm the old beliefs about war," that it is "a crucible of men and events" and "makes a man out of you," (23), he tells readers that he can finally do neither, that all he can do is tell war stories.

Chapters 4–6

The rest of the book will tell these stories in haunting and painful detail. After a brief chapter in which he describes a typical night on combat duty, a chapter that serves as a matched set with the opening chapter, "Days," O'Brien again goes back in time to describe his experiences in basic training at Fort Lewis, Washington, and then in AIT (Advanced Infantry Training) after receiving his assignment as a combat soldier. Despising everything about basic training, from the lack of privacy, to the bullyism, to the mind-numbing routines, O'Brien initially tries to remain as separate from the other trainees as possible. He writes, "I learned to march, but I learned alone. I gaped at

the neat package of stupidity and arrogance at Fort Lewis. I was superior . . . I shunned the herd" (33). Yet, despite his best attempts to keep to himself, O'Brien tells readers that he made a friend at basic training, a fellow draftee named Erik who "talked about poetry and philosophy and travel" (35). The two become extremely close, discussing the morality of violence and their mutual love of literature, and thinking of themselves as fighting a "two-man war of survival" (35) against the army and the other trainees. Even when the pair of friends is humiliated by a drill sergeant who catches them sitting alone together, talking and polishing their boots behind the barracks, their friendship survives. Letters that O'Brien receives from Erik will punctuate the rest of his narrative, often serving as launching points for the philosophic meditations that interrupt the descriptions of the daily violence, cruelty, and monotony that he experiences in Vietnam.

While Erik avoids an infantry assignment by enlisting for an extra year at the beginning of basic training, O'Brien tells readers that he chose to gamble that he would receive a rear job, a risk he loses when he receives his assignment as a foot soldier. The reality of war begins to set in for O'Brien when he undergoes Advanced Infantry Training at Fort Lewis, where all the men know that they will actually be fighting on the ground in Vietnam in a few short weeks. At this point in the story, O'Brien begins to seriously consider desertion as an option. He describes going to the library in nearby Tacoma, Washington, to research escape routes and the life stories of deserters living in Stockholm and PARIS. He visits an army chaplain to discuss his moral objections to the war in Vietnam but is simply told to have faith in his government and country. O'Brien even goes so far as to write down an escape plan, save up his money, compose letters home, and take a bus into SEATTLE, where he plans to desert to Canada and then travel to Sweden. The night he arrives in the city, he checks into a cheap Seattle hotel, then takes a taxi to the University of Washington, where he unsuccessfully tries to finagle a date with a sorority girl. Upon returning to his hotel, O'Brien becomes violently ill and ends up burning his letters home and his escape plan. He writes, "It was over. I simply couldn't bring myself to flee. Family, the hometown, friends, history, tradition, fear, confusion, exile: I could not run" (68). At the end of the weekend, O'Brien takes the bus back to his barracks at Fort Lewis, restless and hopeless, but seemingly resigned to his fate as a soldier.

Chapters 7–19

The next several chapters describe O'Brien's arrival at the CHU LAI COMBAT CENTER in Vietnam, headquarters for the Army AMERICAL DIVISION, his specific assignment to ALPHA COMPANY of the 5th Battalion, 46th Infantry, and his first few weeks at LANDING ZONE GATOR, headquarters of his new infantry battalion. Soon after his arrival at LZ Gator, O'Brien experiences a night mortar attack in which two GIs and eight VIET CONG are killed. Despite the terror of that attack, O'Brien describes his first month with Alpha Company as "mostly a vacation" (79); he spends his days patrolling the beaches around Chu Lai and participates in only a very few night ambushes. During this time, he begins to learn the lingo of war, picking up slang terms such as FNG, FRAG, DINKS and SLOPES, and he also begins to learn about his fellow soldiers, known mostly by their nicknames. He describes Mad Mark, his platoon leader—a first lieutenant and a GREEN BERET who practices what O'Brien calls "an Aristotelian ethic . . . Making war is a necessary and natural profession" but "not a crusade" (82). All in all, O'Brien writes, "it was not a bad war" (83) until the men conduct a night ambush in a village called TRI BINH 4. It is here that O'Brien is introduced to his first war atrocity: Mad Mark and the men slice off the ear of a dead VC and take it back to camp with them as a souvenir. In the morning, O'Brien sees the dead man still lying in the village among slaughtered animals and burning huts. For him, the war has truly begun.

That spring, Alpha Company is moved to a new base called LZ Minuteman, in the middle of the hot, dusty Batangan Peninsula, where the men play chess, write letters home, and wait to be resupplied during the day, while conducting patrols and ambushes at night. O'Brien's worst wartime experiences, however, occur in early summer, when Alpha Company is sent into an area called PINKVILLE to pursue the elusive and feared 48th VIET CONG BATTALION. This is the same area where the MY LAI MASSACRE had occurred over a year previously, in March 1968, although news of the massacre had not yet been reported in the media, so that neither American soldiers nor the public at large yet knew the horrific story. Despite not knowing the facts of the massacre at the time, O'Brien nevertheless senses the animosity of the villagers in the My Lai area, and he witnesses several horrors of his own, from the agonizing death of a pretty VC woman soldier shot in the groin, to the mistreatment of feeble and elderly Vietnamese men, to the numerous deaths of his comrades, mostly by mine explosions and sniper fire. In fact, O'Brien includes in this section of the book an entire chapter that details the different kinds of mines the men encounter and the specific injuries brought on by each.

Under the overwhelming duress of war, O'Brien meditates frequently on courage and cowardice. Citing writers such as Plato, who describes courage as "wise endurance," and ERNEST HEMINGWAY, who views courage as "grace under pressure," O'Brien tortuously wonders whether his own "apparent courage in enduring" is simply "a well-disguised cowardice" (139). He ponders the make-believe heroes of his youth, such as Alan Ladd's character in the movie SHANE, HUMPHREY BOGART in *Casablanca,* and most of all, FREDERIC HENRY in *A Farewell to Arms:* all men who were "hard and realistic," "removed from other men," "wise," and above all, "courageous" (143). Looking for similar heroes in Vietnam, O'Brien finds only one, his beloved Captain Johansen, who he writes, "was separated from his soldiers by a deadfall canyon of character and temperament" (133). Johansen, in O'Brien's view, is courageous not only because he acts bravely but also because he is self-conscious about moral issues. He thinks deeply about bravery, about right and wrong, and tries to act accordingly. O'Brien rejects as potential heroes soldiers who act bravely out of instinct or in an unthinking way.

When Johansen leaves Alpha Company at the end of July, O'Brien describes the new captain, Smith, in much less flattering terms. Openly proclaiming himself a coward, Smith is a green officer who ends up getting several of his own soldiers killed and injured when a group of U.S. armored personnel carriers retreats, crushing several men in their path. O'Brien also depicts a battalion commander who refuses to land his helicopter to evacuate several severely wounded men because the landing zone is not secure. Yet another example of deadly incompetence occurs when Alpha Company is temporarily stationed near a beautiful lagoon to provide security for a small nearby village. One night, while performing a routine firing of mortar rounds designed to calibrate the weapons, 33 villagers are injured and 13 are killed when the mortars are aimed incorrectly.

Chapters 20–23

In the fall of 1969, O'Brien is removed from actual combat when he finally gets the rear echelon job that he had been coveting since his arrival. The final chapters of the memoir explore the differences between life at the front and life in the rear. O'Brien describes the elaborate Thanksgiving and Christmas meals enjoyed by support soldiers, the sexual frustration brought on by floor shows featuring Korean, Japanese, Australian, and Filipino girls, as well as the boredom and bureaucracy of daily life in the rear area. He depicts a particularly gung ho officer named Major Callicles who snaps at reporters come to ask questions about My Lai and who screams at a medic named Tully whom he suspects of deliberately self-inflicting a wound in order to get sent home. In a drunken haze one night, Callicles forces O'Brien to venture out on an unauthorized night patrol to a nearby village. Several nights later, Callicles, in his usual frenzied mission against drugs and prostitutes, burns down the whorehouse catering to the soldiers at LZ Gator and is finally sent away from the base for good. O'Brien himself will leave the base not long after Callicles. The memoir closes with his description of the plane ride he takes back to the United States and home. Attended by a blond-haired, blue-eyed, but uncaring stewardess who seems to represent America to O'Brien, the young soldier writes that "There is no joy in leaving" (205). Yet, as the plane approaches U.S. soil and O'Brien changes clothes in the bathroom, he smiles at himself in the mirror, realizing that he is beginning to be happy at last.

COMMENTARY

Tim O'Brien in *If I Die* like many other Vietnam War writers begins by exploring the ideology and culture he grew up in that eventually prompted him to go to war. Like later Vietnam War memoirists Philip Caputo in *A Rumor of War* and Ron Kovic in *Born on the Fourth of July,* who both discuss the influence of John Wayne movies such as *The Sands of Iwo Jima* on their boyhood beliefs about war, courage, and manliness, O'Brien reveals that he, too, was raised on stories and movies of WORLD WAR II heroism. O'Brien clearly sees himself as a product of the earlier war when he writes that he "grew out of one war and into another" (11). Not only were his mother and father both World War II veterans, but he himself is part of the baby boom generation, "one of millions come to replace those who had just died" (11). He adds that he was "fed by the spoils of 1945 victory" (11). And it is the hallowed aura of that victory that sparks the minds of the young boys of O'Brien's generation. He explains that, "in patches of weed and clouds of imagination," he learned to play army games. The boys buy dented helmets and rusted canteens at the local Army Surplus Store and treat these as holy "relics" of their fathers' history (12). They pretend to fight "Japs and Krauts" along the shores of the local lake and admire their fathers' war decorations. O'Brien even steals a tiny battle star from one of his father's medals and carries it with him in his pocket as a talisman of that earlier war.

Alongside an ideology glorifying America's involvement in World War II, O'Brien is also raised on a general diet of patriotism, on the "careless muscle flexing of a nation giving bridle to its own good fortune and success" (11) during the postwar boom years when he is a young boy. He remembers participating in such all-American activities as Little League baseball games with his father coaching and Fourth of July celebrations in which the whole town would turn out to watch parades of American Legionnaires and fireworks displays that exploded over the lake at night. Some of these memories will work their way into his later fiction, as in the story

"Speaking of Courage" from *The Things They Carried,* in which Norman Bowker drives around and around a lake in the center of his small, midwestern town one Fourth of July while his father watches a baseball game on television. In fact, much of *If I Die,* while standing on its own literary merits, also seems a training ground for O'Brien to experiment with characters, situations, and themes that he will develop in his later fiction. It is possible, for instance, to read the naïve, childish soldier Barney as a model for the future Cacciato and the ironic Bates as the prototype of Doc Peret in *Going After Cacciato.* The partly real, partly imagined girlfriend O'Brien fantasizes about in the memoir shares much in common with Martha from *The Things They Carried,* and O'Brien himself shares qualities with Lieutenant Jimmy Cross. A small Vietnamese girl with hoop earrings whom O'Brien meets by a well in a dusty Vietnamese village perhaps morphs into the young girl that Paul Berlin so desperately tries to explain himself to in *Cacciato,* and even into the Chinese-Vietnamese refugee Sarkin Aung Wan in the same novel. And WORTHINGTON, MINNESOTA, itself appears in only slightly altered form as FORT DODGE, IOWA, in *Cacciato* and as Norman Bowker's small hometown in central Iowa in *The Things They Carried.*

Yet, despite the baseball games and patriotic displays, readers learn quickly that life in Worthington, Minnesota, is not as idyllic as it might seem initially. O'Brien confesses that he did not necessarily fit into small-town life as well as he might have wished. Too small for football and unable to hit a baseball adequately, O'Brien turns from athletics—one of the main defining institutions of manhood in small-town America—to reading. But he confesses that the library was a poor substitute for the football field on an October evening. He watches the athletes from the stands, wishing he were they. The gulf between O'Brien and some of the other townspeople becomes more apparent when he develops an interest in politics while in high school. He drives to a League of Women Voters meeting one evening but asks questions that no one seems able to answer. After reading that the Democrats were liberal, he attends several party meetings but finally is unable to "make out the dif-ference between the people there and the people down the street boosting Nixon and Cabot Lodge" (15). There is a uniformity to prairie life, a blind acceptance of prevailing ideology that O'Brien chafes against even while still in high school. Much later, in a 1991 interview with Daniel Bourne of *Artful Dodge* magazine, O'Brien confirms a lasting bitterness about a certain type of small-town, midwestern, knee-jerk patriotism—a patriotism built largely on ignorance of historical facts—that he first hints at in *If I Die:*

> One aspect [of a midwestern background] is my sense of bitterness about small-town Republican, polyester, white-belted, Kiwanis America. The people who vote and participate in civic events, who build playgrounds and prop up our libraries and then turn around and send us to wars, oftentimes out of utter and absolute ignorance. And I'm bitter about it. I'm bitter about people who say with a knee-jerk reaction, "let's go kill Satan." The Middle America I grew up in sent me to that war. . . . That know-nothing attitude really disturbs and angers me. The Midwest for me is not just a sweet background I naively grew up in full of innocence and romanticism. I have a real bitterness towards it that lasts to this day. . . . And, just to finish this little tirade of mine, above all my bitterness has to do with my hatred of Middle American ignorance. These people didn't know—in my case, in the case of Vietnam—Ho Chi Minh's politics from those of the governor of Arizona. They didn't know Bao Dai from the man in the moon. They didn't know the first thing about SEATO. They didn't know the first thing about French colonialism, about basic history. . . . There's a laziness and a complacency, a kind of Puritan sense of pious rectitude, that you can tell really pisses me off. So when I write about the Midwest, I'm writing about it in part out of a sense of real rage and anger, justifiable rage and justifiable anger.

Although he never expresses his anger as openly in *If I Die* as he does in the 1991 interview, O'Brien does conclude chapter 2, "Pro Patria," by writing that when he went away to college, the town did not, finally, miss him very much.

The theme of patriotic or heroic illusions being punctured by a disappointing reality is a common one in American literature about the Vietnam War. While O'Brien is skeptical about American involvement in Vietnam from the beginning and is drafted into the war rather than being a gung ho recruit like Caputo and Kovic, he is nevertheless raised with a similar cultural ideology and is concerned, as these other writers are, with how reality does not match the country's mythic perception of itself when he gets to Vietnam. One of O'Brien's main objectives, and the concern of almost every Vietnam War writer, is to show that this war is not his father's war. Unlike World War II, which seemed morally imperative in the face of Nazi and Japanese atrocities, and which offered a decisive allied victory, Vietnam turns out to a moral quagmire, a war that the United States finally cannot win. O'Brien drives this point home ironically in the very first chapter when the naïve young soldier Barney asks him the name of the village that ALPHA COMPANY is currently cordoning off and searching. O'Brien replies that the village is called ST. VITH. In cynically citing the well-known location of an American-German encounter during the Battle of the Bulge in World War II, O'Brien draws attention to the differences between St. Vith and the village he and Barney find themselves in. While most American schoolboys growing up in the 1950s had heard about St. Vith, about Normandy, about Stalingrad, about Iwo Jima, and other seemingly heroic World War II battles, in Vietnam the village names are hard for the men to pronounce and to remember. In fact, the villages are often renamed from the original Vietnamese on American military maps and even assigned numbers as identifying monikers.

In addition, while each World War II battle seemed to carry its own mystique, in Vietnam the villages all run together for the men into a dreary sameness as they practice a routine of cordoning and searching, burning huts, blowing tunnels, seldom finding anyone in the villages except the very young and the very elderly. Barney highlights the sameness of this routine when he embarrassedly asks Captain Johansen to confirm that the officers do not expect to find anything in the village.

"That's what O'Brien was saying," Barney tells the captain. "Says it's hopeless. But like I told him, there's always the chance we can surprise old Charlie. Right? Always a *chance*" (5). Captain Johansen does not even respond to Barney's desperate desire for action, and O'Brien writes that he closed his eyes: "Optimism always made me sleepy" (6). Nearing the end of his combat assignment, O'Brien writes about his longing for a rear echelon job. Disillusioned after his time in the country, he writes about himself and the members of his company: "We weren't the old soldiers of World War II. No valor to squander for things like country or honor or military objectives" (175). O'Brien's boyhood dreams of heroically fighting Germans and Japanese like his father have become transformed into a simple attempt to remain inconspicuous and to avoid death.

This war, in fact, often seems absurd to O'Brien and his fellow soldiers, their survival or success in battle based more on luck than on skill or training. In the opening chapter, "Days," O'Brien describes the men unexpectedly taking on sniper fire and mortar attacks while searching a village. One of the men in Alpha Company comments on how lucky they are no one was hurt: "'Nobody hurt,' one of the men said. 'Lucky thing. We was all sitting down—a little rest break, you know? Smokin' and snoozin'. Lucky, lucky thing. *Lucky*. Anybody standing up when that shit hits is dead. I mean gone'" (8). Men survive this war not by valor, but by chance. O'Brien's friend Chip (CHIP MERRICKS) and a squad leader named Tom die, for instance, by triggering a rigged artillery round after the company's most successful and best-executed ambush, when the danger seemed long over. The random nature of the way death is dealt out in Vietnam leads to the men feeling a loss of control. If any single step can trip a wire attached to a mine or sink one's leg into a PUNJI PIT, if VIET CONG SAPPERS can slip through a base's wire perimeter at night while one sleeps, there does not seem to be much a single soldier can do to avoid death. The men cope with this loss of control by adopting a darkly ironic attitude toward the absurdities they witness. In his chapter listing the different kinds of mines encountered in Vietnam, O'Brien writes that he will allow his catalog to stand, "because that is how we talked about them, with a funny laugh, flippantly, with a chuckle. It is funny. It's absurd. . . . Patent absurdity. . . . We slay one of them, hit a mine, kill another, hit another mine. It is funny. We walk through the mines, trying to catch the FORTY-EIGHTH Viet Cong Battalion like inexperienced hunters after a hummingbird" (127).

But the random nature of death in Vietnam is not the only absurdity faced by O'Brien and his fellow soldiers. They repeatedly witness mediocre officers making bad decisions. Captain Smith, for instance, who replaces Captain Johansen, does not understand that it is standard operating procedure (SOP) for U.S. armored personnel carriers to retreat when being fired upon. Thus, he leaves his men in the paths of the reversing vehicles, causing several deaths and severe injuries. Even more absurd is the fact that Smith crows to O'Brien that he will receive a Purple Heart after this operation. The captain has received a tiny scratch from a mine explosion and shows O'Brien a hole in his shirt so small that it looks like it was made by a moth. As in most Vietnam War literature, O'Brien tends to portray the ordinary foot soldier as someone at the mercy of forces greater than himself, as the victim of a bungled American policy in Vietnam, of uncaring or glory-seeking officers and politicians. Readers see another example of this kind of officer when Alpha Company is helicoptered into a burning village as part of a combat assault (CA) mission in mid-July 1969. After the company suffers several severe and life-threatening injuries, the unit's battalion commander, "a tough colonel circling around in his helicopter directing things" (159), refuses to pick up the wounded because the landing zone is not secure. Later the next evening, after even more men are injured and killed in a large mine explosion and the firing and mortar attacks have stopped, the battalion commander finally flies down and picks up the dead and wounded. He receives a Distinguished Flying Cross for this act, even though his participation in the battle occurs only after the personal danger to himself has passed.

The disillusion that accompanies such examples of incompetent and self-serving officers leads to another major difference between Vietnam and the war of the previous generation: a breakdown in military discipline. O'Brien cites several instances of outright disobedience on the part of the enlisted men and lower-ranking officers and even shows officers who are threatened or injured by the soldiers they are supposed to be leading. When Alpha Company's battalion commander, Colonel Daud, orders the men to send out night ambushes while they are on the BATANGAN PENINSULA in April, O'Brien writes, "Sometimes we did, other times, we did not" (105). If the lower-level officers decide that the men are too tired, they call in false grid coordinates, indicating an ambush, which are then blasted with "expensive rounds of marking explosives" (105) from the big guns in the rear. The men then get on the radio each hour, asking for nonexistent situation reports, which they answer themselves by disguising their voices, nervous that headquarters might be monitoring communications. The officers justify the phony ambushes by muttering that "Colonel Daud was a greenhorn, too damn gung-ho" (106). The men come to hate Colonel Daud even more as he orders many dangerous combat assaults in the coming days. When they hear news of his death at the hand of sappers in a midnight raid, the men do not mourn, but rather a lieutenant leads them in song, "a catchy, happy celebrating song: Ding-dong, the wicked witch is dead" (111).

Even more startling is the fact that the men themselves sometimes harm officers considered dangerous. After the incident in which Captain Smith gets several soldiers killed in a retreat of friendly armored vehicles, the men openly ridicule him, some claiming "it was a only a matter of time before someone chucked a grenade into his foxhole" (158). Later in the narrative, O'Brien describes a first sergeant, perceived as dangerously racist by the black soldiers, who is shot by one of his own men with an M-79 round fired off a grenade launcher. In Vietnam, such murders were often called FRAGGING (*see* FRAG)—a term that refers to the most popular method of killing an overzealous officer, which was to toss a fragmentation grenade into his hooch or tent. Fragging left no evidence; the murder weapon was destroyed along with the victim. These killings were a real problem in Vietnam and are estimated to have taken the lives of more than 1,000 officers and noncommissioned officers over the course of the war. It is an issue addressed in many Vietnam War films and literature, including O'Brien's own novel *Going After Cacciato,* in which the main character, Paul Berlin, struggles with his guilt over what the men in his platoon do to their by-the-books lieutenant, Sidney Martin.

Disillusionment, loss of control, and a breakdown of military discipline also lead to the men in Alpha Company becoming hardened to atrocities committed against the Vietnamese, several of which O'Brien describes in vivid detail. Mad Mark's slicing off the ear of a dead Viet Cong soldier, a practice mentioned in numerous later Vietnam War writings, from Michael Herr's *Dispatches* to Bobbie Ann Mason's *In Country,* is only the beginning. In chapter 10, "The Man at the Well," O'Brien relates the story of an old, stooped, and blind Vietnamese farmer who allows the men of Alpha company to bathe in his well, even hauling up buckets of water to help wash the dirty and tired soldiers. When a "blustery and stupid soldier" hurls a carton of milk at the old man from 15 feet away, hitting him squarely in the face and covering the farmer in "perfect gore," no one moves to help him (100). Later, in another village, three gaunt old men are tied to trees, their mouths stuffed with wet rags. The three are left to suffer all night long, in the hopes that they will divulge information about the Viet Cong. In the morning, the men are beaten and whipped before finally being released. But perhaps most disturbing of all is the description of a dying Vietnamese woman, a member of the North Vietnamese Army, who is shot through the groin. O'Brien writes that "blood gushed out of the holes, front and back" made by the bullet (112). He describes her face lying in the dirt, flies crawling all over her, the woman's squirming and moaning as a medic tries to patch her up, and the soldiers' callous comments that she is "pretty for a gook" and that "she's shot dead through the wrong place" (113). O'Brien does not flinch from describing the horror he witnesses in graphic detail.

In such vivid descriptions of violence, O'Brien's own eyewitness account shares much in common with the bulk of Vietnam War literature, which often attempts to grapple honestly with the horror that many Americans experienced in Vietnam. The stories this literature conveys are frequently brutally graphic and shocking, as authors relate atrocities committed both by the Viet Cong and by American soldiers themselves. Vietnam literature tends to describe these atrocities in more excruciating and often brutal detail than we might see in earlier war literature. Part of the reason for this is that honesty, a refusal to blink at the horror witnessed, is a prized virtue of many Vietnam War authors—precisely because of the perceived (and often very real) dishonesty of the U.S. government concerning the war. What really happened with the USS MADDOX in the GULF OF TONKIN that led Congress to authorize LYNDON BAINES JOHNSON to use force in Vietnam? What about secret bombings, secret peace talks, the Pentagon Papers? If the American people cannot trust the U.S. government, these authors attempt to convey the real stories of what happened—to "tell it like it was." O'Brien in the *Artful Dodge* interview makes a similar point when he discusses his own use of violence in literature:

> And I also think that this detailed portrayal of the horrors of violence is a reaction to the myths I grew up with as a kid: John Wayne movies and Audie Murphy movies and the little GI Joe comic books I used to read where death was inconsequential because it didn't seem very horrible at all. No blood, they'd all just "drop" dead. War and violence didn't seem all that horrible as it was portrayed back then. My object is not to wallow in blood and gore. The object is to display it in terms so that you want to stay away from it if possible. (Bourne)

Vietnam War writers like O'Brien, raised on sanitized versions of World War II heroics, insist on fully depicting the human cost of a morally questionable war.

In fact, the dubious morality of this particular war raises the key philosophical question that O'Brien ponders throughout the narrative and also in his later fictional works *Going After Cacciato* and *The Things They Carried*: Is the proper response to an improper war to fight or to flee? Sounding very much like the later Tim O'Brien character in the story "On the Rainy River" from *The Things They Carried*, O'Brien writes about the moral quandary he experienced after receiving his draft notice: "I was persuaded then, and I remain persuaded now, that the war was wrong. And since it was wrong and since people were dying as a result of it, it was evil" (18). Yet, despite the seeming assurance of this pronouncement, O'Brien admits that he lacks the full knowledge to make a truly informed judgment about the war:

> Doubts, of course, hedged all this: I had neither the expertise nor the wisdom to synthesize answers; the facts were clouded; there was no certainty as to the kind of government that would follow a North Vietnamese victory or, for that matter, an American victory, and the specifics of the conflict were hidden away—partly in men's minds, partly in the archives of government, and partly in buried, irretrievable history. The war, I thought, was wrongly conceived and poorly justified. But perhaps I was mistaken, and who really knew, anyway? (18)

The one thing O'Brien is sure of, as he will write later in "On the Rainy River," is that "Certain blood was being shed for uncertain reasons" (*TTTC* 40). Making O'Brien's moral dilemma about whether to go to war or not even more complicated is the fact that his entire upbringing, even more, the whole of Western cultural tradition, is urging him toward war. As he will do later in the short story "The Things They Carried," he uses the metaphor of physical weight to describe the nearly oppressive pull his background and upbringing have on him. "Piled on top of" his doubts about the war's morality, O'Brien writes, "was the town, my family, my teachers, a whole history of the prairie. Like magnets, these things pulled in one direction or the other, almost physical forces weighting the problem, so that, in the end, it was less reason and more gravity that was the final influence" (18).

To help him decide whether to flee or to honor his DRAFT notice, O'Brien looks to his cul-

tural heritage, specifically to classic Greek writers who addressed questions of morality and courage. O'Brien remembers PLATO's dialogue the CRITO, in which the condemned SOCRATES refuses to escape from his prison cell because he had for the 70 previous years of his life consented to live in ATHENS and believed he must follow Athenian law. Following Socrates' example, O'Brien reasons, "I owed the prairie something. For twenty-one years I'd lived under its laws, accepted its education, eaten its food, wasted and guzzled its water, slept well at night, driven across its highways, dirtied and breathed its air, wallowed in its luxuries" (18). Like Socrates, O'Brien questions whether it would be morally just to flee a society he had lived in his whole life when its laws, which he previously had accepted, turn against him. This is a dilemma that O'Brien will return to in the climactic scene of *Going After Cacciato*, in which Paul Berlin decides to stay at the war rather than flee, as urged by the refugee Sarkin Aung Wan. Berlin argues that his prior acts of consent—boarding a plane, putting on a uniform, etc.—bind him to performing subsequent acts. In addition, he explains that he owes a debt to his family, his friends, his town, his country, and his fellow soldiers, and that such obligations to actual people outweigh obligations to abstract principles. Yet, just as the morality of Paul Berlin's decision to stay at the war is open to interpretation—after all, he also admits that what dominates his choice is his fear of being thought of as a coward—Tim O'Brien in *If I Die* never settles the moral dilemma he raises. While he cites the *Crito* in this early scene, later, at basic training, he tries to imagine Socrates as an actual soldier, and he realizes that "Plato may have missed something" (47), noting that Plato recorded nothing about Socrates weeping or about the reluctance he might have experienced, participating in what "could not have been a perfectly just war" (46).

O'Brien looks to the classics as well for a definition of courage that will satisfy him. Unlike other Vietnam narratives, in which authors and characters take on a highly ironic attitude to any notion of courage or bravery, works in which the highest attainable goal often becomes simple survival, O'Brien remains concerned throughout his body of literature with questions of courage and cowardice. Part of the reason that *If I Die* is such an emotionally affecting memoir is that O'Brien continues to grope for morality in this most immoral of wars. Never giving in to complete cynicism, he continues to ask how a person can act honorably, can make good moral choices under extreme duress. As he searches for a workable definition of courage, O'Brien turns again to Plato, who in his dialogue *LACHES*, defines courage as "wise endurance" (137–38). Looking back at his own past behavior, O'Brien has to acknowledge that he has endured. But the stickier question to him is whether or not his endurance has been wise. While Hitler's blitzkrieg and the attack on Pearl Harbor in World War II seem to O'Brien self-evident causes for the use of force, calling for great sacrifice and endurance on the part of American soldiers in that war, the war in Vietnam is being fought for "uncertain reasons" (138), raising the question of whether O'Brien's "apparent courage in enduring" is simply a "well-disguised cowardice" (139). He wonders whether it has been easier for him to simply endure rather than "utter a dramatic and certain and courageous no to the war" (139). When he returns to these same questions in his later story "On the Rainy River," he will offer a more definitive answer for the fictional Tim O'Brien, who asks similar questions: "I was a coward," O'Brien has his narrator state in that story. "I went to the war" (*TTTC* 61).

Unlike his later work and unlike Vietnam War literature in general, in *If I Die* O'Brien offers readers a model for the truly courageous soldier. While he certainly presents numerous incompetent, pompous, or overzealous officers, O'Brien depicts Captain Johansen, his first commanding officer in Alpha Company, as a morally upright and admirable man. Calling Johansen a "living hero" (145), unlike the heroes of his past, who had all been "make believe men" (142) such as Alan Ladd in *SHANE*, CAPTAIN VERE in Melville's *Billy Budd*, HUMPHREY BOGART in *Casablanca*, and, above all, FREDERIC HENRY in Hemingway's *A Farewell to Arms*, O'Brien reflects that one quality that sets Captain Johansen apart is that "he alone cared enough about being brave to think about it and try to do it" (145). O'Brien rejects as courageous those

men who act instinctively or unthinkingly, arguing that wisdom and self-consciousness are necessary parts of courage: "Men must *know* what they do is courageous, they must *know* it is right" (140). Nor, according to O'Brien, is Hemingway's definition of courage as "grace under pressure" adequate, because "it's too easy to affect grace, and it's too hard to see through it" (146). But O'Brien is also a pragmatist who recognizes the difficulty human beings have in acting courageously in all circumstances. Thus, he rejects the cliché that "A coward dies a thousand deaths but a brave man only once" (147). Is a person "once and for always" a coward or a hero, he asks, arguing that it seems more likely to him that "men act cowardly and, at other times, act with courage, each in different measure, each with varying consistency" (147). The definition of courage that O'Brien finally leaves readers with in his memoir is that brave men are those "who do well on the average, perhaps with one moment of glory" (147). He likes this definition because it offers the possibility of redemption to the great mass of men in Alpha Company, those who are neither cowards nor heroes, but those who promise themselves to do better next time.

In *If I Die*, O'Brien touches on other themes that will be developed more fully in his own later works as well as by other Vietnam War writers. As the first fully integrated war, in which troops from different racial backgrounds fought alongside one another, Vietnam was a place where American soldiers were affected strongly by the fight for racial justice back home. O'Brien touches on these issues when he depicts African-American soldiers angry about perceived racism on the part of certain officers who reserve rear echelon jobs for white soldiers. The best route to a rear job, O'Brien writes, is for a soldier to endear himself to the company commander, but that is difficult for black soldiers to do:

> For the soul brothers, that route is not easy. To begin with, the officer corps is dominated by white men; the corps of foot soldiers, common grunts, is disproportionately black. On top of that are all the old elements of racial tension—fears, hates, suspicions. And on top of that is the very pure fact that life is at stake. Not prop-

erty or a decent job or social acceptance. It's a matter of staying alive.

With either the hunch or the reality that white officers favor white grunts in handing out the rear jobs, many blacks react as any sane man would. They sulk. They talk back, get angry, loaf, play sick, smoke dope. They group together and laugh and say shit to the system. (173)

Racism is evident as well in the treatment of the Vietnamese themselves. O'Brien records how the men refer to Vietnamese as "dinks and slopes" (80); it is easier, of course, to shoot an enemy that has been depersonalized in such a way.

In his last chapter, O'Brien comments more fully on the gulfs separating individuals during wartime. He writes that his fellow soldiers never really knew him and that he never really knew the Vietnamese people. The one element of Vietnam that O'Brien does feel he came to know, however, was the land itself. This emphasis on the land is yet another theme that will be developed in the later Vietnam War writing of both O'Brien and others. For American soldiers in Vietnam, the land at times seemed to be their worst enemy. While O'Brien writes that he saw the living enemy only once, he describes the underground tunnels, the jungle terrain, and above all, the broiling sun, which the men of Alpha Company come to accept as their "most persistent and cunning enemy" (102). But the land could also provide protection, as the men would dig in, constructing foxholes to avoid the inevitable mortar fire and sniper fire they would experience while out on patrol at night. As he flies out of the country where he has spent the previous year of his life, O'Brien muses about how well he came to know the land itself: "But the earth, you could turn a spadeful of it, see its dryness and the tint of red, and dig out enough of it so as to lie in the hole at night, and that much of Vietnam you would know" (207). He came to know the land, he says, as one would know a friend's face.

What else does O'Brien know as he leaves Vietnam? As he tells readers earlier, after the war ends, he is left with no great lessons, but only with "simple, unprofound scraps of truth. Men die.

Fear hurts and humiliates. It is hard to be brave" (23). These nuggets of insight might not allow the foot soldier to teach anything important, to relay moral lessons about war, but they do allow him, as O'Brien acknowledges, to tell war stories. And storytelling itself will become the central theme of O'Brien's later trilogy of great war novels: *Going After Cacciato, The Things They Carried,* and *In the Lake of the Woods.*

CHARACTERS

Arizona O'Brien writes that when he thinks about courage, he remembers a young soldier nicknamed Arizona who charges out across a flat piece of land one day, only to be cut down, leaving his "long limp body in the grass" (134). O'Brien muses that Arizona's charge was like "the light brigade with only one man" (134). Later, however, O'Brien rejects the notion that Arizona acted courageously because he did not think or care about courage—he simply acted without thought.

Arnold Arnold is a "tall, skinny" (117) soldier whom Mad Mark carries over his shoulder and deposits into a helicopter during a VIET CONG ambush of ALPHA COMPANY in May. Although readers never find out what happens to the soldier, he is very likely the same Arnold O'Brien had mentioned earlier, when first introducing the men of Alpha Company—a squad leader nicknamed Nestle's Quick who O'Brien says will be killed in two months.

Barker Barker is one of the soldiers in ALPHA COMPANY whom O'Brien meets the morning after a mortar attack his first night at LANDING ZONE GATOR. Barker clowns around with a soldier nicknamed Wolf, and both men claim that the mortar attack was simply "a lark" (78).

Barney Barney is the first war buddy of O'Brien's that readers are introduced to in the memoir. He appears in the opening chapter, "Days," as a rather simple fellow soldier from Cleveland, who good-naturedly argues with O'Brien about whether this particular day is worse than others the platoon has experienced. Described as jumping up "like a little kid on a pogo stick" (2) when ALPHA COMPANY is ready to move out, and as frequently giggling, Barney may be a prototype for Cacciato in O'Brien's 1978 novel, *Going After Cacciato*. Like Cacciato, whose face is described as white and bland like the rising moon, Barney's face "had the smooth complexion of a baby brother" (8). His childlike simplicity, a trait also exhibited by Cacciato, is emphasized when O'Brien adds, "Tickle him and he'd coo" (8). Another soldier named Bates teases Barney at the end of the opening chapter, leading the gullible young man to believe that the enemy may be out of ammunition. Barney appears again in chapter 4, "Nights," when he looks through a STARLIGHT SCOPE with O'Brien and several other soldiers. He is also present near the end of the book, when a group of armored personnel carriers retreats, crushing several members of Alpha Company. Barney proudly shows O'Brien a two-inch hole in his canteen where shrapnel had hit; the canteen protected the simpleminded but lucky soldier from receiving a dangerous injury himself.

Bates   Bates is a fellow soldier of O'Brien's in ALPHA COMPANY, described as a "good friend" (131). Unlike the naïve and childlike Barney, Bates is sophisticated and ironic, someone who, as his name suggests, likes to bait and tease the more gullible soldiers and question the motives of the officers. In this respect, Bates is possibly a model for the philosophic and ironic character Doc Peret in O'Brien's later novel *Going After Cacciato*. Bates is present in *Box Me Up* in the opening chapter, "Days," where he teases the gullible Barney, as well as in the chapter "Nights," where, much to Barney's astonishment, Bates claims to have been dreaming on a long march about undressing a famous politician's daughter on a beach in the Bahamas. Later, O'Brien will describe cooking crayfish at dusk with Bates on a deceptively beautiful lagoon where the men are stationed. The next morning, the water will be sullied by the remains of Peterson, a fellow soldier who had killed himself fishing with hand grenades.

Battalion Commander at AIT   While at Advanced Infantry Training (AIT) at FORT LEWIS,

O'Brien asks to see the unit battalion commander to discuss his moral objections to the war in Vietnam. Although he is first sent to see a chaplain who spews clichés about faith and patriotic duty, O'Brien eventually is able to meet with the commander, who has served in Korea as well as three tours of duty in Vietnam. But rather than listen to O'Brien, the battalion commander launches into tales of his own war experiences. Mistaking O'Brien's moral questions about the war as simple fear, he tries to comfort the young trainee by assuring him that everyone is afraid and that the fear will turn to exhilaration eventually. He then dismisses O'Brien, congratulating himself for talking to one of his men and urging O'Brien to come see him again if other problems, such as bad food or lousy mail service, should crop up.

Battalion Commander of Alpha Company   In mid-July, ALPHA COMPANY is sent on a combat assault (*see* CA) into a burning village. The men immediately take casualties and radio for a helicopter to evacuate the wounded. The company's battalion commander, described as "a tough colonel" (159), refuses to perform this duty because the landing zone has not been secured. The next day, after more fighting and explosions, when the danger has finally passed, the battalion commander agrees to fly down to pick up the wounded and killed. Ironically, he receives a Distinguished Flying Cross for this service. This battalion commander may be Colonel Daud, whom O'Brien mentions earlier in his narrative. Daud was the battalion commander of Alpha Company in April, but is killed by SAPPERS in a midnight raid. Because O'Brien never tells readers exactly when Daud died, it is impossible to be sure whether this battalion commander, who is with Alpha Company in July, is Daud or another man. However, it seems more likely that the winner of the Distinguished Flying Cross is a battalion commander sent to replace Daud, since the narrative implies that Daud died soon after the events O'Brien described taking place back in April.

Blyton, Drill Sergeant   Blyton is the drill sergeant who torments O'Brien and his friend Erik while the pair undergo basic training at FORT

LEWIS. Described as having a "sleek, black, airborne body," Blyton continually "teases, threatens, [and] humiliates" the young recruits (41). Although O'Brien acknowledges that drill sergeants are supposed to play a role, to make themselves hated, he argues that for Blyton the cruelty is more than role-playing. "He is evil," O'Brien writes, "he does not personify the tough drill sergeant; rather he is the army; he's the devil" (41). Erik is the first of the two to have a direct run-in with Blyton, which occurs when he demands a private talk with the drill sergeant. Erik pours out his opposition to the war, but Blyton responds by calling him a coward, a charge that Erik does not reject, but one that he probes philosophically, explaining to O'Brien that he's "not just intellectually opposed to violence," but also "absolutely frightened by it" (36). Already having marked Erik as a troublemaker and a "pansy," Blyton is more than ready to humiliate him and his friend O'Brien when he catches the pair alone together, sitting behind the barracks, polishing their boots and talking. Later, when O'Brien will begin to plan seriously an escape to Sweden during Advanced Infantry Training (AIT), he dreams that his old drill sergeant Blyton is sitting next to him on the bus ride into SEATTLE, grinning and telling O'Brien that he is doomed: "I'll have you in the stockade, in chains, with bread and water. My man never gets away," O'Brien dreams the drill sergeant tells him (65). Blyton, who represents everything that O'Brien hates about the army, seems to win out in the end as O'Brien burns his escape plan and returns to Fort Lewis, his dream of fleeing the military abandoned.

Bully When thinking about courage, O'Brien remembers an eighth grade bully who pushed him out of line while waiting for the school bus. When O'Brien told the boy to "go piss on the principal's desk" (135), a shoving match ensued. Eventually, the two actually fought a few days later at school. Although O'Brien never actually hit the bully, the bigger boy fell down twice, and the fight, "by all accounts . . . ended in a draw" (135).

Callicles, Major Major Callicles is an officer O'Brien meets when he receives his rear echelon job in late August. He is battalion executive officer—second in command—of LANDING ZONE GATOR, headquarters for the 5th Battalion, 46th Infantry. Described as looking like an "ex-light-heavyweight champ," with "a head like a flattened 105 round, a thick brown neck, bristling stalks of hair" and "bloodshot eyes" (191), Major Callicles is a former noncommissioned officer who has worked his way up without attending West Point. He is also a strict disciplinarian who tells the men that he hates "moustaches, prostitution, pot, and sideburns" (191), in that order. When the story of the MY LAI MASSACRE, which had occurred a year and a half previously, breaks in U.S. newspapers, Callicles is interviewed by reporters from all the major news organizations. The major argues that what happened was a natural result of war, in which civilians unfortunately become collateral damage. O'Brien also depicts an incident in which Callicles screams angrily at a medic named Tully, whom he suspects of self-inflicting an injury in order to be sent home. Later that night, a drunk Major Callicles orders O'Brien to accompany him on an ill-advised night patrol into the nearby village of TRI BINH 4. They do not encounter any VIET CONG, and the major is rebuked by the battalion commander the following morning for the escapade. The last readers see of Major Callicles is a few nights later when he burns down the local whorehouse and is kicked out of LZ Gator for good.

Champion During O'Brien's first month with ALPHA COMPANY, as he and his fellow soldiers patrol the beaches outside of CHU LAI, Vietnamese children follow them around, digging their foxholes at night and performing other small, personal services as if they were miniature valets. O'Brien's own helper is a 10-year boy called Champion, who knows how to disassemble and clean rifles as well as how to give back rubs.

Chieu Hoi In chapter 21, "Hearts and Minds," O'Brien tells the story of a Vietnamese man described as a "CHIEU HOI," or an ex-VIET CONG fighter, who serves as a scout for CHARLIE COMPANY. When the man goes to battalion headquarters one day to ask for a pass to visit his sick baby, the captain refuses, insisting that the man is a soldier and must make sacrifices. Less than a day later, the Chieu Hoi goes AWOL.

Chip   Chip is a short, skinny, African-American soldier from Orlando, Florida, who is a member of ALPHA COMPANY. Readers first meet Chip in the chapter "Night" when he tells O'Brien that what seemed to be a night attack was simply a soldier named Turnip Head and a group of friends playing with hand grenades. Chip is killed later in the book, when he "strayed into a hedgerow and triggered a rigged 105 artillery round" (123) after what had seemed to be a successful night ambush. Of Chip's death, O'Brien writes, "He died in such a way that, for once, you could never know his color. He was wrapped in a plastic body bag, we popped smoke, and a helicopter took him away, my friend" (123). Although Chip's last name is never supplied in the memoir, the character is based on O'Brien's real-life friend from Alpha Company, Alvin CHIP MERRICKS, who was killed on May 9, 1960. Merricks is also a partial model for the character Curt Lemon in *The Things They Carried.*

Clauson   O'Brien describes being nearly killed by a hand grenade when ALPHA COMPANY is caught in a VIET CONG ambush in May, in the villages of MY KHE. The force of the grenade is taken by a soldier named Clauson, a "big fellow" (117) who lies on his back and screams, apparently severely injured. O'Brien never tells readers whether Clauson survived the attack or not.

Cop   Cop is the nickname of a young soldier in ALPHA COMPANY who has an Irish background and who wants to join the police force in Danbury, Connecticut. He appears in the narrative when O'Brien discusses the nicknames and slang used by the soldiers.

Czech Student   O'Brien spends the summer of 1967 studying in PRAGUE, CZECHOSLOVAKIA. One evening, he drinks beer with a young Czech student who is an economics specialist. The student invites O'Brien to have a conversation about the Vietnam War with his roommate, a young man

from North Vietnam who is also studying economics at the university. The Czech student facilitates what will be a three-hour conversation, helping to translate.

Daud, Colonel   In April the battalion commander of ALPHA COMPANY, Colonel Daud, described as "a black man, a stout and proper soldier" (106), orders the men to send out numerous night ambushes. O'Brien writes that sometimes the soldiers obeyed Colonel Daud's orders and sometimes they did not. Considering Daud too green and gung ho, the lower-level officers fake the ambushes if they feel the men are too tired, radioing false information back to headquarters. The men truly come to hate Daud when he orders several combat assaults (CA) into the dangerous area of PINKVILLE. Later, when Colonel Daud is killed by SAPPERS in a midnight raid, the men celebrate, led in song by a lieutenant: "a catchy, happy, celebrating song: Ding-dong, the wicked witch is dead" (111).

Doc   Doc is a soldier in ALPHA COMPANY who runs out of his foxhole through enemy fire in order to "wrap useless cloth around a dying soldier's chest" (142). When asked by O'Brien about this incident, Doc replies that he simply reacted without thinking, that his actions did not seem to him either the right or the wrong thing to do. When O'Brien asks whether Doc felt he might die, Doc just laughs and confidently replies that he will not die in Vietnam.

Dream Woman   One night while on an ambush being led by Mad Mark, O'Brien remembers a vivid dream he had as a 14-year-old. In the dream, O'Brien was held captive in a dark prison cell carved into the side of a mountain and forced by his swarthy captors to work with his fellow prisoners all day long in coal mines. Suddenly he is freed, racing from pursuers through dark woods. He comes upon a carnival in a valley, where he sees a beautiful woman, a snake charmer covered with feathers and tan skin, who points out the way home to him. But when he follows the road she indicates, he comes back to the forest, where he sees the woman again, laughing in an embrace with one of O'Brien's original dark captors, and he is taken back to prison.

Drill Sergeant at AIT   When O'Brien forms up for his first inspection at Advanced Infantry Training (AIT) at FORT LEWIS, his drill sergeant tells the group of trainees that every one of them is now a foot soldier, "a grunt in the U.S. Army" (52). When asked by a trainee about rumors that the men would be shipped to Frankfurt, the drill sergeant tells him to forget it, that every single one of the men will be getting on a plane bound for Vietnam.

Edwards   Edwards is an army chaplain whom O'Brien meets during Advanced Infantry Training (AIT) at FORT LEWIS. When he had asked to meet with the battalion commander, a sergeant ordered O'Brien to see the chaplain first, whose job is said to be "weed[ing] out the pussies from men with real problems" (55). Edwards, O'Brien writes, is custom-made "to soothe trainees" (55). He has thick red hair, a firm handshake, a plump belly, and is completely unequipped to deal with the philosophical issues of conscience that O'Brien wants to discuss with him. When O'Brien tells Edwards that he wants to act as a good man, but that he believes the war is wrong, Edwards lectures him on faith and patriotism, eventually losing his temper and shouting at O'Brien, but finally making a phone call to arrange the meeting with the battalion commander as O'Brien had originally requested.

Erik   Erik is the very close friend whom O'Brien meets at basic training at FORT LEWIS, WASHINGTON in the fall of 1968. O'Brien writes that the two young soldiers "formed a coalition" (35) directed both against the army and against the other trainees. An attempt to "save [their] souls" by talking about poetry, philosophy, travel, soldiering, and above all, the morality of violence and war, their coalition becomes a "two-man war of survival" (35) against the small-mindedness and cruelty they experience daily at the camp. When Drill Sergeant Blyton discovers the friends sitting together behind the barracks one day, polishing their boots and talking, he humiliates the men,

calling them "college pussies" and implying that the two have a homosexual relationship. He assigns them extra guard duty that night, although he backs down from his threat to have them serve it "holdin' hands" (48). While Erik has guaranteed himself a noncombat position by signing up for an extra year at the beginning of basic training, O'Brien is assigned to serve as an infantry soldier. Nevertheless, the two remain friends after leaving Fort Lewis, frequently exchanging letters during O'Brien's year-long tour of duty. Erik, working as a transportation clerk at LONG BINH, speaks in these letters about his love of poetry, about his guilt for his own relative safety compared to O'Brien, and about the need for absolute honesty from politicians, friends, lovers, and from themselves. Like several figures in the memoir, Erik is identified only by his first name. The real-life model for this figure is ERIK HANSEN, O'Brien's lifelong friend to whom he dedicated his later novel, *Going After Cacciato.*

First Sergeant in Alpha Company   During his first night with ALPHA COMPANY, O'Brien is assigned to 3rd Platoon by an unnamed first sergeant, who also tells him that he will not be going straight out into the field but will wait at LANDING ZONE GATOR for his company, which will return in a couple of days. Later that night, the same first sergeant comes through the barracks with a flashlight, warning the men to get out because they are under mortar attack. When the sergeant rouses the men out of bed the next morning, they find two dead GIs out on the perimeter and eight dead VIET CONG inside the base. Much later in O'Brien's tour of duty, in early August, Alpha Company's first sergeant is shot by an M-79 round, fired by his own men from a grenade launcher. O'Brien is told by one of the black soldiers in the company that the sergeant was shot on purpose because he refused to give rear assignments to black soldiers, saving them for whites. It is unclear whether this is the same first sergeant whom O'Brien met his first night at LZ Gator.

Forsythe, Captain   Captain Forsythe is an officer who replaces Captain Smith, who himself had replaced Captain Johansen, as leader of ALPHA

COMPANY. Readers do not see much of Captain Forsythe, although O'Brien compares him unfavorably to Johansen, writing that Forsythe "strutted and pretended" (145) to be brave, but that he failed.

Girlfriend   O'Brien mentions an unnamed girlfriend several times in his narrative. Much like Jimmy Cross and his fantasies about Martha in *The Things They Carried*, O'Brien's relationship with his girlfriend seems more a matter of wishful thinking than a real connection. Like Martha, O'Brien's girl back home loves literature. When she sends him a poem by AUDEN, O'Brien memorizes it, merging the poem with thoughts he pretends to be hers and even pretending that she wrote the poem herself, especially for him. The girl then claims in her letters that O'Brien "created her out of the mind" (34), a charge the author never disputes. The status of this relationship is made even more questionable when O'Brien writes about receiving mail during a bad time in Vietnam with ALPHA COMPANY. His girlfriend, he tells readers, was traveling in Europe, "with her boyfriend" (121). Meanwhile, in a pointed contrast, O'Brien dodges sniper fire, radios for helicopter evacuations of the wounded, and prepares to march out to search another village.

Harry the Montanan   Harry the Montanan is a fellow soldier whom O'Brien meets in basic training at FORT LEWIS. When he is told by a squad leader to scrub the commodes, Harry "threatens to use the squad leader's head as a scrub brush" (39). Harry's boisterous nature is again revealed when he demands that his fellow trainees help him smuggle tobacco and Cokes into the barracks and hide the contraband in the footlockers. At the end of training, when the recruits receive their assignments, Harry, like the squad leader and like O'Brien himself, learns that he is to become a combat infantryman in the war.

Johansen, Captain   Captain Johansen is the commanding officer of ALPHA COMPANY from Tim O'Brien's arrival at LANDING ZONE GATOR in January 1969 until he is rotated out at the end of June that same year, and a Tennessean named

Captain Smith replaces him. Described as "blond, meticulously fair, brave, tall, [and] blue-eyed" (148), Johansen, modeled after the real-life CAPTAIN BEN ANDERSON, is the officer O'Brien respects most in Vietnam and the only man he meets whom he considers a true hero. Captain Johansen possesses a SILVER STAR for killing a VIET CONG, but more important to O'Brien, Johansen is a man who thinks about courage and cowardice. While his status as an officer prevents him from discussing the morality of the war itself with his men, Johansen does tell O'Brien at one point that he would "rather be brave than almost anything" (134). Johansen thus fits one of O'Brien's definitions of courage—that a courageous person is self-aware. O'Brien cites PLATO, who says that "without wisdom men are not truly courageous" (140). To be truly courageous, O'Brien speculates, "men must *know* what they do is courageous, they must *know* it is right" (140). When Johansen leaves and is replaced by the cowardly Captain Smith and later the pretentious Captain Forsythe, O'Brien writes that for him and his fellow soldiers it was like the Trojans losing HECTOR. In a foolish war that lacked good political reasons to fight, Captain Johansen motivated his soldiers; he helped "to mitigate and melt the silliness, showing the grace and poise a man can have under the worst of circumstances, a wrong war" (145).

the Kid   One of O'Brien's fellow soldiers in ALPHA COMPANY is nicknamed simply "the Kid." Only 18, but said to be "the best damn shot in the battalion with an M-79" (77), the Kid talks about the eight VIET CONG soldiers killed in a night attack when O'Brien first arrives as LANDING ZONE GATOR. He argues that they should have known better "than to test Alpha company . . . it's like trying' to attack the Pentagon!" (77). Later, after a night patrol erupts into a firefight in a village called TRI BINH 4, the Kid is ecstatic. Upon the patrol's return to base, he tells the lieutenant, Mad Mark, to show the men the ear cut from a dead Viet Cong soldier. The Kid appears in the narrative one more time, when he finds an AK-47 in a village in PINKVILLE in early summer. Three old village men are tied to trees all night and beaten in the morning, in an unsuccessful attempt to get information about the weapon.

Kline   Kline is an overweight, incompetent, and timid trainee whom O'Brien meets during basic training at FORT LEWIS. When Drill Sergeant Blyton catches Kline wearing two left boots one day, he forces the whimpering and terrified young soldier to hang onto his left foot for an hour. When the men receive their assignments at the end of the course, Kline is told he must repeat basic training.

Korean Stripper   In April, soon after learning that ALPHA COMPANY will be sent to PINKVILLE, the men go to a floor show and watch a Korean stripper with big breasts dance to the music of Simon and Garfunkel and the Beatles.

Li   While studying in PRAGUE during the summer of 1967, O'Brien meets a North Vietnamese economics student named Li. The two are introduced through Li's university roommate, a Czech student who is also a friend of O'Brien's. Described as a "cordial," "short," and "reserved" man (95), Li holds a three-hour conversation with O'Brien about the morality of the Vietnam War. The young students soon discover that neither of them views the opposing side in the war as evil, although Li states that he personally believes President LYNDON JOHNSON "was misguided and wrong" (95) in his tactics. O'Brien questions whether the government in Hanoi is totalitarian, but Li argues that it is simply a wartime democracy, necessary to secure stability. As the two men shake hands on parting, Li informs O'Brien that he is actually a lieutenant in the North Vietnamese Army.

Lieutenant on Bus to Seattle   On a bus ride from Advanced Infantry Training (AIT) at FORT LEWIS into SEATTLE, where O'Brien plans to flee the army, he sits next to an unnamed lieutenant who is leaving for Vietnam in two days. The lieutenant explains that he, too, was drafted (*see* DRAFT) into the war, but that he signed up for Officer Candidate School (OCS) in order to delay being sent to Vietnam. The lieutenant ends the conversation by confessing that he is actually look-

ing forward to trying out some of the things he has learned. "I think I'm better than those dinks" (65), he tells O'Brien as the Greyhound bus turns out of the fort and heads for the city.

Lieutenant at LZ Gator   During his first night at LANDING ZONE GATOR, O'Brien and his fellow soldiers experience a mortar attack. When the attack starts, a lieutenant comes by and tells the men to get their gear together, but they ignore him. He comes back later and orders the men out to the perimeter of the camp, where they find two dead GIs.

Little Girl with Hoop Earrings   When the men of ALPHA COMPANY rest at an old farmer's well in a village one afternoon in March, several children gather around. One of them is described as "a little girl with black hair and hoops of steel through her ears" (99), who helps guide the old, blind farmer about. This girl is possibly the model for a small Vietnamese girl with gold hoop earrings whom Paul Berlin desperately wants to understand him—his motives, his good intentions, his hopes for peace—in *Going After Cacciato*.

Mad Mark   Mad Mark is O'Brien's platoon leader in ALPHA COMPANY. A first lieutenant and a GREEN BERET, Mad Mark received his nickname not because of any sort of "hysterical, crazy, into-the-brink, to-the-fore madness," but because he is "insanely calm" and "never showed fear" (81). According to O'Brien, Mad Mark's attitude and manner resemble those of a CIA operative—he loves stealth and has the poise of a "professional soldier," a "hired hand" (81). He does not long for battle, but neither does he fear the prospect of combat. In fact, O'Brien writes that Mad Mark practiced a "more or less . . . Aristotelian ethic . . . Making war is a necessary and natural profession. It is natural, but it is only a profession, not a crusade" (82). The portrait offered by O'Brien of Mad Mark is somewhat contradictory, however. Although O'Brien says that Mark "believed in and practiced the virtue of moderation," that he did only "what was necessary for an officer and platoon leader in war" (82), nevertheless Mad Mark is depicted at the end chapter 8, "Alpha Company," as slicing off the ear of a dead VIET CONG soldier and bringing it back to base as a war trophy, an act that the young, green O'Brien finds anything but moderate. Readers last see Mad Mark in mid-May when Alpha Company is patrolling the area called PINKVILLE around the villages of My Lai. Mark shoots a farmer, wounding him in the leg. Later, he claims the man was a Viet Cong who carried papers in a small satchel identifying him as such. Readers are left unsure about the veracity of this report, although the added claim that the man was "engaged with small-arms fire while trying to evade" clearly does not match O'Brien's description of the shooting, in which the man is shot from 300 meters away while working in a rice paddy. Although Mad Mark's last name is never supplied in the memoir, the real-life Mad Mark was LIEUTENANT MARK WHITE, who killed himself in a rented hotel room not long after returning from the war.

Mail Clerk at LZ Gator Soon after O'Brien is assigned to ALPHA COMPANY at LANDING ZONE GATOR, he meets a mail clerk who sympathizes with how long O'Brien will have to spend in Vietnam. The clerk says that he himself has only 23 days left until his tour is over: "I'm so short I need a stepladder to hand out mail" (73). He also tells O'Brien that Irish guys in Alpha Company are lucky and "never get wasted," unlike the "Blacks and spics" (73).

Martin While providing security for a village outside of a beautiful lagoon, ALPHA COMPANY suffers several casualties from mines. A soldier named Martin, who is described as "a quiet, intelligent Texan, an NCO" (167) steps on a rigged mortar round and dies as the DUSTOFF helicopter lifts him from the beach.

Martinez Martinez is a soldier in ALPHA COMPANY who is close friends with a soldier named Rodriguez. The two spend their time together "snapping Kodak pictures of each other in gallant, machine-gun-toting poses" (171). When a new commander leads the men into a minefield in early August, Martinez is crippled and his friend Rodriguez is killed.

McElhaney McElhaney is a soldier in ALPHA COMPANY who is crushed to death when a group of TRACKS, or U.S. armored personnel carriers, retreats on top of him. McElhaney is unable to move out of the way because he is carrying a radio.

Monk Near the end of July, ALPHA COMPANY is helicoptered onto a mountaintop. Expecting a fight, the men instead encounter a monk in a monastery who brings the soldiers watermelon and other fruit and shows them his gardens and the group of orphan children he takes care of. That night some of the soldiers blow a CLAYMORE MINE, whose fragments destroy a statue of the Buddha outside of the monastery. The monk does not protest when the men leave the next morning.

Mousy Mousy is a fellow soldier who undergoes basic training with O'Brien at FORT LEWIS. Readers see him only briefly when he whines about having to wax the floor as the squad leader commands.

North Dakotan Trainee O'Brien briefly mentions a fellow basic trainee from North Dakota who "bellows out" (39) that O'Brien's platoon may be going to the PX one night during basic training at FORT LEWIS. The North Dakotan's speculation prompts Harry the Montanan to make plans to smuggle tobacco and Coke into the barracks.

O'Brien, Ava Eleanor Schultz Tim O'Brien's mother was a schoolteacher named AVA SHULTZ O'BRIEN, who, readers are told in the memoir, served as a U.S. Navy WAVE (Women Accepted for Volunteer Emergency Service) during WORLD WAR II. O'Brien also mentions that he received letters from home in Vietnam, telling him that his mother and father were worried about him and prayed for his safety.

O'Brien, Greg GREG O'BRIEN is Tim O'Brien's younger brother. He is mentioned briefly in the memoir when O'Brien speculates about the purpose of his book. "It would be fine," he writes, if his book were a plea for peace, if it were written "to persuade [his] younger brother and perhaps some others to say no to wrong wars" (23). Yet,

O'Brien must admit that, finally, his book does not really serve this purpose, any more than it simply confirms old beliefs about war. Greg is mentioned again in a letter O'Brien receives from home while in Vietnam in which he learns that his younger brother is busy playing basketball.

O'Brien, Kathy   Kathy O'Brien is Tim O'Brien's sister. The only time she is mentioned in the memoir is when O'Brien writes that mail came during the bad period that ALPHA COMPANY was on patrol in the My Lai area. His sister is in school while he is a world away, watching his buddies get blown up by mines and sniper fire.

O'Brien, Tim   The memoir is narrated by Tim O'Brien in the first person. Although it is important to remember that memoirs are a somewhat slippery genre—it is impossible for any single account to be entirely factual or fully complete, and readers are getting the memories of a single individual recounted oftentimes long after the events described have taken place—nevertheless, this Tim O'Brien seems to be more of a biographically accurate figure than the Tim O'Brien character who appears in the later, fictional memoir, *The Things They Carried.* In *Box Me Up*, O'Brien recounts snippets of his early life in WORTHINGTON, MINNESOTA, where his family moved when he was 7 years old. He describes the moral quandary associated with receiving his DRAFT notice in the summer of 1968, as well as the plans to flee the country he made while undergoing Advanced Infantry Training (AIT) at FORT LEWIS, WASHINGTON. The bulk of the narrative, however, focuses on the time he actually spent as a foot soldier in Vietnam from January 1969 until March 1970. He describes both the boredom and futility of military life as well as the terror of combat and the horror of witnessing death and atrocity dealt out by both sides in the war. He introduces readers to a wide variety of officers and soldiers, ranging from the childish to the incompetent to the morally reprehensible to the truly heroic. Many of the experiences and characters O'Brien describes in the book, along with many of the themes he explores here, will be revisited and reworked in his later fiction.

O'Brien, William T.   Tim O'Brien's father, WILLIAM T. O'BRIEN, an insurance salesman in small-town Minnesota, is mentioned briefly in the memoir when O'Brien writes that he himself is part of the baby boom generation who "grew out of one war and into another" (11). His father was a WORLD WAR II veteran who saw action in the Pacific theater. Thus, O'Brien is "the offspring of the great campaign against the tyrants of the 1940s" (11). The only other time he mentions his father in the memoir is to write that while in Vietnam he received letters from home saying that his father and mother were afraid for him and were praying for his safety.

Old Lady in Bomb Shelter   In July, soon after Captain Smith replaces Captain Johansen as leader of ALPHA COMPANY, he orders the men to search a village in the My Lai—MY KHE area. The men throw grenades into bomb shelters as they search. One grenade brings a 70-year-old Vietnamese woman, described by O'Brien as an "old lady" (151), out of her shelter. Covered in blood and nearly dead, but still conscious, the woman watches as the medics attempt to patch her up. She is eventually helicoptered away, screaming and hollering, with bandages dangling and blood in her hair and eyes.

Old Lady Hotel Clerk   When O'Brien goes to SEATTLE, planning to flee the army, he checks into a cheap hotel. The desk clerk is described as an "old lady" who hands O'Brien the key "without a glance" (66). She is busy reading the sports page of the *Seattle Times*, which is spread out in front of her.

Old Man at the Well   The men of ALPHA COMPANY meet an old, blind Vietnamese farmer at a well in a small village one day in March. The man smiles and even helps bathe the GIs in buckets of water drawn from the well. The friendly scene is disrupted, however, when a "blustery and stupid soldier" (100) hurls a carton of milk at the old man from 15 feet away, hitting him squarely in the face and covering the old man in blood and milk. Stunned, the old man's eyes roll back in his head, but he eventually smiles and calmly begins showering the soldiers with water again as if nothing had happened.

Old Vietnamese Village Men In chapter 15, "Centurion," O'Brien describes three old Vietnamese village men who are tied up to trees with wet rags stuffed in their mouths all night long after ALPHA COMPANY finds an enemy rifle in their village. The next morning, the old men are beaten and whipped in the hope that they will provide information about the VIET CONG. Although one of the men whimpers, none of them talk, and they are eventually released.

Ortez Ortez is a soldier in ALPHA COMPANY whose leg is broken by U.S. armored personnel carriers (*see* TRACK) when the drivers of the giant vehicles inadvertently retreat over a group of their own soldiers.

Paige Paige is a soldier in ALPHA COMPANY who loses his foot when U.S. armored personnel carriers (*see* TRACK) retreat on top of a group of friendly soldiers after being fired upon.

Peterson When ALPHA COMPANY is stationed at a village near a beautiful lagoon, a soldier named Peterson goes fishing with hand grenades and ends up blowing his own belly away.

Philip When he discusses the different kinds of mines used in Vietnam, as well as the effects these mines had on the men, O'Brien tells the story of Philip, a soldier who is told to "police up one of his friends, victim of an antipersonnel mine" (124). That evening Philip sits in his foxhole and sobs uncontrollably. Eventually, the other men take turns talking to him one at a time, trying to comfort him.

Porter Porter is a fellow soldier of O'Brien's when he receives his rear job at LANDING ZONE GATOR. After the incident in which battalion executive officer Major Callicles screams at a medic named Tully who has shot himself in the foot, Porter agrees with Bates that Callicles is crazy, but

asserts that "he admired the man's pizzazz" (200) and compares him to Heinrich Himmler, head of the SS in Nazi Germany.

Prostitute in Seattle After O'Brien leaves the sorority house at the University of Washington, where he has gone looking for a date during the weekend he spends in SEATTLE during Advanced Infantry Training (AIT), he meets a prostitute on the street who asks if he needs a date. O'Brien declines, explaining that he feels sick. The woman then asks him if he can spare a dollar or two, but O'Brien tells her that he really needs the money himself.

Radio Operator In mid-July, the men of ALPHA COMPANY are helicoptered into a burning village on a combat assault (CA) mission. Very quickly, the radio operator for 1st Platoon calls to report severe casualties. When the battalion commander, directing operations from a helicopter above the fighting, is radioed to evacuate the wounded, he refuses because the landing zone is not secure. When the 1st Platoon radio operator desperately urges the DUSTOFF to land, explaining that the injured men are near death, the battalion commander angrily orders him to stay off the net and relay requests through his commanding officer (CO). The radio operator replies that his CO is unconscious and bleeding.

Ready Whip, Nestle's Quick, and Shake and Bake Ready Whip, Nestle's Quick, and Shake and Bake are the nicknames given to three squad leaders with ALPHA COMPANY's 3rd Platoon. The nicknames derive from the fact that the three are "INSTANT NCOS"—noncommissioned officers who had gone through a crash two-month program to earn their stripes. When Ready Whip and Nestle's Quick, whose real names are Tom and Arnold, are killed two months after O'Brien meets them, he writes that "the tragedy was somehow lessened and depersonalized" (81) by the flippant nicknames and the rough slang used by the soldiers to describe their deaths.

Reno, the Wop, and College Joe Reno, the Wop, and College Joe are nicknames given to young soldiers in ALPHA COMPANY. O'Brien mentions the trio briefly when he discusses the unit's use of slang and nicknames. He writes, "You can go through a year in Vietnam and live with a platoon of sixty or seventy people, some going and some coming, and you can leave without knowing more than a dozen complete names" (81). Reno will figure into the narrative again a bit later, when O'Brien describes him refusing to wake up for his turn at watch when the two are partnered during a night ambush. While he eventually sits up and accepts a CLAYMORE firing device from O'Brien, Reno shortly falls back asleep again, lying on his stomach and wheezing. O'Brien expresses his disillusion when he writes that the man was "a seasoned American soldier, a combat veteran, a squad leader" (96).

Re-Up Officer at LZ Gator   Soon after O'Brien's arrival at LANDING ZONE GATOR, headquarters in Vietnam for the 5th Battalion, 46th Infantry, a noncommissioned officer, whose job is to convince the new men to sign up for another year to guarantee themselves a safe job in the rear, speaks to them about the dangers of combat. He tells the group of new soldiers that one or two of them, without fail, are going to lose their legs or die. Despite the NCO's fear tactics, none of the green soldiers sign the papers to commit to another year.

Rodriguez   Rodriguez is a Radio Transmission Operator (RTO) in ALPHA COMPANY with O'Brien. He is mentioned when the company is on a night ambush led by Captain Johansen. Rodriguez points out three silhouettes of enemy soldiers tiptoeing out of a nearby hamlet. O'Brien writes that this is "the first and only time" he would ever see "the living enemy" (97). This is the well-executed ambush after which O'Brien's friend Chip is killed as he sweeps the village. Rodriguez himself is killed in early August, after a new commander, come to replace Captain Smith, leads the men into a minefield.

Sailor at Seattle Docks   After checking into a cheap hotel in SEATTLE, where he spends a weekend during Advanced Infantry Training (AIT),

O'Brien goes out to look for a place to eat. A sailor near the docks tells him about a good, cheap fish place nearby, then asks for a dime.

Sergeant at LZ Gator   When O'Brien arrives at LANDING ZONE GATOR, headquarters for the 5th Battalion, 46th Infantry, a sergeant welcomes him and the other new soldiers by telling them not to get too used to Gator because they will soon be sent out to see action. The sergeant also tells the new men not to get too scared either because things are not as bad as they were in 1966 in Vietnam.

Shorty   In chapter 14, "Step Lightly," which describes the different kinds of mines used in Vietnam, O'Brien tells the story of a soldier named Shorty, who was so afraid of mines that he went AWOL for a month. In July Shorty returns to the field, only to sit on a booby-trapped 155 round.

Slocum   Slocum is the name of a soldier whose leg is shredded by a mine during ALPHA COMPANY's pursuit of the 48th VIETCONG BATTALION in the PINKVILLE area.

Smith, Captain   Captain Smith is the officer who replaces Captain Johansen as leader of ALPHA COMPANY. Described as a "short, fat ROTC officer" (148) from Tennessee, Smith is not only incompetent, but he openly calls himself a coward. After an incident in which several of his soldiers are killed by U.S. armored personnel carriers (see TRACK) that are retreating, Smith is ignored by his lieutenants and openly ridiculed by his soldiers. He is especially hated by the African-American soldiers, at least one of whom talks about throwing a grenade into the captain's foxhole. Captain Smith is relieved of his duties as commander of Alpha Company in the beginning of August.

Smitty   Smitty is a soldier who loses the toes of one foot to an M-14 antipersonnel mine, a device nicknamed the "TOE POPPER."

Soldier at Well   When the men of ALPHA COMPANY stop to cool off at the well of an old, blind Vietnamese farmer, a soldier, described only as "blustery and stupid," with "blond hair and big belly" (100), throws a carton of milk directly into the kindly old man's face, causing blood and milk to stream down his cheeks.

Soldiers at LZ Gator　When a lieutenant orders a group of soldiers to get their gear on and get out to the perimeter of the base during a mortar attack on O'Brien's first night at Landing Zone Gator, a group of three soldiers refuse his orders, return to the barracks, and go back to sleep.

Squad Leader at Basic Training　O'Brien writes about an unnamed squad leader at basic training, a fellow recruit described as "a peer and a sell-out" (40) who seems to enjoy the power he is able to wield over the other young soldiers. O'Brien describes the squad leader rousing the men out of bed in the morning, ordering one of them to scrub the commodes and another to wax the floors. At the end of chapter 5, "Under the Mountain," readers discover that this squad leader, like O'Brien himself, has been assigned to become an infantry combat soldier.

Sorority Girl　On his weekend in Seattle during Advanced Infantry Training (AIT), when O'Brien plans to desert the army, he first takes a taxi to the University of Washington, where he walks into a sorority house and rings a button at the front desk. A girl with black hair, jeans, and blue-rimmed glasses comes downstairs. O'Brien tells her that he is looking for a date, but the girl replies that she has to study for a big exam that is coming up and that most of her sorority sisters are studying for finals as well. "Besides, this is no way to conduct human relations" (67), she adds, causing O'Brien to leave in embarrassment.

Stewardess　O'Brien mentions two stewardesses in his memoir. The first works on his flight into Vietnam. She wishes the men luck over the loud-speaker and gives out kisses to some of them as they leave the plane, "mainly to the extroverts" (69). The second stewardess serves on the flight home. O'Brien describes her as blond-haired and blue-

eyed and as having a "carefree smile" (205), but also as bored and unable to comprehend the soldiers' experiences as she walks down the airplane aisle spraying sanitizer to kill mosquitoes and diseases.

Tom　Tom is a squad leader in Alpha Company who is killed, along with O'Brien's friend Chip, when sweeping a village after a successful night ambush. Tom is also said to be the real name of one of the "instant non-commissioned officers" nicknamed Ready Whip and Nestle's Quick, whom O'Brien writes about earlier in the narrative. These men are also squad leaders killed in the war. The two Toms are most likely the same man.

Trainee Making Unauthorized Phone Call　When Erik and O'Brien are assigned guard duty as punishment by Drill Sergeant Blyton one night, they stumble upon a fellow trainee who is making an unauthorized phone call. After much debate, the pair decide to turn the soldier in. Though they sympathize with the young man, they are also tired and their feet hurt, and they hope that his punishment will be replacing them on guard duty, which it turns out to be. Although O'Brien and Erik initially feel clever about having escaped duty, they wonder much later "if maybe Blyton hadn't won a big victory that night" (49). Blyton has gotten the pair to unwittingly do his dirty work for him.

Tully　Tully is a medic at Landing Zone Gator who shoots himself in the foot one evening. While he claims the injury was an accident, O'Brien writes that Tully had been scheduled to go the field the next day, so "it was fair to guess [the shooting] had been intentional" (198). Major Callicles, LZ Gator's battalion executive officer, is furious when Tully is brought to him. He repeatedly calls the medic a "coward" (198; 200) and threatens him with a court-martial.

Turnip Head　In the chapter "Nights," O'Brien describes a blond soldier nicknamed Turnip Head, who injures himself by playing with a grenade one night. A group of soldiers, bored all day and night, had agreed to throw grenades outside of the perimeter at a set time, both to amuse themselves and scare the other men, but Turnip Head's grenade hits a tree and bounces back at him, wounding him in the hand.

Viet Cong District Chief In August ALPHA COMPANY is stationed on top of a hill to the north of PINKVILLE. One morning the men chase two VIET CONG soldiers into a bunker, then throw down grenades and rounds from their M-16s. The younger of the two Viet Cong is killed instantly, but the older man emerges, blood-covered and barely alive. Although the medics try to patch him up, the man dies. When his pockets are searched, it is discovered that this man was a Viet Cong district chief. At first, the men are elated by the kill but later acknowledge that it was simply "coincidence and fortune" (177) that caused the death.

Vietnamese Farmer When ALPHA COMPANY is pursuing the 48th VIETCONG BATTALION in the area of PINKVILLE in late spring, Mad Mark shoots a Vietnamese farmer from 300 meters away, who he later claims was a VIET CONG who was "engaged with small-arms fire while trying to evade" (120). Whether or not the man was actually a member of the Viet Cong remains uncertain, but Mad Mark's report is clearly false in its description of how the man was shot.

Vietnamese Scout When ALPHA COMPANY is helicoptered into PINKVILLE during a combat assault (CA) in April, they are accompanied by a scared Vietnamese scout, whom O'Brien says looks younger than his 14-year-old brother back in Minnesota.

Vietnamese Village Women When two popular soldiers from ALPHA COMPANY are blown up by a booby-trapped artillery round while pursuing the 48th VIETCONG BATTALION in the area called PINKVILLE, other soldiers "put their fists into the faces of the nearest Vietnamese, two frightened women living in the guilty hamlet" (119). The soldiers also hack off chunks of the women's hair, crying as they do so.

Vietnamese Woman Soldier In chapter 12, "Mori," O'Brien tells the story of a woman soldier for the North Vietnamese Army who has been shot once through the groin. The soldiers of ALPHA COMPANY gather around the woman as blood pours out of her entry and exit wounds and as a medic tries to help her. Although sympathetic to the suffering woman, who is lying with her face in the dirt, moaning and squirming, the men nevertheless make sexist comments, pointing out that she is "pretty for a gook," but that she has been shot "through the wrong place" (113), implying that she will no longer be able to have sexual intercourse. The woman dies on the floor of the helicopter as she is being airlifted out of the area.

White White is a young recruit whom O'Brien meets during basic training at FORT LEWIS. Possibly from Idaho, since he sings about the state, White's claim to fame is that he was married two days before being inducted into the army.

Wolf One of the members of ALPHA COMPANY whom O'Brien meets during his first days at LANDING ZONE GATOR is nicknamed Wolf. Wolf tells O'Brien that the mortar attack the men undergo during O'Brien's first night was not bad at all: "Look, FNG [Fucking New Guy], I don't want to scare you—nobody's trying to scare you—but that stuff last night wasn't *shit!* Last night was a lark. Wait'll you see some really *bad* shit. That was a picnic last night. I almost slept through it" (77).

FURTHER READING

Bourne, Daniel and Debra Shostak. "A Conversation with Tim O'Brien," *Artful Dodge* 17 (1991): 74–90.
Horner, Carl S. "Challenging the Law of Courage and Heroic Identification in Tim O'Brien's *If I Die in a Combat Zone* and *The Things They Carried.*" *WLA: War, Literature & the Arts* 11, no. 1 (1999): 256–267.
Wesley, Marilyn. "Truth and Fiction in Tim O'Brien's *If I Die in a Combat Zone* and *The Things They Carried.*" *College Literature* 29, no. 2 (2002): 1–18.

"In the Field" (1989)

"In the Field" is a short story first published in *Gentleman's Quarterly* in December 1989. The story depicts a platoon of 18 American soldiers in Vietnam searching a muddy field in the rain for the remains of Kiowa, a fellow soldier who died in the muck during a mortar attack the night before. The story was later revised and included in the collection *The Things They Carried.*

SYNOPSIS

At dawn of a rainy, miserable day in Vietnam, the remaining soldiers of a platoon under the command of Lieutenant Jimmy Cross begin wading through the deep muck of a field alongside the SONG TRA BONG River, probing the ground with their rifles as they search for the body of Kiowa, killed during a nighttime mortar attack. Lieutenant Cross blames himself for the death, realizing that he should have disobeyed orders and camped the platoon on higher ground for the night. As he watches his men search for the body, he composes a series of letters in his head to Kiowa's father, praising the fine young soldier and accepting blame for his death. Meanwhile, a soldier named Azar tries to joke with two platoon members—Norman Bowker and Mitchell Sanders—about Kiowa's death, noting the irony of dying in a "shit field." Norman is not amused at Azar's jokes, and Mitchell Sanders is angry at the lieutenant, blaming him for Kiowa's death. Soon readers are introduced to another member of the platoon—a nameless young soldier who had been a good buddy of Kiowa's and who blames himself for his friend's death as well. The boy had shined a flashlight on a picture of his girlfriend that he was showing Kiowa right before the series of mortars were fired. He believes the light gave away the platoon's position and precipitated the attack. Afterward, he was unable to pull Kiowa out of the muck, despite catching hold of his boot. Yet, the next day, the boy frantically hunts for the missing picture of his girlfriend in the mud rather than for Kiowa's body. The searching men eventually find Kiowa, but it takes considerable effort to pull his body from the sucking mud. Afterward, they rest, feeling bad for Kiowa, but secretly giddy to be still alive themselves. The story ends with Lieutenant Jimmy Cross lying on his back, floating in the river and dreaming of a golf course back home in New Jersey—"a world without responsibility" (225).

COMMENTARY

"In the Field" is, above all, a story about waste: the waste of the war, the unjust death of a promising young soldier whose luck ran out. The "shit field"—the muddy field beside the Song Tra Bong that serves as a toilet for the neighboring village—encapsulates this waste in a single, searing image. O'Brien makes concrete the sorrow and tragedy of the war by having Kiowa literally drown in waste. The fact that Kiowa was "a fine soldier and a fine human being," "brave," and "decent" (217) is telling as well. There is no justice to the deaths brought about by war. Death is unearned and cannot be prevented by good soldiering or by bravery. The best of men die in the worst of ways. In fact, the story repeatedly shows how individual personality traits, such as Kiowa's intelligence and good-heartedness, get swept away in war. Covered in mud, searching for the body, the 18 remaining soldiers in the platoon are described as "identical copies of a single soldier" (217), which is the way Lieutenant Jimmy Cross has been trained to think about them, "as interchangeable units of command" (217), even though he would have preferred to see them as human beings. Later in the story, Cross is unable to recall the name of Kiowa's friend, the young boy who searches in the mud for the lost picture of his girlfriend, further highlighting the dehumanization of soldiers at war, the erasure of individual identities. And Kiowa's death is even more senseless since it is caused by a series of happenstance events: The higher-ups unwittingly order Jimmy Cross to camp for the night in the muddy field; it begins to rain and the river overflows its banks; the unnamed young soldier decides to show Kiowa a picture of his girlfriend, Billie. While the young soldier believes that his flashlight signaled the enemy, giving away the platoon's position, readers can never be sure if this is true or if the mortar attack is mere coincidence. The young soldier is not the only member of the platoon who blames himself for Kiowa's death, after all.

The story is as much about blame and guilt as it is about the waste of war. Lieutenant Cross blames himself for the death because he allowed the men to camp in the field rather than trying to find more defensible ground, even though the order had come from higher up in the chain of command. In fact, Cross would have had to actively deceive headquarters and radio in false coordinates had he moved his men elsewhere. Azar, after the body is found, feels guilty for the jokes he made about Kiowa's death, even explaining to Norman Bowker his strange sensation that if had kept his mouth shut, none of this would have happened, as if the death were his fault. And, of course, the young soldier feels responsible for his friend's death as well. Not only did he shine his flashlight in the night, but he was unable to hold onto Kiowa's boot and prevent him from sinking into the muddy water. Near the end of the story, O'Brien writes, "when a man died, there had to be blame" (225). Blame provides these soldiers with an illusion of control. If someone can be blamed for a death, if someone made a mistake that allowed a death to occur, it stands to reason that things can be done differently next time, that deaths can be prevented by modifying behavior, by correcting past mistakes. But the fact that O'Brien depicts Kiowa's death as the end result of a series of unforeseen circumstances and unwitting actions implies that this sense of control is largely illusory.

The letters that Lieutenant Cross composes in his head to Kiowa's father accentuate the need for control. Cross initially imagines rectifying the death by explaining to Kiowa's father what a decent, upstanding young man the dead soldier was—someone a father could be proud of. He tries to create the illusion of an honorable death in battle. In the second letter Cross imagines writing, he changes tactics, accepting full blame and responsibility for the young soldier's death. Cross seems to believe that if he can explain the death carefully, "not covering up his own guilt" (221), his honesty and acceptance of responsibility will make sense of Kiowa's death—the death would then be a result of a series of blunders on his part. Yet, in the third letter Cross writes in his head, he moves away from

this self-blame and imagines conveying the news in a terse, military manner, no apologies necessary: "It was one of those freak things, and the war was full of freaks, and nothing could ever change it anyway" (225). While Cross thinks to himself that this explanation is the "exact truth," the very fact that he changes the letter so often implies the difficulty in getting at the real truth of an event—a theme that persists throughout O'Brien's entire body of work.

Finally, at the end of the story, Cross gives up on the letter entirely, preferring to retreat into his imagination, where he can exercise the control unavailable to him in Vietnam. He daydreams about playing golf in New Jersey. Like Paul Berlin and his fellow soldiers in *Going After Cacciato* with their endless pickup basketball games, or like Norman Bowker and Henry Dobbins playing checkers in the story "Spin" from *The Things They Carried,* sports are "orderly and reassuring" (*TTTC* 32) to men at war. Tactics are clear; scores are known; the stakes are low. As Cross imagines himself on the golf course, "calculating wind and distance" (220), wondering about whether to use a 7-iron or an 8, he realizes that "all you could ever lose was a ball. You did not lose a player" (220). It is this lack of responsibility that Cross longs for. So, even with the sound of the DUSTOFF helicopter in the background and the young soldier trying to explain his role in Kiowa's death, Cross simply lies on his back in the river, dreaming about a "golden afternoon on the golf course" (225). He finally sees himself as not even bothering to try to explain the inexplicable to Kiowa's father when the war is over but simply knocking his ball down the middle of the fairway and walking off into the afternoon.

Differences in Versions

The version of "In the Field" published in *The Things They Carried* is nearly identical to the original *Gentleman's Quarterly* version. However, like many of the stories first published separately and later included in *The Things They Carried,* the most significant change from the stand-alone version to the revised version of the story includes the additional contextual information given readers when the story appeared as part of the larger book. In

Things, the story of Kiowa's death is told several times. It is presented first in the story "Speaking of Courage" as Norman Bowker's tale, with Norman as the soldier who lets go of Kiowa's boot, allowing his friend to slip under the mud and disappear. This additional context emphasizes the theme of blame and guilt even more fully as the very specific letting go of the boot is attributed to different characters in different places. The additional context provided in the novel also suggests that the young, unnamed boy hunting for the picture of his girlfriend, Billie, in the story is narrator O'Brien himself. In the book, the piece that immediately precedes "In the Field" is a short essay called "Notes," which narrator O'Brien concludes by writing that "Norman Bowker was in no way responsible for what happened to Kiowa. Norman did not experience a failure of nerve that night. He did not freeze up or lose the Silver Star for valor. That part of the story is my own" (*TTTC* 161). The identification of the young soldier as narrator O'Brien is further solidified by the story "Field Trip," which appears in the collection shortly after "In the Field." In this story, narrator O'Brien returns to Vietnam with his daughter, Kathleen, and specifically searches for the field beside the Song Tra Bong where Kiowa had died. Obviously, the narrator feels great sorrow and guilt over this death, and he returns to honor his departed friend.

CHARACTERS

Azar   Azar is an insensitive soldier in the platoon who jokes about Kiowa's death even though Norman Bowker repeatedly asks him not to. Later, after the body is discovered, Azar confesses to Norman that he feels guilty for the jokes: "like if I'd kept my mouth shut none of it would've ever happened. Like it was my fault" (225).

Billie   Billie is the former girlfriend of the unnamed young soldier who was Kiowa's closest friend at the war. The young man blames himself for Kiowa's death because he had shined his flashlight on a photograph of Billie right before the mortar attack that killed Kiowa. The next day, the boy frantically searches for the picture of Billie while the other soldiers hunt for Kiowa's body. He angrily

tells Lieutenant Cross that Billie will not send him another picture because she is "not even [his] girl anymore" (224).

Bowker, Norman   Norman Bowker is one of the 18 soldiers who searches for Kiowa's body in the muddy field. He is disturbed by Azar's repeated jokes about Kiowa's death and asks the loutish soldier to be quiet. When Norman discovers the heel of Kiowa's boot in the muck, he angrily asks Azar what has happened to all his jokes. When the men finally succeed in digging the body out of the mud, Azar confesses to Norman that he feels guilty about the death. Norman simply looks out across the wet field and replies, "Nobody's fault . . . Everybody's" (225).

Cross, Lieutenant Jimmy   Lieutenant Jimmy Cross is the commanding officer of the platoon that camped along the banks of the SONG TRA BONG River and lost a soldier named Kiowa during a nighttime mortar attack. Cross feels guilty for the death and chastises himself for not disobeying orders from headquarters and camping the men on higher ground for the night. As the platoon searches for Kiowa's body in the muddy field the next morning, Cross composes and recomposes letters to Kiowa's father in his mind. At the end of the story, however, he retreats into his imagination, speculating that maybe he would not write a letter at all, but simply enjoy an afternoon on a golf course back home in New Jersey.

Dobbins, Henry   Henry Dobbins is one of the soldiers in the platoon commanded by Lieutenant Jimmy Cross. He helps dig Kiowa's body out of the muck after Norman Bowker finds the dead soldier's boot heel sticking out above the surface.

Jensen, Dave   One of the soldiers who helps dig Kiowa's body out of the muck, Dave Jensen is angry when Henry Dobbins declares that "it could be worse" after the body is finally retrieved. "How man?" he demands, "Tell me *how*" (225).

Kiley, Rat   Rat Kiley is the platoon medic who searches through Kiowa's pockets after the body of the dead soldier is finally dug out of the muddy field. Rat places Kiowa's effects in a plastic bag, tapes the bag to the dead soldier's wrist, then calls in a DUSTOFF helicopter.

Kiowa Kiowa is a Native American soldier from Oklahoma who is killed by drowning in a muddy field during a mortar attack one dark night during the Vietnam War. Described as a devout Baptist and "a splendid human being . . . intelligent and gentle and quiet-spoken" (217), Kiowa was clearly loved by his fellow soldiers, and his death is hard for them to accept, especially since his body has disappeared into the waste and muck of the flooded field. Several characters in the story blame themselves for Kiowa's death, including the platoon's commander, Lieutenant Jimmy Cross, who chides himself for allowing the men to camp on indefensible ground, a brutish soldier named Azar, who makes jokes about Kiowa's death as the men search for the body, and a young unnamed soldier who had been Kiowa's best friend but who could not hold onto his boot and pull him from the muck he sunk into.

Kiowa's Father While Kiowa's father never actually appears in the story, he plays an important role in the imagination of Lieutenant Jimmy Cross, who composes letters to the dead soldier's father in his mind. Initially, Cross imagines writing Kiowa's father about how brave and upright his son had been. The next letter Cross pictures himself writing is a confession of his own guilt in the death—he should have ordered the men to camp on higher ground that night. Cross eventually abandons this tack, however, and imagines a third letter, which announces the death to Kiowa's father in impersonal, military language. This third letter explains the death as simply a freak accident, something that happens in war for no reason. Finally, by the end of the story, Cross remains unsure if he will even write a letter at all; perhaps he will prefer to put the entire war behind him and simply spend his days on the golf course back home in New Jersey.

Mama-Sans When the platoon of American soldiers first begins to set up camp in the muddy field beside the SONG TRA BONG River, two Vietnamese village women, described in the story as "a couple of old mama-sans" (220), come over to warn Lieutenant Jimmy Cross that the spot is not a good one for camping, explaining that it is "Number Ten . . . Evil ground. Not a good spot for good GI's" (220). Later, Cross will discover that the field had been used as the village toilet.

Sanders, Mitchell Mitchell Sanders is one of the members of the platoon who searches for Kiowa's body in the muck. Unlike Norman Bowker, Sanders blames Jimmy Cross for the death, insisting that the young lieutenant should have known better than to camp the men for the night in the village latrine.

Unnamed Young Soldier An unnamed young soldier who had been a good friend of Kiowa's blames himself for the death. The unnamed boy had pulled a picture of his girlfriend, Billie, out of his pocket to show Kiowa right before the nighttime mortar attack. He believes it was the light of his flashlight, which he had shined on the picture, that alerted the enemy to the platoon's position. In addition, in the chaos following the mortar explosions, the unnamed boy had been able to grab hold of Kiowa's boot, but he did not have the strength to pull his friend from the sucking mud, and he eventually had to let go. The next day, however, the young soldier seems more upset over losing the picture of Billie than he does about the death of his friend.

In the Lake of the Woods
(1994)

Published by Houghton Mifflin in 1994, *In the Lake of the Woods* is part thriller, part meditation on love and marriage, and part war exposé. The novel tells the story of John Wade, a Vietnam War veteran and ambitious Minnesota politician running a campaign for the U.S. Senate after having served six years as a state senator and four years as lieutenant

My Lai Massacre *(Photo by Ronald L. Haeberle/Getty Images)*

governor. Wade's campaign, however, comes crashing down around him when his presence at the MY LAI MASSACRE, which he had carefully worked to obscure, is exposed. After suffering a humiliating defeat, Wade and his wife, Kathy, retreat to a cabin in the remote woods of northern Minnesota to recover. When Kathy mysteriously disappears one day, suspicion immediately falls on Wade, but the novel offers several other possibilities for what might have happened to Kathy as well, stubbornly refusing to supply readers with a definite solution to the mystery of Kathy's disappearance. A novel that explores the costs of denying the past as well as the darkness of the human psyche—the thin line separating love, obsession, and madness—*In the Lake of the Woods* was a critical and commercial success, winning the James Fenimore Cooper Prize for Historical Fiction, earning an editor's choice award from the *New York Times Book Review,* and being named the best work of fiction in 1994 by *Time* magazine.

SYNOPSIS

The novel opens at an old yellow cottage on the shore of the LAKE OF THE WOODS in northern Minnesota in September 1986, immediately after the Senate election in which John Wade had been defeated by an embarrassingly large margin. John and Kathy Wade, lying on blankets on the porch of the rented cottage, are dreaming about the future, discussing wild plans to move to VERONA, ITALY, and have a busload of children, and desperately trying to put the election and all the ugliness it entailed behind them. Despite their best efforts, however, John's rage and humiliation and Kathy's hopelessness seep through. An ominous fog moves across the lake, foreshadowing that all is not well with this marriage, and readers are, in fact, told by page 3 that in less than 36 hours Kathy will be gone. The remainder of the novel is divided into four different types of chapters. These include chapters that detail the past, beginning with John's childhood, following him to college and Vietnam, and leading up to the election and the week at the lake before Kathy goes missing; chapters that are set in the present time and follow the large-scale search that is set into motion after Kathy's disappearance; chapters titled "Evidence" that include quotes, documents, and facts relevant to the case; and finally "Hypothesis" chapters that explore several different scenarios for what might have happened to Kathy Wade.

The Past

The chapters that explore the past document John Wade's lonely and unhappy childhood. The son of a charming but alcoholic father who teases him mercilessly, John turns to performing magic as a way to gain attention and feel in control of his life. He spends hours in the basement of his home in small-town Minnesota, practicing magic tricks in front of a full-length mirror. When John is 14, however, his world turns upside down. His father commits suicide by hanging himself in the family garage. At the funeral, John experiences uncontrollable rage, yelling loudly and disrupting the ceremony. For weeks afterward, he comforts himself late at night by pretending that his father is alive again, in his room talking to him, or merely hiding somewhere around the house. John imagines that he has a mirror in his head, like the full-length mirror in the basement of his home, where he can perform illusions to make his life more bearable. In this mirror, he imagines a big blue door and his father walking in and sitting in the rocking chair by John's bed. The mirror father quietly talks with his son, sharing stories and laughing, as the real-life father never did.

While he never gets over the loss of his father, John recovers enough to attend college at the University of Minnesota. In 1966, when he is a senior, he meets Kathy, who is a freshman. The two fall in love and begin dating. But John, insecure

in the relationship and desperately afraid of losing people he loves, begins to secretly follow Kathy around campus, spying on her as she goes about her daily activities. Despite this strange behavior, Kathy and John are deeply in love. They are young and have good times together, inventing silly games like "Dare You," in which each dares the other into titillating or slightly dangerous behavior, such as John removing Kathy's panty hose in a booth at the local bar, or Kathy stealing a bottle of Scotch from behind the counter. John also confides his political ambitions Kathy, mapping out his plans to run for state and eventually national office. Though somewhat skeptical about his motivation, Kathy is at least partially placated when John explains that he wants to do good things for the world.

After he graduates in 1967, John volunteers for service in the Vietnam War. He is sent to Quang Ngai Province, where he joins Charlie Company. While Wade is not much of a soldier, he soon impresses the other young men in the company by performing card tricks and sleight-of-hand. His fellow soldiers give him the nickname Sorcerer and superstitiously begin to see Wade as possessing a kind of magic that will keep them safe. John, who had been a loner growing up, relishes the new sense of belonging he feels and cultivates an air of mystery to go along with his new nickname. Sorcerer's magic, however, runs out in March 1968, when Charlie Company is ordered into the Vietnamese village of Thuan Yen, identified on American maps as My Lai 4. Having lost several comrades in the previous weeks to sniper fire and hidden mines while patrolling the dangerous and hostile territory known as Pinkville, the men are angry, frustrated, and exhausted when they arrive at Thuan Yen. Still, nothing could have predicted the extent of the atrocities that the soldiers of Charlie Company commit that fateful day. Hundreds of men, women, and children in Thuan Yen are raped, sodomized, butchered, and shot. In these sections of the novel, O'Brien mingles fictional characters, such as John Wade and his friend Richard Thinbill, with actual historic figures who participated in the My Lai Massacre, including Lieutenant William Calley, Paul Meadlo, Dennis Conti, and several others. While Wade does not take part in the worst of the atrocities, he does shoot an old Vietnamese villager, mistaking the hoe the man was carrying for a rifle. Traumatized by all the violence he has witnessed, Wade also shoots a fellow American soldier, PFC Weatherby, instinctively firing off his rifle when Weatherby drops into the ditch where Wade is crouching.

Haunted by his memories of the massacre, John Wade signs up for a second tour of duty, during which he performs occasional dangerous and heroic acts, getting injured twice and receiving several medals before eventually being assigned a desk job at the rear. It is here, during his last few months at the war, that Sorcerer again performs magic, carefully deleting his name from any records that place him in Charlie Company and reassigning himself to ALPHA COMPANY. Since so few of his fellow soldiers knew him by anything but the nickname Sorcerer, John Wade's ruse works for many years. He returns home in November 1969 a decorated war veteran, marries Kathy five months later, enrolls in law school, passes the bar in 1973, and takes a job as an assistant legislative counsel with the Minnesota Democratic Farmer Labor Party. On November 9, 1976, he is elected to the Minnesota State Senate, and in 1982 he is elected lieutenant governor. Wade's past is exposed only when he decides to run for national office. One of his opponents in the U.S. Senate race, Edward Durkee, digs into Wade's military career, uncovering the truth about his presence at the My Lai Massacre and exposing his secret to the press. Branded a war criminal and baby killer, Wade loses the election by a landslide.

Claude Rasmussen, an acquaintance of John Wade and an old-time Democratic Party supporter, offers John and Kathy the cottage at the Lake of the Woods as a temporary retreat from the newspaper headlines and public humiliation. It is on their eighth day at the cabin that Kathy mysteriously disappears. John Wade, having had a difficult night, filled with bad dreams and half-memories of boiling water in a teakettle and pouring it on a series of houseplants, sleeps late and wakes up to find Kathy gone. He spends the day puttering about the house, putting things in order, hoping Kathy will return soon, and preparing himself a series of vodka tonics. Not thinking to check the boathouse until it

has grown very late, after midnight, he finds the small Evinrude motorboat missing as well. At this point, John notifies Claude and Ruth Rasmussen, who inhabit a cabin about a mile away from the yellow cottage, about Kathy's disappearance. Ruth calls the local authorities, and the search for Kathy is set in motion.

The Present
On the morning of September 20, shortly after Kathy is reported missing, Sheriff Art Lux flies in from the county seat of Baudette, Minnesota, to orchestrate the search. While the tiny community of ANGLE INLET is the closest town to the yellow cottage, it is too small to have a full-time law enforcement agent. Vinny Pearson, owner of PEARSON'S TEXACO STATION, is paid $80 a month to work part time as a deputy sheriff. While Lux is respectful as the two men question John Wade, Pearson is suspicious, wondering out loud about an argument John and Kathy had at ARNDAHL'S MINI-MART in town the day before her disappearance, and speculating that the Evinrude engine starting up would be too loud for anyone to sleep through. John, tired, dazed, and with a hangover from the night before, does not make a very convincing distraught husband. Nevertheless, a large-scale search, including more than 100 volunteers as well as boats and aircraft from the Minnesota State Police, the U.S. Border Patrol, and the Ontario Provincial Police, is initiated. Patricia Hood, Kathy's sister from Minneapolis and her only close living relative, arrives a few days later, angry that she heard from John only after seeing a television newscast about Kathy's disappearance. The day after Pat's arrival, she and John and Claude Rasmussen join the other searchers on the enormous, remote lake, with its hundreds of miles of inlets, channels, islands, and uninhabited wilderness.

By October 8, approximately two and a half weeks after Kathy had been reported missing, and finding no evidence to explain her disappearance, the Minnesota State Police recalls its three search aircraft. The other official agencies soon follow suit. By October 17 only three private boats still remain actively searching for the missing woman. A few days later, Sheriff Art Lux calls off the official search entirely, informing Claude Rasmussen that the investigation is now going to shift to the cottage itself, its immediate grounds and vicinity. Unable to find any sign of Kathy in the wilderness surrounding the lake, suspicion has begun to settle more firmly on John Wade. Wade, exhausted and depressed from the weeks of fruitless searching, as well as from the Vietnam War memories that have tortured his dreams since his exposure in the media, presses Claude Rasmussen, who still believes in his innocence and is perhaps his only remaining friend, for a boat. The second day after the search has been called off, Wade awakes early to find a key to Claude's Chris-Craft sitting in the middle of the cottage's kitchen table. Having supplied himself with food as well as a compass and map at the Mini-Mart the day before, Wade sets out in the boat, ostensibly to continue searching for Kathy on his own, but in fact intent on losing himself in the vast wilderness of the Lake of the Woods as well. The last contact Wade has with anyone back on shore occurs a few nights later, when, freezing and tipsy on the vodka he has brought along, Wade turns on the boat's radio to ramble incoherently about Kathy and his love for her. At six-thirty in the morning, Wade turns off the radio and heads north into the lake, not to be heard from again. Neither of the Wades' bodies nor either of the missing boats are ever found.

Evidence

Intermingled with the stories of John Wade's past and the search for Kathy Wade are chapters simply titled "Evidence" which include quotes from the novel's fictional characters, such as John's mother, Eleanor Wade; Kathy's sister, Patricia Hood; lawmen Art Lux and Vinnie Pearson; Ruth Rasmussen, the wife of the cottage owner Claude Rasmussen; Myra Shaw, a waitress at Arndahl's Mini-Mart; Wade's campaign manager Tony Carbo; Bethany Kee, a friend from the Admissions Office at the University of Minnesota, where Kathy worked; and several others. These chapters include as well real-life testimony from the court-martial proceedings of Lieutenant William Calley, the only man convicted of crimes committed during the My Lai Massacre. Mixed in with these personal statements

William Calley, April 23, 1971 *(Joe Holloway, Jr./ AP Photo)*

are quotes from published works ranging from biographies of various well-known politicians (such as ROBERT CARO's trilogy on the life of LYNDON JOHNSON), to psychological explorations of war trauma (including JUDITH HERMAN's *Trauma and Recovery* and PATIENCE MASON's *Recovering from the War: A Woman's Guide to Helping Your Vietnam Vet, Your Family, and Yourself*) to treatises on magic (i.e. ROBERT PARRISH's *The Magician's Handbook*), to accounts of previous military atrocities (such as the BATTLE OF LITTLE BIGHORN and the Battles of Lexington and Concord that initiated the American Revolutionary War). These evidence chapters contain as well copious footnotes, documenting the various interviews and sources that the quotes are taken from.

It is in a footnote at the end of the first evidence chapter that readers are initially introduced to the character of the novel's narrator, who speaks about himself only in the footnoted commentary. Calling himself variously a "biographer," "historian," and "medium" (30), this narrator informs readers that he has spent the last four years of his life searching for clues about what might have happened to John Wade. A Vietnam veteran himself and now a writer, the narrator has sifted through mountains of evidence; interviewed numerous friends, family members, and acquaintances of the Wades; and read treatises on magic, politics, psychology, and trauma. The novel, then, purports to be the narrator's attempt to reconstruct, as faithfully and accurately as possible, the story of John Wade. Nevertheless, as he tells readers, "evidence is not truth" (30), and the truth of Kathy's disappearance remains slippery, despite the accumulation of evidence that the readers are presented with.

Hypothesis Chapters
Rather than settling on a single theory for what might have happened to Kathy Wade, the narrator presents instead in chapters given the title "Hypothesis" various speculative theories to explain Kathy's disappearance. There are eight hypothesis chapters in the novel altogether. The first six involve Kathy leaving the cottage on the shore of the Lake of the Woods of her own accord. In the very short, first hypothesis chapter, the narrator speculates that Kathy, fed up with being John Wade's wife, perhaps staged her disappearance to meet a lover. The next five hypothesis chapters, however, imagine Kathy leaving more spontaneously, after waking up on the morning of September 19 to remember a bad night, with John muttering *Kill Jesus!* in his sleep. When she realizes that her husband has boiled the houseplants, Kathy, terribly frightened, may have run from the cottage to the Rasmussens', perhaps getting lost or breaking a leg along the way. Or perhaps she launched the Evinrude into the lake, had a boating accident, and drowned. In a slight variation on this theory, the narrator speculates that maybe, rather than drowning, Kathy simply got lost in the miles and miles of wilderness that the lake encompasses. But the narrator also speculates that her death might not have been accidental. Perhaps she took her medication along with her when she set out in the Evinrude—she had been prescribed both Valium and Restoril—and committed suicide by overdosing after settling herself in a remote spot where she was not likely to be found.

It is not until nearly the end of the novel that the narrator ventures into a much darker hypothesis to explain Kathy's mysterious disappearance. In the seventh hypothesis chapter, he speculates

about the possibility of a "midnight boil"—the idea that John Wade may have horrifically murdered his wife by going into their bedroom late at night and pouring a boiling teakettle of water over her face as she slept. There have been hints earlier in the book that at some point during the night John watched Kathy sleep with the teakettle in his hand, the same teakettle that he had used earlier to boil the houseplants. In this scenario, John would have dragged Kathy's body to the boathouse, launched the Evinrude into the lake, and sunk both the body and the boat deeply enough not to be found before swimming back to the dock near the cottage. However, the narrator himself, in footnote number 131, says that he must reject the theory of "the boil" as "both graceless and disgusting" (300). Therefore, he closes the book with one final hypothesis: the possibility that John and Kathy in an attempt to escape the pain and humiliation of glaring newspaper headlines as well as to evade their mounting pile of campaign debt planned their disappearance together in order to start a new life for themselves somewhere far away. Yet, in the final footnote, the narrator explains that much as he would like John Wade's story to have a happy ending, the "truth won't allow it. Because there *is* no end, happy or otherwise. Nothing is fixed, nothing is solved" (301). Readers are never given a final answer to the mystery of what happened to Kathy or John Wade. We are left only with uncertainty.

COMMENTARY

In the opening chapter of *In the Lake of the Woods*, O'Brien expertly builds suspense, a sense of mystery, that will propel readers through the novel. As many early reviewers pointed out, using words such as *gripping, riveting,* and *electrifying storytelling,* this novel is not only a serious literary meditation on war and marriage, it is also a thriller, a page-turner. O'Brien defends the use of "old-fashioned plot" in an essay on the craft of writing called "The Magic Show," in which he argues that "plot relies for its power on the essential cloudiness of things to come. We don't know. We want to know," adding that "it is the mystery of the future . . . that compels us to turn the pages of a novel, or of a story, or of our own lives" (180). He expertly builds this sense of mystery in *In the Lake of the Woods*. From the first page, readers understand that something bad has happened to the Wades, but O'Brien withholds information in order to build tension, revealing bits and pieces, layer after layer of complexities, much like a magician slowly pulling a series of silk scarves from his sleeve. Yes, the election has been lost, but readers may ask whether that is enough to solicit the "tight pumped-up killing rage" John Wade feels and the terrible cry, *"Kill Jesus!"* (5) that he utters. We are told that, "In less than thirty-six hours [Kathy] would be gone" (3), but we are left to speculate what that phrase means: gone where, gone how? A deliberately ambiguous, flat statement of fact, the phrase raises more questions than it answers. When at the end of the first chapter the narrator writes that John would remember the feel of her hand against his forehead, "its warmth, how purely alive it was" (7), readers begin to suspect that Kathy may no longer be alive, even though, unlike in most thrillers or mystery novels, readers are never even sure that a murder has taken place.

Adding to the tension and buildup of suspense are the novel's dominant images of fog, lake, mirrors, and trapdoors, all of which are introduced in the first few pages. The enveloping fog ominously creeps across the lake, shrouding the cabin and its environs in mystery, seeming almost to "digest" the objects it covers (5) and suggesting the difficulty of seeing clearly, of gaining access to unvarnished truth. This image of fog will be linked later in the novel to the words from First Corinthians read by the minister at John and Kathy's wedding, words that remind their listeners of the incomplete nature of all human knowledge: "For now we see through a glass, darkly; but then face to face: now I know in part; but then shall I know even as also I am known" (45). In addition, in these opening pages O'Brien describes the Lake of the Woods and the surrounding northern Minnesota wilderness as labyrinthine, consisting of "secret channels and portages and bays and tangled forests and islands without names" (1). As in his earlier novel *Going After Cacciato*, labyrinth imagery refers not only to the landscape itself but also suggests the tangled circuitry of the human heart and psyche, the danger of losing one's self in the darkness within.

John Wade, like Paul Berlin in the earlier novel, often seems lost within the tangles of his own life and mind; reconstructing chronology is difficult for Wade as it is for Berlin, and memory is unreliable in both cases.

The lake is described, however, not only as a labyrinth, but also as being "like a great curving mirror, infinitely blue and beautiful, always the same" (1). The mirror of the lake connects not only to the full-length mirror in John Wade's basement, where he practices his magic tricks as a child, but also to the mirrors in his head, where he practices other kinds of illusions—pretending that his father is not dead and that the massacre in Vietnam, because it *"could* not have happened," therefore *did* not happen (109). Mirrors suggest, too, narcissism or turning inward, a key motif in a book in which readers finally have to make up their own minds about the central mystery presented, a choice that may tell us more about ourselves than about what actually happened to Kathy Wade. Trapdoors, associated with the world of magic and illusion just as fog and mirrors are, appear in this opening chapter as well. The narrator describes the sadness Kathy and John experience as a "sudden trapdoor feeling in their stomachs" (2). He further depicts the Wades as imagining the trapdoor dropping open and themselves "falling into that emptiness where all the dreams used to be" (3). Again, as in *Cacciato*, falling is certainly meant to evoke the biblical Fall of Mankind—a fall into sin and evil, a loss of innocence whereby John Wade (and perhaps readers as well) must finally acknowledge the darkness that human beings are capable of as they search for truth armed only with partial knowledge.

The evidence chapters in the novel both aid in and ironically undercut this search for truth. Meant to mimic a trial, in which a jury listens to assembled evidence and arrives at a verdict as to the truth of what happened in a particular case, the evidence chapters provide readers an active role in the novel's proceedings. Readers must assess the evidence for themselves and piece together the disparate pieces of information into some sort of story that explains Kathy's disappearance. In many ways these evidence chapters assert the illusion of "reality"—the quotes and snippets suggest facts that the reader simply has to weave together into a coherent narrative. The irony, however, is that O'Brien freely mixes reality and fiction in these chapters. Readers are presented with remembrances, statements, and opinions from the novel's fictional characters as well as real-life "facts" such as testimony from Lieutenant Calley's court-martial, memories from Revolutionary War soldiers, treatises on psychology and magic, and much more. The mingling of fact and fiction in these chapters illustrates the postmodern view that all truth is mediated by language, that history itself is story, open to endless interpretation. This is true not only of the evidence chapters but of any attempt to get at the past, to write history. The novel's narrator, in the footnote in which he first introduces himself to readers, explains:

> Even much of what might appear to be fact in this narrative—action, word, thought—must ultimately be viewed as a diligent but still imaginative reconstruction of events. I have tried, of course, to be faithful to the evidence. Yet evidence is not truth. It is only evident. (30)

Facts, then, while giving the appearance of reality, do not constitute truth. Conversely, the inclusion of fictional characters and statements in the evidence chapters suggests that the opposite is true as well: Fiction can perhaps be as successful an avenue to "truth" as history can. Or, as O'Brien famously claims in *The Things They Carried:* "story-truth is truer sometimes than happening-truth" (179). These evidence chapters seem particularly postmodern in character as they present a jumble of texts that readers must navigate through and assemble for themselves into some kind of reality, though complete coherence and conclusion remain elusive: "Kathy Wade is forever missing," the narrator tells readers, "and if you require solutions, you will have to look beyond these pages. Or read a different book" (30). In the postmodern world, where we cannot get to absolute truth or reality, the best we can do is interpret texts.

Human character itself in the postmodern view can be another text open for interpretation. And for the narrator, who has been investigating the case for the past four years of his life—interviewing numerous witnesses, chasing down police reports, examining trial testimony from the My Lai Massacre, reading about trauma, politics, love, and sin—the most interesting and puzzling of these texts is John Wade himself. The narrator repeatedly asks the question: What made Wade who he is? Is John Wade's character—his desperate need to be loved, his keeping of secrets, his pretending—the result of his childhood? He was, after all, a lonely, overweight boy able to find comfort only in the world of magic and illusion. Or is his adult personality the outcome of his troubled relationship with his father, an alcoholic who charmed the outside world but who teased his own son mercilessly and later hanged himself in the family garage, a death that filled John with rage? Perhaps Wade's horrifying experiences in Vietnam, where the pressures of daily fear and the frustration of watching his fellow soldiers die led to brutal acts on such a grand scale that it is nearly unimaginable, made him the man he is. Or maybe his relationship with Kathy, his deep, possessive love for her, his fear of losing her, is what shaped John Wade most fully. Or perhaps John Wade was simply born John Wade. As his mother, Eleanor, says in her interview with the novel's narrator, "It wasn't just the war that made him what he was. That's too easy. It was everything—his whole *nature* . . ." (27). Human nature is a complex whole, Eleanor Wade implies. Trying to understand it can be like trying to tease out the thread that makes the cloth, a metaphor O'Brien uses in "How to Tell a True War Story" to describe attempts to find morals or messages in stories: "You can't extract the meaning without unraveling the deeper meaning" (*TTTC* 77). Trying to tease out the secret of John Wade's character may be a hopeless task, like pulling a thread from a piece of cloth—all one may be left with is a collection of lose threads, no more cloth at all.

Just as history in the novel is presented as unknowable, human character, too, is mysterious, enigmatic. In his essay on the craft of writing, O'Brien argues that literary characterization "is achieved not through a 'pinning down' process but rather through a process that opens up and releases mysteries of the human spirit" ("Magic Show" 182). And John Wade in the novel remains a mystery. In a footnote, the narrator writes that John Wade is "beyond knowing. He's an other" (101). He adds:

> For all my years of struggle with this depressing record, for all the travel and interviews and musty libraries, the man's soul remains for me an absolute and impenetrable unknown, a nametag drifting willy-nilly on oceans of hapless fact. Twelve notebooks' worth, and more to come. What drives me on, I realize, is a craving to force entry into another heart, to trick the tumblers of natural law, to perform miracles of knowing. It's human nature. We are fascinated, all of us, by the implacable otherness of others. (101)

The narrator's desire to know and understand John Wade, while indicative of a general human longing to really *know* others, to get inside the skin and the mind of another person, has grown into an obsession. As Ruth Rasmussen advises him in her interview, "You been gnawing on this a long time now, way too long, and sooner or later you should think about getting back to your *own* life. Don't want to end up missing it" (295). The narrator admits the truth of Ruth's words but also acknowledges his "craving to know what cannot be known" (295). In this way the narrator is similar to John Wade himself: His desire to know John Wade parallels John's own desire to know Kathy. John even goes so far as to spy on Kathy in college, trying hard to see the Kathy who exists when he is not around. But even more, this longing to know Kathy fully and completely develops into a desire to actually merge with her, to meld their bodies together. The narrator writes, "There were times when John Wade wanted to open up Kathy's belly and crawl inside and stay there forever. He wanted to swim through her blood and climb up and down her spine and drink from her ovaries and press his gums against the firm red muscle of her heart. He wanted to suture their lives together" (71). O'Brien depicts male characters with similar longings in other works. In the story "The Things They Carried," Jimmy Cross's love for Martha manifests in his wanting to "sleep inside her lungs and breathe her blood and be smothered" (TTTC 11). In "Lives of the Dead," the final story in *The Things They*

Carried, the narrator describes his childhood love for Linda in comparable terms: "Even then, at nine years old, I wanted to live inside her body. I wanted to melt into her bones—*that* kind of love" (TTTC 228). Readers might also be reminded of William Cowling's obsessive love for his wife, Bobbi, in *The Nuclear Age* or of Thomas Chippering's lifelong infatuation with Lorna Sue Zylstra in *Tomcat in Love.*

The problem, of course, with this kind of love is that it becomes possessive and finally destructive. A desire to know the other fully can translate into a desire to eliminate the very otherness that makes two people separate individuals. Thus, in *The Nuclear Age*, William Cowling imprisons Bobbi and comes dangerously close to murdering her when she threatens to leave him, and Thomas Chippering in *Tomcat* cannot let Lorna Sue go after their divorce, spending most of the novel hatching a complicated plan both to gain his revenge on his ex-wife and ultimately to win her back. John Wade's love for Kathy takes this destructive bent as early as his Vietnam years, when he writes her a letter in which he compares their love to a pair of snakes he sees eating each other's tails along a trail near PINKVILLE: "a bizarre circle of appetites that brought the heads closer and closer until one of the men in Charlie Company used a machete to end it" (61). John, though, writes Kathy that he cannot wait to come home and see what would have happened if the snakes actually ate each other's heads, saying that the snakes are a metaphor for how his and Kathy's love feels to him: "like we're swallowing each other up, except in a *good* way . . . I love you Kath. Just like those weirdo snakes—one plus one equals zero!" (61). John Wade's math here is chilling, suggesting that a complete merging of identity eliminates individuals. While the narrator's longing to understand John Wade, and John's longing to understand Kathy so completely that he merges with her, may be part of a natural fascination with "the implacable otherness of others" (101), the danger comes in trying to fully eradicate this otherness. Wade's love for Kathy is so obsessive that it becomes destructive, an urge to actually consume the other person. Although readers never find out definitively what happens to Kathy Wade, the book leaves open the possibility that Wade might actually have murdered his wife in order to possess her completely.

The open-endedness of the novel has intrigued readers and critics, who frequently speculate about whether O'Brien advocates one of the hypotheses about what might have happened to Kathy over the others or whether he deliberately provides evidence to make all of them persuasive. In interviews O'Brien has claimed that as a reader he has the opinion that Kathy simply got in the boat one day and got lost, but that as a writer he is more "neutral" about Kathy's disappearance (Edelman). If he had provided a clear-cut answer to his mystery, he adds, the novel would have been diminished:

> I think that's the way life usually operates. I wanted to write a real mystery, as opposed to a mystery that's solved, and then it's not a mystery anymore. Once you know who done it, you say 'Jack did it to Jane in the dining room with the candlestick,' and then you put down the book and forget about it. What we remember in life is what we don't know. (Edelman)

In an attempt to leave the mystery intact, O'Brien does indeed provide an array of evidence for each of the hypotheses proposed by the novel's narrator.

In support of the theory that Kathy simply ran off, perhaps with a lover, perhaps by herself in the boat, we have the evidence that she herself just found out about John's involvement in Thuan Yen when the story broke in the newspapers, much as John's constituency did. The shock of this revelation, along with her anger at John's keeping of such a troubling secret for so many years, surely could have been enough to drive Kathy away. She clearly had been seething internally for several years over the abortion that John had persuaded her to undergo when she was 34 years old. Her sister and work colleagues provide plenty of evidence that Kathy was unhappy in the role of political wife and that her marriage had been troubled long before John lost the election. Added to these pieces of information is Kathy's habit of making unannounced disappearances in the past. Said to be "fiercely private, fiercely independent," Kathy, at times, would "simply vanish . . . Without rea-

son, usually without warning, she'd wander away while they were browsing in a shop or bookstore, and then a moment later, when [John] glanced up, she'd be cleanly and purely gone, as if plucked off the planet" (33). Kathy also had her own secret history. There is the matter of the dentist, for instance, an affair she kept from John even after it ended. Readers discover, as well, through her memories of a night spent at a casino in the company of Tony Carbo, that Kathy was a compulsive gambler, unafraid to take risks, thriving on the next turn of the cards, which seemed to her to suggest "possibility itself" (220). Would it be so surprising for a woman who relished the "rush in her veins" (220) from the possibility of a jackpot just out of reach, the miracle just around the corner, to gamble on creating a new life for herself, "the rapture of [a] happy ending" (220)? In addition, we have the evidence of what takes place after the disappearance. The day after Kathy vanishes, John seems genuinely surprised, unsure of what happened to her, and worried about his missing wife, even if he does have trouble communicating this bewilderment to Art Lux and Vinny Pearson. The wily Claude Rasmussen, nobody's fool, retains his faith in John's innocence until the end, adding to the plausibility of the hypothesis that Kathy left of her own accord. Finally, no body and no boat are ever found, despite thorough searches of the cabin, the grounds, and the nearby lake. If John had murdered his wife, what has become of the body and the boat? He could have driven the boat out only a short distance into the lake since he had to swim back to the dock. If this were the case, surely the searchers would have recovered it.

Then again, readers cannot dismiss out-of-hand the possibility that John and Kathy planned their disappearance together in an attempt to start a new life. Perhaps a happy ending seems too good to be true in such a dark novel, but many clues in the book point to the possibility of such an ending. The novel opens, after all, with the couple lying on the porch, talking of Verona, a busload of children, and a new life away from politics. So, clearly they had at least imagined the possibility of escape. The mountains of campaign debt, along with the public humiliation John has suffered, suggest the necessity of making a clean break with the past. Staging their own deaths rather than simply struggling to start over would allow them to wipe out the debt and don new identities; they would be free to reinvent themselves in any way they saw fit. Tony Carbo, an experienced politico who understands strategic tactics, seems to accept this theory as the most likely possibility—not only were the couple deeply in debt, but they had cleaned out their bank account before retreating to the cabin in the woods. But even more persuasive, perhaps, is the fact that Kathy in many ways is *like* her husband and has supported him their whole married life. She knew all about the college spying, for instance, and did nothing to stop it. She, too, kept secrets and could be manipulative. In this view Kathy can be seen as the lovely assistant to John's magician, one who aids him in pulling off his tricks and illusions. In one of the Evidence chapters, the narrator includes a quote from a handbook of magic that explains the following terms:

> *Vanish* (noun): A technical term for an effect in which an object or person is made to disappear.
> *Transposition:* A magic trick in which two or more objects or persons mysteriously change places.
> *Causal transportation:* A technical term for an effect in which the causal agent is itself made to vanish; i.e., the magician performs a vanish on himself.
> *Double consummation:* A way of fooling the audience by making it believe a trick is over before it really is. (192)

So, perhaps John Wade has performed an act of causal transportation, a vanish on himself. Moreover, this trick could be said to be a double consummation as well. The witnesses (the Rasmussens, the officers of the law, the friends and family of the Wades) all focus on Kathy's disappearance as the mystery they are interested in. But that may have been just the preliminary "trick" performed by John Wade, with the real illusion being the disappearance of both Wades. The term *double consummation* should bring to mind the image of the two snakes eating each other in Pinkville—one plus one equals

zero. Perhaps John, with Kathy as his assistant, has deliberately made both Wades disappear, Kathy's departure only the first stage in a larger illusion.

While most critics take the view that O'Brien deliberately makes each hypothesis plausible, therefore leaving readers with an unsolvable mystery, a few critics suggest otherwise, arguing that O'Brien does indeed advocate a particular theory of what happened to Kathy, but that this theory is so ugly that readers wish to reject it. H. Bruce Franklin is the critic who makes this case most persuasively, arguing that the novel's main theme is not the inability to get at truth, but rather that the novel is about "denial—both personal and national." According to Franklin, the novel "is not as indeterminate or unresolved as it may seem." He argues that all the possible scenarios for what happened to Kathy Wade, with only one exception, are presented in the novel's eight Hypothesis chapters. The exception is the theory that John Wade murdered his wife, the only theory, according to Franklin, that is supported in non-Hypothesis chapters, including "What He Remembered," "How the Night Passed," and "What He Did Next." While John cannot remember whether or not he murdered his wife, Franklin argues, readers can "reconstruct the gruesome scene" from details provided in these chapters, unless they "would rather indulge in elaborate fantasies of denial," fantasies that the entire nation indulged in after the My Lai Massacre. Just as America tried its best to cover up and forget about My Lai, readers, uncomfortable with the horror of Wade's murder of his wife, choose other, less terrible scenarios to explain Kathy's disappearance.

Certainly the novel offers a great deal of evidence to support the midnight boil theory. John's reaction to loss and death, from his father's suicide onward, has been an unmitigated rage—he wants to kill everyone at his father's funeral, for instance—and he certainly seems unhinged the night of Kathy's disappearance, muttering *"Kill Jesus!"* under his breath. The fact that he boiled the houseplants seems incontrovertible, and he does seem to have dim, deep-down memories of squatting by the sleeping Kathy with the teakettle in his hand as well as of finding himself naked and immersed in the lake later in the night. When he goes to check the boathouse after midnight the day after Kathy's disappearance, Wade knows "exactly what he would find" (83), and late in the novel the narrator himself suggests, not in one of the Hypothesis chapters, that Kathy is indeed at the bottom of the lake, "eyes wide open" (286). While there is no doubt that John loved Kathy deeply, he could have been motivated to kill her by the fear that she would leave him now that the news of Thuan Yen has been made public. As Kathy is washing dishes in the cabin one morning just before her disappearance, Wade notices "the enormous distance" that comes into her face, "a kind of travel," as if she is already gone (17). After their night of lying on blankets on the porch, Kathy pulls away from John after he has reached out to take her hand and walks into the yellow cottage without waiting for him. Afraid that such behavior might indicate Kathy's imminent departure, John might have murdered her to prevent her leaving. Or perhaps John is unable to stand the disappointment that Kathy must surely have felt in him after his involvement in the massacre is exposed. After she is gone, John remembers seeing Kathy's face "turning toward him on the morning when it all came undone. Now she knew. She would always know" (272). John may be unable to live with the idea that he has been forever diminished in Kathy's eyes.

Bruce Franklin's notion that the novel is about denial also seems plausible when we examine the historical web of lies surrounding the Vietnam War. Politicians purposefully lied to the American people over and over again during the prosecution of the war. By the time of JOHN KENNEDY's assassination, before the conflict in Vietnam really appeared on the radar of the American masses, 17,000 so-called advisers were already stationed in Vietnam—these were American soldiers and operatives not officially called soldiers. The attack on the USS MADDOX in the GULF OF TONKIN, which led to a resolution that authorized President Johnson to use military force in Vietnam without a formal declaration of war, turned out to be trumped-up, with no actual attack taking place. Later, Johnson, not wanting to distract from his Great Society domestic agenda, purposefully deceived the public about the extent of American involvement in Vietnam. President RICHARD NIXON behaved deceptively as well, secretly ordering the bombing of Cambodia and entering into peace talks with the North Vietnamese, which were kept hidden from the American public. As the narrator writes about Vietnam, "The war itself was a mystery. Nobody knew what it was about, or why they were there, or who started it, or who was winning, or how it might end. . . . History was a secret. The land was a secret" (72–73). The My Lai Massacre itself was followed by a massive military cover-up. Only one person was ever convicted of a crime—Lieutenant William Calley—and his sentence was reduced from life at hard labor to three years under house arrest. Over and over during the Vietnam years, Americans were lied to by their government. Politicians denied the true atrocities taking place in Vietnam, and the American people seemed content to forget and gloss over the worst of these atrocities.

Even more, the narrator connects the American war in Vietnam to previous events from American history. In the Evidence chapters, the narrator includes testimony concerning previous wars in order to remind readers that Americans tend to whitewash their history, to downplay the real horror of war as they look back. As the French writer GEORGE SAND comments about Shakespeare's Iago, in a quote included as Evidence in the novel, "vice never sees its own ugliness—if it did, it would be frightened by its own image" (256). While Americans tend to romanticize the American Revolution as a heroic struggle for independence, the quotes in the book, from both British infantrymen and colonial militiamen, suggest that horrific atrocities, comparable to those that took place at My Lai, occurred on both sides. British soldiers comment on Americans who scalp and mutilate the bodies of the enemy while also providing eyewitness testimony that the homes of Colonists were invaded and entire families put to death. The narrator includes as well evidence detailing the large-scale massacre of Indian men, women, and children at Sandy Creek—including an account of a three-year-old child being shot that sounds as if it could have come straight from the testimony at Calley's court-martial—alongside accounts of the annihilation of Custer's 7th Cavalry at the Battle of Little Bighorn. It is a mistake, then, O'Brien argues, to see the My Lai Massacre as simply an aberration in American history, as the product of a few bad seeds in an otherwise noble effort to ward off communism in Southeast Asia. While it may be convenient to forget or downplay the details, America has a bloody and violent past.

The narrator comments on our collective national amnesia, lending credence to Franklin's theory about denial, in one his final footnotes when he writes, "it's odd how the mind erases horror" (298). He is talking here about John Wade's ability to repress the secret of Thuan Yen, but this statement can be read as entailing the larger American tendency to overlook the ugly, unpleasant details of history. In addition, the narrator links Wade's "forgetting trick" to his own inability to remember much of his particular experiences in Vietnam: "All these years later, like John Wade, I cannot remember much, I cannot feel much. Maybe erasure is necessary. Maybe the human spirit defends itself as the body does, attacking infection, enveloping and destroying those malignancies that would otherwise consume us" (298). The narrator suggests that denial of atrocity may be a psychological necessity—a survival mechanism. Human beings cannot squarely face the darkness of human nature without being consumed or destroyed by it. It is interesting to note that many of the participants in My Lai who acknowledged their part in the massacre, men such as Varnado Simpson and Robert T'Souvas, whose lives were destroyed by this event, often suffered severe mental anguish and early death. If denial of atrocity is necessary to maintain psychological health, then it seems plausible to suggest that readers perform their own tricks of forgetting, ignoring the ugly evidence that John Wade murdered his wife and choosing instead to believe that Kathy left on her own accord, that her disappearance was an accident, or else that she and John planned a happy ending.

Yet, perhaps what Bruce Franklin overlooks in his otherwise persuasive argument that the novel is about denial, that it weights the evidence to prove that John Wade murdered his wife, is the narrator's early footnote cautioning that even much of what looks like fact in the book is actually "a diligent but still imaginative reconstruction of events" (30). In all of Tim O'Brien's work, history is elusive; full, complete "happening-truth" is unattainable. So it may be a mistake for Franklin to assume that the chapters in the novel that recount the past are necessarily to be more fully believed or trusted than the chapters that freely admit their own speculative nature. Just like *The Things They Carried, In the Lake of the Woods* is controlled by a specific narrative voice, by a writer who is shaping and influencing the history that he presents to readers. And just as in that earlier collection what readers are left with is story itself. *Lake,* while it is a novel about secrets, about war, about love, is also a novel that, like *The Things They Carried* and like *Going After Cacciato,* is a metafictional (*see* METAFICTION) meditation on the nature of storytelling. Readers, like the narrator, must choose, with only partial knowledge, the story that they find most plausible. "Finally," the narrator comments, "it's a matter of taste, or aesthetics . . . a judgment call" (300). O'Brien deliberately leaves the novel open-ended because, as he writes in his essay "The Magic Show," a satisfying plot ultimately "involves not a diminution of mystery but rather a fundamental enlargement" (181). Writers, according to O'Brien, are akin to magicians as they perform illusions with words, as they create "a new and improved reality" (175). And the magician's credo, like the writer's credo in this novel, must be: "Don't give away your secrets" (182). "Once a trick is explained," O'Brien argues, "once a secret is divulged—the world moves from the magical to the mechanical" (182). O'Brien as master magician who uses words as his medium both manipulates his audience and keeps them guessing.

CHARACTERS

Note: Historical figures who appear as characters in the novel are cited in this section. Historical figures who do not actually appear as characters in the book but who are mentioned by other characters or cited in the evidence chapters appear in the "Related People, Places, and Topics" section of this volume.

Boyce, Allen Allen Boyce, a private first class in CHARLIE COMPANY, is a real-life figure who was present during the MY LAI MASSACRE. In some accounts he was told to guard crowds of Vietnamese villagers alongside Paul Meadlo, although he was not actually ordered to shoot into the crowds as Meadlo was. Boyce appears as a minor character in the THUAN YEN sections of *In the Lake of the Woods*. He is riding in the back of the chopper that flies the men into the village on the morning of March 16, 1968, and later, when LIEUTENANT CALLEY menacingly asks the men whether they had seen any babies back in the village, Boyce replies, "No way . . . Not the breathing kind" (205).

Brandt, Mrs. Mrs. Brandt was Kathy Wade's girl scout leader when Kathy was a child. In one of the Hypothesis chapters in the novel, in which the narrator speculates that Kathy took the Evinrude out on the lake and became hopelessly lost in the dense wilderness, Kathy remembers Mrs. Brandt and the long list of proverbs she always had at the ready, banal statements like *"Good thought for good girls"* (169). While Mrs. Brandt had "a jingle for every occasion: birthdays, menstruation, first love" (169), none of the old lady's truisms help Kathy as she finds herself "lost and totally alone" (170).

Calley, Lieutenant William LIEUTENANT WILLIAM CALLEY is a real-life figure who was the only person ever convicted of a crime for his actions during the MY LAI MASSACRE. The commanding officer of CHARLIE COMPANY on March 16, 1968, Calley, after a contentious court-martial, was convicted of the premeditated murder of 22 Vietnamese civilians. Although originally sentenced to life imprisonment at hard labor, Lieutenant Calley actually served only three and a half years under house arrest. Calley, along with several other actual historical figures, appears as a character during the Vietnam scenes in the novel, where he is depicted as a callous, violent, and racist officer who insists that "gooks [are] gooks" (205) and who menaces any of the men who question the actions of Charlie Company on that ill-fated day. Snippets from the actual proceedings of Calley's court-martial are scattered through the Evidence sections of

the book as well. Taken out of the context of the horror of the war, these excerpts—such as Calley claiming that the "only means" with which he could have evacuated people would be "a hand grenade" (135)—seem particularly grotesque and chilling.

Carbo, Tony Tony Carbo is John Wade's campaign manager when he runs for the U.S. Senate. A fat, sloppy, cynical political operative who seems at least half in love with Kathy Wade himself, Tony Carbo has no illusions about John Wade's intentions. Carbo believes that his boss is ruthlessly ambitious, that his first goal is to get elected, and that policies and programs for change—the idealism of politics—are only a secondary concern for him. While Tony Carbo appears in the chapters detailing John Wade's past political life, as well as some of the Hypothesis chapters that speculate about what might have happened to Kathy, readers find out that he was also interviewed by the novel's narrator, on July 12 and 13, 1993, in St. Paul, Minnesota. Thus, many of his comments appear in the Evidence chapters of the book as well. In these comments, Carbo compares magicians to politicians, arguing that both are performers who will do anything for love. He is astonished that John Wade thought he could keep his war past hidden but speculates that Wade did not set out to tell an intentional lie, but rather simply kept quiet about his past until he had "probably talked himself into believing it never happened at all" (196). Tony Carbo, at the end of the novel, seems to believe most strongly in the theory that John and Kathy worked together to orchestrate their disappearance, pointing out in the interview that "they were in debt up to their necks," that their bank account was "cleaned out slick as a whistle even before they headed up north," and that "nobody ever found *either* boat" (296). He concludes by musing that neither John nor Kathy had "a damn thing to come *back* to—reputation shot, no more career, bills up the gazoo" (296). "Christ," he adds, "I'd run for it too" (296).

Carbo's Secretary While John and Kathy Wade are staying at the cabin on the shore of the LAKE

OF THE WOODS, he puts in a call to his former campaign manager, Tony Carbo, only to find out he is unavailable. Half an hour later, he calls back, only to be told by Carbo's secretary that her boss has gone out for the day. It is after this phone call that Wade unplugs the telephone and tosses it in the cupboard below the kitchen sink. Clearly, Tony Carbo is now refusing to take Wade's calls, which infuriates the former Senate candidate.

Conti, Dennis Dennis Conti was a real-life member of CHARLIE COMPANY who testified about the killings in the village of My Lai 4 during LIEUTENANT WILLIAM CALLEY's court-martial. Conti claimed that Calley had ordered his men to round up villagers into tightly huddled groups in the rice paddies, and to then fire automatic weapons into the crowds. In cross-examination, Conti was accused of raping Vietnamese women on several occasions, including on March 16, 1968. It also came out in trial that he was taking penicillin for a venereal disease. Portions of Conti's actual testimony during the court-martial are included in some of the Evidence chapters of the novel, and Conti himself appears as a character in the chapters that recount the My Lai atrocities. In the rear of the chopper that carries the men into the village that day, Conti is said to be "off in some mental whorehouse" (104), clearly an allusion to his sexual activities as reported in Calley's court-martial. O'Brien then depicts Conti watching Calley and Paul Meadlo spraying gunfire into a crowd of villagers a little later that morning. The next day, when members of the platoon, who have marched within a kilometer of Thuan Yen, see that several huts are still smoking in the distance, the fictionalized Conti laughs and calls himself and his fellow soldiers "Grave robbers" (207). A few minutes later, he says, "Zombie patrol . . . that's us" (207), and lets out a ghoulish howl right before Paul Meadlo's left foot is torn off by a land mine.

Cox, Sergeant George Sergeant George Cox was an actual historical figure, a beloved squad leader in CHARLIE COMPANY killed by a land mine just before the MY LAI MASSACRE. Cox becomes a character in the novel when the narrator explains

that he accounts for one of the many casualties taken by Charlie Company in the area of PINKVILLE. On March 14, just two days before the American soldiers lose control in the village of THUAN YEN, a booby-trapped 155 round blows Sergeant Cox "into several large, wet pieces" (103), according to the narrator.

Doherty, William William Doherty is another of the actual historical figures who appears in the novel. An infantry rifleman assigned to the Second Platoon of CHARLIE COMPANY, Doherty was present at the MY LAI MASSACRE and was one of the informants cited by Ronald Ridenhour in the long letter the ex-serviceman wrote to Congress that prompted the PEERS COMMISSION investigation. In the novel, Doherty is said to be "finishing off the wounded" (107) after the atrocities in the village of Thuan Yen are committed.

Dyson Dyson is a soldier in CHARLIE COMPANY who loses both legs two days before the MY LAI MASSACRE when the unit inadvertently explodes a booby-trapped 155 round while on patrol in the area of PINKVILLE. The blast kills another soldier, Sergeant George Cox, and severely injures a third man as well, Hendrixson.

Durkee, Ed Ed Durkee was John Wade's closest rival in the race for U.S. Senate, who ends up handing Wade a humiliating defeat, beating the former lieutenant governor as much as four-to-one in some parts of Minnesota. Described as "an old war horse" (158), Durkee and his political team uncover Wade's past participation in the MY LAI MASSACRE and publicize it in the press. Durkee explains, "The Peers Commission people weren't looking for him. We were. Nothing to it really . . . Once we got wind of this so-called Sorcerer, it was only a matter of time. I put the boys on it. No sweat" (292). Durkee's team may have first learned the name Sorcerer from the testimony of Wade's old friend Richard Thinbill during LIEUTENANT WILLIAM CALLEY's court-martial proceedings.

Ehlers, Lawrence While John Wade is shooting baskets during gym class at his junior high school one day when he is 14 years old, the gym teacher walks up to him, puts his arm around John's shoulder, and tells the boy to take a shower because his mother is there to pick him up. Mrs. Wade has come to the school to inform John of his father's suicide. The teacher, Lawrence Ehlers, is interviewed by the novel's narrator on March 1, 1994. In the interview, Ehlers calls both the school principal and himself cowards for not breaking the news about his father's suicide to John themselves.

Harmon   Harmon is the name of a dentist whom Kathy Wade has an affair with during her marriage to John. In the summer of 1983, Kathy had flown off to meet Harmon in Boston, telling John she was going to visit an old high school friend. Harmon picks her up at the airport, and the two drive north to a resort in Maine called LOON POINT, where they spend four days and three nights together. On the morning of the fourth day, Kathy tells Harmon that the relationship is a mistake, that she still loves her husband. She flies home to Minneapolis earlier than expected, but John does not even notice the change in her flight plans. Depressed by John's self-centeredness, she decides not to tell him about the affair. Nevertheless, he somehow finds out about it. At the LAKE OF THE WOODS, shortly after the election, when Kathy asks her husband if what the papers are saying about his past is true, he replies, "It's history, Kath. If you want to trot out the skeletons, let's talk about your dentist" (56). The two spend the rest of the evening in silence, "pretend[ing] not to know the things they knew" (57).

Hendrixson   Hendrixson is the name of a soldier in CHARLIE COMPANY who loses an arm and a leg in an explosion two days before the MY LAI MASSACRE. While the unit is patrolling in the PINKVILLE area, a booby-trapped 155 round blows up, killing Sergeant George Cox and severely wounding both Hendrixson and another soldier named Dyson. This incident scares and frustrates the other members of Charlie Company; two or three men cry afterward, but "others couldn't remember how" (103). The resulting rage over the explosion is one of the factors leading to the atrocities the Ameri-

can soldiers will commit in the village of THUAN YEN.

Hood, Patricia   Patricia Hood, described as a tall, muscular, well-built woman who owns several health clubs in Minneapolis and its surrounding suburbs, is Kathy Wade's sister. She arrives at ANGLE INLET by airboat a few days after Kathy's disappearance to help with the search efforts. Suspicious of men in general following her two divorces and string of live-in boyfriends, Pat is no friend of John Wade. In an interview conducted on May 6, 1990, Pat Hood seems reluctant to talk about John and Kathy, but she does reveal that Kathy had confided in her about John's nightmares—the fact that he would often wake up in the night shouting foul language. Pat is also privy to the fact that Kathy hated "the political wifey routine" (184), the pasted-on smiles and devoted behavior expected of the candidate's spouse, information that she does not hesitate to share with John Wade soon after her arrival at the yellow cottage on the lake. Pat is suspicious of John Wade from the beginning and seems inclined to believe that her brother-in-law, whom she openly calls a "war criminal" (185), was fully capable of murdering his wife.

Hutson, Max   A real-life member of CHARLIE COMPANY's Second Platoon, Max Hutson was one of the nine enlisted men originally charged with murder for his participation in the MY LAI MASSACRE, even though LIEUTENANT WILLIAM CALLEY was the only person ever convicted of a crime. A fictionalized version of Hutson briefly appears in the novel, during the slaughter at THUAN YEN, when he is said to be taking turns on a machine gun with a fellow soldier named Wright.

Hutto, Charles   Sergeant Charles Hutto was one of the soldiers who underwent a court-martial for his actions during the MY LAI MASSACRE. Under oath, Hutto testified that he had simply followed the orders of his superiors, which had been to kill every living thing in the village. Like the other enlisted men who faced a court-martial, Hutto was acquitted of all charges. Charles Hutto appears only briefly as a character in the novel. In chapter

13, "The Nature of the Beast," which describes the atrocities committed at THUAN YEN, Hutto is said to be "shooting corpses" (107).

Karra, Sandra Sandra Karra, whom John Wade as a young boy calls the "Carrot Lady" because of her bright orange hair, is the owner of Karra's Studio of Magic, a shop that John frequented in his childhood. Although he is half-afraid of the Carrot Lady, who shouts *"You!"* at him whenever he enters the store, John is still fascinated by the tricks and illusions that Karra stocks. One day near Christmas, when John is 11, his father takes him to Sandra Karra's store to pick out his own Christmas present. John, significantly, chooses the "Guillotine of Death," a piece of equipment that foreshadows many events in John's later life, including his father's suicide, his involvement in the MY LAI MASSACRE, and his possible murder of his wife. Sandra Karra, interviewed by the novel's narrator on December 16, 1991, explains that, as a child, "John had slick hands . . . And he knew how to keep his mouth shut" (191). Although Karra does not speculate specifically on what became of John as other interviewees do, she sees him as an accomplished magician, able to keep secrets, suggesting, perhaps, her view that John Wade was capable of planning a double vanishing act on Kathy and himself, their likely deaths being an illusion that John has skillfully arranged.

Kee, Bethany Bethany Kee, whom the novel's narrator interviews on September 21, 1991, is the associate admissions director at the UNIVERSITY OF MINNESOTA, where she worked closely with Kathy Wade before her disappearance at the LAKE OF THE WOODS. Kathy has clearly confided in Bethany certain details about John's strange behavior, including the fact that John used to spy on her. Although she calls John a "creep" (12), Bethany does not subscribe to the theory that John Wade murdered his wife. She tells the interviewer that she initially believed Kathy drowned, but she says that on further reflection she realized Kathy seemed perfectly fine before her disappearance. "Right after the election," she adds, Kathy "was almost carefree. Incredibly happy. Like I'd never seen her before" (297).

Bethany surmises that Kathy either ran away by herself—"I'll bet she's on a Greyhound bus somewhere" (12)—or that she and John planned their vanishing act together. Kathy "had the guts," Bethany insists, "And she wanted changes" (297).

Lindquist, Deborah Deborah Lindquist was a classmate of Kathy Wade's at the UNIVERSITY OF MINNESOTA. In an interview that the narrator conducts with her on April 2, 1993, Deborah talks about John's spying on Kathy during their college years, adding that Kathy was fully aware of it and even used to call John "Inspector Clouseau" (191) behind his back. This testimony adds evidence to the idea that Kathy was more complicit in the strangeness of her relationship with John than it might first appear.

Lux, Arthur J. County Sheriff Arthur J. Lux, who is stationed in Baudette, Minnesota, is the full-time officer of the law closest to the small cottage in the LAKE OF THE WOODS, where the Wades had been staying. He flies in on the morning of September 20, 1986, immediately after Kathy is reported missing, to set up search headquarters at PEARSON'S TEXACO STATION in ANGLE INLET. Described as "a short gaunt man in his late fifties, tanned and windburnt, dressed in gray trousers and a soiled gray shirt" (119), Art Lux looks more like a dairy farmer than an officer of the law to John Wade when he first meets him. Lux, unlike part-time deputy Vinny Pearson, works hard to remain polite and sympathetic as he interviews John Wade. He retains this sympathy when he informs Wade, Pat Hood, and the Rasmussens 18 days later that the official search for Kathy is being called off. In an interview with the novel's narrator, conducted on January 3, 1991, in Baudette, Lux explains that the case is still wide open. Although reluctant to commit himself to a particular theory of what happened to the Wades, he does say that, while he can buy one missing person, two in a row begin to make him "get antsy" (297). He adds that certain things John Wade did after Kathy's disappearance, such as spending the afternoon paying bills and not getting that upset, have always bothered him. Yet, he also admits that an extremely thorough search of the house and grounds turned up nothing. Lux even brought in divers to search the lake, who never found anything either.

Maples, Robert   Robert Maples was an actual machine gunner in CHARLIE COMPANY who was present during the MY LAI MASSACRE. At LIEUTENANT CALLEY's court-martial, Maples testified that he had been ordered to fire his gun into a crowd of Vietnamese men, women, and children, but had refused to do so. This piece of testimony is included in chapter 16 of the novel, one of the Evidence sections. Maples also appears as a character riding in the back of the chopper that brings the men into the village of THUAN YEN, and as one of the soldiers who returns to the village on March 17, 1968, the day after the massacre has occurred. When he sees a young Vietnamese woman with both breasts cut off, and the letter C carved into her stomach, Maples along with a fellow soldier named Boyce, "[goes] off to be sick" (210).

Meadlo, Paul   Paul Meadlo was a real-life soldier who participated in the MY LAI MASSACRE. In a television interview with CBS news, he publicly admitted to firing his rifle into groups of Vietnamese civilians when ordered to do so by LIEUTENANT WILLIAM CALLEY. Two days after the My Lai tragedy, Meadlo stepped on a mine and lost his foot, an injury for which he was awarded the Purple Heart. In the novel, Meadlo appears as a character during the Vietnam chapters. He is depicted sobbing and spraying gunfire into a crowd of villagers, a description that squares with Meadlo's real-life confession of his crimes. The novel's Evidence chapters also include snippets of Meadlo's actual testimony during William Calley's court-martial, the most infamous of which involves Meadlo's assertion that babies "in their mother's arms" might "make a counterbalance" at any moment (136).

Minister   John and Kathy Wade are married in an outdoor ceremony in the yard of her family's house a few months after John's return from service in the Vietnam War. During the ceremony, the minister speaks about "the shield of God's love, which warded off strife" (45), a topic drenched

in irony for readers who believe that Wade murdered his wife. The minister also reads the following passage from First Corinthians in the Bible: "For now we see through a glass, darkly; but then face to face: now I know in part; but then shall I know even as also I am known" (45). This passage echoes what may be the major theme of the novel: All human knowledge must be partial and incomplete. Human life and character remain essential mysteries that we can never untangle, at least not in this life.

Mitchell, Sergeant David   Sergeant David Mitchell was a real-life soldier charged with participating in the MY LAI MASSACRE. Accused of firing into crowds of unarmed civilians, mostly consisting of women and children, Sergeant Mitchell underwent the first My Lai court-martial but was acquitted. Mitchell appears briefly as a character in the novel in the chapters that describe the atrocities committed at THUAN YEN. He is first depicted sitting in the rear of a chopper in the early morning hours of March 16, 1968, alongside other real-life figures such as Paul Meadlo and Dennis Conti as well as the fictional Richard Thinbill. Later, Mitchell is one of the soldiers to whom LIEUTENANT CALLEY asks, "You troopers notice any VC babies back there?" (205), as he attempts to deny the atrocities that took place in the village.

Narrator   The novel's narrator is first introduced to readers in footnote 21 of chapter 6, the second Evidence chapter. Referring to himself as "biographer, historian, medium," the narrator explains that he has been investigating John Wade's disappearance for four years, but that all he has to show for his hard labor is "little more than supposition and possibility" (30). While readers might be tempted to take the chapters that explore Wade's past at face value, to read them as objective truth, the narrator warns his audience that "Even much of what might appear to be fact in this narrative— action, word, thought—must ultimately be viewed as a diligent but still imaginative reconstruction of events" (30). The narrator's occasional comments, like the ones cited above, about the research and writing of the book, are found sprinkled throughout the novel's 133 footnotes. This commentary constitutes a metafictional (*see* METAFICTION) meditation on the process of writing itself and on the unreliability of history, thus linking *In the Lake of the Woods* to earlier O'Brien novels, including *Going After Cacciato* and *The Things They Carried.*

In footnote 88, readers discover that this narrator himself is a Vietnam veteran, who, like the real-life Tim O'Brien, served in and around PINKVILLE a year after the MY LAI MASSACRE occurred. As such, he can understand the "wickedness that soaks into your blood and slowly heats up and begins to boil" (199). But the narrator also explains that his job is not to justify the actions of CHARLIE COMPANY on that day, but rather to "bear witness to the mystery of evil" (199). The narrator argues that what human beings find fascinating is the unknown: "The human desire for certainty collides with our love of enigma" (266). It is the mystery of the Wade case that propels the narrator in his investigation—the "craving to know what cannot be known" (295). He speculates about how well human beings can truly know other human beings, even themselves, and he discusses his own inability to access his darkest secrets about the war, about his life. "It's odd," he writes, "how the mind erases horror" (298), suggesting a reason for his failure to remember much about his own war experiences as well as readers' unwillingness to accept the hypothesis that John Wade murdered his wife in a brutal and horrifying way. In footnote 131, after all, the narrator writes that he himself rejects the possibility of the midnight boil as "both graceless and disgusting" (300), although he also adds that it comes down to a matter of aesthetics and that some readers might "hear her screaming," might "see steam rising from the sockets of her eyes" (300). Finally, in his last footnote, the narrator concludes that there can be no ending to his story, happy or otherwise: "All secrets lead to the dark, and beyond the dark there is only maybe" (301).

Old Man with Hoe   During the massacre at THUAN YEN, John Wade shoots to death a Vietnamese villager who is described as "an old man with a wispy beard and wire glasses and what looked to be a rifle" (109). What initially appears to be a

rifle, however, turns out to be a hoe; the man is a farmer, not an enemy soldier. Wade shoots the man nearly reflexively, and afterward he is haunted by a vision of the old man's wooden hoe "spinning like a baton in the morning sunlight" (109). The old man is the only Vietnamese citizen that Wade kills that day, although he also shoots to death a fellow American soldier, PFC Weatherby.

Pearson, Vincent   Vinny Pearson is a part-time deputy in the small town of ANGLE INLET, Minnesota, who also owns the local Texaco gas station. When Kathy Wade is reported missing, Vinny aids County Sheriff Art Lux in the investigation. Unlike Lux, Vinny is suspicious of Wade from the beginning and impatient in his questioning of the former lieutenant governor. The two men nearly get in a fistfight at the Angle Inlet boatyard a few days into the search. Wade calls Pearson an "albino fetus," and Vinny, who served as a Marine during the Vietnam War, retorts that he never "mass murdered nobody" (237). In his interview with the novel's narrator on June 9, 1993, Pearson is adamant in his belief that John Wade killed his wife, stating plainly that "The guy offed her" (12).

Rathmussen, Claude   Claude Rathmussen is a nearly 80-year-old man who owns the yellow cottage on the LAKE OF THE WOODS, where John and Kathy Wade retreat after the election loss. Described as an old time Democratic Party contributor who hides his sharp intelligence behind a "hick caretaker" act (87), Claude is in fact a wealthy man who owns seven miles of shoreline and 12,000 acres of timber in northern Minnesota. Although only an acquaintance of John Wade, not a close friend at all, Claude calls him after the election to offer the cottage for a two-week getaway. After Kathy's disappearance, Claude is one of the few people in the area who supports John and seems to believe in his innocence. He takes Wade and Wade's sister-in-law, Patricia Hood, out searching on the lake for many days unsuccessfully. When the search is called off, Claude Rathmussen understands John's desire to get back out on the lake and leaves Wade a key to his Chris-Craft on the kitchen table, with a note explaining that the boat is equipped with a radio and a chart book under the seat. He seems to believe that Wade is planning to start a new life for himself in Canada. When the sheriff's men find nothing after tearing apart the yellow cottage after John Wade's disappearance, including ripping the boards up from the floor, Claude cackles with delight. Readers discover, from the interview the narrator conducts with Claude's wife, Ruth, that the old man died in 1988.

Rathmussen, Ruth   Ruth Rathmussen is the practical, no-nonsense wife of wily old Claude Rasmussen, who owns the cottage on the LAKE OF THE WOODS, where the Wades stay briefly. Described as a "large, sturdy woman in her mid-fifties, tall and rugged looking, with a graceful way of carrying the extra thirty pounds at her hips and belly" (84), Ruth becomes deeply involved in John Wade's life after Kathy's mysterious disappearance, calling the police to report the missing person, serving coffee, and staying with Wade at the cottage, along with Claude, until the arrival of his sister-in-law, Patricia Hood. Ruth, interviewed by the novel's narrator on June 6, 1989, steadfastly affirms John Wade's innocence, speculating that John and Kathy might be in Hudson Bay now, or someplace similar. She insists that John and Kathy were deeply in love—"Honest love—just like Claude and me. You could see it plain and obvious" (296)—and tells the interviewer that she expects a note in the mail or for the couple to show up and walk through her door any day.

Reinhart   In the first months of 1968, when John Wade is patrolling the PINKVILLE area of Vietnam with CHARLIE COMPANY, the war turns terribly dangerous for his unit. The men take many casualties, including a sergeant named Reinhart, who is shot dead by sniper fire while eating a Mars candy bar in the second week of February. Wade, feeling cold inside and acting as if he has no control over his own body, will glide through deep brush until he comes upon the sniper. He puts his rifle against the man's cheek and pulls the trigger. Later, Wade and other members of his unit will drag the body into a nearby village and hang it upside down from some trees as a warning.

Reinhart's death, coupled with the loss of several other men, enrages and frustrates the soldiers of Charlie Company, who will vent their anger in atrocities committed on the villagers of THUAN YEN a month later.

Roschevitz, Gary   An actual American soldier who took part in the MY LAI MASSACRE, GARY ROSCHEVITZ was said to have used an M-79 grenade launcher to kill a group of nude Vietnamese women whom he had originally planned to rape. The novel includes in one of the Evidence chapters testimony to this effect given by the soldier Leonard Gonzalez during LIEUTENANT CALLEY's court-martial. During the fictionalized scenes of slaughter at THUAN YEN in the novel, Roschevitz appears as a character and is said to have "shot people in the head" (108).

Shaw, Myra   Myra Shaw is a plump, 18-year-old waitress who works at ARNDAHL'S MINI-MART in ANGLE INLET, Minnesota, six miles away from the cabin the Wades stay in at the LAKE OF THE WOODS. Interviewed by the novel's narrator on June 10, 1993, Myra discusses the argument she witnessed between John and Kathy when they came into the store for coffee the day before Kathy disappeared. Myra Shaw is also the girl behind the counter when John Wade returns to the Mini-Mart to purchase bread, sandwich meat, vodka, a tourist map, cans of Sterno, and a plastic compass before he sets out on the lake in Claude Rasmussen's Chris-Craft the following morning. She is distrustful of Wade and locks the door after he leaves. In her interview, Myra expresses doubt that John Wade killed himself, pointing to the tourist maps he bought: "If he's out to zap himself, why tourist maps? Sounds to me like a tour" (297).

Simpson, Varnado   Varnado Simpson was a soldier in CHARLIE COMPANY who participated in the MY LAI MASSACRE and who later confessed to personally killing several Vietnamese villagers, including women and children. In later life, his own 10-year-old son was shot to death by random gunfire, and Simpson interpreted this as punishment for his actions in Vietnam. Simpson, suffering from paranoia and other psychological disorders, committed suicide in 1997 by shooting himself in the head. In the THUAN YEN chapters of the novel, Simpson is depicted "killing children" (107). Quotes from Simpson that originally appeared in a documentary called *Four Hours in My Lai* are also included in the Evidence chapters of O'Brien's novel. In one of these, Simpson claims to have been personally responsible for killing about 25 people, as well as for other atrocities committed against the Vietnamese villagers, such as "scalping them," "cutting off their hands," and "cutting out their tongues" (257). Because Simpson was heavily medicated for his psychological problems and racked by guilt at the time he made this confession, and because he had earlier admitted to killing only eight people, there is some doubt as to the veracity of these later claims.

Sledge, Charles   Charles Sledge was an African-American radioman in CHARLIE COMPANY who testified during the court-martial hearing of Sergeant David Mitchell. Sledge claimed to have seen Mitchell shoot into a crowd of men, women, and children cowering in a ditch that day. Under cross-examination, some inconsistencies in Sledge's testimony were exposed. In earlier interviews and accounts, he had seemed less certain of Mitchell's involvement than he was at the trial. Sledge appears only briefly as a character in *In the Lake of the Woods*. He is said to be fiddling with his radio in the rear of the chopper as the men of Charlie Company are flown into the village the morning of March 16, 1968.

Sniper   After Sergeant Rinehart is shot dead by a sniper in the PINKVILLE area of Vietnam in February 1968, John Wade, or Sorcerer, slips and glides through deep brush until he comes upon the sniper: "a little man in black trousers and a black shirt" (40). Wade puts his rifle muzzle up against the man's cheekbones and pulls the trigger. Later, the men of CHARLIE COMPANY drag the sniper's body into a nearby hamlet, where "Sorcerer and his assistants performed an act of levitation, hoisting the body high into the trees, into the dark, where it floated under a lovely red moon" (41).

T'Souvas, Robert   Robert T'Souvas, a high school drop-out from San Jose, California, was a real-life participant in the MY LAI MASSACRE who was charged with two counts of premeditated murder against Vietnamese civilians. After the first two trials of enlisted men ended in acquittals, charges against T'Souvas and several others were dropped. Robert T'Souvas later became a homeless drifter. At the age of 39, he was shot to death by his girlfriend during an argument over a bottle of vodka under a bridge in Pittsburgh. In the novel the fictionalized T'Souvas is said to be "shooting children" (107) during the carnage that takes place in the village of THUAN YEN. This piece of information squares with accounts from actual soldiers who testified that T'Souvas shot injured children to death during the massacre, possibly to end their suffering. A report from the *Boston Herald* concerning T'Souvas's death is included in one of the novel's Evidence chapters.

T'Souvas, William   In a newspaper account of the death of the homeless Vietnam veteran and MY LAI MASSACRE participant Robert T'Souvas, which appears in chapter 25 of the novel (one of the Evidence sections), WILLIAM T'SOUVAS, Robert's father, states that his son "had problems with Vietnam over and over," adding that "he didn't talk about it much" (261).

Terry, Michael   A real-life soldier in CHARLIE COMPANY who was present during the MY LAI MASSACRE, Michael Terry claimed to have come upon the scene after most of the killings were ended. Terry is one of the soldiers who later talked about the atrocities in PINKVILLE with serviceman Ronald Ridenhour, who took it upon himself to investigate disturbing rumors he had heard about the massacre, and whose long letter sent to high-ranking politicians broke the case open. In the novel the fictionalized Terry is depicted at the village of THUAN YEN. He is said to be "finishing off the wounded" (107) along with a buddy, William Doherty.

Thinbill, Richard   Richard Thinbill is a full-blooded Chippewa Indian who served with John

Wade in Vietnam. Interviewed by the novel's narrator on July 19, 1990, Thinbill's comments appear primarily in the Evidence chapters of the book, where he frequently mentions the millions of flies that infested the dead and dying in THUAN YEN. The flies, frequently a symbol of evil because of their association with Beezlebub in the Christian Bible, whose name is commonly translated as "Lord of the Flies," are Thinbill's most prominent memory of that ill-fated day. Thinbill also appears as a character in the chapters that recall the Vietnam War portions of John Wade's past. While Thinbill is a fictional character, he and John Wade interact with real-life figures who participated in the MY LAI MASSACRE, including LIEUTENANT WILLIAM CALLEY, Paul Meadlo, Dennis Conti, and others. Unlike these other men, Thinbill does not participate in the massacre, is horrified by what he witnesses, and urges John Wade to join him in reporting the atrocity. When Wade is overcome by a fit of hysterical giggling at Thinbill's suggestion, the young Chippewa soldier concedes that Wade has "the right attitude" (216). "Laugh it off. Fuck the spirit world" (216), Thinbill adds, and the two men keep the horrifying incident to themselves. Later, when Thinbill is questioned as part of Lieutenant Calley's court-martial proceedings, he briefly mentions his friend Sorcerer. Readers are led to believe that this minor reference might be the thread that unravels Wade's cover-up, the clue that eventually leads Ed Durkee to the truth about John Wade's past.

Wade, Eleanor   Eleanor Wade is John Wade's mother. Her comments appear frequently in the Evidence sections of the book. A footnote at the beginning of chapter 2 explains that these comments come from an interview conducted on December 4, 1989, in St. Paul, Minnesota (presumably by the novel's narrator, a character whom readers will be introduced to later in the novel). In her interview, Mrs. Wade discusses John's childhood, explaining that he was "always a secretive boy" (8), and that he used to practice magic tricks for hours on end, shut up in the basement of the family home. Mrs. Wade also discusses her husband's alcoholism and the effect it had on the fam-

ily. She explains that the summer John was 11 years old she got up the nerve to check her husband into an alcohol treatment center. While Mrs. Wade describes her relief at having Mr. Wade out of the house temporarily, things did not get much better after his return home. John's father continued to tease him cruelly and ended up committing suicide when John was 14 years old. Eleanor Wade is the one who finds her husband hanged in the garage. Mrs. Wade hints as well in the interview that her son lost control of himself at his father's funeral, yelling and raging wildly. Nevertheless, she steadfastly refuses to believe that John hurt his wife, Kathy. Her final comment in the book suggests that she believes the two mutually planned their disappearance and are living a new life together somewhere: "A person has to hope for *something*. So I hope they're happy. They deserved a little happiness" (297).

Wade, John   John Wade, the novel's main character, is a Vietnam veteran and a former Minnesota state senator and lieutenant governor, who has just suffered a humiliating election defeat for the U.S. Senate when the novel opens. Wade's political aspirations are destroyed when his secret involvement in the MY LAI MASSACRE is discovered and made public by Edward Durkee, an opposing Senate candidate. As a temporary haven from the public humiliation caused by this news, John and his wife, Kathy, have retreated to a remote cottage in the wilderness at the LAKE OF THE WOODS on the U.S.-Canadian border. However, eight days after their arrival at the cottage, Kathy Wade mysteriously disappears. A full-scale search for the missing woman lasts for 18 days, but when no trace of Kathy is found, suspicion falls firmly on John Wade, whom local officers suspect of murdering his wife. While nothing is ever proven one way or the other, John Wade only adds to the mystery when he himself goes missing after taking a boat out onto the lake a few days after the search for Kathy has been called off.

Intermingled with the story of the disappearance of both Wades is the story of John's past. Readers discover that John Wade was a lonely, chubby boy with an alcoholic father who hanged himself in the family garage when John was 14 years old. When he meets Kathy as a senior at the UNIVERSITY OF MINNESOTA, John seems to have found the love he had been seeking his whole life. Yet, John's love takes a strange turn when he begins to spy on Kathy at school, and when, after volunteering for service in Vietnam, he writes disturbing letters home to her. In Vietnam John continues to practice the magic tricks that had brought him comfort and a sense of control as a young boy growing up in Minnesota, soon earning the nickname "Sorcerer" and a grudging respect from the other young soldiers in CHARLIE COMPANY, where he has been assigned. But events spiral out of Sorcerer's control on the morning of March 16, 1968, when the members of Charlie Company rampage through the village of THUAN YEN, known as My Lai 4 on American maps, brutalizing and killing hundreds of civilians. While John Wade participates only minimally in the savagery, he nevertheless carefully works to erase his name from Charlie Company's records before he leaves Vietnam after serving a second tour of duty.

Once home, John marries Kathy, attends law school, and launches his political career. Despite some rough patches in his marriage, John is largely successful and happy until his world comes crashing down around him when he is exposed in the newspapers. After Kathy's disappearance from the cottage, the novel turns to the question of whether John Wade murdered his wife or not. The novel's unnamed narrator, who has investigated the case for four years, provides ample evidence on either side. Certain facts work against the theory of homicide: It is clear that John loved Kathy deeply; no boats or bodies are ever found; and the wily and clever Claude Rasumussen retains his faith in John Wade to the end. As John was a magician, it is possible that he performed a vanishing act on both his wife and himself in an attempt to start life fresh. On the other hand, John's love for Kathy is unhealthy and possessive. Perhaps he murdered her because he was afraid of losing her. He was, after all, in a strange psychological state the night and early morning of her disappearance, muttering "*Kill Jesus!*" and boiling numerous houseplants to death with water from a teakettle. In addition, he seems to have dim but real memories of going to the boathouse and being in the lake very late that night. He does not seem surprised by her disappearance, and it takes him quite a while to join the actual search to find Kathy.

John Wade's character remains enigmatic in the novel. Were his psychological problems the result of a weak and needy personality, an unhappy childhood, or his Vietnam experiences? Was his political career an admirable attempt to do good in the world, to make amends for past sins, or simply an expression of his deep need to be loved and admired? Finally, was he "a monster" or "a man" (303)? Readers are left to try and answer these questions for themselves.

Wade, Kathy Kathy Wade is the wife of U.S. Senate candidate and Vietnam War veteran John Wade. She mysteriously disappears while the couple is staying temporarily at a small, remote cottage on the shore of the LAKE OF THE WOODS in northern Minnesota, where they have gone to escape the humiliation of John's recent election defeat as well as his exposure in the newspapers as having participated in the MY LAI MASSACRE. In an excerpt from the official Missing Persons Report, filed on September 21, 1986, readers discover that Kathy was 38 years old when she disappeared, that she worked as the director of admissions for the UNIVERSITY OF MINNESOTA, that she had an abortion four years previously, and that she was currently prescribed the medications Valium and Restoril. As the novel unfolds, readers discover more about Kathy's past, although the mystery of her disappearance is never conclusively unraveled.

Kathy first met John when she was 18 years old and a freshman at the University of Minnesota. They soon fall deeply in love, despite Kathy's knowledge of John's sometimes strange behavior—he frequently spies on her as she goes about her daily campus life, following her to class, to the library, to volleyball practice, and elsewhere. After graduation, John volunteers for service in Vietnam, and Kathy stays in close touch with him by writing frequent letters and cards, although some of John's letters from Vietnam are quite troubling, especially one in which he describes witnessing two snakes eating each other's tails and declares that this is a metaphor for his and Kathy's love for each other. After his second tour of duty, John returns home, marries Kathy, goes to law school, and begins a political career. While the Wades begin their lives together happy and in love, as the years pass Kathy grows increasingly dissatisfied with her role as a politician's wife and has a brief affair with a dentist named Harmon at some point during the marriage. She also seems to be extremely depressed by the abortion she undergoes at the age of 34 since she longs for children and a stable home. When the news of John's Vietnam past breaks, Kathy seems to be at least partly relieved that his political career has ended but also disturbed about the secrets that John has been keeping all these years.

The novel's narrator provides abundant supporting evidence for each of the hypotheses he proposes to explain Kathy's disappearance. The previous affair with Harmon, which Kathy has kept secret from John, lends credence to the notion that she might have planned to meet a lover. However, John's erratic behavior, especially the boiling of the houseplants, could easily have frightened his wife, who may have left the cottage in a panic that morning and either had a boating accident or gotten lost in the remote wilderness. Kathy's depression and her reliance on the tranquilizers Valium and Restoril, as noted in the Missing Persons Report, suggest the possibility of suicide. Homicide, though, cannot be ruled out either, especially in light of John's rage that night, his psychological difficulties, and his fear that Kathy might leave him. Finally, the notion that the two planned their disappearances together in order to start a new life is supported by the wild plans they hatch for VERONA, ITALY, at the beginning of the book, by their staggering campaign debt, and by the fact that Kathy in many ways seems to act as her magician-husband's beautiful assistant, enabling him to perform the many tricks and illusions that he does so well. Readers, finally, are left only with speculation—Kathy's disappearance remains an unsolved mystery to the end.

Wade, Mr. John Wade's father, whose first name readers never learn, is a temperamental alcoholic who hangs himself in the family garage when John is 14 years old. Although he teases his son mercilessly about his weight and his love of magic, Mr. Wade could also be a charming man: smart, funny, and good company. The neighborhood kids frequently stop by the Wade house to toss a football around with John's father and listen to his jokes and stories. And at school one day, a boy named Tommy Winn gives a speech about how he wishes that Mr. Wade were *his* father. Alone with his family, however, Mr. Wade shows another side to his personality, often behaving in an unkind and even cruel way to his wife and son. It is a relief to both Eleanor and John, in fact, when Mr. Wade checks into an alcohol treatment center for a few months when John is 12 years old. Eleanor Wade, in an interview with the narrator, says that her husband was basically "a sad person underneath" (195), although she is unsure what had caused his sadness. In this respect, Mr. Wade represents the book's concern with the mystery that lies at the heart of all human relationships: the impossibility of fully knowing another human being.

Weatherby, PFC PFC Weatherby is a fellow soldier of John Wade's in CHARLIE COMPANY, whom Wade, dazed and terrified by the atrocities he witnesses during the MY LAI MASSACRE, shoots in the face. Weatherby drops alongside Wade into a ditch where Wade is crouched and hiding, says "Hey Sorcerer" (64), and starts to smile when Wade shoots him dead. The shooting seems to be involuntary—a gut, instinctive reaction on Wade's part to the horror all around him. Readers find out later that Weatherby had been a full participant in the worst of the violence of THUAN YEN, "killing whatever he could kill" (107).

Weber Weber is a fictionalized member of CHARLIE COMPANY who is shot through the kidney while the unit is patrolling in the area of PINKVILLE one day. When John Wade, in the persona of Sorcerer, kneels down to comfort him, the wounded soldier believes he will be all right because Sorcerer will work his magic: "I'm aces, I'm golden," he claims (37). Despite this, the young man dies "of an exploding kidney" (39), and some of Sorcerer's magic seems to wear off in the eyes of his fellow soldiers.

Winn, Tommy   Tommy Winn is a boy in John Wade's sixth-grade class who gives a speech about John's father and "what a neat guy he was" (66). Tommy talks about how Mr. Wade is always friendly and "full of pep and willing to spend time just shooting the breeze" (66), concluding that he wishes Mr. Wade were *his* father and shooting John a reproachful look. Clearly, Tommy Winn is unaware of the fact that John's father has another hidden side that is not so charming and likeable as the self that he shows to the neighborhood children.

Wright   A soldier named Wright appears briefly in chapter 13: "The Nature of the Beast," which describes the carnage committed by CHARLIE COMPANY at THUAN YEN. Wright is said to be taking turns on a machine gun with a fellow soldier named Hutson. This character is most likely a fictionalized version of Floyde Dale Wright, an actual member of Charlie Company.

FURTHER READING

Edelman, David Louis. "Tim O'Brien Interview: The Things He Carried." *Baltimore City Paper*. 19 October 1994. Available online. URL: http://www.davidlouisedelman.com.

Franklin, Bruce. "Kicking the Denial Syndrome: Tim O'Brien's *In The Lake of the Woods*." In *Novel History: Historians and Novelists Confront America's Past (and Each Other)*, edited by Mark C. Carnes, 332–343. New York: Simon & Schuster, 2001.

Melley, Timothy. "Postmodern Amnesia: Trauma and Forgetting in Tim O'Brien's *In the Lake of the Woods*," *Contemporary Literature* 44, no. 1 (2003): 106–131.

Piwinski, David J. "My Lai, Flies, and Beelzebub in Tim O'Brien's *In the Lake of the Woods*," *WLA: War, Literature, and the Arts* 12, no. 2 (2000): 196–202.

Worthington, Marjorie. "The Democratic Meta-Narrator in *In the Lake of the Woods*," *Explicator* 67, no. 2 (Winter 2009): 67–68.

Young, William. "Missing in Action: Vietnam and Sadism in Tim O'Brien's *In the Lake of the Woods*," *The Midwest Quarterly* 47, no. 2 (2006): 131–143.

"July '69" (2000)

"July '69" tells the story of Lieutenant David Todd, who is severely injured along the SONG TRA KY River in an attack in Vietnam that kills everyone else in his platoon. The story was first published in *Esquire* magazine in July 2000 before being revised and published as chapter 2 of O'Brien's 2002 novel, *July, July*.

SYNOPSIS

The story opens on July 16, 1969. Second Lieutenant David Todd is lying in the grass along a river called the Song Tra Ky, shot through both feet. He is surrounded by the dying members of his platoon, killed in a surprise VIET CONG attack. As David lies there in great pain, unable to move, he thinks about his college girlfriend back home, Marla Dempsey, and about his baseball career—he had aspirations of making it to the big leagues. Amid the noise of the dying men around him, he also hears a voice coming from a transistor radio that had been owned by one of the dead soldiers. A deejay talks about the APOLLO 11 Moon landing, scheduled for July 20. Eventually, David begins to hear the deejay speaking to him personally, telling him that it is time to move out. The following day, David finds 12 Syrettes of morphine in the medical pouch of the platoon's dead medic. He injects himself and is able to drag himself down to the river and soak his feet. Over the next few days, David, in a daze of pain, drifts in and out of consciousness, sometimes lost in his memories, sometimes hallucinating. The radio deejay, who identifies himself as Master Sergeant Johnny Ever, continues to speak to him, eventually offering David a deal: If David is willing to live out the rest of his life with the foreknowledge that his baseball career will be destroyed, that Marla will divorce him after several years of marriage, and that he will suffer survivor guilt from his war experiences, Ever will send in a helicopter to save him. Much to Ever's surprise, David, after experiencing "a bounce of joy" (109) when he hears on the radio that the *Eagle* had landed on the Sea of Tranquility, finally agrees to the deal. Deciding to live, he asks Ever to send the helicopter.

COMMENTARY

"July '69" highlights the terrible irony of the *Apollo 11* Moon landing set alongside David Todd's agonizing experiences in Vietnam. While the radio deejay talks about how the Moon landing has "brought the world together" (104), David Todd is frighteningly alone, and his world is falling apart all around him. He panics at the beginning of the story when he realizes he is almost certain to die in Vietnam, even though, a mere hour before, "the universe had still been a universe" (104). Clearly, after the surprise Viet Cong attack, David Todd's universe has shattered. Even the name of the planned landing spot for the *Apollo* spacecraft has ironic echoes—the Sea of Tranquility seems like a naïve, hopeful dream in the grim meadow where David is lying injured. He himself might as well be on the Moon—the astronauts seem closer to the rest of the world, even though they are hurtling through space, hundreds of thousands of miles away from Earth, than does David.

Just as the idyllic-sounding Sea of Tranquility contrasts the body-strewn clearing in Vietnam, other images of innocence clash with reality in the story. David himself is a naïve young second lieutenant before the Viet Cong attack, who allows half his platoon to march up the river for a swim, who does not set out proper flank security, and who permits Hector Ortiz to listen to the news on his transistor radio, perhaps drawing the enemy's attention to the position of the American platoon. Although nominally an officer, David does not truly know how to behave like one and considers himself a baseball player rather than a soldier. The innocence of the game of baseball, in which one tries to make it home after running around the bases, contrasts with David's despair at making it home as a severely injured soldier. Even more, on the second day of his ordeal, when David finds the other half of his platoon, all the men dead in the water or on the riverbank, the brutality of the stinking, disfigured and swollen bodies contrasts with the butterflies that flutter along the riverbank in the sunshine. David realizes that the men had been killed while swimming naked in the river, "frolicking, like a Boy Scout troop" (105). And

even the young door-gunner, whom he imagines looking at closely with his All-American, "prep-school blue" eyes is nevertheless caught up "in the murder of it all" (106). The grisly details of the war scenes seem even more horrifying when contrasted with the wholesome images that O'Brien evokes in the story.

The story asks, as well, how much one would be willing to give up to hold onto life. Master Sergeant Johnny Ever, at least in the original story version of "July '69," seems to be most likely a figment of David Todd's imagination. The young soldier, after all, is nearly out of his mind with pain and fear, and is injecting himself repeatedly with the morphine Syrettes that he finds in Doc Paladino's medical pouch. As the pain becomes unbearable in the late afternoon of the third day, David begins to "converse with his feet. He talked baby talk. He made ludicrous bargains with God" (108). It seems likely that David's invention of the Johnny Ever figure is his attempt to bargain with God. He imagines Ever as God's "middleman," someone who can facilitate the deal that David would like to make for his life. Insecure about his relationship with Marla Dempsey anyway—although she had agreed to marry him, she had also been scrupulous about her language, confessing that she cared for David but she was not sure their relationship would last forever—and realizing that the injuries to his feet will likely put an end to his burgeoning baseball career, David imagines trading Johnny Ever the realization of his very worst fears in exchange for his life.

But at the same time, the story leaves open the possibility for miracles. Perhaps David is not simply a pathetic, self-deluded failure of a soldier destined to die in Vietnam. The year 1969, after all, was not only the year of the seemingly impossible Moon landing, but it was also the year of the MIRACLE METS. The radio announcer calls the Mets' success "a season for the ages . . ." (108). "Bunch of has-beens and never-will-bes," he adds, "they're surprising all of us, even ol' Master Sergeant Johnny Ever. And I'll guarantee you, this here is one hip ten-thousand-year lifer who don't *get* surprised" (108). David Todd, with his baseball obsession, would be keenly aware of the unexpected good fortune experienced by the Mets that year. In addition, when David finally decides that he wants to live, despite his forbidding future, his choice is motivated by hearing the news on the transistor radio that the *Eagle* had actually landed on the Moon. While Johnny Ever delivers the news of the Moon landing along with the interpretation that it is a sad comment on how the world has turned away from the war in Vietnam, David himself feels "a bounce of joy . . . almost elation, almost awe" (109) as he hears of the craft touching down safely on the Sea of Tranquility. Reading the miraculous Moon landing in terms of his own situation, he wonders if Armstrong and Aldrin and Collins will make it home. He seems to determine that if the "raggedy-ass Mets" and if the daring astronauts can experience miracles, perhaps he can too. David asks Johnny Ever to send the medi-vac rescue helicopter at the end of the story, despite the deejay's advice that he simply cut his losses, that he give up and avoid a future sure to be filled with hurt and pain. David sticks to his decision despite Johnny Ever's chiding and even earns in the final line a grudging admiration of his bravery from this enigmatic figure.

Differences in Versions
The original story as published in *Esquire* magazine is nearly identical to the version published as chapter 2 of the novel *July, July*. O'Brien made only minor changes when he revised, including describing Happy James's injury as a shot to the neck rather than the throat, lowering David Todd's age from 24 in the original story to 22 in the novel, and having David find only seven rather than 12 Syrettes of morphine in Doc Paladino's medical pouch. In addition, when Johnny Ever discusses what has amazed him over the years, he mentions ESTHER WILLIAMS along with SPARTACUS, rather than Davy Crockett as in the original story. O'Brien might have made this change to highlight the absurdity of Ever's statement, and to highlight the deejay's constant half-joking demeanor. Perhaps a more significant change is the addition of the detail in the novel that the bodies of Alvin Campbell, Tap Hammerlee, and Van Skedarian are not only missing their feet but have had their scalps stripped away

as well. This detail draws heightened attention to the true brutality of the war. Finally, in the novel O'Brien expands slightly on David Todd's reaction to Marla Dempsey when she originally agrees to marry him. David in the novel acknowledges that he had known, from the day he met Marla that the odds against their relationship "were poison," maybe "one in a thousand" (*July* 35), but he refuses to give up nevertheless.

Despite the minor nature of these revisions, the story as it appears in the novel has a very different feel to it from the story as originally published, mostly because of the larger context surrounding the novel's version. Readers of the original *Esquire* version of "July '69" are much more likely to assume that Master Sergeant Johnny Ever is simply a figment of David Todd's pain-riddled imagination or of his morphine-induced hallucinations than are readers of the novel. This is because the figure of the strange, nearly omniscient Ever appears multiple times in the novel, sometimes in different guises such as that of retired Marine Corps Colonel Fred Engelmann, the neighbor of Dorothy Stier. Fred seems to have intimate knowledge of Dorothy's life, and Dorothy, unlike David Todd, does not seem prone to hallucinating. The repeated appearance of this seemingly supernatural figure to multiple characters over the course of the book lends credence to the view that David does not simply invent Johnny Ever into being. In addition, while the original story ends with David asking to be saved, the novel makes it clear that David *is* miraculously saved. He survives his four-day ordeal in Vietnam, makes it home, and pretty much lives out his life as Ever had predicted.

CHARACTERS

Bond, Buddy Buddy Bond is a soldier in David Todd's platoon who is killed in the first burst of gunfire that is fired by the VIET CONG in their surprise attack on the American soldiers. David will later see Buddy Bond's body lying near the river, in a rough semi-circle formation with other dead American soldiers.

Campbell, Alvin; Tap Hammerlee; and Van Skedarian Alvin Campbell, Tap Hammerlee, and Van Skedarian are three former members of David Todd's platoon in Vietnam. The day after the surprise VIET CONG attack, when David is able to drag himself down to the river, he sees the bodies of the three men lying side-by-side along the bank, "as if on display" (105). The boots have been stripped away and their feet are gone as well, their legs ending in stumps that appear shiny and "reddish-purple in the lurid sunshine" (105).

Dempsey, Marla Marla Dempsey is David Todd's college girlfriend. An art major who has trouble understanding David's love of baseball, Marla is apparently more lukewarm about their relationship than David is. As he lies suffering in the Vietnamese heat, David imagines marrying Marla and living a comfortable suburban life. Yet, at the same time, he listens to the radio deejay Master Sergeant Johnny Ever make predictions about his future with Marla that conflict with David's dreams. Ever claims that, although Marla will indeed marry David, she will eventually leave him for a stockbroker who drives a Harley Davidson motorcycle.

Dexter, Staff Sergeant Bus Staff Sergeant Bus Dexter is one of the American soldiers severely injured in the VIET CONG attack along the SONG TRA KY River. David Todd hears Dexter yelling something and watches him crawl toward a clump of boulders. The large man pushes himself to his feet and begins to run, but after only a few steps, an explosion just behind him catches Dexter and drops him to the ground, dead.

Door Gunner On the morning of July 18, two days into his ordeal as the only surviving member of his platoon in Vietnam, David Todd sees a pair of American helicopters sweep in low over the SONG TRA KY River. Whether it is his imagination or the result of morphine, David believes for an instant that he is looking into the eyes of a young door gunner, which are described as "rapt, prepschool blue, caught up in the murder of it all" (106). When David tries to raise a hand to signal the door gunner, he passes out and the image fades away.

Ever, Master Sergeant Johnny The voice on the radio that David Todd listens to as he lies severely injured in a grassy clearing in Vietnam, the only survivor of his platoon, belongs to a deejay who identifies himself as Master Sergeant Johnny Ever. O'Brien leaves Ever's identity open for interpretation. It is possible that David Todd simply hallucinates that the deejay is addressing him personally. After all, he is suffering tremendously from his injuries, only half-conscious most of the time, and doped up on the morphine that he is injecting himself with. On the other hand, it is possible that Johnny Ever is a supernatural being watching over David. When David asks the deejay if he is God, Ever laughs and tells the injured solder that he is "like a middleman. Billy Graham without the sugar, Saint Christopher without the resources" (108). He certainly seems to know quite a bit about David's future, although David, could just be projecting his own worst fears onto the radio voice. The story ends without readers ever finding out if David is actually rescued by a helicopter or not. Thus, we remain unsure about whether Ever actually fulfills his promise to the young man, or whether the rescue is simply a morphine-induced bit of wishful thinking on David's part, typical of the bargains with God often made by people in stressful and dangerous situations.

Hammerlee, Tap See CAMPBELL, ALVIN.

James, Happy One of the soldiers in David Todd's ill-fated platoon, Happy James is shot through the throat during the VIET CONG surprise attack.

Maples, Kaz Killed along with Buddy Bond in the first burst of gunfire in the VIET CONG attack, Kaz Maples's body lies alongside the riverbank of the SONG TRA KY River. To David Todd, Kaz, like the other dead men, seems to be made of plastic, almost as if he had never been alive to begin with.

Manning, Borden When David Todd drags himself down to the river after the surprise VIET CONG attack on his platoon, he sees the body of an American soldier named Borden Manning bobbing on its back in the water, his face gone.

Mustin, Vince   As David Todd is lying in the grass in excruciating pain, he hears one of the men in his platoon, Vince Mustin, crying, having been shot in the stomach. Vince, like all the other members of Todd's platoon, will soon die of his injuries, leaving David as the only survivor.

Ortiz, Hector   Hector Ortiz is one of the soldiers in David Todd's platoon who is killed in the VIET CONG attack. After Hector is shot in the face, his transistor radio continues to crackle with the evening news. David will take the radio with him as he drags himself through the grass and down to the river in the following days.

Paladino, Doc   The medic of David Todd's platoon, Doc Paladino, seems to disappear entirely during the surprise VIET CONG attack. Later, David will find what is left of his body lying in the grassy clearing along the SONG TRA KY RIVER. The injured lieutenant will remove 12 Syrettes of morphine from Doc's medical pouch, which help him survive during his four-day ordeal.

Reiss, Gil   Sergeant Gil Reiss is one of the dead American soldiers who had separated from the rest of the platoon to go swimming just before the VIET CONG attack. The day after he is severely injured, David Todd drags himself down to the river, where he sees Reiss's body, lying on the riverbank.

Skedarian, Van   *See* CAMPBELL, ALVIN.

Stockbroker   Toward the end of the story, Master Sergeant Johnny Ever, whose voice David Todd listens to over a transistor radio, predicts that David's girlfriend, Marla, will marry him but will eventually divorce him, leaving the former lieutenant heartbroken. According to Ever, Marla will "take off with this slick stockbroker on a Harley" (109), and David will not hear a word from her for the next six years.

Todd, David   David Todd is a 24-year-old second lieutenant in the army in Vietnam who is seriously injured in both feet in a surprise VIET CONG attack that kills all the other members of his platoon. As

he lies in the grass near death for four long days after the attack, David thinks about his past, especially his college girlfriend, Marla Dempsey, and his burgeoning career as a baseball player. He also begins to hear strange things over the transistor radio that he is listening to—a deejay named Master Sergeant Johnny Ever begins to address him personally. Readers are never sure whether this voice is simply a figment of David's morphine-ridden and pain-addled brain or some supernatural figure that somehow seems to be watching over David. Either way, David believes that the deejay gives him the choice to live or die at the end of the story. If David is willing to accept a devastating future in which he will lose a leg, ending his baseball dreams, Marla will divorce him, and his war memories will haunt him, Johnny Ever will send in a helicopter to save him. David agrees to the bargain, finally choosing to live.

Todd, Mr. and Mrs; Mickey   While David thinks mostly about baseball and about Marla Dempsey as he lies severely injured in the tall grass in Vietnam, he also thinks about his family. He pictures his mother hanging up laundry in the backyard of the Todd family home and his father planting a lilac bush. He also imagines his younger brother, Mickey, tossing a baseball at the garage. But these images come to David like flashes of fireworks; he is unable to hold onto them for any length of time.

July, July (2002)

Published in 2002 by Houghton Mifflin, *July, July* tells the story of a group of old friends from the DARTON HALL COLLEGE class of 1969 who have gathered in July 2000, a year and a month late, to celebrate their 30th reunion. The novel moves back and forth between the past and present as it explores how the idealistic hopes and dreams of a group of 22-year-olds have been transformed into the divorces, disappointments, and compromises made by 53-year-olds. While some of the characters' lives will end happily and some will end in tragedy, the novel explores the persistence of faith in the face of disappointment and loss, the possibility of miracles in a secular age.

SYNOPSIS

The novel opens in the gymnasium of Darton Hall College in Minnesota on Friday night, July 7, 2000. The members of the class of 1969 have gathered a year late for their 30th reunion dance. Former roommates Amy Robinson and Jan Huebner, both 53 years old and divorced, drink vodka together and discuss the recent murder of Karen Burns, another one-time roommate. Marv Bertel, an overweight mop and broom entrepreneur, lusts after crazy, sexy Spook Spinelli, just as he did 30 years ago. Billy McMann, a DRAFT dodger during the Vietnam War, plots revenge against his old girlfriend, Dorothy Stier, who had promised to run away with him to WINNIPEG, CANADA but changed her mind at the last minute. Dorothy, now suffering from breast cancer, talks about her sweet husband and two terrific sons in conversation with Paulette Haslo, a Presbyterian minister who has been kicked out of her church. Vietnam War veteran David Todd longs to reunite with his ex-wife, Marla Dempsey, who cannot love David the way he deserves. And Ellie Abbott holds herself slightly apart from the rest of the group, depressed about the death of Harmon Osterberg, a dentist and former classmate who drowned while the two

Macalester College, model for Darton Hall College in *July, July* (Courtesy of Macalester College)

were engaged in an extramarital fling at a northern Minnesota resort. After introducing its large cast of characters in the opening chapter, the novel reverts back to the past to explore the history and background of each major character in more detail. Chapters set in the present, which depict various events over the long reunion weekend, alternate throughout the novel with chapters that describe the past, so that readers gain a deepening understanding of the friendships, betrayals, loves, and enmities that percolate below the surface of this group of old college friends.

David Todd

The first flashback chapter tells the story of David Todd, who dropped out of Darton Hall College after his junior year and was subsequently drafted into the Vietnam War. On his 19th day in-country, on July 16, 1969, David finds himself lying on the bank beside the SONG TRA KY River, shot through both feet and listening to the sounds of the rest of his platoon dying all around him. For four days, he feverishly pulls himself through the rough bush, periodically shooting Styrettes of morphine into his pain-addled body and listening on a small, transistor radio to news updates about the APOLLO 11 Moon landing. Nearly out of his mind with pain and with the drugs, David thinks about his college girlfriend, Marla Dempsey, whom he never expects to see again, and his budding baseball career, which will be cut short by his severe injury. Eventually, though, he begins to hear a voice coming over the radio—a deejay named Master Sergeant Johnny Ever, who has an uncanny knowledge of David's life as well as his hopes and dreams, seems to be talking directly to the injured soldier. Ever, perhaps an angel, perhaps a devil, perhaps a product of David's own feverish imaginings, offers the young man a deal at the end of the chapter. He foretells David's future, letting him know that Marla will leave him for another man and that David will never play baseball again. But he also promises to send a helicopter to rescue him if David still wants to live with the foreknowledge of the difficult life ahead of him. David, strangely elated when the *Apollo* rocket actually touches down on the Moon, agrees to be rescued at the end of the chapter.

Amy Robinson and Jan Huebner

The next series of flashbacks highlight the lives of Amy Robinson and Jan Huebner, inseparable drinking buddies and cocommiserators. In a flashback, readers learn of Amy's brief marriage to a math teacher named Bobby. On their honeymoon, the two experience an amazing streak of luck playing blackjack at an Indian casino, winning nearly $230,000. Nevertheless, Amy is depressed by the experience, fearing that she has used up all her luck in this one, short night. On the drive home to Minneapolis, when Bobby stops the car at a gas station outside the Twin Cities, Amy calls a cab, leaving both Bobby and her marriage behind. Jan Huebner has been similarly unlucky in love. In her chapter, readers discover that Jan spent the summer after her college graduation posing for pornographic pictures snapped by men she picked up on the streets of Minneapolis. She is first introduced to this profession by Andrew Henry Wilton, an angry young man, short and misshapen enough to be a dwarf, whom she meets on the street following a performance of her guerrilla theater troupe. A homely young woman herself, Jan is flattered by the male attention, first from Andrew and then from other men. Later, when Andrew introduces Jan to his tall, good-looking brother, Richard, she falls deeply in love, only to suffer through a nearly 30-year-long abusive marriage to a man who refuses to be faithful to her.

Spook Spinelli

While Amy and Jan are both recently divorced, Spook Spinelli suffers from the opposite problem. She is overly married—married, in fact, to two men at once. A free spirit who refuses to live by the conventions of society, Spook marries James Winship, an associate professor of philosophy one year after her marriage to Lincoln Harwood, a lawyer. Because she loves both men, Spook insists that the threesome invent their own rules. Lincoln and James agree, and the three live happily in the same suburb outside the Twin Cities for 13½ years, Spook dividing her time between the home she shares with Lincoln and the one she shares with James. Things go fairly smoothly until Spook meets another man she feels she cannot live without—a

young lawyer in Lincoln's firm named Baldy Devlin. When Baldy finds out about Spook's strange marital arrangement, he refuses to return her phone calls and e-mails, sending the love-struck woman into a tailspin of depression. Readers also discover in this chapter that Spook grew up a twin— "Caroline to her sister's Carolyn" (96). When Carolyn contracted renal disease at the age of five and died at the age of six, Caroline Spinelli stopped speaking and took on an otherworldly character, thus earning the nickname Spook. Spook Spinelli's desperate need for "absolute and unqualified love" (97) stems from this deep childhood loss.

Billy McMann and Dorothy Stier

The next tale from the past belongs to Billy McMann, who, like David Todd, was drafted into the Vietnam War shortly after leaving college. Billy, however, chooses the opposite path from David; he flees to Winnipeg, Canada, to evade serving in the war. While forging a new life in a foreign country is difficult, Billy's biggest disappointment lies in the fact that his college girlfriend, Dorothy Stier, had promised to accompany him in his exile but never showed up at the airport to catch the plane to Winnipeg. Unwilling to live a nonconformist life, Dorothy ends up marrying a man named Ron, a close friend of Billy's, and eventually has two sons. Billy reacts bitterly to Dorothy's defection and subsequent marriage, even throughout his own marriage to a librarian, the birth of his daughter, and his wife's unexpected death in a hit-and-run accident. Despite building a successful life for himself in Winnipeg as the owner of a chain of hardware stores, Billy holds a lifelong grudge against Dorothy. One of the reasons he attends the reunion is to express his hurt to his former girlfriend. Dorothy, however, is already suffering from her own life traumas. Diagnosed with breast cancer several years earlier, Dorothy has undergone a mastectomy, and she worries that her husband, Ron, is no longer attracted to her. Although she is still drawn to Billy and seems to feel guilty for her behavior back in 1969, she nevertheless justifies her actions by reminding her former boyfriend that she had been a Republican in college and could not face living as an exile from the country she loved.

While Dorothy's chapter will end with her surprisingly knowledgeable neighbor Fred Engelmann—a character much like Johnny Ever in the David Todd chapter—informing her that her cancer will return and she has only five more years to live, Billy McMann will wind up much happier. He finds a new love during the reunion weekend with the disgraced Presbyterian minister, Paulette Haslo.

Paulette Haslo and Ellie Abbott

Paulette has her own shameful secret from the past, which she shares with Ellie Abbott on a long walk the two women take together the morning after the reunion dance. Paulette, single her whole life, but a dedicated and compassionate minister, relates the story of how she struck up a close friendship with an aging and married parishioner named Rudy Ketch. While the affair was never physically consummated, the pair flirted together and eased each other's loneliness. After Rudy's death from heart disease, Paulette is caught breaking into the Ketch house one late night by Rudy's unpleasant and vengeful wife, Janice. Paulette had merely intended to retrieve love letters between herself and Rudy, but Janice fears the minister means to harm her. The next day, Janice notifies police and church officials about the break-in. Paulette is not only arrested and briefly jailed but also fired from her job. In turn, Ellie Abbott confesses that her past also involves an illicit relationship and a brush with the law. Borrowing language, characters, and locations from O'Brien's earlier novel *In the Lake of the Woods,* in which John Wade's wife, Kathy, has an affair with a dentist named Harmon, Ellie confides to Paulette that she had been having an affair with former college classmate and dentist Harmon Osterberg, who unexpectedly drowned while the two were spending several days together at Loon Point Resort in northern Minnesota. Deeply ashamed and guilt-ridden by the death, Ellie is questioned by a young policeman before she returns home to Boston and to her husband, Mark, who has failed to even notice that Ellie was gone longer than expected. At Paulette Haslo's urging, Ellie eventually confesses her secret to her husband, who leaves the reunion abruptly. The last readers see of Ellie, she has packed her suitcase to head home for Boston in the hope of winning back her husband's love.

Karen Burns and Marv Bertel

Two classmates perennially unlucky in love are the subjects of the next tales from the past. On the afternoon of July 8, the Darton Hall graduates hold a memorial service for Harmon Osterberg and for another classmate who has recently died—Karen Burns. Karen, while working as the director of a retirement community in Tucson, Arizona, is murdered by a 36-year-old part-time bus driver named Darrell Jettie. Romantically attracted to the younger man and fantasizing a relationship with him, Karen had hired Jettie to take the community residents on short outings. One day, on a purported trip to Nogales, Mexico, Jettie drives Karen and four elderly residents of the retirement community far beyond their destination, eventually meeting up with another young man in the remote Mexican wilderness in order to conduct an apparent drug smuggling operation. Back in the United States in the barren desert 40 minutes west of Tucson, Jettie orders Karen and the four old people out of the van, abandoning them to die of thirst in the isolated location.

Marv Bertel, the broom and mop entrepreneur, while more financially successful than Karen Burns, has also had an unhappy romantic life. Deeply in love with the unattainable Spook Spinelli since college, Marv is overweight and self-deprecating. In his chapter, however, readers discover that Marv had actually lost a great deal of weight about 10 years ago, enough that he became attractive to women. Marv celebrates by divorcing his first wife and starting up a relationship with his much-younger executive secretary Sandra DiLeona. In order to impress Sandra, Marv invents a secret life for himself; he tells the young woman that he is actually Thomas Pierce, a famous and reclusive writer. While Sandra eventually finds out the truth, she marries Marv anyway, demanding that he keep up the Thomas Pierce charade for her friends and family and that he support her lavishly in a separate house. Trapped in a loveless marriage with a beautiful but mercenary new wife who largely despises him, Marv hopelessly moons over Spook throughout the reunion weekend.

David Todd and Marla Dempsey

The final chapter to detail the past circles back to the story of David Todd, this time focusing on his marriage and divorce from Marla Dempsey rather than on his Vietnam experiences. The two are married on Christmas Day, 1969, after David has returned from the war with an amputated leg. Marla makes it clear before the marriage that, while she loves and respects David, she is not *in* love with him. In fact, the only time Marla ever was in love was during her junior year at Darton Hall when she had a brief affair with a former high school teacher, a married man, who breaks off the relationship after a month. Marla's marriage to David lasts 10 years, until she leaves him on Christmas Day, 1979, for a stockbroker who drives her away on a Harley Davidson motorcycle. In 1987 Marla returns to the Twin Cities, divorced from her stockbroker husband, and she and David become fast friends, although David still longs for a deeper relationship.

Ending

The novel ends in the present, a little more than 24 hours after it began. The reunion has ended. Jan and Amy continue to talk deep into the night in the dorm room that they are sharing, eventually venturing out to look for an all-night diner. David Todd takes a tab of LSD and offers one to Dorothy Stier, who begins her first acid trip 30 years after the sixties have ended. Billy McMann and Paulette Haslo happily spend the night together in his hotel room. Ellie Abbott decides to go home to Boston to try to set things right with her husband, Mark. Marla returns to the Darton Hall banquet room to look for David, finally asking him to tell her about his experiences along the Song Tra Ky River in Vietnam when she finds him. Dorothy walks the six blocks back to her house, stoned and enjoying the beautiful night. Marv Bertel boards a flight home to Denver, astonished to find that Spook Spinelli, who had accompanied him to the airport, has slipped into the seat beside him, having had a premonition that something bad would happen on this flight. At 3:11 A.M. on July 9, the plane begins to make a shearing noise, presumably crashing as it flies over the Pawnee National Grassland near Fort Collins, Colorado.

COMMENTARY

July, July is largely about the disappointment and disillusion that overtake the formerly idealistic 1960's generation as they age. While characters in their younger days were intent on changing the world—Amy Richardson, for instance, was a campus radical; Jan Huebner participated in guerrilla theater on the streets of Minneapolis; Billy McMann fought the draft by fleeing to Canada—by the year 2000, these same characters have settled into life, with all of its dissatisfactions and compromises. Amy talks about her former college friends as the "golden generation" (7), kids who had big dreams. She laments to Jan Huebner that in college the group of friends used to "talk about the Geneva Accords, the Tonkin Gulf [Gulf of Tonkin] Resolution," but that now their talk centers on "liposuction and ex-husbands" (18). Their politics have become personal, as interest in world events fades when individual tragedies and losses intercede. O'Brien points out that at the dance the first night of the reunion conversations across the darkened gym are all about "death, marriage, children, divorce, betrayal, loss, grief, disease" (7). As Amy argues, the friends must accept the fact their "old-fogy parents," who "didn't know jack about jack" and "couldn't spell Hanoi if you spotted them the vowels" (18), did know more than their children in some ways: They knew that aging and loss were inevitable, that bodies fail, love fades, idealism gives way. While the friends tried to change the world in their younger days, they must accept the tired cliché that the world changed them instead.

The generational conflict that once existed between the children of the revolutionary sixties and their more practical, conformist parents, members of the World War II generation, now occurs between the aging baby boomers and younger characters who appear in the novel. The new bride of Minnesota's lieutenant governor, for instance, 26 years younger than he, is not interested in reunions or in funerals. Moreover, she despises what she considers to be the sloppy nostalgia displayed by the Darton Hall class of 1969, viewing the reunion attendees as a "crowd of alcoholic, pot-bellied, whatever-happened-to-us old folks" who dance to "crappy songs about barricades and paranoia" (186). Sandra DiLeona, the much younger wife of Marv Bertel, does not have patience with the lapsed idealism of the older generation, either. Presenting an aura of professionalism even in the bedroom, Sandra, who holds an MBA degree, displays a "profit-and-loss shrewdness in her eyes" (257) as well as a "calculating, what's-in-it-for-me posture toward the world" (256), very unlike the Darton Hall young people who, in 1969, wanted to save the world. Another representative of the younger generation is the boy, most likely a current Darton Hall student, whom the reunion attendees encounter in the Red Carpet bar on the second day of the festivities. Wearing "baggy jams" (242) and several silver studs in his nose, the boy approaches the group to request that "the jukebox be rescued from 'all that soupy sixties bullshit'" (243). The younger generation views the children of the sixties as wallowing in sentimental nostalgia about the past—how special they were, how morally pure, how idealistic. Amy Robinson's response to the boy—she tells him to go kill himself—suggests that her generation does not sympathize with or understand the current generation of college students any better than the baby boomers' parents understood them. They have become as insular and judgmental as their own parents, mired in their personal griefs and betrayals.

And nearly all of the characters at the reunion do suffer from disappointment and loss. David Todd is haunted by his war experiences and the baseball career that his injury forced him to abandon, but most of all by his overwhelming love for Marla Dempsey and Marla's inability to love him back. Amy and Jan are both divorced and lonely. They face down middle age by cracking jokes and drinking too much. Spook Spinelli, while in love with both her husbands, is still not satisfied, always needing more attention, the death of her twin sister having left her feeling incomplete. At the reunion she seems too tightly wound and frequently contemplates committing suicide by drinking out of a fire extinguisher, a metaphor for her longing to extinguish her own pain and unfulfilled desires. Billy McMann cannot let go of the past, harboring a hatred and resentment, mingled with love,

for his old girlfriend, Dorothy Stier, that has lasted more than 30 years. Paulette Haslo, never married and never even having been involved in a serious relationship, has recently been fired from a job she loved and is at loose ends, unsure about her future. Ellie Abbott is consumed by guilt over her illicit affair with Harmon Osterberg. Dorothy has been diagnosed with breast cancer and despite trying to put on a brave front by talking incessantly about her wonderful husband and terrific sons, she is frightened about her future and unsure about Ron's continued attraction to her. Marv Bertel, trapped in a loveless marriage to a beautiful but scheming and ambitious wife, has gained back all the weight he lost a few years back. Filled with self-loathing, he moons hopelessly over Spook Spinelli. Marla Dempsey also despises herself, worrying that she is less than human because of her incapacity to love.

Along with their disappointments in life, these characters also carry around what they consider to be shameful secrets. Secret guilt and the need to confess link the characters of *July, July* to earlier O'Brien novels, particularly *The Things They Carried,* in which a young Tim O'Brien confesses to readers a story about spending six days at the TIP TOP LODGE on the RAINY RIVER deciding whether or not to flee the draft, a story he claims never to have told in its entirety before, as well as *In the Lake of the Woods,* in which the aspiring senator John Wade is personally and politically destroyed by the exposure of his secret involvement in the MY LAI MASSACRE. Secrets kept and secrets confessed are an important theme in this novel as well. David Todd, like many Vietnam veterans, keeps his war experiences bottled up inside of himself, especially his burden of guilt for the mistakes he made as a young officer—mistakes that he believes caused the deaths of 16 of his platoon members: "It was his own fault" (26), David thinks to himself as he lies near death on the banks of the Song Tra Ky River. Jan Huebner carries the secret of her flirtation with the seedy street life of sexual exploitation when she worked as "Veronica" the summer after graduation. Paulette Haslo and Ellie Abbot both maintained secret relationships with married men. Paulette bears the additional shame of her subsequent arrest and firing, while Ellie is burdened by guilt over Harmon's death. Billy McMann also feels "guilt and fear" (112) about his decision to flee to Canada, and Dorothy Stier, even though she is open in speaking about her cancer, nevertheless hides the true state of her marriage as well as her feelings of regret for not accompanying Billy to Winnipeg.

As in many O'Brien novels, the burden of carrying secrets is perhaps worse than the shame of revealing them. Ellie Abbott, for instance, tells Paulette Haslo that Harmon's death has created an unbearable heaviness inside of her: "The secrecy," Ellie explains, "It weighs a ton. I wake up with it, lug it around all day. Can't ever relax" (183). So, along with secrets comes the need to confess. The act of confession, in religious terms, suggests not only the possibility for atonement—when one admits to sins, one can be absolved or cleansed of them—but also a continued faith or profession of belief as opposed to an entry into despair. In an age that has lost or abandoned traditional religious values, as the children of the sixties certainly have, the small community of friends nevertheless perform their own versions of traditional religious rituals, serving as secular priests for one another, hearing confessions and offering absolutions. Many of the secrets of the Darton Hall class of '69 are revealed at the Red Carpet bar in the late afternoon on the second day of the reunion, when the old friends agree to play a game called Truth that had originated in their college days. Amy Robinson lays out the rules, asserting that each participant must "confess the most terrible thing ever" about himself or herself, something each did or did not do, "Something monstrous. Evil" (241). As the game progresses, the friends confess their secret sins to one another. While seldom exactly "monstrous" or "evil," these secrets do signify the darker selves each of the college graduates hides deep inside, the moral compromises they have settled into over the years, again linking the novel to other O'Brien works, in which characters such as William Cowling and John Wade desperately try to hide the depths of their own depravity from the world around them. Just as the novel *In the Lake of the Woods* asks how well human beings can really know one another, *July, July* suggests that these

friends, despite their college closeness, do not really understand one another or even themselves, their friendships based largely on the surface selves that each is willing to show. The confessions bring them closer together.

Religious overtones in the novel continue in the mysterious characters of Johnny Ever, Fred Engelmann, and several others who seem to have almost supernatural knowledge of the inner secrets carried by the college friends. Similar to the mystifying voice Norman Bowker hears over the intercom at the A&W root beer stand in the story "Speaking of Courage," a voice that seems to understand Bowker and his suffering, David Todd hears a puzzling voice over a transistor radio when he is severely injured in Vietnam. The voice, which identifies itself as belonging to deejay Master Sergeant Johnny Ever, not only knows intimate details from David's past—his budding baseball career, his love for Marla Dempsey—but he also seems able to predict the future. Ever informs David that his baseball career is over and that Marla will leave him, and he also predicts David's rescue by helicopter. Johnny Ever claims to be 10,000 years old, suggesting that he knew Spartacus from ancient Rome and that his name is Ever because, as he puts it, "I could go on. I do" (42), suggesting that he has lived forever. David, responding to Ever's seeming omniscience, asks the voice, "Are you God?" (32). Ever laughs and then curses, replying that he is not God, but that he is "like a middleman" (32) to God. Yet, David has trouble deciding if Ever is an angel or a devil. Does Ever provide the miracle of salvation to David, or does he deceive the grievously injured young soldier into pessimism and self-destruction, into making sure that all of Ever's grim prophecies come true?

Ever is a character, as well, who manifests in various forms to several of the other college friends. Telling David that he is a "jack-of-all-trades," he adds, "Disc jockey. Cop. Duck whittler. Retired colonel, USMC. Not to mention hit-and-run artist and pharmacist and bigshot keyboard player. Even dealt some blackjack in my day" (42). This list of occupations corresponds to similarly omniscient characters met by other Darton Hall graduates. After Harmon Osterberg's death, Ellie Abbott is driven to the police station by a young cop who has uncanny knowledge of her emotional state, who also mentions ancient Sparta, and who finally tells Ellie that he is what she has instead of a conscience. Rudy Ketch, the aging companion of the minister Paulette Haslo, who understands her in ways that no previous man has been able to, whittled ducks in his spare time. Dorothy Stier's next-door neighbor, Fred Engelmann, who mysteriously knows all about Dorothy's secret troubles with Ron and who predicts her death from cancer in five years, claims to be a retired colonel in the U.S. Marine Corps. The hit-and-run driver referred to by Ever is Alexandra Wenz, who enters Billy McMann's life in Winnipeg after accidentally killing his wife. Alexandra also has access to secret knowledge—to the unhappiness of Billy's librarian wife, whom Alexandra claims jumped in front of the car. The pharmacist mentioned by Ever is encountered by Dorothy on the second day of the reunion when she stops in a drugstore to buy perfume. One of Spook Spinelli's previous boyfriends was a "bigshot" keyboard player for a well-known rock'n'roll band in Los Angeles, and Amy Robinson interacts with a young blackjack dealer on her honeymoon who understands that luck comes in finite quantities and can be used up. And finally, even though Johnny Ever does not explicitly list the character, Andrew Henry Wilton, the misshapen young man who first snaps a nude photograph of Jan Huebner, also seems to have overly intimate knowledge of Jan, asking if he should call her Veronica the second time he meets her and knowing that she wears a police whistle around her neck.

What is O'Brien doing with these strange omniscient characters? Do they interject an element of the mysterious, of the supernatural even, of God and fate and destiny, into the otherwise mundane, disappointing, secular lives of these children of the 1960s? Are they ambassadors of God sent to punish moral lapses and reward virtuous behavior? Or perhaps these figures play a more prosaic role. O'Brien suggests, alternatively, that they may simply represent the college graduates' own secret selves, their inner voices, that these seemingly mysterious figures may serve as manifestations of the guilt carried around by nearly every one of the Darton Hall friends. After all, David Todd first hears Ever's voice when he is high on morphine and nearly out of his mind with pain from his injuries. And the VA psychiatrist whom David goes to see when his marriage to Marla Dempsey begins to fail assures David vigorously that "Master Sergeant Johnny Ever was no angel, no devil, no ghost, no middleman; that in fact, the man at the microphone was none other than David himself" (294). Clearly, the psychiatrist reads Ever as a manifestation of David Todd's survivor's guilt over his Vietnam experiences. The fact that Ever's prophecies have come true is simply evidence that David has been sabotaging himself ever since the war—he expects the worst and behaves in a way to make his expectations come true. And even more, this version of Ever makes sense to David. O'Brien writes, "In a way, somewhere deep inside him, he'd known all along. He slept better. His dreams went foggy and bland. Only rarely did he hear Ortiz's transistor radio, or yipping sounds, or the murderous drone of the Song Tra Ky" (294). Similarly, psychological explanations can be offered for the manifestations of others of these omniscient characters as well. Ellie Abbott's overwhelming feelings of guilt and shame may cause her to conjure up a policeman who forces her to face up to her own role in Harmon's death, who serves as the conscience she had been suppressing during her extramarital affair. Dorothy may be projecting her own innermost doubts about her marriage and the fears of her cancer returning onto the voice of her neighbor, afraid to admit these troubling thoughts even to herself.

Whether these strange figures are manifestations of angels and demons, or whether they are psychological projections of inner guilt and fear, they nevertheless suggest the mystery inherent in everyday life. Whether we call it luck or miracles, strange, inexplicable events occur—events that are unexpected, unlikely, and nearly unbelievable. As David spends his four days injured and suffering in Vietnam, he listens to news on the transistor radio of the 1969 Miracle Mets, who won the World Series that year despite having been a mediocre team their whole existence and coming from behind to face a much stronger Baltimore Orioles squad. David listens as well to news of the *Apollo 11* Moon landing, a miraculous feat of technology. In fact, it is the "bounce of joy" (34) David feels when the *Eagle* finally touches down on the Sea of Tranquility that motivates his choice to survive in the jungle, to ask Johnny Ever to "send in the bird" (35) despite being told of the disaster that his future life will entail. David's own survival, alone out of his 17-member platoon, is in itself, nothing short of miraculous. Other lucky or miraculous events occur in the novel as well. For instance, the winning streak of Amy Robinson and her husband, Bobby, at the Indian casino on their honeymoon is unprecedented. Yet, at the same time, the novel suggests that miracles do not come through for everyone and that belief in miracles might be naïve and misguided. Jan Huebner comments that her "whole generation" kicked off with the Monkees' song, "I'm a believer," a conviction she claims is "so naïve" it makes her "want to cry" (7). And Karen Burns and Harmon Osterberg, the two characters honored in a memorial service at the reunion, are both said by Paulette Haslo to have "believed in miracles" (212) 31 years ago. Yet, these two characters wind up dead before their time, more unlucky than any of the others. Amy Robinson even comments that hope itself is what killed Karen. According to Amy, hope is "lethal" (8). Her own miracle of good luck at the casino leads to the dissolution of her marriage. And hope did indeed seem to be deadly for Karen, whose misplaced trust in Darrell Jettie and fervent wish for a romantic relationship with him led to her murder.

In *July, July* then, O'Brien explores the human tendency to hope for miracles in the midst of great suffering and loss, the tenacity of the desire to believe in the future, the human will to survive. Whether such hope is lethal or not, whether it harms or saves us is a question left open at the end of the novel. Lucky endings exist for some characters, but not for others. Miracles do not occur according to merit or worth; they are not apportioned to the most deserving, but rather arise out of grace. The novel ends with a pair of incidents that illustrate this tenet. Marv Bertel and Spook Spinelli, seemingly on the verge of a miracle, about to get together after more than 30 years of Marv's one-sided longing for Spook, wind up in a plane crash over the Colorado grasslands, the victims of storm clouds that had started to pile up over the Dakotas many hours before, lending the "scent of a coming storm" (183) to the air at the reunion. Yet, at the same time, Billy McMann and Paulette Haslo discover the miracle of new love with each other at the end of the reunion, something completely unexpected by either of them. And the final lines in the novel suggest as well the prevalence of hope in the lives of these characters. Even the two most cynical of the reunion attendees—Amy Robinson and Jan Huebner—lonely, divorced, middle-aged, set out at 3:11 A.M. on the morning of July 9 for an all-night diner known for its great pancakes and cute waiters. "Maybe we *will* score," Amy comments, and Jan replies, "Not even maybe . . . Follow me, sweetheart. We're golden" (322). Despite repeated disappointments, despite their own acknowledgment that hope is naïve and possibly even lethal, the two women retain their faith in miracles and march out into the night.

CHARACTERS

Abbott, Ellie   One of the members of the DARTON HALL class of 1969, Ellie Abbott is haunted and depressed by the death the previous summer of classmate Harmon Osterberg. Harmon, a dentist, had drowned while he and Ellie were spending a few days together at a northern Minnesota resort called LOON POINT. The two were involved in an extramarital affair, each of them cheating on their respective spouses. Shaken by the drowning, Ellie is questioned by a young policeman who, like Johnny Ever from David Todd's past and Fred Engelmann from Dorothy Stier's past, seems to know Ellie more intimately than possible. Ellie's relationship with Harmon is strikingly similar to an episode from an earlier O'Brien novel, *In the Lake of the Woods*, in which Kathy Wade also has an affair with a dentist named Harmon at the Loon Point resort. While the dentist does not drown in the earlier novel, the return home of the two women is described in similar terms. Each lies to her husband, telling him she is visiting old friends. Each extends her trip by a few days, leaving a message on the answering machine that her husband does not receive. Both husbands seem somewhat negligent of their wives, not even noticing the delayed return home. In *July, July,* Ellie seems to have been traumatized by keeping the secret of her relationship with Harmon from everyone for the past year, including her husband, Mark. She eventually confides in the Presbyterian minister Paulette Haslo, who urges her to confess the affair to her husband. When Ellie does, Mark becomes angry and leaves the reunion early. The novel ends with Ellie deciding to fly home to Boston as well to try to repair her relationship with Mark.

Abbott, Mark   Mark Abbott is the husband of DARTON HALL graduate Ellie Abbott. Until Ellie confesses her affair with Harmon Osterberg to him, Mark seems fairly oblivious to his wife, not even noticing when she came home several days late from supposedly visiting friends the year before, following Harmon's death. Angry at Ellie's revelation, Mark leaves the reunion abruptly, flying home to Boston early.

Anderson, Jim   Jim Anderson is a married former high school teacher of Marla Dempsey, whom she has a short-lived affair with in 1967, during her junior year at DARTON HALL COLLEGE. Described as "a blond, dark-eyed, poisonously handsome specimen" (286), Anderson breaks up with Marla after four weeks, as the two are sitting in his antique red Cadillac in the parking lot of Marla's dorm. Distraught, Marla goes to Anderson's house later that afternoon, only to be greeted at the door by the teacher's wife, who is dressed in blue jeans and wearing her hair in pigtails. This relationship seems to ruin Marla's later attempts at romance. Feeling that this was the only time in her life she was truly in love, Marla describes herself as cold and inhuman inside, unable to love her first husband, David Todd, as he deserves and leaving her second husband, the Harley Davidson-riding stockbroker, after only a brief marriage.

Anderson, Mrs.   The wife of high school teacher Jim Anderson, who has a month-long affair with Marla Dempsey when she is a junior in college, is described as an "emaciated, brittle-looking creature, thirty-five or so, her reddish brown hair

arranged in a pair of pigtails secured by rubber bands" (287). When Marla rings the Anderson's doorbell late one afternoon after Jim has broken up with her, Mrs. Anderson answers the door. "Aren't we cute?" she says to Marla, "Awful young to be a husband fucker" (287). Overcome with guilt, Marla turns away, realizing that "this woman's sad, unsurprised, washed-out face offered exactly what she'd needed, everything she'd run three miles for, which was to know she would never be forgiven" (287).

Basketball Star   An unnamed mother of three who is a former star point guard for the DARTON HALL women's basketball team is one of the reunion attendees. Over the weekend, she has a love affair with a prominent physician. The couple appears periodically, described briefly as background color for the more important characters. The middle-aged mother often seems giddy with happiness, giggling over the physician's "bedside manner" (139) and thoroughly enjoying herself, despite knowing that this relationship will not last.

Bertel, Marv   Marv Bertel is a grossly overweight mop and broom entrepreneur who has been in love with Spook Spinelli since college. He drinks heavily at the reunion, flirts hopelessly with Spook, and watches her seduce other men. "Too Skinny," the chapter that details Marv's past, describes a diet he undertakes in March 1998. By August of that year, he has lost 41 pounds, and the weight continues to fall off. Marv celebrates his new self by divorcing his first wife—their marriage had been a lackluster affair—purchasing a new wardrobe, moving into a new apartment, and beginning to date beautiful young women who would not have looked his way earlier. He eventually becomes involved with his own executive secretary, an ambitious and dazzling 26-year-old MBA named Sandra DiLeona. Desperate to impress Sandra, Marv impulsively tells her that he is actually the famous, reclusive writer Thomas Pierce. Although Sandra eventually discovers Marv's lie, she has already told the secret to her family and friends. Sandra agrees to marry Marv, provided he will keep up the Thomas Pierce pretense and support her lavishly in her own separate house. Marv soon puts back on all the weight he had lost and finds himself trapped in another loveless marriage. Nor does his luck improve during the reunion weekend. Just when it looks like he might win Spook at last—she unexpectedly slips into the seat beside his on the plane that Marv is taking home to Denver—the plane begins to shear violently during a thunderstorm. While O'Brien never definitely explains what happens to Marv and Spook, readers are left to assume that the plane crashes into the Colorado countryside early in the morning of July 9, 2000.

Blackjack Dealer   A young Native American woman deals blackjack to Amy Robinson and her new husband, Bobby, as they gamble at an Indian casino during their honeymoon. The girl, "who was perhaps twenty-two or twenty-three, slim-hipped, with braided black hair and black eyes and brown skin" (48), talks to Amy about luck and weddings, mentioning that she herself is engaged to be married in October and urging the couple repeatedly to take the money they have already won and "start honeymooning" (49). Like Johnny Ever and Fred Engelmann, this young woman seems to have an uncanny knowledge of the future, warning Amy that she might use up all her luck in the casino that night and have none left for the honeymoon or the marriage.

Bobby   Bobby is a math teacher who is briefly married to Amy Robinson. Although he is rumored to be a "decent guy" (8) by the other reunion attendees, Bobby's marriage to Amy lasts only two weeks. She leaves him on the drive back to the Twin Cities after having spent their honeymoon gambling at an Indian casino, where they had an unprecedented run of luck, winning nearly $230,000. While Bobby is exhilarated by their winnings, Amy is depressed, afraid that she has used up all the luck allotted her in this one night.

Bond, Buddy   Buddy Bond is a soldier in David Todd's platoon during the Vietnam War. When the unit is ambushed by a group of VIET CONG soldiers on July 16, 1969, Buddy Bond dies in the very first burst of gunfire.

Boy at the Red Carpet Bar   When the old college friends gather at the Red Carpet bar, a former college hangout, on the afternoon of July 8, 2000, a young man in baggy pants "and with a silver-studded nose" (242) approaches their table and asks that the group stop playing "all that soupy sixties bullshit" (243) on the jukebox. In reply, Amy Robinson tells the boy to go kill himself.

Burns, Karen   Karen Burns is a former roommate of Amy Robinson and Jan Huebner, who is murdered outside of TUCSON, ARIZONA in 1998 by a part-time bus driver named Darrell Jettie. Karen had hired the 36-year-old man to drive the residents of HOMEWOOD ESTATES, a retirement community which Karen directs, on short daytrips into Mexico and surrounding areas. Trusting and naïve, as well as harboring a crush on the flashy, younger man, Karen had accompanied Jettie and four residents of Homewood Estates on a planned trip to NOGALES, MEXICO. Jettie, however, had driven the bus not into Nogales, but onto a barren back road deep in Mexico, where he transacted a drug smuggling deal with another man. After driving the residents back across the U.S. border, he abandons them in an isolated portion of the Arizona desert, leaving Karen and her four elderly charges to die of thirst and exposure. The DARTON HALL class of 1969 holds a memorial service to remember Karen and another dead classmate during their reunion weekend.

Campbell, Alvin   *See* HAMMERLEE, TAP.

Chemist   One of the unnamed background figures at the DARTON HALL reunion, mentioned periodically during the chapters set in July 2000, is a "tall, silver-haired chemist" (41) who dances with a retired librarian who had been a prom queen in college. The chemist, now a Nobel Prize prospect, has prospered in life since college, while the former librarian has suffered, having now become "a recipient of insufficient alimony" (41).

Cowboys   Also delayed at the airport where Marv Bertel and Spook Spinelli wait for his flight back home to Denver are a pair of "improbable cowboys in fancy shirts and feathered Stetsons" (301) who try to decide whether to wait out the delay or find a hotel for the night. The pair must have decided to wait, since they reappear at the rear of the plane as the flight attendants prepare for take-off. The cowboys cuddle together high over Nebraska, blissfully unaware of the plane's impending crash.

Dempsey, Marla Marla Dempsey, one of the DARTON HALL graduates from 1969, worries throughout the reunion weekend that something is wrong with her—that she cannot feel things the way other human beings can. Marla is divorced from the Vietnam War veteran David Todd, a decent man whom she likes and respects, but whom she cannot love in the way he deserves. Readers, in fact, discover that Marla had been in love only once in her life, during her junior year in college when she had a month-long affair with a married high school teacher. When the man breaks up with her, Marla goes to his house distraught, only to be greeted at the door by his skinny 35-year-old wife, who is cooking dinner with the television blaring, her hair in pigtails. When David returns from the war after college, Marla agrees to marry him but warns him that she will need her space. She ends up leaving him on Christmas Day, 1985, for a stockbroker who drives her away on a Harley Davidson motorcycle. But that marriage is short-lived as well. Marla returns to the Twin Cities, where she and David become fast friends. The novel ends by suggesting that Marla and David will try to give their romance another chance. The last time readers see the couple, Marla asks David to tell her about his Vietnam experiences for the first time.

Devlin, Baldy Baldy Devlin is a young lawyer recently hired by the firm where one of Spook Spinelli's husbands, James Winship, works. Described as "half Spook's age, a long-distance runner, cowboy-rugged, smart, well spoken, far from bald" (91), Baldy flirts with Spook at a New Year's Eve party and ends up spending the night with her. Spook falls hard for the young man, but when he learns about her unconventional living arrangements, Baldy no longer answers her phone calls and e-mails. Spook, deeply depressed at losing her

"unblemished record for sovereignty over the male gender" (94), has trouble sleeping and gains four pounds. Her lack of success with Baldy still bothers Spook at the DARTON HALL reunion that summer, where she thinks repeatedly about the possibility of suicide.

Dexter, Bus Bus Dexter is a staff sergeant in David Todd's platoon during the Vietnam War. During the July ambush by VIET CONG soldiers, Todd sees Dexter crawling toward a clump of boulders. The big man almost makes it, but after he pushes himself up and begins to run, something explodes behind Dexter, lifting him up and dropping him down dead on the riverbank.

DiLeona, Sandra Sandra DiLeona is a beautiful 26-year-old business school graduate and the executive assistant of Marv Bertel at his mop and broom company. After Marv loses a great deal of weight, he asks Sandra out on a date. In order to keep her interest, he tells her that he is really the reclusive novelist Thomas Pierce. Marv keeps the charade going for several months, but after he asks Sandra to marry him, she realizes that he has been lying to her. Sandra agrees to go ahead with the marriage anyway, provided that Marv support her lavishly in a separate residence and that he keep up the Thomas Pierce façade for her friends and family members. Sandra and Marv are still married when he attends the DARTON HALL class reunion in July of 2000.

Door Gunner Just after dawn on July 18, 1969, the second day after his platoon in Vietnam was wiped out by a VIET CONG ambush, David Todd sees a pair of helicopters sweep in low over the SONG TRA KY River. For a moment, he looks into the bright blue eyes of a young door gunner. Unsure whether the vision is real or whether he is imagining it in a morphine daze, David tries to raise a hand to request help, but becomes dizzy. The gunner's face turns into a blur and the helicopters disappear.

Engelmann, Alice Alice Engelmann is the wife of Fred Engelmann and next-door neighbor of Dorothy and Ron Stier. When Dorothy wanders out of her house drunk and topless one afternoon, Fred tells her that Alice took a peek out the window and probably took to her bed.

Engelmann, Fred   Fred Engelmann is the next-door neighbor of Dorothy and Ron Stier. A retired Marine Corps colonel and dear friend of Dorothy's, Fred is outside watering his garden when Dorothy walks out of her house and into her driveway one July afternoon, half-drunk and without a shirt or bra, in an attempt to make her husband, Ron, look at her after her mastectomy. While Ron quickly retreats to the back patio of his house, Fred chats casually with Dorothy as she joins him in her garden. It soon becomes clear from the conversation that he has an uncanny knowledge of Dorothy—of her past as well as her hopes and fears. Like Johnny Ever, Fred Engel-mann even seems able to predict the future. As he and Dorothy take a swim together in his pool, Fred tells Dorothy that her cancer will return and that she has only five more years to live. Doro-thy challenges Fred's assertion, however, telling him to stick around and that she plans to survive much longer than that.

Ever, Johnny   Master Sergeant Johnny Ever is the name of the deejay whom David Todd hears—or imagines he hears—broadcasting over a transistor radio after he has been severely injured during an ambush in Vietnam. Identifying himself at times as God's "middleman" (32) and as an "angel" (187), Johnny Ever seems to know more about Todd than humanly possible, about both his past and his future. He prophesies that the young soldier's baseball career is over and that Marla Dempsey will leave him for another man. But he also offers David a bargain: If the severely injured young man still wants to be rescued after learning of his tragic future, he will send a helicopter. Buoyed by the miracle of the APOLLO 11 Moon landing, which he has just heard broadcast over the radio, David Todd agrees to be saved. After leaving Vietnam, David continues to hear Johnny Ever speak to him periodically. Later in life, a VA psychiatrist will tell David that Master Sergeant Johnny Ever "was no

angel, no devil, no ghost, no middleman; that, in fact, the man at the microphone was none other than David himself" (294). David's disappoint-ments in life, then, can be read as the result of his own self-sabotage, his expectations of failure, his survivor guilt following the war. Many of the main characters in the novel have their own version of Johnny Ever who speaks to them, a character or a voice who knows their deepest secrets: Fred Engel-mann for Dorothy Stier, the Loon Point policeman and later a television evangelist for Ellie Abbott, and Andrew Henry Wilton for Jan Huebner. In a novel that is largely about friendship, about the ways that people hide from and expose themselves to others, these mysterious characters, whether finally angels or demons, or simply versions of peo-ples' own inner selves, force secret, hidden desires and fears into the light.

Hammerlee, Tap; Skederian, Van; and Camp-bell, Alvin   Tap Hammerlee, Van Skederian, and Alvin Campbell are three dead American soldiers from David Todd's platoon in Vietnam. The bod-ies of the three dead men, killed in the VIET CONG ambush in which David is severely injured, are lined up along the bank of the SONG TRA KY River. All three men have had their scalps stripped away and their feet amputated. The stumps are said to be "shiny and reddish purple in the lurid sunshine" (26). The men had been killed naked, after frolick-ing in the river "like a Boy Scout troop" (26).

Harwood, Lincoln   Lincoln Harwood is Spook Spinelli's first husband, a lawyer whom she marries in 1985. When Spook falls in love a year later with James Winship, an associate professor of philoso-phy, she marries him as well. Lincoln, not wanting to lose Spook, accepts the bigamous relationship. Spook divides her time between two houses in a single Minnesota suburb—one she shares with Lin-coln and one with James. The three live amicably for more than 13 years until Spook falls in love again, this time with a young lawyer from Lincoln's firm named Baldy Devlin. Scared away by Spook's strange living arrangement, Baldy ends the rela-tionship, driving Spook into a deep depression and worrying both Lincoln and James.

Haslo, Paulette One of the group of old college friends attending the DARTON HALL reunion, Paulette Haslo is a Presbyterian minister who has recently lost her job in a shameful way. She had struck up an extremely close friendship with an older married parishioner, a lonely man named Rudy Ketch. After Rudy dies of heart disease, Paulette breaks into the home of his widow, Janice, one night to retrieve embarrassing love letters she and Rudy had written each other. Caught in the act by the vindictive Janice, Paulette is arrested, briefly jailed, and drummed out of her position at the church. Despite this humiliation, the reunion ends well for Paulette. She and Billy McMann fall in love and make plans to spend their future together.

Hollander, Bess and Ed Bess and Ed Hollander are elderly residents of the HOMEWOOD ESTATES retirement home in TUCSON, ARIZONA. Bess is described as "a balding, partly deaf eighty-year-old" (218), while her husband Ed is 76. Both Hollanders take part in the planned outing to NOGALES, MEXICO, and both are murdered along with Karen Burns when the bus driver Darrell Jettie abandons them in the desert 40 miles outside of Tucson.

Huebner, Jan Jan Huebner is a member of the 1969 graduating class of DARTON HALL COLLEGE who returns for her 30th reunion. Described as someone who "had never been perky," who had "never been pretty, or cute, or even passable," Jan is a 53-year-old divorcée with "bleached hair and plucked eyebrows and Midnight Plum lipstick" (4). In college Jan adopted the role of class clown, joking away her misery and her lack of success with men. Good friends with criminal lawyer Amy Robinson, Jan spends the reunion weekend drinking vodka and lamenting her deplorable 30-year marriage and recent divorce. In the chapter "Little People," which describes Jan's past, readers find out that she worked as part of a guerrilla street theater group the summer after graduation. When an extremely short and bitter young man offers her $50 to take her photograph, Jan complies, leading to a reckless summer spent as "Veronica," a street name she adopts when she poses for erotic photos snapped by a variety of men she thinks of

as "losers, one all . . . mostly old, mostly fat, uniformly creepy" (63). Nevertheless, Jan is flattered by the male attention and feels relatively safe as Veronica, at least until she reconnects with the dwarf who initially enticed her into the business, Andrew Henry Wilton. Bitter about Jan's college education and the way that middle-class girls think they can "skinny-dip into the sewers for a couple months . . . then hustle back to Main Street with lots of scary stories to tell" (67), Andrew threatens to blackmail Jan. But he gains a more lasting revenge when he introduces her to his good-looking younger brother, Richard. Jan ends up marrying Richard Wilton, leading her into a life of misery with an unfaithful and abusive husband.

Ickles, Norma Norma Ickles is one of the four elderly residents of the HOMEWOOD ESTATES retirement community in TUCSON, ARIZONA, who accompanies Karen Burns and the bus driver Darrell Jettie on a supposed outing to NOGALES, MEXICO. When Jettie abandons the small group in the desert far from Tucson, Norma is relieved, commenting, "At least they didn't murder us" (229). But Elaine Wirtz sets her friend straight, replying, "Oh, they did" (229). Jettie has abandoned Karen and the four elderly residents to die of thirst and exposure in the remote locale.

Immigration Officer After a month in Canada, during which time he secures a decent job at the WINNIPEG Public Library, Billy McMann discovers that in order to stay in the country he must secure "landed immigrant status" (116), which requires that he return to the United States, then recross the border into Canada with evidence of employment. In a small office on the Canadian border, an immigration officer brings him a cold Pepsi and has him fill out paperwork. The officer seems to understand that Billy is a DRAFT dodger, acknowledging that the young American is in a difficult position and hesitantly asking him if he is sure about what he is doing.

James, Happy Happy James is an American soldier fighting in Vietnam who dies when he is shot in the neck during a VIET CONG ambush in July

1969. James had been a member of David Todd's platoon.

Jettie, Darrell   Darrell Jettie, described as "thirty-six, blond, excessively polite, a chain smoker" (218) is the part-time bus driver hired by Karen Burns to take the residents of HOMEWOOD ESTATES, a retirement community she directs in TUSCON, ARIZONA, on short outings. Karen, 51 and lonely, fantasizes that Darrell is romantically interested in her. On a planned trip to NOGALES, MEXICO, however, Darrell drives Karen and a small group of retirees not to the tourist town as planned but to a remote locale off a dusty Mexican road, where he conducts what seems to be a drug deal with younger man. Although Darrell drives Karen and the small group of elderly residents back over the United States border, he abandons them in the Arizona desert 40 miles outside of Tucson, leaving the luckless group to die of thirst and exposure.

Jimmy the Gardner   A gardner named Jimmy, who works at the wealthy suburban home of Dorothy and Ron Stier, witnesses Dorothy leave the house topless and tipsy one summer afternoon, angry about her recent mastectomy and about her husband's lack of sexual interest in her since then. When Dorothy nods at him, Jimmy looks uncomfortably down at his hedge clippers, as if inspecting them.

Kepler, Tommy and Eddie   Tommy and Eddie Kepler are twin boys who live next door to Janice and Rudy Ketch in a Minneapolis suburb. When Janice hears noises in the middle of the night shortly after Rudy's death, she gets up from bed, expecting that the Kepler twins are to blame. The noises, however, turn out to have been made by Paulette Haslo, the minister at Janice's church. Paulette has broken into the Ketch house to retrieve letters she had written to Rudy before he died.

Ketch, Janice   Janice Ketch is the sour, cross, aging wife of Rudy Ketch. After Rudy's death from heart disease, Janice is awakened one night by sounds in her house. She gets out of bed to discover the minister of her church, Paulette Haslo,

dressed in black bicycle shorts and a skimpy white halter top, rummaging through Rudy's old desk. Paulette eventually confesses that she and Rudy had developed an extremely close friendship—an emotional if not a physical affair. She is in Janice's house searching for compromising letters she and the lonely, elderly man had written each other. Janice, who never liked Paulette's clothes, her demeanor, or her liberal politics, vindictively calls the police. She reports Paulette's transgressions as well to church officials at St. Marks. Paulette is arrested, briefly jailed, and loses her position as minister.

Ketch, Rudy   Rudy Ketch was a 64-year-old parishioner at St. Marks, the Presbyterian church in Minneapolis where Paulette Haslo was hired as the first female minister. A lonely man with a spiteful and unloving wife named Janice, Rudy strikes up a close friendship with Paulette. The two often have drinks together on a Saturday night, while Janice thinks Rudy is at the Legion Hall. When Rudy dies of heart disease, Paulette breaks into his house to try to retrieve love letters the two had written each other. When she is caught red-handed by Janice, Paulette loses her job at St. Marks.

Librarian   Among the unnamed figures who serve as background color at the DARTON HALL reunion is a former prom queen, now a retired librarian and divorcée. The woman dances with a chemist who had been bookish in college but is currently a Nobel prospect. O'Brien writes, "Nobody mentioned it, but the years had leveled their bumpy playing field" (41).

Lieutenant Governor of Minnesota   One of the DARTON HALL graduates who attends the class reunion is Minnesota's lieutenant governor. Although the man is never given a specific name in the novel, he is described as a "handsome, well pickled, newly married compromiser" (41) who seems entranced by his ex-fiancée, a Lutheran missionary. The lieutenant governor had broken off their engagement as a young man, explaining that the missionary life was not for him. However, at the last night of the reunion he is filled with regrets for choosing politics over romance, having lived his career as a "political bridesmaid" (313) rather than a major player.

Lieutenant Governor's New Bride The new bride of Minnesota's lieutenant governor is 26 years younger than her husband. She is not interested in reunions or in funerals, and she especially detests the "crowd of alcoholic, pot-bellied, whatever-happened-to-us old folks" (186) that she meets during the DARTON HALL reunion weekend, her husband having been a member of the class of 1969. She also seems jealous of her husband's ex-fiancée, a Lutheran missionary, whom the lieutenant governor dances with and talks to at length during the various reunion activities.

Lutheran Missionary One of the DARTON HALL COLLEGE class of 1969 reunion attendees is a Lutheran missionary who is also the ex-fiancée of the lieutenant governor of Minnesota. He had broken off their engagement when the two were young, explaining to the "lovely, big hearted" (313) girl that the missionary life was simply not for him. Yet, at the reunion, the two still seem attracted to each other, sharing several dances together under the cardboard stars in the Darton Hall gymnasium.

Manning, Borden Private Borden Manning is a soldier in David Todd's platoon, killed with the others in a VIET CONG ambush. After David drags himself to the SONG TRA KY RIVER, he sees Manning lying on his back, caught in the current. The dead man's nose is gone, and his body is being pushed against a big gray boulder.

Maples, Kaz Kaz Maples is a soldier in David Todd's unit during the Vietnam War. He dies in the first burst of gunfire when a group of VIET CONG guerrillas ambush the platoon.

McMann, Billy Billy McMann is drafted into the Vietnam War immediately after graduating from DARTON HALL COLLEGE in 1969. Unlike David Todd, however, who goes to the war, Billy decides to flee to Canada to evade the DRAFT. He convinces his college girlfriend, Dorothy Stier, to accompany him on his journey, but Dorothy never shows up at the airport for the flight to WINNIPEG, a betrayal that wounds Billy for the next 30 years. Despite the difficulty of having abandoned his home, his family and friends, and his country, Billy starts a new life in Winnipeg, opening a chain of hardware stores and eventually marrying a librarian and having a daughter named Susie. After 10 years of marriage, Billy's wife is killed by a hit-and-run driver, who turns out to be a woman named Alexandra Wenz. Racked with guilt over her secret, Alexandra takes a job as Billy's account manager, and the two have a brief romantic relationship after she confesses her role in his wife's death six years earlier. Despite his financial success, his marriage and the birth of his daughter, Billy never forgives Dorothy Stier for abandoning him so many years ago; he attends the reunion mostly in an attempt to explain to Dorothy the complicated love and hate he feels for her at the same time. While Billy winds up spending the first night of the reunion with Spook Spinelli, he falls in love with Paulette Haslo the second night. The novel ends with Billy and Paulette planning a new life together for themselves.

McMann, Billy's Wife After Billy McMann has been in Canada for six years, he marries a librarian from Calgary and has a daughter. While Billy wants to be a good family man, he feels that he is pretending with his new wife. Ten years later, the wife, whose name readers never learn, is killed in a hit-and-run accident.

McMann, Mr. and Mrs. When Billy McMann calls his parents from Canada to let them know that he has evaded the DRAFT, his mother is bewildered at first, then angry. "It's your life," his mother tells him, "and I suppose you're entitled to ruin it" (111). Billy's father is more understanding and promises to wire his son money. When Billy's mother dies in September 1992, he attends the funeral in Minnesota, stays with his father a few days in his old hometown, then drives north to the Twin Cities, where he meets his old girlfriend, Dorothy Stier, for a few unsatisfying hours in a hotel coffee shop.

McMann, Susie   Susie McMann is the daughter of DRAFT dodger Billy McMann and a Canadian librarian from Calgary. Her mother is killed by a hit-and-run driver when Susie is still a young child, leaving Billy to raise his daughter alone. On the last night of the DARTON HALL COLLEGE reunion in July 2000, Billy calls Susie to tell her about Paulette Haslo, a former classmate whom he has fallen in love with during the tumultuous reunion weekend.

Mustin, Vince   Vince Mustin is an American soldier who is shot in the stomach when David Todd's platoon is ambushed in July 1969. As David lies next to the SONG TRA KY River, badly wounded himself, he can hear Vince crying. Eventually, the young soldier stops sobbing, presumably having died along with all of the other platoon members except David himself.

Niece of Sandra DiLeona   At his wedding to Sandra DiLeona, Marv Bertel flirts with one of Sandra's teenage nieces, "who came equipped with a suggestive smile and largely bared breasts" (265). During the wedding toasts, however, Sandra leans over and whispers to Marv that, if he ever puts the moves on her niece again, he will wind up "just a dirt-poor ex" (265).

Organist   While gambling at an Indian casino during her honeymoon, Amy Robinson becomes depressed despite an unprecedented winning streak. She closes her eyes at one point during the long night and pictures the organist from her recent wedding: "a frail old woman in a crepe dress and crocheted white sweater" (53). Something about the memory gives Amy "the creeps" (53); she recalls that the wedding had been her husband Bobby's idea, that he had planned the event and chosen the music entirely by himself. While Amy likes Bobby, she recognizes that she does not love him, and she ends up walking out of the marriage after barely two weeks.

Ortiz, Hector   Hector Ortiz is a member of David Todd's platoon during the Vietnam War. On July 16, 1969, when the unit is ambushed by a group of VIET CONG soldiers, Hector Ortiz is shot in the face. The transistor radio that Ortiz had carried, however, continues to blast out the evening news from DA NANG. The radio becomes Todd's only companion during the next four days as he crawls alone through the jungle before finally being rescued by a helicopter.

Osterberg, Harmon   Harmon Osterberg, a member of the DARTON HALL class of 1969, is a dentist who drowned the year before the class reunion is held. He had been conducting an extramarital affair with former classmate Ellie Abbott and drowned while the two were spending a few days together at the LOON POINT resort in northern Minnesota. The class of 1969 holds a memorial service for Harmon and for another recently deceased former classmate, Karen Burns, on the second day of the reunion weekend. Interestingly, Harmon Osterberg closely resembles a minor character in a previous O'Brien novel, *In the Lake of the Woods*. In that book, Kathy Wade, the missing wife of politician John Wade, also has an affair with a dentist named Harmon. Just like Ellie Abbott, Kathy meets her dentist at the Loon Point resort. However, the dentist does not drown in the earlier novel as he does in *July, July*.

Paladino, Doc   Doc Paladino is one of the soldiers in David Todd's platoon during the Vietnam War who is killed in the ambush on July 16, 1969. The last time David sees Doc, he is kneeling in the grass, listening to Hector Ortiz's transistor radio broadcast news about the APOLLO 11 Moon landing when he is "sucked away into the powdery grass" (22), vanishing entirely.

Pale Old Woman   One of the passengers on Marv Bertel's flight back home to Denver is a pale, elderly woman who dozes in her seat, mumbles in her sleep, and remains completely unaware of the tragedy about to unfold: the fast-approaching plane crash into the Pawnee National Grassland far below.

Pharmacist   Before the final night of the reunion, Dorothy Stier stops at a drugstore to buy the perfume that she used to wear as a college student and that Billy McMann had liked. She cannot, however, quite remember the brand name and asks for help from the pharmacist on duty. The pharmacist looks in the back without success. When he returns, he studies Dorothy intently, then says, "Perfume won't do it," as if he, like Dorothy's neighbor Fred Engelmann, somehow has knowledge of her deepest secrets.

Physician   An unnamed "prominent physician," who develops a relationship with a former star point guard of the women's basketball team over the course of the weekend, is one of the attendees at the DARTON HALL COLLEGE reunion. While the affair might not last, both feel "miraculous happiness" (139) as they spend the weekend together.

Pierce, Thomas   Thomas Pierce is the name of a famous, but very reclusive writer, whose identity Marv Bertel adopts in order to impress his young girlfriend and executive assistant, Sandra DiLeona. Clearly based on real-life writer THOMAS PYNCHON, the Thomas Pierce character is the well-regarded author of novels that no one seems to actually read. As Marv keeps up the pretense for several months, his life begins to take on the quality of Thomas Pierce's "most grotesque fictions, freakish and scary, ruled by entropy, a madhouse of make-believe looping back on itself in infinite ellipses" (262).

Policeman   After Harmon Osterberg drowns at LOON POINT, a young policeman drives Ellie Abbott into town for questioning. On the ride Ellie asks if her involvement with Harmon can be kept confidential, confessing that she is married to someone else. Sensing the policeman's disapproval, Ellie lapses into silence. Later, after driving her back to Loon Point, the policeman asks Ellie if she needs anything else, offering to stay and talk with her. Like Johnny Ever with David Todd and Fred Engelmann with Dorothy Stier, this young policeman seems to know Ellie better than she knows herself, explaining that he is what Ellie has instead of a conscience. Even after returning home to Boston, Ellie believes she sees the policeman get out of a car parked on the street opposite the neighbor's lawn. She confides in Paulette Haslo

her fear that the man is following her and possibly spying on her.

Reiss, Gil   As David Todd lies tangled up in a web of tree roots along the bank of the SONG TRA KY RIVER after his platoon has been ambushed in Vietnam, he notices the body of Sergeant Gil Reiss lying dead on the riverbank.

Robinson, Amy   Amy Robinson is the close friend of Jan Huebner. Former college roommates, the two women now live seven blocks apart in the Twin Cities suburb of EDEN PRAIRIE. Amy is a criminal lawyer who still has the "boyish figure," as well as the "button nose and freckles" of her younger self, but whose "collegiate perkiness has been replaced by something taut and haggard" (4). She spends most of her time at the DARTON HALL reunion drinking vodka with Jan and lamenting her single status. In her chapter from the past, "The Streak," readers discover that Amy had been married briefly to a math teacher named Bobby. On their honeymoon, the two experience an extended streak of luck while gambling at an Indian casino, winning nearly $230,000. Amy, however, is depressed by the experience. She is not in love with Bobby, and she fears that the couple will use up all the luck apportioned them for the marriage at the black jack table, as the pretty young dealer warns. At a gas station on the drive back to the Twin Cities, Amy calls a cab and leaves her marriage behind.

Skederian, Van   *See* HAMMERLEE, TAP.

Spinelli, Carolyn   Carolyn Spinelli had been the twin sister of Caroline "Spook" Spinelli. When Carolyn died at the age of six from renal disease, her twin sister stopped speaking for more than a year, earning her the nickname "Spook" because of her silent and ghostlike demeanor. While Spook grows up to become a beautiful, popular and outgoing young woman, an outrageous flirt, she secretly remains haunted by her sister's death, having occasional relapses into deep melancholy and strange behavior. Perhaps the reason that Spook marries two husbands in later life is because she feels as if she is living as both Carolyn and Caroline.

Spinelli, Spook A good-looking woman who loves men, Spook Spinelli is known for posing topless on the cover of the DARTON HALL yearbook back in 1969. During the class reunion in July 2000, she seduces the DRAFT dodger Billy McMann all the while flirting shamelessly with Marv Bertel, the overweight broom and mop entrepreneur who has been in love with her for the past 30 some-odd years. Desperate to be loved, Spook is married to two different men, each of whom knows about the other and has accepted their bigamous marriage. She married lawyer Lincoln Harwood in 1985, then a year later, she fell in love with and married James Winship, an associate professor of philosophy. Spook shares a separate house with each man in a suburb of the Twin Cities, dividing her time between households. This arrangement works well for more than 13 years, until she meets another man she feels she cannot live without: a young lawyer in Lincoln's firm named Baldy Devlin. Baldy, when he finds out about Spook's unconventional living arrangements, refuses to return her phone calls and e-mails, sending the older woman into a deep depression. Spook's neediness arises at least partially from childhood trauma. She had been a born a twin, but her sister, Carolyn, died when she was only six years old. Spook is haunted by the death and remains mute for more than a year, earning the nickname "Spook" because of the otherworldly quality she displays. During the reunion weekend, Spook seems wound too tightly; she is out of control and nearly suicidal. At the end of the novel, readers are left to presume that she dies in a plane crash after unexpectedly appearing on Marv Bertel's flight home to Denver after having urged Marv to cancel the flight because she has a "weird, creepy feeling" (303) about it.

Stier, Dorothy Dorothy Stier is the lone Republican among her group of college friends at DARTON HALL in 1969. When her boyfriend, Billy McMann, decides to flee to Canada in order to evade the Vietnam War DRAFT, Dorothy agrees to accompany him, but is unable to give up her vision of a comfortable future in the country she loves and changes her mind at the last minute. She never meets Billy for the flight to WINNIPEG as she had promised, a betrayal that Billy takes to heart for the next 30 years. Dorothy marries instead a man named Ron, who had been a friend of Billy's, moves with her new husband to a wealthy suburb a few blocks away from Darton Hall, and gives birth to two sons. Her life unfolds comfortably until 1996, when she is diagnosed with breast cancer. After undergoing a mastectomy, Dorothy worries that Ron is no longer attracted to her. The chapter that details Dorothy's past is called "Half Gone"; it takes place on July 19, 1997, 9½ months after Dorothy's surgery and describes a morning when the angry and tipsy middle-aged woman goes out to her driveway topless in order to force her husband to look at her. During this episode, Dorothy talks with her close friend and neighbor Fred Engelmann, a character similar to Johnny Ever in David Todd's chapters, who seems to know more about Dorothy and her life than humanly possible. The chapter ends with Fred telling Dorothy that her cancer will return and that she has only five years to live. In July 2000, at the Darton Hall reunion, Dorothy loosens up enough take a tab of acid from David Todd. The last readers see of her, she is walking home from the college, stoned and enjoying the beautiful night.

Stier, Ron Ron Stier is the man Dorothy Stier marries after she jilts Billy McMann, not showing up at the airport to accompany him to WINNIPEG as she had promised. Ron had apparently been a close friend of Billy's in college. In later years, he goes on to become a senior vice president at a company called Cargill. While Dorothy tells everyone at the reunion what a sweet, supportive husband she has, her relationship with Ron is not as simple as she pretends. After her mastectomy following a diagnosis of breast cancer, Dorothy feels that Ron cannot bear to look at her or touch her, that he no longer finds her attractive. He seems more interested in taking care of his cherished twin Volvos than in his wife's difficult recovery. When Dorothy strolls down the driveway of her suburban home topless one afternoon, Ron does not know how to behave. She ignores his entreaties to return inside, causing Ron to angrily retreat inside himself, leaving Dorothy to chat with their next-door neighbor, Fred Engelmann.

Stockbroker Marla Dempsey leaves David Todd after a 10-year marriage on Christmas Day, 1979, for a stockbroker whose name readers never learn. The younger man picks her up on a Harley Davidson motorcycle that morning. Marla had met the stockbroker the previous spring and had started up a relationship with him, thinking she might be in love. Even though she marries the man after her divorce from David is finalized, Marla realizes that she is not in love with him. She worries that something is missing inside of her and that she is incapable of feeling real love. Marla returns to the Twin Cities in 1987, having divorced the stockbroker. She and David Todd take up their friendship again, leaving all their friends to wonder what went wrong in the marriage since they seem to be such "a perfect fit" (297) for each other.

Tabor, Larry Paulette Haslo, in explaining to Ellie Abbott how she lost her job, tells Ellie about the time she and Rudy Ketch went to a retreat camp together in northern Minnesota run by an "absolute lunatic" (163) named Larry Tabor, a retired hippie who leads nude yoga exercises in the morning. Rudy, over 60 years old, plays along, telling Paulette he never knew that religion could be so much fun.

Television Evangelist When Ellie Abbott returns to her downtown hotel room at the end of the DARTON HALL reunion, after her husband has flown home to Boston without her, angry about her affair with Harmon Osterberg, she is "shepherded through her sorrows by a TV evangelist, a man with a pot belly and doughy skin and colorless eyes and large, jowly, almost featureless face" (311). The evangelist seems to be speaking to Ellie Abbott personally from the television. Like other mysterious characters in the novel such as Johnny Ever and Fred Engelmann, he seems to have supernatural knowledge of Ellie's life and her situation. It is the "wise counsel" (320) of the TV evangelist that encourages Ellie to fly home to try to patch things up with her husband, Mark.

Todd, David David Todd is a member of the DARTON HALL class of 1969 who drops out of college after his junior year and is subsequently drafted into the Vietnam War. As a young, inexperienced second lieutenant, having been in the country for only 19 days, David is severely injured when his platoon is ambushed by VIET CONG soldiers. The lone surviving member of a platoon originally containing 17 men, David lies by the SONG TRA KY River, listening to the moans and cries of his dying fellow soldiers while nearly going out of his mind with the pain from his own foot and leg injuries. After dragging himself alone through the harsh terrain for four days, David begins to hallucinate that he hears a voice speaking to him over the transistor radio he carries. The voice identifies himself as deejay Johnny Ever and seems able to foretell David's future. Ever informs David that if he survives he will lose his leg, never play baseball again, and that the love of his life, his girlfriend Marla Dempsey, will eventually leave him for another man. When Ever offers him the choice of dying in the jungle or being rescued, with the foreknowledge of how difficult his life will be, David, elated by the miraculous Moon landing he has just heard reported on the radio, chooses to live, and he is choppered out of the jungle. As Ever had predicted, David loses his leg and his baseball career. He marries Marla, but she leaves him for a stockbroker who rides a Harley Davidson motorcycle on Christmas Day, 1985. David eventually returns to Darton Hall and graduates with the class of 1992, but his divorce from Marla as well as his memories from the war continue to haunt him and make him unhappy. Whether the events of David's life are fated to occur or whether he sabotages his own life because he expects failure is difficult to discern. The end of the novel, however, does offer some hope for the psychologically damaged veteran, as Marla returns to the reunion banquet hall to find David, and the two seem to have a chance of getting back together.

Todd, Mickey Mickey Todd is the name of David Todd's brother. While severely injured and hallucinating in Vietnam, David imagines he is back in his childhood and that he sees Mickey tossing a baseball at the garage. But the present interferes with the memory when David thinks the sound the baseball makes is like getting shot.

Todd, Mr. and Mrs.   Nearly out of his mind with pain and guilt after the ambush on his platoon in Vietnam, David Todd drifts back into memories of his childhood, imagining that he can see his mother hanging up clothes to dry in the backyard and his father planting a lilac bush.

Veterans Administration Psychiatrist   During the last four years of his marriage to Marla Dempsey, David Todd goes to see a Veterans Administration psychiatrist, described as "a woman his own age, also a veteran of the sixties" (293). The psychiatrist assures David that Master Sergeant Johnny Ever is neither an angel nor a devil, but is, in fact, a manifestation of David himself. David agrees that this assessment makes sense, and he sleeps better after the sessions, his memories of the war tamed at least temporarily. When his divorce from Marla is finalized in April 1980, David begins dating the psychiatrist, a relationship that lasts for six weeks.

Wenz, Alexandra   In October 1991, Billy McMann, who by that time owns a chain of four hardware stores plus a lumberyard and roofing company, hires a young woman named Alexandra Wenz to handle his accounts. Described as "tall and quiet and smart, very efficient, very grave, with slate-blue eyes and red hair" (120), Alexandra begins to date Billy. On their fourth night out, she confesses that she was the hit-and-run driver who killed Billy's wife back when she was 17 years old. She applied for the job because she felt she had to face up to her past. Alexandra also tells Billy that his wife jumped out in front of her car purposefully. The couple dates for five months, but Alexandra ends up leaving Billy because he is still obsessed with Dorothy Stier after all these years.

Wenz, Mrs.   When Alexandra Wenz and Billy McMann are dating, she tells him stories about her crazy mother, whose only goal in life was for Alexandra to become a majorette. Her mother called her Allie, not Alexandra, the young woman explains to Billy, "because the last thing she wanted was a *complicated* majorette" (122).

Wilton, Andrew Henry   Andrew Henry Wilton, described as a "diminutive, large-headed young man" (60), offers Jan Huebner $50 if she will pose naked for a personal photo shoot after he sees her perform in a piece of guerrilla theater the summer after she graduates from DARTON HALL COLLEGE. Jan, flattered by the offer and judging the young man to be harmless, agrees. The session with Andrew Henry Wilton leads to similar experiences with a variety of other men over the summer, Jan even adopting the street name of "Veronica" as she earns a great deal of extra money through the photo shoots. One night, however, Andrew Wilton returns to her apartment, drunk and belligerent. Calling Jan "Snow White" and himself a dwarf, he threatens to blackmail the young woman by mailing some of the erotic photos to her mother. Wilton is angered by the fact that Jan, a nice girl from a middle-class suburban family, believes she can "skinny-dip in the sewer for a couple of months, fraternize with the scum, then hustle back to Main Street with lots of scary stories to tell" (67). He ends up gaining his revenge on Jan not through blackmail as he had originally threatened but by introducing her to his good-looking younger brother, Richard, who will be an abusive and unfaithful husband to Jan for 30 years.

Wilton, Richard   Richard Wilton is the handsome younger brother of the diminutive Andrew Henry Wilton, whom Jan Huebner meets on the streets of Minneapolis in July 1969. After spending the summer as "Veronica," posing for nude photographs, Jan is introduced to Richard at Andrew's birthday party. Readers suspect that the bitter, misshapen Andrew is exacting revenge on Jan by setting her up with his brother. The chapter titled "Little People," which describes Jan's adventures that summer, ends with Andrew saying, "Can't say I never stuck it to Snow White" (76). As Andrew knows, Richard is chronically unfaithful and even abusive. Jan's marriage turns out miserably.

Winship, James   The second husband of Spook Spinelli, James Winship is an associate professor of philosophy whom Spook marries in 1986, a year after she had married Lincoln Harwood. James, like

Lincoln, accepts the bigamous relationship. He and Spook share a house in WHITE BEAR LAKE, Minnesota, a few blocks from the house she shares with her other husband, Lincoln. Spook divides her time between her two houses and her two husbands in an unconventional relationship that nevertheless seems to work fairly well for more than 13 years.

Wirtz, Elaine   Elaine Wirtz is a feisty 79-year-old resident of the HOMEWOOD ESTATES retirement community directed by Karen Burns in TUCSON, ARIZONA. She is one of the four elderly residents who accompany Karen and the bus driver Darrell Jettie on an outing planned for NOGALES, MEXICO. On the bus ride, Elaine announces that she was a jaguar in a past life, a fact she knows as surely as the fact that she ate a bagel for breakfast that morning. Elaine is the first of the small group to realize that Darrell Jettie plans to murder them. While her accusations at first seem overblown and somewhat hysterical, Elaine is proven right when Jettie abandons Karen and the four old people in a dry creek bed in the desert 40 miles from Tucson.

Young Man in Mexico   When the part-time bus driver Darrell Jettie takes Karen Burns and a small group of elderly retirement community residents into NOGALES, MEXICO for a day of sightseeing, he bypasses the center of town and instead drives the small group straight south for almost an hour into the interior of the country. He stops the van on a dusty dirt road in a remote location, pulling up beside an old red pickup. A young man dressed in coveralls and a white baseball cap, who looks to be in his mid-20s, emerges from the truck to speak with Darrell. Eventually, the two remove several shoe boxes from under the floorboard of the van, which Ed Hollander presumes is evidence of drug smuggling. The young man accompanies the group on the trip back over the United States border and aids Darrell Jettie in abandoning Karen and the four elderly travelers along a dry creek bed in the remote Arizona desert.

FURTHER READING

Dayley, Glenn. "Familiar Ghosts, New Voices: Tim O'Brien's *July, July*," *War, Literature, and the Arts* 15, nos. 1–2 (2003): 316–322.

Stocks, Claire. "Acts of Cultural identification: Tim O'Brien's *July, July*," *European Journal of American Culture* 25, no. 3 (2006): 173–188.

"Keeping Watch By Night" (1976)

Published in December 1976 in *Redbook* magazine, "Keeping Watch By Night" is a story that pits faith against reason. On a night ambush in Vietnam, the religious Jim Pederson tells the skeptic Doc Peret a story about Christ's healing powers as a third soldier, Paul Berlin, bears silent witness. While the story involves characters who will be central to the 1978 novel, *Going After Cacciato*, the particular events detailed in the story do not appear in the novel.

SYNOPSIS

"Keeping Watch By Night" is a story about an exchange that occurs between two soldiers, Jim Pederson and Doc Peret, as they set up an ambush one dark night in Vietnam. Pederson, a tall, sincere Texan who had been a missionary in KENYA before being drafted (*see* DRAFT), tells the skeptical Doc a story about religious faith. When he had been serving in Kenya, two young boys arrived at his missionary headquarters. The boys' father was dead from cholera and the mother was on the verge of dying as well—she had sores all over her face, a terribly high fever, eyelids swollen open, and she was slipping in and out of a coma. Pederson sits up with the woman through the night, bathing her forehead and talking to her about his family, his boyhood in Houston, his belief in God, and how he came to do missionary work. As Pederson talks, he sees the woman begin to smile. He asks her about her own faith, but as she is unable to speak, Pederson answers for her, affirming that she believes in Jesus Christ and that her faith is strong. The woman's fever drops that night, and in five weeks she is completely healed. Doc, meanwhile, remains skeptical, telling Pederson when he is finished that that there are simply too many uncertainties in the story for him to accept the woman's healing as a result of religious faith or spiritual strengthening. Paul Berlin, who has been silently listening to Pederson's story, and who both admires and envies Pederson's faith, understands that in the morning he, too, will be skeptical about Pederson's tale.

COMMENTARY

"Keeping Watch By Night" is a story that illustrates the disjunction between religious faith and scientific reason as Jim Pederson tells the skeptical Doc Peret about a near-miracle he witnessed in Kenya. But it is also a story, as are so many of O'Brien's works, about the nature of storytelling itself—about how stories work and what their effect is on a listener. The story opens with a discussion of miracles. (This is a theme that O'Brien will return to in later works such as the 2002 novel, *July, July,* in which the injured soldier David Todd in July 1969, the same year that the MIRACLE METS win the World Series, listens to the astonishing APOLLO Moon landing on a transistor radio before undergoing his own miraculous rescue and recovery.) While Pederson likes to talk about "the powers of Christ as Healer," Doc Peret, a man trained in science, has "his own theories about healing, none of which involved Jesus Christ" (65). Doc is willing to concede the impact of psychology on a patient's recuperative process, but he denies that any true spiritual transaction or supernatural intervention takes place in such cases. Pederson, who is careful to point out that he is *not* speaking specifically about miracles, which "would involve the reversing of natural law, or at least its temporary suspension" (65), nevertheless insists that the natural laws of healing can be accelerated when patients are strengthened by their faith in Jesus Christ. Pederson also acknowledges that faith is something that cannot "be argued into a man" (65), but rather must be absorbed into his thoughts and behavior. Interestingly, although he is talking to Doc Peret, Pederson looks at Paul Berlin as he speaks, as if his comments are directed more toward the silent, frightened young soldier than the experienced medical man. And Berlin absorbs Pederson's story into himself, much as Pederson claims a man must absorb faith.

Of course, O'Brien also wants readers to notice the irony of the fact that Pederson, a man who performed missionary work in Africa, who stopped his fellow soldiers from burning a village, and who takes a "moral stance" to his soldiering, is unwinding wires, planting CLAYMORE MINES, and positioning hand grenades as he speaks, carefully preparing for the night ambush that the men will undertake. Talk of ambush configurations, with their "reliable killing zones" (66) sits uncomfortably next to Pederson's words about kindness, faith, and salvation in Kenya. Pederson is a complicated man, whose strong religious beliefs do not prevent him from being a good soldier—patient, smart, and in control, as well as brave and respected by the other men in the platoon despite their cynicism about his Christian tenets. Doc Peret is a complex figure as well. A skeptic who believes in science over miracles, Doc nevertheless respects Pederson's moral stance, and he listens to Pederson's tale carefully and with an open mind, as if he is truly trying to learn something, not just find holes to pick apart.

As Paul Berlin watches Pederson set up the ambush and as he listens to the two men talk, he holds himself somewhat apart, not quite sure whose side to take. Berlin, as his name signifies, is a divided character. He envies Pederson's firm beliefs and his bravery, but he knows that he could never have sat up all night with the woman in Kenya the way Pederson did. Berlin, "whose only passion was for survival" (68), is torn between the desire to be brave and a recognition of his own lack of bravery, just as he will be in the later novel, *Going After Cacciato*. It is almost as if the two men are battling for Berlin's soul as they talk through the night. And Berlin, as the night grows longer and darker, anticipates what is to come:

> Paul Berlin . . . could feel the springy compression of the ambush. He knew the feeling. It would erode, he knew, with the progress of the night, and with his own thoughts and imaginings, but now there was the feeling of balance and precision and stored energy, like a mousetrap pulled back and latched, dangerous, and he could feel all this without having to see it.

The dark was part of it. And the waiting, and the sense of mystery. (66)

The set ambush in this passage is akin to Pederson's setting up of his story. Doc believes he knows the ending—that the priest will save the Kenyan woman: "And so the priest saved her," he cynically comments to Pederson. But Pederson arms his trap with his quiet response to Doc's supposition: "No, Pederson, said. "I did" (66). With that, Pederson has set up the story that will follow. Berlin's musings about the rigged ambush apply equally well to his anticipation of the story to come—the feeling of balance and precision and stored energy at the beginning of the story, the waiting and sense of mystery for what is about to come, the knowledge that the mystery will erode as the story is told and as the listener mulls it over in his own thoughts and imagination.

And just as miracles require faith, so, too, does narrative. When Pederson's story has ended, Doc questions him about it, asking if the woman understood English, suggesting that Pederson might have made up the answers when he asked the woman about her faith, wondering if she was really awake or if she was in a coma. Finally, the story itself comes down to a matter of faith. If he is to believe Pederson's story, Doc must accept the Texan's word about what he witnessed, his judgment about whether the woman actually understood what was happening or not. Narrative, like faith, "isn't a commodity to be traded by reason" (65). Like faith, a story is an experience that must be absorbed into a person. Pederson refuses to debate his tale with Doc Peret, exacting a promise before he begins that he will just tell the story, that Doc will not require him to argue about it or to defend it. As O'Brien will later point out in "How to Tell a True War Story," one must "feel the truth" of a story; a listener must believe a story "by the raw force of feeling" (TTTC 74). But Paul Berlin, the silent listener whom the story in many ways seems directed toward, finally cannot make this leap of faith. Despite his nighttime belief in Pederson's narrative, despite his best attempts to feel the story, to accept its truth, Berlin knows that in the morning he will agree with Doc Peret that

there "were too many uncertainties" in the story, "too many spots for misinterpretation" (68). Berlin cannot find the faith to believe in Pederson's narrative any more than he can summon up Pederson's bravery or moral stance as a soldier. Courage is directly connected to faith in this story as Pederson's bravery seems to stem from his morality. When Pederson stops the men from burning down Tri Nuoc 2, nobody resents him afterward. The soldiers understand and respect his deep moral convictions. Pederson, therefore, is "splendid in the night; there was no one better" (68), but Berlin, afraid of possible "misunderstandings" in Pederson's story, is also afraid in the night. He will remain a divided character, feeling both envy and admiration for Pederson but unable to summon the faith that sustains the other soldier.

CHARACTERS

Berlin, Paul   Paul Berlin, the main character in the 1978 novel, *Going After Cacciato*, plays a minor but important role in the story. While he is mostly a silent witness to the extended conversation between Jim Pederson and Doc Peret concerning religious faith, Berlin himself is frightened during the night and wishes he had the same convictions Pederson does. But he knows that in the morning if he survives the night without incident, he, too, will become a skeptic like Doc.

Cacciato   During the long, dark night spent on ambush in Vietnam, Jim Pederson tells a story about a woman saved by faith in Kenya. When the story has ended, Paul Berlin stays awake listening to the noises of the men and the jungle. Once, very late, he hears a fellow soldier named Cacciato whistling until someone hisses at him to be quiet. Cacciato's whistling will also make Berlin nervous in the later novel, *Going After Cacciato*.

Harris, Stink   Stink Harris is a fellow soldier of Jim Pederson, Doc Peret, and Paul Berlin. He is mentioned very briefly in the story when the narrator writes that Pederson never lectured Stink or any of the other men about his faith. Stink will play a larger role in the later novel *Going After Cacciato*.

Kenyan Mother and Father   Jim Pederson tells the story of working as a missionary in KENYA when two boys, possibly of the Indandis tribal group, arrive at his camp. Their father has just died of cholera, and Pederson helps to bury the man. The mother, while still alive, is at death's door. Pederson stays awake through the night with the woman, bathing her face and talking to her about his own childhood and about his religious faith. He believes that he witnesses the woman's spiritual awakening during the night, which he feels gives her the strength to recover from cholera. To Pederson the woman is beautiful, despite the ugly sores and the high fever.

Johnson, Oscar   Oscar Johnson, a buck sergeant in ALPHA COMPANY in the novel *Going After Cacciato*, appears briefly in the story when the narrator is discussing the advantages of the classic L-shaped ambush configuration, which Pederson, Peret, Berlin, and the other men are setting up. Noting the L-shape's "reliable killing zone," the narrator comments that Oscar Johnson had once said that if anything within the ambush zone "moves . . . it dies" (66). But the narrator then goes on to list the configuration's disadvantages: "poor rear and flank security, no perimeter, vulnerability to counterambush" (66).

Lazzutti, Eddie   Eddie Lazzutti is an American soldier in Vietnam who serves in a unit with Jim Pederson, Doc Peret, Paul Berlin, and several other recurring O'Brien figures. Although he plays a more important role in the novel *Going After Cacciato*, Eddie is only briefly mentioned in "Keeping Watch By Night"—the narrator explains that Pederson "never lectured Stink or Eddie or any of the others" about his spiritual beliefs. Rather, he "listened to them, expressed his own convictions and let it go at that" (65).

Pederson, Jim   Jim Pederson is an American soldier in Vietnam with deep Christian convictions. A handsome, clean-shaven Texan who is also a good, steady soldier, calm and brave, Pederson does not proselytize but rather takes what Doc Peret calls a "moral stance" (65) in his life and in his soldiering.

"Keeping Watch By Night" revolves around a story that Pederson tells Doc Peret one night about a Kenyan woman suffering from cholera when he was a missionary in Africa. Pederson claims the woman was healed by the strength of her faith in Christ, an assertion about which Doc remains skeptical. Pederson appears as well in the novel *Going After Cacciato*, where he dies from friendly fire. He is shot by the door gunners on an American helicopter during a combat assault (CA) mission.

Peret, Doc   Doc Peret is a medical man who subscribes to science and reason rather than faith. While he admires Jim Pederson's moral stance and while he listens to the Christian soldier's account of a woman in KENYA saved by her faith in Christ, Doc remains skeptical about Pederson's story, claiming that there are too many uncertainties for him to believe it. Did the woman truly have cholera to begin with? Did she understand English? Was Pederson merely witnessing what he wanted to see? In other O'Brien works, such as the short story "Where Have You Gone, Charming Billy?" and the novel *Going After Cacciato*, Doc is something of an amateur philosopher, explaining that it is possible for a man to die of fright on the field of battle and arguing with an Iranian colonel about the nature of war.

Priest   A priest who serves the mission in KENYA where Jim Pederson is stationed before the Vietnam War helps to bury the Kenyan father who dies of cholera, but he stays away from the man's still-living wife, who is also on the verge of death from the disease. Pederson speculates that the priest was afraid of contagion.

Ruth, Doctor   Doctor Ruth is a medical doctor who works at the mission headquarters where Jim Pederson is stationed when he is working as a missionary in KENYA before he is drafted (*see* DRAFT) into the Vietnam War. When a woman suffering from open sores, an extremely high fever, and slipping into and out of a coma arrives in the camp, Dr. Ruth pronounces her chances of survival to be zero. According to Pederson's story, the doctor says the woman is as good as dead and that there is "no known medical cure" (66) for her symptoms. When the woman miraculously survives, Pederson attributes her recovery to her faith in Jesus Christ.

Two Boys Jim Pederson tells the story of two young boys who arrived at his camp when he was a missionary in KENYA. Their father had just died of cholera, and their mother is near death. In Pederson's story, the mother survives the disease and is eventually able to care for her boys again because she is strengthened by her faith in Jesus Christ.

"Landing Zone Bravo" (1975)

Originally published in *Denver Quarterly* in August 1975, "Landing Zone Bravo" tells the story of the Vietnam War soldier Jim Pederson, who is killed by friendly fire from a U.S. helicopter after being deposited with his platoon members in a hot landing zone. The story was reworked slightly and included as a chapter with the same title in O'Brien's 1978 novel, *Going After Cacciato*.

SYNOPSIS

The story opens aboard a CHINOOK helicopter that is ferrying a group of American soldiers into battle in Vietnam. While the story is told in the third person, the point of view is that of the young soldier Paul Berlin, who is shivering in the cold air of the helicopter and fighting feelings that something is not right. The various platoon members bite their nails, sweat, drink Cokes, and even pass around a joint of marijuana as the helicopter door gunners fire loudly and repeatedly and the Chinook bounces and makes abrupt drops in altitude. As the helicopter approaches its destination, Jim Pederson, a soldier who had been a former Christian missionary in KENYA, holds his stomach and squeezes his eyes shut. Flying scares Pederson more than the war does. The helicopter crew chief counts off the remaining minutes until the men will be forced to jump out in the hot

landing zone, while bullets begin to whiz into the metal hull and tear openings in the ceiling and floor. The Chinook shakes violently, throwing the men against one another and even onto the floor. When the crew chief signals it is time, the soldiers, all except for Pederson, jump out one by one into the marshy rice paddy below, bullets hurtling around them from the door gunners' incessant firing. As the Chinook begins to rise, the crew chief drags Pederson to the ramp and throws him into the paddy as well. But before he can wade very far out, Pederson is cut down by several rounds of the bullets. He is shot by friendly fire first in the legs, then in the groin and stomach. Lying on his back in the paddy, Pederson calmly raises his rifle, takes careful aim at the departing helicopter and fires at it several times before it disappears into the distance, only the sound of its rattling guns remaining.

COMMENTARY

"Landing Zone Bravo" is a story that clearly illustrates the extremes of warfare. The icy cold that Paul Berlin experiences while far above the ground in the Chinook helicopter contrasts the hot landing zone that the copter is flying into as well as the sweltering landscape of the jungles and rice paddies of Vietnam where the men fight. The overwhelming machinery of war—the automatic weapons; the "greasy and mechanical" (72) smells of the helicopter; the roaring metal blades of the rotor; the sharp, high-pitched whine of bullets tearing into the sides of the Chinook —contrast with the natural muck of the paddies, the clumps of rice bent double in the wind, and the fragile flesh of the human body. The racket of the guns fired continually by the door gunners punctuates nearly every paragraph of the story, serving as a chorus that emphasizes the unnatural and forbidding environment that Paul Berlin finds himself in.

It is in this environment that Berlin and his fellow soldiers attempt to control their fear. Berlin tells himself that it is the cold he objects to, that the cold, rather than fear, is responsible for the "bad feeling" (73) he has as the men are transported into battle. Other soldiers are depicted trying to distract themselves by ordinary activities such as inspecting their fingernails or drinking Cokes. They are leery of making eye contact with one another, since, as in many O'Brien works, the shame of being thought a coward may be even worse than being a coward. When Pederson visibly displays his fear, clutching his stomach and squeezing his eyes tightly shut, the other men "tried not to look at him" (72), reluctant to shame him further, or perhaps afraid of being unable to hold in their own fear any longer. Oscar Johnson attempts to inject an air of ordinariness into the scene by lighting up a joint of marijuana and passing it down the row of soldiers lining the Chinook's belly. Perhaps Oscar hopes as well that the marijuana will mellow the mens' fear, much as the tranquilizers Ted Lavender ingests in "How to Tell a True War Story" calm his nerves.

The story depicts, as well, the randomness of war deaths, a common theme in the literature of the Vietnam War. Jim Pederson is a good man, a moral man. He had served previously as a Christian missionary in KENYA, and Berlin thinks to himself that there is nothing "zealous or stupid" (73) about Pederson. Berlin, in fact, likes the man as much as he likes any of the other soldiers. Pederson's basic decency is highlighted even more when O'Brien rewrites the story for inclusion in *Going After Cacciato*. Except for his fear of noise and machines and height, Pederson in the novel version of "Landing Zone Bravo" is described as being "otherwise a fine soldier" (GAC 127). Elsewhere in the novel, he is said to be the most trusted member of Third Squad, and thus he is given the responsibility for triggering ambushes. He is a compassionate man as well, who offers aid to a dying VIET CONG woman and who writes a letter home to Billy Boy Watkins's parents after the young man dies of fright. It seems unjust that a basically brave and moral soldier should die as a result of his fear and even more unjust that he should be cut down by friendly fire when he represents in many ways the exemplary American soldier. But, as is often the case in Vietnam War literature, death comes randomly and indiscriminately and is more a matter of bad luck than of bad soldiering.

Pederson's essential helplessness against the machinery of war is depicted when he calmly lies on his back, mortally wounded, and fires up at the giant, departing helicopter. The bullets from his rifle ricochet harmlessly off the helicopter's "great underside" (77), a single gunner ineffective against the automatic weapons from the large metal bird that strafes the paddy, turning it into a frothy, boiling cauldron. The might of the machinery is driven home when the sound of the automatic weapons can still be heard even as the helicopter itself has disappeared from sight. Pederson's turning of his weapon against the American military machine is indicative of another common trope in Vietnam War literature: that of the war being fought essentially among American soldiers themselves rather than against a Vietnamese enemy. As Katherine Kinney points out in her fascinating book-length study, *Friendly Fire: American Images of the Vietnam War,* the common scenes of fragging (*see* FRAG), friendly fire deaths, and fights between doves and hawks, which appear in American literature about the war, suggest the country's internal turmoil and divisions over Vietnam. The war, Kinney argues, is often depicted as a battleground that pits Americans against Americans and elides the Vietnamese presence. One of the books she examines in her study is *Going After Cacciato,* which revolves around the fragging of a young lieutenant named Sidney Martin. Jim Pederson's story in "Landing Zone Bravo" introduces the trope of friendly fire that will figure so prominently in the later novel.

Differences in Versions
The story "Landing Zone Bravo" appears in *Going After Cacciato* with only minor changes. Some of the characters who appear in the story are missing in the novel's version. No soldier named Dakota or Toby Hiffler appears anywhere in the novel. And Bernie Lynn, who appears on the Chinook in the story version, is omitted in the version that appears in *Cacciato,* most likely because he seems to have died in the tunnels *before* Jim Pederson dies during the combat assault (CA). The novel's version also adds a soldier on the Chinook

who does not appear in the story—Rudy Chassler. Other than these minor character changes, most of O'Brien's later edits work to tighten and condense the original language of the story. For instance, the novel omits the details of Pederson having served as a missionary in Kenya (Pederson's Christian background has already been established elsewhere in the novel) and this version of the story is generally less explicit and more suggestive than the earlier version. Pederson's getting shot is also condensed quite a bit in the novel. In the story readers see bullets hit him four distinct times, while in the novel he is shot only twice by the door gunners. Language that could perhaps be considered too flowery, such as the phrase about the helicopter blades stirring "creamy white caps" (76), which appears at the end of the story, is removed as well. At other times, details and dialogue are expanded somewhat to make the story more realistic and specific. For example, the crew chief's magazine is specifically identified as *Newsweek* in the novel, and some of his language more clearly utilizes G.I. slang. As the helicopter approaches the landing area, for instance, the chief says, "She's hot kiddies . . ." and he orders the men not to display any "dilly-dally shit" (GAC 129), language that does not appear in the original story.

But perhaps the most interesting addition to the story in the novel occurs not in the story itself but later in the book, when readers see how much Paul Berlin is affected by his war memories. Despite his best attempts to repress these memories, they constantly arise and work their way into his mind, shaping his imagined story.

CHARACTERS

Berlin, Paul Paul Berlin is the protagonist of *Going After Cacciato*, the 1978 O'Brien novel that portrays Berlin's memories and imagination during a long night on guard duty in November of 1968. In "Landing Zone Bravo," Berlin is a young, frightened soldier who witnesses the death by friendly fire of fellow soldier Jim Pederson after their unit is choppered into a firefight during a combat assault (CA) mission. The story, only slightly rewritten,

appears as one of Berlin's war memories in the later novel.

Buff Mentioned only briefly in "Landing Zone Bravo," Buff is a soldier who sits between Doc Peret and Nystrom on the CHINOOK combat assault (CA) helicopter. His role is expanded a bit when the story is rewritten as part of the novel *Going After Cacciato*, where he bites his nails nervously as the big helicopter dips and sways.

Cacciato The title character who simply walks away from the war in O'Brien's 1978 novel, *Going After Cacciato*, planning to march all the way to PARIS, Cacciato is mentioned only twice in the story "Landing Zone Bravo." He first appears in the opening paragraph of the story sharing a Coke on the CHINOOK transport helicopter with another soldier named Vaught. He is later depicted following a fellow soldier named Dakota out of the helicopter and into a Vietnamese rice paddy as bullets fly all around.

Crew Chief A fat crew chief who has jiggling flesh under his neck, reads a magazine while the Chinook helicopter dips and rattles. As the time approaches for the men to jump out of the helicopter into the rice paddy below, the crew chief puts his magazine away in his pocket and begins counting down the remaining minutes. The ride gets rougher, however, and the wind sucks the man's magazine out of the ramp of the helicopter. When they reach the landing zone, the crew chief pushes the men toward the ramp and shoves them off the chopper, his face green. He screams at someone to pull Pederson off when the frightened soldier remains seated with his eyes shut.

Dakota Dakota is one of the American soldiers on the CHINOOK helicopter. Readers see Bernie Lynn passing him a marijuana cigarette originally lit up by Oscar Johnson, and he is said to exit the helicopter into the rice paddy just before Cacciato. Dakota, however, no longer appears in the story when it is rewritten as part of *Going After Cacciato*.

Door Gunners   As the American squad of soldiers is choppered into a firefight in a hot landing zone, unnamed door gunners on the CHINOOK transport helicopter repeatedly fire their automatic weapons. The firing guns become almost a chorus to the story, punctuating everything else that happens. The door gunners themselves wear sunglasses and have black arms; they seem almost inhuman in their relentless firing, not stopping even after they accidentally shoot down soldier Jim Pederson in the Vietnamese rice paddy below.

Harris, Stink   Stink Harris nervously clicks his teeth together aboard the CHINOOK as the American soldiers are being transported to the firefight. When the helicopter crew chief signals it is time for the men to jump out, Stink is the first one on the ground. In the novel *Going After Cacciato*, Stink Harris serves as the point man in the squad that follows Cacciato out of Vietnam.

Hiffler, Toby   Toby Hiffler is an American soldier who is mentioned only once in the story, when he is said to jump off the assault helicopter after Buff and right before Paul Berlin. Hiffler does not appear in the novel *Going After Cacciato*.

Johnson, Oscar   One of the soldiers aboard the CHINOOK helicopter, Oscar Johnson is said to be "sweating silver on his black face" (72) during the rough transport. Oscar is also the soldier who lights a marijuana cigarette and passes it down the row of men on either side of the Chinook's belly. In *Going After Cacciato*, Oscar Johnson is the buck sergeant for Third Squad who takes charge of the men after he organizes the fragging (see FRAG) death of Lieutenant Sidney Martin.

Lazzutti, Eddie   Eddie Lazzutti is mentioned only briefly in the story as being one of the soldiers aboard the CHINOOK helicopter that is making its way into a hot landing zone in Vietnam. Lazzutti is described as twisting his neck around on his shoulders, "as if loosening up for a race" (72). In *Going After Cacciato*, Eddie Lazzutti is a member of Third Squad, the group that chases deserting soldier Cacciato all the way to Paris. He is renowned for his beautiful singing voice in the novel.

Lynn, Bernie   Bernie Lynn is mentioned in "Landing Zone Bravo" as one of the men who takes a puff on the marijuana cigarette that Oscar Johnson passes around. Bernie gets up from his row, crosses the aisle, and hands the joint to a soldier named Dakota, sitting across from him. Bernie is also said to be one of the last men who gets off the combat assault (CA) helicopter, following Paul Berlin into the bullet-riddled rice paddy. When O'Brien rewrites the story for the novel *Going After Cacciato*, however, Bernie Lynn no longer appears. Bernie Lynn most likely died in the tunnels near the SONG TRA BONG River before Pederson died in the combat assault.

Murphy, Harold   Harold Murphy is one of the American soldiers aboard the assault helicopter. He takes the marijuana cigarette from Dakota, then passes it down the row of men until it eventually comes to Paul Berlin. When the helicopter begins to dip and shake violently as it is fired upon, Murphy falls down onto the floor and cannot get up. He shakes his head and smiles as he makes it to his knees, only to fall down again. Nevertheless, Murphy does make it off the helicopter when it reaches the landing zone. He is the last soldier off except for Jim Pederson, who has to be dragged to the ramp and thrown down by the crew chief. In *Going After Cacciato*, Harold Murphy is the member of Third Squad who carries "the big gun." He disappears from the group chasing Cacciato, apparently having decided to return to the unit's base in CHU LAI, shortly after the squad crosses into LAOS and commits themselves to the pursuit of the AWOL soldier.

Nystrom   One of the American soldiers on the assault helicopter, Nystrom is mentioned only once in the story, when he is said to be sitting next to a soldier named Buff. In *Going After Cacciato*, Nystrom is a radio operator who gets sent home from the war after shooting himself in the foot.

Old Lieutenant In "Landing Zone Bravo," the officer commanding the squad of men that is being transported on the CHINOOK helicopter is described as an "old lieutenant" who sits on the floor, "leaning low and wiping dust from his rifle, his lips moving as if talking to it" (73). In the novel version, the word *old* is removed, suggesting that the lieutenant in the novel version is Sidney Martin, not Lieutenant Corson, who replaces him. This makes sense, since Martin is still in command when Pederson dies. Martin will be fragged (*see* FRAG) by his own men later in the novel after they march up the mountains and into LAKE COUNTRY.

Pederson, Jim Jim Pederson is a soldier who is deathly afraid of flying. A man who had formerly been a missionary for the Church of Christ in KENYA, Pederson remains seated, clutching his stomach, licking his lips, and squeezing his eyes tightly shut, seemingly unaware of the chaos surrounding him, as the CHINOOK helicopter transporting the American soldiers on a combat assault (CA) missions dips and rattles and gets struck by sniper fire. When the crew chief orders the soldiers to jump out into the rice paddies below, Pederson remains curled into himself and has to be dragged to the ramp and thrown off the helicopter. He is struck repeatedly by friendly fire from the helicopter's door gunners as he begins to wade out into the paddy. Eventually lying on his back in the muck, Pederson carefully aims his rifle into the sky and shoots at the belly of the departing helicopter until it disappears from view. Pederson dies the same way in *Going After Cacciato*, but his character is more fully developed in the novel, where he is depicted as a deeply moral man who gives aid to a dying VIET CONG woman and writes a letter home to the parents of Billy Boy Watkins, who dies of a heart attack on the field of battle.

Peret, Doc While Doc Peret is one of the most important characters in the later novel *Going After*

Cacciato, into which the story "Landing Zone Bravo" is incorporated, he plays only a minor role in the story as initially published. Doc is depicted sitting next to Jim Pederson on the CHINOOK assault helicopter, and he later tells the soldier Vaught to shut up when he begins to giggle uncontrollably. Doc Peret is the second man out of the helicopter, right behind Stink Harris, when it lands briefly to discharge the American soldiers.

Vaught Vaught is one of the men aboard the CHINOOK helicopter that is transporting a group of American soldiers into a firefight in Vietnam. He is originally depicted sharing a Coke with another soldier named Cacciato. Later, as the flight becomes increasingly tense and dangerous, Vaught will begin giggling uncontrollably, unable to stop even when told to shut up by Doc Peret. In *Going After Cacciato*, Vaught is Cacciato's friend who is sent to a hospital in Japan after developing an infection in his arm.

"Little People" (2001)

Originally published in *Esquire* magazine in October 2001, "Little People" tells the story of recent DARTON HALL COLLEGE graduate Jan Huebner, who, in the summer of 1969, begins a secret career as a nude model in pornographic photographs. The story was later revised and included as chapter 5 of the novel *July, July*.

SYNOPSIS

Jan Huebner, a homely young woman who graduated from Darton Hall College in June 1969, spends the summer after her graduation performing street theater with a group of anti–Vietnam War protesters. When she is approached one day by an extremely short young man with an unusually large head, who offers her $50 if she will pose for erotic photographs, she is suspicious at first but pleased to earn the extra money. After this initial session, word on the street gets around, and Jan begins to take on many new clients. She eventually buys some professional photography lights and adopts the street name Veronica, earning a tidy sum from her new business. One night in late July, the short young man who had originally propositioned Jan, Andrew Henry Wilton, shows up at her apartment and threatens to send compromising pictures of her to her mother unless she pays him a large sum of money. In the course of their conversation, Andrew drops his blackmail scheme and instead invites Jan to his upcoming birthday party, with the condition that she pose as his date. At the party Andrew introduces Jan to his tall, good-looking younger brother, Richard. Jan and Richard begin to date, and eight months later, the couple marry. Jan spends the next 29 years of her life being ridiculed by her cruel and philandering husband.

COMMENTARY

The title "Little People" certainly plays on the height of Andrew Henry Wilton since he is, literally, a very small man, standing only four feet, seven inches tall, whose abnormal shortness has rendered him bitter and angry. But the title suggests that the characters in the story are small-minded, selfish people as well. The story is set against the large, wide-ranging backdrop of political, cultural, and historic changes taking place in the summer of 1969. There is a war raging in Vietnam, in which more than 3,000 American soldiers and more than 7,000 Vietnamese will have been killed that summer alone. By the end of summer, Neil Armstrong will have landed on the Moon. Sharon Tate will have been murdered. The Woodstock music festival will be shaping up. Yet, the characters in the story, as people everywhere are wont to do, care more about their minor, petty dramas than these large events sweeping the nation and the world. As O'Brien writes, "But for Jan Huebner, as for most others, the late summer of 1969 would later call to mind not headlines, nor global politics, nor even a war, but small, modest memories of small, modest things—rumpled beds and ringing telephones and birthday cakes and dirty pictures and catchy tunes about everyday people" (188).

While O'Brien does not condemn his characters for living ordinary lives in the midst of tumultuous times, he does point out the troubling ironies in what the Vietnam War means for both Jan Huebner and Andrew Henry Wilton. Jan feels that the new connections she makes to a group of antiwar protesters her senior year in college save her life. For the first time, she meets a group of people who genuinely seem to like her and whom she likes and respects in turn. The war for Jan is a "miracle" (100). The "morbid irony" of her situation is that "indiscriminate slaughter had given her a life. Napalm had made her happy" (100). Despite the fact that one of her college friends will be severely injured in Vietnam later in the summer and that another will grow increasingly bitter and hate-filled after fleeing to Canada, she secretly wishes that the war would never end. While Jan is a sympathetic character in many ways, she profits personally from the war, and her antiwar activities thus seem hypocritical, as Andrew Henry Wilton will suggest with his condemnation of "goo-brain liberal[s]" (105) and his labeling of Jan as "just one more pigeon from the burbs" (104).

But Andrew himself, with all his tough talk and scorn for peaceniks and liberal politics, is no better than Jan herself. His short stature gives him something of a Napoleon complex. He has, in fact, longed to be a warrior his whole life, to hurt others. He attempts to enlist in the war more than once, not because of patriotism or because he believes in fighting Communists but because he wishes to perpetrate mass violence: He is "dying to kill people, dying to get killed," to "cut off testicles and grease folks every which way" (105). While Jan uses the war for emotional fulfillment—she cries over events in Vietnam and is comforted by good-looking men in her group of friends, Andrew sees the war as a way to fulfill his emotional neediness as well and to express his rage for his physical deformities. Both Jan and Andrew are, indeed, "little people" in this respect. And Andrew's brother, Richard, as Andrew well knows, despite his service in the war, despite his good looks and his medals, is a little person as well. Intrigued by Jan's adventures in pornography, he never really looks carefully at his fiancée until their honeymoon in Hawaii, when he sees for the first time through the lens of his camera her "sunken jaw and muddy brown hair and scrawny legs" (188). He will make her pay for her unattractiveness throughout the 29 years of their marriage, mocking her cruelly, sleeping with other woman, and finally walking out on her in 1999.

A story about how fantasies do not match up to real life, O'Brien in "Little People" writes a fractured fairy tale. Jan Huebner is not any more the beautiful Snow White of the children's story than Andrew Henry Wilton is one of the charming and grateful dwarves who set up house with the beautiful princess. Richard Wilton is anything but the handsome Prince Charming, come to awaken the princess with a kiss, to marry her, and to whisk her away to live happily ever after. The sexy, tough Veronica of Jan's alternative life turns out to be a fantasy as well. While Jan might not experience the "Jack the Ripper" treatment from one of the "street scum" (104) that she poses for as Andrew predicts, she nevertheless ends up paying a very high price for her summer fantasies. As the last sentence of the story suggests, the dwarf "sticks it to" (188) Snow White in the end.

Differences in Versions
The changes that O'Brien made to the original story when it was published as part of *July, July* involve mostly small alterations to specific words and phrases here and there. The menace presented by Andrew Henry Wilton is toned down a bit in the novel; O'Brien removes much of the profanity that the character uses in the original story during his first two meetings with Jan Huebner. Other minor changes involve Jan losing 15 pounds in college after meeting the antiwar crowd rather than the 12 pounds she loses in the original story; Richard Wilton becomes nine years rather than seven years younger than his brother, Andrew; and Jan drives a Chrysler in her married life rather than a Volvo. O'Brien, as well, changes some historical references. In the section where Andrew invites Jan to his birthday party, for instance, he refers to liberal girls as "RFK babes" rather than "Clean Gene babes" as he does in the original story, and he says that he sleeps with more women than

"Mick Jagger" rather than "Martin Luther King." The only other significant change is that Andrew's desire for revenge is motivated a bit more fully in the novel since Jan insults him more directly when she believes he is asking her for sex. In the novel, Jan says she doesn't "do that . . . Not if you grew ten inches. Not if you came up to my belly-button" (*July* 69), while in the original story, she replies "Not in ten billion years" (104), not making a specific comment about Andrew's height.

CHARACTERS
Haslo, Paulette Paulette Haslo is mentioned only briefly in the story as one of the antiwar movement friends that Jan Huebner makes her senior year at DARTON HALL COLLEGE.

Huebner, Jan Jan Huebner is a 22-year-old woman performing guerrilla theater on the streets of the Twin Cities during the summer of 1969 when readers first meet her. A recent graduate of DARTON HALL COLLEGE, Jan is a homely young woman who learned early in life to survive by making jokes and being a clown. During her senior year in college, though, she had become involved in the antiwar movement. For the first time in her life Jan felt she belonged with a group of people she genuinely liked and admired. Making a living as a street performer turns out to be difficult, however, and Jan is tempted into posing nude in exchange for quick money when an abnormally short young man named Andrew Henry Wilton propositions her on the street one day. This photography session eventually leads to steady work with a number of seedy clients who pay her $50 per photo shoot. Jan soon adopts the street name Veronica and starts to build an impressive bank account. One night in late July, however, Andrew Henry Wilton arrives at Jan's apartment drunk and angry and threatening extortion—he says that he will send erotic photographs of Jan to her mother unless she pays him a large sum of money. Andrew eventually retreats on his threat, though, instead making Jan promise to attend his birthday party, which is to take place in a few days. At the party, where Jan initially poses as Andrew's date, the short young man introduces her to his younger, taller, better-looking brother,

Richard. Jan eventually marries Richard and lives a hellish life for the next 29 years as her husband continually taunts her for being ugly and sleeps with numerous other women. Jan often wonders whether Andrew had set her up all along—gaining his revenge for her lack of interest in him not through blackmail as he had originally planned, but by introducing her to Richard and effectively ruining her life.

Huebner, Mrs. Jan Huebner's mother, recognizing that comedy was her daughter's "special gift," used to brag that her girl was "Ugly as North Dakota," but that she could "squeeze a laugh out of a Lutheran" (98).

McMann, Billy Billy McMann is one of the close friends that Jan Huebner makes her senior year at college when she becomes involved in the antiwar movement. Billy is part of a group of people who sincerely liked Jan and "whom she genuinely liked back" (100).

Robinson, Amy Amy Robinson is a member of Jan Huebner's antiwar group of friends at DARTON HALL COLLEGE. After becoming involved with this group of people that she genuinely likes and admires, Jan drops several pounds, develops a new sense of self-confidence, and feels almost attractive for the first time in her life.

Veronica Veronica is the street name that Jan Huebner adopts when she begins to lead a double life in the summer of 1969 posing for pornographic photographs.

Wilton, Andrew Henry Andrew Henry Wilton is the name of the extremely short, large-headed young man who initially approaches Jan Huebner on the streets of Minneapolis and offers her $50 for a nude photo session. Standing only four feet, seven inches tall, Andrew is bitter about his handicap, and he seems to have developed a special hatred for activists in the antiwar movement, particularly naïve young suburban women whom he feels treat him condescendingly. He himself had wanted to enlist as a soldier in Vietnam but had been laughed at by army recruiters because of his size. Andrew expresses his anger in self-deprecating comments; he refers to himself as a "dwarf" and to Jan as "Snow White," although he also taunts the young woman for her own unattractiveness. Initially, he plans to punish Jan by blackmailing her but soon schemes instead to introduce her to his younger brother, Richard, understanding his brother's appeal to women. When Richard and Jan marry, Andrew's revenge against "Snow White" is complete—Jan's new husband turns her life into a living hell. He constantly belittles his wife and sleeps with any number of other women during their 29-year marriage.

Wilton, Mrs. The son of normal-sized parents, Andrew Henry Wilton tells Jan Huebner a story about his mother looking down at him when he was a child and saying, "Oh, well, no big deal" (102) in a sad attempt at comedy.

Wilton, Richard Richard Wilton is a decorated Vietnam War veteran who is seven years younger than his brother, Andrew Henry Wilton, as well as tall, tan, good-looking, and charming. Andrew manipulates Richard and Jan Huebner into getting married, hoping to gain revenge on both of them—his brother for having the looks and service record that Andrew desires for himself, and Jan for what he considers her politically liberal naivety and lack of sexual interest in him. Richard seems surprised during his honeymoon to find himself married to a homely woman, and he proceeds to fulfill Andrew's scheme by tormenting Jan with cruel comments about her looks and cheating on her throughout their long marriage.

"The Lives of the Dead" (1989)

First published in January 1989 in *Esquire* magazine, "The Lives of the Dead" tells the story of narrator Tim O'Brien's first days in the Vietnam War. This story is juxtaposed with memories of his nine-year-old girlfriend who died of a brain tumor when

O'Brien was in fourth grade. "The Lives of the Dead" was later revised and included as the final story in the collection *The Things They Carried*.

SYNOPSIS

The story begins by describing the fourth day in the Vietnam War of an American soldier named Tim O'Brien. His platoon takes some sniper fire from a small village near the SOUTH CHINA SEA. None of the American soldiers are hurt, but Lieutenant Jimmy Cross calls in an air strike, which ends up killing an old Vietnamese man, who is found lying faceup near a village pigpen. The American soldiers prop the man up in a sitting position and one by one go up to shake the dead man's hand. O'Brien, new to the war and sickened by the death, refuses to participate in the ritual. When another soldier named Kiowa praises him for not joining in with the others, O'Brien replies that the old man reminds him in a strange way of a nine-year-old girl he used to know, named Linda.

The story then moves into the past, to 1956, when O'Brien is in the fourth grade. He tells readers about Linda, a girl in his class at school whom he loved deeply. Linda is the first girl he ever went on a date with; Tim's parents take the nine-year-olds to the movies one night, where they see the WORLD WAR II film THE MAN WHO NEVER WAS. Although Tim does not realize it at first, Linda is sick with a brain tumor, and she wears a stocking cap everywhere she goes to hide her stitches and her loss of hair. O'Brien writes about being ashamed when he fails to protect Linda when a class bully pulls off her stocking cap at school. A few months after this incident, Linda dies of brain cancer. Tim has a difficult time accepting the death, even though he asks his father to take him to the funeral home, where he sees Linda's body in the casket. He spends the next several months imagining that Linda is alive again and speaking to her in dreams. Linda tells him that being dead is not that bad—that it is like being in a book high up on a library shelf that no one is reading. Eventually the story circles briefly back to the war, where O'Brien remembers piling dead bodies onto a truck. The story concludes in the present time, when O'Brien is a 41-year-old writer who is "still

Cliffton Webb and Josephine Griffin in a scene from *The Man Who Never Was* (Courtesy of Twentieth Century Fox Pictures)

dreaming Linda alive" (142) through the stories he writes.

COMMENTARY

As its title suggests, "The Lives of the Dead" is a story about death. It explores how human beings, both at war and on the home front, deal with the death—how they face it, how they try to manage their fear of it, and how the human imagination can possibly even overcome death. The portion of the story that takes place in Vietnam in 1969 depicts scared young American soldiers who have witnessed the deaths of enemy soldiers as well as of their platoon members and friends. These soldiers have learned to contain their fear and horror by laughing at their own mortality and that of others, by making jokes in order to control the enormity of death, such as the ritual of greeting when the soldiers shake the hand of an old Vietnamese man killed in a U.S. air strike. This gruesome ritual seems less callous when O'Brien explains that such joking is a way the soldiers retain their sanity amid the death and destruction they see all around them:

> In Vietnam, we had ways of making the dead seem not quite so dead. Shaking hands, that was one way. By slighting death, by acting, we pretended it was not the terrible thing it was. By our language, which was both hard and wistful, we transformed the bodies into piles of waste. Thus, when someone got killed, as Curt Lemon did, his body was not really a body, but rather one small bit of waste in the midst of a much wider wastage. (138)

And the American soldiers do not spare their own fallen comrades the jokes and hard language. When Ted Lavender dies, for instance, Mitchell Sanders holds an imaginary conversation with him, in which Lavender says the war is "mellow" (137) that day. While the story opens with narrator Tim O'Brien experiencing only his fourth day at war and thus unused to the men's joking and sickened by it, readers can see that the narrator has undergone some of the same hardening by the time that he is 41 years old and writing the story. While he says that he never shook hands in Vietnam— "not that" (142)—he does adopt what may seem a coarse and unsentimental way to describe death, writing that while at the war, "he climbed a tree and threw down what was left of Curt Lemon" and that he helped dig his friend Kiowa "out of the muck along the Song Tra Bong" (142).

These flat, nearly emotionless statements about the realities of death help to deglamorize war. In this respect, O'Brien shares much in common with a writer like ERNEST HEMINGWAY, whose character FREDERIC HENRY from A Farewell to Arms famously muses on the words *sacred, glorious, sacrifice,* and *in vain* after his experiences in World War I: "We had heard them . . . and had read them . . . and I had seen nothing sacred, and the things that were glorious had no glory and the sacrifices were like the stockyards at Chicago if nothing was done with the meat except to bury it. There were many words that you could not stand to hear and finally only the names of places had real dignity." The Tim O'Brien character in "The Lives of the Dead" simi-

larly works to debunk notions of heroism or self-sacrifice often associated with war. When Kiowa praises Tim for refusing to shake hands with the dead Vietnamese man, saying that such an action took guts, O'Brien disagrees: "It wasn't guts. I was scared" (136). Kiowa recognizes the slippery nature of courage and fear when he replies, "Same difference" (136). As in many O'Brien works, the line between courage and fear is fine and difficult to determine. Men act bravely sometimes because they are simply afraid or ashamed not to. In this instance in Vietnam, O'Brien's fear makes him behave morally, but earlier, when he was in fourth grade, his fear prevented him from standing up to Nick Veenhof, the boy who bullied Linda. The nine-year-old Tim watches Nick's actions as a spectator and wishes he could "do things" (137) he simply cannot not bring himself to: i.e., stand up to Nick. Further, O'Brien's inaction haunts him and still matters to him as a middle-aged writer: "I should've stepped in; fourth grade is no excuse. Besides, it doesn't get easier with time, and twelve years later, when Vietnam presented much harder choices, some practice at being brave might've helped a little" (137). Again, O'Brien deconstructs normal ideas of bravery and cowardice. For him, bravery is not something one is born with; a person is not simply either brave or a coward. Bravery is a learned behavior, a trait that requires practice and reflection and perhaps even conscious intent, as he suggests in his 1973 memoir, *If I Die in a Combat Zone, Box Me Up and Ship Me Home.*

While the story depicts soldiers who attempt to diminish death by mocking it, as well as those who desire to behave bravely, thus controlling their fear of death, storytelling is the method of containing death that O'Brien is most interested in. "The Lives of the Dead" opens with the sentence: "But this, too, is true: stories can save us" (134). It is an odd opening line, suggesting an offstage argument already in progress that readers enter into the middle of. We might wonder: What is the first true thing that this statement refers to? Perhaps it is the very fact of death itself, implied in the title of the story, so that the interrupted train of thought might run like this: Death is true, death is inevitable, or, as Mitchell Sanders asserts later in the story: "Death sucks" (142). But if this is true, it is also true that stories can offer some kind of redemption. After "The Lives of the Dead" was revised and appeared in the longer collection *The Things They Carried,* this opening line could be read as a response or a counterargument to the proposition O'Brien puts forth in the collection's opening story, that "Imagination was a killer" (*TTTC* 11). In that story, Lieutenant Jimmy Cross feels that he must dismiss and close down his imagination because he was dreaming of Martha, a girl back home, when Ted Lavender was shot. In "The Lives of the Dead," however, imagination has been transformed from a killer into a savior, as O'Brien is able to bring people back to life through storytelling. "The thing about a story," O'Brien writes, "is that you dream it as you tell it, hoping that others might then dream along with you, and in this way memory and imagination and language combine to make spirits in the head. There is the illusion of aliveness" (136).

Discussing the writing of *The Things They Carried* in an interview with Michael Coffey of *Publishers Weekly,* O'Brien elaborates on the way that stories can create this feeling of aliveness:

> What I discovered in the course of writing this book is the reason I love story; not just for its titillation, its instant gratification of what next, what next, but for the livingness that's there as you read and that lingers afterward. Jake Barnes is alive for me. Though he is a fictional character in the taxicab at the end of *The Sun Also Rises,* he is alive in that cab with Brett. That's what I love about writing them and reading them—that quality of immortality that a story is—doesn't contain—just is.

As O'Brien tells stories of Curt Lemon and Kiowa and Linda, it is as if they are alive again, at least for a little while.

But O'Brien is also careful to make it clear that his stories are fiction and are to be read as such. Storytelling is different than memory. Rather than simply remembering his dead friends, O'Brien creates them anew in his stories. The Linda he describes in "The Lives of the Dead," O'Brien cautions readers, is "not the embodied Linda" (142).

Although she may be based on a real little girl who died of a brain tumor in WORTHINGTON, MINNESOTA, in 1956—LORNA LUE MOELLER—Linda in the story is "mostly made-up, with a new identity and a new name, like the man who never was" (142). O'Brien, throughout his fiction, insists on the value of pretending, of the human imagination as a creative agent.

In the film *The Man Who Never Was,* which Tim's parents take him and Linda to see in the story, a creative act of pretense actually helps win World War II for the allies. The main character in the film, O'Brien writes, "was a corpse" (137), a dead British soldier. But the Allies make a false identity for him, dressing him up like an officer and planting false documents in his pocket. The fiction is effective enough to fool the Germans and lead to an easier Allied landing in Italy. O'Brien in "The Lives of the Dead" is very much like the Allies in that his story also has corpses for main characters: the dead Vietnamese man, Kiowa, Ted Lavender, Linda, and others. But through fiction, O'Brien, too, can make these characters real and important people who can influence happenings in the actual world outside of the story.

While O'Brien in the Coffey interview demurs somewhat about his ideas concerning storytelling and aliveness—he apologetically concedes at one point that "These are hard things to talk about. It sounds mystical, and I'm not a mystical person"—he nevertheless concludes by expressing his hope that a story will preserve a life or even a constellation of lives that would otherwise have been lost, "like most lives are." And for O'Brien this is a miraculous happening, analogous, perhaps, to a religious miracle. In a story, O'Brien writes, he can "steal [Linda's] soul. . . . In a story, miracles can happen. Linda can smile and sit up. She can reach out, touch my wrist, and say, 'Timmy, stop crying'" (138). Through storytelling, O'Brien achieves an almost godlike power. As a young boy he loved Linda so intently that he "wanted to live inside her body" so that he and Linda could merge together and become like one person, with "no skin between" them (136). As a 41-year-old writer, O'Brien can indulge this human desire to completely know another person, to merge identities with a fellow human being. Through writing about Linda, he creates a new Linda, who is also part of himself. And finally, O'Brien tells readers in the story, it is himself that he is trying to save. His nine-year-old self, he writes, is, deep down, the same as his older self: "Inside the body, or beyond the body, there is something absolute and unchanging. The human life is all one thing: like a blade tracing loops on ice: a little kid, a twenty-three-year-old infantry sergeant, a middle-aged writer knowing guilt and sorrow" (138). By resurrecting his nine-year-old self, O'Brien can imagine that self healed and the healing extending into the life he lives now. While storytelling cannot embody Linda or Timmy physically, it can reimagine and recreate them.

Differences in Versions

O'Brien made very few changes in "The Lives of the Dead" when he revised the original *Esquire* story for publication in *The Things They Carried*. Perhaps most noticeable is the change of the story's present time from 1988 to 1990 and the age of the Tim O'Brien narrator from 41 to 43. In addition, he toned down a bit the language that appeared in the original story about wanting to sleep with Linda, live inside her skin, and become her. The revised version deletes a good portion of this passage, leaving only the lines: "Even then, at nine years old, I wanted to live inside her body. I wanted to melt into her bones—*that* kind of love" (*TTTC* 228). Finally, after the passage in which Ray Kiley describes Curt Lemon's Halloween trick-or-treating at the HOOTCH of a Vietnamese "Mama-san" and the narrator says that listening to Rat's stories one would never know that Curt was not alive, O'Brien adds a simple sentence: "But he was dead" (240). The only other changes are extremely minor and involve some new paragraph breaks and single words either deleted or substituted occasionally.

CHARACTERS

Cross, Lieutenant Jimmy   Lieutenant Jimmy Cross is the leader of Tim O'Brien's platoon during O'Brien's first days in the war in Vietnam. One afternoon in 1969, on O'Brien's fourth day in the war, the platoon receives sniper fire from a small village near the SOUTH CHINA SEA. Lieutenant

Jimmy Cross calls in an air strike, which ends up killing an old Vietnamese farmer.

Dobbins, Henry   Henry Dobbins is one of the soldiers in Tim O'Brien's platoon during his first days in the Vietnam War. When a U.S. air strike on a village kills an old Vietnamese man, who is found lying near a pigpen, Henry Dobbins is one of the American soldiers who goes over to shake the dead farmer's hand. He tells the dead man that he is "pleased as punch" (134) to meet him as he performs the hand-shaking ritual.

Jensen, Dave   Dave Jensen is one of the American soldiers in the platoon commanded by Lieutenant Jimmy Cross. Jensen is the first to go over to the old Vietnamese man, killed in the U.S. air strike, and shake his hand. He also badgers the raw young soldier, Tim O'Brien, to shake the man's hand as well: "Be polite now . . . Go introduce yourself. Nothing to be afraid about, just a nice old man. Show a little respect for your elders" (134). When O'Brien continues to refuse, Jensen suggests that maybe the death is "a little too real for him" (134) and O'Brien agrees.

Kiley, Rat   Rat Kiley is another of the soldiers in the Vietnam War platoon under the command of Lieutenant Jimmy Cross. Rat Kiley, following the lead of Dave Jensen, shakes the hand of the old Vietnamese farmer killed in a U.S. air strike. "Gimme five," he jokes as he bends over the corpse, telling the man that it is "a real honor" to meet him (134). Later in the story, O'Brien explains that the soldiers' joking is a way of slighting death, making it seem less important. He tells readers that the men used hard language to make death easier to handle. Rat Kiley, for instance, refers to a Vietnamese baby, burnt to death, as a "crunchie munchie" (138).

Kiowa   Kiowa is a fellow soldier in Tim O'Brien's platoon in Vietnam. After O'Brien refuses to shake the hand of the dead Vietnamese farmer, Kiowa offers the new and bewildered soldier a Christmas cookie and praises him for not participating in the ghoulish hand-shaking ritual. When Kiowa tells O'Brien that what he did "took guts," O'Brien replies, "It wasn't guts. I was sacred" (136). Kiowa shrugs and responds, "Same difference" (136). O'Brien then tells Kiowa that the dead farmer reminded him, strangely, of a girl he went to the movies with once, his first date. "Man . . . that's a bad date," the soldier replies. While Kiowa's death is not described in any detail in "The Lives of the Dead," the O'Brien narrator does inform readers that Kiowa died in the war. He recalls helping dig the soldier's body "out of the muck along the Song Tra Bong" (142). Kiowa is one of the soldiers that Tim O'Brien, as a 41-year-old writer can imagine alive again though telling stories.

Lemon, Curt Curt Lemon is one of the soldiers in Tim O'Brien's platoon who is killed in Vietnam. O'Brien writes that at the war the soldiers tried to make light of death by making jokes and using language that was "both hard and wistful" (138). When Lemon dies, then, "his body was not really a body, but rather one small bit of waste in the midst of a much wider wastage" (138). Later, readers discover a bit more about how Lemon died when O'Brien describes climbing a tree and throwing down "what was left of Curt Lemon" (142). Curt is also one of the soldiers that O'Brien, as a 41-year-old writer can imagine alive again through the stories he tells.

Linda Linda is a nine-year-old girl whom the Tim O'Brien narrator describes going on a date with in the fourth grade. Despite suffering from a brain tumor, Linda shows extreme composure, even when teased by her classmates about the stocking cap she wears to hide her baldness and the stitches from surgery. Linda dies a few months after going to the movies with Tim, but the young boy pretends through his imagination and his dreams that she is still alive. The character of Linda is based on a real 10-year-old girl whom the author knew growing up in WORTHINGTON, MINNESOTA, who died of brain cancer: LORNA LUE MOELLER.

O'Brien, Mr. and Mrs. The narrator's mother and father take Tim and Linda on a date to see THE MAN WHO NEVER WAS in the spring of 1956, when the children are in fourth grade. Later, Tim's mother will explain to him that Linda has a brain tumor and will not get better. Mr. O'Brien will take his young son to see Linda's body at the funeral home after her death.

O'Brien, Tim Tim O'Brien is the name of the first-person narrator who tells the story of his first few days at the war as well as of Linda's death from a brain tumor. The Tim O'Brien character, however, (as will be made clear when the story is included in *The Things They Carried*), should not be confused with the real-life author Tim O'Brien, even though he, too, knew a girl in fourth grade who died of a brain tumor. But "The Lives of the Dead" is fiction, not autobiography. In many ways the O'Brien character in the story is like "the man who never was" in the movie that he and Linda watch. He is an invented character who connects his experiences before, during, and after the war in order to comment on the heartbreak and sorrow of human life in general but also on the power of the imagination to resurrect the dead and bring them back to life through memory and storytelling.

Sanders, Mitchell After an old Vietnamese villager is killed in a U.S. air strike on a small village, the soldiers in Tim O'Brien's platoon shake the dead old man's hand and prop him up against a fence. Mitchell Sanders places a can of orange slices in the old man's lap, saying gently, "Vitamin C . . . A guy's health, that's the most important thing" (134). Later, Sanders will also make jokes about his own dead friends. After Ted Lavender is shot, he looks over at the body wrapped in the green plastic poncho and says, "Hey Lavender . . . how's the war today?" (136). He continues to talk to the body until it is choppered away, with fellow soldiers responding in the supposed voice of Lavender. As O'Brien writes immediately after this incident, "That's what a story does. The bodies are animated. You make the dead talk" (137). The last time Mitchell Sanders appears in the story occurs when O'Brien remembers what he calls his "worst day at the war" (142). He and Sanders are assigned to load 27 dead enemy soldiers onto a truck. The two men work together to heave the bloated, smelly corpses up and into the truck bed.

When they finally complete this gruesome chore, Sanders quietly tells O'Brien that he just realized something: "Death sucks" (142).

Teacher The teacher of Tim O'Brien's fourth grade class is unable to stop Nick Veenhof from pulling off Linda's stocking cap because he carefully plans his assault by breaking his pencil and asking to use the sharpener. When the teacher tells Nick to hustle up, the boy begins to walk with an exaggerated limp, as slowly as possible. On the way back to his seat, Nick intentionally drops his pencil by Linda's desk and pulls off her cap after stooping to retrieve the fallen pencil.

Veenhof, Nick Nick Veenhof is the class bully who pulls Linda's stocking cap off her head in the fourth grade, exposing her bald head and dark black stitches to the entire class. Later, Nick and Tim will walk Linda home. Nick Veenhof is based on a real-life boy whom O'Brien knew in WORTHINGTON, MINNESOTA: MIKE TRACY.

Vietnamese Man When Lieutenant Jimmy Cross calls in an air strike on a small village near the SOUTH CHINA SEA after his platoon receives sniper fire, the only person killed is an old Vietnamese villager, who is found lying faceup near a pigpen at the center of the village. The American soldiers, as they attempt to make light of death, prop the old man up against a fence and take turns shaking his hand, asking about his health, and putting small gifts in his lap. Tim O'Brien, a raw young soldier who is only on his fourth day in the war, is sickened by the ritual and refuses to participate in it. He later tells a fellow soldier, Kiowa, that, in a strange way, the dead old Vietnamese man reminded him of a girl he dated in the fourth grade, Linda.

Vietnamese Woman Rat Kiley tells a story about his dead friend Curt Lemon going trick-or-treating in a Vietnamese village one Halloween. Wearing a ghost mask and painting his naked body all different colors, Curt goes into the HOOTCH of a young Vietnamese woman, whom Rat describes as a "cute little Mama-san" (138). Curt holds an

M-16 to the woman's head, strips off her pajamas, and takes them away with him. After telling this story, Rat grins and comments admiringly, "Lemon—there's one classy guy" (139). Readers clearly are meant to view this episode less admiringly than Rat does. Although never made clear in the tale, there exists a distinct possibility that Curt Lemon raped the young woman.

FOR FURTHER READING

Coffey, Michael. "Tim O'Brien." *Publisher's Weekly* 16 Feb. 1990: 60–61.

"Loon Point" (1993)

Originally published in *Esquire* magazine in January 1993, "Loon Point" tells the story of Ellie Abbott's affair with a dentist named Harmon who drowns in the waters off LOON POINT, Minnesota, during a secret tryst. The story was later revised and included in O'Brien's 2002 novel, *July, July*. Elements from the story are also included in the 1994 novel, *In the Lake of the Woods*, in which the political wife Kathy Wade also has an affair with a dentist named Harmon.

SYNOPSIS

One summer, when Ellie Abbott is 37 years old, she flies to Minneapolis from her home in Boston to spend a week at a resort called Loon Point with her lover, a married dentist named Harmon. Although Ellie still loves her husband, Jack, the romance has gone out of the marriage. Jack no longer pays much attention to Ellie, distracted by his working life. On the morning of their sixth day at Loon Point, Harmon drowns in the waters of the lake. Ellie feels more angry than sad, as if nature is conspiring against her. She is driven to the courthouse by a young policeman, whom she asks to be discreet about the extramarital affair, but sensing the young man's disapproval, Ellie remains silent for the remainder of the ride. Unable to answer questions from the coroner about whether Harmon had a history of heart trouble, she suggests that the dead man's immediate family would know more about the state of his health. The same young policeman drives Ellie back to her hotel and advises her to leave early the next morning because Harmon's family is scheduled to arrive. Back in Boston, Ellie feels empty and tired. During dinner, Jack asks polite, forced questions about her trip, easily accepting her lies about a high school reunion. Eventually, Ellie realizes that her husband never received her message that she would be a day late returning home—he did not even notice the delay. The story ends with Ellie standing outside in the twilight in her suburban garden, "wanting and wanting" (94), but unsure what it is that she wants.

COMMENTARY

While Harmon literally drowns in the waters off Loon Point, Ellie Abbott is figuratively drowning in a dying marriage and a passionless life. Her relationship with Harmon, in fact, seems to have been simply a distraction from the depression and lack of direction she feels in her Boston life. O'Brien writes that after Harmon's death it was hard for Ellie "to imagine a future for herself" (93). He adds, "In a way, it seemed, she was drowning in the flow of her own life, its little pools and currents. Ellie wanted something—she wanted it very badly—but she didn't know what" (93). The story, like the novel *July, July,* where it would later appear in a revised version, is largely about middle-aged disappointment, the compromises people make in life as they grow older, the dashed hopes and expectations of youth. No longer sure about what she wants, Ellie seems paralyzed by indecision. Things seem to simply happen to her; she is bereft of will. The affair itself "started almost by accident" (92), Ellie refusing to accept responsibility for her betrayal of her husband. In fact, she seems to be left without a moral compass altogether in the story, an ability to judge her own actions or the actions of others according to their rightness or wrongness. Ellie's initial reaction to Harmon's death illustrates this. Rather than sorrow, the overwhelming emotion she feels is one of being mistreated by the world: "She blamed the lake and Harmon and the morning sunlight. A conspiracy of nature, it seemed, and there was no sense of moral participation"

(92). Ellie feels like a passive victim rather than an active moral participant in her own life.

Ellie's refusal to judge the morality of her behavior makes her conversations with the young policeman in the story awkward and uncomfortable. As a representative of the law, and perhaps of conventional morality and authority, as well as a young man who has not yet experienced the disappointments and compromises associated with growing older, the policeman seems to disapprove of Ellie and refuses to let her off the hook for what happened. When she requests that Harmon's death be kept "confidential" (92), the young policeman deliberately misunderstands her meaning, replying that the police force does not often hide bodies. In addition, he reminds her of the risks that she took in engaging in the affair in the first place: "People play games, people get hurt" (92). Later, when he drives her back to Loon Point, the policeman insults Ellie by offering her money, implying, at least in Ellie's interpretation, that she was with Harmon for mercenary reasons. As he sits on the porch with her to drink tea, the policeman suggests that she strung Harmon along, evoking at least a partial agreement from Ellie. He seems skeptical, as well, when Ellie claims to love Jack, and he remains silent, "examin[ing] a spot over her shoulder" when she makes a second request that he keep her out of the investigation into Harmon's death. The policeman's youthful, upright, moral idealism contrasts with the older married woman's slide into moral ambiguity.

But while readers may judge Ellie Abbott harshly in the opening pages of the story, when she returns home to Boston they see the sad state of her marriage. Jack Abbott seems to be a decent man—he is kind to his wife and playful with her—but he also seems extremely self-centered, talking about his own work difficulties as Ellie prepares dinner, able to muster up only a polite, forced interest in her trip, and most tellingly of all, not even noticing that she has returned home from Minnesota a full day late. When she remembers a New Year's Eve dance 18 years ago, Ellie pictures the couples' younger selves and their excitement over new love. Jack kissed her back then as if "nothing else had mattered" (94). As a 37-year-old woman who has engaged in her second extramarital affair, however, Ellie realizes that "the reality of love was not what she had imagined it to be" (94), despite her repeated insistence to herself that she loves Jack and that she had also loved Harmon. The problem is not that she is with the wrong man; it is deeper than that. Ellie's problem is that she can no longer believe in the promise of love that she once felt.

Although the story ends in the garden of the Abbotts' suburban Boston home, amid the nasturtiums, astilbes, and phlox that Ellie had planted there, these growing things no longer give her the pleasure they once did. As Ellie has descended into the moral uncertainty and disappointment of middle age, flowers are no longer the right emblem to symbolize her marriage and her life. Rather, the dead thing that Harmon has become—the wet, fishy-white corpse that she saw—is a more fitting signpost for her. She is "feeling pretty soggy herself" as she is "struck by the terror of growing old and silly and insignificant" (94). While unburdening herself to Jack, discussing these feelings with him might have led to some relief, Ellie is unable to do so. When he comes out into the garden, teasingly calling her "gorgeous" and completely oblivious to how she is now more concerned with dead things than with growing things, Jack asks her, "How's the crop?" (94). Ellie, consumed with desire for something, but unsure what that something is, simply tightens her robe around her and replies that things are fine. Readers are left without much hope for the resurrection of this dying marriage.

Differences in Versions

O'Brien incorporates details of "Loon Point" into two of his later novels. Kathy Wade in *In the Lake of the Woods* has an affair with a dentist named Harmon just as Ellie Abbott does in this story. While the dentist in the novel does not drown, Kathy does meet him at a resort called Loon Point, although it is located in Maine rather than in Minnesota. Like Ellie, Kathy lies to her husband about her trip. And like Jack Abbott in the story, John Wade does not notice that his wife's travel plans have changed, although Kathy in the novel returns home earlier than expected rather than later. The scene from the story in which Ellie cooks hamburg-

ers and speaks to Jack appears in nearly identical form in the novel, with only the names of the characters and a few minor plot details changed.

O'Brien would later revise the story again and include it as a chapter titled "Loon Point" in the novel *July, July*. In this second version, which is set specifically in the summer of 1999, Ellie Abbott is 52 rather than 37 years old, and her husband's name is changed from Jack to Mark. Readers of the novel also find out a bit more background about Ellie, discovering that she is a DARTON HALL COLLEGE graduate, that she knew Harmon back in college, and that she worked as a waitress and a dance instructor before marrying Mark. But the most significant change in the novel *July, July* involves the character of the young policeman who drives Ellie to the courthouse, then back to the resort later in the day. While the policeman in the original story is interested in Ellie and seems to disapprove of her morality, the revised version of the character takes on a larger and more menacing significance in Ellie's life. After drinking tea with her on the porch of her cabin, he stands up and says, "Don't take this the wrong way, but I think you'd sleep with me in a flash. Down and dirty" (*July* 174), an incident that does not occur in the original *Esquire* story. Like other mysterious characters that appear throughout *July, July*, such as radio deejay Johnny Ever and ex-marine Fred Engelmann, the young policeman seems privy to Ellie's innermost secrets. He even tells her at one point that he is "what [she's] got instead of a conscience" (*July* 175). In addition, revised in *In the Lake of the Woods*, when Ellie sees a slim, neatly dressed young man get out of a car in her neighborhood, she believes it might be the policeman, somehow having mysteriously followed her home from Minnesota to Boston.

CHARACTERS

Abbott, Ellie   The story is told from the point of view of Ellie Abbott, a 37-year-old married woman from Boston whose husband's career seems to have taken on more importance to him than his marriage. Dissatisfied with her life, Ellie starts an affair with a dentist from Minneapolis named Harmon. The two arrange to spend a week together at a Minnesota resort called LOON POINT, where on the sixth day of the tryst Harmon drowns in the lake. Feeling more anger than sorrow and embarrassed about her awkward situation, Ellie asks a local policeman to be discreet about her affair. She leaves early in the morning the day after Harmon's death, wanting to avoid the dentist's wife and family, who are scheduled to arrive later that day. Back in Boston, Ellie is unsure how to feel. She is immensely tired and briefly considers confessing the entire affair to her husband, Jack. But when Jack arrives home from work, he does not even notice that Ellie has returned home a day late. She ends the evening despairingly, filled with desire for something, but not sure what it is that she wants.

Abbott, Jack   Readers never learn exactly what business Jack Abbott is in. He may be a lawyer or a businessman—he deals with important contracts and earns a six-figure salary. But, in any case, he seems so completely caught up in his career that he no longer has time for his wife. While Ellie repeatedly claims to still love Jack throughout the story, their love has changed from the romance of their early years together. After nearly 18 years of marriage, the two exist in separate worlds. Jack never suspects Ellie's unhappiness in the story; he remains ignorant about her affair and about the trauma of Harmon's death. He fails to even notice that his wife returns from her trip to Minneapolis a full day late.

Coroner   After Harmon's autopsy, the local coroner stops by to ask Ellie if the dentist had a history of heart trouble. When Ellie is unable to answer, not knowing enough about the man to respond, the coroner assesses the situation by studying Ellie's legs. He eventually nods and suggests that Harmon's health is something he "might better discuss with the immediate family" (92).

Harmon   Readers do not learn much about Ellie Abbott's lover, Harmon, in the story—only that he is a married dentist from Minneapolis whom Ellie has been having an affair with for the past seven months. When Harmon drowns off the waters of LOON POINT during a week-long tryst with Ellie

at a resort in northern Minnesota, his body seems repulsive to Ellie: "His eyelids were half open, his pupils like quartz. His arms and legs seemed oddly shrunken, out of proportion to the heavy chest and stomach. . . . Ellie wondered how she had ever come to care for such a man, someone so wet and dead, whose swimming trunks had slipped below the knees and whose buttocks looked wrinkled and fishy-white in the bright morning sunlight" (91). The coroner suspects that Harmon might have had a heart attack in the waves, but readers are never told more about why the man drowned so suddenly. Ellie is unsure about the condition of his heart and leaves his family to answer questions about the dentist's health.

Nancy   Nancy is the name of Jack Abbott's secretary at work. When he arrives home late for dinner the day Ellie returns from Minneapolis, Jack tells a story about Nancy mixing up a pile of contracts, which caused him to have to drive the contracts across town himself. "I'm a six-figure delivery boy," Jack complains.

Policeman   A young policeman drives Ellie Abbott to the courthouse to answer the coroner's questions about Harmon's death after he drowns off the waters of LOON POINT. Although the young man is polite and correct with Ellie, she suspects that he disapproves of her when she asks him to be discreet about the extramarital affair. Later, the policeman drinks tea with Ellie on the porch of her cabin at the resort, where Ellie tells him that she still loves her husband and claims to have loved Harmon as well.

"The Magic Show" (1991)

O'Brien's essay "The Magic Show" appeared in a 1991 book called *Writers on Writing,* an anthology that grew out of the annual Bread Loaf Writer's Conference in Middlebury, Vermont. In the essay, O'Brien compares the writer's craft to that of the magician. Both art forms rely on a sense of drama and enduring mystery.

SYNOPSIS

The essay begins with O'Brien reminiscing about his childhood love of magic. He liked the power associated with performing magic tricks, the ability to make miracles happen. He liked working on the craft of magic as well as the solitude of the magician. While he writes that he understood he was not performing "real" magic, but merely "trickery" (175), O'Brien nevertheless points out that when doing magic as a child, for a while at least, "what seemed to happen became a happening in itself" (175). But what most appealed to O'Brien about magic was the sense of "abiding mystery" it offered, a universe that seemed "infinite and inexplicable" (176), in which anything is possible. When he grew up, O'Brien gave up magic and took up a new hobby, writing stories, but he argues that the fundamentals of the two pursuits are the same: "Above all, writing fiction involves a desire to enter the mystery of things: that human craving to know what cannot be known" (176). A writer uses the power of language to create a "magic show of the imagination" (177); a writer can make the dead sit up and talk and can shine light into the mysteries of what it means to be human.

O'Brien goes on to argue that in many cultures the magician and the storyteller are embodied in a single person. In Christianity, for instance, Jesus was both a miracle worker and a teller of parables. Stories for O'Brien, then, are not mere entertainment, they serve a moral and spiritual function; they provide models for how humans might or might not live their lives. Good stories, he points out, also create a sense of "aliveness" for their characters, who are like spirits. While characters such as Jake Barnes or HUCK FINN were never embodied, they nevertheless live in the mind, just as "a dead father lives in the memory of his son" (178). Well-written characters live outside of ordinary reality, in the extraordinary realm of memory and imagination. The writer is the medium between these two different worlds. Writing, O'Brien continues, is "essentially an act of faith" (179). Writers must have faith in the power of the imagination, in the "fertility of dream" (179), in the notion that writing will lead to some kind

of enlightenment or understanding unavailable through empirical means.

The essay then moves on to examine more closely how two specific elements of fiction—plot and character—participate in an exploration of the deep mysteries of human life. Plot, according to O'Brien, revolves around mysteries of fact: a reader's desire to know what happened and what will happen next. "In this sense," O'Brien writes, "plot involves the inherent and riveting mystery of the *future*" (180). While acknowledging that he is arguing in defense of "old-fashioned plot" (180), O'Brien nevertheless argues that plots need not give an impression of finality. While readers crave knowledge, they also crave enigma, unsolved puzzles that raise new questions. Satisfying plots, for O'Brien, involve not a diminution of mystery but an enlargement of it. Character, in O'Brien's view, is similarly related to the mysterious—the human desire to truly know and understand other people, as well as the fundamental impossibility of doing so. Like plot, good characterization enhances mystery. Interesting, compelling characters are not achieved by a process of "pinning down" (182) what a person is like but through deepening and enlarging the riddle of human character. "What intrigues us, ultimately," O'Brien writes, "is not what we know but what we do not know and yearn to discover" (182). Like a good magician who does not give away his secrets, a good writer retains mystery. When tricks are explained, just as when plots or characters are tied up neatly, the world "moves from the magical to the mechanical" (182). For O'Brien, then, the object of a story is not to explain or resolve the mysteries of human existence, but "to create and perform miracles of the imagination" (183), to finally look into the self and pull up the mysteries in one's own heart.

COMMENTARY

The magic of fiction that O'Brien discusses in this essay—its ability to conjure possible worlds and give life to disembodied characters—is very much a theme that O'Brien explores throughout his fiction. It is perhaps first apparent in the 1978 novel, *Going After Cacciato,* in which much of the story takes place only in Paul Berlin's imagination. Berlin's ability to imagine characters and events in rich, vivid detail makes his story seem "real"—so real, in fact, that readers are usually not aware until many chapters into the novel that the pursuit of Cacciato is a story invented by Berlin during his night on the observation tower. Through the magic of his imagination, Berlin is able to make a character such as the young refugee Sarkin Aung Wan seem like a living, breathing human being, even though she is doubly fictional: invented by Berlin, who, in turn, is invented by O'Brien. Fiction's capacity to render a sense of aliveness to characters, to make the dead sit up and talk, is a theme O'Brien explores particularly in *The Things They Carried*. The final story of that collection, "The Lives of the Dead," begins with the sentence: "But this too is true: stories can save us" (225). The narrator, a 43-year-old writer also named Tim O'Brien, tells readers how he keeps dreaming his long-dead fourth grade girlfriend, Linda, alive again through stories. He is able to do the same for his dead friends and enemies from the Vietnam War—Ted Lavendar, Kiowa, Curt Lemon, a slim young Vietnamese man, and an old villager sprawled beside a pigpen. In a story, he writes, "which is a kind of dreaming, the dead sometimes smile and sit up and return to the world" (225). The writer, then, becomes more than just a storyteller. He is also a miracle worker who can resurrect the dead and create new life through the word.

Yet, the book of O'Brien's that this essay most fully illuminates and explicates is most likely the 1994 novel *In the Lake of the Woods*. In *Lake*, the young John Wade is an aspiring magician who loves the power and possibility of magic, just as in the essay O'Brien claims he did as a youth. Magic becomes a theme that runs throughout the novel, with the narrator citing sources such as ROBERT PARRISH's *The Magician's Handbook* in several of the evidence chapters, and speculating on the parallels between magic and politics—both of which are about transformations, trying to change existing realities. John Wade, who obtains the nickname "Sorcerer" during the war, also brings together the figure of the magician and the storyteller. He literally rewrites history, cutting and pasting actual documents from the war, in order to cover up the fact

that he was a member of CHARLIE COMPANY who participated in the MY LAI MASSACRE, magically making his own past disappear. The novel, as well, retains the enigma of plot that O'Brien discusses in the essay. Readers never discover what happens to Kathy Wade—the essential mystery of the novel is never tied up neatly for readers. It is enlarged rather than diminished by the multiple hypotheses the narrator provides to explain Kathy's disappearance.

But the central mystery at the heart of *In the Lake of the Woods* seems to be not so much its obvious refusal to resolve the plot but the perhaps even deeper mystery of human character. John Wade loves his wife, Kathy, intensely, so much so that he desires to *become* Kathy, to inhabit her body and mind, to know her more fully than is humanly possible. The narrator of the novel writes, "There were times when John Wade wanted to open up Kathy's belly and crawl inside and stay there forever. He wanted to swim through her blood and climb up and down her spine and drink from her ovaries and press his gums against the firm red muscle of her heart. He wanted to suture their lives together" (71). And the narrator himself, the self-proclaimed "biographer" or "historian" whom readers are introduced to in the novel's footnotes, has a similar desire to truly *know* John Wade. "What drives me on," he writes, "is a craving to force entry into another heart, to trick the tumblers of natural law, to perform miracles of knowing. It's human nature. We are fascinated, all of us, by the implacable otherness of others" (101). However, the narrator, like readers, winds up with a character who cannot be pinned down, just as O'Brien urges in the essay. Readers are left to wonder what made John Wade the man he became. Is John Wade's character—his desperate need to be loved, his keeping of secrets, his pretending—the result of his childhood? He was, after all, a lonely, overweight boy able to find comfort only in the world of magic and illusion. And his father was an alcoholic who hanged himself in the family garage. Or perhaps it was Wade's experiences in Vietnam, the death and brutality he witnessed on a daily basis, that made him the man he was. Or maybe his relationship with Kathy, his deep, possessive love for her, his fear of losing her, is what shaped John Wade most fully. The novel also raises the possibility that John Wade was simply born John Wade. As his mother, Eleanor, says in her interview with the novel's narrator, "It wasn't just the war that made him what he was. That's too easy. It was everything—his whole *nature* . . ." (27). In the essay O'Brien writes that "successful characterization requires an enhancement of mystery . . . What intrigues us, ultimately, is not what we know but what we do not know and yearn to discover" (182). *In the Lake of the Woods* not only enhances the mystery of John Wade's character, it self-reflexively draws attention to its own characterizations through the metafictional (*see* METAFICTION) commentary of its narrator/biographer.

"A Man of Melancholy Disposition" (1974)

First published in *Ploughshares* magazine in 1974, "A Man of Melancholy Disposition" tells the story of the Minnesota preacher Paul Perry, who comes to the aid of a young, unmarried, pregnant woman and attends the birth of her child. Paul Perry and his wife, Grace, will later appear as main characters in the novel *Northern Lights*, although the incidents described in the story do not appear in the novel.

SYNOPSIS

The story opens with the Lutheran minister Paul Perry meeting young, unwed Ruby Stjern in his church office, where she signs papers agreeing to give her unborn child up for adoption. It is winter in northern Minnesota, and Paul seems deeply depressed, suffering a painful toothache and feeling that his Sunday sermons have become stale and boring. Several weeks later, Paul pays a home visit to Ruby, where he discovers that she had found his name in the phone book after deciding that she needed spiritual guidance to help her through her unplanned pregnancy. Paul and Ruby engage in a mild flirtation while he is at her apartment, but Paul is chastened by thoughts of his wife, Grace, at home, who badly wants to have a child, although Paul does not feel ready to take such a step.

When it comes time for Ruby to have her baby, Paul meets her in the hospital room and witnesses the traumatic birth scene. The baby is turned sideways in the womb; there is a great deal of blood; and Ruby even falls off the examination table at one point. Nevertheless, Ruby makes it through the ordeal, although she never sees the baby, which is immediately whisked away. Paul chooses not to tell Ruby that the baby had been born dead. He later performs a service for the dead baby, with only Grace and a mortician as witnesses. He and Grace then drive to a cemetery in St. Paul to bury the child. The story ends with Paul and Grace back at home in their own bed, Grace awake and looking at the ceiling as Paul falls asleep.

COMMENTARY

The toothache that Paul Perry suffers throughout the story is emblematic of his general feelings of pain and despair concerning his life and his ministry. While the toothache is painful, he chooses to do nothing about it, putting off a visit to the dentist, just as he does nothing to solve the problems in his marriage or to reinvigorate his religious life. Clearly, Paul and his wife, Grace, are having difficulties. She wants a baby, but Paul does not. When Paul asks Grace what she would think if he stopped being a minister, she tells him simply to stop being silly, assuring him that he is a "fine minister" (48), but not taking Paul's unhappiness seriously. The marriage seems to be as stale as Paul's sermons have become, which is at least partly why he seems to be attracted to the young Ruby Stjern.

Much like the free-spirited, part-Indian young woman Addie in the novel *Northern Lights*, Ruby Stjern, in contrast to Paul, seems full of life and energy. Unlike Paul, who seems bound by duty, plodding through his sermons, remaining loyal to his wife, Ruby is a rule breaker. Not only does she have a baby out of wedlock, but she also flirts unabashedly with the young minister. She does not attend church, and she is unafraid to voice her curiosity about what God is like or her fear of ministers with their "black robes and collars and wizened faces" (50). Ruby's very name suggests a certain fiery brightness, and her face is said to "glow" (50) in the sun that shines in through the window of her apartment. It is no wonder that she is appealing to Paul, who seems icy in contrast to Ruby's fire. He is frozen in inaction, much like the cold, forbidding winter landscape that surrounds him. While Ruby remains strong and slender everywhere except her belly, Paul feels that he is aging, growing soft and fat from lack of exercise.

Paul's uncertainty about becoming a father seems motivated at least partly by his failure to live up to the example of his own father, who was a minister as well. While Paul, in the words of Ruby, is "not much of a minister" (47), the senior Perry apparently excelled in his vocation. The Christmas sermon written by Paul's father "had real strength and simplicity" (52). The only time Paul feels genuinely successful as a minister, the only time he feels "a glow" (52) while preaching is when he delivers his father's sermon, which he does "forthrightly" and "with authority" (52). In contrast, when Paul attempts to write his own sermon, he feels that he is "preparing a message for people he barely knew, whose lives he had no knowledge of and no real concern for, nor love" (48). He chooses to forge the sermon around a quote from Revelation that reads, *Blessed are they that do his commandments, that they may have right to the tree of life, and may enter in through the gates into the city.* Paul is a man struggling to fulfill commandments, not only from God but from his father as well. It is possible that Paul has chosen his profession based not on his own wishes but in an attempt to live up to his father's expectations for him.

Paul's ambivalence about fatherhood is expressed in the trauma of Ruby's giving birth. The scene in the hospital room is unnatural and frightening. Ruby lies on her back on a steel table, the room glistening "in chrome and white enamel," chilly and too bright from the "banks of lights" shining from the ceiling (52). She comments that the doctors "have a lot of tools for the job" (52) of delivering the baby, again suggesting that this most primal of human experiences has been turned into something unnatural and artificial. Ruby feels restrained by her hospital gown, begging the doctor and nurses to remove it, but she is told that "it's not allowed" (53). Although the nurse says that "she wants natural" (54), implying that Ruby has

requested a natural childbirth experience, the doctor insists on a sedative and an X-ray machine, and she is strapped down to the table after she falls off. When she is asked whether she can feel the baby, Ruby insists that the lump in her uterus is a "bomb" (57), not a baby. Witnessing the scene, Paul wonders why Grace wants a baby so badly.

While Ruby's baby is born dead, Paul's experience with the young woman does seem to offer a rebirth to his relationship with Grace. Paul does not tell Ruby that the child died, seeing no reason to since she had agreed to give up the baby in any case. But he does tell his wife about the dead child, and Grace not only attends the service, she weeps a great deal and plants flowers on the baby's mound in the cemetery where it is buried. In bed together later that night, the room is cool and good for sleeping. Paul seems to have unfrozen somewhat as he playfully nuzzles his nose against Grace's throat and under her ear and asks her if she is "the prettiest woman in the world" (60). The husband and wife are able to laugh together and even talk about their own future plans for a child, Paul telling Grace he knows she would like to have a baby of her own, and Grace replying that she does not want to rush him. While nothing is settled by the end of the story, it does not exactly end on a hopeful note. Paul falls asleep while Grace is awake and looking at the ceiling. Nevertheless, he does seem to have recommitted himself to his marriage and wife.

CHARACTERS

Doctor An unnamed doctor, who seems both incompetent and uncaring, oversees the birth of Ruby Stjern's baby. As the delivery begins, the doctor sits under a white light in the hospital room, reading a copy of *Sports Afield*. Later, as things begin to go wrong with the delivery, he asks the nurses to bring in several other doctors, only to be told that they are on vacation or in surgery. He eventually delivers the baby by cesarean section, but the child has died in the womb.

Grave Diggers At the cemetery where Paul Perry takes Ruby Stjern's baby to be buried, three "Negro grave diggers" (59) stand respectfully to one side while Paul says the Lord's Prayer for the dead newborn. The grave diggers then lower the coffin into the grave and fill in the hole, and Grace plants flowers on the mound.

Mortician   After Ruby Stjern's baby is born dead, Paul Perry performs a brief service, attended only by his wife, Grace, and a mortician. This mortician will later drive with Paul and Grace to the cemetery to bury the infant.

Nurses   Several nurses participate in the delivery of Ruby Stjern's baby. One is described as older and "hefty" and as someone who "looked like she knew her job" (52). In many ways this nurse seems more competent than the attending physician. Another nurse in the room, who is named Amy, is said to be "slender" and younger.

Perry, Grace   Grace Perry is the wife of the Lutheran minister Paul Perry. Although she longs to have a baby, Paul is not yet ready to become a father. At the end of the story, Grace accompanies Paul to the cemetery to bury the baby of Ruby Stjern, a young, unwed mother whom Paul had befriended. Grace weeps over the dead infant and plants flowers on its grave, perhaps thinking about her own future children. Grace Perry is also a major character in *Northern Lights*, O'Brien's first published novel. In that book Grace is a schoolteacher who also longs for a child.

Perry, Paul   A Lutheran minister in northern Minnesota who befriends a young, pregnant girl named Ruby Stjern, Paul Perry begins the story with a bad toothache, depressed about his sermons, his marriage, and his life in general. Ruby seems to bring needed energy into Paul's cold, wintry existence, however, and he agrees to accompany her to the hospital when it is time for her to have the baby. After witnessing a traumatic birth scene, Paul returns to his wife, Grace, and seems to recommit himself to the marriage. Paul Perry is also the main character in O'Brien's 1975 novel *Northern Lights* in which Paul Perry's father was minister of the DAMASCUS LUTHERAN CHURCH, but Paul is not a minister himself, working instead as an agent for the U.S. Department of Agriculture.

Perry, Paul's Father   Paul Perry's father is mentioned only briefly in the story and is never given a specific name. Readers do find out, though, that he had been a minister like his son. Unlike Paul, however, Mr. Perry wrote sermons that "had real strength and simplicity" (52). The only time Paul feels at all worthwhile as a minister is when he is delivering his father's Christmas sermon.

Stjern, Ruby   Ruby Stjern is a young, free-spirited unwed mother-to-be who meets the Lutheran minister Paul Perry after she looks up his name in the phone book, having decided she needs spiritual guidance to help her through her pregnancy. The first time readers see Ruby, she is in Paul's church office, signing papers agreeing to give up her unborn child for adoption. In contrast to Paul, Ruby is lively and flirtatious, much like the part-Indian girl Addie in O'Brien's 1975 novel about Paul Perry, *Northern Lights*. In the second part of the story, Ruby undergoes a traumatic birth experience. Her baby is born dead, but she is never told this, left to believe at the end that the child has been adopted.

Young Man in T-shirt   (Tony)   At one point during the traumatic birth scene in which Ruby Stjern delivers a dead baby, a young man in a T-shirt and mask arrives in the hospital room carrying pints of blood and clear-solution bottles. After dumping his load on the table, he stands with his hands on his hips, watching Ruby. The young man is most likely named Tony, since the doctor had previously asked one of the nurses to "Tell Tony to get blood ready" (55).

"Nogales" (1999)

First published in the *New Yorker* magazine in March 1999, "Nogales" tells the story of a desperately lonely woman named Karen Burns, who directs a retirement community in TUCSON, ARIZONA, and sexually fantasizes about the new bus driver she has hired to take the residents on outings. The story was later revised and published as a chapter in the 2002 novel, *July, July*.

SYNOPSIS

Karen Burns is a lonely, middle-aged woman who runs a retirement community called HOMEWOOD ESTATES in Tucson, Arizona. The story opens with Karen leading several of the retirees on a walking tour of a desert park just outside the city. She is also accompanied by a blond, 36-year-old man named Darrell Jettie, whom she has recently hired as a bus driver for the retirement center. As she reads from a brochure, Karen concocts romantic fantasies about Darrell inside her head, imagining the two of them honeymooning on an exotic island. When they return to the center for lunch, Darrell suggests a trip for the next day to NOGALES, MEXICO. Karen, who realizes that Darrell has been hired as a bus driver, not a tour leader, and is thus overstepping his authority, is nevertheless so enamored of the younger man that she agrees.

The next morning, Karen sets out in a van with four elderly Homewood Estates residents in the back and Darrell behind the wheel. He drives the group over the border into Mexico, through the town of Nogales, but he does not stop there as planned. Instead, he continues farther out into the desert, telling Karen that he is taking the little assembly to see "the real Mexico" (70). After driving many miles into the desert, the little group meets up with a young man in a red pickup truck on a deserted dirt road. Clearly, the point is no longer a carefree tourist trip to the Mexican countryside. Darrell and the young man work to unscrew the floorboards of the van, then carry six yellow shoe boxes from the truck and hide them in the floor of the van. Ed Hollander, a 76-year-old resident of the retirement community, recognizes that the pair is smuggling drugs. Elaine Wirtz, another resident, expects the two men to murder her and the others at any moment, but Darrell Jettie orders Karen and the old folks back into the van in order to divert suspicion as he drives back over the border into the United States. However, Darrell does not return the group to Homewood Estates, driving them instead into the deep desert west of Tucson. Karen Burns, despite Darrell's cruel behavior, still continues to fantasize about the man as he and his friend drive away, abandoning her and the four old people to die of thirst in the desert.

COMMENTARY

Somewhat reminiscent of the famous Joyce Carol Oates short story "Where are You Going, Where Have You Been?," which was inspired by three murders that took place in Tucson, Arizona, in the early 1960s by a man named Charles Schmid, "Nogales" also depicts a rather silly woman who is attracted to the danger and threatened violence of a highly sexualized male figure. While 15-year-old Connie in the Oates story is seduced by black-haired, gold jalopy–driving Arnold Friend, O'Brien has made his female character an aging and lonely middle-aged woman rather than an overly confident and rebellious teenager. Nevertheless, both women are torn by their own sexuality—both longing to experiment but at the same time afraid of their own sexual urges. The male figures in both stories have mysterious backgrounds, are very charming but also manipulative and threatening, and both use the women's own insecurities against them. O'Brien has even retained the original Tucson setting where the actual Schmid murders took place, although the action of Oates's story takes place in a mid-1960s suburbia whose exact location is never specified. Interestingly, Charles Schmid's adoptive parents ran a nursing home in Tucson called Hillcrest, which might be the inspiration for Homewood Estates, and Schmid killed the first young woman in the desert, where he also disposed of all three bodies of the women he murdered.

In "Nogales," Karen Burns is a dreamer and pretender like many other O'Brien characters, particularly Paul Berlin in *Going After Cacciato*. Both Karen and Berlin concoct elaborate fantasies that take them away from the unbearable circumstances of their actual lives—Berlin from the war in Vietnam and Karen from the desperate loneliness of middle age. Both fantasies, as well, end in domestic bliss. Berlin imagines renting an apartment in PARIS with the beautiful young refugee Sarkin Aung Wan, while Karen fantasizes about honeymooning on an exotic island with Darrell Jettie. But O'Brien also drops hints in the story that Karen Burns might be more mentally unbalanced than she seems at first. While Paul Berlin clearly recognizes that he is creating a story in his mind—the chase after Cacciato—the narrator of "Nogales" tells readers that "since childhood [Karen Burns] has had trouble separating the world of fantasy from the world of here and now" (69). She hears voices in her head, the voices of the men she develops crushes on, but unable to recognize these voices as fantasy, she actually acts on them, making overtures to the men and receiving "curt and absolute and crushing" rejections in turn, twice even ending up in "hospitals"—presumably mental hospitals—because of these rejections.

In addition, the trip to Nogales with Darrell Jettie replays Karen's earlier high school experience with a boy she had adored who abandoned her at a Dairy Queen restaurant the night of her 16th birthday, telling her to walk home after he had performed sexual acts with her in the back seat of his car. In that earlier relationship, the easily manipulated Karen seems blind to the true character of the boy she develops a crush on. Mistakenly believing that the boy is interested in her romantically after drawing "graphic, exhilarating pictures in a book she had dropped" (72), Karen pursues the boy relentlessly, leaving "many, many love letters" in his school locker (72). Later, when Karen remembers this incident, she tries to rewrite the past by telling herself the high school boy was simply too shy to return her affection. Nevertheless, she clearly has conflicted memories about that night. The boy nearly "broke her in half" and "almost suffocated her" (72) in the backseat of his car before abandoning her at the Dairy Queen, perhaps leaving Karen with the impression that sexual experience is inherently violent.

In her fantasies about Darrell, Karen attempts to rewrite this earlier cruelty, pretending that Darrell, unlike the high school boy, wishes to marry her. But just as she had fooled herself earlier, the older Karen ignores Darrell's atrocious behavior, wanting only to please him. She dresses carefully for the trip to Nogales, selecting a black bra and panties that she believes will appeal to the younger man. She seems dreamy and far away when the trip begins to go bad, even seizing Darrell's hand in her own after the drug smuggling has been exposed, still able to

fool herself that Darrell is romantically interested in her rather than simply interested in using her and the others to make his border crossing easier. Karen also imagines the bus driver performing sexual acts upon her—"all the bestial things she has read about in magazines, back-seat things, gynecologist things, all those things she herself so desperately wants to do to him" (72)—but she also recognizes that these are things she "doesn't want to do, never again, or only on her wedding night, only on an exotic island with soft winds and flower smells" (72). Karen longs for a kind of sexual violence, but then dresses the longing up in romantic fantasies of honeymoons and exotic islands, making her own sexual desires more acceptable to herself.

The story becomes even more chilling, set as it is amid the ordinary, mundane details of life in a retirement community. The old people bicker and misunderstand one another, speaking of jaguars and bagels, unaware of the extent of the danger they are actually in. Even after it becomes clear that this will be no carefree trip to Nogales as promised, the old people remain totally trusting. Norma Ickles and Ed Hollander continue to argue in the backseat about the meaning of the word *mesa*. Bess Hollander seems more concerned about her need to use the "conveniences" (72) than she is about the intentions of Darrell and his drug-smuggling buddy. And Norma even praises the bus driver as being "very polite" (71). Karen herself, responsible for the safety and well-being of her small group, refuses to face reality, continuing to dream of a relationship that has a fairy-tale happy ending. Thus, when things turn suddenly brutal, such as Darrell striking Karen on the forehead with his free fist after she takes his hand, or his friend in coveralls telling him he "should've fucked" (73) the retirement community director, these small acts of violence are all the more shocking.

By the end of "Nogales," as violence creeps into the ordinary, unexceptional lives of its characters, readers might be reminded of another famous story that involves the murder of a small group of people by a polite but ruthless lawbreaker: Flannery O'Connor's "A Good Man Is Hard to Find." In that story an escaped murderer named the Misfit kills an entire family who have been delayed by the side of the road by a small car accident in Georgia while on their way to Florida. The self-centered grandmother of the family, who has talked nonstop during the family's entire trip, instigates the killings when she unthinkingly proclaims her recognition of the escaped criminal. Readers may hear echoes of the O'Connor story at the end of "Nogales" when Darrell Jettie's partner orders Elaine Wirtz to sit on a flat boulder, adding "and don't flap those old-bitch lips of yours" (73). After all, it is the grandmother's flapping of her lips that gets the family into so much trouble in "A Good Man Is Hard to Find." But while the grandmother in that story eventually begs for her life, the old people in O'Brien's story continue to remain nonplussed at the end, even as Elaine Wirtz recognizes what is happening to them. After the two men drive off in the van, leaving the four retirees and Karen alone in the desert, Bess Hollander complains simply that she is "totally pooped," almost as if she had actually spent the day shopping as planned. When Norma says, "At least they didn't murder us," Elaine calmly responds, "Oh, they did" (73), even though the news does not seem to affect anyone very much. Karen Burns, meanwhile, continues to fantasize that Darrell will return to take her away, maybe to a pretty old house in New Hampshire with lace curtains in the kitchen. Her desperate loneliness finally trumps any fear or regret she might have experienced in trusting Darrell Jettie. These characters' lives are so drab and uneventful that they cannot be excited even by their own impending deaths.

Differences in Versions

When O'Brien revised the story for inclusion in *July, July*, he made numerous small but significant changes. Karen's age, for instance, is changed from 43 in the original story to 51 in the novel version—to better fit the time frame of the novel. In *July, July* she is murdered shortly before her 30th college reunion. O'Brien changes as well the series of men that Karen had dreamed of since her girlhood. In the story, the list includes a high school art teacher, two college professors, and a gynecologist. The novel changes this assortment to a lifeguard at summer camp, a sociology professor, and a gynecologist. In the novel's version,

Darrell Jettie is somewhat more explicit in both his comments to Karen and his behavior toward her. In the story, he simply puts his hand on Karen's thigh at the truck stop in Mexico, but in the novel he actually slips his hand into her black panties. In addition, when he talks to Karen about driving in the story, he tells her that he lets the road take him where it will—"Like relationships, I guess" (71). In the revised version, however, the word *relationships* is replaced by the more explicit word "sex"—"Like sex, I guess," Darrell tells Karen, "Enjoy the ride, kick back, let the road drive *you*" (*July* 223). Other small changes include the alteration of the color of the drug-containing shoe boxes from yellow to green, and Darrell's telling Elaine Wirtz that he will shoot her in the face rather than in the "titties" as he threatens in the original story.

The novel also presents the elderly retirement community residents as being slightly more alarmed about the fate that awaits them than they seem to be in the original *New Yorker* story. In the novel, Elaine Wirtz begs Darrell Jettie not to kill her as soon as Ed Hollander announces that the men are smuggling drugs, an incident that does not happen in the original story. In addition, Darrell's friend, the young man in white coveralls, is presented as even more crude and shocking in his comments about Karen toward the end. While in the story version he tells Darrell he "should've fucked" Karen, the man more pointedly mocks Karen's girth in the novel version when he says, "Shoulda holed her, man. Reamed off some lard" (*July* 228). Karen's longing for a fairy-tale ending to her imagined romance is highlighted more fully in the novel as well when Darrell orders the young man to "Cut it out," saying that Karen is his "princess" (*July* 228), when in the original story he had called her his "doll" (73). But perhaps the most significant change between versions is that in *July, July* O'Brien completely omits the final paragraph of the original story, in which Karen imagines Darrell taking her to a pretty house in New Hampshire with lace curtains in the kitchen. The novel's version ends flatly, with Norma Ickles saying, "At least they didn't murder us," and Elaine Wirtz responding simply, "Oh they did" (*July* 229). O'Brien might have thought the original ending was too obvious, too pat. After all, readers have already been provided many glimpses into Karen's fantasy world. The novel version certainly ends on a more chilling note than the original story. The surrounding context of the novel makes it clear, as well, that Karen is actually murdered in the desert, that she does not manage to escape, while the original story leaves her fate more open-ended. Readers never find out what actually happens to Karen and her elderly charges in the original story.

CHARACTERS

Burns, Karen Karen Burns is a 41-year-old single woman, described as a "sturdy, graying redhead, bashful with men, undistinguished of face and figure" (69), who runs the HOMEWOOD ESTATES Retirement Community outside of TUCSON, ARIZONA. An intensely lonely woman, Karen has begun to fantasize extensively about Darrell Jettie, the new bus driver she has just hired to take the retirees on short outings. Completely seduced by the man's good looks and pleasant manners, Karen allows Darrell to talk her into taking a few residents on a day trip to NOGALES, MEXICO, although she realizes that he is overstepping his job description by organizing the outing. When Darrell turns out to be a drug smuggler, Karen, blinded by her attraction to the man, does not give up her romantic fantasies about him, even pretending to herself that he will come back to pick her up after he has abandoned her and four retirees in the desert west of Tucson to die of thirst and exposure.

High School Boy When things begin to go very wrong on the trip to Nogales, Karen barely listens to the murmuring of the elderly HOMEWOOD ESTATES residents, preferring instead to continue to fantasize about Darrell Jettie, who reminds her of a boy she had adored back in high school. The boy used to smile at her in the cafeteria and once drew graphic pictures in a book she had dropped. But the relationship ended badly, the boy almost breaking her in half in the backseat of his car on the night of her 16th birthday, before pulling into a Dairy queen and telling her to walk home.

Hollander, Bess Bess Hollander is one of the retirees at HOMEWOOD ESTATES who goes along on the supposed outing to NOGALES, MEXICO. Described as a "balding, partly deaf eighty-year-old," Bess, too, flirts with Darrell Jettie when he first proposes the trip. But Bess seems to have trouble following what is going on as Darrell drives the small group deep into the Mexican backcountry in order to collect smuggled drugs from an accomplice. Her deafness prevents her from following what the others are saying.

Hollander, Ed Ed Hollander is the 76-year-old husband of HOMEWOOD ESTATES resident Bess Hollander. Unlike his wife, who seems incapable of understanding what is happening on the trip to Nogales, Ed figures out that Darrell Jettie and the young man in coveralls are planning to smuggle drugs back into the United States. Ed also understands that Darrell needs the old people with him to make his border crossing easier. When the three elderly ladies look to him to "*do* something" (72) to stop Darrell, however, Ed replies that he is an "old man . . . and not stupid" (72). Like the others, he remains quiet at the border, which allows Darrell to cross easily.

Ickles, Norma Norma Ickles is one of the three elderly women who accompany Karen Burns, van driver Darrell Jettie, and Ed Hollander on what is supposed to be a day trip to NOGALES, MEXICO. When Elaine Wirtz chastises Karen for hiring Jettie, who turns out to be a "monster," Norma defends the man, commenting that he is "very polite, though" (71).

Jettie, Darrell Darrell Jettie is the slick new HOMEWOOD ESTATES bus driver hired by Karen Burns. Described as "thirty-six, blond, excessively polite," and a "chain-smoker" (69), Darrell flirts shamelessly with Karen and even 80-year-old Bess Hollander, trying to worm his way into their good graces. Karen is completely smitten by the man and repeatedly concocts romantic fantasies about the two of them. Darrell, however, turns out to be a drug smuggler who will use the old people in order to cross the U.S.-Mexican border without suspicion, then dump them in a deserted area west of TUCSON, ARIZONA. Although he hits Karen on the head in the van when she takes his hand and will not let go, he seems aware of her feelings for him and even defends her later in the story. When his accomplice, the man in the coveralls and white baseball cap, tells Darrell he should have "fucked" Karen, Darrell replies that Karen is his "doll," his "sweetie pie" (73), feeding her romantic fantasies even as he leaves her in the desert to die.

Man in Coveralls When Darrell Jettie drives through NOGALES, MEXICO, and on into the desert, he eventually meets up with a man dressed in coveralls and a white baseball cap who is waiting on a dirt road by a red pickup truck. The young man, whose face is sunburned and whose left cheek is discolored by a birthmark, is possibly Jettie's younger brother, since he, too, is blue-eyed, and except for the birthmark, could pass for Darrell's twin. The two men work together to load six shoe boxes of drugs under the floorboard of the HOMEWOOD ESTATES van before driving back across the border. The young man in coveralls is more brutal than Darrell himself, making fun of Karen Burns's weight and telling Darrell that he should have "fucked" her. At the end of the story, the young man drives away in the van with Darrell, leaving the old people and Karen alone in the desert.

Wirtz, Elaine Seventy-nine-year-old Elaine Wirtz is the feistiest of the retirees who goes on the trip to NOGALES, MEXICO, with Karen Burns and Darrell Jettie. Insisting that she was a jaguar in a previous life at the start of the trip, Elaine says what comes into her head without worrying about politeness. She chides Karen Burns for hiring Jettie, whom she calls a "monster" (71), and she is also the first of the bunch to realize that the two young men plan to murder the bunch of old people. When at the end of the story Norman Ickles comments, "At least they didn't murder us," Elaine replies, "Oh, they did" (73), understanding the full implication of what it means to be abandoned in the desert with no water.

Northern Lights (1975)

Published in 1975 by Delacorte Press, *Northern Lights* is Tim O'Brien's first novel. The story of two brothers, Paul and Harvey Perry, one who fought in the Vietnam War and one who stayed home in northern Minnesota, the novel explores family relationships as well as the hold that the harsh, unforgiving Minnesota landscape has on the Perry family. While *Northern Lights* initially seems very different from Tim O'Brien's later trio of Vietnam War novels—*Going After Cacciato* (1978), *The Things They Carried* (1990), and *In the Lake of the Woods* (1994)—it nevertheless introduces what will become one of the major themes of this later fiction: the conflict between leading a peaceful, productive, domestic life and living up to traditional notions of courage and manhood. Paul Perry is a character torn between two extremes. Symbolized by repeated imagery of heat and cold, the motherless Paul is attracted to the warmth, domesticity, and security offered by his wife, Grace, but he also longs to live the more adventurous, daring life of his brother, Harvey, and is influenced by the cold hardships and stern theology of his male forebears. The novel's form illustrates this conflict as it begins as a domestic drama, morphs into a harrowing adventure story for approximately 150 pages, just under half the book's length, then reverts to domesticity again for the final 50 pages.

SYNOPSIS

Part One

Northern Lights tells the story of one year in the life of Paul Milton Perry, a young agent for the U.S. Department of Agriculture, who lives in the tiny town of SAWMILL LANDING, Minnesota. Set in an indeterminate year in the mid to late 1960s, the novel opens on a hot July night. Paul, unable to sleep, battles mosquitoes in the large, family farmhouse he shares with his wife, Grace. Adding to Paul's insomnia is the fact that his younger brother, Harvey, is due to return home from his stint in Vietnam the following day. Harvey has been seriously injured in the war, losing an eye, and Paul is unsure exactly what to expect when he and Grace drive into town the next day to pick Harvey up at the local drugstore and Greyhound bus depot. Harvey, upon his arrival, however, seems to be his old self—joking about his injuries, asking why there is no parade to greet him. Paul drives Harvey home, and the next few weeks are spent close to home, playing Scrabble, listening to Harvey's dreams about the future—especially the exotic places where he would like to travel.

While Harvey is readjusting to civilian life, Paul's restlessness with his job and marriage become increasingly apparent. Fascinated by and attracted to a young, free-spirited, part-Indian girl named Addie who works at the local library, Paul halfheartedly pursues her during the day while accepting at night the comforting of his accommodating, motherly wife, Grace, a schoolteacher and homebody who wants nothing more than a child and a comfortable domestic life, a routine existence that Paul is profoundly ambivalent about. When the brothers go out drinking at a local tavern one evening, Harvey meets Addie, and the two begin a relationship, although the young woman continues to tease and flirt with Paul. The two couples—Paul and Grace and Harvey and Addie—spend the late summer and fall months together. Grace throws a large birthday picnic for Harvey the last day of July, and later, the injured veteran finally gets his parade when he is honored by the entire town at the halftime celebration of a local high school football game.

Interspersed with these events, O'Brien supplies background information about the Perry brothers and their forebears. Paul and Harvey have spent their whole lives in Sawmill Landing, growing up in a house built by their grandfather, Pehr Peri, who immigrated to the United States from Finland when he was 16, and who lived a rough life in lumber camps and the deep backwoods of northern Minnesota for the next five years. At the age of 22, Pehr Peri appeared in Sawmill Landing, unmarried, but with a young son, whom he named Pehr Lindstrom Peri. After having his arm crushed in a lumber accident, the elder Pehr Peri became a stump preacher, and his son, who later anglicized his name to "Perry," followed in his father's footsteps, becoming the minister of the DAMASCUS LUTHERAN CHURCH and father to Paul and Harvey, whose mother died giving birth to the younger boy. After an isolated and lonely childhood, Paul eventually went to college at the University of Iowa, where he met Grace, then briefly attended divinity school before dropping out in favor of advanced studies in agricultural science. Harvey, meanwhile, became very close to his father, hunting, camping, and trekking through the deep woods with him. The old minister died a few years before Harvey was drafted (*see* DRAFT) into the Vietnam War. The house the two brothers now share is the house they grew up in.

In the present time, fall advances into winter, and Harvey, still jobless and fantasizing about foreign travel many months after his return home from the war, plans a skiing trip for the two couples shortly after Christmas in the not-too-distant town of GRAND MARAIS, MINNESOTA, where yearly ski races are held in conjunction with a winter carnival. While Grace, true to her nature, goes to bed early their first night in the hotel, Harvey and Addie have a late-night, hard-drinking party in their own room, a party that Paul attends. As the night wears on, Addie leaves the party with a young, handsome ski racer named Daniel. In the coming days, Harvey is clearly depressed by Addie's defection. Although she continues to eat meals and watch races with Paul and Grace, Addie is also seen quite frequently with Daniel, who ends up winning the top prize in the races. One evening in the hotel lobby, Addie confesses to Paul that Harvey has asked her to marry him, even after her new relationship with Daniel had begun. Paul, himself disappointed in Addie and at least partially jealous of Daniel, spars with her a bit before she goes off with her new boyfriend.

Part Two

Following the disastrous vacation, the two brothers make preparations to ski back to Sawmill Landing, an outdoor adventure that Harvey had planned in advance and persuaded Paul to participate in. They have sleeping bags, maps, and rucksacks with enough supplies for a few days, the time they estimate it will take them to reach their hometown. The first two days of the planned trip go well, but it begins snowing in the evening of the second day, when the brothers set up camp for the night. In the next few days, it begins to snow in earnest, and the brothers become increasingly disoriented in the woods, the maps they have brought not helping much. Soon the two are hopelessly lost. As the food runs out, they continue on, but Harvey becomes seriously ill, making it difficult to cover much ground. After an indeterminate number of days lost out in the woods with no food and having grown increasingly cold and exhausted, Paul finally stumbles upon a small hunter's shack in the woods. Even though they now have shelter and Paul is able to kill a woodchuck, the two men are still starving. As Harvey's condition worsens in the following days, Paul realizes that he will have to leave his brother alone to go for help. He skis back out into the woods, and after a day and a half of travel he meets a little girl pulling a sled who leads him to her parents' isolated home. Carla, the girl's young mother, is home alone—her husband, Arild, is away for a few days in town with the couples' pickup truck. Carla feeds Paul, draws a bath for him, and urges him to rest. She has no phone or means of transportation, however, so after spending the night with mother and daughter, Paul sets out again for a nearby town. He eventually comes to a gas station/café where he calls the state police and informs them of Harvey's location. One of the troopers arrives to drive Paul back home to Sawmill Landing, explaining that there had been a large manhunt for the missing brothers. Harvey, meanwhile, is helicoptered out of the woods and taken to a hospital to recover.

Following their return to Sawmill Landing, the brothers do not talk much about their experience in the woods. That spring things at the Perry farmhouse seemingly return to normal, with Harvey and Addie back together again, the two couples playing games and drinking gin in the evenings, and Harvey making idle plans for future travel. In summer Paul begins packing up his office, having been laid off from his position as agricultural agent since the government has decided his minuscule office is a waste of taxpayer's money. When Harvey disappears for several days in a row, Paul worries about him, but the younger brother returns home

to report that Addie has moved to Minneapolis and he had been to the city to see her. Harvey tells Paul that he again asked Addie to marry him, but she refused, preferring instead to stay in her new apartment in Minneapolis with a new roommate. As Paul officially closes his office on the first day of July, Harvey instigates a discussion about the possibility of selling the old farmhouse, and the brothers begin to seriously consider the possibility. However, when a young couple makes an offer on the house, Harvey gets cold feet, insisting that Paul is betraying him by selling out.

As July wears on, Paul has another restless night like the one that opens the novel. Depressed and irritated, he gets up in the middle of the night to go for a walk in the woods, eventually wading into PLINEY'S POND, an algae-ridden spot he had always feared since his father had tried to force Paul to learn to swim there when he was a young boy. This night Paul does swim. When he emerges from the pond, he sees the Northern Lights rippling in the distance and feels much more quiet and peaceful. He returns to the house and makes love to Grace, the two finally trying to conceive the child that Grace had wanted for so long. In the morning Paul finds out that the house has sold. Harvey is unhappy, but half-drunk later that evening, he insists that Paul drive into town with him to have a beer at the local tavern to celebrate. When the brothers discover that the tavern is closed, they take a walk through tiny Sawmill Landing instead. Harvey, angry about the sale, accuses Paul of being a coward and of not truly loving their father, but he eventually apologizes, and Paul confides that he and Grace are considering moving back to Iowa. The novel ends with the two brothers putting their arms around each other as they resume their walk, Harvey continuing to make wild, unrealistic plans for exotic travel, this time begging Paul to consider a trip to Mexico City.

COMMENTARY

The tension between domesticity and adventure is depicted in the opening pages of the book when Paul wakes up in the night to battle mosquitoes. In this scene, Paul is described as a warrior; he is "thinking murder" and wielding his black can of poison as if it were a weapon (4). Yet, Paul's aggression is contained inside of the stiflingly hot bedroom, with Grace whispering softly in the background. Repeatedly throughout the novel, Grace is described as a mother figure to Paul. In this opening scene, Grace comforts her husband by telling him to roll onto his "tummy" (6) so that she can rub him, sounding more like a mother with a young child than a woman soothing a grown man. As she rubs him, Grace is said to whisper "like a mother" (6), and readers soon find out that Paul's father had objected to his marriage, muttering that Grace "looks like somebody's mother . . . like somebody's goddamn mother" (9; 12), a comment that Paul remembers frequently. When Paul first met Grace back in college at the University of Iowa, it was Grace's "heavy-breasted sympathy" that initially attracted him (12). The narrator writes that Grace had taken Paul in "like an orphan" and offered him her "sympathy that oozed like ripe mud" ever after (12–13). Marrying her had been "as easy and natural as falling asleep in a warm bath" (13). Later in the novel, Paul looks at Grace and believes that she resembles his mother, whom he knows only from photographs.

Grace's motherliness, however, both attracts and repels Paul. Her warm domesticity offers him something that he has been missing in his previous life. Paul has been raised by a stern and distant father, and his earliest memories all suggest a cold, forbidding childhood. Paul's first memory of his father involves a wintry holiday with a snowstorm blowing outside. In this memory, Paul's mother is "only a pleasant shadow" sitting beside her husband (73), an insubstantial figure in the face of the dominating Pehr Perry. His second childhood memory also occurs in a snowstorm and includes a baby crying, a sobbing sound, and his father wiping bloody hands. Apparently, something has gone wrong as Paul's mother is giving birth to his younger brother, Harvey. This suspicion is confirmed when the narrator tells readers that Paul's third memory "was of great loss. The house was stone cold. His father was holding a child, rocking before the fire, and the sobbing sound ran through the house like the wind" (73). Coldness, then, is associated for Paul with the loss of his mother at such a young age. Grace, who offers warmth and motherly comfort,

counteracts Paul's early loss, the coldness associated with these early memories. Yet, her all-encompassing warmth also threatens to stifle Paul, just as the unrelenting July heat depicted in this opening chapter, "Heat Storm," stifles the town of Sawmill Landing. Ambivalent about Grace's desire to have a child, and at times chafing under her motherly touch, Paul frequently has to leave the house at night, taking walks into the woods alone and visiting natural haunts such as Pliney's Pond, which his father had originally introduced him to.

Paul's younger brother, Harvey, suggests a different path than that offered by Grace. Associated with the hard, cold world of masculine courage and endurance visualized by his father and grandfather, Harvey lives out what might be considered the expected and admired trajectory for young men in traditional small-town America. He goes to war and comes home a hero in the eyes of the townspeople, having been severely wounded in service to his country. His nickname, in fact, given to him by his father, is Harvey the Bull. The original Pehr Peri's hero is said to have been the BULL OF KARELIA, a mythic figure from his Finnish homeland. While bulls are prominent figures in world mythology, often suggesting masculine fertility, such as the Egyptian bull-god Osiris and the Greek Dionysus, and associated with ritual killing and resurrection, the Bull of Karelia seems to represent endurance in a cold, harsh environment. The Bull of Karelia, described as "a moose with antlers gone and head down in the dead of winter" (71), is a fitting emblem of Pehr Peri's worldview. Not only does Paul think of his grandfather as having a "frozen spirit," but the novel's narrator informs readers that Pehr Peri's sermons "offered no hope of salvation," that his only promise was "that things would get worse," that his "theme was apocalypse" (71). In the face of such a bleak outlook, Peri's sermons "called merely for heroism," which he defined as the Finnish *Urbo*: "Practiced endurance, silent suffering, fortitude" (71). Harvey, drafted into the Vietnam War and refusing to talk about his injury upon his return home, displays the masculine qualities most admired by his father and grandfather.

Harvey, unlike Paul, had a close relationship with his father growing up. He learned to hunt and fish and camp from Pehr Perry, and he enjoyed challenging himself in the harsh Minnesota wilderness. Paul, however, preferred the indoors as a boy, refusing to accompany Harvey and their father on their outdoor adventures. Paul rejected other traditional emblems of masculinity as well. Lost in the blizzard, Harvey reminds Paul of the rifle that the younger brother received as a gift from his father one Christmas. At first frightened of the gun and reluctant to touch it, Harvey eventually becomes adept at shooting, a portent of his later participation in the Vietnam War. Paul never received such a gift, though. Harvey remembers the boys' father telling Paul he "hadn't finished the dishes" (262) before sitting down and showing Harvey how to oil his new rifle. Paul seems to reject his father and grandfather's bleak, apocalyptic outlook as well when he refuses to help Harvey build a bomb shelter in the farmhouse yard during the CUBAN MISSILE CRISIS of 1962, even though it is the old man's dying request. Even Paul's adult job as an agricultural extension agent involves taming and domesticating the vast wilderness of northern Minnesota rather than testing himself against it as his male relatives have traditionally done. When Harvey initially suggests a winter ski trip, calling snow "God's own stuff . . . Clean and pretty and white," Paul responds, "Snow, cold freeze. They go together. They give me the creeps" (36), suggesting a vacation to Iowa instead. Associated with the traditionally feminine and domestic from his boyhood, Paul is both attracted to Harvey's more adventurous side and repelled by it, much as he is by Grace's warm domesticity.

Paul's fascination with the young, free-spirited Addie arises from the part of his character that longs for a more adventurous life. The "lean and athletic" (32) Addie, who loves to dance and swim and drink and flirt, not only suggests a contrast to the motherly Grace, but because she is part-Indian she is tied as well to the mythic past of the ARROWHEAD, the pointed peninsula of land where Sawmill Landing is located. The summer that Harvey returns home, Paul begins paying more attention to his surroundings. The narrator writes that "he was searching in a vague way for the first elements. Complexity to elementals, a backward

tracing" (81). As he considers his own past, Paul also thinks about the past of Sawmill Landing itself—how the first people to arrive in the area were the Sioux, then the Chippewa. Later came French trappers, then Swedish farmers who tried to plant corn in a land meant for spruce trees, and finally Germans who opened taverns and shops. While the later settlers attempted to domesticate the landscape, Indians, described in racist terms as having "sour faces, bad teeth, and greasy hair" (20) in present-day Sawmill Landing, nevertheless suggest an adventurous, romanticized frontier past. The town mayor Jud Harmor half-jokingly calls Addie "Geronimo," the name of a fiercely independent and daring Apache military leader in the 19th century who escaped capture by both the U.S. and Mexican armies numerous times. And Addie teases Paul endlessly about the two of them running away together for the BADLANDS of South Dakota, a place connoting outlaws, Indians, and the Wild West.

But at the same time that these daring notions of adventure and heroism pull at Paul, the novel also questions what true heroism consists of. Harvey, returning from service in Vietnam, is called a hero by Jud Harmor. Herb Wolff, the druggist, is dismayed that no crowd is waiting to cheer Harvey's arrival, and Harvey himself, immediately upon stepping off the bus, asks about parades and refers to his reception by only Paul and Grace as "some awful hero worship" (23). Yet, there is an uneasiness among the men about all this talk of heroics. Jud laughs so hard after calling Harvey a hero that he begins coughing, and later, when he tells Paul and Grace to inform Harvey how proud the town is, that everyone views him as a hero, he adds, "Tell him anything you want. A pack of lies, anyway" (30). Harvey echoes this language when he discusses the article about him in the local newspaper, calling the story "a pack of lies" (34). Part of the town's uneasiness is due to the nature of the Vietnam War itself—it was an unpopular war half a world away, fought in a country most Americans knew almost nothing about. O'Brien, as he does in his memoir, *If I Die in a Combat Zone,* criticizes the small-town ignorance that propelled Harvey to fight in an unjust war. He writes that "no one in Sawmill Landing knew a damn about the war anyway" (20). Yet, the town leaders send Harvey off with "optimism and good humour, a little sympathy," all the while in a "sleepwalking, slothful" state of political unawareness, so that Harvey's departure is driven by a "blinding foggy invisible force" (20), not unlike the blizzard the brothers will encounter in Part Two of the novel. The theme of blindness, in fact, is key in *Northern Lights*. Not only has Harvey lost an eye in the war, thus becoming half-blind and directionless, but when the brothers set out on their ski trip, Paul feels "that they rushed too blindly to the forest" (160). Later, he will be blinded by the blizzard itself as well as by the darkness when night falls. Characters in this novel seem blinded as well by their allegiance to a heroic past that might not have been as heroic as they imagine. The brothers' grandfather Pehr Peri, after all, while preaching heroic endurance, ended up hanging himself from the rafters of the Damascus Lutheran Church in 1919.

As O'Brien wrestles in the novel with these issues of heroism and courage, he pays homage to another great 20th-century war writer whom he very much admires: ERNEST HEMINGWAY. In his earlier memoir, *If I Die in a Combat Zone*, O'Brien speaks of his affection for Hemingway, especially of his admiration for FREDERIC HENRY in *A Farewell to Arms*, whom he describes as "hard and realistic," "removed from other men," "wise," and above all, "courageous" (*If I Die* 143). While it is possible to see Hemingway's influence in all of O'Brien's works, *Northern Lights* is the novel in which this influence is most extensive and explicit. Like Nick Adams in "Big Two-Hearted River," and Jake Barnes in THE SUN ALSO RISES, Harvey Perry is a wounded veteran who tries to heal in nature. But just as Nick initially walks through a burned-out countryside and the impotent Jake moves through a spiritual wasteland of ennui and decadence, Harvey's injuries are reflected in the landscape around him. O'Brien, like Hemingway, relies on a myth frequently evoked in 20th-century literature, especially by the modernists: that of the Fisher King. Perhaps best known from T. S. Eliot's epochal poem "The Wasteland," the Fisher King myth derives from medieval legends describing the quest for the

Holy Grail. The Fisher King is said to be the keeper of the Grail relics, including the spear of Longinus, used to wound Christ as he hung on the cross. The King suffers from a wound inflicted by the same spear, and this wound not only destroys the Fisher King's virility, but by a sympathetic transference turns his realm into a wasteland. Harvey's injuries, brought on by his being drafted into a war the town does not understand or comprehend, are mirrored in his small hometown. Sawmill Landing is described as a dying town, with "rusting machinery, uncut weeds, unpainted buildings, unstopped forest" (72). Images of decay abound in the novel, from the bacterial waste and decaying plant life that clog Pliney's Pond, to mayor Jud Harmor's slow submission to the cancer that is eating away his body. The inevitability of death and decay is evoked as well in the apocalyptic tone that permeates the book. The epigraph from Revelation paints a picture of a natural world turned toxic: great earthquakes, the Sun as black as sackcloth and the Moon like blood. Pehr Peri's sermons preach apocalypse, and the political situation in 1962 with the Cuban missile crisis raises the threat of real, imminent atomic annihilation.

While Harvey Perry resembles Jake Barnes from *The Sun Also Rises*—a man deeply wounded in an unpopular and wasteful war who moves through a physical or spiritual wasteland upon his return—his brother, Paul, takes on characteristics of Jake as well, especially in his ongoing flirtation with Addie, who can be read as a stand-in for Lady Brett Ashley from the Hemingway novel. Repeated imagery of bulls and bullfighting also connect the two novels. Much of the action in *The Sun Also Rises* revolves around the culture of bullfighting, while Addie in *Northern Lights* is described as able to ride "Harvey the Bull" with ease, to guide him effortlessly "like a matador" (96). But the point at which *Northern Lights* most resembles Hemingway's 1926 masterpiece is when O'Brien describes the ski races at Grand Marais. Just as Jake Barnes travels with a group of friends to a sporting event—the bullfights at Pamplona—in what can be read as an attempt to revitalize himself, to reconnect with the great mysteries of life and death in an increasingly decadent and meaningless world, Paul travels with Grace,

Harvey, and Addie to the ski races, at least partly so that the brothers can renew and test themselves against the harsh natural landscape, both by entering the races and through the planned cross-country skiing and camping trip back home to Sawmill Landing. Harvey devises the trip as an alternative to the safe, comfortable routine of evenings spent by the fireside playing Scrabble and spinning dreams of foreign travel that the two couples have settled into since Harvey's return from the war.

But events in Grand Marais do not work out as Harvey had planned. Just as the free-spirited Brett Ashley in *The Sun Also Rises* begins an affair with the young bullfighter Romero, calling herself a "bitch" for doing so, Addie deserts Harvey for Daniel, the young, handsome ski race champion. In her talks with Paul, Addie refers to herself as "terrible" and "a witch" (148) for what she has done to Harvey, but like Brett, Addie refuses to conform to standard domestic rules governing women's behavior. Unlike Grace, Addie does not want to be tied down, and her continued affair with Daniel seems at least partly motivated by the fact that Harvey had proposed to her, as she confesses to Paul. The older brother, secretly in love with Addie himself, as Jake Barnes is with Brett Ashley, may be as concerned for his own feelings as he is for Harvey when he says to Addie, "You're such a sweetie . . . Some sweetie to ruin it all" (155). What exactly has Addie ruined here? Her relationship with Harvey? Her flirtation with Paul? The delicate balancing act wrought by the two couples as they sidestep around their uneasy ties to one another, deliberately blinding themselves to the deep feelings of betrayal, hurt, and fear lurking below the surface?

Hemingway famously wrote his novel about a lost generation, and the theme of being lost is a recurring one in *Northern Lights* as well as in many of O'Brien's works. In *Going After Cacciato*, Paul Berlin imagines himself falling into an underground maze of tunnels, lost in the tangled complexities of war, while Kathy Wade is literally lost, become a missing person, in *In the Lake of the Woods*. In *Northern Lights*, Harvey and Paul's getting lost in the blizzard suggests the aimlessness and dissatisfaction with which these characters live their lives. They exist under the spell of forebears who

preached apocalypse; they lost their mother at a young age; they are scarred by an unjust and senseless war; and they live in a town that is decaying around them. The following passage drives home the point that being lost works on more than a simple literal level in the novel:

> . . . When Harvey returned, they had a cigarette, threw their butts into the fireplace and helped each other into their packs, breathed in the warm hotel air, then went outside.
> Perry was lost.
> He stepped into his skis, pulled up the woolen leggings. (161)

Paul Perry is described as lost the moment he steps outside, before the brothers venture into the woods and snow, before the blinding blizzard even arrives.

In fact, the novel suggests that both brothers are not only lost—scarred, aimless, frightened—but that they are potentially suicidal as well. It is possible to read Harvey's planned excursion into the woods as a halfhearted suicide attempt. Part of Harvey's hurry to get started on the trip seems to be driven by Addie's deserting him at the winter games. And at one point out in the woods, after Harvey has grown increasingly ill, Paul rouses him and tries to make him get up. Harvey replies that "This is the end," chiding Paul for "not facing it" (238). He says that he is not going on, that he is too sick, adding, "this is the whole purpose of it, don't you see that?" (239), possibly suggesting that Harvey never planned to make it out of the wilderness. After all, the maps he brings along are inadequate, and he overlooks the likelihood of snow in the forecast—not smart decisions for a man so experienced and adept in the wild. Paul's own dissatisfaction with life also blossoms into near-suicide at times. When Jud Harmor finds Paul at Pliney's Pond late one night the summer before the ski trip, the eccentric old town mayor confesses that he "expected to find [Paul] floatin' face down" (91). Jud urges Paul to take a swig of liquor in order to help him "see clearer" (91) after he had hurried "blindly" (90) out of the house and down to the pond. And at the end of the novel, Paul is once more awakened by mosquitoes and feels the urge to rush out of the house and visit the pond. In language that evokes the blizzard scene, Paul is described as being "blind and cold in the steaming woods," despite the heat of the summer night, and he is said to be "thinking suicide" (347).

Perhaps part of the problem facing the Perry brothers is the macho code of silent suffering expected of them by their father and grandfather. Harvey never talks about his war injury, despite Addie's repeated attempts to get him to describe how it occurred. Although courage and heroism in the form of stoic endurance are expected of the brothers, the novel questions just how useful that code is. Paul, returning from his ordeal in the woods, is described in terms similar to those used to depict Harvey returning from war. At the gas station, where he waits for the state police to take him home, Paul is depressed. "There ought to have been crowds," waiting to welcome him home, he thinks. "The highway should have been jammed with well-wishers" (310). But Paul's homecoming is as quiet and uneventful as Harvey's return from the war. And neither brother talks about their ordeal after it is over. Finally reunited with Grace, Paul tells his wife that he is "okay," but adds, "There's nothing I can say" (313). And as the routine at the Perry farmhouse returns to normal as the spring wears on, Harvey "did not talk about the long days of being lost" either, "the same way he never talked about the war, or how he lost his eye, or other bad things" (315). Paul and Harvey both have to accept the fact that their encounter with nature did not change things for them. O'Brien writes:

In the winter, in the blizzard, there had been no sudden revelation, and things were the same, no epiphany or sudden shining of light to awaken and comfort and make happy, and things were the same, the old man was still down there alive in his grave, frozen and not dead, and in the house the cold was always there . . . everything the same. Harvey was quiet. Like twin oxen struggling in different directions against the same old yoke, they could not talk, for there was only the long history: the town, the place, the forest and religion, partly a combination of human beings and event, partly a genetic fix, an alchemy of circumstance." (317)

As long as the brothers live out the stoic, masculine code they have been raised with, change is not possible for them. They are still haunted by the memory of their father, "frozen and not dead" in his grave, and the past seems to overwhelm the present.

The epiphany that Paul had expected and not received during his adventure in the wilderness finally does come to him in the end, however. On the night at the end of the novel when he ventures out to Pliney's Pond, when he is thinking about suicide, Paul actually enters the waters of the pond:

He shed his clothes and at last went in.
At last.
He glided inch by inch into Pliney's Pond.
It seemed almost a ritual . . .

The pond is the sight of childhood trauma for Paul. It is where his father forced him to learn to swim, saying "No back talk, just jump in" (62). In that earlier scene, Paul is overwhelmed by the stink of the pond, by the rot and sewage and strange, frightening creatures that greet him when he wades in. This time, though, Paul enters the pond willingly, and his immersion into the water seems to be a baptism ritual. He faces his fears head-on, even taking a handful of slime from the bottom of the pond and squeezing it between his fingers. When he emerges, it is as if Paul has been reborn. He notices the beautiful Northern Lights, which he had been blind to earlier, and these lights seem to dispel his bad childhood memories: "He had no more memories. Not so bad, he thought. Not so bad, at all. . . . The old man *was* crazy" (348). Paul is able to accept his father's flaws here, and with acceptance comes a putting to rest of the old man's ghost.

Paul's epiphany in the pond is prefigured by his earlier experiences with the young mother Carla after emerging from the blizzard. Carla's home, which provides shelter, food, and warmth to the starving Paul, contrasts with the cold and unforgiving wilderness he had been wandering through for so many days. Like Paul's wife, Grace, Carla is a nonstop talker, a motherly woman who challenges the masculine code of silent endurance espoused by Pehr Peri and his son. Carla even draws a bath for Paul, offering him a ritual cleansing that invites him back into civilization. The night at Pliney's Pond when he sees the Northern Lights completes Paul's baptism. Upon emerging from the pond, Paul thinks immediately of Grace. He returns home that night, and he and Grace make love, trying to conceive the child that Grace has wanted for so long. At this point Paul seems to have made his choice between the two forces that have pulled at him throughout the novel. He reembraces all that Grace represents—warmth, domesticity, family love—over the stern, cold, apocalyptic, heroic vision preached by his father and grandfather. This choice allows him to leave his old life behind at the end of the novel as he sells the family farmhouse and makes plans to move back to Iowa with Grace. While Harvey remains half-blind and directionless at the end, still spinning his adventure fantasies, Paul ends the novel content, having found the grace that he had been seeking.

CHARACTERS

Addie Addie is the young, free-spirited, part-Indian girl whom both Paul and Harvey Perry are attracted to. She works as a part-time librarian in SAWMILL LANDING and lives in a boardinghouse on Acorn Street. Readers first see Addie swimming in the local lake as Paul is waiting for her on the beach. Described as "athletic," as "very slender," and as having skin that is "walnut-coloured and shining" (32), Addie never speaks to Paul in this scene, although he feels better just watching her dive deep into the lake. The next time readers see Addie, she is dancing in FRANZ'S GLEN tavern with a group of friends. This is where she meets Harvey for the first time. The two soon begin dating, with Paul watching their growing relationship ambivalently. When the two couples, Paul and Grace and Harvey and Addie, attend the ski races and winter carnival in GRAND MARAIS, Addie becomes involved with a handsome ski racer named Daniel, leaving Harvey depressed and Paul disappointed. It is on the way home from Grand Marais that the brothers become lost in the blizzard. After their eventual return home, it initially seems as if things will be back to normal at the Perry farmhouse—that Addie and Harvey will reunite. But as spring

advances Addie unexpectedly moves to Minneapolis, where she lives an apartment with a new roommate. Although she tells Harvey he can visit her and that they can remain friends, it is clear that the romantic relationship has ended. Addie's departure is one of the incidents spurring Harvey and Paul's decision to sell the old farmhouse and start new lives somewhere else.

Arild Arild is the husband of the young mother named Carla who takes Paul Perry in after he has been lost in the woods for countless days. Readers never actually meet Arild because he has taken the couples' only working car—a pickup truck—into town for a few days, so he is not at home when Paul arrives. Despite hinting that Arild might not like it, Carla allows Paul to spend the night before he continues on his journey into town the next day.

Bennett, Hal Hal Bennett is the local dentist in SAWMILL LANDING. He gives a speech at the rainy Memorial Day ceremony held at the cemetery near the end of the novel. Later, after Paul Perry learns from Bishop Markham that the town mayor Jud Harmor has died of cancer, Paul goes to Hal Bennett's office to have a tooth repaired. Bennett also announces Jud's death to Paul, as does Paul's wife, Grace, when he returns home that evening.

Borg, Ole Ole Borg was a farmer of Swedish extraction who lived in SAWMILL LANDING in the mid-19th century. In 1860 he shot dead two Indians whom he caught stealing corn from his farm. In 1862 Ole Borg himself was killed when three "Chippewa renegades" (66) slipped into his house and used a hatchet to crack his skull. The Chippewas were later captured by cavalry troops and hanged. The town began celebrating Ole Borg Day the following year, in 1863, a holiday they observed until the timber companies changed the name to Paul Bunyan Day many years later.

Carla (little girl) After Paul and Harvey Perry have been lost for many days in the woods, starving and weak, Paul eventually leaves Harvey in an old hunting shack and skis out to find help. He meets a little girl named Carla, who is out hunting for her lost dog. The nonchalant child signifies civilization and rescue for Paul, who follows her home to her isolated house. There he is given food and a bath by the little girl's mother, also named Carla. Paul spends the night with the two Carlas before heading into town the next day.

Carla (mother) The mother of the little girl whom Paul Perry follows home after being lost so long in the woods is named Carla, just like her young daughter. When he arrives at the isolated house, the mother and daughter are home by themselves, Carla's husband, Arild, having taken the couples' pickup truck into town for a few days. The house is so isolated and primitive that Carla does not even have a phone for Paul to call for help. Yet, Carla kindly feeds Paul and draws a warm bath for him, perhaps a symbol of Paul's baptism back into domesticity and civilization after having been lost in the wilderness. After allowing Paul to spend the night in her bed, while Carla and her daughter sleep on the floor, she sends him off the next morning with directions to the nearest town.

Daniel Their first night at the ski races in GRAND MARAIS, Harvey Perry and Addie have a party in their hotel room, which they convince Paul to attend. When the older brother arrives, he sees a drunk, handsome boy asleep on the bed. Addie tells Paul that the boy's name is Daniel and that he is going to ski in the Olympics some day. After Daniel wakes up, Addie insists on helping him back to his own room. Apparently, she never returns that night. The following morning Paul sees Addie with Daniel, and the two continue to spend time together in the following few days. When Daniel wins the ski races, Addie is delighted, but the boy himself seems somewhat embarrassed by his position as interloper in the relationship between Harvey and Addie. When the games end, the Perry brothers set out to cross-country ski all the way home to SAWMILL LANDING, the relationship between Harvey and Addie and Daniel never resolved.

Fifteen-Year-Old Ski Racer At the ski races in GRAND MARAIS, a 15-year-old boy who is a native

to the town and a crowd favorite wins the final championship heat. The raucous and joyful crowd celebrates wildly, with the boy's drunken father spilling beer everywhere. Eventually, Addie's new boyfriend, Daniel, will defeat the 15-year-old in the championship race.

Forest Service Agent During the height of July heat in SAWMILL LANDING, a Forest Service agent comes to speak with Paul Perry at his office. The danger of fire is so great that Forest Service firefighters have checked into a local motel and are on alert. The agent tells Paul that the firefighters will have to use his office for a headquarters until the threat diminishes.

Franz Franz is the owner of a tavern in SAWMILL LANDING known as FRANZ'S GLEN. The night that Harvey first meets Addie at the tavern, Franz plays polkas on his accordion so that the crowd of young people can dance.

Girl in Yellow Sweater At the ski races in GRAND MARAIS, while Harvey and Addie are dancing in the hotel bar, Paul Perry talks briefly to a girl in a yellow sweater who seems interested in him. The girl tells Paul that she works for the port authority in Duluth and has been coming to the winter games for years although she does not ski herself. She also lets Paul know that she is recently divorced. When Paul asks the girl to dance, however, she refuses, and gets up to dance with a man in a blue and gold sweater instead, leaving Paul to sit by himself.

Harmor, Jud Jud Harmor is the eccentric mayor of SAWMILL LANDING, who is dying of cancer throughout the novel. Annoyed at not being informed of Harvey Perry's return from the Vietnam War, Jud promises to organize a parade to honor the war hero. Perhaps as a result of his illness, Jud often seems confused when speaking with Paul Perry, not remembering if Paul's parents are living or dead, accusing Paul of selling out and leaving Sawmill Landing, and generally mixing up the past and the present. Yet, there is also a certain wisdom to the old man. He predicts that the storm that ends Harvey's birthday party will bring nothing but heat, no rain; he detects Paul's dissatisfaction with his life, even worrying at one point about finding Paul "floatin' face down" (91) in PLINEY'S POND; and his suspicions of Paul selling out seem justified in the end. Jud Harmor eventually dies of the cancer that has been eating his body. Bishop Markham brings the news of Jud's death to Paul late in the novel, when Harvey has disappeared to Minneapolis. Jud's death seems to mark the end of an era in Sawmill Landing and perhaps jolts Paul into finally deciding to move away from the town.

Librarian   When Paul Perry goes to the SAWMILL LANDING library to look for Addie, he falls asleep at a desk. He awakens to a librarian stacking books who looks at him sourly and tells him that he was snoring. When he asks about Addie, the librarian informs Paul that Monday is her day off, adding, "You oughta know that by now, Mr. Perry" (26).

Lorna   Lorna is a young waitress with a beehive hairdo who works at FRANZ'S GLEN, a local tavern. Harvey Perry flirts with her the night he and Paul go drinking in the tavern—the same night that Harvey meets Addie. When Lorna tells Harvey that she had seen his picture in the paper, Harvey pretends to be a dentist and asks her to open her mouth so he can look at her teeth, but he frightens her away when he treats her too roughly.

Maglione, Dick and Wife   The Magliones are a wealthy young couple from St. Paul who eventually buy the old Perry farmhouse at the end of the novel. Dick Maglione had been a bonds broker back in the city but is giving up that career in order to become an abstract painter. Mrs. Maglione is described as "extraordinarily pretty" (341), and Paul Perry speculates that she had once worked as a stewardess or model. Although Harvey was the one to first suggest selling the house, he becomes angry when Bishop Markham, the real estate agent, calls one morning to say that the Magliones have agreed to buy the place. He especially resents having to say good-bye to the bomb shelter he had built with his own hands. The shelter, though, is exactly what

sold the Magliones on the farmhouse, according to Bishop Markham. Dick Maglione plans to turn it into a painting studio.

Markham, Bishop   Bishop Markham is a SAWMILL LANDING resident who was a classmate of Paul Perry's in high school. Markham grew up to be a life insurance and real estate salesman who periodically runs against Jud Harmor for town mayor but always loses. He sits on the Sawmill Landing Chamber of Commerce, chairs the Kiwanis Club, and serves on the DRAFT board that good-naturedly sent Harvey Perry off to fight in the Vietnam War. In this capacity, he represents the small-town ignorance that O'Brien complains of in essays and interviews. It is Bishop Markham who serves as the real estate agent for the Perry brothers at the end of the novel, finding a young, artistic couple to purchase the old Perry farmhouse.

Men at Gas Station   When Paul Perry finally arrives at a gas station after his ordeal in the wilderness, he encounters two men inside wearing flannel shirts and jeans who are drinking beer and playing an electronic bowling game. The men, themselves having participated in the search for Paul and Harvey, treat Paul derisively, asking what he was doing out in the wilderness, and explaining how they would have been clever enough to be rescued by building a giant fire in the woods. The two also seem suspicious of the fact that Paul has left Harvey behind. They try to bait Paul as he drinks his beers and eats his hamburgers, but Paul simply agrees with them when they call his actions stupid. The two men, one of whom is apparently named Bill, and the other whose name readers never learn, drive away in their pickup truck while Paul is still waiting for the state police to arrive.

Nielson, Lars   Early in the novel, Paul Perry in his position as agricultural agent types out a loan application for SAWMILL LANDING resident Lars Nielson, described only as a "dumb-eyed farmer" (25). Paul generally does not have much to do in his office; this is one of the few times readers see him conduct actual business. After typing out the application, however, Paul makes coffee, reads the newspaper, and leaves the office around noon to go look for Addie.

Peri, Pehr The original Pehr Peri, grandfather to Paul and Harvey Perry, was born in a fishing community north of Helsinki and emigrated from Finland to the United States when he was 16 years old. After spending a year in Baltimore, he traveled west, then up the Mississippi River into Minnesota, where he lived a rough life working in lumber camps for the next five years. At age 22, Pehr Peri appeared in SAWMILL LANDING with a young son, named Pehr Lindstrom Peri, although no one in the town ever knew who the mother was or how the young man gained custody of the child. When Pehr Peri's arm was crushed in a sawmill accident in 1901, he took up life as an itinerant stump preacher, eventually becoming minister of the DAMASCUS LUTHERAN CHURCH in Sawmill Landing, a job his son would inherit when Pehr Peri hanged himself from the church rafters in 1919.

Perry, Grace Grace Perry is a schoolteacher from Iowa who is married to Paul Perry. A kind, sympathetic, and "full-breasted" (37) woman, Grace serves as a substitute mother figure to Paul, whose own mother died when he was a young boy. In many ways Grace competes with Harvey and with Addie for Paul's attention. While the younger couple appeal to Paul's more adventurous side, Grace longs to have a child with Paul and to settle more fully into their comfortable domestic routine. At the end of the novel, after Paul sees the Northern Lights at PLINEY'S POND, he seems to consciously recommit himself to Grace and the life she represents. The book closes by suggesting that the couple will move back to Iowa, where they had met while in college.

Perry, Harvey Harvey Perry, the younger brother of Paul Perry, has just returned from serving as a soldier in the Vietnam War as the novel opens. During his tour of duty, Harvey suffered a serious eye injury, although he refuses to speak to friends and family about how the injury occurred. In the months after his return, Harvey is restless and aimless, spending his time at the old farm-house he shares with Paul and Paul's wife, Grace, and spinning dreams about future travel, but making no attempt to get a job. He soon begins dating a young, half-Indian girl named Addie, whom Paul is also infatuated with. When Harvey plans an after-Christmas ski trip for the two couples in a town several hours drive away from the Perrys' own hometown of SAWMILL LANDING, he insists that he and Paul cross-country ski and camp on the way home. The trip turns nightmarish for Havey when Addie becomes involved with a handsome ski racer named Daniel, and the brothers lose their way in a blizzard on the return journey. Initially optimistic, Harvey becomes increasingly weak and ill as he and Paul run out of food and spend day and after day in the woods. Eventually Paul has to leave Harvey in an abandoned hunting shack the brothers stumble upon while he goes for help. Although Harvey is finally rescued and returns to Sawmill Landing, his relationship with Addie never recovers. Her move to an apartment in Minneapolis especially depresses the young veteran. When Paul loses his job with the U.S. Department of Agriculture, Harvey suggests selling the farmhouse that both brothers have grown up in, but becomes angry and resentful when the deal is actually closed. The novel ends with Harvey's future undetermined. As Paul and Grace plan to move to Iowa, Harvey is still talking in wild, extravagant ways about foreign travel and adventures, proposing to Paul a canoeing and fishing trip to Canada, then urging that his brother accompany him to the mountains outside of Mexico City.

Perry, Mrs. Readers never learn the first name of Paul and Harvey Perry's mother, the woman once married to Pehr Perry. Paul himself does not remember his mother very well since she died giving birth to Harvey when Paul was very young. He thinks of her now as merely a "pleasant shadow" (72) sitting by his father one wintry holiday, and he imagines that she resembled Grace, his wife.

Perry, Paul Milton Paul Milton Perry, the novel's protagonist, works as a county farm extension agent for the U.S. Department of Agriculture in the tiny town of SAWMILL LANDING, Minnesota. He and his wife, Grace, a schoolteacher, live together outside of town in a large, old farmhouse built by Paul's grandfather, a Finnish immigrant. They are soon joined by Paul's younger brother, Harvey, who has just returned from serving in the Vietnam War. As the novel opens, Paul seems to have grown restless with his marriage and his job. He is attracted to a young, part-Indian woman in town named Addie, whom he spends his summer days flirting with. When Addie begins dating Harvey, Paul is mildly jealous, but he and Grace nevertheless spend their evenings with the young couple, drinking, playing games, and listening to Harvey's fantasies about world travel. Shortly after Christmas, the two couples take a vacation together to attend ski races in another small town. Paul and Harvey plan to ski home, camping along the way, but this return trip turns disastrous when the brothers become lost in a blizzard. They wander in the deep woods for many days, having run out of food and with Harvey growing increasingly ill. Paul, the less adventuresome of the two brothers, is eventually forced to go for help on his own. Both men survive to return to Sawmill Landing, where their life returns to normal for a few months. But big changes are in store for the Perry brothers. Paul loses his job when the Department of Agriculture decides to close down his office, Addie leaves Harvey to move to Minneapolis, and the brothers decide to sell the house they have lived in their entire lives. At the end of the novel, Paul announces his plans to move back to Iowa with Grace, where he had gone to college and where she had grown up.

Perry, Pehr   Pehr Perry is the father of Paul and Harvey Perry. Initially baptized Pehr Lindstrom Peri, Perry never knew his own mother, having been raised by a single father—a stern Finnish immigrant, lumberjack and preacher, also named Pehr Peri. When the first Pehr Peri hanged himself in the rafters of the DAMASCUS LUTHERAN CHURCH, his son anglicized the family name to "Perry" and took over as minister of the church. Although Pehr Perry later married, his sons never knew their mother since she had died giving birth to Harvey, the younger brother. Following his wife's death, Perry grimly raised the boys alone in a farmhouse

his father had built outside of SAWMILL LANDING, maintaining a close relationship with Harvey, whom he taught to swim and camp and hunt, but never getting along as well with his older son, Paul, whom he considered soft. The old man died soon after the CUBAN MISSILE CRISIS in October 1962, having on his death bed instructed Harvey to build a bomb shelter in the yard of the farmhouse in the face of impending atomic war.

Silent Andy   On the first day of July, several months after his ordeal in the woods, Paul goes to the barber shop in SAWMILL LANDING for a haircut and shave. The barber's name is Andrew, but everyone in town calls him Silent Andy. Andy tells Paul that he has been "looking forward to this a long time," referring to the fact that Paul has apparently been letting his beard grow ever since getting lost that winter. The two men also briefly discuss the fact that Paul is selling his house. Silent Andy had seen the real estate advertisement in the newspaper.

State Police Officers   Upon arriving at a gas station after being lost in the woods for many days, Paul Perry borrows a phone and calls the state police. He first talks to an older officer who tells Paul they have been looking for him. He then repeats his story to a younger officer, who is less friendly but more efficient. Paul describes to this officer as best he can the location of the hunting shack where he had left Harvey. The young officer tells Paul that a police car is being dispatched from GRAND MARAIS. An agreeable patrolman eventually arrives and drives Paul home to SAWMILL LANDING.

Stenberg, Reverend   Reverend Stenberg is the minister who has taken over the pulpit at the DAMASCUS LUTHERAN CHURCH after Pehr Perry's death. Paul Perry, at one point, regrets not becoming a preacher himself like his father and grandfather, and thinks of Stenberg as a "crusty usurper" (25). Reverend Stenberg appears briefly in the novel at Harvey's birthday picnic the last day of July and at the Memorial Day parade and cemetery ceremony the following May.

Stjern, Elroy Elroy Stjern is the local mailman in SAWMILL LANDING. When the town mayor Jud Harmor finds Paul Perry's mail lying in the snow outside of his office one day, he determines to have a talk with Stjern.

Waitress at Gas Station A waitress at the gas station where Paul Perry goes for help after his long ordeal in the woods, who is said to speak with a "frontier Swedish" accent (306), serves Paul beer and hamburgers as he waits for the state police to come and pick him up. At first suspicious of Paul, the woman refuses to let him use the phone but relents when he tells her that it is an emergency situation. Eventually she seems to warm up to Paul, bringing him beer and a second hamburger unbidden.

Wolff, Herb Herb Wolff is a German immigrant who operates a drugstore in SAWMILL LANDING. Described as "pure German—impeccable and stiffly manicured, greedy eyes, a bristling crewcut and a voice that rose like deep magic from his sunken little torso" (15), Herb is dismayed that Paul and Grace Perry have planned no large-scale celebration for Harvey Perry's homecoming from the Vietnam War. Wolff, readers soon discover, is a town stalwart, challenging Jud Harmor for the office of mayor periodically and serving on the DRAFT board that had cheerfully sent Harvey off to war.

Wolff, Sr. Herb Wolff, a local drugstore owner, brings his elderly father to the birthday picnic that Grace holds for Harvey Perry on the last day of July. Wolff pushes the old man onto the Perry property in a wheelchair.

FURTHER READING

Herzog, Tobey C. *Tim O'Brien*. New York: Twayne, 1997.

Kaplan, Stephen. *Understanding Tim O'Brien* Columbia: University of South Carolina Press, 1995.

Nelson, Marie. "Two Consciences: A Reading of Tim O'Brien's Vietnam Trilogy: *If I Die in a Combat Zone, Going After Cacciato,* and *Northern Lights.*" In *Third Force Psychology and the Study of Literature,* edited by Bernard J. Paris, 262–279. Rutherford, N.J.: Farleigh Dickinson University Press, 1986.

The Nuclear Age (1985)

Published by Alfred A. Knopf in 1985, Tim O'Brien's third novel, *The Nuclear Age,* explores what it means to live under the very real threat of nuclear devastation. The novel is narrated in the first person by William Cowling, a 49-year-old geologist living outside of FORT DERRY, MONTANA, who has been obsessed with nuclear war his whole life. The present time is 1995, when William has begun digging an enormous bomb shelter in his yard. But like *Going After Cacciato,* much of the novel's action takes place in flashbacks as William tells his life story, from his boyhood in small-town Fort Derry during the COLD WAR to his college protest years in the late 1960s and DRAFT evasion of the Vietnam War, through his involvement in increasingly radical politics, to his eventual return to Fort Derry, where his discovery of a uranium deposit in the hills outside of town allows him to move into a comfortable conformity in a handsome new house, with a beautiful blond wife and a young daughter. But the threat of losing this hard-won nuclear family, as much as the continuing threat of nuclear apocalypse, has begun to unhinge William. His behavior in the present time grows increasingly strange as the novel unfolds. Possibly unbalanced himself, William nevertheless questions the sanity of a world peopled by human beings who are able to go blithely about their business despite the very real possibility of human extinction hanging over them. The novel explores the tenuous balance between fear and repression, between action and withdrawal, between obsession and oblivion, as the world edges ever closer to apocalypse in the waning days of the 20th century.

SYNOPSIS

Chapters 1–3
The novel opens in 1995 as William Cowling rises from bed in his home in Fort Derry, Montana, after midnight and begins digging obsessively in his yard, intent on building a fallout shelter to protect himself, his wife, Bobbi, and his 12-year-old daughter, Melinda, in case of a nuclear war. The story soon circles back in time to the year

1958, when William was a child about Melinda's age. Despite growing up with loving parents—his father sells real estate and his mother keeps house—and despite being a "happy kid" (10), living a regular childhood in a typical small town, William develops an overwhelming fear of nuclear attack, prompted largely by the news of the day filtered through his own overactive imagination. Overcome by his fears, William wakes up in the middle of a night in early May and heads for the basement, where he begins converting the family Ping-Pong table into a bomb shelter. His father finds him there several hours later, lumber and bricks and old rugs piled atop the table, walls built out of cardboard boxes filled with newspapers, rations from the kitchen pantry stacked inside the makeshift enclosure, and William's face covered by a paper bag filled with charcoal briquettes and sawdust—a homemade fallout mask.

Worried about their son's strange behavior, William's father and mother call in the old family doctor, Doc Crenshaw, to examine their son. The doctor finds nothing physically wrong with William, and, suspecting that the boy is simply trying to play hooky from school, orders him to cut out "the crap" (20). Later, William rides his bicycle to the town library, where a sympathetic librarian sees the boy thumbing through back issues of news magazines, studying pictures of real fallout shelters. Commenting that these are frightening times and that most people just "want to forget" (22), the librarian unleashes William's inner turmoil, and he begins sobbing uncontrollably, until his parents arrive to pick him up. That night, William runs for the basement again to take shelter under the Ping-Pong table. This time, when his father discovers him there, he challenges his son to a game of Ping-Pong. Working together, the father and son clear all the lumber scraps, bricks, and other detritus off the table in order to play. After William beats his father several games in a row, his father suggests it its time for bed and offers to help him rig up the shelter again. William yawns, says he can get to it in the morning, then forgets his debilitating fear for the next several years.

The novel then jumps ahead to October 1962, during the period of the CUBAN MISSILE CRISIS. Wil-

liam is now in high school. Although he has tamed his obsessive fears of nuclear war, he admits to not fitting in at school or in his town, to being a loner who hates high school and has few friends. To appease his parents' worries, William sometimes pretends to call friends on the phone, talking to them for long periods of time in made-up, one-sided conversations. The threat of nuclear devastation produced by the October missile crisis, perhaps the closest the world has ever come to nuclear war, makes William physically sick. He suffers from constipation and severe headaches. Although he tries to hide his unpopularity and his fears from his parents, they realize that something is wrong and soon take William to see a psychiatrist named Charles Adamson in Helena, Montana. The family books rooms at the Holiday Inn and stays in Helena for a week while William undergoes long, daily sessions with Adamson, a wily doctor who encourages William to speak about his problems by reeling off his own litany of complaints about the world—the inane, hierarchical pecking order of high school, his own failings as a child, his lack of friends, etc. During the last session, Adamson talks about his own despair for the future, pointing out that the world is doomed, the universe is eventually going to expire, and that there is nothing anyone can do about it. William responds by talking about bombs, missiles, radioactivity, and thermal blasts—all of his own worst fears. While the psychiatrist does not completely turn William's life around, the headaches and constipation clear up after the week in Helena, and William is able to return to his ordinary life and routines.

Chapters 4–6

The narrative, as it will do periodically throughout the book, then switches back to 1995 again. Readers find out that William has been digging his hole in the yard for two weeks now. Melinda tells her father that he's "nutto" (57), and Bobbi spends most of her time in the bedroom, writing poems. One morning at breakfast, William loses his temper after reading one of Bobbi's poems. There is "some bad language, some table-thumping" (58), but more disturbingly, Melinda claims to see William eat the poem, to actually put the piece of paper in his mouth and swallow it. That night Bobbi and Melinda move into the master bedroom together, locking William out. He stretches out in a sleeping bag in the hallway outside the bedroom door, soon discovering that pinned to the pajamas that Bobbi has laid out for him is another poem, this one suggesting that Bobbi will seek a divorce.

Readers are then transported back in time again, to the autumn of 1964, as the first rumblings of the Vietnam War—the GULF OF TONKIN, Marines in DA NANG—are making themselves heard in the country. William is a freshman at Peverson State University in Montana. He is studying geology, having developed a love of rocks as a child back in Fort Derry. Still a loner, William spends much of his time fantasizing about Sarah Strouch, a high school cheerleader from Fort Derry who has also gone on to Peverson State. As his college years progress, William becomes increasingly depressed and frightened by the news from Vietnam. He even calls his old psychiatrist, Chuck Adamson, whose number he has held onto for all these years. When no one answers the phone, William invents a conversation with the psychiatrist, which seems to comfort him for a time. By the autumn of his junior year, October 1966, the United States has 325,000 troops in Vietnam, and, under OPERATION ROLLING THUNDER, has begun dropping tons of explosives on North Vietnam. One Monday morning William purchases poster paper and writes on it in simple block letters, THE BOMBS ARE REAL. He positions himself in front of the school cafeteria at noon, silently holding his poster aloft, a practice he repeats every Monday for the next two months, until he is joined in his protest by Ollie Winkler, a pint-sized fellow student obsessed with explosives. An obese young woman named Tina Roebuck soon joins the group, which now calls itself THE COMMITTEE. In February 1967, William dances with his longtime fantasy girlfriend, Sarah Strouch, at Peverson's annual Winter Carnival. The two end up spending the entire night together, and the following Monday Sarah joins the Committee's protests outside the cafeteria.

With Sarah aboard, the Committee becomes much more active, arranging teach-ins, classroom boycotts, and parades in the spring of 1967. Wil-

liam, who started the whole thing with his simple poster, hangs back, both in his growing relationship with Sarah, and in the Committee's activities, afraid of losing control in the face of Sarah's uncompromising passion. He participates only reluctantly when the group sets off an explosion in the dean of students office in May 1967. The next school year, activities continue to escalate, with Ollie Winkler sabotaging the university's stadium lights during a football game, and the group seizing the campus radio station in January 1968. In March the group obtains a new member when Ned Rafferty, an old boyfriend of Sarah's, joins the group. William feels nothing but hate for Ned, jealous of his past relationship with Sarah but forced to concede Ned's basic decency. After graduation in May 1968, the group of co-conspirators breaks up temporarily, Ned Rafferty heading back to his father's ranch in Idaho, Ollie Winkler and Tina Roebuck heading west to work for the EUGENE MCCARTHY presidential campaign, and Sarah going to Florida for mysterious "appointments." William returns home to his parents' house in Fort Derry, where he spends a summer watching the assassination of ROBERT KENNEDY unfold on television, but paralyzed with indecision about his level of commitment to the increasingly radical group he helped form. In late August, William receives his draft notice to the Vietnam War.

Chapters 7–9
Meanwhile, back in the present time, 1995, William's wife, Bobbi, has packed suitcases, intending to separate from her husband. William has been digging his hole for two months now, and it is 15 feet deep. When Melinda tells her father that Bobbi plans to leave the next day, taking Melinda with her, William is initially calm, telling his daughter not to worry, that he will not allow that to happen. That night William cuts the phone lines to the house, waits until Melinda and Bobbi are in the bedroom, then methodically and quickly nails two-by-fours across the door, barring their exit. He next places a ladder outside the house, climbs up, and nails boards across the window as well. He spends the night cleaning the house and thinking about the war and his old friends. In the morning

Melinda cries and begs to be allowed to go to the bathroom, but William just cheerfully tells her to use a bottle and that he will figure something out.

When the narrative shifts back to the past, it is September 1968, and William's parents are supplying him with money and warm clothes, supportive of his decision to flee the draft. William takes a flight for Chicago, then another plane to New York, and finally, a red-eye to Miami. On this final leg of his journey, he is comforted by a TWA stewardess named Bobbi, who pins a poem titled "MARTIAN TRAVEL" to William's pocket before he leaves the plane. In Miami William spends two days in a hotel with his old girlfriend, Sarah Strouch, before being driven in a rented van to KEY WEST, FLORIDA, where Sarah has been living with the former members of the Committee. The group stays in Key West for several weeks, passing time, waiting for some kind of assignment from Sarah's mysterious contacts, and bemoaning the election of President RICHARD NIXON in November. During this period, the Committee members pressure William, who is still ambivalent about radical politics, for some kind of commitment, which he seems to make when the group takes a speed boat to Cuba shortly after the election.

After a week spent in relative luxury at a retreat compound in Cuba called SAGUA LA GRANDE, the young men and women begin undergoing a brutal and terrifying training period. Two ex-marines, with the unlikely names of Ebenezer Keezer and Nethro, lead the punishing physical fitness exercises and nightly lessons in radical politics. William, terrified of guns and war, defecates on himself one day on the weapons range and later collapses during a realistic nighttime exercise in which real bullets are fired at the trainees. Diagnosed with acute anxiety, William spends nine days in a hospital on the outskirts of HAVANA. Because of his inability to handle "the rough stuff" (193), William is eventually assigned a position as a network delivery boy in the shadowy organization. When The Committee performs its first major operation on March 6, 1969, a night raid on a Selective Service office in Miami, William is out of the fray, safe on a plane headed for some kind of pickup in SEATTLE.

Chapters 10–12
Back in 1995, William has kept Bobbi and Melinda locked in the master bedroom of their house for two weeks. He has cut a small rectangular opening in the boarded-up door to allow food trays and chamber pots to be slid in and out. Melinda pleads with her father to let her out, asking him what would happen if she got really sick, accusing him of being a kidnapper, and shouting "Loony" at him (197). William stays remarkably calm, and Bobbi remains remarkably silent through all this; William constantly reiterates his love for his wife and daughter, while Bobbi composes poem-messages for her estranged husband. Meanwhile, William continues to dig his hole in the yard, using dynamite to aid his efforts. While he tells himself that he is working to eventually save the lives of Bobbi and Melinda, he is clearly growing more and more deranged, even believing by this point that the enormous hole he is digging is speaking to him, urging him on, reciting nursery rhymes, inciting him to ever more extreme behavior. One late afternoon, he puts sleeping pills in the drinks he brings for Bobbi and Melinda. Later that night, he uses a crowbar to remove the boards from the bedroom door, carries the sleeping woman and girl out of the house, and places them in sleeping bags on hammocks he has rigged up in the giant hole in the earth.

Back in his radical past, William continues to serve as courier for the Committee, logging 200,000 miles on airplanes between early March 1969 and April 1971. Between trips he comes home to the bungalow in Key West that is headquarters for the group. When Sarah brings sealed crates of M-16 automatic weapons into the house to store in the attic, William is disturbed, but as usual, too ambivalent to protest much. In October 1969 William watches the MORATORIUM TO END THE WAR IN VIETNAM, a giant, global war protest, from a television in a Kansas City motel room. He spends Thanksgiving and Christmas of that year on the road as well, calling home once but saying nothing when his mother answers the phone. Lonely on his travels and still remembering the stewardess he had met on the original TWA flight to Miami, William begins looking for Bobbi in May

1970, making inquiries of airport personnel. He eventually discovers that she has become a graduate student in creative writing in New York. Following the trail to New York after many dead ends, William finds out that Bobbi has left the airline navigator she went to New York with for a famous poet-translator named Scholheimer. William finds a listing in the phone book and calls Bobbi, who says she is flattered but who also tells William she is happy and that she is moving to Germany with Scholheimer.

Back in Key West, Sarah is jealous of William's obsession with Bobbi, but she has been distracting herself with Ned Rafferty, who has been in love with her for years. As 1970 passes into 1971, William becomes more friendly with Ned as well, who seems to share some of his own reservations about the Committee's activities. On April 21, 1971, William's father back in Fort Derry dies. While it is considered too dangerous to attend the funeral, Sarah and Ned accompany William back to his small hometown, where he watches the graveside ceremony through binoculars from a nearby hilltop. The next day William calls his old psychiatrist, Chuck Adamson, who urges the young man to make a clean break from the Committee. Adamson promises to help William with the logistics of a new life. But before he leaves the group completely, William makes one final trip to Key West to pack up his things and say goodbye. While there, he and Ned Rafferty, after drinking heavily one night, remove the weapons crates still stored in the attic of the bungalow and dump their contents into the Atlantic Ocean.

Following this symbolic act of parting, William returns to Fort Derry, where Chuck Adamson sets him up in small cottage in the foothills outside town. William lives quietly for the next several years. On October 1, 1976, his 30th birthday, he gives himself up to the authorities as a draft dodger. While there are formalities and papers to sign, he is not given any jail time, and in fact, he receives a blanket pardon, along with all the other Vietnam draft evaders, which President JIMMY CARTER issues on January 21, 1977. William begins graduate studies in geology in February of that same year and completes his master's degree in June

1979. In late summer and fall of 1979, he begins seriously exploring the hills around his cottage with his Geiger counter, realizing from his studies of geology that there must be uranium in these Montana mountains. When the former Committee members—Sarah, Ollie, Tina, and Ned—come to visit on New Year's Day, 1980, William tells them about the uranium, and they begin searching in earnest. The friends find an actual ore deposit their 12th day out and buy the mountain on February 4, 1980. Several months later, they sell the mining rights to Texaco for $25 million in cash. William uses part of his money to continue his search for the elusive Bobbi, who has haunted his memory for the past decade. Sarah, whose love for William seems to grow in proportion to William's own obsession with Bobbi, insists on accompanying William to Germany, where over the course of several weeks the two make inquiries and track down leads. Eventually, their search leads them back to the United States, to Minneapolis, where Bobbi had reenrolled in graduate school for a time, and on to New York after a professor at the UNIVERSITY OF MINNESOTA tells Sarah and William that Bobbi had left to work as a tour guide at the United Nations.

It is in Manhattan at the UN building that William finally finds the ex-stewardess who has occupied his thoughts for so long. He persuades her to come west with him, back to Montana, where they eventually marry. Melinda is born in 1983, and the young family uses part of their fortune to build a beautiful house in the SWEETHEART MOUNTAINS, where Bobbi writes her poetry and William continues to stew about the arms race and the threat of nuclear destruction. In the early nineties, three events happen that contribute to William's extremely aberrant behavior in 1995. His mother dies in January 1993; Bobbi disappears for two weeks that summer, taking her diaphragm with her, and refuses to tell her husband where she was; and Sarah Strouch dies of encephalitis in March 1994 at the home of William and Bobbi, where she had been staying since becoming ill during a Christmas visit. In autumn of 1994, William suffers what he calls a "minor breakdown" (295), and that winter Bobbi suggests a trial separation.

Chapter 13

The final chapter of the book returns to the present time—1995. While Bobbi and Melinda sleep in their hammocks underground, William imagines the hole urging him to set off a dynamite explosion. Despite trying to silence the irrational urgings from the hole, William finds himself rigging wires and blasting caps into the granite that lines the giant cavity in the earth. When Melinda wakes up unexpectedly, she sees her father with the firing device at her feet. Eventually managing to take the firing device into her own hands, Melinda threatens to blow them all up if her father does not take her out of the hole. However, as William crawls toward her and lifts the device from her hands, she is unable to carry out her threat. When William touches his daughter's skin, he feels as if "a kind of miracle" (311) happens. He carries her up the ladder and into the house and goes back for Bobbi, whom he also carries to safety. The novel ends with William acknowledging the certainty that his wife will leave him, that his daughter will one day die, and that the world will surely end. But in the final paragraph he claims that despite this knowledge he "believe[s] otherwise" (312). He tells himself that life will go on as usual, that at night he will "sleep the dense narcotic sleep of [his] species" (312), forgetting his troubles and madness, forgetting the inevitable sentence of doom that the world lives under.

COMMENTARY

The novel is divided into three parts, titled "Fission," "Fusion," and "Critical Mass." The term *fission* refers to a nuclear reaction in which the nucleus of an atom splits into smaller parts, and the first portion of the book deals with William Cowling's split from his family and from his supposedly normal, small-town, all-American upbringing. William describes Fort Derry, Montana, as "a typical small town," and he describes himself, at least initially, as a "happy kid," who "grew up in a family that pursued all the ordinary small-town values" (9–10). Continuing to insist on the complete normalcy of his childhood during the conformist 1950s, he adds,

> I played war games, tried to hit baseballs, started a rock collection, rode my bike to the A&W, fed the goldfish, messed around. Normal, normal. I even ran a lemonade stand out along the sixth fairway at the golf course, ten cents a glass, plenty of ice: a regular entrepreneur. (10)

Sounding not unlike WORTHINGTON, MINNESOTA, Tim O'Brien's own hometown, Fort Derry fits the stereotype of small-town America in the 1950s, with its requisite cast of eccentric but lovable locals like the curmudgeonly Doc Crenshaw, who nevertheless makes house calls and knows his patients and their past histories intimately, as well as the lovely town librarian who sympathizes with an overwrought 12-year-old William and knows exactly whom to call when the young boy breaks down in tears. William's family matches the 1950s ideal as well: His mother stays home to take care of the house, and his father, who sells real estate, is kind and patient with his son, well-respected in his local community, and with his tall and straight posture and bright blue eyes possesses all-American good looks. Describing his father early on, William writes, "I worshipped that man" (10). The Cowlings are an intact and loving nuclear family, living the good life during the postwar boom years of the 1950s.

Yet, as the title of this first part of the novel suggests, small-town American life in the 1950s is not as ideal or normal as it seems. Hanging over this nuclear family is the constant threat of nuclear war. The children in this supposedly safe and idyllic small town practice duck-and-cover drills at school, William sees pictures of H-bombs in *Life* magazine, reads about the radioactive chemical STRONTIUM 90 in the milk that he drinks, and is haunted in dreams by the whining drone of ICBM missiles. From his earliest years, William writes, he understood "that there was nothing make-believe about doomsday. No hocus-pocus. No midnight fantasy. . . . It was real, like physics, like the laws of combustion and gravity" (11–12). This insistence on the reality of the threat of nuclear annihilation marks William's mental state throughout the novel. While others may view him as paranoid or cowardly, William repeatedly insists on his own sanity in recognizing the very real danger lurking behind the façade of normalcy with which postwar Americans go about their lives. To William it is the world around him that is crazy; he marvels at his fellow citizens' ability to repress and ignore the dire consequences that the cold war could very well bring about.

Hints of death and apocalypse seep through the facade of small-town normalcy as well in the weekend celebration called CUSTER DAYS, during which the residents of Fort Derry stage an annual historical reenactment of the BATTLE OF LITTLE BIGHORN, popularly known as Custer's Last Stand. William's adored father plays the role of the doomed GEORGE ARMSTRONG CUSTER in the yearly ritual, bravely riding into battle again and again, the outcome already known, his death a foregone conclusion. Not only does this ritual evoke death over and over for the young William, it also drives home the inevitability of destruction on a massive scale. Although William "crave[s] the miracle of a happy ending" (11), just as he longs for a miraculous escape from the nuclear war he feels certain will come, he knows that his father "didn't stand a chance" (11). The script of history is inexorable; the U.S. 7th Cavalry will be wiped out and Mr. Cowling as Custer will lose his scalp to CRAZY HORSE year after year. Perhaps even more significant, though, the historical reenactment evokes the apocalypse facing western Indian tribes. While the Battle of Little Bighorn represents the pinnacle of the Indian Wars for tribal members, it also suggests the eventual annihilation of the tribes' traditional cultures and ways of life, a near cultural genocide. The town, while seeming to celebrate the triumph of the Indians at Little Bighorn, is really commemorating the obliteration of an entire previous culture. The pacification of the western tribes, after all, is what allowed white settlement of places like Fort Derry, Montana, to take place. Witnessing this yearly spectacle teaches the young William Cowling that wholesale destruction of a previous culture is not only possible but historically inevitable. Nonetheless, the residents of Fort Derry fail to register the true significance of their Custer Days celebration, calmly eating ice cream and cotton candy in the grandstands and heading out for late night root beers at the A&W when the spectacle ends.

What William learns from the behavior of those around him is the necessity of telling lies in order to survive. He claims that by the time he reached high school in 1960 he had become "something of a loner . . . a hermit: William Cowling, the Lone Ranger" (35). His interest in geology, in fact, stems from his enjoyment of the solitude he experiences while wandering the cliffs and canyons surrounding Fort Derry and the fact that rocks seem "safe" to him; they never talk back (35). In order to cover up his solitary existence and to comfort his parents, who are understandably worried about him, William begins to tell lies about his social life: "A few fibs here and there," he explains, "Quite a few, in fact" (37). One of his favorite tricks is to pretend to call up high school cheerleader Sarah Strouch on the telephone and invent one-sided conversations with her, which his parents can overhear. William's games escalate when he begins to pretend to go on dates with Sarah. These small lies that William lives are connected, of course, to the big lie that he sees his family and friends in Fort Derry living every day: They go about their ordinary lives as if the world is not under a death sentence, doomed to end in a horrible and violent way. Just as his parents in an attempt to shelter William never discuss the nuclear arms race, he tries to shelter his parents from the reality of his own disturbed mental state: "I loved [my father] too. Which is why I didn't blurt out the facts. To protect him, to beef up his confidence" (36). Small-town America in the 1950s and 1960s teaches that repression and pretense are the ways to deal with frightening political realities. Readers here might sense some of the same frustration with the blindness and willed ignorance of small-town life that O'Brien expresses in his memoir, *If I Die in a Combat Zone,* and in a 1991 interview with Daniel Bourne in which he discusses his "bitterness about small-town Republican, polyester, white-belted, Kiwanis America."

It is not until the Cuban missile crisis of October 1962 that William's fellow Fort Derryians are forced to at least partially acknowledge the reality of the nuclear threat hanging over them. During this month, U.S. spy planes confirmed that Cuba, fearing a U.S. invasion and with full Soviet support, had begun to build offensive missile bases in the country, which lies a mere 90 miles off the Florida Keys. Historians generally view the Cuban missile crisis as the point at which the cold war came closest to erupting in actual nuclear attack. During this tense period, William looks at his father and asks, "There, you see?" (38). He adds that he is not being a smart aleck: "It was a serious question: Did he finally *see?*" (38). Despite the fear William experiences, it is also something of a relief for him that others around him are finally having to recognize the dread he has been living with since he turned the family Ping-Pong table into a makeshift bomb shelter at the age of 12. While William's parents, as well as his acquaintances in town, continue to go about their lives, repressing the terror underlying the current political situation, nevertheless the repression is now acknowledged as exactly that—his mother asks him about college plans, pointing out that they "have to trust" there will be a future. The high school principal delivers "a speech about the need for courage and calm," and adults attempt to reassure themselves by repeating that world leaders "aren't madmen" (39–40). This sense of shared fear, of an entire community finally experiencing a nuclear anxiety comparable to his own, allows William to get through the crisis relatively unscathed. "I wasn't haunted by the nuclear stuff, I didn't lose control," he states (40). Yet, his fears become manifested in actual physical symptoms. He soon develops headaches and constipation. When William says that he "couldn't shit" (40), readers understand that on the metaphoric level William simply cannot "bullshit"—repress his fears—as the other members of his community seem so able to do.

The theme of lies and pretense continues when William is taken by his parents to see the psychologist Chuck Adamson. William confides in Adamson his belief that the "whole counseling game was a waste of time. A racket . . . A total charade" (45). Following this confession, Adamson obliges William by acting out a charade with him. Adamson expresses hatred and anger about his personal high school experiences, encouraging William to open up about his own problems. While William is somewhat suspicious, speculating that Adamson's

declarations "could've been an act of some sort—I wasn't naïve" (46), he nevertheless is taken in, and the two seem to exchange roles as William eventually begins to give Adamson advice about dealing with his problems:

> "I'm no expert," I told him, "but the first thing is to take a good look at yourself. Stop covering up. Stop pretending." I waved the ruler at him. "You might not believe me, but I've had some experience with this sadness stuff, and there's one thing I know for sure. Self-deception, that's the killer. You can't get well if you don't admit you're sick." (51)

William, although no good at repression, is a master at pretending for the sake of his parents and teachers to be well and happy when he is not. Clearly, this advice that he gives Adamson is actually meant for himself. Yet, at the same time, William could also be speaking here about the U.S. political situation in the early 1960s. If the country refuses to admit that it is sick, that the arms race is a dangerous and pathological game, how can it ever expect to achieve a true, lasting peace? If the world continues to cover up the very real and frightening danger of nuclear war, to pretend such a danger does not exist, it can never address this danger in a productive way. The novel asks which kind of self-deception is worse: a lonely, scared, and friendless young man, possibly becoming mentally unhinged, who pretends to be "normal," or a world on the brink of nuclear apocalypse that pretends no real threat exists?

And even beyond the threat of nuclear war, the fear driving William is at least partly plain old existential angst about the inevitability of death itself. In his final session with Adamson, the psychologist explains to the boy that he gave up his hobby of astronomy because it brought home to him the ultimate death sentence that all mankind lives under: "Doom! End of the world, end of everything!" (52). William writes that Adamson was not shy about laying it all out: "How someday the sun would begin cooling down, losing energy, and how our pretty little planet would freeze up into a shining ball of ice" (52). Adamson goes on to argue that all the ways human beings have of coping—"Our children. The genetic pool" (54)—are basically lies, pretenses, as well:

> The things we've made, books and buildings and inventions. Doesn't Edison still live in his light bulb? Switch it on and there he is. Immortality, in a way. A kind of faith. We plant trees and raise families, and those are ways of seeking—I don't know—a kind of significance. Life after death. That's what civilization *is:* life after death. But if you wipe out civilization— (54)

Adamson's remarks suggest that all human life is a pretense to some extent. We must somehow continue to live with the painful knowledge of our impermanence and even the impermanence of ourselves as a species. As William leaves Adamson's office for the last time, the psychologist looks away from the boy, then laughs and says, "A charade, you were right" (55). While Adamson is speaking about his own behavior in their sessions, his technique of getting William to open up about his problems, he is also speaking about the superficiality of the high school experience, the tendency of people to ignore frightening political realities, and in the largest sense, the human will to survive in the face of certain doom. The word *fission* in the title of this section of the novel suggests William's real split with his family and community: his willingness to recognize and think about these charades that human beings live every day.

William's increasing separation from those around him only escalates when he graduates from high school and leaves home to attend PEVERSON STATE COLLEGE. Arrogant in his feelings of intellectual superiority when writing home about the antics of his fellow students—"Stereos that blew your brains out at 3 a.m. Coeds who pondered the spelling of indefinite articles. Elaborate farting contests in the school library" (67)—William recounts his love of geology, not only for the solitude it provides him but also because of the sense of permanence that rocks offer. He sometimes even sleeps in the lab at night, enjoying the "brilliant twinklings" of the rocks that surround him and contemplating the physical earth: "*Terra firma,* I'd think. Back to the elements. A hard thing to explain, but for me geology represented a model for how the world

could be, and should be. Rock—the word itself was solid. Calm and stable, crystal locked to crystal, there was a hard, enduring dignity in even the most modest piece of granite. Rocks lasted" (68). It is no wonder that William's reaction to the threat of losing Bobbi and Melinda in the novel's present time, spring of 1995, is to dig deep into the earth as he desperately seeks the permanence that eludes him in human relationships.

William manages to survive his first year and a half at college, but his mental state grows increasingly precarious as news of the Vietnam War begins to filter home. He has nightmares involving marines dying along a paddy dike near CHU LAI, planes dropping napalm bombs, and villages burning to the ground. While William Cowling will become a radical war protester rather than a foot soldier like so many other O'Brien characters, the war nevertheless affects him profoundly, shaping his future just as it molds the lives and personalities of characters such as Paul Berlin, Jimmy Cross, Norman Bowker, and John Wade. As the war escalates, so does William's inability to repress his fear. He eventually hand-letters a sign with the words THE BOMBS ARE REAL, which he holds aloft outside the college cafeteria at noon every Monday. Although he is soon joined in his protest by two other students, Ollie Winkler and Tina Roebuck, William, ever the loner, remains ambivalent about his involvement with the group that the students name the Committee, especially Ollie's penchant for bomb making. To William, who so dreads the specter of nuclear war, bombs on either side are frightening and dangerous.

William's ambivalence becomes, if anything, even more deep-seated when his longtime fantasy girlfriend, Sarah Strouch, joins the Committee. Both attracted and repelled by Sarah's outgoing nature—she is a former high school cheerleader—and by her daring bravado, William's reaction to Sarah's recklessness is to become more careful, more controlled, a response metaphorically illustrated by the return of his constipation. Sarah's personal intimacy with death is another factor that seems to both repel and attract William. Her father was a mortician in Fort Derry, and the home she grew up in also served as her father's place of business—the STROUCH FUNERAL HOME. While William is afraid to act, despite his strong antiwar beliefs, Sarah goes to the opposite extreme. She acts vigorously, at times seeming to act solely for the sake of action itself, setting into motion boycotts, teach-ins, and parades, arranging for a small explosion in the dean's office, and sabotaging the stadium lights during a college football game. Not only does Sarah make things happen; the vocabulary she uses is military: "It's combat, she'd say. Philosophy's fine, but you don't hem and haw on the front lines. You haul in the artillery" (100). William ponders the easy continuity in Sarah's transformation from cheerleader to rabble-rouser:

> It was a smooth, almost effortless transition. Surprising, maybe, and yet the impulse was there from the start. In a sense, I realized, cheerleaders *are* terrorists. All that zeal and commitment. A craving for control. A love of pageantry and crowds and slogans and swollen rhetoric. Power, too. The hot, energizing rush of absolute authority: *Lean to the left, lean to the right.* And then finally that shrill imperative: *Fight—fight—fight!* Don't politicians issue the same fierce exhortations? (100)

Here William notes that the line separating the radical war protesters from the politicians who committed the country to war is a very fine one. Both groups enjoy the power they wield over others, and both advocate violence as a solution to world problems. This observation will grow even more pertinent when, along with his fellow Committee members, he undergoes paramilitary-style training in Cuba after his college graduation.

The next section of the novel, titled "Fusion," depicts William becoming more fully cemented into the radical politics he had flirted with as a college student. Just as fusion is a nuclear reaction that bonds lighter atomic nuclei together, the members of the Committee, which now include Sarah's previous boyfriend, Ned Rafferty, move to a bungalow in Key West, Florida, forming a "heavy nucleus" for their radical operations. William's decision to evade the draft notice he receives for Vietnam War duty is what propels him to leave Fort Derry and finally join Sarah and their friends

in Key West. While his parents support his decision to flee, William and his father both recognize that such a solution is not the best one. Mr. Cowling understands that his son does not want to die in such a morally confused war and thus sees the practical need for William to leave, yet William acknowledges that his father also doubts the morality of his decision: "It wasn't cowardice exactly, and he understood that, too, and it wasn't courage" (140). In many ways, William Cowling here resembles the young Tim O'Brien, who will appear in the later short story "On the Rainy River" from *The Things They Carried.* Both are paralyzed by an impossible choice: whether to accept the call to fight in a war in which "certain blood" is being shed "for uncertain reasons" (140). Both recognize that fleeing the draft means they will be losing a great deal of what they have been taught to value their whole lives: "Little things, like backyard barbecues, but big things, too, family and history, all of it" (139–140). Both decisions—O'Brien's to go to war and William Cowling's to flee the draft and join the protest movement—are at least partially nondecisions. While Tim O'Brien is so paralyzed by uncertainty that he cannot bring himself to jump out of Elroy Berdahl's boat and swim the few remaining feet to the Canadian border, William Cowling in his preparations to leave Fort Derry seems to be acting in a near-somnambulistic state, allowing his father to make arrangements and telling Sarah on the phone that he is "pretty sure" (140) about his commitment to the group. The two books, *The Things They Carried* and *The Nuclear Age,* work nearly as companion pieces as each explores the outcome of different decisions made in response to the basic moral quandary faced by numerous thoughtful young men in the late 1960s.

But while the later novel would be nearly unanimously hailed as a masterpiece by critics, early reviewers of *The Nuclear Age* were much less congratulatory. The "Fusion" section of the book is the portion that most bothered these reviewers, who argued that O'Brien's depiction of the radical left of the late 1960s and early 1970s does not ring true. John Romano, writing in the magazine *Atlantic,* called "the protagonist's long involvement in the radical left . . . the book's most errant (and lengthy) nonsense" (105), while Grace Paley in the *New York Times Book Review* opined that in this section of the book O'Brien settled for "mockery," which "usually means easy, narrow characterization" (7). O'Brien's depiction of the Committee members was disparaged as well by David Montrose in the *Times Literary Supplement*, who wrote that the book's principal flaw was "O'Brien's inability to create believable urban guerillas: Cowling's anti-war brothers and sisters come across as tepid cartoons" (342). Perhaps the most cartoonish of these figures are the two radical commandoes who oversee the Committee members' training in Cuba: Ebeneezer Keezer and Nethro. Both African Americans, whose blackness alone seems enough to intimidate these young college graduates from Montana, Ebeneezer Keezer and Nethro are also former marines who have seen action in Vietnam. During the training sessions, Ebeneezer acts like a marine drill sergeant, humiliating the young recruits in order to toughen them up. When Ebeneezer reminds the protesters that they are "soldiers . . . Like in wartime" (177), and when he forces them to perform endless calisthenics and mock war games, William thinks to himself that he has actually come face-to-face with everything he had tried to escape. He complains to Sarah about the training sessions, pointing out that he "can't tell the good guys from the bad guys" (183). O'Brien is satirizing the antiwar movement here, showing again that the motives and tactics of the radical protesters are not that different from the motives and tactics of those who supported the war.

And just as many of O'Brien's characters, including Paul Berlin and John Wade, are scared and incompetent soldiers, so William Cowling turns out to be a scared and incompetent revolutionary. While Paul Berlin loses control during the ambush of Cacciato, firing his rifle wildly and urinating on himself, William Cowling undergoes a similar experience during a simulated night raid in Cuba, panicking, squealing, shooting off his rifle, and finally defecating into his pants. Yet, William reasons that such a reaction should perhaps be considered a sane response to insane circumstances: "If you're sane, you see madness. If you see madness,

you freak. If you freak, you're mad. What does one do?" (184). Just as Tim O'Brien in "On the Rainy River" is caught in a no-win situation, facing exile and loathing from his family and community if he flees the war but injuring his own sense of morality and self-respect if he goes, William Cowling also faces a catch-22. If he is sane enough to notice the madness around him, he will respond with the appropriate fear, and thus be labeled mad. This is the dilemma that has faced William his whole life and that has shaped his personality.

William's obsession with Bobbi, the stewardess he initially meets on his TWA flight from New York to Miami as he is fleeing the draft, grows out of the feeling of escape she seems to offer from the muddled world of politics, protest, and war. It is no accident that William's introduction to Bobbi occurs 10,000 feet above the earth; in William's mind, Bobbi belongs to an ethereal realm, a world of the imagination far removed from the bombs that threaten to destroy the world. She speaks to William about books and travel and poetry, explaining that poems "do not *mean* . . . that meanings are merely names, just as grass is a name, but that grass would still be grass without its name" (152). For a young man obsessed with naming reality, with pointing out that THE BOMBS ARE REAL, Bobbi's ideas are confusing but liberating, at least initially. As the critic Daniel Cordle argues, William has believed that words simply reflect reality, that there is a one-on-one correlation between the word and the thing. Bobbi, however, sees the metaphoric possibilities of language; she notes the instability between words and the things that words describe. As a poet, she suggests a world of metaphoric, suggestive meaning, in which the imagination has the power to shape reality. The idea that imaginative literature—poetry and stories—can reform the world we live in is a continuing theme in much of O'Brien's work, from Paul Berlin's attempts to imagine himself out of war in *Going After Cacciato,* to the narrator's assertion that "stories can save us" in *The Things They Carried,* to the biographer's attempt to imaginatively reconstruct what happened to Kathy Wade in *In the Lake of the Woods.* William Cowling, like many O'Brien characters, is torn between what, on the one hand, seem to be the inescapable pressures of reality and, on the other, the capacity to invent new realities. He is instinctively aware of this dilemma when he muses earlier in the book about the nature of the imagination:

> Our lives are shaped in some small measure by the scope of our daydreams. If we can imagine happiness, we might find it. If we can imagine a peaceful, durable world, a civilized world, then we might someday achieve it. (70)

Throughout O'Brien's work he suggests that it is the paucity of the human imagination that traps people into war and other unendurable circumstances. Bobbi, like Sarkin Aung Wan in *Cacciato*, suggests the power of the imagination to create new worlds, new realities. William Cowling in his desperation to escape the only reality he knows becomes obsessed with finding the poet again.

Yet, *The Nuclear Age*, while exploring the dark political realities of the cold war and the radical protest movement of the late 1960s, also exposes the murky underside of individual human relationships. William's obsession with Bobbi transforms into a desire to possess her completely. In physics, the term *critical mass* refers to the smallest amount of material needed to set off a nuclear reaction. It is in this third and final section of the novel that William himself reaches critical mass. What pushes William over the edge in this section is Bobbi's threatened departure coming so soon after the deaths of William's mother and of Sarah Strouch. After losing both parents and all of his Committee comrades, William simply cannot bear another loss. The fear of impermanence has haunted him throughout his life. So, when Bobbi mysteriously disappears for two weeks, taking her diaphragm with her, and later asks for a separation, William desperately attempts to make her stay, digging deep into the earth, working among the seemingly permanent rocks that he loves, as he attempts to protect himself from another devastating loss. To avoid letting Bobbi and Melinda go, William is willing to imprison them and even kill them by the end of the novel.

The fine line between love and possession is a theme that O'Brien will continue to explore in

later works as well, especially *The Things They Carried* and *In the Lake of the Woods,* in which he depicts characters who become so obsessed with the objects of their desire that they imagine the self and the other merging into a single being. In "Sweetheart of the Song Tra Bong," from *Things,* Mary Anne Bell's necklace of tongues suggests her own nearly ravenous desire to consume and destroy the other. "I want to *eat* this place," she explains. "Vietnam. I want to swallow the whole country— the dirt, the death—I just want to eat it and have it there inside me. That's how I feel. It's like . . . this appetite" (111). Her desire to know and understand the Vietnamese people has grown into a perverse longing to actually incorporate them into her own body. Surely suggestive of America's desire to create a capitalist Vietnam in its own image while largely ignoring the other country's culture and history, Mary Anne's appetite is reflected in personal relationships presented elsewhere in the novel. Lieutenant Jimmy Cross in "The Things They Carried" is so overwhelmed by his love for Martha that "he wanted to sleep inside her lungs and breathe her blood and be smothered" (11). The narrator in the final story describes his childhood love for Linda in similar terms: "Even then, at nine years old, I wanted to live inside her body. I wanted to melt into her bones—*that* kind of love" (228). These male characters' desire to know and understand the female other is imagined in terms of a literal blending of physical bodies.

But the character who most resembles William Cowling is Senator John Wade in *Lake of the Woods.* In that novel O'Brien writes:

> There were times when John Wade wanted to open up Kathy's belly and crawl inside and stay there forever. He wanted to swim through her blood and climb up and down her spine and drink from her ovaries and press his gums against the firm red muscle of her heart. He wanted to suture their lives together. (71)

Wade's love for his wife, Kathy, is so obsessive that it becomes destructive, an urge to actually consume the other person. Although readers never find out definitively what happens to Kathy Wade, the book leaves open the possibility that Wade might actually have murdered his wife in order to possess her completely. Just as John loves Kathy and is afraid of losing her, William Cowling in the final chapter of *The Nuclear Age* reflects that all his actions are motivated by love of his wife and the fear that she will leave him: "Certain truths appear. I love my wife. I loved her before I knew her, and I love her now, and I will not let her go. I'm committed. I believe in fidelity. I will not be separated. One thing in my life will last and keep lasting and last forever. Love is absolute" (296). William's statement that he loved Bobbi before he even knew her suggests that like other O'Brien characters he is perhaps more in love with the *idea* of the other, of finding a soulmate, than with the real woman herself. Just as Jimmy Cross in "The Things They Carried" imagines a relationship with Martha that does not really exist, William Cowling is in love with the idea of romantic love, with finding an other to complete him and make him whole, with the idea that love can deliver the happy ending he has longed for his whole life.

But just as the novel depicts the very real nuclear threat hanging over the sweetly nostalgic small-town world of Fort Derry, Montana, it also shows that human relationships themselves are impermanent and that others must remain, to a certain extent, unknowable and unattainable. The narrator of *In The Lake of the Woods* will muse on just this dilemma when he considers his own desire to fully understand John Wade: "What drives me on, I realize, is a craving to force entry into another heart, to trick the tumblers of natural law, to perform miracles of knowing. It's human nature. We are fascinated, all of us, by the implacable otherness of others" (101). Bobbi cannot complete and fulfill William anymore than Sarah Strouch could. It is only in fantasy that these women can expel his ultimate aloneness. The hole in the ground that William is digging, then, which he imagines as a nearly womblike safe place, where the dangerous world can be kept at bay, becomes more a grave than a womb by the end of the novel. The only thing that prevents William from actually using the firing device to set off the dynamite lining the walls of this deep, underground chasm is his holding his daughter, Melinda, tight to him and touching her

skin after she has threatened to blow them all up herself:

> When I get to my feet, Melinda whimpers and says, "Stay *away* from me." But I'm willing to risk it. I'm a believer. The first step is absolute. "Daddy," she says, "you better not!" But I have to. I cross the hole and kneel down and lift the firing device from her lap and hold her tight while she cries. I touch her skin. It's only love, I know, but it's a kind of miracle. (310–311)

The miracle here is not the "miracle of knowing" that the narrator of *Lake* longs for—it is a miracle of repression. William tells himself that "it isn't real," not Sarah, whom he imagines speaking to him at the end, nor the Bomb itself: "just a fault line in the imagination. If you're sane, you accept this" (311). William removes both Melinda and Bobbi from the hole in the ground, where he had placed them and carries them inside the house.

Although his wife and daughter will live, the novel does not conclude happily. William admits that he knows the ending of his own story: "One day it will happen. One day we will see flashes, all of us. One day my daughter will die. One day, I know, my wife will leave me" (312). Despite knowing all this, however, William consciously makes the decision to "believe otherwise," to pretend, as other people seem able to do, that "all things are renewable, that the human spirit is undefeated and infinite," that his marriage will last, that he will endure (312). While earlier William had mused that human beings could perhaps produce a peaceful, happy world if they could only imagine it, nevertheless at novel's end William's willful act of pretending seems more delusion than a constructive imagining of a better world. Readers surely know that Bobbi and Melinda cannot stay with a man who imprisoned them in their home for weeks and who tried to murder them. And his claim that he will "hold to a steadfast orthodoxy, confident to the end that E will somehow not quite equal $mc2$ (312), should sound delusional to readers as well. The tragedy of the novel is not that one man has gone mad or that life in 20th-century America involves living with nuclear dread. The tragedy is that when human beings refuse to face the consequences of their actions, when they repress the very real dangers facing them, they will not be able to imagine a way out of the nightmare politics of the cold war they themselves have created. But even more tragic is the fact that, even if the nuclear threat disappeared, it would not take away with it the instability and temporality that is a fact of human existence. The real tragedy of the novel is that in order to survive in a fleeting and impermanent world, people must pretend a belief in the permanence of human life that is not really justified.

CHARACTERS

Adamson, Charles C. Charles C. Adamson is the name of the psychologist whom William Cowlings' parents take him to see in Helena, Montana, after the boy passes out in a high school study hall. Worried about William's reclusiveness, his lies, and his anxieties about nuclear war, Mr. and Mrs. Cowling hope that Chuck Adamson will help their son recognize and share what is troubling him. Described by William as being "all nerves," Adamson is "a reasonably young man, maybe thirty-five or so" who seems much older because he is "weary-looking," especially around the eyes, which are the saddest that William has ever seen (44). Adamson uses an interesting technique during his sessions with William. Never contradicting the teenager's assertion that the profession of psychology is a "charade," Adamson draws William out by launching into a litany of his own complaints about high school, the phoniness of most people, and the ultimate doom that hangs over the entire earth and everyone on it. William plays the role of counselor, chiding Adamson for his insecurities, but in the process diagnosing himself. While William does not leave Helena completely cured, nevertheless he seems to have made real progress; his physical symptoms improve, and he is able to graduate from high school and move on to college without further incident. Later, Chuck Adamson will help William disentangle himself from the radical leftist group he has been involved with for years. He will find a place for his former patient to rent on the outskirts of FORT DERRY, MONTANA, spend time with the troubled young man, and even arrange for him to turn himself in to the authorities for DRAFT

evasion when William turns 30 years old. The last time readers see Chuck Adamson is on November 8, 1988. He has just been elected mayor of Helena and holds a drunken victory party at his home. Despite his initial flush of success, however, Adamson spends the final minutes of the party alone with William in a stairwell, melancholic as the night winds down, leading readers to wonder how much of Adamson's woebegone recitals as William's psychologist were an act.

Air Force Adjutant On William Cowling's trip to Europe to search for the stewardess Bobbi Haymore, he is told that she left BONN, GERMANY, to become a schoolteacher on an American Air Force base in Wiesbaden. There he and Sarah Strouch question an adjutant who recognizes Bobbi from a photograph William shows him. The adjutant describes Bobbi as an angel, "the sweetest thing on earth" (279). He tells William that Bobbi had been his daughter's teacher and that he loved her. He explains that Bobbi used to slip poems under his pillow at night and shows one of them to William. The poem is "MARTIAN TRAVEL," the same poem that Bobbi had pinned to William's coat after his night flight to Miami. Finally, the adjutant tells William that the last he had heard, Bobbi was back in graduate school, this time at the UNIVERSITY OF MINNESOTA.

Cowling, Bobbi Haymore Bobbi Cowling is the beautiful poet who is married to William Cowling in the novel's present time: 1995. William had first met Bobbi on a night flight to Miami as he was fleeing the DRAFT in September 1968. She worked as a stewardess for TWA Airlines and had comforted him during the long night, leaving a poem called "MARTIAN TRAVEL" pinned to William's coat pocket when he walked off the plane. William never forgets this night with Bobbi, and during the years he spends as a messenger for the radical political group THE COMMITTEE, he tries to track her down, questioning airline personnel about the mysterious stewardess. Acting on a tip that Bobbi has left the airline business to attend graduate school in creative writing in New York City, William follows her there, only to discover that she has abandoned Andy Nelson, the airline navigator she went to New York with, for a poet-translator named Scholheimer. When William calls Bobbi on the telephone, she tells him that she is flattered by his interest in her but that she has married Scholheimer, is happy, and is moving to BONN, GERMANY. After the uranium discovery in 1980 makes William a wealthy man, he and his former girlfriend, Sarah Strouch, travel to Germany in pursuit of Bobbi, where William discovers that she and Scholheimer have broken up. His search next brings him to Minneapolis, where Bobbi had returned to graduate school at the UNIVERSITY OF MINNESOTA, then on to Manhattan, where he has heard she is working as a tour guide at the United Nations. It is there that William finally finds the woman he has thought about obsessively for so many years. He persuades Bobbi to travel back west with him, and the two eventually marry, have a child together, Melinda, and build a house in the SWEETHEART MOUNTAINS outside of FORT DERRY, MONTANA. While the two lead a comfortable existence, their marriage is not perfect. It is after Bobbi disappears for two weeks, taking her diaphragm with her and refusing to tell William where she has been, that her husband snaps and begins digging the enormous hole in the yard. William goes so far as to imprison Bobbi and Melinda in the master bedroom of their home to prevent Bobbi's leaving him. During this time, Bobbi is strangely silent, communicating with her husband only through the poems that she periodically leaves for him. The novel's climax occurs when William carries his drugged and unconscious wife and daughter into the deep pit he has dug in the yard and seems poised to blow them all up, until Melinda wakes up prematurely. Although he allows Bobbi and Melinda to safely return to the house, readers know at the end that the marriage is over, that one of William's worst fears has come true: He will lose his wife and daughter.

Cowling, Melinda Melinda Cowling is the 12-year-old daughter of William and Bobbi Cowling. While she clearly loves her father, she is confused and angered by his erratic behavior at the novel's beginning when he starts digging the enormous hole in the yard of the family's house. Yet, Melinda still trusts William enough to confide in him the night before Bobbi's planned departure. It is this information that prompts William to board up the master bedroom with Melinda and Bobbi inside, preventing them from leaving. While Melinda had desperately wanted to keep her family together, being made a prisoner is not what she had in mind, and she alternately threatens and pleads with her father to let her go. Events escalate when William drugs her root beer, carries her out to the granite-lined pit in the yard, and places her in a hammock next to her unconscious mother. The young girl, however, wakes up before William expects her to. The scene that confronts her is terrifying—the walls of the enormous hole are rigged with wires and blasting caps and her father is standing over a detonator. The courageous 12-year-old manages to take the firing device into her own hands but is unable to follow through on her threat to blow them all up if her father comes closer. When William touches his daughter's skin, he describes it as "a kind of miracle" (311). He allows Melinda to climb the ladder out of the hole, then goes back for his wife, Bobbi. While a horrific murder/suicide has been averted, the novel suggests that the family will be torn apart in the aftermath of this incident.

Cowling, Mr. William Cowling's father is a real-estate agent in FORT DERRY, MONTANA, who plays the role of GENERAL GEORGE ARMSTRONG CUSTER every year in the town's historical recreation of the BATTLE OF LITTLE BIGHORN during their annual CUSTER DAYS celebration. A loving, kind man who worries about his son's obsession with nuclear war, Mr. Cowling nevertheless does not initially understand the seriousness of William's fear, and, to William's mother, he subtly mocks his son's attempts to protect himself with a Ping-Pong table and pencil lead. Yet, Mr. Cowling also gently prods William to temporarily forget his fears by challenging his son to a game of Ping-Pong, which causes William to dismantle his makeshift fallout shelter. Mr. Cowling will also prove himself to be very supportive of his son when he takes William to see a psychiatrist in Helena during his high school years and when he provides William money and clothing to help him flee the DRAFT in September 1968. William is greatly affected by his father's death a few years later. Although he is unable to attend the funeral because of his fugitive status, he watches the proceedings from a nearby hillside, focusing his binoculars on his father's grave, which is described as "a hole" in the ground (248). William's having to watch his father die as Custer every summer and his focus here on the hole that his father is placed into perhaps contribute to his continuing obsession with doom and his later digging of the giant hole in his own yard in 1995.

Cowling, Mrs.   William's mother is a housewife who is concerned about her son's erratic behavior, both when he turns the family Ping-Pong table into a fallout shelter when he is 12 years old and even more when he grows into a lonely high school student who pretends to talk to friends on the phone and who leaves the house on phony dates. Mrs. Cowling is not fooled by William's pretenses, and she is the one who insists on taking her son to see Chuck Adamson in Helena. After college, when William is drafted, Mrs. Cowling, like her husband, tells her son she will support him in whatever decision he makes: "Whatever happens . . . we're with you all the way. A thousand percent" (120). Later, during William's years traveling on secret business for the COMMITTEE, he calls his mother on the telephone in the middle of the night. Even though he is silent when she answers the phone, she knows that it is her son calling and repeats his name several times, "without question, softly yet absolutely" (225). Mrs. Cowling will see her son regularly again after he moves back to FORT DERRY, MONTANA, following his split with the Committee. She dies on January 10, 1993, one of the losses that will unhinge William by the end of the book.

Cowling, William   The novel's protagonist, who tells his own story in the first person, William Cowling grows up in small-town FORT DERRY, MONTANA, the son of a stay-at-home mother and a real-estate broker father. Despite growing up in a loving, middle-class family during the prosperous American postwar boom years, William cannot shake his fear of nuclear war, even attempting to turn the family Ping-Pong table into a fallout shelter when he is 12 years old. He becomes a loner in high school, fantasizing a social life for himself and worrying his parents, who eventually take him to nearby Helena for a week to speak with a psychologist named Chuck Adamson. Although Adamson does not completely cure William of his fears, he does help ease the teenager's physical symptoms—constipation and headaches. William stays in Montana after high school, attending PEVERSON STATE COLLEGE, where he studies geology. Rocks seem comforting and permanent to him in the face of a world poised on the brink of nuclear disaster. When the Vietnam War breaks out, William's fears erupt to the surface again. He hand letters a poster with the words THE BOMBS ARE REAL, and holds it up outside the college cafeteria every Monday at lunch time for several weeks. This silent protest garners the attention of a few other students who join with William to form a leftist group called the COMMITTEE. Eventually, they are joined by Sarah Strouch, a former high school cheerleader also from Fort Derry, whom William had fantasized about as a teenager. He and Sarah soon start a relationship, which will last in an on-again, off-again manner throughout college and for many years afterward. When William receives his DRAFT notice after graduation, he flees to KEY WEST, FLORIDA, with Sarah's help and becomes deeply enmeshed in radical politics, serving as an errand-runner for the Committee's murky dealings. He eventually extricates himself from the protest movement and returns to Fort Derry, where he lives quietly for several years before turning himself in to authorities as a draft evader when he is 30 years old. Like other draft dodgers, he receives a blanket pardon from President JIMMY CARTER in 1977. William, who has continued his geological studies, eventually discovers uranium in the hills outside of Fort Derry, a find that makes him a wealthy man. He uses this newfound wealth to track down an ex-stewardess named Bobbi, whom he had been obsessed with ever since meeting her on a late-night flight to Miami when he was fleeing the draft. He and Bobbi marry, build a beautiful house in the SWEETHEART MOUNTAINS outside of Fort Derry, and have a daughter named Melinda. But after suffering the death of his mother in January 1993, the disappearance of Bobbi for two weeks that summer, then the death of Sarah Strouch in March 1994, William grows increasingly unhinged. In spring 1995, he begins digging an enormous bomb shelter in his yard, working on it night and day, much to the bewilderment of his wife and daughter. When Bobbi packs her suitcases to leave, William imprisons her and Melinda in the master bedroom of their house. He eventually drugs their drinks and carries them out to his giant hole in the ground, which he has rigged with dynamite. When Melinda wakes up unexpectedly, William ends up carrying his wife and daughter back inside rather than blowing them up as he had threatened. The novel ends with William insisting that his story will have a happy ending, despite the fact that readers know better.

Crenshaw, Doc Doc Crenshaw is the cynical and mean-spirited old doctor who examines William Cowling when he is a 12-year-old boy claiming to see "flashes" in small-town FORT DERRY, MONTANA. Described as a "butcher" whose breath smells like "a mixture of formaldehyde and stale chewing tobacco and foot rot," and who has "warts and wrinkles and liver spots" dotting his "mushy yellow skin" (18), Doc Crenshaw had treated William several years ago after an embarrassing bicycle accident, in which the boy's penis was severely injured. Unsympathetic to William during both incidents, Doc Crenshaw tells the boy that he is full of "crap" about seeing flashes. William will go to see Doc Crenshaw again when he is 22 years old and receives his DRAFT notice into the Vietnam War. His parents hope that the doctor will be able to find a reason for William to fail his physical exam. But the old doctor tells William that he is healthy and that as a doctor he cannot fake an excuse for the young man. Doc Crenshaw remains alive in the novel's present time, 1995. Although William reports that his old enemy is over 90 and out of the doctoring business, he adds that that the old man "hangs in there like the town itself, cantankerous and stubborn" (202).

Cuban Compadre In November 1968, after the COMMITTEE members have been living together in KEY WEST, FLORIDA, for several months, Ollie Winkler shows up one evening aboard a sleek, 38-foot cabin cruiser, accompanied by "a slim, mustachioed Cuban without a name. Compadre, Ollie called him" (168). This is the boat that will transport the Committee members to Cuba, with the young, unnamed Cuban at the helm. In Cuba the group of radicals will undergo tough military and political training sessions intended to prepare them to participate in the underground antiwar political movement in the United States.

Dean of Faculty at Bonn University William Cowling in his search for Bobbi Haymore questions the dean of faculty at Bonn University in Germany, who remembers Bobbi as the young wife of the poet-translator Scholheimer who had served briefly on the faculty. Described as a "portly old gentleman," the Dean remembers Bobbi fondly, but tells William that the marriage had broken up after only a couple of months and that Scholheimer had returned to the states while Bobbi was teaching school on a U.S. Air Force base in Wiesbaden, Germany.

Ex-Buddy When William Cowling's father offers to buy him a chemistry set, hoping this will help distract his son's attention from his nuclear fears, William remembers an ex-buddy of his who was a "chemistry set fanatic" (25) back in fourth grade. The boy, whom William describes as a "turd" (25), used to perform experiments for friends who came over to his house. William, secretly insulted by his father's offer, thinks to himself that chemistry sets, in fact, were probably "originally invented for turds. . . . weirdos and losers and poor chumps who couldn't play baseball" (25).

High School Principal During the CUBAN MISSILE CRISIS of October 1962, William Cowling's high school principal in FORT DERRY, MONTANA, delivers a speech about the need for courage and calm at a convocation in the high school gym. The missile crisis is the first time that William actually sees the adults around him display fear about the possibility of nuclear war, a fear that William himself has been crippled by for years.

Janet   On a TWA flight from Denver to Salt Lake City in 1970, William Cowling asks a stewardess wearing the nametag "Janet" about the elusive Bobbi, a flight attendant he had become obsessed with during his night flight to Miami while he was fleeing the DRAFT. Janet is able to tell William that Bobbi's last name is "Haymore," and that she passed out "those poems of hers . . . like peanuts," to male passengers especially (227). Janet calls Bobbi a "tone deaf little tramp" (228) and admits she did not like the poetry-writing stewardess at all. Nevertheless, she reveals that Bobbi had left TWA with a navigator named Andy Nelson in order to go to New York for graduate school.

Johnson   William Cowling discovers that Bobbi Haymore had run off with a professor named Johnson shortly after she finished her master's degree at the UNIVERSITY OF MINNESOTA. Professor Johnson had given Bobbi B's in her classes, claiming that she "needed incentive" (281). Another professor, Rudolph, tells William that Bobbi dumped Johnson, however. The last he heard, she was working as a tour guide at the United Nations in New York.

Johnson, Leonard B.   Leonard B. Johnson is the alias that William Cowling travels under when he flees the DRAFT. It is a name that Sarah Strouch has chosen for him, seeing the humor in William's having to use the initials LBJ. Later, he will obtain a driver's license, two credit cards, and a Social Security card all made out in the phony name.

Keezer, Ebeneezer   Ebeneezer Keezer, an intimidating former marine who has seen action in Vietnam, acts as both drill sergeant and political instructor for the COMMITTEE members when they undergo training in Cuba. A no-nonsense African American who dresses in a black beret, combat fatigues, and jungle boots during the daily calisthenics and military exercises, Ebeneezer changes personas to lecture the group members about politics and history during their evening classes. For these sessions, Ebeneezer wears "a dark blue suit,

a blue tie, a crisply starched white shirt with gold cuff links" (176). His voice changes as well: "There were no dropped consonants, no ghetto slurrings; it was the precise, polished voice of a corporate executive" (176). When the training in Cuba finishes, Ebeneezer will continue to make periodic visits to KEY WEST, FLORIDA, including one memorable occasion on October 1, 1969—William Cowling's birthday—when Ned Rafferty stands up to him, insisting that the crates of guns stored in the attic not be used. Much later, long after William has dropped out of the radical leftist movement, Sarah Strouch visits him in Montana and hints that upon Ebeneezer Keezer's orders the group has stolen a nuclear warhead. Like most of the other radicals that William knows well, Ebeneezer Keezer will die in the SWAT team raid on the Key West bungalow, burnt to death in the resulting fire.

Librarian   After William Cowling's father shows Doc Crenshaw the young boy's makeshift bomb shelter, both men laughing about it, William becomes angry and rides his bike down to the town library, where he thumbs through back issues of *Time* and *U.S. News,* studying photographs of real fallout shelters. He is interrupted by a pretty librarian with "smooth skin and greenish eyes and a thick tangle of black hair" (22), who looks over William's shoulder at the magazine pictures he is studying and comments that people want to forget about the frightening state of political affairs. She says as well that she is pleased to see William taking an interest in such problems, which she says should be a "top priority . . . crucial" (23). William starts to like the woman after this comment, recognizing that she takes his fears seriously and will not laugh at him as the doctor and his own father had done. Several minutes after the librarian returns to her desk, William begins sobbing uncontrollably. The woman gently takes him into her office and calls William's parents to come pick him up. When Mr. Cowling arrives at the library, he winks over his son's head at the librarian, who does not wink back. William writes, "I loved her for that. I wanted to crawl into her lap and curl up for a long sleep, just the two of us, cuddling, that gentle hand on my knee" (24). This unnamed librarian in FORT

DERRY, MONTANA, then, is the first of the string of women, including Sarah Strouch and Bobbi Haymore, whom William will fantasize about in order to comfort himself and assuage his loneliness.

Motel Night Clerk After the COMMITTEE members sell uranium mining rights on their land in the SWEETHEART MOUNTAINS to the Texaco corporation, they drive to Helena to deposit their $25 million check. Arriving at midnight on a Saturday, they check into a motel to wait for Monday morning. The night clerk is a smug kid who demands cash up front, mostly because of the hippyish appearance of the group members. Before he leaves for BONN, GERMANY, to hunt for Bobbi, William Cowling buys the motel in Helena and fires the night clerk.

Muggs Muggs is a three-legged dog that belonged to Sarah Strouch as a child. The dog lost one of its legs after being hit by a car. But even after the accident, Muggs still loved to run fast and chase cars. Sarah tells William the story of Muggs during one summer vacation from college when the couple is camping in the SWEETHEART MOUNTAINS outside of FORT DERRY, MONTANA. She explains that she both hated and loved the dog, which seems to sum up her feelings for William as well.

Nelson, Andy William Cowling learns during his search for the stewardess Bobbi Haymore that she had quit her job at TWA and left for New York with a former TWA navigator named Andy Nelson. Later, William calls Nelson in New York. Reluctantly, the navigator tells him that Bobbi had walked out on him for her creative writing teacher at NYU, a poet-translator named Scholheimer.

Nethro Nethro is the name of Ebeneezer Keezer's sidekick at SAGUA LA GRANDE, CUBA. Together, the two African-American radicals train the COMMITTEE members in military and political strategy during the late fall and early winter of 1968. Readers do not find out much background information about Nethro, although it seems likely that he, like Ebeneezer, is a former U.S. marine who served in Vietnam. The novel never reveals

Nethro's final fate, either. His name is not mentioned when William Cowling remembers watching the SWAT team raid in KEY WEST, FLORIDA, unfold live on television, in which Ollie Winkler, Tina Roebuck, Ned Rafferty, and Ebeneezer Keezer are killed.

Pastor of the First Baptist Church When Fort Derry High School holds a convocation during the CUBAN MISSILE CRISIS of October 1962, the pastor of the First Baptist Church offers "a punchy prayer" (39–40) in an attempt to reassure the worried students that everything will be all right.

Rafferty, Ned Ned Rafferty is the fifth and final student at PEVERSON STATE COLLEGE to join William Cowling's war protest group, the COMMITTEE. A former boyfriend of cheerleader Sarah Strouch, Ned is a football linebacker whom William hates even though he has to admit that Ned is "a truly nice guy" (114). William's feelings for Ned are tainted by jealousy over his popularity as well as his former relationship with Sarah. After graduation, Ned heads back to his father's ranch in Idaho but eventually winds up living with the other Committee members in the bungalow at KEY WEST, FLORIDA, that becomes their center of operations. Later, Ned will admit to William that he is not particularly politically engaged but that he's stuck with the radical movement so long because of his love for Sarah and need to be close to her. Ned, like William, is also leery of the violent tactics espoused by the group. On a night in early summer of 1970, Ned helps William drop crates of automatic rifles that the Committee had been storing in the bungalow's attic into the Atlantic Ocean. Like most of William's other colleagues in the radical group, Ned Rafferty will die in the SWAT team raid on the Committee's Florida headquarters, burned to death in the resulting fire.

Rafferty, Mr. Ned Rafferty, like William Cowling, flees the DRAFT for the Vietnam War. Ned tells William the story of his leaving the ranch in Idaho. When his father asks him where he is going, Ned tells him the truth, insisting to his father that he is doing the right thing. But Mr. Rafferty simply gives his son a long look, then says "Pussy" and nothing else.

Roe, Rancher William Cowling and his COMMITTEE friends buy the piece of land in the SWEETHEART MOUNTAINS, where they had discovered uranium from a local rancher named Roe on February 4, 1980. Rancher Roe, according to William, believes the friends plan to set up a commune, but even so, he is anxious to unload the property.

Roebuck, Tina Tina Roebuck is the second PEVERSON STATE COLLEGE student to join William Cowling in his antiwar protests. Described as a "large, tent-shaped coed" who is a "home-ec major" and a "chronic overeater" (80–81), Tina responds when William and Ollie take out an ad in the *PEVEE WEEKLY*, the college newspaper, asking for volunteers for their newly formed organization, the COMMITTEE. Later, when the Committee holds a meeting in Tina's cluttered, dirty dorm room, William notices that all the walls are papered over with photographs of models from fashion magazines, with little hand-printed notes below each picture, saying things such as "This can be you!" or "Tiny Tina—think lean!" (115). A social misfit like the other Committee members, Tina nevertheless proves to be a dependable and hardworking member of the group. She will become romantically involved with Ollie Winkler, move to KEY WEST, FLORIDA, after graduation, train in Cuba, and stick with the radical protest movement until her violent death in the fiery inferno of the Key West bungalow after it is raided by a police SWAT team.

Rudolph During his search for Bobbi Haymore, William Cowling discovers that she left Germany to enroll in graduate school at the UNIVERSITY OF MINNESOTA. He and Sarah Strouch travel to Minneapolis, where William meets a professor named Rudolph, "a tall and very bitter man" (281) who had given Bobbi A's in all of the classes she took with him. Although he insists she deserved the grades, Professor Rudolph was clearly infatuated with Bobbi and angry that she had run off with another professor named Johnson.

Scholheimer Scholheimer is a well-known poet and translator who was Bobbi Haymore's teacher at NYU. When William Cowling tracks down Bobbi in New York in 1970, he discovers that she has married Scholheimer and that the couple is planning to move to BONN, GERMANY. Later, continuing the hunt after the uranium discovery in 1980, William learns that Bobbi had left Scholheimer after two months together in Bonn. Scholheimer had returned to the United States, and Bobbi had taken a job teaching sixth-graders on an American Air Force base at Wiesbaden.

Strouch, Mr. and Mrs. Sarah Strouch's mother is dead, and her father is a mortician who owns the STROUCH FUNERAL HOME. Thus, Sarah has had a close relationship with death her whole life, a characteristic that seems to both fascinate and repel William Cowling. This close acquaintance with death also seems to encourage Sarah's flamboyance and daring recklessness. When William asks her if she would mind toning down her personality a bit, she replies that "Discretion . . . is for *dead* people" (105).

Strouch, Sarah Readers first meet Sarah Strouch when she is a high school cheerleader in FORT DERRY, MONTANA, whose father is a mortician and owner of the STROUCH FUNERAL HOME. William Cowling pretends to call her on the phone, fakes one-sided conversations with her, and even leaves the house on make-believe dates in order to reassure his parents that he is not as lonely as they fear. When William passes out during study hall after taking a double dose of a laxative in an attempt to relieve his constipation, the real Sarah leans over him and fans him, seemingly impressed with the drama of the moment. William and Sarah meet up again at PEVERSON STATE COLLEGE, where William studies geology and Sarah is a "campus superstar—a cheerleader, of course—vapid, vain, cruel, and beautiful" (69). After spending the whole night with William during Winter Carnival in February 1967, Sarah joins the COMMITTEE, William's dismal little war protest group, and the two begin a long-term love affair. With Sarah's energy and involvement, the Committee is revitalized. She organizes parades, teach-ins, and even small bombings and acts of sabotage during her remaining two years at Pevee State. After graduation, Sarah moves to KEY WEST, FLORIDA, where she becomes involved in the radical leftist movement. When William receives his DRAFT notice for the Vietnam War, she arranges for him to flee to Key West, where she is living with the other Committee members: Ned Rafferty, Ollie Winkler, Tina Roebuck. The fall after college graduation, she uses her contacts to organize a trip to Cuba, where the budding revolutionaries undergo a brutal, boot camp–type training period under the supervision of former U.S. marines. While William is still ambiguous about the Committee's political activities and is assigned as an errand boy, where he will be out of the main action, Sarah remains gung ho. Displaying a strange mixture of bravado and neediness, Sarah's romantic interests during this period alternate between her former boyfriend, Ned Rafferty, and William, who continually frustrates her with his unwillingness to make a real commitment to the movement. Her love for William seems most intense during the periods when he becomes obsessed with Bobbi Haymore, a stewardess he met on a night flight from New York to Miami while fleeing the draft. Although William eventually leaves the protest movement, Sarah remains deeply involved. When the war ends and William discovers a rich uranium deposit in the hills outside of their small hometown, Sarah insists on accompanying him to Germany, where he goes to track down Bobbi. While William will eventually marry Bobbi and build a house in the mountains outside of FORT DERRY, MONTANA, Sarah's later life remains shadowy; a self-described "terrorist," she hints that she is wanted by the police and has to live on the run. Sarah becomes very ill after visiting William and Bobbi in Fort Derry during Christmas of 1993. She dies of encephalitis in March 1994, one of the events that triggers William's psychotic breakdown the following year.

Teacher   When William Cowling is 12 years old and paralyzed by his fright of nuclear weapons, he hits on what he calls his "Pencil Theory." Sitting in school one day when the idea comes to him, he says "Pencils" out loud, causing his teacher, who remains unnamed, to jerk her head toward William and give him "a long stare" (15). When he gets home that day, William, believing that ordinary pencils contain lead, which can protect him from radiation, lines up dozens of pencils atop his family Ping-Pong table, which he has converted into a makeshift bomb shelter.

TWA Clerk   When William Cowling is fleeing his DRAFT notice, he takes a bus from FORT DERRY, MONTANA, to Chicago. In Chicago he takes a taxi to O'Hare Airport, where he tells the TWA clerk working the counter that his name is Johnson. Although William is frightened, the girl hardly notices him, counting out the tens and twenties he has given her for his ticket, waving him on to the gate, and wishing him a "safe trip" (145).

Winkler, Ollie   Ollie Winkler is the first student at PEVERSON STATE COLLEGE to respond to William Cowling's silent protest outside the school cafeteria on Mondays at lunch. Described as "very short, very plump . . . a Friar Tuck facsimile in a white cowboy hat and fancy high-heeled boots" (75), Ollie, who is obsessed with bombs himself, offers to help William after he sees his fellow student holding up the sign reading THE BOMBS ARE REAL. William responds coldly at first, simply moving away from the flamboyantly dressed young man. But Ollie is persistent, following him into the cafeteria and pointing out that no one likes William, that people laugh at him, and arguing that the protester needs to change his style, to become more radical, more violent: "You don't make a revolution without breaking a few legs" (78). Although William insists that his relationship with Ollie Winkler is not "friendship, just an alliance" (78), this is the start of the COMMITTEE, the radical political group that will persist through the late 1960s and into the 1970s. Ollie will eventually die for his politics, shot through the mouth when SWAT teams raid the bungalow in KEY WEST, FLORIDA, that had been the center of operations ever since college graduation. Long after his departure from the movement, William Cowling watches the raid and resulting deaths unfold live on television.

FURTHER READING

Bourne, Daniel, and Debra Shostak. "A Conversation with Tim O'Brien," *Artful Dodge* 17 (1991): 74–90.

Cordle, Daniel. "In Dreams, in Imagination: Suspense, Anxiety and the Cold War in Tim O'Brien's *The Nuclear Age*." *Critical Survey* 19, no. 2 (2007): 101–120.

Montrose, David. Review of *The Nuclear Age,* by Tim O'Brien. *Times Literary Supplement* [London], 28 March 1986, 342.

Paley, Grace. "Digging a Shelter and a Grave." Review of *The Nuclear Age,* by Tim O'Brien. *New York Times,* 17 November 1985, Section 7, 7.

Romano, John. Review of *The Nuclear Age,* by Tim O'Brien. *Atlantic* 256 (October 1985), 105–106.

Schwininger, Lee. "Ecofeminism, Nuclearism, and O'Brien's *The Nuclear Age*." In *The Nightmare Considered: Critical Essays on Nuclear War Literature,* edited by N. Anisfield, 177–185. Bowling Green, Ohio: Bowling Green State University Press, 1991.

"The Nuclear Age" (1979)

First published in *Atlantic* magazine in June 1979, "The Nuclear Age" tells the story of a group of disaffected 1960s radicals who discover uranium in a Montana hillside and later sell the land to Texaco for a huge profit. The story's narrator, William, accompanied by a former college cheerleader and rabble-rouser named Sarah, uses some of his new wealth to finance a trip to Germany to search for a woman he had met and fallen in love with over a decade ago. The story, revised significantly, forms the basis for the second half of O'Brien's novel of the same name, published in 1985.

SYNOPSIS

The first section of the story, titled "Fission," depicts a group of eight friends, former campus radicals during the 1960s, who locate a uranium deposit deep in the mountains of Montana. They soon arrange to buy the land from an old rancher, and a few months later, sell the claim for $25 million to Texaco after instigating a bidding war among the world's major oil companies. Because no local bank will handle such a large check, the friends drive to Helena. Arriving late on a Saturday night, they elect to stay at a small motel with a swimming pool and sauna to wait for the banks to open on Monday morning. The night clerk, apprehensive of the motley group of aging hippies, demands that they pay cash up front. When Monday comes, the money is split up, each of the eight friends receiving just over $3 million. The various members of the group go their separate ways, with only the story's narrator, William, and one other friend, Sarah, staying behind. William intends to travel to BONN, GERMANY, to search for a woman he had once been in love with, and Sarah asks to come along.

The second section of the story, called "Fusion," details William and Sarah's trip to Bonn in search of William's former girlfriend, Bobbi Haymore. First, though, William buys the motel where his friends had been treated rudely by the night clerk and fires the young man. Once in Germany, the search for Bobbi proves more difficult than William had expected. Not only did she arrive in Germany a decade ago, but Bobbi has also married and William does not know her new last name. His relationship with Sarah is somewhat strange and awkward as well. More than friends, the two share a bed, but Sarah clearly wants a deeper relationship. The search for Bobbi eventually leads the two back to the United States, first to the UNIVERSITY OF MINNESOTA, where Bobbi had earned a master's degree in Germanic Studies, then to Manhattan, where they finally find William's elusive former girlfriend working at the United Nations. This section ends with Sarah walking out the door of the UN building, telling William she is headed for Rio.

In the story's final section, "Critical Mass," William marries Bobbi, the two move back to Montana, build a beautiful house in the SWEETHEART MOUNTAINS, and eventually have a daughter together. Yet, despite his comfortable life, William is uneasy. As a hobby, he begins to dig a bomb shelter in his yard. When it is finished, Bobbi decorates the interior, and the family often uses it as a weekend retreat. Their life progresses uneventfully until one winter day when Sarah arrives in a jeep with a black bodyguard named Nethro. Reengaged in radical activities, Sarah has with her an armed warhead that she has stolen from her revolutionary cohorts, who she claims had planned to use the warhead to blow up Fairbanks, Alaska. Not long after arriving in Montana, however, Sarah is diagnosed with cancer. She dies in March, and the old gang of radicals shows up for her funeral, but no one asks about the warhead. The story ends on a note of loss as several of the old radicals die of gunfire in Minneapolis, and as William finds a poem in his bomb shelter, signaling that Bobbi has left him.

COMMENTARY

The deep irony in this story concerns the fact that this group of former political radicals realize their fortune by selling uranium—the essential material in making nuclear weapons. While the friends most likely would have protested nuclear arms in college, none of them, at least in the beginning of the story, seems much bothered by what might be considered their "selling out," both literally and ideologically. The friends conduct a ceremony along the banks of the Little Bighorn on the way into Helena, in which each drops a chunk of near-pure uranium into the river. The Little Bighorn River, suggesting CUSTER's Last Stand and the Indian wars of the 19th century, represents some of the worst aspects of U.S. history—the imperialism and greed that devastated the western tribes. And the eight friends, despite their idealistic 1960s past, continue this historic trajectory. Financial profit motivates them to find and sell the uranium, which may well be shaped into nuclear weapons that will continue to spread America's power the world over. Rather than leaving a better world for future generations, as they might have wished to do when they were back in college, they leave instead, on the banks of the river, "two clickers . . . as a gift for the next generation" (58). The treatment of the motel night clerk goes hand-in-hand with the group's loss of idealism. William uses his newfound wealth to gain revenge on the clerk, who is "just a kid" (59), working in what must be a low-paying job and understandably suspicious of a check for $25 million. While the friends do not seem particularly troubled by this new morality—William says that each of the friends "blessed the bomb without

guilt" (59)—readers nevertheless get a hint near the end of the first section of the story that William may be a bit uneasy. Standing in the middle of Helena, he thinks about the far-off mountains that the friends had "plundered" (59), and he smells "horse dung" everywhere in the air, suggesting that there is something foul or unsavory about the bit of business that has just taken place.

William's quest to find Bobbi Haymore, his former girlfriend, is perhaps an attempt to redeem himself from the dark, morally murky business he and his friends have been involved in. William idealizes Bobbi, who, with her love of German poetry, seems separate and apart from the world of politics. If he can no longer believe in political idealism, William falls back on romantic ideals of true love. He tells himself that in the chase after Bobbi he is "still an activist, only now it was aimed at something truly critical" (61), his winning back of Bobbi Haymore. The more practical Sarah is suspicious—when William claims that he loves Bobbi, she answers "perhaps" (59) and insists that love is as much a gamble as finding the uranium was. His relationship with Sarah seems odd in the face of William's idealization of Bobbi. More than mere friends, Sarah and William share a bed and act like lovers as they explore the city of Bonn. Clearly, Sarah would like a deeper relationship, but it is difficult to assess William's true feelings for her. He is sexually attracted to the former cheerleader, but he remains obsessed with Bobbi, even though he feels that she betrayed him long ago, first by switching political loyalties from EUGENE MCCARTHY to ROBERT KENNEDY, and later by getting married without telling him. Even when William learns that Bobbi has left a trail of men behind, often sending the same poem to each man in turn, he is undeterred in his search, in his determination to cling to romantic ideals.

Although William does eventually find and marry Bobbi, the fulfillment of this long-held desire is not enough to satisfy him completely. One day, while floating in the motel pool in Helena, he hears a Piper Cub airplane flying low and thinks that the world is "coming unzipped" (65), that nuclear war has finally arrived. Although William claims that this reaction is a product of fear, not guilt, it still seems that his dealings in uranium might be responsible for the anxiety that grips him in later life. The bomb shelter that he builds in his yard in Montana is an attempt to ward off this fear—not only fear of nuclear devastation but also fear of retribution, perhaps, for the sins of his past, for "turning nature against herself" (65) as he tells Bobbi he did when he shows her the landscape where the uranium-pocked hillside used to be. He hopes to keep his "nuclear family" (66) safe from nuclear war by spending weekends in the decked-out and well-stocked bomb shelter.

But William is unable to escape his past, which turns up in the form of his old girlfriend, Sarah, with her black bodyguard Nethro and an armed warhead in tow. The formerly charming birthmark below her lip has grown ugly just as her revolutionary activities have. Her radical comrades have turned into terrorists and want to use the stolen warhead to blow up Fairbanks, Alaska. Ironically, Sarah and William hide the warhead in the bomb shelter, the very locale that is supposed to be safe from the penetration of nuclear weapons. Sarah, recognizing the irony, claims that they are helping to preserve the peace, "Maintaining equilibrium" (67). The very same people who originally found the uranium that helped to build such warheads are now burying one of them deep underground. Symbolically, the bomb does devastate William's home and family, though not in the way that he had feared. Sarah dies of skin cancer a few months after arriving in Montana, her past finally seeming to have caught up with her. "Rio did it," she says. "Too much time in the sun" (67). But it is almost as if the radical activities she took up in Rio are what cause her death. And in the end Bobbi leaves William as well, just as he always feared she would do. The poem she leaves behind in the bomb shelter reads, "The balance of power, our own, the world's, grows ever fragile" (67). Perhaps an allusion to the COLD WAR and the belief that the arms race brings a balance of power among nations, the line also suggests that such a delicate balance will have to give way in the end. Despite William's attempts throughout the story to cling to ideals, he cannot do so. He abandons the political principles he held in college, while his supposed

true love abandons him at the end, leaving him fragile and alone.

Differences in Versions
The story version of "The Nuclear Age" is much more compressed than the novel version. Essentially, the story as originally published in the *Atlantic* is expanded and revised to become the entire second half of the novel *The Nuclear Age*. When O'Brien rewrote the story as a novel, he reduced the number of former college ex-radicals involved in the discovery of the uranium. The story lists eight friends—William, Sarah, Ned, Ollie, Janet, Steve, Ben, and Richard—while the novel depicts only five members of the politically radical group who work together to discover the uranium deposit—William, Sarah, Ollie, Tina, and Ned. In addition, the novel fleshes these characters out much more fully than the story does. Ollie Winkler in the novel is a social misfit obsessed with bombs; Tina Roebuck is an overweight former home-economics major, and Ned Rafferty is a one-time college football player who is in love with Sarah Strouch, the radical ex-cheerleader. While the search for Bobbi Haymore in the story remains much the same in the revised version, Bobbi in the novel not only translates German poems; she is an accomplished poet herself. In the novel William first meets her when she is the stewardess on William's airplane flight to Miami as he is escaping the DRAFT. But perhaps the most significant change in the novel version is the addition of the chapters set in 1995 in which William Cowling, obsessed with the fear that Bobbi will leave him, imprisons her and his daughter, Melinda, first in the master bedroom of their home and later in the bomb shelter that he has dug in his yard. In the novel readers watch William Cowling go slowly insane as he digs the shelter and locks up his family members. The William of the story, while uneasy about the future and perhaps guilt-ridden about the past, is a much less ominous character than the William of the novel.

CHARACTERS

Air Force Adjutant   William and Sarah, as they search all over Germany for any sign of the elusive Bobbi Haymore, eventually come across an Air Force adjutant who recognizes Bobbi from a photograph. He tells them that Bobbi, whom he calls "the sweetest thing on earth" (63), used to teach sixth grade at a U.S. Air Force base south of the city. One of Bobbi's students was the adjutant's own daughter. The man also informs William and Sarah that he had had a brief affair with Bobbi after her husband left her.

Assistant Registrar   When William's search for Bobbi Haymore leads him to the UNIVERSITY OF MINNESOTA, he bribes the assistant registrar at the school for access to his former sweetheart's college records. It turns out that Bobbi had enrolled at the university in 1975 and earned a master's degree in German Studies 10 months later.

Ben   One of the friends who become rich after discovering uranium in Montana, Ben lounges in the swimming pool of the motel in Helena, wearing a cowboy hat and long underwear. Like Ollie and Ned, Ben plans to return to graduate school after the Texaco money is divided up. Nevertheless, at the airport after receiving his $3-million share, Ben follows Richard and several others to British Columbia, presumably on a quest to discover more valuable mineral deposits. Ben, like several of the others, returns to radical politics after he becomes a millionaire. Sarah mentions that he was in on the plot to steal an armed warhead. The last readers see Ben, he is at Sarah's funeral, genuinely saddened by the death of his longtime comrade.

Benson, Professor   Following Bobbi Haymore's trail to the UNIVERSITY OF MINNESOTA, William discovers that she ran off with a professor named Benson, who had given her all B's in her courses, not because she deserved them, but because "she needed incentive" (64). Another professor named Rudolph explains that he heard that Bobbi had dropped Benson, who now translates German comics for a living.

Daughter   The story's narrator, William, eventually has a daughter with his wife, the former Bobbi Haymore. The daughter is never named, but Wil-

liam claims that he and Bobbi raised her "with discipline and love" (66) and that the family, by and large, is happy. Nevertheless, it should strike readers as somewhat strange that this happy nuclear family spends its weekend getaways in a bomb shelter that William has dug in their yard.

Haymore, Bobbi Louise   Bobbi Haymore is the former girlfriend whom the story's narrator, William, searches for all over Europe. A beautiful German language student who loves poetry, Bobbi has had relationships with numerous men, all of whom she eventually leaves after honoring them with her translations of German poems. Although the search is difficult, William eventually finds Bobbi working at the United Nations in New York. She moves back to Montana with him, where the two get married and build a beautiful home in the SWEETHEART MOUNTAINS. Bobbi eventually gives birth to a daughter. However, as she has done with all her previous husbands and lovers, Bobbi will eventually abandon William, leaving behind in the bomb shelter he has built on their land only a poem that contains the line, "The Balance of Power, our own, the world's, grows ever fragile" (67).

Irving   Irving turns out to be the last name of the man Bobbi Haymore had married and gone to BONN, GERMANY, with. William and Sarah, during their search for Bobbi, eventually come across an American Air Force adjutant who recognizes Bobbi's photograph and who knows the woman as Bobbi Irving. He informs the couple that Bobbi's husband was a "bastard" who had "left her for some Jamaican broad" (63).

Janet   Janet is a member of the group of eight former campus radicals who discover uranium in Montana. A well-educated woman with a Ph.D., Janet departs for British Columbia with Richard and several others after the group divides up the money they receive for selling the Montana claim. Apparently, she becomes reinvolved in radical political activities. Many years later, when Sarah shows up in Montana with an armed warhead, she tells William, the story's narrator, that Janet was part of the group that had stolen the warhead.

Motel Clerk When the group of friends drives to Helena to deposit the $25 million Texaco check in the bank, they stop for the night in a motel that advertises a heated swimming pool and sauna. The night clerk, described as "just a kid" (59), eyes the group suspiciously and demands that they pay cash up front for the one room that they all share. Later, after the money is divided up, William buys the motel and fires the clerk.

Ned One of the group of eight radical friends, Ned is most often depicted driving the others around in a van. After the money from the uranium discovery is divided, Ned says he plans to return to graduate school. At the airport, where several members of the group depart for British Columbia, Ned suggests that he is heading west, to Portland or SEATTLE. He is not seen again in the story after this, not being among the political radicals who show up at Sarah's funeral at the end.

Nethro Nethro is the name of the black bodyguard who shows up with Sarah when she returns to Montana to visit William and Bobbi near the end of the story. It turns out that Sarah and Nethro actually need a hideout since they have a stolen warhead in the jeep with them. When Sarah dies of cancer a few months later, Nethro, a usually silent man, "bawled all night long" (67) and departs the morning after her death, not even waiting for the funeral.

Ollie Ollie is one of the eight friends who become rich after discovering uranium. He plans to return to graduate school after the money is divided up. Yet, despite this desire, Ollie is one of several members of the group who follow their friend Richard to British Columbia, after they hear stories of "rich lodes" (59) in that area. Ollie evidently becomes engaged once again in radical politics since he is one of the friends Sarah names who had been involved in the theft of an armed warhead. Ollie later shows up at Sarah's funeral and sincerely grieves over his dead friend.

Richard Richard, described as a "brave, movie-star-looking guy" (59) is one of the eight friends who find uranium in Montana. Richard heads for British Columbia with several of the other friends after the huge Texaco check is divided. At the end of the story, Sarah tells William that Richard owns a gold mine in Lesotho.

Roe, Rancher Rancher Roe is the original owner of the hillside in Montana where the eight ex-radical friends discover uranium. Unaware of the rich mineral deposit in his hillside, he is eager to sell the land to the group of friends. Later, William will buy Rancher Roe's place in the SWEETHEART MOUNTAINS as a home for himself and his wife, Bobbi.

Roommate Once, back during the days of their love affair, when Bobbi and William were living far apart, she sent him a complicated German poem in the mail. William, in Mexico at the time, drove up to Veracruz to call Bobbi. The phone is answered by Bobbi's roommate, who tells William that the young woman had gone to BONN, GERMANY, to teach school. However, William can hear Bobbi conferring quietly in the background with the roommate while he is on the line. Later, he discovers that Bobbi had gotten married and really did intend to go to Bonn.

Rudolph, Professor A professor named Rudolph at the UNIVERSITY OF MINNESOTA, described by William as "an old coot with a cane" (64), had been Bobbi Haymore's teacher when she was a graduate student in 1975. He gave the young woman all A's in her courses and speaks fondly and regretfully of the beautiful young woman and of the fact that she ran off with another professor who had given her B's.

Sarah Sarah is a former college cheerleader and campus radical, now become a lawyer, who is among the group of friends that discover uranium on a hillside in Montana. After the money is split up, she insists on accompanying William, the story's narrator, to BONN, GERMANY, as he searches for an old girlfriend. Sarah herself is in love with William and hopes that the search will prove to be a dead end. When Bobbi Haymore is eventually located working at the United Nations in New York, Sarah leaves for Rio de Janeiro, where she becomes involved in radical politics once again. Many years later, she shows up at the home of William and Bobbi in Montana with an armed warhead in tow and a wild story about comrades who want to blow up Fairbanks, Alaska. She is soon diagnosed with skin cancer, however, and dies a few months later.

Steve Steve, like William and Janet, is a former campus radical who holds a Ph.D. in some science-related field. The friends' technological savvy helps them locate a rich vein of uranium in a Montana mountainside. After the money is divided, Steve departs along with several others for British Columbia. He is not mentioned again in the story.

William William, the story's narrator, is one of a group of eight friends—former campus radicals—who discover uranium in a Montana hillside. When the money obtained from selling the uranium deposit is divided up, William chooses to use a portion of his newfound wealth to travel to BONN, GERMANY, to search for an old girlfriend, Bobbi Haymore. Accompanied in his travels by a friend and sometime lover named Sarah, William searches unsuccessfully for Bobbi in Europe. Eventually, the trail leads him back to the United States, where he eventually discovers his former love working at the United Nations. William marries Bobbi and moves back to Montana, where the two buy a home in the SWEETHEART MOUNTAINS and have a daughter together. But William is uneasy, not least because of the betrayal to his ideals suggested by the fact of a former war protester and radical making a fortune selling uranium—an essential material in the making of nuclear weapons. His political unease eventually leads him to build a bomb shelter at his home, which his small family begins to use as a weekend retreat. At the end of the story, William is abandoned by both of the meaningful women in his life. Sarah, his intimate friend, dies of cancer, and his wife, Bobbi, leaves him.

"On the Rainy River" (1990)

"On the Rainy River" is a short story told in the first person by a young college graduate in Min-

nesota named Tim O'Brien, who receives a DRAFT notice in the summer of 1968 and is unsure how to respond. He travels to a remote fishing lodge in the northern part of the state but is unable to flee to Canada despite his belief that the war in Vietnam is wrong. The story first appeared as part of the 1990 collection, *The Things They Carried*. Unlike the other short stories covered in this section of the book, it was never published separately as a magazine story. Nevertheless, it is included here because it has been anthologized as a stand-alone short story in a number of fiction collections.

SYNOPSIS

When 21-year-old Tim O'Brien is drafted in June 1968, he experiences a feeling of moral paralysis; he is unable to decide whether to report for duty or flee to Canada. He describes for readers his opposition to the war in Vietnam—the intellectual stand he made against the war in college, his doubts about its morality. He describes as well the job he held that summer working at an ARMOUR MEATS plant in his hometown of WORTHINGTON, MINNESOTA. O'Brien's job title is "Declotter," and the work consists of his standing on an assembly line, using a giant water gun suspended from the ceiling to remove blood clots from pig carcasses as they pass by on a conveyer belt. One day at his job, O'Brien writes, he "cracked" (46). Unable to continue spraying dead pigs any longer, he leaves work in midmorning, returns home, and writes a short note to his parents before getting in his car and heading north.

Although he has no real destination in mind, just a strong urge to escape, O'Brien winds up pulling into an old, decrepit fishing resort that is closed for the season. The proprietor, an 81-year-old man named Elroy Berdahl, invites O'Brien in. The narrator spends the next six days at the TIP TOP LODGE doing odd jobs, going on long hikes, and playing Scrabble with the old man. On the sixth day of his stay, Elroy Berdahl takes O'Brien out fishing on the RAINY RIVER, which separates the United States from Canada. Berdahl stops the boat 20 yards away from the Canadian shore. But O'Brien, despite his desire to slip overboard and swim to Canada, is overcome by a feeling of helplessness. He hallucinates that he sees himself as a young boy, along with members of his family, townspeople from Worthington, and an assortment of politicians, celebrities, historical figures, and fictional characters on the Minnesota side of the Rainy River, cheering and urging him "toward one shore or the other" (59). At this point O'Brien realizes that the shame of being thought a coward should he choose to flee to Canada would be more than he could bear. He stays in the boat, acknowledging that he will go to war.

COMMENTARY

"On the Rainy River" is a story that is structured like a mythical hero's journey, such as the cross-cultural monomyth described in Joseph Campbell's influential 1949 book, *The Hero With a Thousand Faces,* or the reformulated version presented by David Adams Leeming in his 1981 book, *Mythology: The Voyage of the Hero.* A young man on the brink of adulthood is separated from his ordinary existence, from his comfortable home and family. He enters into a liminal space, outside of ordinary time and place, where he is morally tested. He has a spiritual guide who helps him on the journey, and he receives a vision at the end of his quest. However, O'Brien's twist on the conventional mythological structure is that the narrator presents his story as a failed hero's journey. Unlike the typical protagonist of myth who passes the moral test and dons the mantle of hero, O'Brien's narrator in the story describes himself as a coward at the end. Nevertheless, O'Brien suggests that the problem might actually be not so much with his young protagonist as with traditional western notions of courage in the first place. The story offers the possibility of redemption to its failed hero/narrator through his honest confession of his own moral failings and his willingness to communicate these failings to others through the process of storytelling.

In most formulations of hero tales, the hero's journey begins with a call to action, something that spurs the potential hero to leave his ordinary world and surroundings behind. Sometimes the hero ventures out on his journey of his own volition, but often the hero is called by forces beyond his control or understanding, such as when Harry Potter is summoned by messenger owl to report to the Hogwarts School or when Luke Skywalker finds an urgent message from Princess Leia hidden inside a droid. In "On the Rainy River," the potential young hero, Tim O'Brien, is called to action by the draft notice he receives in the mail on June 17, 1968. While some heroes are eager to take up the call, others, such as Bilbo Baggins in Tolkien's *The Hobbit,* are reluctant, fearful of leaving behind the safe, comfortable world they have grown up in. O'Brien is this second type of figure. Upon receiving his draft notice, he remembers "feeling the blood go thick" behind his eyes and a sound going off inside his head: "It wasn't thinking, just a silent howl" (41). O'Brien feels that he is "too *good* for this war. Too smart, too compassionate, too everything" (41). One of the problems with this particular hero's journey, and with definitions of courage and heroism in general in small-town America of the late 1960s, O'Brien points out, is the lack of a clear-cut moral imperative attached to the quest he is being asked to undertake. While O'Brien admits the difficulty of knowing what the right thing to do in Vietnam consists of—"smart men in pinstripes could not agree on even the most fundamental matters of public policy"—he also recognizes that "certain blood was being shed for uncertain reasons" (40), and he argues that when a nation goes to war, "it must have reasonable confidence in the justice and imperative of its cause. You can't fix your mistakes. Once people are dead, you can't make them undead" (41). O'Brien rails in this story, as he does elsewhere in his work, about the small-town ignorance that sends him to war without understanding or even wanting to understand the first thing about the complexities of Vietnamese nationalism, the country's long history of French colonialism, or even the more recent tale of NGO DINH DIEM's tyranny.

O'Brien's summer job at the Armour MEATS plant demonstrates that despite his reluctance to answer the call to action as his society demands, forces larger than himself have been preparing him for war. The job, in which he is required to use a giant water gun suspended from the ceiling in order to flush blood clots out of pig carcasses, has trained O'Brien in the weaponry of war and accustomed him to the gore associated with war wounds. In the evenings as he drives aimlessly around town, O'Brien thinks to himself that his whole life "seemed to be collapsing toward slaughter" (43). But O'Brien is more than a warrior-in-training in these scenes describing his summer job. He images himself as well in the likeness of one of the slaughtered animals when he tells readers a portion of the story he has never told before—how he cracked. He describes being at work one morning and feeling "something break open" inside his chest, a feeling he says was "real," an actual "physical rupture—a cracking-leaking-popping feeling" (46). He quickly removes his apron and drives home but continues to feel a "leaking sensation" deep in his chest, "something very warm and precious spilling out" (46). Covered with blood and hog-stink," he takes a hot shower. O'Brien images himself here as a declotted pig, whose bodily fluids leak out under the warm shower just as the blood clots are removed from the pig carcasses by the spray gun. Psychologically torn apart by the draft notice he has recently received, O'Brien feels as if he is being led to slaughter by the U.S. government. The pressures placed on him by a community and country that urge him to war cause O'Brien's own volition and desires to leak out of his body like the blood from the pigs, rendering him, too, an empty carcass, seemingly unable to act but only to be acted upon. The cracking or breaking open that O'Brien describes in this scene can be read as indicative of the breaking-down of the former self often seen in the hero's journey. The former self must fall away in order to make way for the rebirth that will occur.

Suffering from what he calls a kind of moral "schizophrenia" (44), O'Brien enters into the next stage of the hero's journey when he drives north to the old-fashioned, decrepit fishing resort, the Tip Top Lodge, on the U.S. border with Canada. Once removed from their routines of daily life, heroes often enter into some kind of liminal space, a disorienting in-between locale, often outside of ordinary time and place. The Tip Top Lodge, situated as it is along the Rainy River, which O'Brien describes as not only separating Minnesota from Canada, but even more, as separating "one life from another" (47) for him, serves as just such a liminal space. The lodge is located in the midst of a vast, wild, untamed nature, with the countryside unfolding in "great sweeps of pine and birch and sumac" (47), very unlike the safe, small-town world O'Brien is accustomed to. Further, although it is still August when O'Brien arrives, "the air already had the smell of October, football season, piles of yellow-red leaves, everything crisp and clean" (47). The lodge seems to exist outside of the normal passage of the seasons. Looking back on this experience 20 years later, O'Brien muses about whether "the events of that summer didn't happen in some other dimension, a place where your life exists before you've lived it, and where it goes afterward" (54). Clearly, in O'Brien's memory, the Tip Top Lodge represents a space outside of ordinary existence, even a vaguely supernatural or magical locale that seems otherworldly. It is in such liminal spaces that protagonists in mythical stories are tested and undergo trials to prove their worthiness as heroes.

Quite often, potential heroes meet magical helpers or spiritual guides who present them with magical talismans to aid them in their journey. In "On the Rainy River," the old man Elroy Berdahl serves as just this kind of spirit guide for the young O'Brien. Looking back on Berdahl from his mature vantage point, the narrator describes the old man as "the hero of [his] life" because he offered O'Brien exactly what he needed at the time, "without questions, without any words at all . . . a silent, watchful presence" (48). O'Brien remembers that Berdahl, upon their initial meeting, carried in one hand "a green apple" and that he had "a small paring knife in the other" (48). While Berdahl does not specifically offer O'Brien the apple or the knife, nevertheless, these items do seem to work as magical talismans. The apple can be read as signifying forbidden knowledge, a key to the whole other realm of existence O'Brien might experience as a draft evader in Canada. The paring knife represents the weapon traditionally given the hero by the spirit guide—it suggests a way to access the hidden knowledge represented by the apple. Later in the story, Elroy will actually offer O'Brien money, another equivalent of the magical artifact from mythic stories that can aid the young hero in his quest. Elroy Berdahl seems otherworldly as well in the narrator's description of his physical self. He is said to be "skinny and shrunken and mostly bald," but his bluish gray eyes are the color of a razor blade and equally sharp. O'Brien writes, ". . . as he peered up at me I felt a strange sharpness, almost painful, a cutting sensation, as if his gaze were somehow slicing me open" (48). With his keen vision—what seems to be an ability to see beyond ordinary physical sight—Berdahl immediately peers into O'Brien's soul and guesses his situation. The old man is further associated with the supernatural realm when he is linked with gods or godlike figures three times in the course of the story. Reflecting on his first meeting with Berdahl, the narrator writes that "the man saved me" (48). Later, one evening just at sunset, the old man points out to the confused young narrator an owl circling overhead and says, "Hey, O'Brien . . . There's Jesus" (50). At the end of the story, O'Brien describes Berdal as being like "a witness, like God, or like the gods" (60) who silently observe the choices that individuals make in their lives. While Berdahl never talks to O'Brien about the draft or his future, he clearly provides the means and the opportunity for him to escape to Canada. As spirit guide, he silently nudges O'Brien toward the unconventional but brave choice to flee an unjust war.

It is at the Tip Top Lodge that O'Brien undergoes the phase of the hero's journey that includes moral testing and overcoming obstacles. On his sixth and last day at the old fishing resort, O'Brien is taken fishing by Elroy Berdahl. The old man stops the boat within 20 yards of the Canadian shore, providing an easy opportunity for his young visitor to swim to Canada. The young narrator has come to the biggest moral test of his young life. Throughout his boyhood, as O'Brien explains in the beginning of the story, he had always imagined that, "in a moral emergency," he would behave like the heroes of his youth, "bravely and forthrightly, without any thought of personal loss or discredit" (39). He envisions courage as being like an inheritance or money in the bank, something one could save up and draw upon "if the stakes ever became high enough—if the evil were evil enough, if the good were good enough" (39). Further, O'Brien

imagines that this inheritance consists of traditional western notions of courage—that he would fulfill the role of the solitary warrior fighting for justice. He imagines himself, in fact, as the LONE RANGER, a western hero that he grew up watching on television. Looking back 20 years later, O'Brien understands that the economic metaphor he previously used to think about courage was inadequate: "It dispensed with all those bothersome little acts of daily courage; it offered hope and grace to the repetitive coward; it justified the past while amortizing the future" (40). Part of O'Brien's problem, as well, is that his inheritance of courage, everything he had been taught about heroism and cowardice as a boy, does not apply in a situation like the war in Vietnam, where the moral imperative is so hopelessly murky. Even if courage is like an inheritance, it is like a foreign currency that cannot be spent in O'Brien's current situation.

The past, then, which O'Brien had long thought of as providing him his inheritance of courage, by the end of the story becomes the millstone around his neck, preventing him from passing the moral test and becoming a true hero. Like many figures in mythic hero journeys, O'Brien experiences a vision. As he sits in Elroy Berdahl's fishing boat on the Rainy River, the dividing line between his two possible futures, O'Brien realizes that he will not be the hero of his childhood dreams. Filled with sorrow, he feels "a sudden swell of helplessness come over [him], a drowning sensation" as if he had "toppled overboard and was being swept away by the silver waves" (57). It is here, when his old self seems most fully broken down, that his vision begins. O'Brien first sees chunks from his own history, images of himself as a seven-year-old dressed as the Lone Ranger, as a 12-year-old Little League shortstop, and a 16-year-old dressed for the prom. These key moments from a seemingly idyllic all-American boyhood then transform into images of his parents, his siblings, and the townsfolk of Worthington gathered on the far shoreline, cheering and shouting for him. While O'Brien speculates that these images are simply "an hallucination," he nevertheless acknowledges that they "are as real as anything" (58) he would ever feel. As the vision advances, the people O'Brien knew growing up are gradually joined by historical figures such as ABRA-HAM LINCOLN and SAINT GEORGE, political figures as diverse as ABBIE HOFFMAN and LYNDON JOHNSON, and fictional characters such as HUCK FINN. O'Brien even begins to observe characters from his own fiction such as Jimmy Cross and a an old Vietnamese man sprawled beside a pigpen as well as figures from his imagined future, including a wife, an unborn daughter, and two sons. O'Brien's vision carries the weight of the entire western culture he has been raised with—its past, its present, and its projected future. These cultural traditions associate true manhood and heroism with a warrior mentality, and they press down so heavily on O'Brien that he cannot escape them. In his vision he hears all the congregated figures from western history and culture and from his own upbringing and imagination begin to yell at him: "Traitor! . . . Turncoat! Pussy!" (59). The shame is so much for O'Brien that he submits. He writes, "I would go to the war—I would kill and maybe die—because I was embarrassed not to" (59). As O'Brien cries in the boat, Elroy Berdahl quietly comments, "Ain't biting," and pulls in his fishing line, realizing that the young narrator has failed his test. When O'Brien packs his things to leave the lodge, the old man has simply disappeared, and O'Brien cannot find him to say good-bye. As in many mythic hero stories, the spirit guide dies or vanishes after the moral crisis has passed, his services no longer needed.

Traditional hero tales, in the formulation of Joseph Campbell and others, often conclude with the hero returning home to deliver a boon that may be used to improve the world or to benefit those left behind. While O'Brien at the end of "On the Rainy River" does not return home immediately—the story ends with the lines "I survived, but it's not a happy ending. I was a coward. I went to the war" (61)—nevertheless, the story suggests a possibility of redemption or healing through O'Brien's ability to share his story with readers many years afterward. It is important to note that O'Brien presents the story as a confession. The first lines read, "This is one story I've never told before. Not to anyone. Not to my parents, not to my brother or sister, not even to my wife" (39). Right away, then, readers feel as if they are being let in on a secret, and

most likely a shameful one at that. O'Brien's use of the word *confession* in the third sentence of the story suggests that this secret may even be sinful or criminal since we are most used to hearing about confessions in either religious or criminal justice contexts. But alongside this idea of a sinful secret is also the notion that a confession can be a cleansing ritual. O'Brien writes that "by this act of remembrance, by putting the facts down on paper," he is hoping "to relieve at least some of the pressure on [his] dreams" (39). O'Brien suggests that the writing of stories can be a way of beginning to heal from the wounds of war. Confession in the religious sense can lead to absolution or forgiveness, and the narrator of the story seems to hope that his own confession will similarly bring about a lightening of the burden of guilt he carries with him.

Psychotherapists who work with American Vietnam veterans have noted that the ability to talk about war experiences can aid former soldiers in processing trauma and becoming reintegrated into their former communities. While "On the Rainy River" depicts a failed hero's journey, it still leaves open the possibility of the communal reintegration that most traditional mythic heroes undergo at the end of their tales. For O'Brien this reintegration is best achieved through storytelling. Although "On the Rainy River" is a piece of fiction disguised as a painful, heartfelt, and honest confession, its fictional status does not undermine the emotional truth at the story's core—the paralyzing moral schizophrenia experienced by a young man facing a nearly impossible decision. This theme of the redemptive power of storytelling links "On the Rainy River" to other stories in the collection, such as "Speaking of Courage" and "Notes," in which Norman Bowker's inability to speak about his war experiences leads to his suicide, and "The Lives of the Dead," which opens with the line, "But this too is true: stories can save us" (225).

CHARACTERS

Berdahl, Elroy Elroy Berdahl is the 81-year-old owner of the TIP TOP LODGE, where the young Tim O'Brien spends six days in August 1968 as he decides how to respond to his DRAFT notice. Berdahl serves in the role of spiritual guide for O'Brien, offering him money and opportunity to flee to Canada, but remaining nonjudgmental when the young man cannot bring himself to do so.

O'Brien, Mr. and Mrs.   While the narrator Tim O'Brien's parents appear only briefly in the story, the fear of his parents' reaction if he decides to flee the DRAFT is partly what paralyzes O'Brien into inaction. On June 17, 1968, when O'Brien receives his draft notice, he writes that he had just come in from a round of golf and that his mother and father "were having lunch out in the kitchen" (41). At dinner that night, Mr. O'Brien asks his son what his plans are, but Tim can only reply, "Nothing . . . Wait" (42). Later in the story, O'Brien imagines the reactions of his parents should he decide to flee to Canada: "I could see particular shapes and images, the sorry details of my own future—my father's eyes as I tried to explain myself over the telephone. I could almost hear his voice, and my mother's" (44). Before he drives north, O'Brien writes his parents a brief note explaining that he is "taking off" and "will call" (46). Later in the story, the older O'Brien imagines himself as a young man at the TIP TOP LODGE composing a long letter to his parents, explaining his feelings about the war, his reasons for leaving, and asking them not to be angry. But because O'Brien could not bring himself to flee to Canada, this letter was never sent.

O'Brien, Tim   Tim O'Brien is the story's narrator who is writing as a middle-aged man looking back on his experiences during the summer of 1968, when he was drafted to fight in the Vietnam War. He recounts for readers how the DRAFT notice left him morally paralyzed, how he worked at an ARMOUR meatpacking plant that summer, and how he eventually left WORTHINGTON, MINNESOTA, to drive north, where he stayed for six days at the TIP TOP LODGE, an old-fashioned fishing resort on the RAINY RIVER. O'Brien recounts as well how he was finally unable to bring himself to flee to Canada, a decision that he believes made him a coward. While the narrator of the story shares a name and many biographical details with the real-life Tim O'Brien, nevertheless this story should not be read as autobiography. The actual Tim O'Brien never worked at a meatpacking plant and never spent time at the Tip Top Lodge with an old man named Elroy Berdahl. As he does throughout the collection *The Things They Carried*, O'Brien blurs the lines between fact and fiction in this story, drawing readers' attention to the difficulty of getting at objective truth and the ability of stories to convey emotional truth.

"The People We Marry" (1992)

"The People We Marry," a story about the college romance between John and Kathy Wade, who meet at the UNIVERSITY OF MINNESOTA when he is a senior and she is a freshman, and which endures during John's service in Vietnam after his graduation, was first published in the *Atlantic* magazine in January 1992. The story was later published as chapter 7, "The Nature of Marriage," in O'Brien's 1994 novel, *In the Lake of the Woods*.

SYNOPSIS

The story begins by quickly painting a picture of important scenes from John Wade's childhood—the magic tricks he loved to perform as a 12-year-old and the death of his father when John was 14, among others. It then moves to the autumn of 1967 when John meets Kathy at the University of Minnesota. He is a senior and she is a freshman, and the two fall deeply in love, although John remains fearful that Kathy will someday leave him. He begins to spy on her, following her around campus as she goes about her daily business. By spring semester, the pair is making plans to be married, and John is dreaming of a future political career. But first he serves a tour of duty in Vietnam, where his ability to perform card tricks and his aloof, somewhat mysterious demeanor earn him the nickname "Sorcerer." Initially, John seems like a good luck charm to the men, someone who can protect them from harm with his magic. But when bad times come and several men die, it is as if Sorcerer has lost his touch, and the men begin to partly blame him for the spate of casualties. When a soldier named Reinhart is shot in the head by a sniper in mid-April, something inside of John breaks. In a state of intense agitation, in which he seems to lose touch with his own body, John advances on the enemy and shoots the sniper through the cheekbone. The American soldiers later string the body up in a tree to serve as a warning to a group of Vietnamese villagers.

As his war experience grows increasingly more violent and troubling, John's letters home to Kathy become more and more disturbing as well. Her letters, in response, become colder and more distant. When John is finally discharged, he returns to Minneapolis without informing Kathy of his arrival, choosing instead to spy on her for nearly 48 hours straight. John's worst fears are confirmed when Kathy does not return to her dorm room at all the second night that he keeps watch. Despite the betrayal, the couple marry anyway. The story closes by briefly describing the wedding, held in the landscaped backyard of Kathy's family's suburban home in the Twin Cities, and the honeymoon at the St. Paul Ramada Inn. But readers are left uneasy as John carries Kathy over the threshold of their new apartment. He determines to be vigilant in the relationship, to "guard his advantage" (98), and above all, not to let Kathy know about the tricks that he plays.

COMMENTARY

"The People We Marry" is a story largely about the human desire to regain control in the face of overwhelming sorrow and loss. Even as a young boy, John Wade seems to be somewhat lonely, practicing magic tricks by himself in the basement of his family's home, with only a full-length mirror for company. The magic provides John a measure of control over his environment, or at least the temporary illusion of control. Even though the 12-year-old boy understands that he is performing "trickery" rather than "true magic," he sometimes pretends otherwise because he is a dreamer and because, "for a time what seemed to happen became a happening in itself" (90). So, the imaginary reality John creates through his tricks takes

on the status of actual reality, at least for a short time. By pretending that his tricks are real, John is able to control and change the world around him in small ways.

When John turns 14 and his father dies, his pretending becomes more desperate. Just as Paul Berlin in *Going After Cacciato* deals with the deaths he has witnessed by escaping into his imagination, by inventing a complex tale about his platoon following a deserting soldier all the way to PARIS, John Wade prefers to live in his imagination rather than the real world immediately after his father's death. He pretends that his father comes into his bedroom at night to talk to him, and he even imagines his father referring jokily to his own death—"'Well I'm back,' his father would say, 'but don't tell your mom—she'd kill me'" (90). Like many of the soldiers in O'Brien's earlier works about Vietnam, including the men of ALPHA COMPANY in *The Things They Carried*, John Wade uses jokes, a kind of dark irony, to wrestle with the enormity of death. And his father's death does have an enormous effect on the teenage boy. The devastating loss creates a powerful feeling of rage in John, so much so that he wants to kill everybody at the funeral—"everybody who was crying and everybody who wasn't . . . the minister . . . the choir . . . the skinny old lady at the organ . . . the flowers . . . he wanted to grab a hammer and crawl in to the casket and kill his father for dying" (97). Unable to act on his violent fantasies, John is reduced to simply feeling helpless. After the service, he goes down into the basement and practices magic, pretending to perform "miracles of love and healing" (97).

But John not only feels a helpless sort of rage in response to his father's death, he feels abandoned as well, betrayed. Thus, as a young man attending college, he expects betrayal from the people he loves. He expects to be abandoned. That is why he begins secretly spying on Kathy. Initially, he looks "for signs of betrayal" (90) in Kathy's behavior. But he soon begins to enjoy the new trick of spying for itself, which is explicitly linked to the magic tricks he performed as a boy: "It was sleight-of-body work, or sleight-of-mind, and over those cold winter days he was carried along by the powerful, secret thrill of gaining access to a private life"

(91). John feels more powerful, more in control as he begins to gain secret knowledge about Kathy. When Kathy is amazed by how well John knows her and comments that it is almost as if he can read her mind, John takes her in her arms and tells her that their closeness is "a miracle" (91). John feels that he can finally perform the miracles of love and healing that he so desperately practiced after his father's funeral.

Yet, despite his best attempts to know Kathy completely and to control their relationship, John Wade must recognize that Kathy has her own secrets as well. She is described as an intensely private and intensely independent young woman who sometimes vanishes completely from John's presence in unexpected and unannounced ways. In addition, Kathy is "hard to fool" (92). When John tells her about his political ambitions, Kathy comments that his plans feel calculated, manipulative, and he notices "something flat and skeptical" in her eyes, "something terrifying" (92). What John is terrified by here is the specter of his inability to control the relationship as he would like. He also realizes, as he tries to persuade Kathy that he wants to live a good life, do good things in the world, that he is not telling her the full truth. Politics, John admits to himself, does involve manipulation: "Like a magic show: invisible wires and secret trapdoors. He imagined placing a city in the palm of his hand, making his hand into a fist, making the city into a happier place. Manipulation, that was the fun of it" (92). John's entire life has been built upon the magic tricks he practiced as a young boy, his need to control the daunting uncertainties of life.

When John gets to Vietnam, he finds himself in an environment in which control over his daily life is taken almost completely out of his hands. Not only is he a soldier who must obey the orders of his superiors, but death in Vietnam arrives in unexpected and seemingly random ways—men get shot in the head by snipers or step on booby-trapped mines, blowing themselves apart. Such an environment is anathema to a young man who has struggled so hard for control throughout his life. It is small wonder, then, that John's reliance on trickery and illusion begins to take on sinister undertones in Vietnam. While at first he performs harmless card

tricks and other sleight-of-hand for the men in his unit, enjoying the nickname "Sorcerer" with which the men dub him, soon the men come to believe in the reality of his magical powers, superstitiously touching his helmet before going out on patrol or ambush and asking his advice "on matters of fortune" (92). John, as Sorcerer, again seems to take on almost godlike abilities. While he had earlier assured Kathy that his ability to know her so well was a "miracle," the men in his platoon in Vietnam file past him to perform the "ritual" of touching his helmet "as if at communion" (92). Of course, the men begin to turn on their Sorcerer-god when bad times come, when things begin to go wrong and men begin to die. John Wade feels betrayed and lost by this behavior, as he had felt earlier when his father died. But Sorcerer has one more trick up his sleeve. When he charges on the enemy sniper following Reinhart's death, John Wade seems to act without volition, as if he no longer has control over his physical body. But when later that night he and the other soldiers string the body up in a Vietnamese village, a group of villagers summoned to watch at gunpoint, Sorcerer is clearly in charge again. The raising of the sniper's body into the tree is described as "an act of levitation" performed by "Sorcerer and his assistants" (97). During the war, John is able to act upon the feelings of murderous rage he had to suppress as a 14-year-old, and he is rewarded for doing so. The men in his unit are amazed by Sorcerer's new trick and cannot stop talking about it.

Upon his return home, John is still propelled by his fear of Kathy's betrayal. Unable to live with the unknown, with the heartbreaking uncertainties and ambiguities of human life, John does not inform Kathy of his return but again spies on her. Although he is dimly aware that he could choose to "simply love her, and to go on loving her," he is terrified by uncertainty: "The ambiguity of it all seemed intolerable" (98). Further, he realizes that "Nothing could ever be certain, not if he spied forever, because he would always face the threat of tomorrow's treachery, or next year's treachery, or the treachery implicit in all the years beyond that" (98). Even though John's worst fears are confirmed when Kathy does not return to her dorm room at all the second night he spies on her, they marry anyway. The minister at the Wades' wedding affirms what for John lies at the heart of the tragedy of the human condition when he quotes from the Bible: "For now we see through a glass, darkly; but then face to face; now I know in part; but then shall I know even as also I am known" (98). Human beings live in a world with limited knowledge. Their lives are rife with ambiguity and uncertainty. Full knowledge is the realm of the eternal, of God, not of human beings. Only in death, in another world, will human beings take on this godlike knowledge. John Wade's fatal flaw is that he simply cannot accept the minister's words. During his honeymoon, he reassures himself that he is Sorcerer, in control of the world he lives in. John resolves to "guard his advantage" (98) in the marriage and to keep his tricks secret from his wife. Readers assume that he will continue to play God in his desperate attempts to control his fear of loss and betrayal. Although Kathy insists that she knows the couple will be happy, the future does not bode well for the Wades.

Differences in Versions

While the story remained largely intact when O'Brien revised it for inclusion in *In the Lake of the Woods*, he did make a few significant changes, mostly to better fit the story into the My Lai subtext that it is so important to the novel. The original story does depict John Wade's service in Vietnam, his adopting of the nickname "Sorcerer," and his killing of the Vietnamese sniper, but the time line of Wade's service puts him in Vietnam about a year after the MY LAI MASSACRE. Thus, when O'Brien revises the story, he pushes all the dates back a year, so that John meets Kathy at the University of Minnesota in the autumn of 1966, graduates in the spring of 1967, and is a member of CHARLIE COMPANY in March 1968, when the massacre actually took place (Wade had been a member of Bravo Company in the original story). O'Brien also changes the name of the soldier killed by a sniper from Reinhart to Weber. This change is significant because an American soldier named Bill Weber was actually shot by a Vietnamese sniper near one of the villages of My Lai on February 12, 1968. Some

of the men who later participated in the massacre cited Weber's death as partial motivation for their actions. In addition, O'Brien makes John Wade's behavior in Vietnam seem even more ominous in the novel version than in the original story version. He adds the detail that swallowing his jackknife is one of the tricks that Sorcerer initially performs for the men of Charlie Company, and he adds the comment that "Much could be done . . . with his jackknife and a corpse" (*Lake* 38) a bit later when the narrator tells readers that Wade, when pressed, would sometimes do a trick or two using the everyday objects he found around him. The revised version also more directly addresses the book's theme of sinfulness when it lists "sorrow" and "evil" (*Lake* 40) among the emotions Wade feels after Rinehart's death, replacing "humiliation" and "despair" (94) in the original version.

Other changes involve John twice repeating how much he loves his father the night he spends at a hotel and has nightmarelike visions immediately after his return from Vietnam. The novel version of this scene clearly links John's experience at his father's funeral to the massacre at THUAN YEN as well, as John imagines seeing the mourners at the funeral squatting near a Vietnamese village irrigation ditch, and these mourners slowly dissolve into John's own mother, and then into a minister who shouts out "Sin!" (42). The scene after Kathy spends the whole night away from her dorm room is slightly changed, too. While the original story concludes this scene with John simply waiting for Kathy, in the revised novel version the two actually speak—Kathy saying simply that she "was out" (44), and John smiling secretly and flatly repeating her statement. Finally, the very end of the story is slightly altered as well. While the original story says that "John" carried Kathy into their new apartment after their marriage, the novel version changes the name to "Sorcerer," perhaps suggesting more of a threat than is implied in the original. John also resolves at the end even more explicitly to keep from Kathy "the things he'd seen, the things he'd done" (*Lake* 46), an addition that sets readers up for the nearly 20-year secret of his My Lai involvement that John will keep in the novel.

CHARACTERS

Henderson Henderson is a fellow soldier of John Wade's who is shot through the stomach in January. When John kneels down to press a towel against the wound and comfort the boy, Henderson starts to giggle and declares, "Hey, no sweat . . . I'm aces. I'm golden" (92), as he urges "Sorcerer" to do his magic. Later, during March, which is described as a "wretched month" (94), Sorcerer seems to lose his magic, and Henderson dies in a hospital.

Minister at Funeral John remembers the minister at his father's funeral saying words "that made him want to search for his father in the pews and aisles as if for a lost nickel" (94, 97). Later, when John kills the enemy sniper in Vietnam, he will reexperience the rage he felt when he was 14 at his father's funeral and he wanted to kill everyone present, including the minister.

Minister at Wedding A second minister appears in the story as well. This one, contrasting with the first minister, who speaks at the funeral of John's father, officiates at John's wedding. The wedding minister cites a passage from First Corinthians that reads, "For now we see through a glass, darkly; but then face to face; now I know in part; but then shall I know even as also I am known" (98). This passage encapsulates the ambiguity that makes up the human condition. Despite John's desperate desire for certainty and permanence, human life is made up of the unknown. As he enters a marriage that is already filled with secrets and the burden of past betrayals, he has no idea how the future will turn out, despite Kathy's insistence that she "knows" she and John will be happy together.

Reinhart Reinhart is a soldier in John Wade's unit in Vietnam who is shot in the head by an enemy sniper as he is eating a candy bar. The death fills John with coldness inside, mingled with rage, humiliation, illness, and despair. He is so filled with emotion, in fact, that he unthinkingly surges forward to discover the sniper's hiding place and shoots the man to death through the cheekbone.

Vietnamese Sniper After a Vietnamese sniper shoots an American soldier named Reinhart in the head, John Wade loses control of himself. He unthinkingly glides forward toward the sniper's position, circles it, and comes up behind the sniper. The man turns to face John, and their eyes meet before Wade puts the muzzle of his rifle against the Vietnamese soldier's cheekbone and pulls the trigger. Later, the American soldiers will string the body up in a Vietnamese village to serve as a warning.

Wade, John John Wade is a troubled young college student and Vietnam War soldier in the story, whose love for his girlfriend, Kathy, nearly overwhelms him. Traumatized and enraged by his father's death when he was only 14 years old, the 21-year-old John is emotionally needy and terrified of experiencing the loss of another loved one. His insecurity is apparent in the way that he spies on Kathy, expecting her to betray him at any moment. John's political aspirations also seem to be a symptom of his emotional neediness and his desire to control and manipulate his surroundings. As a soldier in the Vietnam War, John earns the nickname "Sorcerer" from his platoon mates, enjoying the attention and the aura of mystery that surrounds him, at least until things begin to go terribly wrong and the men feel that Sorcerer has lost his magic. While John could be considered brave for his killing of the enemy sniper, this incident is described in a disturbing way—it is almost as if he loses touch with his physical self, he is so out of control with rage. After his return home, he has even more secrets that he must keep from Kathy. The two marry despite John's worst fears about Kathy being confirmed—she stays out all night soon after he returns from Vietnam, presumably spending the time with another lover. The story ends ominously as Kathy and John embark on a marriage already filled with secrets and haunted by past betrayals.

Wade, Kathy Readers meet 18-year-old Kathy, later to become Kathy Wade, when she is a freshman at the UNIVERSITY OF MINNESOTA and begins to date John Wade. A smart, athletic young woman who loves John but who is also an intensely private and independent person, Kathy does not seem to realize the extent of John's neediness and psychological damage—he spies on her as she moves around campus, secretly following her every move. When John tells Kathy his dreams of a political career, she skeptically asks him what all his ambitions are *for,* and when he writes disturbing letters home from Vietnam, she coolly expresses her hope that the war is not part of his political game plan. Kathy obviously has her own secrets as well; she starts a new relationship while John is in the war, which he discovers while spying on her after his return home. While the lack of trust in the relationship between John and Kathy seems ominous to readers, the couple marry anyway. Despite Kathy's final comment that she knows they will be happy, readers suspect the opposite may be true, as the story closes with John determining to keep his secrets through the course of their marriage.

Wade, Mr. John Wade's father dies when John is a boy of 14. While readers do not find out much about Mr. Wade, they understand the devastating effect this death has on John as he simply cannot accept the loss, imagining his father alive again and coming into his room at night. Readers discover, as well, that John was filled with rage at the funeral, wanting to kill everyone there—everybody who was crying and everybody who was not—the minister, the organist, and even his father for dying and leaving him. This early loss and the resulting sense of betrayal seem at least partially responsible for John's later insecurity in his relationship with Kathy, his intense fear that she will leave him, and his need to manipulate the relationship so that he will retain her love.

Wade, Mrs. Mrs. Wade, John's mother, is mentioned only briefly in the story. She is depicted weeping at her husband's funeral, then sleeping after the service while John practices magic tricks in front of the full-length mirror in the family's basement.

"Quantum Jumps" (1983)

The short story "Quantum Jumps," about a Vietnam War DRAFT evader and former political radical named William, who slowly loses his mind as he digs a bomb shelter in his yard in Montana, was first published in *Ploughshares* magazine in 1983. The story was revised and divided into three separate chapters (chapters 1, 4, and 7) when it was included in the 1985 novel, *The Nuclear Age.*

SYNOPSIS

It is after midnight in mid-April of the early 1980s when the story opens. A 45-year-old man named William—whose last name readers never learn in the original story version—is digging an enormous hole in his yard in Montana, planning to build a bomb shelter to protect his wife, Bobbi, and daughter, Melinda, from the threat of nuclear war. Readers soon discover that William is a Vietnam War draft dodger who was heavily involved in radical politics back in the late '60s. Now, over a decade later, he is a family man whose sole desire is to protect himself and his nuclear family. However, William's 12-year-old daughter, Melinda, and his wife, Bobbi, a poet, think that William is going crazy as he obsessively digs and digs and even uses dynamite to blast through the deep underground rock. Bobbi refuses to speak to her husband directly during this period, communicating with him only through poems she writes. As the weeks pass, Melinda becomes increasingly upset, eventually telling her father that her mother is planning to leave him. But the night before Bobbi and Melinda are scheduled to depart by taxi, William hammers pieces of lumber across the door and window of the master bedroom, where they are sleeping, effectively imprisoning them inside the house. The story ends with Melinda angrily shouting at her father that he is crazy.

COMMENTARY

In physics, the term *quantum jump* refers to an electron that almost instantaneously changes from one energy level to another. The term in popular use has come to refer to any abrupt and dramatic change as contrasted to a change that occurs gradually or incrementally. The story "Quantum Jumps" catalogs several such dramatic changes. When William begins digging his hole in the yard, it seems like a quantum jump to his wife and daughter. He does not spend time contemplating the digging, not does he enter gradually into his new pursuit; rather, he leaps into it obsessively, spending entire nights and days in his hole over the next two months. In addition, William's alteration from political radical to near-survivalist seems abrupt as well, at least to readers; they are never given a description of how the change came about and see only snapshots of his life in the late '60s versus his life in the early '80s, almost like before-and-after photos. William's transition from a nonviolent war dodger to an angry, menacing figure whose every move threatens violence to his wife and daughter is a quantum leap as well, especially in the magnitude of the change that he seems to have undergone.

The main question that the story asks as it details these dramatic changes is whether William has actually gone crazy or not. He himself brings up the possibility that he has gone mad several times in the opening paragraphs of the story, acknowledging that readers might interpret his actions as insane: "Crazy, you think? Maybe, maybe not, but listen. This is the hour of mass murder" (11). Yet, William also protests—perhaps too vehemently at times—that he is not losing his mind: "Crazy? Not likely, not yet," he admonishes readers early on, adding a few paragraphs later: "Crazy, my ass" (11). While his own family members and the world at large might label William crazy for his obsession with nuclear war, he sees things differently. To him the rest of the world is crazy for ignoring real, concrete scientific facts. Other people, he believes, simply close their eyes to the possibility of nuclear devastation. He scorns those who view the end of the world as mere metaphor, insisting that "the bombs are real" (12), a slogan that he will actually print on a poster and hold up outside the college cafeteria in the version of the story included in a novel.

This conflict between metaphor and reality marks William's relationship with his wife, Bobbi, as well. Bobbie is a poet who deals in metaphor,

whose poems compare her husband to a blind mole and who writes about divorce as being like nuclear fission, but William reads a preference for metaphor "over the real thing" as simply "coyness and indirection" (18). Metaphor, he thinks to himself in mid-June as the hole gets deeper and deeper, is "the opiate of our age" (30). Literature, he seems to believe, lulls people into a fall sense of beauty and security in the world. Rather than waste time writing, poets, he believes, should dig. William specifically mulls over in his mind two famous poems about the end of the world: ROBERT FROST's "Fire and Ice," in which the speaker playfully contemplates what kind of doomsday scenario he would prefer, and T. S. Eliot's "The Hollow Men," which concludes with the image of the world ending quietly and pathetically, with a "whimper" rather than a "bang." A literal-minded man who values scientific fact over poetic allusion, William feels that these two poets hide behind "sugar-coated bullshit" (30). His wife, Bobbi, he believes, hides behind her own beauty and the beauty of her poems. He writes that she "makes the deadly mistake of assuming that her beauty is armor against the facts of fission" (18–19). Again, William insists on the real over the metaphoric, believing that metaphor is a kind of blindness.

While William maintains that he is simply reacting to fact—to the looming threat of nuclear war—it is possible that he is motivated not only by his fear of a doomsday scenario. He is also a middle-aged man who longs to regain his youth, particularly what he remembers as the idealistic politics of the late 1960s. During long nights digging in his hole, William remembers "that old gang" (35) of his: Sarah, Ollie, Tina, and Ned, and he wonders what happened to his old friends and radical cohorts. He recalls his youth fondly and thinks that the current historical period is one of "disillusion" as he considers "the loss of energy, the slow hardening of a generation's arteries" (35) that he believes has occurred over the past decade and a half. Further, he bemoans what he considers a lack of passion in the world of the early 1980s: "There are no more heroes, there are no more public enemies," he muses, "Villainy itself has disappeared . . . leaving a world without good or bad, without passion, and the moral climate has turned mild and banal. We've been homogenized, I fear" (35). Part of William's increasing mental instability seems to involve his own disappointment in his current life. He has a sort of midlife crisis as he romanticizes his 1960s past, which may at least partially motivate him to the extreme action he takes, although he believes his action is based simply on the scientific facts surrounding him and that he is able to see through the metaphors that others hide behind.

But perhaps William's insistence on the emptiness of metaphor, his dogged literalness, is what hinders him most. While he can imagine the end of the world in great detail, he seems unable to imagine the effect that his actions have on his wife and daughter, how terrifying his behavior seems to them, or even how close to the edge he really is. Thus, as Bobbi suggests in her poem "THE MOLE IN HIS HOLE," William himself is blind in many ways. When he eats the poem titled "FISSION" that he finds stapled to the Cheerios box one morning, William tells the story in a strangely matter-of-fact way, as if this were completely normal behavior. His daughter's outraged and incredulous reaction seems much more sane to readers than William's own calm detailing of the "awesome dignity" he displayed as he chewed and swallowed the piece of paper. While on some deep psychological level William does seem to sense the dirtiness, the messiness of his own behavior—after all, he cleans the house obsessively after boarding up the bedroom—he is nevertheless unable to clearly see the insanity in his decision to actually imprison his wife and daughter inside a room in the house. While he believes he is preparing for a nuclear future, he overlooks how he is completely alienating and frightening the very people he loves and most hopes to save. He is blind to the fact that he is destroying his family in his attempt to protect them. A fallout shelter, despite his assertions to the contrary, is not a home. Melinda thus seems justified in shouting "Crazy, crazy!" (44) at her father at the very end of the story. William, while exactly right about the scientific facts, while refusing to ignore that $E=mc^2$ and that the possibility of nuclear annihilation is all-too real, nevertheless seems to have stepped off the tightrope that all human beings must walk: the

delicate balancing act between acknowledging and repressing fear, the "balance of power" that Bobbi writes about in her poem, both psychological and political.

Differences in Versions

Although O'Brien makes numerous small changes when he revises the story "Quantum Jumps" for inclusion in *The Nuclear Age,* most of these alterations are fairly minor—new paragraph breaks, insertion of substitute words and phrases, and tightening up of the language. More substantive revisions involve the division of the story into three separate chapters in the novel, with tales of William's childhood and college days inserted between them, and the raising of his age from 45 to 49 to mesh with the time line presented elsewhere in the novel. In addition, William, in the revised novel version, thinks earlier and more often of his old radical group of friends—Sarah and Ned and Tina and Ollie than he does in the story, mostly likely to introduce these characters' increased importance in the book. But perhaps the most significant change in the novel is that William actually imagines the hole speaking to him, urging him to continue digging. In the story, William never personifies the hole; he never sees the hole as a separate entity with a volition of its own. This change draws more attention to William's possible insanity. If he is actually hearing voices, if he really believes the hole is speaking to him, it seems more clear to readers that he is losing mental control. Finally, the novel omits a long paragraph that occurs at the very end of the story in which William speculates about the ordinary life he would live if possible— the cocktail parties he would attend, the long summer days he would enjoy, the trips he would take (43–44). While the language is changed quite a bit, the general direction and content of this paragraph is moved to the very end of the novel, when William claims that he will force himself to repress his fears and live an ordinary life.

CHARACTERS

Bobbi Bobbi is the name of William's wife in the story. She is described as a gorgeous, blue-eyed blonde, a poet who deals in metaphors on a daily basis. Clearly frightened by her husband's new obsession with digging a fallout shelter and his increasingly odd behavior, Bobbi has stopped talking to him, choosing to communicate instead by leaving poems for him to read. As William continues to act stranger and stranger, Bobbi retreats to the master bedroom with their daughter, Melinda, and makes preparations to leave. However, Melinda betrays her mother's plans to William, and he boards up the bedroom, effectively rendering them prisoners. The story ends unresolved, readers unsure of what will happen to Bobbi and Melinda.

Melinda Melinda is the spunky 12-year-old daughter of Bobbi and William. Unable to understand her father's fear of nuclear war or his strangely obsessive behavior in digging the bomb shelter, she begs him to return to normal. Unlike her mother, who simply shuts down and stops talking to William, Melinda is unafraid to tell her father what she thinks—that he is "nutto" (15) and "crazy" (44). The young girl desperately tries to show William how sad and afraid she is, but her father steels himself to her complaints, insisting that everything is perfectly normal. When Bobbi decides to leave her husband, Melinda tells her father of the plan, still hoping against hope that he will do something to stop it. But she certainly does not expect what actually happens—that her father imprisons her and her mother in the master bedroom of their home, boarding up the door and window of the room with two-by-fours in order to prevent their departure. Melinda gets the last word in the story when she shouts at her father through the door that he is crazy.

Rafferty, Ned Ned Rafferty is one of the group of radical friends that William associated with in his youth. While digging the hole, William becomes nostalgic for the '60s, telling himself that Ned, like his other old friends, really *cared* about the world.

Sarah While digging for countless hours in the hole in his yard, William thinks about an old radical friend from his youth named Sarah, who stuck with her revolutionary politics longer than the other members of William's old group of friends.

In his imagination, Sarah, a gutsy operative who "made a career out of sabotage" (35), encourages him when he cuts the telephone line and imprisons his wife and daughter in the master bedroom, telling him "Terrorism isn't all that difficult—just takes some getting-used-to" (35).

Tina Tina is another member of the gang of radical friends from the '60s whom William thinks about as he digs the bomb shelter in his yard. He wonders what has happened to these old friends from the past, just as he wonders what has happened to the idealism and political outrage that motivated a generation.

William William, who narrates the story in first person, tries to rationalize his obsessive and erratic behavior as he spends hours and hours digging a fallout shelter in his yard. At times, he himself does not seem to understand that he is acting strangely, downplaying outbursts of temper and odd actions such as eating one of the poems that his wife, Bobbi, writes to him. He misses the radical days of his youth, lamenting that his generation has become complacent and disillusioned. Readers learn that after college he had evaded the DRAFT for the Vietnam War, become involved in radical political activities, and spent "ten years on the run, dodging danger, dodging the feds, hopping from hideout to hideout like a common criminal" (16). While William seems justified in his claims that "the bombs are real" (12)—that nuclear war is an actual possibility—he nevertheless also seems like a man out of control. But when he goes so far as to imprison Bobbi and his daughter, Melinda, in a bedroom inside their home, readers realize that William is verging on insanity. The story ends menacingly, readers unsure what happens to William's wife and daughter or what lengths he will go to in order to keep them from leaving him.

Winkler, Ollie Ollie Winkler is one of a group of former radicals that made up William's "old gang" (35) from the late 1960s. William informs readers that he learned how to use dynamite from Ollie, who was a bomb expert of some kind, ironically manufacturing "Bombs for Peace" (23).

"Speaking of Courage" (1976)

The story "Speaking of Courage," which depicts Vietnam War veteran Paul Berlin driving aimlessly around the lake in his small hometown in Iowa on a hot Fourth of July, was first published in the *Massachusetts Review* in the summer of 1976. The story was later revised significantly and included in the 1990 book, *The Things They Carried*, with a soldier named Norman Bowker rather than Paul Berlin as its protagonist.

SYNOPSIS

"Speaking of Courage" opens with Paul Berlin, a young soldier just returned home from the Vietnam War, driving his father's big Chevy around and around a seven-mile loop circling a lake in his rural Iowa hometown. It is a hot Sunday afternoon on July 4th, and Berlin has nowhere to go and no one to talk to about his war experiences. As he repeatedly circles the lake, Berlin thinks about his old high school friend Max Arnold, a budding philosopher who avoided serving in the war when he drowned in the lake. He thinks about his old girlfriend Sally Hankins, who is now married. Berlin imagines as well having conversations about the war with his father, a WORLD WAR II veteran, who in real life does not want to talk about Vietnam. Mostly, he pictures himself explaining to his father how he almost won the SILVER STAR for valor after going down into a Vietnamese tunnel where a fellow soldier named Frenchie Tucker had just been shot. Eventually, Berlin pulls into an A&W root beer stand, where he is ignored by the young carhop because he does not know the correct way to order, until she grudgingly shows him how to use the intercom system. The story ends with Berlin completing several more circuits around the lake before finally pulling into SUNSET PARK and standing on the beach with his arms folded to watch the town's Fourth of July fireworks display.

COMMENTARY

The story opens with an image of futility as Paul Berlin makes repeated circuits around the lake, having "no place in particular to go" (243). As

the critic John Timmerman points out, the circular imagery in the story is connected to "the weary circularity of [Berlin's] own life and mind" (106). Berlin's memories keep returning to the war, despite his attempts to fit back into the small-town life he had left behind. Later in the story, the Chevy is said to circle the lake "like an electron spinning forever around its nucleus" (244). As the center of Berlin's small hometown, the lake functions like the dense nucleus of an atom, the part that contains the atom's weight. The lake represents the values of small-town life—the expensive, well-cared for houses on the lake side of the road suggesting the American dream fulfilled and the kind of life Berlin might have aspired to before he left home to fight in the war. Now that he has returned, things in the town seem "pretty much the same" (243) to him. The problem is that the town has remained the same while Berlin himself has changed dramatically as a result of his wartime experiences. He no longer fits in, and so he spins endlessly around the lake, both drawn to and repelled by the world he left behind.

What Berlin has to face upon his return home is that the town and the people in it are not interested in listening to his war stories. Berlin's inability to talk about his experiences and the town's silence in the face of his need to communicate are the main themes of the story. As Berlin drives around the lake, he reflects that it is nice to look at. But he also realizes that the lake is not as clean or refreshing as it first seems. Despite its pleasant appearance, Berlin understands that, fed by neither springs nor streams, "it was a tepid, algaed lake that depended on fickle prairie rains for replenishment" (243–44). The stagnant lake suggests a town with stagnant values as well. Berlin muses that despite the fact that he knows many war stories, "nobody was there to listen, and nobody knew a damn about the war because nobody believed it was really a war at all" (250). The traditional values of Berlin's small hometown demand that war stories include "talk of valor" (250) rather than details about how afraid a soldier could be or whether it hurts to be shot, which are the lessons Berlin actually learned during the war. While the town will make a dazzling show of patriotism every Fourth of July, and

Berlin imagines the fireworks reflected in the lake, he also comes to understand that the town is more concerned with reflections or images—with holding onto illusions about war and projecting illusions of patriotism—than with the reality of Berlin's own wartime experience. Thus, the young soldier feels separate from the town after his return home. The action on the lake is "all distant and pretty" (248) as he observes it through his car windows, through which "the town shined like a stop-motion photograph, or a memory" (247). Again, the town is associated with an image, a photograph. While Berlin was raised in this town, now he looks at it nostalgically, as something from a distant past that he can no longer be part of.

Paul Berlin struggles throughout the story with defining his own behavior in the war against conventional definitions of heroism—was he brave or was he a coward? According to the conventional small-town definitions of bravery and valor that he grew up with, the seven medals he brings home should suggest that he acquitted himself well, that he was brave. Yet Berlin knows, as does his veteran father, that "many brave men did not win medals for their bravery, and that others won medals for doing nothing" (245). Readers might think back to the 1973 memoir, *If I Die in a Combat Zone, Box Me Up and Ship Me Home,* in which O'Brien describes a tough colonel, a battalion commander, who wins the Distinguished Flying Cross after bringing a helicopter in to pick up the dead and wounded following a combat assault (CA) mission in July 1969. The irony is that the commander had initially refused to fly into the hot landing zone, agreeing to pick up the injured men only after the personal danger to himself had passed. While Berlin wishes he had won the Silver Star or the Medal of Honor, he still understands that even these medals, awarded for valor, tell only partial stories. The medal that Berlin is most proud of in his collection is the COMBAT INFANTRYMAN'S BADGE, because it means "that he had seen the war as a real soldier, on the ground" (247). The medal signifies that Berlin had "had the opportunity to be brave" (247) whether he was actually brave or not.

And the memory that Berlin keeps circling back to during his drive around the lake concerns just this question of bravery. In his imagined conversation with his father, he repeatedly asserts, "I wasn't brave . . . but I might have been" (247). Apparently, after Frenchie Tucker was shot through the neck, Paul Berlin was sent down into the same tunnel, perhaps to retrieve the injured soldier, a job performed by Bernie Lynn in the later novel *Going After Cacciato.* While both Frenchie and Bernie die in the novel version of the story, in the 1976 version of "Speaking of Courage," Paul Berlin seems to have become overwhelmed with fear in the tunnel and backed out. Berlin imagines explaining his tunnel experiences to a sympathetic listener,

> . . . how, after crawling into the red-mouthed tunnel, you close your eyes like a mole and follow the tunnel walls and smell Frenchie's fresh blood and know a bullet cannot miss in there, and how there is nowhere to go but forward or backward, eyes closed, and how you can't go forward, and lose all sense, and are dragged out by the heels, losing the Silver Star. (250)

But part of Paul Berlin's difficulty in telling this story is that he finds it shameful. As in many of O'Brien's works, a soldier's bravery or cowardice is closely tied with shame and embarrassment. Not only does Berlin return to a town that "could not talk" and "would not listen" (247), he himself is unable to confess his most shameful memories. O'Brien writes that, while Berlin could talk about his terror in the tunnel, and talk about emerging to see sunlight, "he could not feel the warmth, or see the faces of the men who looked away, or talk about his shame" (253).

So, the story ends with silence: "There was no one to talk to, and nothing to say" (253). With this conclusion, Berlin exits the car in Sunset Park to watch the fireworks: "For a small town, it was a pretty good show" (253), he thinks to himself. Thus "Speaking of Courage" is, finally, a story about putting on shows—on maintaining appearances at all costs. The town wants to hold onto its illusions about war and valor, which would be disrupted by talk about Vietnam or by recognizing that Vietnam was not simply an anomaly, but "a war the same as any war" (250). And Berlin hides his inner turmoil behind the seven medals displayed on his uniform, putting on a "pretty good show" upon his return and not speaking about his fear or shame.

Differences in Versions

In the chapter titled "Notes," which immediately follows "Speaking of Courage" in *The Things They Carried*, O'Brien explains that the story was originally written in 1975 in response to a long letter he received from a fellow soldier named Norman Bowker in which Norman described working in dead-end jobs and feeling out of place since he left the war. O'Brien explains that after receiving the letter he immediately sat down and began writing "Speaking of Courage," which he originally thought would be a chapter in *Going After Cacciato*, the novel he was working on at the time. But he tells readers that he realized the story "had no proper home in the larger narrative" because *Going After Cacciato* was a "war story" while "Speaking of Courage" was a "postwar story" (*TTTC* 159). So, he removed it from the novel. He informs readers as well that he sent the story as initially written to Norman Bowker, who wrote back, "It's not terrible . . . but you left out Vietnam" (160). Eight months later, O'Brien explains, Norman hanged himself in a neighborhood YMCA, suggesting that perhaps O'Brien's own silences, his own failure to tell the story properly, contributed to Norman's death.

When O'Brien rewrites the story for inclusion in *The Things They Carried*, he removes Paul Berlin and substitutes Bowker himself as the story's protagonist. He also deletes the death of Frenchie Tucker in the tunnel, an incident that *does* appear in *Going After Cacciato*. Instead, the death that haunts Norman as he drives around and around the lake in his Iowa hometown is that of a soldier named Kiowa, who drowned in a muddy "shitfield" where the men had been encamped during a nighttime firefight. Norman feels terribly guilty about the death since he had hold of Kiowa's boot as he sank into the dark swampy field, but he simply could not hold on. As in the original version, Norman imagines explaining all this to his father, who is the idealized listener who does not really exist for the young veteran. The inclusion of Kiowa's death in the rewritten story connects "Speaking of Courage" to several pieces that come later in *The Things They Carried*. The story of Kiowa is retold in "In the Field," but in that story, the soldier who cannot hold onto the boot has switched from Norman to a young version of Tim O'Brien. The death of Kiowa plays an important role as well in the story "Field Trip," in which the fictional version of Tim O'Brien describes returning to Vietnam with his daughter, Kathleen, to visit the site of Kiowa's death.

In addition, Sally Hanson in the earlier story transforms into Sally Kramer Gustafson and is given a larger role in the rewritten story, when Bowker imagines her objecting to his use of obscenity to describe Kiowa's death. This addition ties the story more firmly to the theme of war and obscenity that O'Brien had developed in "How to Tell a True War Story," an earlier piece in *The Things They Carried*. In that story, he writes, ". . . you can tell a true war story by its absolute and uncompromising allegiance to obscenity and evil. . . . If you don't care for obscenity, you don't care for the truth . . . Send guys to war, they come home talking dirty" (*TTTC* 69). Norman's imagined version of Sally Gustafson does not understand the link between war and obscenity in the rewritten version of the story, but it is important to remember that Norman never actually speaks with Sally—his whole conversation with her exists only in his mind and tells readers more about Norman than about Sally herself. This aspect of Sally's expanded role works to emphasize the theme of gender relations in the longer narrative. Sally is one of many women—women back home like Martha and like Curt Lemon's sister—whom the soldiers in the novel resent because they did not participate in the war and therefore cannot understand what the soldiers experienced. But the rewritten version of the story makes another imagined listener—the young veteran's father—slightly less sympathetic as well. In the later version, Norman's father is more interested in watching a baseball game on television than in listening to his son, a detail not included about Berlin's father in the earlier story.

When O'Brien rewrote the story, he also enlarged the role of the order taker at the A&W root beer stand near the end. In the revised version, the order taker, speaking over the intercom, very clearly uses G.I. lingo and seems possibly to be a veteran himself, someone willing to listen to Norman if only Norman were willing to give him a chance. But the rewritten story also leaves open the possibility that Norman imagines or fantasizes this potential listener, or that the intercom voice might be some kind of inexplicable, omniscient presence like radio deejay Johnny Ever in the 2002 novel, *July, July*. In any case, the order taker's expanded role emphasizes even more strongly Norman's desire for a listener, as well as Norman's own inability to communicate his shame to another person. O'Brien rewrites the end of the story in another way as well when he has Norman not simply stand with his arms folded to watch the town's Fourth of July fireworks display, as Paul Berlin does, but actually wade into the lake, as if he is attempting to cleanse himself, to wash away the sins of the war in the waters of the lake. O'Brien seems to want to leave open more of a possibility for redemption for the young soldier in the rewritten version of the story—while the original story described the lake as "tepid" and "algaed" (243), the revised version adds the word *often* in front of the descriptors it uses for the lake, suggesting that it is not always this way, that there is at least a possibility of clean, purifying water at times. The discovery in the following essay, "Notes," that Norman hanged himself, is rendered even more powerful by these small hints that the possibility of redemption or renewal existed for Norman Bowker.

CHARACTERS

A&W Carhop   When Paul Berlin pulls up at an A&W root beer stand in the early evening of July 4th, a "slim, hipless, deft young blonde" (251) carhop is delivering food to the parked cars. The carhop ignores Berlin, preferring instead to flirt with four boys in a Firebird. When Berlin finally leans on his horn to get her attention, the girl grudgingly walks over, taps on his window and gestures toward the intercom where customers are supposed to place their orders, rudely commenting, "You blind or something?" (252). Berlin's ignorance about how to order is indicative of his separation from the town and his inability to fit in after the war.

A&W Order Taker   Toward the end of "Speaking of Courage," after Paul Berlin has pulled into an A&W root beer stand and finally figured out how to order a meal over the intercom, he is greeted by a "tinny voice" (252) that repeats his order and tells him to "Stand by" (252). When Berlin finishes eating, he buzzes the intercom again, to tell the speaker on the other end that he is done with his meal. The disembodied voice replies, "Roger-dodger, over n' out" (253). In the revised version of the story that appears in *The Things They Carried*, this order taker is given a slightly larger role. When Norman Bowker buzzes his order in, the voice uses even more marked G.I. lingo and offers to listen if Norman needs someone to talk to.

Arnold, Max   Max Arnold was a high school friend of Paul Berlin's who drowned in the Iowa lake that Berlin repeatedly drives around in his father's Chevy. Berlin remembers Max as a thoughtful, philosophical young man who used to worry "eagerly about the existence of God and theories of causation" (243). While Max might have made an appropriate, appreciative listener for Berlin's Vietnam stories, he is gone now, highlighting Berlin's loneliness and his inability to talk in any meaningful way about his wartime experiences.

Berlin, Paul   Paul Berlin is a veteran recently returned from the Vietnam War. Listless and with no one to talk to on a hot Sunday afternoon on the Fourth of July, he drives repeatedly around the lake in his small Iowa hometown, holding imagined conversations with his father about his war experience. Berlin is concerned with bravery and cowardice. Although he won seven medals in Vietnam, none of them were for valor, and this fact bothers him. He imagines himself telling his father how he almost won the SILVER STAR for going down a tunnel after a gravely injured fellow soldier, but how, at the last minute, he could not be brave. Berlin seems separate and distant from his fellow townspeople after his wartime experiences. His hometown seems to him almost a relic from a past life, and he watches the firework display with an air of objective detachment at the end. Paul Berlin will later become the protagonist in O'Brien's 1978 novel, *Going After Cacciato*. This story, however, does not appear in that novel, but rather in the 1991 collection, *The Things They Carried*, where it is heavily revised and no longer includes Berlin as the main character, but rather a soldier named Norman Bowker.

Berlin's Father   Paul Berlin's father is a WORLD WAR II veteran who does not want to talk about the Vietnam War. O'Brien writes that Berlin's father "had been in another war, so he knew the truth already, and he would not talk about it, and there was no one left to talk with" (244). Nevertheless, Berlin imagines himself having conversations with his father about his war experiences, particularly about the seven medals he won as well as the medals he did not win—the SILVER STAR or the Medal of Honor, both given for uncommon valor. In his imagined conversation, Berlin pictures himself confessing to his father that he was not brave. His imagined father is a sympathetic and understanding listener who reassures his son by replying, "That's all right" (245). Berlin's imagined father "know[s] full well that many brave men did not win medals for their bravery, and that others won medals for doing nothing" (245). But like Max Arnold who has died, Berlin's imaginary father highlights the fact that Berlin has no real listener, no one in his small, sleepy hometown who will allow Berlin to talk about his wartime experiences.

Hankins, Sally   As Paul Berlin drives around the lake, he remembers doing the same thing back in high school, although the car then would have been filled with his friends and with pretty girls like Sally Hankins. Berlin remembers that he used to spend time wondering whether Sally "would want to pull into the shelter of Sunset Park" (243), presumably for a romantic interlude, in those more innocent days before there had been a war. Now Sally is married, and the other girls are all gone as well. In the revised version of "Speaking of Courage" that appears in the novel *The Things They Carried*, Sally Hankins morphs into Sally Kramer Gustafson, who plays a much larger role than in the 1975 version of the story. In the story as it appears in the novel, Norman Bowker imagines Sally Gus-

tafson living in one of the large houses by the lake and becoming offended by his use of obscenity. Sally represents the overly nice sensibilities of those Americans, particularly women, who did not go to war and who refuse to listen to or understand the war experiences of returned soldiers.

Harris, Stink   Stink Harris is a soldier who figures into Paul Berlin's memories about his Vietnam experiences as he drives around and around the lake in his Iowa hometown. Berlin imagines telling his father the story of Frenchie Tucker, who gets shot through the neck in a Vietnamese tunnel. As whole platoon stands around in a circle near the mouth of the tunnel to watch Frenchie go down, Stink Harris tells him, "Don't get blowed away" (248), but Frenchie is already inside the tunnel and does not hear him. Stink Harris appears as a character as well in the novel *Going After Cacciato*, where he is the point man for Third Squad, the small group of men that chases an AWOL soldier out of Vietnam, across LAOS, India, Turkey, and all the way to PARIS.

Peret, Doc   Doc Peret, one of the main characters in the novel *Going After Cacciato*, appears briefly in the story "Speaking of Courage" when Paul Berlin remembers some of the "simple unprofound things" (249) he learned in Vietnam. Doc is the medic who announces that Billy Boy Watkins died of a heart attack caused by fright. This diagnosis teaches Berlin that it is possible for a man to literally die of fright.

Tucker, Frenchie   Frenchie Tucker is a fellow soldier of Paul Berlin's who is shot through the neck after being ordered to search a Vietnamese tunnel. Frenchie proves to the other men that the old tale about not hearing the bullet that shoots you is a lie—he excitedly tells his fellow soldiers that "he'd heard it coming the whole way" (249) as he lies wounded on the ground, just before he begins bleeding heavily through the mouth. The dead soldier figures prominently in Berlin's memories of the war, particularly in the story Berlin imagines telling his father of how he almost won the SILVER STAR for valor. Apparently Berlin had been sent into the tunnel after Frenchie, but became afraid and backed out before he made much headway. Frenchie Tucker appears as well as a character in the 1978 novel, *Going After Cacciato*. In that book Frenchie also dies in a tunnel after being threatened with a court-martial by Lieutenant Sidney Martin if he refuses to obey the order to search it. Another soldier, Bernie Lynn, dies as well when he is sent into the tunnel to retrieve Frenchie's body. These two deaths inspire the fragging (*see* FRAG) of Lieutenant Sidney Martin by the men under his command; Martin is considered overly gung ho and therefore dangerous. When O'Brien later revised "Speaking of Courage" as part of *The Things They Carried*, Frenchie Tucker no longer appears in the story. The dead soldier transforms into Kiowa, who dies in a "shitfield" rather than in a tunnel.

Watkins, Billy Boy Billy Boy Watkins is a soldier who dies of a heart attack in Vietnam. Paul Berlin remembers what happened to Billy Boy as he drives around the lake in Iowa. He reflects that Billy Boy's death taught him one of the simple, unprofound truths about war that he learned during his time in Vietnam: that a man can literally die of fright. Billy Boy appears in several other works by O'Brien as well, most notably the 1975 short story "Where Have You Gone, Charming Billy?" and the 1978 novel, *Going After Cacciato*.

FURTHER READING

Kaufmann, Michael. "The Solace of Bad Form: Tim O'Brien's Postmodernist Revisions of Vietnam in "Speaking of Courage." *Critique: Studies in Contemporary Fiction* 46.4 (2005): 333–343.
Timmerman, John H. "Tim O'Brien and the Art of the True War Story: 'Night March' and 'Speaking of Courage.'" *Twentieth Century Literature* 46.1 (2000): 100–114.

"The Streak" (1998)

First published in the *New Yorker* magazine in September 1998, "The Streak" tells the story of a newly-married couple, Amy and Bobby, who experience an amazing streak of luck at a small Indian casino on their honeymoon, winning nearly $240,000 playing blackjack. The story was later revised and included as chapter 4 of the 2002 novel, *July, July*.

SYNOPSIS

Amy, a 36-year-old lawyer, married once previously, and her new husband, 51-year-old junior high school math teacher, Bobby, impulsively stop at a small, lakeside Indian casino on a weekend in late summer after they have been married for three and a half days. The couple plays blackjack, winning $2,500 before lunch. As the day wears on, they continue to win hands, while the pretty young blackjack dealer complains about her own rotten luck—she breaks on hand after hand. Amy soon becomes uncomfortable with the gambling, although Bobby is excited by their winning streak and urges her to keep betting. She remembers back to their wedding a few days ago. The old woman organist playing show tunes at the ceremony now seems creepy to her, and she wonders how she ever let Bobby talk her into the marriage. Late that night, Amy goes to bed while Bobby continues to play and win. The next morning Amy and Bobby drive away from the casino, $240,000 richer than the day before. Bobby, exhilarated by their winnings, speaks of a new car, early retirement, and perhaps a condo in Arizona, but Amy remains depressed, fearful that she has used up all her luck. When they stop at a gas station just outside the Twin Cities, Amy calls a cab to pick her up. The story ends ambiguously, Amy herself unsure whether she will depart with Bobby in his car and finish her honeymoon or take the cab, abandoning her new husband and her marriage.

COMMENTARY

"The Streak" is a story about a woman nearing middle age who lives life cautiously, who has settled for a marriage that is not based on love, and who comes to regret this decision over the course of a night spent gambling. O'Brien hints at tension in the marriage between Amy and Bobby early in the story. Although the couple has been married for only three and a half days, their early interaction is marked by disagreement. Amy is reluctant to continue gambling from the beginning, repeatedly suggesting they quit and that the amounts Bobby is risking are too high. Amy would clearly prefer to have a honeymoon in which love rather than money is the highlight. Bobby promises her early on that if they win again they'll go to bed, but when they do win, he breaks his promise and they continue to play cards. The pretty young blackjack dealer emphasizes as well that the couple is not focusing on what should be the point of the honeymoon. When she suggests that Amy and Bobby "go upstairs and pull back the sheets and start honeymooning" (88), Bobby ignores this advice, instead ordering her to deal the cards.

As the night wears on and Amy becomes more tired and depressed, she thinks back to the wedding. Not only did Bobby choose the music—show tunes from Rodgers and Hammerstein—but the wedding itself was his idea. Amy remembers that she had assented to the marriage "mainly out of guilt" (89). They had been dating four years, and Bobby has been decent to her—"assiduously decent—decent without flaw" (89)—but Amy does not love Bobby. Although she truly likes him, Amy has settled on this marriage. At the age of 36 and once divorced, "she no longer expected fairy-tale romance" (89). Amy recognizes this lack of romance in her new marriage when she accuses her brand-new husband of staring at the pretty blackjack dealer when she asks why she and Bobby are not in bed together if they are celebrating.

The blackjack dealer herself is about to be married as well in a few months. While her future does not seem much more promising than Amy's—she expects that she will honeymoon in her fiancé's Winnebago, a vehicle she already knows every square inch of, and her engagement ring seems cheap and gaudy—nevertheless she has youth and good looks on her side. Each woman seems slightly jealous of the other. Amy believes that the young woman's good looks can captivate Bobby's attention in a way that she herself cannot, and the blackjack dealer resents the well-off white city folks coming into the casino and throwing their money around so loosely. When Bobby bets $6,000 on two separate hands at one point, she tells him

that it is enough to buy a car or "two real decent used cars" (88), and later, when he places an even larger bet, she chides him that the money he is risking is enough to pay for "half a house" (89). The dealer, as well, imagines the "big, ritzy wedding" that the two most likely had and suggests they save their money "for a rainy day in the suburbs" (89). Clearly, she is aware that this couple enjoys a very different lifestyle than the one she is accustomed to. Amy and Bobby, after all, are middle-class professionals, Amy a lawyer and Bobby a teacher. And the two display their class privilege rather callously, Amy commenting that the dealer should not want them to lose, that dealers "aren't supposed to think that way. It's a job, that's all" (89). And Bobby snidely remarks that while the girl is pretty now in 10 years she will be ruined by "Babies and Winnebagos" (89).

Bobby, even though he is the one that pressed the marriage on Amy, does not seem particularly consumed by a burning love for his new wife. He is somewhat condescending to Amy, scolding her for not being happy "as if she were a student in his junior-high algebra class" (89). In addition, he is more interested in the streak of gambling luck and in possibly leaving his job and the wintry Minnesota weather behind than he seems to be interested in Amy herself. During the long night at the casino, Bobby speaks of his age and of the fact that he is "a lousy math teacher" (89). His dreams involve a new car and a new life in an Arizona condo. When Amy announces late at night that she is going to bed and Bobby can choose to do what he wants, he decides to ride out his lucky streak. In his conversation with Amy, Bobby claims that this choice does not mean the couple is "splitting up" (90). Even though on the surface he is speaking about splitting up for the evening, Bobby's decision forecasts the ultimate doomed state of this marriage. The math is sure to catch up with this couple—their luck will run out when the night of gambling draws to a close. While the math that Bobby is obsessed with this night involves the multiplication of their winnings, math for Amy involves loss, subtraction. After Bobby chooses to stay in the casino, Amy goes up to her hotel room, where she lies down on the balcony, mentally "subtracting things" (90) from her life, including the wedding, the flowers, the creepy old organist, and even Bobby and herself.

Although the story ends ambiguously, readers left unsure about whether Amy will leave Bobby or continue with her honeymoon, neither choice offers much hope for this couple. If she stays with the marriage, Amy imagines it will be like stopping on a 16 in blackjack—a cautious decision, a way of playing it safe and avoiding risk. Bobby in many ways is a safe choice for Amy even though she does not love him. As readers have seen throughout the story, Amy is not much of a gambler. But perhaps she will choose to take another card in the deck of life—to risk everything on a future that could give her much bigger gains, particularly the romance she longs for. The danger is that such a decision also carries a large risk of breaking, of going over 21 and being left with an unplayable hand.

Differences in Versions

When O'Brien revised the story for inclusion in the novel *July, July*, he made several small, surface changes. For instance, Amy's age is changed from 36 in the original story to 52 so that she can credibly be attending her 30th college reunion. Bobby is aged as well, from 51 in the original story to 56 in the novel version. The amount of winnings in the novel is lowered slightly, from $240,000 to $230,000, and Bobby dreams about buying a new Mercedes at the end of the revised version rather than a Buick. A few changes, however, are more significant. O'Brien adds in the novel's version a paragraph in which Amy tells Bobby, "we're not a couple of idiots, we don't chase pipe dreams. We settle for . . . I don't know. We take what comes our way" (*July*, 51). This addition further emphasizes the theme of the marriage being a compromise on Amy's part, a case of resigned acceptance rather than romance. This point is further highlighted when O'Brien adds the very explicit line in the novel, "She was not in love" (*July*, 55). In addition, the class differences between the blackjack dealer and the middle-class professional couple are highlighted more fully in the novel version when O'Brien has Amy say that dealing cards in a casino is a "stupid robot job" (*July* 52), a phrase that does not appear in the original story. Finally, O'Brien

alters the ending of the story slightly, moving the paragraph that describes Amy considering telling Bobby that the marriage had been a terrible mistake even closer to the end, and expanding it slightly as well. In the revised paragraph, Amy remembers back to the crocheted white sweater of the organist at her wedding, and she thinks about a condo in Arizona. As she sits down on the toilet in the ladies' room of the gas station, she looks for a sign signaling her what to do, but all the graffiti on the bathroom wall is written by 16-year-olds. These revisions again emphasize Amy's disillusionment with Bobby—the wedding was his idea and his imagined future does not appeal to her. They also emphasize Amy's middle-aged status—the world of sex and romance seems reserved for 16-year-olds rather than a middle-aged woman such as herself.

CHARACTERS

Amy Readers see the events of the story as filtered through the consciousness of a woman named Amy, a 36-year-old lawyer on her honeymoon in Minnesota. Uncomfortable with her new marriage in general—she likes Bobby and considers him a decent man, but she does not love him—Amy is depressed rather than excited by the streak of luck the couple experiences in the Indian casino where they impulsively stop to gamble. Amy has been married once before and seems skeptical of weddings and happy endings in general. Despite Bobby's exhilaration after they win nearly $240,000 playing blackjack, Amy toys with leaving her new husband and her marriage behind, feeling that she may have made a big mistake.

Bobby Bobby is a 51-year-old junior high school math teacher who clearly experiences one of the biggest thrills of his life when he and his new wife, Amy, win nearly $240,000 playing blackjack in an Indian casino on their honeymoon. Bobby rides his luck, oblivious to his new wife's depression and her ambivalence about the marriage in general. He excitedly talks to her about a new car and a golf condo in Arizona, having no idea that Amy may be planning to leave him even before the honeymoon has ended.

Dealer The blackjack dealer at the Indian casino is described as a pretty young woman, "twenty-two or twenty-three, slim-hipped, with braided black hair and black eyes and brown skin" (88). The good luck experienced by Bobby and Amy as they play cards clearly points out to the young woman her own bad luck as the house loses hand after hand. The dealer herself is engaged to be married, although she is skeptical about her future. "With my luck," she says, "I'll probably end up honeymooning in my fiancé's Winnebago . . . as if I don't already know every square inch" (88). Bobby, too, imagines a dead-end future for the girl. Although Amy comments that the young dealer is very pretty, her new husband responds, "Give it ten years. . . . Babies and Winnebagos" (89). Despite their very different circumstances, the dealer and Amy seem to share a connection—both suspicious of good luck, both unexcited about their marriages and future prospects.

Pit Boss As Amy and Bobby continue to win big sums at the Indian casino, the blackjack dealer glances briefly at a pit boss, who simply shrugs, indicating that she should continue to allow the honeymooning couple to play. When the girl curses about her own bad luck, the pit boss murmurs something and she apologizes. A few minutes later, the pit boss announces that he will buy everyone a round of drinks "on the Chippewa nation" (89).

"Sweetheart of the Song Tra Bong" (1989)

"Sweetheart of the Song Tra Bong" tells the story of 17-year-old Mary Anne Bell, a former high school cheerleader who is brought to Vietnam by her boyfriend, Mark Fossie, a medic stationed outside of CHU LAI. After her arrival, Mary Anne becomes fascinated by the war and by the country. She changes from an all-American high school girl into a tough young woman who assists in bloody operations and accompanies Special Forces soldiers on night ambushes in the jungle before eventu-

ally disappearing into the mountains, never to be seen again. The story was originally published in *Esquire* magazine in July 1989 before being revised and included in the 1990 collection, *The Things They Carried*.

SYNOPSIS

Mary Anne Bell's story is told to the men of ALPHA COMPANY by Rat Kiley, a medic who was part of a small unit stationed in the mountains outside of Chu Lai before being assigned to LANDING ZONE GATOR. He recounts how the men in the unit were joking one night about importing "a few mama-sans from Saigon" to "spice things up" (96). A medic named Mark Fossie takes the conversation seriously and soon makes complicated arrangements to bring his high school girlfriend, Mary Anne Bell, from Cleveland to Los Angeles to Bangkok, then on to Saigon, to Chu Lai, and finally to the remote medical detachment in the mountains. When Mary Anne first arrives, she is a friendly, long-legged blonde, wearing a pink sweater and white culottes. She is naïve, but Rat is careful to point out that she is not stupid. She is, in fact, curious and a quick learner. She learns how to assemble and shoot an M-16 rifle; she soon begins to assist in gory medical operations; she visits the South Vietnamese soldiers who live along the perimeter of the camp; and she demands that Mark take her into the VIET CONG–controlled village at the foot of the mountain.

When Mary Anne does not return to Mark's bunker one night, the young soldier panics, suspects she is sleeping with another man, and he wakes up Rat to help him search for his missing girlfriend. It turns out that Mary Anne was out all night in the jungle, on ambush with a group of six mysterious GREEN BERET soldiers who live at the edge of the encampment. Although the young lovers briefly reconcile, the girl disappears again when Mark begins to make plans to send Mary Anne back home to Cleveland. This time she is out in the jungle for three weeks with the Greenies. When she returns, Mark Fossie stations himself outside the Greenies' tent as he listens to weird music and high singing coming from inside. He eventually enters the tent, followed closely by Rat and a soldier named Eddie Diamond. The three are astonished by what they see: The tent is filled with a nonhuman, animal-like stench. The head of a leopard is mounted on a post, and piles of bones, both animal and human, are stacked in a corner. The strange singing is coming from Mary Anne herself, who is wearing a necklace of human tongues. Soon after this, Mary Anne disappears. While Rat never sees her again and is unsure what happens to her, the Greenies say that one morning she simply walked into the mountains, never to return.

COMMENTARY

"Sweetheart of the Song Tra Bong" is a story about transgressing boundaries, particularly gender boundaries, but also racial distinctions, lines separating moral from immoral behavior, and even rules governing narrative. O'Brien evokes boundaries from the story's opening sentence: The tales about Vietnam that will last forever, the narrator tells us, "are those that swirl back and forth across the border between trivia and bedlam, the mad and the mundane" (94). The first conventional boundary line that the story overturns is the narrative distinction separating truth and fiction. The narrator immediately tells readers that he heard the story of Mary Anne Bell from Rat Kiley, "who swore up and down to its truth." Yet, among the men in Alpha Company, "Rat had a reputation for exaggeration and overstatement, a compulsion to rev up the facts" (94). So, the veracity of the story is in doubt from the very beginning. But, as he frequently does in his work, O'Brien plays with the notion of the accessibility of historic truth in the first place, the idea that one can easily separate fact from fiction or have access to the simple truth of another's experience. The narrator informs readers that most of the men automatically discounted "sixty or seventy percent of anything [Rat] had to say. If Rat told you, for example, that he'd slept with four girls one night, you could figure it was about a girl and a half" (94). Of course, the joke here is that the "truth," derived after subtracting for Rat's exaggeration, is harder to believe than the fiction. It is, in fact, impossible. So, the "truth" becomes simply another story.

Author O'Brien, in using this particular example, draws attention to the fact that the soldiers' relationships with women are based not on hard and fast realities but are largely products of their own imaginings and socialization. And in the beginning of Rat's story about Mark and Mary Anne, gender roles are carried out in accordance with traditional Western stereotypes about men and women. Initially, the men at Chu Lai conceive of women in a conventionally dichotomous way: either as sex objects or as emblems of a kind of innocent domesticity. Eddie Diamond first suggests bringing women onto the base to serve the men's sexual needs: "What they should do," he suggests, is "pool some bucks and bring in a few mama-sans from Saigon, spice things up. . ." (96). Asian women, in particular, are viewed as sex objects by the American soldiers. Mitchell Sanders, who is listening to Rat tell the story, voices a similar view of women. Rat's story "don't ring true," he says: "I mean, you just can't import your own personal poontang" (94). Sanders, in many ways, serves as a spokesman for obeying traditional distinctions in the story. Not only does he talk about women as "poontang," he insists throughout that Rat stick to narrative convention as he tells the story. Even Mark Fossie, who keeps returning to Diamond's suggestion, uses sexualized language when he asserts that bringing a woman to the base could be done: "A pair of solid brass balls, that's all you'd need" (96). When Mary Anne actually arrives at the base, she is described as coming in "by helicopter along with the daily resupply shipment out of Chu Lai" (96). She is simply another supply, whose purpose is to fulfill the mens' needs.

Yet, Mary Anne, unlike the "mama-sans" suggested by Eddie Diamond earlier, turns out to be an all-American girl. When the men actually see her for the first time, they switch narratives; Mary Anne is transformed from whore to innocent. Rat describes her as a "a tall, big-boned blonde . . . seventeen years old, fresh out of Cleveland Heights Senior High. She had long white legs and blue eyes and complexion like strawberry ice cream. Very friendly, too" (96). Later, she is described as a "doll" and as a "cheerleader visiting the opposing team's locker room" (98). We find out that she and Mark Fossie "had been sweet-hearts since grammar school" who plan to marry and to live "in a fine gingerbread house near Lake Erie, and have three healthy yellow-haired children, and grow old together, and no doubt die in each other's arms and be buried in the same walnut casket" (96).

While Mark and Mary Anne initially try to make their dream work in Vietnam—they "set up house" and stick together "like a pair of high school steadies" (96)—Mary Anne soon begins to transgress her domestic role. She is curious about weaponry; she asks intelligent questions and soon learns to assemble and use an M-16. She helps out in the surgery, seems fascinated by casualties, and is unafraid of getting her hands bloody. She also crosses traditional boundaries separating the American soldiers from their Vietnamese allies. Rat, as he's telling the story, emphasizes a separation between the Vietnamese and American soldiers. He describes the compound at Chu Lai:

> Surrounding the place were tangled rolls of concertina wire, with bunkers and reinforced firing positions at staggered intervals, and base security was provided by a mixed units of RFs, PFs, and ARVN infantry. Which is to say virtually no security at all. As soldiers, the ARVNs were useless; the Ruff-and-Puffs were outright dangerous. (96)

While Rat reiterates American stereotypes of the South Vietnamese soldiers as lazy or cowardly, Mary Anne actually spends time with the ARVNs out along the perimeter, "picking up little phrases of Vietnamese, learning how to cook rice over a can of Sterno, how to eat with her hands" (98). She insists upon visiting the village of TRA BONG as well, wanting "to get a feel for how people lived, what the smells and customs were" (98). Mary Anne behaves quite differently toward the villagers than American soldiers frequently depicted in other O'Brien stories. There is no threat of violence in her visits. We might compare Mary Anne's attitude to that of Curt Lemon and Rat Kiley himself who praises Curt for "lighting up villes and bringing smoke to bear every which way" (*TTTC* 68) in "How to Tell a True War Story."

The demise of Mark and Mary Anne's relationship is foreshadowed when Rat tells us that the bunker the two have chosen as their new home is "along the perimeter, near the Special Forces hootch" (96). The Greenies are also boundary transgressors. Set up along the very edge of the perimeter, they operate in a shadowy, ethically murky world. The Green Berets or Special Forces were first organized as counterinsurgency specialists in the 1950s. The critic John Hellmann in his book *American Myth and the Legacy of Vietnam*, claims that the group "became a leading symbol" of President KENNEDY's idea of the New Frontier (37). In Kennedy's vision, Hellmann argues, America could revive the virtues of its frontier mentality, spreading liberty to the darker races of Indochina while redeeming itself from the destructive excesses of its earlier westward expansion. The Green Berets, then, served a strange, dual purpose; they were highly trained professional killers with the mission of toppling the Communist government who, at the same time, "engaged in the missionary work of the Peace Corpsman" (Hellmann 47). In "Sweetheart of the Song Tra Bong," the Greenies retain the covert nature of their origins. They "sometimes vanish[ed] for days at a time or even weeks," on their secretive missions, suddenly reappearing "just as magically" (96). None of the medics dare ask questions about their operations; contact between the Greenies and the medics is minimal. O'Brien uses the Green Berets to suggest the tension between America's overt mission in Vietnam—to save the Vietnamese from Communist oppression—and the covert, often grotesque and horrifying methods used. With their savage, animalistic den, their piles of bones, and their sign welcoming visitors to "ASSEMBLE YOUR OWN GOOK!!," the Greenies in the story disrupt the myth of the decent, upright American soldier, much as Mary Anne Bell disrupts myths about traditional womanhood.

As Mary Anne becomes more accustomed to life at Chu Lai, she begins to question the earlier narrative of domestic bliss that she had shared with Mark Fossie: "Not necessarily three kids, she'd say. Not necessarily a house on Lake Erie. 'Naturally we'll still get married,' she'd tell him, 'but it doesn't have to be right away. Maybe travel first. Maybe live together. Just test it out, you know?'" (98–100). Mary Anne changes physically as well in ways that make Fossie distinctly uncomfortable: "Her body seemed foreign somehow—too stiff in places, too firm where the softness used to be. . . . Her voice seemed to reorganize itself at a lower pitch" (100). Author O'Brien's repetition of the word *seemed* in this passage draws attention to the fact that readers are observing Mary Anne through Mark Fossie's perceptions of her (perceptions that are then reinterpreted by Rat Kiley and finally by narrator O'Brien). When Mary Anne transgresses Fossie's narrow expectations of what a woman should be, he can only imagine her as becoming more like a man. Fossie's discomfort reaches its climax one night when Mary Anne does not return to their shared bunker. Rat describes Fossie on the point of collapse: "He squatted down, rocking on his heels, still clutching the flashlight. Just a boy— eighteen years old. Tall and blond. A gifted athlete. A nice kid, too, polite and good-hearted, although for the moment none of it seemed to be serving him well" (100). At this point, the sweethearts have exchanged gender roles. Fossie is described in terms similar to those initially used for Mary Anne—he is young, tall, blond, nice, polite and good-hearted. When the power in the relationship shifts from Mark Fossie to Mary Anne Bell, so do the men's perceptions of their gender attributes.

At first, when Eddie Diamond and Rat go to check on Mark Fossie, who has stationed himself outside the Greenies' hootch, they hear only a weird sort of music, with lyrics that "seemed to be in a foreign tongue" (102). Mark insists that the voice is Mary Anne's. When he bursts into the bunker, his suspicions are confirmed. The men find Mary Anne amid a horrific scene—piles of bones and animal skins, lit candles, the smoke of incense, and an appalling, animal stench. The voice that the men could not understand is indeed Mary Anne's. But "the grotesque part," Rat tells us, "was her jewelry. At the girl's throat was a necklace of human tongues" (102). As the critic Katherine Kinney points out, the necklace of tongues "testifies to [Mary Anne's] violently earned right to tell war stories" while at the same time showing that she earns this right at the expense of the Vietnamese who "are literally dismembered, figured only as pieces of skin and the tongues Mary Anne has appropriated to voice her own experience" (*Friendly Fire* 155; 156). When Mary Anne tells Mark Fossie and Rat Kiley that they're in a place "where [they] don't belong" (102), she means much more than the Greenies' bunker. She questions the very presence of Americans in Vietnam. Mary Anne finally speaks in what Rat describes as "a language beyond translation" (103) because she points up the many contradictions and paradoxes of the American experience in Vietnam, both on the home front and in the paddies and jungles of Vietnam. American women are supposed to be innocent and pure emblems of home and domesticity, symbols of what will be lost if too many dominoes (see DOMINO THEORY) fall in the COLD WAR, but Mary Anne is not. American soldiers are supposed to be the good guys, there to save the Vietnamese people from the evils of Communist oppression, but Mary Anne's necklace of tongues signifies otherwise.

O'Brien has reiterated both in his fiction and in interviews his belief that war stories are about more than war. In a lecture at Brown University in April 1999, O'Brien said, "War stories aren't always about war, per se. They aren't about bombs and bullets and military maneuvers. They aren't about tactics, they aren't about foxholes and canteens. War stories, like any good story, are finally about the human heart." "Sweetheart of the Song Tra Bong" works on both a political and a personal level; the story not only exposes the darkness at the heart of the American political and military mission in Vietnam (critics such as Lorrie Smith and Katherine Kinney argue that the story alludes to Conrad's novel), it also explores human relationships on a more individual level. Mary Anne's necklace of tongues suggests her nearly ravenous desire to consume and destroy the other. "I want to *eat* this place," she explains. "Vietnam. I want to swallow the whole country—the dirt, the death— I just want to eat it and have it there inside me. That's how I feel. It's like . . . this appetite" (102). Her desire to know and understand the Vietnamese people has grown into a perverse longing to actually incorporate them into her own body. Surely suggestive of America's desire to create a capitalist Vietnam in its own image while largely ignoring the other country's culture and history, Mary Anne's appetite is reflected in personal relationships presented elsewhere in O'Brien's work. Lieutenant Jimmy Cross in "The Things They Carried," for instance, is so overwhelmed by his love for Martha that "he wanted to sleep inside her lungs and breathe her blood and be smothered" (*TTTC* 11). The narrator of "The Lives of the Dead" describes his childhood love for Linda in similar terms: "Even then, at nine years old, I wanted to live inside her body. I wanted to melt into her bones—*that* kind of love" (*TTTC* 228). These male characters' desire to know and understand the female other is imagined in terms of a literal blending of physical bodies.

This is a theme that O'Brien develops further in his 1994 novel, *In The Lake of the Woods*. A desire to meld completely with another also motivates O'Brien's main character in this book, Senator John Wade. The narrator writes:

> There were times when John Wade wanted to open up Kathy's belly and crawl inside and stay there forever. He wanted to swim through her blood and climb up and down her spine and drink from her ovaries and press his gums against the firm red muscle of her heart. He wanted to suture their lives together. (*Lake* 71)

Wade's love for his wife, Kathy, is so obsessive that it becomes destructive, an urge to actually consume the other person. Although readers never find out definitively what happens to Kathy Wade, the book leaves open the possibility that Wade might actually have murdered his wife in order to possess her completely. Yet, O'Brien seems careful not to present this longing to meld completely with another person as simply a male desire to dominate a feminine other. The male characters in each of the previous examples imagine themselves being incorporated into rather than consuming the female body. Further, the narrator of *In The Lake of the Woods*, in his pursuit to find out the truth surrounding Kathy's disappearance, muses on his own desire to fully understand John Wade: "What

drives me on, I realize, is a craving to force entry into another heart, to trick the tumblers of natural law, to perform miracles of knowing. It's human nature. We are fascinated, all of us, by the implacable otherness of others" (*Lake* 101). In order to support his view that gender differences are largely cultural and situational rather than biological and innate, O'Brien carefully orchestrates parallels between Mary Anne and certain male characters, both in *The Things They Carried* and elsewhere in his writing. Mary Anne Bell is not so different from Jimmy Cross, from nine-year-old Timmy, or from John Wade. She falls prey to the same malady that affects these characters—she wishes to destroy boundaries separating one individual from another, to merge so completely with the other that she herself "burn[s] away into nothing" (102).

Rat's story about Mary Anne Bell stops "almost in midsentence" (103) after his description of her in the Greenies' bunker. Once Mary Anne fully transgresses established social codes—rules codifying not only gender behavior but racial and national differences, conduct of war, and ethical mores as well—she moves out of the world that Rat Kiley, the medics at Chu Lai, and the soldiers of Alpha Company know and understand and try to cling to despite their chaotic, confusing, and often horrific experiences in Vietnam. Mitchell Sanders's outrage at Rat's pause in his story suggests just such an attempt to adhere to established order:

> Mitchell Sanders stared at him.
> "You can't do that."
> "Do what?"
> "Jesus Christ, it's against the *rules*," Sanders said. "Against human *nature*. This elaborate story, you can't say, Hey, by the way, I don't know the *ending*. I mean, you got certain obligations." (103)

Sanders's insistence on the rules of proper storytelling is linked to the men's expectations about proper gender conduct. When he says "it's against the rules," he is referring to gender rules as well as narrative rules. Sanders sees both as natural and innate rather than as socially constructed.

In order to provide an end to his story, Rat must turn to his imagination, to guesswork:

Rat gave a quick smile. "Patience, man. Up to now, everything I told you is from personal experience, the exact truth, but there's a few other things I heard secondhand. Thirdhand, actually. From here on it gets to be . . . I don't know what the word is."

"Speculation." (103)

Rat goes on to tell about Mary Anne's love for night patrols, how she takes crazy chances— "things that even the Greenies balked at" (115). Finally, he concludes that Mary Anne "had crossed to the other side," a phrase heavy with implication in this story. Mary Anne has crossed many boundaries: those separating men from women, home front from front line, and "civilized" behavior from savagery. But in the context of a war story, perhaps the primary suggestion of this phrase is that Mary Anne has indeed switched sides, joined the enemy: the Viet Cong or the North Vietnamese Army. In Rat's ending, Mary Anne is described in terms often used by American soldiers to characterize the Viet Cong: She is shadowy and ghost-like, an unseen but felt presence who seems to be watching the Greenies intently when they go out on ambush. Rat's ending, then, suggests the possibility that Mary Anne has switched political allegiance. A character who refuses to follow rules, to stay where she "belongs," Mary Anne deconstructs American imperialistic tendencies as well as traditional gender imperatives.

Yet, with this ending, O'Brien also makes a point about "the human heart"—the story shows that it is only through imagination that we can ever begin to penetrate what the narrator of *In the Lake of the Woods* calls the "implacable otherness of others." It is exactly Rat's act of imaginative speculation that allows him to proclaim his love for Mary Anne in the end, to move beyond attitudes toward women he expresses in other stories, such as when he calls Curt Lemon's sister a "dumb cooze" in "How to Tell a True War Story." Thus, when Rat recounts this story to the men after the fact, he, too, questions established definitions. He disrupts the conventional rules of storytelling with his "tendency to stop now and then, interrupting the flow," his desire "to bracket the full range of meaning,"

despite Mitchell Sanders's admonishments to "get the hell out of the way and let [the story] tell itself" (101). He also breaks the logic of traditional gender boundaries. Unlike most of the other men, Rat is aware of gender as a socially constructed category. He insists that Mary Anne wasn't dumb, just young: "Like you and me," he argues. "A *girl,* that's the only difference, and I'll tell you something: it didn't amount to jack" (98). And later, Rat argues for the verisimilitude of his story:

> "I know it sounds far-out . . . but it's not like *impossible* or anything. . . . She was a girl, that's all. I mean, if it was a guy, everybody'd say, Hey, no big deal, he got caught up in the Nam shit, he got seduced by the Greenies. See what I mean? You got these blinders on about women. How gentle and peaceful they are. All that crap about how if we had a pussy for president there wouldn't be no more wars. Pure garbage. You got to get rid of that sexist attitude." (101)

Author O'Brien surely wants readers to notice the juxtaposition of Rat's own sexist language with his admonition that the men lose their "sexist attitudes." Rat is struggling to overcome his own earlier views, but, like the other men in Alpha Company, he is a product of his society and time. When these men are presented with a woman who transgresses traditional gender roles, they are uncomfortable, unsure how to react. But they are finally unable to contain her or reincorporate her into the normative world through their stories about her. Mary Anne Bell both *escapes* the limits of their imaginations and expands their notions of what is possible.

Differences in Versions

"Sweetheart of the Song Tra Bong" was republished in *The Things They Carried* in a version virtually identical to its original *Esquire* form. A few phrases in the story are rearranged, a few words that might have been considered redundant in the original story are removed, and a few paragraph breaks fall in different places. The only significant addition is a sentence included near the end, when Rat describes some of the crazy chances Mary Anne took when out on ambush with the Greenies. "She was lost inside herself" (*TTTC* 115) O'Brien writes in the novel, a sentence that does not appear in the original *Esquire* version of the story. The only other significant alteration occurs in the final sentences of the story, which are slightly reordered. The original version ends with the lines: "She was part of the land. She was dangerous, she was ready for the kill. She was wearing her culottes, her pink sweater, and a necklace of human tongues" (103). The novel version, however, is rearranged to read as follows: "She was part of the land. She was wearing her culottes, her pink sweater, and a necklace of human tongues. She was dangerous. She was ready for the kill" (*TTTC* 116). The ending of the revised version seems stronger and more emphatic, with its two short, simple, blunt sentences and the final word changed to *kill*. The focus is shifted from what Mary Anne is wearing to her altered state of being.

CHARACTERS

Bell, Mary Anne Mary Anne Bell is a 17-year-old, fresh-faced all-American girl from Cleveland when she first arrives in Vietnam, wearing white culottes, a pink sweater, and carrying a plastic cosmetics bag. However, she soon sheds her girlish innocence as she becomes increasingly fascinated by Vietnam. She not only learns how to assemble and shoot an M-16 rifle, she also learns to assist with bloody medical operations. Unlike the American soldiers, who hold themselves apart from the native Vietnamese, Mary Anne visits the South Vietnamese soldiers stationed outside the encampment as well as the small VC-controlled village at the foot of the mountain where the medical detachment is situated. As Mary Anne adapts to life in country, she also abandons her initial dreams of marrying her high school sweetheart Mark Fossie and settling down in a cute gingerbread house with three healthy, blond-haired children. "Not necessarily three kids," she begins to say, "Not necessarily a house on Lake Erie. . . . Maybe travel first. Maybe live together. Just test it out, you know?" (98, 100). Mary Anne is clearly defying conventional gender boundaries here, just as she defies boundaries separating the Vietnamese from the Americans and, eventually, boundaries separating moral from immoral behavior. Readers know that

the naïve high school girl is gone for good after Mary Anne begins to go out on ambush with a group of Special Forces soldiers. When Mark Fossie begins to make plans to send her back to Cleveland, Mary Anne disappears for three full weeks. The last time Mark sees her, she is in the Greenies' tent, singing in strange, high-pitched tones and wearing a string of human tongues around her neck. She tries to explain her fascination with Vietnam, telling Mark and the other soldiers that the transformation she has gone through is "not bad" and that she wants to "swallow the whole country—the dirt, the death" (102). Although readers never find out definitely what happens to Mary Anne, one of the GREEN BERETS tells Eddie Diamond, who tells Rat Kiley, who reports to the men of ALPHA COMPANY, that she simply walked into the mountains and disappeared one morning.

Diamond, Eddie Eddie Diamond is the highest-ranking noncommissioned officer in the small medical detachment near CHU LAI where the story of Mary Anne Bell takes place. One of the reasons that Mary Anne is able to be flown in is that the rules in the remote outpost are lax since no regular officers are part of the unit. Eddie himself, "whose pleasures ran from dope to Darvon" (94), does not enforce military discipline, and in fact he is the one who first jokingly suggests that the men should "bring in a mama-sans from Saigon" to "spice things up" (96). Eddie Diamond, along with Rat Kiley, follows Mary Anne's boyfriend, Mark Fossie, into the Greenies' tent the night they hear weird singing and chanting noises emerge from it. Thus, Eddie is one of the witnesses to Mary Anne's complete transformation—he sees the young girl step from the stench and shadows of the tent, wearing a necklace of human tongues. Eddie is also the soldier who conveys to Rat Kiley rumors of what finally happened to Mary Anne Bell: that she disappeared into the mountains one morning and that the Greenies think she is still out there, living in the jungle with her culottes and necklace of body parts.

Fossie, Mark Mark Fossie is the young medic who schemes to bring his high school girlfriend,

Mary Anne Bell, to Vietnam. When Mary Anne first arrives in country, the two behave like high school steadies—always together, holding hands, making plans to get married and live in a gingerbread house on Lake Erie with three perfect children. However, Mark gets more than he bargained for when Mary Anne adapts quickly to life at the war, shedding her high school sweetness for a deep fascination with Vietnam. As she becomes increasingly competent and assured, Mark seems to shrink, becoming more like a schoolboy. He panics when Mary Anne does not return to their shared bunker one night, only to find that she has been out on ambush with a group of mysterious Special Forces soldiers. Although Mark begins to make plans to send Mary Anne back home to Cleveland, he cannot contain her. She disappears again, away for three weeks with the Greenies this time. Following her return, Mark finds her nearly unrecognizable in the Greenies' tent, singing in a strange, high, seemingly nonhuman voice and wearing a necklace of human tongues. When Mark Fossie begs Rat to "do something," insisting that he "can't just let her go like that," Rat replies, "Man, you must be deaf. She's already gone" (103).

Green Beret Soldiers   Rat Kiley reports that a squad of six GREEN BERETS, or Special Forces soldiers, used the small medical detachment in the mountains outside of CHU LAI, where Rat was originally stationed after arriving in Vietnam, as a base of operations. Mary Anne Bell, the young girl Mark Fossie arranges to bring to the war, eventually begins to spend time with this group of soldiers, even going out on night ambush in the jungle with them. The Greenies camp on the perimeter of the base, but they live on the border in other ways as well, their mysterious missions ethically murky. When Mark, Rat, and Eddie Diamond enter the Greenies' tent one night, searching for Mary Anne, they witness a bizarre scene: The tent is filled with an animal-like stench, stacks of bones are piled up in the corner underneath a sign reading "ASSEMBLE YOUR OWN GOOK!! FREE SAMPLE KIT!!," and a leopard skull is mounted on a post. The Green Berets have succumbed to the violence and savagery of the war.

Kiley, Rat   Rat Kiley, a medic for ALPHA COMPANY, tells the story of Mary Anne Bell, a girl fresh out of CLEVELAND HEIGHTS SENIOR HIGH, who is flown to Vietnam by her boyfriend. Rat claims he witnessed the events of the story firsthand when he was stationed in a small medical detachment in the mountains outside of CHU LAI before being assigned to Alpha Company. While the story's narrator admits that Rat "had a reputation for exaggeration and overstatement, a compulsion to rev up the facts" (94), the medic insists that the story of Mary Anne Bell is absolutely true, that it really happened. Toward the end of his tale about Mary Anne's transformation from a sweet, all-American cheerleader into a ferocious jungle fighter, Rat confesses that he loved the girl, largely because unlike all the other girls back home Mary Anne can truly understand the war, what it is like for the men in country: "She was *there*," Rat says, "She was up to her eyeballs in it" (103). Because he is transferred to Alpha Company a few days after witnessing Mary Anne singing in the GREEN BERETS' tent with a string of human tongues around her neck, Rat is never sure what became of her. He can only report rumors—that Mary Anne disappeared into the mountains one day and is out there still.

O'Brien, Tim   Although never identified by name, the narrator of the story is presumably the character Tim O'Brien, who narrates most of the other stories that will later be collected into *The Things They Carried*. "Sweetheart of the Song Tra Bong" opens with this narrator, a soldier in ALPHA COMPANY, informing readers about a story he heard from the company's medic, Rat Kiley. The narrator admits that Rat cannot always be relied upon to tell the full, unvarnished truth—that he is a master of exaggeration—but he also asserts that Rat never backed down from his claims that the story about Mary Anne Bell is entirely true, that he was an eyewitness to most of the events he describes. While the Tim O'Brien narrator largely steps aside after the first few paragraphs and relates the story as Rat told it, he nevertheless does not allow readers to forget that this story is filtered through several layers of perception, reminding readers of this frequently with phrases such as, "As Rat described it" (94) and "Rat said" (96). O'Brien also breaks into Rat's story on occasion to describe the reaction of the men from Alpha Company who listen to it, particularly Mitchell Sanders, who demands that Rat tell the story according to established narrative rules.

Sanders, Mitchell   Mitchell Sanders is one of the men in ALPHA COMPANY who listens to Rat Kiley's tale about Mary Anne Bell. Skeptical of the story from the beginning, Sanders stands with his arms folded and looks over at the Tim O'Brien narrator, not quite grinning, when Rat insists that Mary Anne arrived in Vietnam wearing white culottes and a sexy pink sweater. Undeterred, Rat insists that his story is "no lie" (94), that the girl was indeed wearing culottes. As Rat's story progresses, Mitchell Sanders frequently interrupts, often to remind Rat to stick to the rules of good storytelling. He guesses that when Mary Anne is missing all night long, she is found with the GREEN BERETS because, he argues, that is how stories work: "That stuff about the Special Forces—how they used the place as a base of operations, how they glide in and out—all that had to be there for a *reason*. That's how stories work, man" (100). Sanders also objects at the end, when Rat claims not to know what happened to Mary Anne after she was seen singing in a strange, high voice in the Greenies' tent one night: "You can't do that," Sanders complains, "Jesus Christ, it's against the *rules!* . . . Against human *nature*. This elaborate story, you can't say, Hey, by the way I don't know the *ending*. I mean, you've got certain obligations" (103). Yet, despite Sanders's insistence that stories must be told a certain way, that the narrator must get out of the way and let the story tell itself, Rat flouts the conventions of realistic narrative, breaking in and commenting on his tale frequently, just as author Tim O'Brien does throughout *The Things They Carried*, where the story will appear after its initial publication as a standalone work in *Esquire* magazine.

FURTHER READING

Bulla, Elizabeth. "Tim O'Brien's *Sweetheart of the Song Tra Bong:* the Woman Warrior Tale Updated," *Overland Review* 31, nos. 1–2 (2003): 57–63.

Ciocia, Stefania. "Conradian Echoes in Vietnam War Literature: Tim O'Brien's Rewriting of Heart of Darkness in 'Sweetheart of the Song Tra Bong,'" *Symbiosis:* 11, no. 1 (2007): 3–30.

Hellmann, John. *American Myth and the Legacy of Vietnam.* New York: Columbia University Press, 1986.

Kinney, Katherine. *Friendly Fire: American Images of the Vietnam War.* Oxford (England); New York: Oxford University Press, 2000.

Martin, Terry J. and Margaret Stiner. "*Sweetheart of the Song Tra Bong:* Tim O' Brien's (Feminist?) *Heart of Darkness,*" *Short Story* 9, no. 2 (2001): 94–104.

O'Brien, Tim. Transcript of President's Lecture. Brown University, Providence, R.I. (21 April 1999). Available online. URL: http://www.stg.brown.edu/projects/WritingVietnam/obrien.html. Accessed April 26, 2011.

Smith, Lorrie. "'The Things Men Do': The Gendered Subtext in Tim O'Brien's *Esquire* Stories," *Critique: Studies in Contemporary Fiction* 36, no. 1 (Fall 1994): 16+.

"Telling Tails" (2009)

O'Brien's essay "Telling Tails" appeared in the Fiction 2009 edition of the *Atlantic* magazine. In this short piece, O'Brien explains what in his view separates good fiction from bad fiction.

SYNOPSIS

O'Brien begins the essay with an anecdote about his two young sons, TIMMY and TAD O'BRIEN, and their recent habit of wearing pretend tails wherever they go. Worried that the family is entering into a state of "reverse evolution" and haunted by an image of Tad, currently three years old, showing up for his own wedding "with a large powdered tail quivering aloft," O'Brien gently warns his sons that pretending, while a good thing, can be dangerous when carried too far. When his son Timmy tells O'Brien that he understands what pretending is, that he sometimes pretends his father is still there after he has gone away on a trip, O'Brien's fears shift to worries about being away from home too often, missing out on conversations with his son like this one.

This opening anecdote leads into O'Brien's main point in the essay, which is that imagination is absolutely central to good fiction writing. A creative writing teacher for many years, O'Brien worries that classroom discussions of student writing focus far too frequently on issues of verisimilitude: the believability of characters and their motives, the desire to know more details about a character's appearance, surroundings, or back story. O'Brien himself believes that a far greater problem in fiction writing is the danger of simply boring readers. Too many details, included only for the sake of verisimilitude rather than to advance the story, are clutter that can distract from the main event. According to O'Brien, a "well-imagined story" is not generic, predictable, or melodramatic. It does not rely on overwrought language in an attempt to puff up ordinary events. A well-imagined story, he argues is "organized around extraordinary human behaviors and unexpected and startling events, which help illuminate the commonplace and the ordinary." That is not to say that a story must contain elements of the supernatural or fantastic. But the *events* of a story should be themselves interesting. In addition, a well-imagined story must contain a thematic weightiness. In other words, it must *matter*, it must illustrate something about human behavior—illuminate a "corner of the human soul."

O'Brien includes a long quote from Jorge Luis Borges's "The Aleph" as an example of a story that fits his definition of a well-imagined piece of fiction. The events in this story are unexpected and startling—a disappointed lover mourning for a long-dead woman named Beatriz is invited by his rival to view an Aleph, a point in space that contains all other points, in the basement of the dead woman's home. O'Brien praises Borges's use of specific detail in the story, the way he describes the objects glimpsed in the Aleph so as to suggest the infinite. But what truly catches the reader's attention are the detailed, obscene love letters the narrator sees in the Aleph—letters that Beatriz had written to the narrator's pompous rival. This detail, O'Brien argues, moves the story out of the realm of the merely clever; it gives the story emotional heft. We can all imagine beholding something forbid-

den and the pain that could result. O'Brien concludes his essay by circling back to the story of his young sons. He decides to let them keep their tails. He pictures a future in which they will *need* their imaginations, in which they are grown up and they imagine their father alive and in their lives again just as he sometimes imagines his own father.

COMMENTARY

While critical discussion of Tim O'Brien's work often defines him as a postmodern writer who is interested in the intersections between narrative and the real world, the essay "Telling Tails" reminds readers that O'Brien also considers himself an old-fashioned storyteller who refuses to eschew traditional plot in favor of literary trickery. In the essay, he insists that good writing must contain plots whose events are inherently interesting. O'Brien's own novels do indeed play with literary form. They tend to provide metafictional (*see* METAFICTION) commentary on the stories they tell. But the key point is that they *tell* stories as much as they comment on them. Readers of *The Things They Carried* are concerned not only with O'Brien's struggle to find a form in which to tell a "true" war story, they also care about his fictional characters—Lieutenant Jimmy Cross, Kiowa, Ted Lavendar, Rat Kiley, and the others—and they want to know what becomes of these characters. Readers of *In the Lake of the Woods* may understand that human nature is complex and some mysteries have no answer, but they still *care* about what happened to Kathy Wade and long for a solution to the mysteries that O'Brien presents in the novel. If O'Brien were not a good storyteller, if his plots and characters were not themselves compelling, readers would not be frustrated by his refusal to provide closure—they would not care whether John Wade killed his wife, whether she left him, or whether they planned their disappearances together from the beginning. In this essay, as in his 1991 essay, "The Magic Show," O'Brien makes a case for old-fashioned plot. As he writes in the earlier essay, plot is "often discredited as a sop to some unsophisticated and base human instinct," but he says that he sees nothing base in the desire of readers to know what will happen next: "I'm suggesting that plot is grounded in a high—even noble—human craving to *know*, a craving to push into the mystery of tomorrow" (*The Magic Show* 180). Failure to invent interesting plots, for O'Brien, is a failure of imagination.

The other main concern voiced in this essay, which also works its way into O'Brien's fiction, has to do with thematic heft or weightiness. O'Brien believes that good writing must explore moral issues, must suggest something about human behavior. Again, this is a sentiment he delineated earlier, in the essay "The Magic Show," in which he argues that storytelling involves "the conjuring up of spirits," in the form of characters, who "make implicit moral claims" on readers, "serving as models of a sort, suggesting by implication how we might or might not lead our own lives" (177–178). O'Brien's own fiction often provides the moral weight that he argues for in this essay. As several critics have pointed out, his novels and stories frequently tackle complex moral and philosophical issues. The novel *Going After Cacciato*, for instance, enters into the imagination of a young soldier in Vietnam debating whether to stay at war or desert, and the story "On the Rainy River" depicts a similar dilemma for a young man fresh out of college who receives a DRAFT notice. While these works do not provide definitive answers to moral quandaries, they present the philosophical complexities of the situations their characters find themselves in, never diminishing the difficulty of making moral decisions in an imperfect world.

Finally, this essay illustrates as well O'Brien's ongoing concern throughout his work with the relationship between fathers and sons. From his first novel, *Northern Lights*, in which two brothers are raised by a stern, apocalyptic minister, through works such as *Going After Cacciato* and the story "Speaking of Courage" in which Vietnam War soldiers imagine speaking to their fathers, themselves veterans of WORLD WAR II, about their wartime experiences, to *In the Lake of the Woods*, in which the suicide of John Wade's father, a charming alcoholic, fills the teen-age boy with rage, O'Brien has examined fathers' interactions with their sons. O'Brien's own father shared some characteristics with Mr. Wade—he, too, was a charming man, but

an alcoholic whose marriage and family suffered because of it. O'Brien was very close to his father, and on the lecture circuit he talks frequently about his father's death, explaining, as he does in this essay, that his father lives on in his own memory and imagination, a disembodied spirit, like a character in a story. O'Brien, whose first son was born very late in his life, when he was approaching 60, has written movingly about the experience of fatherhood and his overwhelming love for his son Timmy in a short essay published in *Life* magazine in 2004, called "A Letter to My Son." As an older father, he realizes that he will not be around to enjoy his son as long as he would like, much as he speculates in "Telling Tails" about living only in his sons' imaginations in the future.

The Things They Carried (1990)

A genre-defying blend of short story, novel, autobiography, and essay collection, *The Things They Carried* was published to great critical acclaim by Houghton Mifflin in 1990. The book consists of a series of interconnected stories that follow the fortunes of a group of soldiers in ALPHA COMPANY during the Vietnam War. Narrated by a 43-year-old writer named Tim O'Brien, who intersperses critical commentary about the stories and about the art of writing in general amid the stories he tells, the book's goal is to communicate to readers the raw emotional truth of men at war. The collection explores themes of courage and cowardice, asking what makes men go to war in the first place and what keeps them there fighting even in the most horrendous circumstances. It explores the trauma of soldiers who witness unspeakable atrocity as well as the lingering feelings of guilt and responsibility that haunt them long after the war is over. But above all, *The Things They Carried* is a book about storytelling, a book that explores how the most devastating trauma can be transformed into something alive and beautiful through art.

O'Brien in January 1989, during the period in which he wrote *The Things They Carried (Harry Ransom Humanities Research Center. The University of Texas at Austin)*

SYNOPSIS

"The Things They Carried" and "Love"

The book opens with the story "The Things They Carried," which details the guilt felt by a young lieutenant, Jimmy Cross, over the death of Ted Lavender, one of the men serving under his command in QUANG NAI PROVINCE during the Vietnam War. Lavender is shot in the head by a sniper after briefly separating from the rest of the men in his platoon to urinate. Lieutenant Cross, who had been daydreaming about Martha, a girl back home in New Jersey, when Lavender was shot, blames himself for the death. The men of Alpha Company subsequently burn the nearby village of THAN KHE, and Cross burns his two pictures of Martha, resolving not to daydream any longer, but to be a model officer. Intermingled with the story of Lavender's death is a running commentary on the men of Alpha Company and the things each man carries. The list starts with concrete items, including helmets, canteens, and mosquito repellent, as well as weapons and ammunition described according to their exact weight. But the men also carry personal items that mark them as individuals. Kiowa,

for instance, a Native American from Oklahoma City, carries a New Testament and an old hunting hatchet, while the big man Henry Dobbins carries a pair of his girlfriend's panty hose wrapped around his neck. The burdens the men carry are also spiritual and metaphorical. They carry fear and shame and other emotional baggage—intangibles that "had tangible weight" (21). Jimmy Cross carries both his unrequited love for Martha as well as guilt over Lavender's death. The ensuing stories in the collection will explore in more detail the ramifications of the things these soldiers carry and the effect that the war has on their psyches.

The next story, "Love," introduces readers to the book's first-person narrator, a 43-year-old writer named Tim O'Brien, who served as a foot soldier in Vietnam on a one-year tour of duty in 1968 and 1969. Although the two share much biographical background, narrator Tim O'Brien should not be confused with author Tim O'Brien. Narrator O'Brien is a fictional character with a fictional 10-year-old daughter named Kathleen, who wonders if her father ever killed anyone. Including the writer/narrator as a character in his book is a device that allows O'Brien to offer metafictional (*see* METAFICTION) commentary on the events that take place in the various stories. In "Love," Jimmy Cross comes to visit O'Brien many years after the war has ended and tells his friend about meeting Martha again at a college reunion in 1979. When O'Brien suggests to Cross that he'd like to write a story about Cross and Martha, readers understand that "The Things They Carried," which opens the collection, is the story that narrator O'Brien has written. Throughout the rest of the book, narrator O'Brien will continue to tell his own stories, to repeat stories he heard from other soldiers, and to comment on his style and purpose in writing these war stories.

"Spin" and "On the Rainy River,"

After "Spin," a story consisting of a series of brief vignettes highlighting some of narrator O'Brien's fleeting, fragmentary, and even "sweet" (31) memories of the war, he tells a story called "On the Rainy River," about his experience as a recent college graduate drafted (*see* DRAFT) into Vietnam in the summer of 1968. He describes working that summer at an ARMOUR MEATS plant, in a job that requires using a giant, gunlike water-spraying device to declot blood from slaughtered pigs as they move along a conveyer belt. Opposed to the war in principle, but paralyzed by indecision about how to respond to his draft notice, O'Brien feels as if his whole life is "collapsing toward slaughter" (43). He eventually leaves home, unsure of his destination, but stops at a nearly deserted fishing resort near the Canadian border called the TIP TOP LODGE, run by an 81-year-old man named Elroy Berdahl. O'Brien stays at the lodge for six days, helping with chores around the place. On his last day, Berdahl takes O'Brien out fishing on the RAINY RIVER, cutting off the boat's engine a mere 20 yards from the Canadian border. Sensing his opportunity to flee, O'Brien looks across to the Canadian shore and imagines seeing his friends and family members;

people from his small hometown of WORTHINGTON, MINNESOTA; fictional characters from books and movies; and even iconic figures from history, all waving and cheering to him. Unable to take the plunge and leave behind everything he knows and loves, O'Brien concludes the story with the sentences, "I was a coward. I went to the war" (61).

"Enemies," "Friends," and "How to Tell a True War Story"

The next two stories are very short and detail the troubled relationship between Alpha Company soldiers Dave Jensen and Lee Strunk. In "Enemies," Jensen breaks Strunk's nose during a fistfight, then must live with the fear of Strunk's eventual retribution. In "Friends," the two soldiers have called a truce, even making an agreement that if one is terribly injured—"a wheelchair wound" (65)—the other will shoot him. When Lee Strunk steps on a

U.S. medic in Vietnam searches the sky for a Medevac helicopter to evacuate his wounded buddy, 1967. *(Courtesy of the National Archives)*

rigged mortar round and loses his right leg though, he begs Dave Jensen not to carry out the pact. Strunk later dies in the helicopter on the way back to the base at CHU LAI. These brief pieces are followed by "How to Tell a True War Story," in which narrator O'Brien relates the death of Curt Lemon, a young soldier who also steps on a mine and whose body is blown up into a tree. Curt's friend, a medic named Rat Kiley, writes a letter home to Curt's sister, explaining what a "great, great guy" (67) her brother was. When the sister never writes back, Kiley calls her a "dumb cooze" (68). Soon after Curt's death, Rat and his fellow soldiers shoot up a baby water buffalo, aiming their guns to hurt the animal as much as possible. This outer story frames an inner story told by the soldier Mitchell Sanders, in which a six-man patrol hikes into the mountains circling Quang Nai Province, where they begin to hear all kinds of eerie noises, including music that seems to emanate from the landscape itself, and a "gook cocktail party" (74), complete with champagne corks, martini glasses, and small talk, among other things. The men, completely spooked, call in an air strike, and the countryside is napalmed and strafed. Sanders concludes his tale with a moral: "just listen" (77). Intermingled with the tale of Rat and Curt and the six-man patrol in the mountains is metafictional commentary from narrator O'Brien about the art of telling war stories and the importance of listening to such stories carefully. Good war stories, "true" war stories, O'Brien muses, must "make the stomach believe" (78). They must affect readers emotionally, give them the feel of what war is like, even though the events related in a "true" war story might never actually have happened. Readers soon find out that events in both the inner and outer tales of "How to Tell a True War Story" are invented. Mitchell Sanders confesses to making up many of the details in his tale about the patrol going up into the mountains, while narrator O'Brien tells readers at the very end of the story that he invented Rat Kiley, Curt Lemon, and the baby water buffalo—all of it, "every goddamn detail" (85). In order to make readers listen to his stories, O'Brien says that he must patiently tell them again and again, adding and subtracting details in order to get at the "real truth" (85).

"The Dentist" and "Sweetheart of the Song Tra Bong"

After a brief vignette called "The Dentist," which provides some more details about Curt Lemon—his fear of having his teeth examined and the lengths he goes to in order to overcome that fear—O'Brien includes a long story narrated by Rat Kiley called "Sweetheart of the Song Tra Bong." In this story, which Rat repeatedly insists is exactly true, a soldier named Mark Fossie, part of a small medical detachment in the mountains west of Chu Lai, schemes to bring his high school girlfriend, Mary Anne Bell, to Vietnam. When the 17-year-old arrives, she is fresh from CLEVELAND HEIGHTS SENIOR HIGH, a pretty blonde wearing white culottes and a pink sweater. While she is young and naïve, Mary Anne is a quick learner who soon becomes fascinated with the war. She learns to help out in the operating room, to clean and assemble weapons, and she even spends time with Vietnamese soldiers and villagers, entranced by the foreignness of the new world she has entered. Mary Anne eventually begins to spend time with a group of GREEN BERETS, intense and secretive soldiers who live on the perimeter of the medical unit, even going out on ambush with them. One night Mark Fossie discovers Mary Anne in the Greenies' tent, singing in a strange, high-pitched nonhuman voice and wearing a necklace of human tongues. What happens to Mary Anne after that is pure speculation. She walks off into the mountains one morning and does not come back. Said to "have crossed to the other side" (116), Mark Fossie's former high school sweetheart is transformed completely; she has surrendered to the madness and evil of war.

"Stockings," "Church," and "Style"

Continuing the pattern of short vignettes linking the longer stories, the next two pieces involve the soldier Henry Dobbins. The first describes the good luck charm that Dobbins wears around his neck—a pair of panty hose sent him by his girlfriend back home that Dobbins believes have kept him safe during his months in the bush. When the girlfriend breaks up with him, Dobbins continues to wear the panty hose, claiming that the "magic doesn't go away" (118). Readers see another side of Dobbins in the next story, "Church," in which the men of Alpha Company have set up camp in a nearly abandoned Buddhist pagoda, maintained only by a pair of monks who develop an affectionate relationship with the big American soldier. Dobbins talks with Kiowa, a devoutly Christian soldier from Oklahoma, about his own earlier desire to be a preacher, insisting that the monks should be treated decently but not recognizing his own condescension toward them. Dobbins will appear again in another brief vignette a bit later in the book, "Style," in which a 14-year-old Vietnamese girl dances quietly and intensely amid the ruins of her burning village. When the American soldiers enter her house, they find her family members dead and badly burned. Later, one of the Americans, a loutish soldier named Azar, mocks the girl's dancing, performing clumsy twirls and leaps. Angry, Henry Dobbins picks Azar up from behind and threatens to dump him into a deep well, insisting that the soldier "dance right" (136).

"The Man I Killed," "Ambush," and "Good Form"
These brief stories about Dobbins frame two stories about the narrator O'Brien himself and a young Vietnamese man he may or may not have killed during his tour of duty. O'Brien describes the delicate young man's dead body—a starlike hole where his eye should have been, one cheek missing, his neck torn open to the spinal cord—and he also describes his own guilt following the death. He had thrown a grenade at the young man out of fear when the soldier posed no serious threat to him. Subsequently, O'Brien imagines a history for the dead young man, speculating that he may have been a mathematics student, repelled by war but forced to fight because of cultural traditions. Later in the collection, in a very brief essay called "Good Form," however, O'Brien is a bit more cagey about whether he actually killed the young Vietnamese man or not, reassuring his daughter, Kathleen, that he did not kill anyone but also claiming that he could honestly answer either yes or no to her question since the truth is that he is "left with faceless responsibility and faceless grief" (180) after the war.

"Speaking of Courage," "Notes," "In the Field," and "Field Trip"
A quartet of stories that explore the death of O'Brien's good friend Kiowa in a muddy field

alongside the SONG TRA BONG River make up the next part of the collection. "Speaking of Courage" tells the story of Norman Bowker, returned from the war but unable to fit in back in his small midwestern hometown. One Fourth of July, Bowker drives around and around the lake in town, imagining conversations with his old girlfriend, Sally Kramer, and with his father. While Norman imagines that Sally refuses to listen to his war stories, he pictures himself explaining to his father how he was responsible for Kiowa's death—how Kiowa sank into the muddy field one night and how Norman could not pull him out despite catching hold of his boot. The following piece, "Notes," more an essay than a story, provides commentary on "Speaking of Courage." O'Brien explains that Bowker wrote him a long letter after the war in which he discussed his trouble returning to a normal life. O'Brien writes a story based on Bowker's letter but leaves out the "shitfield" where Kiowa died. Later, Norman will hang himself at the local YMCA. O'Brien concludes this essay by suggesting that Kiowa's death was, in fact, his *own* responsibility, not Norman's. The next story, "In the Field," retells the tale of Kiowa's death. This time, however, the guilt for the death lies with an unnamed young soldier, presumably O'Brien himself, who had pulled out a flashlight to show his friend a picture of his girlfriend back home. The young soldier believes it was the light that drew enemy fire, causing Kiowa to be shot and to sink into the muddy field. The final story in this portion of the book details a return trip the narrator O'Brien made to Vietnam with his daughter, Kathleen, many years later. One of the sites he visits is the field where Kiowa died. To his daughter's bewilderment, O'Brien wades out into the Song Tra Bong River and wedges an old pair of Kiowa's moccasins into the muck at the river bottom, trying to bring resolution to the events of that tragic night so many years before.

"The Ghost Soldiers" and "Night Life"
"The Ghost Soldiers," appearing next in the book, details O'Brien's anger at a young, raw medic named Bobby Jorgenson who fails to treat O'Brien properly after he is shot for the second time. O'Brien nearly dies of shock, and his wound

becomes borderline gangrenous because of Jorgenson's incompetence. Transferred from the field to battalion headquarters after the shooting, O'Brien plots revenge against Jorgenson when the men of Alpha Company arrive at headquarters for a stand-down. Discomfited to find that he no longer fits in with his former comrades since his transfer to the rear, while Jorgenson has now become a bona fide member of the group, O'Brien discovers that the only soldier willing to help him in his plan to terrify Jorgenson is the unhinged Azar. Together, the two men rig up an elaborate ruse, complete with noise-makers and ghostly apparitions, to frighten Jorgenson while he is on night guard duty. Although the plot is largely successful, O'Brien becomes disgusted with himself while carrying it out. The following story, "Night Life," explains why Alpha Company's previous medic, Rat Kiley, who had bravely ministered to O'Brien the first time he was shot, is no longer with the outfit. In the words of the soldier Mitchell Sanders, Kiley had "lost his cool" (219). The medic had become increasingly agitated and paranoid, believing insects were crawling all over his body and imagining his fellow soldiers reduced to mere body parts. Eventually, unable to bear the strain any longer, Rat Kiley shoots himself in the foot and is sent to recover in Japan.

"The Lives of the Dead"
The book closes with a story called "The Lives of the Dead," which mingles war memories with events that occurred to the narrator O'Brien long before he was sent to Vietnam. On O'Brien's fourth day in the war, Alpha Company comes upon an old Vietnamese man lying dead and faceup in a village pigpen. O'Brien's fellow soldiers prop the man up into a sitting position, then take turns shaking hands with him and joking about his condition. Repulsed, O'Brien refuses to participate. But he later tells his friend Kiowa that strangely the old man reminded him of a girl he used to know when he was a fourth-grader back in WORTHINGTON. The girl's name was Linda, and O'Brien says that as nine-year-olds he and Linda were deeply in love. When the young girl dies of a brain tumor, O'Brien partly imagines, partly dreams that she comes back to visit him. Linda explains that being dead

is not "so bad," that it is "like being inside a book that nobody's reading" (245). In this final piece, O'Brien muses on the power of storytelling, arguing that "stories can save us" (225) as they work to bring the dead back to life. In stories, he writes, Ted Lavender and Kiowa and Curt Lemon and the slim, young Vietnamese man, as well as Linda herself, can sit up and smile and return to the world, at least until readers close the book and put it back on the shelf.

COMMENTARY
The Things They Carried is an unsettling book in many ways, not just for the violent wartime experiences that it describes, the suffering and sorrow of the American soldiers who fought in Vietnam, but also because its very form creates and then undoes readers' expectations, even before the story proper begins. While the title page carries the label, "a work of fiction by Tim O'Brien," and while the copyright page proclaims the usual caution: "This is a work of fiction . . . all the incidents, names, and characters are imaginary," other elements of the introductory material belie these assertions, suggesting the book's status as a true account. In a move more reminiscent of autobiography than of fiction, *The Things They Carried* is dedicated to the characters that appear in it: "This book is lovingly dedicated to the men of Alpha Company, and in particular to Jimmy Cross, Norman Bowker, Rat Kiley, Mitchell Sanders, Henry Dobbins, and Kiowa." In addition, the epigraph consists of a quote from JOHN RANSOM's *ANDERSONVILLE DIARY*, the real-life account of a 20-year-old Union soldier during the Civil War who became a prisoner in 1863, which concludes with the words: "Those who have had any such experiences as the author will see its truthfulness at once, and to all other readers it is commended as a statement of actual things by one who experienced them to the fullest." With its claim about the veracity of the book that is to follow, this epigraph leads readers to expect a real-life account. But most important, readers who know anything about Tim O'Brien are probably aware of his own year-long tour of duty in Vietnam, an experience publicized by the success of his earlier award-winning novel *Going After Cacciato*. When

they encounter a narrator named Tim O'Brien who describes himself as a 43-year-old writer currently living in Cambridge, Massachusetts, who had grown up in Worthington, Minnesota, and had published an earlier book called *Going After Cacciato,* it is entirely understandable that they read the narrator of the book as the real-life Tim O'Brien and believe that O'Brien is describing experiences that actually happened to him.

Even critics and interviewers have found themselves confused about the book's status as fiction or nonfiction. In an interview with *Publishers Weekly,* conducted just before the release of *The Things They Carried,* O'Brien picks up the writer Michael Coffey at the airport and comments: "I was wondering if you'd ask us where our daughter is," suggesting that other interviewers had mistaken the fictional 10-year-old, Kathleen O'Brien, for a real person. O'Brien goes on to explain to Coffey that his own experience "has virtually nothing to do with the content of the book," adding that he remembers "maybe a week's worth of stuff" from the whole time he spent in Vietnam. In the interview, O'Brien clarifies, as well, his decision to name the book's narrator after himself:

"All along, I knew I wanted to have a book in which my name, Tim, appeared even though Tim would not be me; that's all I knew. Over the course of, I'd say, 12 years, I was developing courage, which was the whole problem. The conception was pretty clear. But if you can imagine putting your name down doing horrible things you've never done or witnessed, it was something I had to find the guts to do. Even though in the broader sense of the world it's no big act of courage, when you face it in that room"—he points to the large, book-lined study just off the kitchen—"it's a scary feeling."

Tim O'Brien is not alone among American authors lending their actual names to fictional characters in their books. Norman Mailer, for instance, whose first book, *The Naked and the Dead,* is a realistic war novel set in the pacific theater of World War II, created a fictionalized, buffoonish version of himself as a Vietnam War protester in the 1968 volume *The Armies of the Night,* a work of

New Journalism that bore the subtitle "History as a Novel, The Novel as History." And the writer Phillip Roth released two novels in the early 1990s (*Deception: A Novel* in 1990 and *Operation Shylock: A Confession* in 1993) as well as another in 2004 (*The Plot Against America*) that featured characters named Phillip Roth. Why do contemporary writers sometimes choose to name characters after themselves? One reason may be that such a move tends to blur the line separating reality and fiction. Skeptical about the objectivity of traditional history, postmodern writers understand that history is dependent on narrative. Since we cannot recreate historical events except through the stories we tell about these events, it stands to reason that experience, or at least the human ability to understand and communicate experience, is always mediated by language. In addition, as O'Brien writes in "How to Tell a True War Story," memory itself is unreliable: "In any war story, but especially a true one, it's difficult to separate what happened from what seemed to happen. What seems to happen becomes its own happening and has to be told that way. . . . When a guy dies, like Curt Lemon, you look away and then look back for a moment and then look away again . . ." (71). So, if objective or "true" history is unattainable, what we are left with is story. In naming characters after themselves, writers such as Mailer, Roth, and O'Brien are reminding readers that the hard-and-fast boundaries separating history and fiction, the real and the invented, are not as strong and impermeable as we may like to think.

Yet Tim O'Brien carries his postmodern blurring of the line between fact and fiction even further than most contemporary writers. Even in interviews and in speaking engagements, O'Brien sometimes works to undermine readers' and listeners' desire for the truth, as he refuses to settle their questions about which portions of his book are "real" and which are invented. A writer who is popular on the lecture circuit, O'Brien will often begin his talks by telling a story about his war experiences. This story will often be heartfelt and emotionally moving, affecting audience members deeply. Then, as he frequently does in *The Things They Carried,* he will follow up by telling his listeners that the story they just heard was completely made up. Unsure whether they are more angry or intrigued about O'Brien's confession, audience members are usually left unsettled, not knowing quite what to think. O'Brien purposefully muddles the question of reality in interviews as well. In an exchange with Martin Naparsteck, for instance, published in *Contemporary Literature*, O'Brien talks about the source for his story "Speaking of Courage":

> "Speaking of Courage," for example, came from a letter I received from a guy named Norman Bowker, a real guy, who committed suicide after I received his letter. He was talking to me in his letter about how he just couldn't adjust to coming home. It wasn't bad memories; it was that he couldn't talk to anybody about it. He didn't know what to say: he felt inarticulate. All he could do was drive around and around in his hometown in Iowa, around this lake. In the letter he asked me to write a story about it, and I did. (7)

When Naparsteck asks whether this was someone O'Brien knew, the writer answers, "Yeah, in Vietnam. I sent him the story after it was published, and he said he liked it. Then I didn't hear from him for a long time. His mother finally wrote me . . . saying he committed suicide by hanging himself in the locker room of a YMCA" (7–8). Yet, a few sentences later, O'Brien adds:

> *The Things They Carried* is my best book. There's no doubt in my mind about it. When I was writing *Cacciato* I had that feeling; I have that feeling now. I can tell by the strangeness of it. It's a new form, I think. I blended my own personality with the stories, and I'm writing about the stories, and yet everything is made up, including the commentary. The story about Norman Bowker is made up. There was no Norman Bowker. The point being, among others, that in fiction we not only transform reality, we sort of invent our lives, invent our histories, our autobiographies." (8)

Here O'Brien reverses the expected order of things. Rather than real-life events inspiring stories, he surmises that stories invent reality: that fiction calls

history and autobiography into being. Like other postmodern writers, O'Brien sees the world as constructed through language, through the stories we tell about it.

This is a lesson repeated over and over in *The Things They Carried*. The book's title story, which opens the collection, is narrated in the traditional third person, lending weight and authority to the narrative voice. And in many ways the story initially seems as if it will be an objective, realistic account of the experiences of a group of soldiers fighting in the Vietnam War. The flat, realistic details of the lists of items the men carry, often enumerated down to their specific weights—"As PFCs or SPEC 4s, most of them were common grunts and carried the standard M-16 gas-operated assault rifle. The weapon weighted 7.5 pounds unloaded, 8.2 pounds with its full 20-round magazine" (5)—suggest that this story will provide an objective "truth" to its readers, a kind of ultrarealistic description of weapons and battle. Yet, other stories mingle with the hard, concrete lists that O'Brien provides. These are the stories of the personal items the men carry with them, from Kiowa's feathered hatchet and New Testament to Mitchell Sanders's brass knuckles and Jimmy Cross's pictures of Martha. But the death of Ted Lavender and Jimmy Cross's feelings of guilt for this death constitute the real heart of the story. Structurally, the tale of Lavender's death spirals around the lists of items that the men carry. The narrator refers to the death early on, reporting on page 2 the bare fact that Lavender "was shot in the head outside the village of Than Khe in mid-April." About a page later, he returns to the death again, this time writing, "In April . . . when Ted Lavender was shot, they used his poncho to wrap him up, then to carry him across the paddy, then to lift him into the chopper that took him away" (3). The narrator continues to periodically return to the subject of Ted Lavender's death throughout the story, providing readers incrementally more information each time, so that the story of the death has the same effect that O'Brien is striving for in the lists of items that the men carry—a piling up of weight on top of weight. The literal heaviness of the physical burdens the men carry is reflected in the amassing of emotional details concerning Lavender's death.

"The Things They Carried" is the most frequently anthologized story from the longer book, appearing in many short story anthologies, collections of readings for college composition courses, Vietnam War literature compilations, and the like. But taken by itself, the story, while a tremendously moving tale about American soldiers in Vietnam dealing as best they can with their war-induced fear and guilt, lacks the metafictional component that so defines the rest of the book. Metafiction, a key element of postmodern literature, refers to fiction that is at least partly about the process of writing fiction itself, about the ways that narrative shapes reality. According to the critic Patricia Waugh:

> Metafiction is a term given to fictional writing which self-consciously and systematically draws attention to its status as an artifact in order to pose questions about the relationship between fiction and reality. In providing a critique of their own methods of construction, such writings not only examine the fundamental structures of narrative fiction, they also explore the possible fictionality of the world outside the literary fictional text. (2)

The second story in the collection, "Love," adds this metafictional element, working to further complicate readers' views of "The Things They Carried." Placed as it is immediately after the opening story and involving two of the same central characters (Martha and Jimmy Cross), "Love" comments on and draws attention to the fictive status of the previous story. In "Love," readers are first introduced to the character of the narrator Tim O'Brien, who remembers Jimmy Cross coming to talk to him at his home years after the war ended. After Jimmy confides in O'Brien about meeting up with Martha again at a college reunion, the narrator O'Brien suggests that he would like to write a story about Cross and Martha. When Jimmy Cross agrees, readers are led to assume that "The Things They Carried," the story that opens the book, is the story that narrator O'Brien has written. Author O'Brien deliberately juxtaposes these two stories to make readers question the perceptions presented

in the previous story. Mostly readers must question the seeming authority and omniscience of the third-person narrative voice of "The Things They Carried." "Love" teaches readers that the events surrounding Ted Lavender's death are filtered not only through Cross's subjective and guilt-laden recollections but are then shaped into fiction by the Tim O'Brien character who may or may not be a reliable narrator.

In fact, O'Brien's friendship with Cross and his desire to please his fellow soldier might have influenced the portrait of Cross in "The Things They Carried." As Cross is driving away from O'Brien's house at the end of "Love," he makes a specific request of the author:

> He got into his car and rolled down the window. "Make me out to be a good guy, okay? Brave and handsome, all that stuff. Best platoon leader ever." He hesitated for a second. "And do me a favor. Don't mention anything about—"
> "No, I said, "I won't." (29)

Cross's unfinished sentence raises several questions. Readers might first assume that Cross is referring to the death of Ted Lavender, in which case the narrator O'Brien shows a lack of integrity as he breaks his promise to his friend, relating the incident in the previous story. Such a reading suggests that this is a narrator who cannot be entirely trusted. But perhaps Cross is referring here to another incident, one that remains unspoken in the course of the book. In this case, the narrator O'Brien keeps his promise to Cross, but readers must begin to accept the contingent nature of truth—we realize that we may never know exactly what it was like to be a soldier in Vietnam as we see that there are incidents that remain unspoken, uncommunicated. All we have is story, and stories are always incomplete.

Further, in stories soldiers like to think of themselves as fulfilling traditional notions of masculine virtue. In the exchange between the narrator O'Brien and Jimmy Cross cited above, O'Brien also draws attention to the shaping of the previous story when he tells readers about Cross's desire to come off as handsome and brave, the "best platoon leader ever." This statement should deconstruct for readers Cross's macho resolves at the end of "The Things They Carried," just as O'Brien works to undo traditional expectations about women in the story "Sweetheart of the Song Tra Bong." Among other things, Cross determines not to fantasize about Martha anymore, to think about her only as belonging elsewhere. A new "hardness" (24) develops in his stomach along with a new firmness to carry out his duties. He resolves to "be a man" (25) about his responsibility for Lavender's death, confessing his culpability to his troops. He determines to love his men more than he loves women, yet to remain strong and distant from them, "leaving no room for argument or discussion" (25) when he issues orders. Cross's intent here is to become in many respects the traditional American John Wayne–type hero, an icon of American individualism and courage. As the critic John Hellmann points out, this iconic figure appears frequently in Vietnam War literature, moving in the American mythic imagination from the western frontier to the "new frontier" of Vietnam. In fact, the story ends with explicit frontier imagery as Jimmy Cross pictures his men "saddling up" and moving "west" under his command in the last line of the story. Even if narrator O'Brien is trying to fulfill Cross's request to come off as a stereotypical war hero, author O'Brien exposes the falseness of such constructs by laying bare his own devices. Traditional masculine heroism must be questioned, seen as a construct rather than an absolute.

This technique of telling readers a story, then in a following commentary or story either taking back what he just said or drawing attention to the previous story as fiction, is one that O'Brien uses throughout *The Things They Carried*. While the story "Love" ask readers to look back at the collection's opening story and reconsider it as less objective, less realistic than they might have first imagined, later stories work in similar ways. "How to Tell a True War Story," for instance, relates the death of Curt Lemon as well as his friend Rat Kiley's anger and frustration at the death, which he expresses by shooting a baby water buffalo repeatedly, aiming to cause as much pain and suffering as possible. But at the end of the story, the narrator O'Brien claims that the moving tale he just told was "all made up," beginning to end, "Every goddam detail—the mountains and the river and especially that poor dumb baby buffalo. None of it happened. *None* of it" (85). Similarly, in "The Man I Killed" O'Brien will describe in grisly detail the body of a dead Vietnamese soldier he killed with a hand grenade while on ambush. Later, however, in the short commentary "Good Form," he will cast doubt on whether he actually ever killed anyone in Vietnam. The story of Kiowa's death in the "shitfield" alongside the Song Tra Bong River is equally ambiguous. The story is first told in "Speaking of Courage," where Norman Bowker relives his guilt over letting go of Kiowa's boot and allowing his friend to slip into the mucky field. But when the story is retold in "In the Field," the person who let go of Kiowa's boot is no longer Bowker but a young soldier who seems to be a version of the narrator O'Brien himself. Readers are left unsure exactly what to believe.

O'Brien's unsettling form of the book not only continues the metafictive project of blurring the line between fact and fiction, between history and story, which began with the book's cover, copyright page, dedication, etc., but it also invites greater reader participation than a straightforward war narrative might do. As the critic Catherine Calloway argues, the novel's fragmented form forces the reader "to piece together information, such as the circumstances surrounding the characters' deaths, in the same manner that the characters must piece together the reality of the war, or, for that matter, Curt Lemon's body." In this respect, O'Brien shares much in common with other American writers of Vietnam War literature who must grapple with a question underlying much literature of the later 20th century: How does one write about atrocity? As Kurt Vonnegut puts it in *Slaughterhouse-Five*, a World War II novel actually written and published during the height of the Vietnam War: "There is nothing intelligent to say about a massacre." That's why his book is so "short and jumbled and jangled," Vonnegut explains to his editor. Similarly, Vietnam War writers often use forms that may at first appear confusing, fragmented, or disordered to readers.

Such formal experimentation may be designed to mimic the chaos and confusion felt by soldiers in Vietnam, who were often unsure about the politics and morality of the war, the history and motivations of the people they were fighting, or even the basic strategy of their commanders as their patrols and ambushes often seemed futile and repetitive. The critic Lloyd Lewis argues that it is the duty of the Vietnam War writer to incorporate the seeming illogic of the war into the structure of his work. The reader, according to Lewis, should be "obliged to live like the soldier, adrift in an alien universe in which the familiar . . . landmarks [have] disappeared." Giving readers a small taste of the confusion and chaos of the war may be the best writers can do as they explore the potential for art to communicate or even transform the trauma of war experience into something meaningful and "true."

For O'Brien, at least, the truth of the war experience is best communicated through storytelling. In the short chapter "Good Form," he justifies to readers his own formal choices, explaining that for him form is much more than "a game" and insisting that readers understand why "story-truth is truer sometimes than happening truth" (179). O'Brien's goal is to attain a kind of emotional honesty in his work. "A true war story," he writes, "if truly told, makes the stomach believe" (78). Mitchell Sanders, in "How to Tell a True War Story," must make up details about the six-man patrol sent into the mountains because he wants O'Brien, his listener, "to feel the truth, to believe by the raw force of feeling" (74). For Sanders, as for O'Brien, whether the events described actually happened or not is irrelevant so long as the raw emotion of the experience is understood. The moral of his story, Mitchell explains, is "just listen" (77).

If readers listen carefully to the stories in *The Things They Carried*, they will feel, at least partly, the sense of "faceless responsibility and faceless grief" (180) that the U.S. soldiers are left with. In the story "In the Field," Jimmy Cross acknowledges that "When a man died, there had to be blame" (177). Assigning blame is a way of erasing the randomness of death and the chaos of the wartime experience. The soldiers wish to find a reason for the deaths they witness in order to give themselves the illusion of control, to make these deaths seem less frightening, less random and meaningless. Blame can provide the illusion that war deaths are preventable, if only someone behaves differently, more responsibly, in the future. This is why O'Brien has Jimmy Cross burn Martha's pictures in the opening story. Cross feels guilty for Ted Lavender's death despite the fact that the death was largely out of his control—the soldier was "zapped while zipping" (17), shot unexpectedly by sniper fire after separating briefly from the other men to urinate. In Vietnam War literature death comes randomly and illogically. Lee Strunk had just survived his very dangerous exploration of the Vietnamese tunnel when Lavender is killed while going about the ordinary business of living. Similarly, O'Brien retells the death of Kiowa so many times in the book in order to illustrate the sense of guilt felt by three separate men, Norman Bowker, Jimmy Cross, and a younger version of himself, all of whom claim responsibility for the death. Both Bowker and the young soldier specifically remember letting go of Kiowa's boot as their friend sinks into the muck, while Cross blames himself for ordering the men to set up camp in the muddy field, even though he was following orders in doing so. When the narrator O'Brien casts doubt on whether he actually killed the slim, young Vietnamese man with a hand grenade, he emphasizes again that the actual historic truth of the event does not matter as much as the feelings that accompanied the man's death. In their longing for control and in their grief over the loss of friends, these soldiers blame themselves when death occurs. But O'Brien's metafictive shaping and retelling of the stories should lead readers to see further than the characters themselves. The point is not to determine individual guilt or innocence but for readers to recognize the ways that human beings respond emotionally to trauma, to acknowledge the lingering feelings of guilt and responsibility that never leave the men who fought in Vietnam.

Along with guilt, the book also explores the shame and fear that the American soldiers carry with them into battle. Like Paul Berlin in *Going After Cacciato*, the soldiers in *The Things They Carried* are often afraid:

For the most part they carried themselves with poise, a kind of dignity. Now and then, however, there were times of panic, when they squealed or wanted to squeal but couldn't, when they twitched and made moaning sounds and covered their heads and said Dear Jesus and flopped around on the earth and fired their weapons blindly and cringed and sobbed and begged for the noise to stop and went wild and made stupid promises to themselves and to God and to their mothers and fathers, hoping not to die. In different ways, it happened to all of them. (19)

Afterward, the men reassemble themselves, make jokes about their fright, and go on. Although the soldiers are afraid of dying, "they were even more afraid to show it" (20). In fact, O'Brien suggests that it is this "common secret of cowardice barely restrained" (21) that motivates the men and keeps them HUMPING and fighting in the worst of circumstances. They do not want to be considered cowards by their fellow soldiers. "Men killed, and died, because they were embarrassed not to" (21) O'Brien writes, deconstructing an entire western tradition of manly courage in battle. Ironically, in *The Things They Carried,* courage is displayed by men who are "too frightened to be cowards" (22).

This complex undoing of traditional notions of courage and valor is perhaps best seen in the story "On the Rainy River" when the young Tim O'Brien contemplates fleeing the draft. The story opens as something of a confession, with O'Brien examining his early notions of heroism. "All of us," he tells readers, "like to believe that in a moral emergency we will behave like the heroes of our youth, bravely and forthrightly, without thought of personal loss or discredit" (39). O'Brien goes on to explain that as a boy he had thought of courage as almost being like money in the bank, like an inheritance carefully saved for a rainy day. His metaphor here suggests the notion that Americans believe they inherit courage from the heroes and icons of their mythic past— O'Brien as a boy thinks of himself as the LONE RANGER, a "secret hero" (39). Yet, this economic metaphor for courage is morally suspect. View-

ing courage as an inheritance to be hoarded up for a time when the evil is evil enough, when the good is good enough, to justify the account being drawn down allows one to dispense with "all those bothersome little acts of daily courage" (40). It is, as O'Brien explains, a theory that offers "hope and grace to the repetitive coward" (40). By the end of the story, readers see that O'Brien does not inherit courage from the past, as if courage were a generous legacy left him by a departed relative. Rather, O'Brien feels himself to be trapped by the past. When Elroy Berdahl takes the morally paralyzed young man out fishing and turns off the boat's motor near the Canadian bank of the Rainy River, O'Brien has a vision of family members, townspeople, and assorted characters from American history and myth as well as from western cultural tradition who all cheer and yell to him from the shore. The unbearable weight of the past, of all that he has been taught to feel and believe, along with the burden of all the people he would disappoint, are simply too much for O'Brien to overcome. Rather than make an active decision about whether to flee to Canada or honor his draft notice, O'Brien writes that he "submitted" (59), that he could not make himself be brave: "It had nothing to do with morality. Embarrassment, that's all it was . . . I would go to the war—I would kill and maybe die—because I was embarrassed not to" (59). Just as Paul Berlin in the earlier novel *Going After Cacciato* is unable to imagine a way out of traditional models of masculine courage, the young Tim O'Brien is trapped by the weight of cultural tradition. "I was a coward," the story ends. "I went to the war" (61).

Yet, elsewhere in the book, O'Brien speculates about a theory of courage different from the inheritance model he adhered to as a young boy. While he previously viewed courage as something to be saved up, believing that courage was like money in the bank that would draw more interest and grow the less it was used, in the story "Speaking of Courage" he suggests that it might be exactly the little daily acts of courage—acts that his previous theory dispensed with—that make for true bravery. Norman Bowker imagines explaining to his father that the seven medals he won in Vietnam were not for uncommon valor but only for the common variety: "The routine, the daily stuff—just humping, just enduring—but that was worth something, wasn't it?" (141). Later, Bowker thinks again about the little things he remembers from the war: "How the rain never stopped. How the cold worked into your bones. Sometimes the bravest thing on earth was to sit through the night and feel the cold in your bones" (147). Courage, O'Brien suggests, might not be a definable quality but a matter of degree. Rather than accepting the Socratic notion of courage from the LACHES—knowing how to act wisely in spite of fear—as Paul Berlin seems to do in *Going After Cacciato*, both Norman Bowker and the narrator O'Brien suggest that courage might be at least partly a matter of simple endurance, of being able to stand more hardship than you imagined you could. But courage is also represented in this collection as an elusive ideal that can never be fully attained. Bowker in his longing to explain his war experiences to a sympathetic listener remembers how "he had been braver than he ever thought possible, but how he had not been so brave as he wanted to be" (153). Human beings strive to live up to virtuous ideals, but O'Brien also acknowledges that we live in a fallen state. For O'Brien, the experience of fighting in a war is a way to represent this move from innocence into sin. He ends the story "Speaking of Courage" by having Norman Bowker walk into the lake that he had been circling repeatedly in his car, put his head under, and taste the water against his lips, in an attempted baptism or cleansing ritual. But as readers find out in the essay "Notes," which immediately follows "Speaking of Courage," Norman is unable to wash away his sins or his feelings of guilt and sorrow. Just as he is unable to save Kiowa from drowning in the terrible waste of the shitfield, Norman Bowker is unable to save himself. In 1978 he hangs himself at the local YMCA.

The dark, sinful nature of war is a theme explored frequently by American writers of Vietnam War literature. The critic Tobey Herzog calls this trend the "Heart of Darkness" theme, after Joseph Conrad's 1902 novel. According to Herzog, Vietnam narratives often offer moral explorations of individuals stripped of civilization's restraints, confronting evil, primal emotions, chaos, and savagery. These narratives, Herzog adds, ask two key questions: What spiritual darkness resides in us? And what do we possess to hold off this darkness? Like other Vietnam War writers, Tim O'Brien explores the human fascination with horror, the allure of war. In "How to Tell a True War Story," he writes:

> The truths are contradictory. It can be argued, for instance, that war is grotesque. But in truth war is also beauty. For all its horror, you can't help but gape at the awful majesty of combat. You stare out at tracer rounds unwinding through the dark like brilliant red ribbons. You crouch in ambush as a cool, impassive moon rises over the nighttime paddies. You admire the fluid symmetries of troops on the move, the harmonies of sound and shape and proportion, the great sheets of metal-fire streaming down from a gunship, the illumination rounds, the white phosphorous, the purply black glow of napalm, the rocket's red glare. It's not pretty, exactly. It's astonishing. It fills the eye. It commands you. You hate it, yes, but your eyes do not. (181)

The awesome nature of combat itself is alluring and forces the eye to appreciate its majestic beauty even though the mind might consciously hate everything that war stands for. When Mary Anne Bell in "Sweetheart of the Song Tra Bong" succumbs to the darkness of war, wearing a necklace of human tongues and living in a tent with animal skins dangling from the rafters and piles of bones lining the corners, she, too, describes war as alluring, as seductive. "Sometimes I want to *eat* this place. Vietnam. I want to swallow the whole country—the dirt, the death—I just want to eat it and have it there inside of me" (111). Mary Anne desires to feel the darkness inside of herself because it makes her seem more fully alive than she ever has been before: "When I'm out there at night, I feel close to my own body, I can feel my blood moving, my skin and my fingernails, everything, it's like I'm full of electricity and I'm glowing in the dark—I'm on fire almost . . . You can't feel like that anywhere else" (111).

O'Brien depicts other characters seduced by the dark allure and horror of war as well, including Azar, the soldier who straps a puppy to a CLAY-MORE MINE and squeezes the firing device, and who never wants to leave Vietnam because he "*love[s] this shit*" (212), and Curt Lemon, who possibly rapes a young Vietnamese woman when he goes trick-or-treating in a village at Halloween, dressed only in boots, his body weirdly painted all over. Dave Jensen and Lee Strunk are unable to control their own violent impulses and get into a fistfight so vicious that Jensen cannot stop hitting Strunk even after the man's nose is badly broken. It takes three other soldiers to pull him off the injured soldier. But O'Brien really drives home the heart of darkness theme when in the story "Ghost Soldiers" he shows the Tim O'Brien narrator to be infected by the sinful nature of war. After the new young medic Bobby Jorgenson botches treating O'Brien when he is shot for the second time, the collection's narrator writes that he "turned mean inside" (200). He plans an elaborate revenge against Jorgenson, recognizing that soldiers on night guard are particularly vulnerable to being terrorized because sitting alone hour after hour one has "nothing to do but stare into the big black hole at the center of your own sorry soul" (205). The narrator O'Brien then describes in detail the darkness at the center of *his* soul:

> I was part of the night. I was the land itself— everything, everywhere—the fireflies and pad-dies, the moon, the midnight rustlings, the cool phosphorescent shimmer of evil—I was atrocity—I was jungle fire, jungle drums—I was the blind stare in the eyes of all those poor, dead, dumbfuck ex-pals of mine—all the pale young corpses, Lee Strunk and Kiowa and Curt Lemon—I was the beast on their lips—I was Nam—the horror, the war. (209)

Sounding very much like Mary Anne Bell here, O'Brien imagines himself merging with the land-scape itself, which American soldiers often saw as their real enemy, largely because of the hostile jungle terrain, the overwhelming heat and drench-ing monsoons, the treacherous mines and tripwires embedded it, and the elaborate system of under-ground tunnels used by VIET CONG soldiers. Fur-

ther, his own surrender to the darkness of war is at least partially brought on by the deaths of his fellow soldiers—"all the pale young corpses" that he cannot forget. As O'Brien writes in "How to Tell a True War Story," one way to tell a true war story is "by the way it never seems to end. Not then, not ever" (76). The effects of war, of witness-ing repeated death and atrocity, are lingering and traumatic and not easily overcome.

While Norman Bowker is unable to cleanse himself of sin and guilt, and while even the narra-tor O'Brien feels himself so dirtied by the war that he has grown mean and cold inside, *The Things They Carried* nevertheless suggests that perhaps the best way to deal with this internalized darkness is to expose it to the light of day. Psychotherapists who work with American Vietnam veterans, such as Jonathan Shay in his moving and heartbreaking account *Achilles in Vietnam: Combat Trauma and the Undoing of Character,* have argued that nar-rative itself—telling one's story, communicating it to others who listen respectfully—can aid in the healing process. We have already seen that listen-ing is an important theme throughout the collec-tion: Mitchell Sanders says that the moral of his story about the six-man patrol that goes up into the mountains is "just listen" (77), and the narrator O'Brien faults the kindly, humane, older woman at the end of "How to Tell a True War Story" for not listening. Norman Bowker imagines girlfriends back home who refuse to listen and invents an idealized father figure who does listen, though his real-life father is distracted by watching a baseball game on television and seems more concerned that Norman win medals than purge his guilt by talking about his experiences. Is all of this not listening indicative of the incommunicability of trauma, of the war experience? Does O'Brien succumb to an old cliché about Vietnam War literature: "If you weren't there, you can't possibly understand"? The answer to these questions seems to be a resounding no. While O'Brien acknowledges that it may be impossible to ever reach the "full and exact truth" (159) about human experience, he suggests that it is imperative that we try, that we work diligently to get the story right, that the writing (or the reading, the listening) does not simply come "quickly and easily" (159), as O'Brien said it did for him in his first version of "Speaking of Courage." This is the version that O'Brien sends to Norman Bowker, an incident he describes in "Notes." Abruptly following this information is the sentence, "Eight months later [Norman] hanged himself" (160), suggesting that Norman's death almost seems to result from O'Brien's failure to tell the story properly.

But while stories told poorly to listeners who refuse to hear can be dangerous, good stories told under good conditions are different. O'Brien begins the last story in the collection, "The Lives of the Dead," with the words, "But this, too, is true: stories can save us" (225). In the interview with Michael Coffey, O'Brien says about *The Things They Carried*:

> What I discovered in the course of writing this book is the reason I love story: not just for its titillation, its instant gratification of what next, what next, but for the livingness that's there as you read and that lingers afterward. Jake Barnes is alive for me. Though he is a fictional character in the taxicab at the end of *The Sun Also Rises,* he is alive in that cab with Brett. That's what I love about writing them and reading them—that quality of immortality that a story is—doesn't contain, just is.

In his stories, O'Brien points out, he can bring the dead back to life again. Kiowa and Ted Lavender and Curt Lemon and the nine-year-old Linda, a little girl who died of a brain tumor when O'Brien was in the fourth grade, can sit up and talk and dream and return to the world of the living, at least temporarily, in the stories that he writes about them. Perhaps the reason that O'Brien chooses to conclude his collection with this story about Linda—a tale that takes place long before his Vietnam experiences—is to show the connection between war experience and human experience in general. While Kiowa is dumbfounded that the dead old Vietnamese man in the pigpen, whom the soldiers in Alpha Company shake hands with, reminds O'Brien of a girl he used to know, his first date in fact, readers see that the experience of death and trauma is not exclusive to war. All human beings will have to face sorrow and loss during their lives. O'Brien has reiterated, both in his fiction and in interviews, his belief that war stories are about more than war.

In a lecture at Brown University in April 1999, O'Brien said, "War stories aren't always about war, per se. They aren't about bombs and bullets and military maneuvers. They aren't about tactics, they aren't about foxholes and canteens. War stories, like any good story, are finally about the human heart." While much Vietnam War literature expresses the "incommunicability" of war trauma, O'Brien's work expresses the exact opposite. *The Things They Carried* suggests that through imaginative acts of storytelling and reading, through the patient telling and retelling of stories, and through active, sympathetic listening, the atrocity of war can begin to be understood and thus healing can begin.

CHARACTERS

A&W Intercom Voice In the story "Speaking of Courage," Norman Bowker pulls up to an A&W root beer stand after driving his car aimlessly around and around the lake in the center of his small hometown one Fourth of July. After a carhop rudely tells Norman how to order, he buzzes the intercom outside his window and is answered by a faceless voice that seems to speak in military lingo. When Norman asks for a Mama Burger and fries, the intercom voice replies, "Affirmative, copy clear" (151). Later, when Norman is done eating, he buzzes the intercom again, and this time the disembodied voice asks Norman what he really needs, and then offers to listen to anything Norman has to say. But Norman backs off and refuses to speak. The voice signs off with the words, "Over an' out" (152), again evoking military idiom. Possibly, the A&W worker who speaks to Norman over the intercom is a fellow veteran, who might have been able to listen to and understand Norman's problem. But it is also possible that Norman simply fantasizes the conversation, just as he imagines elsewhere in the story speaking with both Sally Kramer Gustafson and his own father about his war experiences.

Arnold, Max Max Arnold, an old high school friend of Norman Bowker's, appears in the story

"Speaking of Courage." A budding philosopher who loved to argue about the existence of God, Max drowned in the lake that Norman drives around and around on the Fourth of July. Norman imagines Max as a possible listener for his story of almost winning the SILVER STAR—the story of Kiowa's death in the muddy field alongside the SONG TRA BONG RIVER. While Norman believes that Max would have liked the story, "its irony in particular," he also notes that Max "had become a pure idea" (146) and is unable to listen to Norman's stories.

AWOL Soldier and his Buddy in Danang   In "Spin," the narrator Tim O'Brien tells what he calls "a quick peace story" (35). He describes a soldier who goes AWOL (Absent Without Leave) and shacks up with a nurse in DA NANG. Although he has a great time, he eventually rejoins in his unit in the bush. When a buddy asks what happened with the nurse, the soldier replies, "All that peace, man, it felt so good it *hurt*. I want to hurt it *back*" (35).

Azar   Azar is a cruel, loutish, war-loving soldier in ALPHA COMPANY. Readers first meet him in the story "Spin" when he hands a bar of chocolate to a one-legged little Vietnamese boy and comments insensitively that "War's a bitch . . . One leg, for Chrissake. Some poor fucker ran out of ammo" (31). In the same story, Azar straps an orphaned puppy that had been adopted by Ted Lavender to a CLAYMORE MINE and squeezes the firing device. When his fellow soldiers become angry, Azar asks, "What's everybody so upset about? . . . I mean, Christ, I'm just a *boy*" (37). Azar infuriates the soldier Henry Dobbins as well in the story "Style" when he mocks the dancing of a 14-year-old Vietnamese girl whose family has been killed. Finally, Azar plays an integral role in the story "Ghost Soldiers." He is the only member of Alpha Company willing to help the narrator Tim O'Brien gain revenge on the incompetent medic Bobby Jorgenson. But in Azar O'Brien unleashes a monster—the soldier refuses to stop the psychological torture of Jorgenson even when O'Brien himself has had enough.

Bell, Mary Anne   Mary Anne Bell is the title character in the story "Sweetheart of the Song Tra

Bong." A pretty, 17-year-old blonde wearing a pink sweater and white culottes when she first steps off the resupply helicopter after her high school boyfriend, Mark Fossie, has made elaborate arrangements to transport her to Vietnam, Mary Anne quickly sheds her innocence. She cuts her hair, adapts to field hygiene practices, and learns to assist in the operating room as well as how to handle and shoot a weapon. Insatiably curious about this new world she had become part of, Mary Anne even begins spending time with the South Vietnamese soldiers along the camp's perimeter, as well as pestering Mark to take her into the nearby Vietnamese village to interact with the locals. As Mary Anne changes—her body even becoming more "stiff in places" and her voice "reorganiz[ing] itself at a lower pitch" (99)—her previous plans with Mark Fossie for the future change as well. Rather than getting married right away, she says, maybe they will travel first, maybe live together for a while. Eventually, Mary Anne is drawn to a group of six GREEN BERETS who live in a HOOTCH outside the medical unit and who often disappear for days and weeks at a time on mysterious missions in the jungle. One night, she does not return to the bunker she had shared with Mark Fossie, having spent the night out on ambush with the Greenies. Although she and Mark get back together for a short time, Mary Anne soon disappears again; this time she is out on a mission with the Greenies for three whole weeks. When Mark Fossie finds her in the Greenies' tent a few nights after her return, wearing a necklace of human tongues and singing in a weird, high voice, Mary Anne explains to him her transformation as best she can: "When I'm out there at night, I feel close to my own body, I can feel my blood moving, my skin and my fingernails, everything, it's like I'm full of electricity and I'm glowing in the dark— I'm on fire almost—I'm burning away into nothing" (111). Although Rat Kiley, who tells this story, is unsure of what happened to Mary Anne after that night, he reports hearing from Eddie Diamond, the unit's ranking noncommissioned officer, that the girl had gone into the mountains one day and never returned. "She had crossed to the other side" (116), Rat concludes, suggesting that she has transgressed not only gender boundaries but also the line separating the Americans from enemy soldiers and even the border between human and nonhuman, between the sane and the insane.

Berdahl, Elroy   Elroy Berdahl is the skinny, bald, 81-year old owner of the TIP TOP LODGE in the story "On the Rainy River." O'Brien calls Berdahl "the hero of [his] life" (48), confiding that the man saved him by providing him a safe sanctuary to think over his situation after he was drafted (*see* DRAFT). If the story is interpreted as a hero's journey, in which a young man at a crossroads in his life enters into a liminal space, receives a vision, then changes forever, Berdahl acts in the role of mentor/guide during O'Brien's journey. The old man seems almost godlike as he understands O'Brien's troubles without every being told them and offers the emotionally distraught young man the money and opportunity to make his own decision about whether to flee to Canada or not, even taking him within 20 yards of the border in his fishing boat, like the Greek ferryman Charon, who rowed souls across the river into Hades. Both figures are marked by eyes of a distinct bluish gray color. O'Brien writes that Elroy Berdahl "was a witness, like God, or like the gods, who look on in absolute silence as we live our lives, as we make our choices or fail to make them" (60). Berdahl seems to understand the young man's failure to act when he says "Ain't biting" (60) and turns the fishing boat back toward the U.S. side of the river.

Blyton   A drill sergeant named Blyton, who is among the crowd on the Canadian riverbank in the narrator O'Brien's vision at the end of "On the Rainy River," is said to sneer, shoot up a finger at O'Brien, and shake his head in disgust as the young man contemplates fleeing the DRAFT. Blyton appears as well in O'Brien's 1973 memoir, *If I Die in a Combat Zone, Box Me Up and Ship Me Home.* He is the tough, sadistic drill sergeant who torments O'Brien and his friend Erik as the two thoughtful young soldiers undergo basic training at FORT LEWIS, WASHINGTON.

Billie   Billie is the girlfriend of the young, unnamed soldier from the story "In the Field" who

feels responsible for his friend Kiowa's death. The soldier had pulled out a picture of Billie in the dark night to show Kiowa. He believes that the light from his flashlight had drawn the enemy fire that slammed into Kiowa and caused him to sink deep into the muck of the "shitfield" where the men were camped that night. This story parallels the collections' opening story, in which Lieutenant Jimmy Cross feels responsible for Ted Lavender's death because he had been looking at pictures of a girl named Martha and daydreaming about their relationship when Lavender was shot. While neither man might actually have been guilty of causing the death, the narrator O'Brien makes it clear that they each blame themselves: "When a man died, there had to be blame" (177). Assigning blame for deaths erases their randomness and gives the men hope that they can prevent similar incidents in the future, by behaving more carefully, more correctly.

Bowker, Norman   Norman Bowker is a soldier in ALPHA COMPANY who carries a diary in the field, along with his standard-issue equipment and weapons. Although he is described as "a very gentle person," he also carries a thumb from a dead Vietnamese soldier, a souvenir given to him by Mitchell Sanders. The stories in which Bowker figures most prominently are "Speaking of Courage" and "Notes." In the first of these, Bowker is back after the war in his small, midwestern hometown. Unable to fit into civilian life, Bowker drives aimlessly around and around the town's central lake one Fourth of July. Although he is unable to speak about his wartime experiences, he imagines holding a conversation with his father, in which he explains how he almost won the SILVER STAR by saving his friend Kiowa from a muddy death in a field alongside the SONG TRA BONG RIVER. But Norman had to let go Kiowa go at the end, unable to pull his fellow soldier out of the muck in which he drowns. In "Notes," the narrator O'Brien explains that Bowker had written him a 17-page-long letter after the war, discussing his troubles and suggesting that O'Brien write a story about them. Although O'Brien takes Bowker's advice and writes a story, it remains unsatisfying because, as Norman points out in a second letter, O'Brien has left out Vietnam and Kiowa and the "shitfield" in which Kiowa died. Eight months after receiving this letter, O'Brien discovers that Norman Bowker hanged himself at the local YMCA. O'Brien later revises the story to include the elements he had left out previously.

Bowker's Father   In the story "Speaking of Courage," the ALPHA COMPANY soldier Norman Bowker imagines explaining his wartime experiences to his father, who listens carefully and encourages his son to continue talking. Norman particularly imagines telling his father about almost winning the SIL-VER STAR by pulling Kiowa out of the muck in the field alongside the SONG TRA BONG RIVER. In Norman's imagination, his father understands that medals themselves are not that important, "that many brave men do not win medals for their bravery, and that others win medals for doing nothing" (141). In real life, however, Norman's father contrasts with the imagined father. Rather than listening to his son's war stories, Mr. Bowker is home watching baseball on national TV while Norman drives around and around the lake. And in the story "Spin," Norman confesses to the narrator O'Brien that his father is obsessed with Norman winning medals: "If I could have one wish, anything, I'd wish for my dad to write me a letter and say it's okay if I don't win any medals. That's all my old man talks about, nothing else. How he can't wait to see my goddamn medals" (36).

Bowker's Mother   While Norman Bowker's mother is never mentioned in the story "Speaking of Courage," she appears in the essay "Notes" that immediately follows that story. In this essay, O'Brien tells readers about receiving a brief note from Norman's mother in August 1978, explaining that Norman had hanged himself after playing basketball at the local YMCA. There was no suicide note, Norman's mother explains, because he "was a quiet boy" whom she speculates did not want "to bother anybody" (160).

Bronx Cabbie   A cab driver from the Bronx is said to be among the crowds cheering and jeering the narrator Tim O'Brien at the end of the story "On the Rainy River" when he is deciding whether or not to flee to Canada and avoid the DRAFT. While seemingly an inexplicable addition to the list of family, friends, historical figures, and fictional characters who appear in O'Brien's vision, this cab driver might possibly be meant to evoke the taxi driver from O'Brien's 1973 memoir, *If I Die in a Combat Zone, Box Me Up and Ship Me Home,* who ferries O'Brien to the sorority house in SEATTLE, where he has fled from FORT LEWIS on an aborted attempt to escape to Canada. The earlier account never mentions where the cabbie is from, but both instances revolve around the point at which O'Brien comes closest to fleeing the draft.

Carhop   When Norman Bowker pulls into the parking lot of an A&W root beer stand after spending the afternoon and early evening driving aimlessly around the lake in his small hometown, he sees a "slim, hipless young carhop" (150) who initially ignores him when he hits his car's horn to gain her attention. When Norman leans on the horn, the young girl walks over to his window, asks "You blind?" (151), and points to the intercom over which Norman is supposed to place his order. This incident illustrates Norman's inability to fit in after his return from the war as well as the cruel indifference that his fellow townspeople feel toward Norman's troubles.

Cross, Jimmy   A 24-year-old first lieutenant from New Jersey, Jimmy Cross is the commander of the fictional ALPHA COMPANY platoon whose members include Tim O'Brien, Rat Kiley, Henry Dobbins, Mitchell Sanders, Kiowa, and others. During his sophomore year at MOUNT SEBASTIAN COL-LEGE, Cross had signed up for the Reserve Officer Training Corps in preference to being drafted (*see* DRAFT). But Cross is essentially uninterested in the war, has no desire to command, and feels unprepared once he is in Vietnam. He spends his days dreaming about a girl named Martha, whom he loves, but who was not exactly his girlfriend back at college in New Jersey. Cross feels great guilt for the deaths that occur under his command, especially those of Ted Lavender and Kiowa. After Lavender's death, he resolves to be a better officer and to follow strict military regulations. After Kiowa's death, Cross composes in his head letters home to Kiowa's father in which he accepts full responsibility for stationing his men in the muddy field next to the SONG TRA BONG RIVER, indefensible ground. Cross is one of the few characters readers see after the war. He comes to visit the narrator O'Brien at his home in Massachusetts many years after the war has ended and tells a story about meeting Martha again at a 1979 college reunion. When O'Brien suggests writing a story about Jimmy Cross and Martha, Cross agrees, but requests that his friend not mention something which is never named, leading readers to believe that there is still much left unsaid in this collection, that the war holds secrets that cannot perhaps ever be fully communicated.

Dentist When an unnamed army dentist, "a tall, skinny young captain with bad breath" (87), is choppered into CHU LAI to check the men's teeth and do minor repair work, Curt Lemon, terrified of dentists, faints in the examination chair before even opening his mouth. Later that night, Lemon will wake up the sleeping dentist in his tent and demand that the captain remove a perfectly good tooth.

Diamond, Eddie Eddie Diamond is the highest ranking noncommissioned officer at the medical detachment in the mountains west of CHU LAI in the story "Sweetheart of the Song Tra Bong." O'Brien writes that Eddie's "pleasures ran from dope to Darvon" and that, as a result, "there was no such thing as military discipline" (91) in this particular unit. Eddie Diamond is the soldier who first brings up the possibility of bringing women into the camp, suggesting that the men pool their money in order to import "a few mama-sans from Saigon" (93). This half-joking suggestion will lead to Mark Fossie's very real determination to bring his high school girlfriend, Mary Anne Bell, to Vietnam. Later, when Rat Kiley runs into Eddie Diamond on R&R (rest and rehabilitation) in Bangkok, Diamond fills Rat in on the end to Mary Anne's story—her disappearance into the surrounding mountains.

Dobbins, Henry Henry Dobbins is a soldier in ALPHA COMPANY. A big man, he carries extra rations and is assigned duty as a machine gunner, carrying the squad's large M-60 weapon. As a good-luck charm, Dobbins wears a pair of panty hose tied around his neck, sent to him by his girlfriend back home. When she breaks up with him, Dobbins claims that the magic protection contained in the panty hose still works, and he continues to wear them. Described as a "good man" and a "superb soldier," but as not "sophisticated" (117), Dobbins as a boy had considered becoming a minister since he is interested in being nice to people, in treating others decently. However, as he tells Kiowa, he decided that he was not smart enough for such a position. More sympathetic to the Vietnamese than some of the other soldiers, Dobbins bonds with two Vietnamese monks who live in a nearly abandoned pagoda where Alpha Company sets up camp temporarily, and he becomes angry at Azar for mocking a young girl whose family has been killed.

Dobbins's Girlfriend The ALPHA COMPANY soldier Henry Dobbins has a girlfriend back home who sends him a pair of panty hose to wear around his neck as a good-luck charm. Even when the girlfriend breaks up with him, Dobbins superstitiously continues to wear her panty hose.

Fat Bird Colonel In Mitchell Sanders's story about a six-man patrol that hears eerie, strange noises while on patrol in the mountains, an officer described as a "fat bird colonel" (75) calls the men in after they return to camp and questions their decision to call in an air strike. As Sanders explains, "I mean, they spent six trillion dollars on firepower, and this fatass colonel wants answers, he wants to know what the fuckin' story is" (75). But all the men in the patrol can do is stare silently back at the colonel, dumbfounded by his lack of understanding. Sanders relates this tale in "How to Tell a True War Story."

Fossie, Mark Mark Fossie is a young medic stationed with Rat Kiley in a small detachment outside of CHU LAI before Rat joins the other soldiers of ALPHA COMPANY. In the story "Sweetheart of the Song Tra Bong," Rat relates the tale of Mark Fossie arranging for his high school girlfriend, a young, tall blonde named Mary Anne Bell, to come to Vietnam. Mary Anne and Mark have been sweethearts since grammar school. They plan to be married and "live in a fine gingerbread house near Lake Erie, and have three healthy yellow-haired children, and grow old together . . ." (94). These plans are interrupted, however, by the war. Once in Vietnam, Mary Anne soon sheds her girlish innocence, learning to assist during medical operations, to assemble and use weapons, and to cook rice over a can of Sterno. When Mary Anne does not return to the bunker she shares with Mark one night, he discovers the next day that she had been out on ambush with a group of six GREEN BERETS who lived on the perimeter of the medical camp. Although Mark and Mary Anne temporarily make up, she soon disappears again, out on patrol with the Greenies for three weeks. Mark Fossie is so overwhelmed by grief during this time that he is unable to function. Mark's last communication with his former sweetheart occurs after her return to the camp, when he goes to the Greenie's bunker one night and finds Mary Anne singing in an eerie, high-pitched voice and wearing a necklace of human tongues. The story is a study in the transgression of traditional gender roles as Mark seems increasingly young, naïve, and helpless in the face of Mary Anne's hardening.

Four Soldiers and Grenade In "How to Tell a True War Story," the narrator Tim O'Brien relates a story that "we've all heard" before: "Four guys go down a trail. A grenade sails out. One guy jumps on it and takes the blast and saves his three buddies" (83). While O'Brien says that such an event may have actually happened, he adds that this tale does not have the ring of a true story. He then revises the tale, to go like this: "Four guys go down a trail. A grenade sails out. One guy jumps on it and takes the blast, but it's a killer grenade and everybody dies anyway. Before they die, though, one of the dead guys says, 'The fuck you do *that* for?' and the jumper says, 'Story of my life, man,' and the other guy starts to smile but he's dead" (84). O'Brien

claims that this version is "a true story that never happened" (84). This story is more truthful than the previous version because it expresses the emotional truth of war—the irony and futility and dark humor of the Vietnam experience.

Four Workmen In the story "Speaking of Courage," Norman Bowker, as he aimlessly drives around the lake in his Iowa hometown, sees four city workmen laboring to set up a platform that will be used for that evening's fireworks display. The men, "dressed alike in khaki trousers, work shirts, visored caps, and brown boots" (144), are oblivious to Norman, even though the young veteran imagines telling the four men about the SILVER STAR he almost won.

Gustafson, Sally Kramer Sally Kramer Gustafson is an old girlfriend of Norman Bowker's who appears in the story "Speaking of Courage." As Norman is driving around and around the lake in his hometown on the Fourth of July after returning home from the Vietnam War, he remembers driving around the same lake with Sally Kramer back in high school. In the story's present time, however, Sally Kramer has married and become Sally Gustafson, and she lives "in a pleasant blue house on the less expensive side of the lake road" (139). Norman had seen her out mowing the lawn on his third day home from the war. As he aimlessly drives, Norman imagines himself speaking to Sally Gustafson, explaining Kiowa's death to her. When he mentions the *shitfield,* Norman imagines Sally closing her eyes and asking him not "to use that word" (145). "Clearly," Norman concludes, "this was not a story for Sally Kramer" (146).

Harris, Stink At the end of "How to Tell a True War Story," the narrator Tim O'Brien claims that the story he had just told, about Curt Lemon, Rat Kiley, and the death of a baby water buffalo, was entirely invented from start to finish. Then he adds that even if it did happen it took place not in the mountains but in a village on the BATANGAN PENINSULA, when it was "raining like crazy" one night, and "a guy named Stink Harris woke up screaming with a leech on his tongue" (85). While this is the only mention of the character in *The Things They Carried,* Stink Harris is a prominent figure in O'Brien's earlier novel *Going After Cacciato.*

Jensen, Dave One of the soldiers in ALPHA COMPANY, Dave Jensen is noted for practicing field hygiene. He carries with him a toothbrush, dental floss, and several bars of soap. He also carries night-sight vitamin tablets that are high in carotene. In the story "Enemies," Dave Jensen gets into a fistfight with fellow soldier Lee Strunk, breaking the other man's nose. Tired of living in fear about Strunk's eventual retribution, Jensen uses a pistol like a hammer to break his own nose, then shows Strunk what he has done, asking if everything is now square between them. In "Friends," Jensen and Strunk have declared a truce, each agreeing to shoot the other if one of them should suffer a terrible injury. But when Lee Strunk steps on a mine and blows off his leg, he begs Jensen not to shoot him. Although Jensen swears he will not kill Strunk, the injured man dies in the evacuation helicopter on the way to the hospital.

Jorgenson, Bobby Bobby Jorgenson is a young medic who replaces Rat Kiley in ALPHA COMPANY after Rat shoots himself in the foot and is sent to Japan to recuperate. When the narrator Tim O'Brien is shot for the second time during the war along the SONG TRA BONG RIVER, Jorgenson, green and scared, takes 10 minutes to "work up the nerve to crawl over" (190) and treat the injured soldier, neglecting as well to notice that O'Brien is suffering from shock. Infuriated and humiliated by his injury—he has been shot "in the butt" (190)—O'Brien develops a strong hatred for Jorgenson, whose incompetence nearly killed him. After he is rotated to the rear, O'Brien becomes obsessed with gaining revenge on the medic. When the men of Alpha Company rotate into the Landing Zone for a stand-down, O'Brien is dismayed to discover that Jorgenson has become part of the group now, while he, O'Brien, feels distanced by his former comrades. Subsequently, no one will help him with his plan to terrorize Jorgenson when the medic is on night guard duty, save for the brutal Azar, whom O'Brien has trouble

reining in. O'Brien is ashamed after spooking Jorgenson during the night, largely because the medic reacts "quietly, almost with dignity" (216) to the terror campaign and shakes hands with his antagonist when the ordeal is over, asking if the two men are "even now" (217).

Kiley, Rat Bob "Rat" Kiley is the medic for ALPHA COMPANY. Along with his weapons and medical equipment, Rat carries comic books into the field as well as brandy and M&M candies for especially bad wounds. In "How to Tell a True War Story," Rat's best friend in Vietnam, Curt Lemon, is killed by stepping on a booby-trapped 105 mortar round while the two soldiers are simply "goofing" around (83). After the death, Rat writes a letter to Curt's sister, explaining his love and respect for Curt. When the sister never writes back, Rat refers to her obscenely as a "dumb cooze" (68). Later, Rat will lead the men of Alpha Company in shooting to death a baby water buffalo, driven to the act by grief and anger over the loss of his friend. Rat Kiley also figures prominently in "Sweetheart of the Song Tra Bong," a story that he narrates to O'Brien, insisting that he witnessed the events he describes first hand. At the end of the story, Rat confesses to loving Mary Anne Bell, the high school girl whom soldier Mark Fossie had arranged to bring to Vietnam, because, unlike other girls back home, Mary Anne would be able to understand what the war was like and what the men went through. In "Ghost Soldiers," readers discover that Rat, unlike the new Alpha Company medic, Bobby Jorgenson, was a courageous soldier who calmly risked his life to check on and attend to O'Brien the first time he was shot in the field, using humor and skill to ease O'Brien's pain. However, Rat's job finally exacts an unbearable toll on him. Increasingly paranoid and beginning to imagine bugs crawling on him and to visualize his friends as simply body parts, Rat shoots himself in the foot to avoid further service, an act detailed in the collection's penultimate story, "Night Life." As O'Brien explains, none of the men of Alpha Company blame Rat for his decision. They send him off to the hospital in Japan, promising to vouch that Rat's injury was accidental.

Kindly Older Woman At the end of "How to Tell a True War Story," the narrator Tim O'Brien explains that he will often tell the story of Curt Lemon, Rat Kiley, and the death of the baby water buffalo during speaking engagements. Now and then, when he tells the story, he reports, someone will come up to him afterward to say she liked it. O'Brien writes that this person is "always a woman," adding that, "Usually it's an older woman of kindly temperament and humane politics" (84). The woman will explain that she hates war stories but that she liked the story about the poor baby buffalo. Then she will suggest, much as O'Brien's daughter, Kathleen, had suggested earlier, that he stop writing war stories, that he find new stories to tell. O'Brien reports that in response he will picture Rat Kiley's face and think, "You dumb cooze" (85). The woman, he explains, was not listening: "It *wasn't* a war story. It was a *love* story" (85). While this incident may be off-putting to readers, who have most likely been reading the story as a war story as well (and whose title implies that the story is meant to be taken that way), it nevertheless highlights the difficulty of communicating the trauma of war. True war stories are not easy to tell, nor are they easy to listen to. In many ways this incident explains O'Brien's methodology in the book as a whole: He must patiently keep telling and retelling stories, adding and subtracting details, "making up a few things to get at the real truth" (85). The moral of this story, then, might be "just listen" (77), the same moral that Mitchell Sanders claims for the tale of the six-man patrol in the mountains, the story within a story.

Kiowa Kiowa is a Native American soldier in ALPHA COMPANY who comes from Oklahoma City. In the field, he carries with him a New Testament given to him by his father as well as his grandmother's distrust of the white man and his grandfather's old hunting hatchet. He wears moccasins so that he can walk silently when on ambush. A kind and decent young man who is a good friend to the narrator O'Brien, comforting him when he kills a young Vietnamese soldier with a hand grenade and praising him for not mocking death by shaking hands with the dead Vietnamese man early in

his tour of duty, Kiowa dies an undignified death in a muddy field when Alpha Company is camped alongside the SONG TRA BONG River one murky night. Several men claim responsibility for Kiowa's death. Norman Bowker imagines telling his father the story of Kiowa getting shot and sinking into the muck, with Norman letting go of his friend's boot at the last moment, unable to pull Kiowa out of the dark swampy field. The story "In the Field" retells the story of Kiowa's death, this time with responsibility lying on the shoulders of a young, unnamed soldier who seems to be the narrator O'Brien himself. This young soldier believes that he is responsible for drawing enemy fire when he turned on his flashlight to show Kiowa a picture of his girlfriend from back home. In this version of the story, it is the young soldier who takes hold of Kiowa's boot but is unable to pull him from the bubbling mud. Lieutenant Jimmy Cross feels responsible for the death as well, having made the decision that the men camp for the night in the muddy field, which served as the village toilet.

Kiowa's Father The father of Kiowa, the young Native American soldier who dies after sinking into a muddy field alongside the SONG TRA BONG RIVER, is a Baptist Sunday school teacher in Oklahoma City, Oklahoma, who gives his son an illustrated version of the New Testament to carry with him in Vietnam. After Kiowa's death, Lieutenant Jimmy Cross composes in his head several versions of a letter that he plans to write to Kiowa's father. In the first version, Cross imagines leaving out the specific details of Kiowa's death, telling the father only what a fine soldier and fine human human being Kiowa had been. In the second version, Cross imagines apologizing to Kiowa's father and taking full responsibility for his son's death. The third imaginary letter that Cross composes has an impersonal tone as he simply informs Kiowa's father of the death, without apology, but explaining it simply as a freak accident. Readers never discover whether or not Cross actually writes or mails any of these letters to Kiowa's father.

Kiowa's Grandfather One of the items that the Native American soldier Kiowa carries in Vietnam with him is an old hunting hatchet that had belonged to his grandfather. The weapon contrasts with the illustrated New Testament given Kiowa by his father.

Kiowa's Grandmother   As "a hedge against bad times," the Native American soldier Kiowa is also said to carry with him in the field his grandmother's "distrust of the white man" (3). This distrust reminds readers that although Kiowa is a devout Baptist whom his fellow soldiers in ALPHA COMPANY respect and admire, he is also a member of an oppressed minority back in the United States and has good reason to be suspicious of the very government whose army he is fighting in.

Lavender, Ted   Ted Lavender is a soldier in ALPHA COMPANY who is shot in the head by a sniper in the book's opening story, "The Things They Carried." Known for carrying tranquilizers because he was scared, Lavender would "give a soft, spacey smile" to men who asked him how the war was going and reply, "Mellow, man. We got ourselves a nice mellow war today" (33). After Lavender's death, the men ease their pain and fright by joking that Lavender's mind was blown because of the tranquilizers. "There's a moral here," Mitchell Sanders says, "Stay away from drugs. No joke. They'll ruin your day every time" (20).

Lemon, Curt   Curt Lemon is an African-American soldier in ALPHA COMPANY who is good friends with the medic Rat Kiley. He figures most prominently in "How to Tell a True War Story," which details Lemon's death from stepping on a booby-trapped 105 mortar round while he is playfully tossing smoke grenades back and forth with Rat. Lemon's body is blown up into a tree, and Tim O'Brien is one of the soldiers assigned to climb up and retrieve the parts. O'Brien specifically remembers Dave Jensen singing "LEMON TREE" as the men throw down the body parts. After Lemon's death, Rat Kiley writes a letter to his friend's sister, expressing his love and respect for Curt. But the sister, perhaps frightened by the violence hinted at throughout the letter, never writes back. One story that Rat relates in the letter and that gets retold

in the book's final story, "The Lives of the Dead," depicts Curt trick-or-treating in a Vietnamese village, wearing only a ghost mask, body paint, and his combat boots, but armed with an M-16 rifle. Rat tells of Curt stripping the pajamas from a "cute little mama-san" in the village (239–240), suggesting that a rape might have occurred. Curt is also the central figure in the story "The Dentist." Terrified of getting his teeth checked after having had bad experiences with dentists in high school, Lemon faints in the chair before the examination begins. Later that night, mortified by his earlier behavior, Curt wakes up the dentist, who is sleeping in his tent, and demands that the man remove a perfectly good tooth. O'Brien has stated that Curt Lemon is based partially on ALVIN "CHIP" MERRICKS, a real-life friend of his from Alpha Company, who was killed by a rigged artillery round in May 1969.

Lemon's Sister   After Curt Lemon's death, the medic Rat Kiley writes a long, heartfelt letter home to the dead soldier's sister, explaining what a "great, great guy" (67) Curt was. He tells the sister about the good times he and Curt had together, "lighting up villes and bringing smoke to bear every which way," using a crate of hand grenades to blow up "gook fish," and going trick-or-treating in a Vietnamese village "almost stark naked" (68). When the sister never writes back, readers should not be surprised, especially since Rat claims to be just like Curt and promises to look the sister up when the war is over. Rat, however, fails to see the effect his violent letter might have on a woman back home, and he calls Curt's sister a "dumb cooze" (68) for failing to respond.

Linda   Linda was the nine-year-old girlfriend of the narrator Tim O'Brien when he was a boy in fourth grade in WORTHINGTON, MINNESOTA. She appears in the story "The Lives of the Dead," which details her death from a brain tumor and the young Tim's willful dreaming that she is alive again. Linda comes to Tim and reassures him that being dead is not that bad—it is like "being inside a book that nobody's reading" (245), she explains. O'Brien's relationship with Linda sets the tone for his later war experiences. When he does not step in to help Linda after the bully Nick Veenhof pulls off the stocking cap she wears to hide her baldness, O'Brien worries about being a coward, writing that, "twelve years later, when Vietnam presented much harder choices, some practice at being brave might've helped a little" (234). This earlier experience with death also forecasts the deaths O'Brien will witness in Vietnam; he comments specifically that the old Vietnamese man found lying dead in a pigpen on his fourth day at the war reminds him of Linda. Finally, it is his experience with Linda that leads O'Brien into becoming a storyteller. In order to perform the miracle of making Linda alive again, O'Brien says that he began "to practice the magic of stories" (244), a skill he will use in the book to bring fellow soldiers such as Curt Lemon and Kiowa alive again as well. In his personal papers, housed at the Harry Ransom Humanities Research Center at the University of Texas, O'Brien confirms that the character of Linda is based on LORNA LUE MOELLER, an actual fourth-grade classmate of his in Worthington, Minnesota, who died of a brain tumor on September 11, 1956, when she was 10 years old.

Man in Motorboat In the story "Speaking of Courage," Norman Bowker, as he drives aimlessly around and around the central lake in his small, midwestern hometown, sees a man in a stalled motorboat in the middle of the lake. The man is "bent over the engine with a wrench and a frown" (140). Norman will continue to see this man several more times as he continues his circuits around the lake.

Martha Martha is a friend of First Lieutenant Jimmy Cross and a junior at MOUNT SEBASTIAN COLLEGE in New Jersey. An English major, Martha writes Jimmy letters about her love of Chaucer and Virginia Woolf. She also sends him a pebble that she found on the Jersey Shore, at the point where the water meets the land. Cross carries the pebble in his mouth as a good-luck charm. While Jimmy Cross is deeply in love with Martha, the young woman seems less sure of the relationship, holding herself distant and aloof. After the death of Ted Lavender, Cross burns the pictures Martha had

sent him, resolving to no longer daydream about her. Readers meet Martha again in the collection's second story, "Love," when Cross tells the narrator O'Brien about running into her at a college reunion in 1979. Martha had become a nurse after graduation, had worked as a Lutheran missionary in Ethiopia, Guatemala, and Mexico, but had never married. While she reacts negatively to Cross's confession that he had wanted to tie her up in college and stroke her kneecap all night long, Cross still maintains that he loves Martha even after so many years have passed.

Nurse in Danang In a story that O'Brien remembers and recounts in the chapter "Spin," an AWOL soldier "shacks up in Danang" (35) with a Red Cross nurse. Although the relationship is great—the nurse is said to love the soldier "to death" (35)—he eventually leaves her to rejoin his buddies in the bush, unable to handle the pleasures of peacetime.

O'Brien, Kathleen Kathleen O'Brien is the narrator Tim O'Brien's 10-year-old daughter. A completely fictional character—the real-life author Tim O'Brien had no children when the book was published in 1990—Kathleen tells her father that he is obsessed with the war and that instead of writing war stories he should write about "a little girl who finds a million dollars and spends it all on a Shetland pony" (34). Kathleen appears again at the end of "On the Rainy River." Even though she has not yet been born, O'Brien imagines Kathleen among the group of friends and family waving to him from the other side of the river. In the story "Ambush," O'Brien recounts how when she was nine Kathleen had asked him whether or not he killed anyone during the war. O'Brien confesses that he could respond either "yes" or "no" to his daughter's question, and that both would be honest answers since he is "left with faceless responsibility and faceless grief" (180) after the war. Kathleen appears most prominently in the story "Field Trip," in which O'Brien recounts a return trip he made with his daughter to Vietnam, to visit some of the places that had haunted his memory since the war, especially the muddy field where his friend Kiowa had died. Unable to understand exactly what is happening, Kathleen watches, puzzled, as her father wades into the shallow, muddy SONG TRA BONG and wedges a pair of Kiowa's old moccasins into the muck at the bottom of the river.

O'Brien, Tim   Tim O'Brien is the 43-year-old writer and former Vietnam soldier who narrates *The Things They Carried*. Although he shares much biographical information with the actual author of the book, including his name; his hometown of WORTHINGTON, MINNESOTA; his experience being drafted into the war in the summer of 1968 after graduating from college; and his career as a writer who has published a novel called *Going After Cacciato*, this narrator should nevertheless not be mistaken for the author O'Brien. In interviews author O'Brien insists that narrator O'Brien is a fictional character, pointing out that he himself never had a daughter named Kathleen, that he never worked at an ARMOUR MEATS plant, and that in reality he can remember little of his wartime experiences. Naming the book's narrator after himself, however, allows O'Brien to cement some of the book's main themes: the tenuous line between fiction and history, between the real and the imagined, and the difficulty of getting at truth. In this book, "truth" is shown to be multiple and various, with invented stories sometimes expressing more truth than actual historical events, a difference O'Brien emphasizes when he writes that "story-truth is truer sometimes than happening truth" (179). The narrator O'Brien presents himself as a thoughtful young man who opposed the war in principle but who could not bring himself to flee the DRAFT because of the shame and ostracism that would result. He feels tremendous guilt for his time in Vietnam, blaming himself for the death of a delicate young Vietnamese soldier as well as for his best friend, Kiowa, who drowns in a muddy field. During his tour of duty, O'Brien is shot twice. He is sent to a job in the rear after the second shooting, where he plots revenge on the incompetent medic who failed to treat him for shock. The narrator describes himself as changing during his time in Vietnam, as growing mean and cold inside. He concludes by telling a story about his deep love as a nine-year-old boy for a girl named Linda who died of a brain tumor. While death is inescapable, whether in war or in ordinary life, stories, O'Brien concludes, are his way of trying to save his own life, to preserve the self that used to be.

O'Brien's Brother, Sister, Aunts, Uncles, and Grandfather   The narrator Tim O'Brien tells readers that his brother and sister, all of his aunts and uncles, and his grandfather, along with all the townspeople of WORTHINGTON, MINNESOTA, appear in his vision of crowds waving and cheering from the riverbank at the end of "On the Rainy River." This is the only place in the book where these relatives are mentioned.

O'Brien's Father and Mother   The first time that the narrator Tim O'Brien mentions his father and mother occurs in the story "On the Rainy River." Mr. and Mrs. O'Brien are quietly having lunch when Tim receives his DRAFT notice in the mail, and his world irrevocably changes. Later in the same story, O'Brien imagines what it would be like if he fled to Canada to escape the draft. He pictures his father's eyes as he tries to explain his decision over the telephone and imagines hearing the voices of both parents. The O'Briens make another appearance in the book's final story, "The Lives of the Dead," in which they take nine-year-old Tim and his young girlfriend, Linda, to the movies to see a WORLD WAR II feature called *THE MAN WHO NEVER WAS*. Later, Tim's mother will explain to her young son about Linda's brain tumor, and his father will take the boy to the funeral home to see Linda's body after she has died.

O'Brien's Sons   In his vision of crowds waving at him from the Canadian shore at the end of "On the Rainy River," the narrator Tim O'Brien includes a description of his "two sons" who "hopped up and down" (59). These sons are not mentioned anywhere else in the book, unlike the narrator's daughter, Kathleen, who plays a significant role in several stories.

O'Brien's Wife   While she is never given a name or described in any detail in the book, readers know that the narrator Tim O'Brien is married. At the beginning of the story "On the Rainy River," he confesses that this is one story he has never told before, not even to his wife. Later in the story, his wife, presumably Kathleen's mother, will appear in O'Brien's vision of family, friends, historical figures, and fictional characters waving and cheering for him along the banks of the RAINY RIVER.

Phillips, Morty   Morty Phillips is a soldier in ALPHA COMPANY who makes a brief appearance in the story "Ghost Soldiers" when Norman Bowker tells about how the young man used up his luck. Morty had disappeared from his platoon to go by himself for a swim in the dangerous area surrounding MY KHE one day, worrying his fellow soldiers tremendously, only to reappear at nightfall, alive and soaking wet. Yet, several days later, Morty comes down with a serious, disabling disease contracted from his surreptitious swim. The men of Alpha Company deem Morty a fool for using up his luck on a lark and see the disease he contracts as reasonable retribution.

Radio Announcer   As Norman Bowker drives around the lake in his small Iowa hometown in the story "Speaking of Courage," he listens to a tired announcer on the radio who periodically reports on the time and temperature and cautions drivers to be careful on this Fourth of July.

Sanders, Mitchell   Mitchell Sanders is the radio operator for ALPHA COMPANY. In the field, he carries condoms and brass knuckles along with the heavy PRC-25 radio and his standard weapons and gear. Sanders is known for drawing morals out of nearly every situation the soldiers encounter, joking that the moral of Ted Lavender's death is to stay away from drugs. In the story "Spin," Sanders is depicted picking lice off his body and depositing them in an envelope that he addresses to his DRAFT board back home in Ohio. Mitchell Sanders is also a storyteller who in "How to Tell a True War Story" relates the tale of a six-man platoon that goes up into the mountains west of CHU LAI and hears spooky, uncanny noises all night long, then calls in an air raid on the landscape itself. The

moral of that story, Sanders says, is "just listen" (77). Even though Sanders admits to inventing certain elements of the tale, the narrator O'Brien understands that he does this in order to make his listener "feel the truth, to believe by the raw force of feeling" (74). Later, in "Sweetheart of the Song Tra Bong," Mitchell Sanders becomes angry when Rat Kiley deviates from the rules of proper storytelling, insisting that Rat must provide a satisfying ending for his story about Mary Anne Bell.

Six Green Berets   In "Sweetheart of the Song Tra Bong," six GREEN BERETS live in a HOOTCH on the perimeter of the medical detachment where Rat Kiley is assigned in the mountains west of CHU LAI. These Greenies are secretive men who disappear for days or weeks at a time on mysterious missions in the jungle. Mary Anne Bell, the initially sweet and innocent high school girl whom Mark Fossie arranges to transport to Vietnam, eventually begins to spend time with these soldiers, even going out on ambush with them. One night Fossie discovers Mary Anne in the Greenies' tent, singing in a weird, high voice and wearing a necklace of human tongues. The tent itself is like an animal's den, emitting a raw, wild smell of moldering flesh, containing stacks of bones, and boasting a neat sign propped against a wall, which reads: "ASSEMBLE YOUR OWN GOOK!! FREE SAMPLE KIT!!" (110).

Six-Man Patrol   In "How to Tell a True War Story," Mitchell Sanders relates a tale about a six-man patrol sent into the mountains west of QUANG NAI PROVINCE on what was supposed to be a "basic listening-post operation" (72) in which the men were simply to lie low and listen for enemy movement. However, alone in the eerie landscape, the men begin to hear strange, inexplicable noises, including strange music, the murmurings and clinking glasses of a cocktail party, and even an entire glee club singing in the dark. Terrified, the men call in an air strike on the landscape itself, leaving the mountains and trees scorched and smoking. When the men arrive back in camp, a colonel asks them what happened out there, but all the men in the patrol can do is stare silently back at him, amazed at his lack of understanding. At the end of this tale, Sanders confesses to the narrator Tim O'Brien that he made up some of the details in the story in order to give him the real feel of what the experience was like for the men. The moral of the story, Sanders adds, is "just listen" (77).

Slim, Young, Dead Vietnamese Soldier In the story "The Man I Killed," the narrator Tim O'Brien recounts the death of a "slim . . . dainty young man," a Vietnamese soldier of about 20, who is killed when O'Brien throws a hand grenade at him along a trail while the American soldiers are lying in ambush. Feeling tremendous guilt over the death, O'Brien invents a history for the soldier, imagining that he was a mathematics student, a serious scholar who abhorred the war, but who was forced to participate in it by family and cultural expectations. The image of this dead young soldier, a starlike wound where his eye should have been, will recur throughout the book. He will even appear among the friends, family, historical figures, and imaginary characters who congregate on the bank of the RAINY RIVER to wave and cheer at O'Brien as he contemplates fleeing the DRAFT. Talking with his daughter, Kathleen, in later stories, particularly "Ambush" and "Good Form," O'Brien will raise doubts about whether he actually killed the man, telling readers that he could answer honestly either yes or no to his daughter's question about whether he had killed anyone during the war. His point, though, is that he is left with feelings of responsibility and grief no matter what the happening-truth of the event might have been.

Slim Young Soldier's Father and Uncles In the invented history that the narrator Tim O'Brien makes up for the slim, young Vietnamese soldier he kills with a hand grenade, the man's father and uncles had joined the struggle for Vietnamese independence from the French following WORLD WAR II. Their brave deeds in battle resonate in family stories, and the young man feels pressured to become a soldier during the American war as his family members had been before him.

Slim Young Soldier's Mother While Tim O'Brien imagines that the slim young Vietnamese

soldier in "The Man I Killed" was pressured into battle by his father and uncles, he speculates that the frightened young man's mother prayed with him that the war might end soon—that it might not take her son from his family and village, from his university studies in mathematics.

Slim Young Soldier's Wife In "The Man I Killed," the narrator Tim O'Brien imagines that the delicate young man he kills with a hand grenade had before becoming a soldier fallen in love with a 17-year-old girl, a classmate of his during his final year at university. "One evening, perhaps, they exchanged gold rings," O'Brien speculates, "Now one eye was a star" (129). The war has claimed this peace-loving young scholar, as it had claimed so many of O'Brien's friends and comrades.

Soldier Lying in the Mud Norman Bowker in the story "Speaking of Courage" has returned from the war damaged but unable to speak to anyone in his small Iowa hometown about his disturbing experiences. As he drives around and around the town's central lake one Fourth of July, he imagines telling the story of the night Kiowa died to an unnamed, silent listener. Norman imagines describing the "crazy things he saw" that night. "Like how, at one point he noticed a guy lying next to him in the sludge, completely buried except for his face, and how after a moment the guy rolled his eyes and winked at him" (148). Later, Kiowa will be shot and disappear beneath the filthy mud in the field, Norman unable to pull him out.

Strunk, Lee Lee Strunk is a soldier in ALPHA COMPANY who carries a slingshot into the field with him, which he calls "a weapon of last resort" (7). In the opening story, "The Things They Carried," Strunk is the unfortunate soldier who draws the number 17, indicating that he must search the VIET CONG tunnel the men discover right before Ted Lavender dies. Although Strunk emerges alive from the tunnel, grinning and filthy, Ted Lavender is shot in the head just as Strunk makes a funny ghost sound to mock his own fear at going down the tunnel. Lee Strunk will also figure prominently in the later stories "Enemies" and "Friends." In the first of these, Strunk gets into a fistfight with fellow soldier Dave Jensen, who believes Strunk stole his jackknife. Jensen breaks Strunk's nose in the fight, then lives in fear for many days that Strunk will retaliate. He eventually uses a pistol to hammer his own nose, announcing to Strunk that the two men are now even. At the end of the story, Strunk cannot stop laughing, admitting that he actually did steal Jensen's jackknife. "Friends" depicts the soldiers after they have made up and learned to trust each other. They even make a pact that if one of them should ever be grievously injured, the other will shoot him to end his misery. When Lee Strunk steps on a rigged mortar round, however, which blows off his right leg at the knee, he begs Jensen not to shoot him. Jensen swears he will not, but Strunk dies anyway in the evacuation helicopter on his way back to the field hospital in CHU LAI.

Vietnamese Boy with Plastic Leg The story "Spin" opens with O'Brien asserting that the war "wasn't all terror and violence" (31). In fact, "things could almost get sweet" (31), he argues, then proceeds to tell an anecdote that is anything but "sweet." He remembers a little Vietnamese boy with a plastic leg who asks Azar for a chocolate bar. Azar hands over the candy, and as the child hops away on one leg, he comments, "War's a bitch. . . . One leg, for chrissake. Some poor fucker ran out of ammo" (31).

Veenhof, Nick Nick Veenhof is a fourth-grade classmate of nine-year-old Tim O'Brien who teases Linda for weeks in the story "The Lives of the Dead," trying determinedly to pull off the stocking cap that hides the stitches and scars from her brain surgery. As he recalls this story, O'Brien faults himself for not having been brave enough at the time to stand up to the bully: "I should've stepped in; fourth grade is no excuse. Besides, it doesn't get easier with time, and twelve years later, when Vietnam presented much harder choices, some practice at being brave might've helped a little" (234). When Nick Veenhof finally succeeds in pulling off the cap one day in class, the other students are shocked by the bald whiteness of Linda's skull, marked by patches of grayish brown fuzz where her

hair had begun to grow back, a large Band-Aid at the back of her head, and a row of black stitches. After school that day, Nick Veenhof and O'Brien will gently walk Linda home together. According to a letter written to O'Brien by MARVIS MOELLER in September 1991, Nick Veenhof is based on MIKE TRACY, a real fourth grade classmate of O'Brien's in WORTHINGTON, MINNESOTA. Marvis Moeller was the mother of LORNA LOU MOELLER, a 10-year old Worthington girl who died of a brain tumor in 1956 and the real-life model for Linda in the story.

Vietnamese Dancing Girl In the story "Style," O'Brien recounts the tale of a 14-year-old Vietnamese girl whom the soldiers of ALPHA COMPANY encounter dancing silently in front of her burned-down house in the midst of her smoking village. When the soldiers enter the girl's house, they discover her dead and badly burned family members. The girl continues dancing, her hands over her ears, as the American soldiers drag her dead family members from the house and lay them out on the ground. Later that night, the brutal soldier Azar mimics the girl, crudely moving his body in turns and leaps, until Henry Dobbins grabs him from behind and threatens to throw him into a deep well.

Vietnamese Farmers The narrator Tim O'Brien describes returning to Vietnam with his 10-year-old daughter, Kathleen, many years after the war in the story "Field Trip." When they visit the site of Kiowa's death, they see two old Vietnamese farmers standing in ankle-deep water and repairing the dike where O'Brien and his fellow soldiers had laid out Kiowa's body after pulling him from the muck so many years ago. One of the old men watches as O'Brien wades into the river and sinks Kiowa's moccasins into the mud that lies at the bottom. When Kathleen asks her father whether the old man is mad about the war, O'Brien replies, no, explaining, "All that's finished" (188).

Vietnamese Government Interpreter When the narrator Tim O'Brien and his daughter, Kathleen, travel to Vietnam in the story "Field Trip," they ride in a jeep to the field where O'Brien's friend Kiowa had died, accompanied by a Vietnamese government interpreter who becomes fast friends with Kathleen. The man demonstrates magic tricks for the young girl in the back of the jeep, causing her to giggle while her father is distracted by his memories of the war.

Vietnamese Mine Field Guide In the story "Spin," O'Brien remembers the time that ALPHA COMPANY hired "an old poppa-san" to lead the men through the minefields on the BATANGAN PENINSULA. The old man has a real feel for the land beneath him and is able to keep the men safe as they traverse the dangerous ground. As the soldiers play their "ruthless game of follow the leader" (33), Rat Kiley makes up a rhyme that goes, "Step out of line, hit a mine; follow the dink, you're in the pink" (33). Soon all the soldiers begin chanting along with Rat. When the soldiers part ways with the old man, there is a sad scene. The men of Alpha Company have learned to love him, and the old Vietnamese man has tears in his eyes at the parting. "Follow dink . . . you go pink" (34), he says to each of the soldiers in turn.

Vietnamese Monks In the story "Church," the men of ALPHA COMPANY set up a temporary camp in a nearly abandoned Buddhist pagoda, manned only by a pair of Vietnamese monks. The soldier Henry Dobbins befriends the monks, who do not seem to mind the American soldiers' presence. The two monks obligingly bring the soldiers buckets of water each morning to wash themselves, and they learn to disassemble and clean Dobbins's machine gun for him. While Dobbins speaks to his fellow soldier Kiowa about treating the Vietnamese decently, he is blind to his own condescension when he tells the holy men to "*didi mau*" or "beat it" (122–23) after they are finished performing services for him.

Vietnamese Old Dead Man In "The Lives of the Dead," the narrator O'Brien describes seeing on only his fourth day at the war an old Vietnamese man lying dead and faceup beside a pigpen at the center of a village. O'Brien's fellow soldiers make a joke of the old man's death, going up to the body one-by-one and shaking hands with the dead man, a ritual that O'Brien refuses to participate in. When Kiowa praises O'Brien for having the "guts" not to follow the other soldiers in their disrespect, O'Brien replies, "It wasn't guts. I was scared" (227). He then tells Kiowa that strangely the dead old man reminded him of a girl he used to know back home . . . his "first date" (228). This memory introduces the story of Linda, a nine-year-old girl whom O'Brien loved but who died of a brain tumor.

Vietnamese Old Mama-Sans As Norman Bowker remembers Kiowa's death in the story "Speaking of Courage," he recalls that the men of ALPHA COMPANY bivouacked for the night in a field along the SONG TRA BONG River. As the men prepare to set up camp, "a dozen old mama-sans ran out and started yelling . . . yapping away about how this field was bad news. Number ten, they said. Evil ground. Not a good spot for good GIs" (144–45). Although Lieutenant Jimmy Cross fires off his pistol to shoo the old women away, he will later regret not listening to them since the field turns out to have been used as the village toilet, and Kiowa, after getting shot, sinks to his death in the smelly, filthy muck.

Woman in Pedal Pushers As Norman Bowker drives around the lake in his hometown one Fourth of July, he sees a woman wearing pedal pusher pants casting for bullheads off the municipal docks. As Norman continues to circle the lake aimlessly, he sees the woman several more times, patiently rebaiting her hook as she casts for fish.

Young Boys Hiking In "Speaking of Courage," as Norman Bowker is driving around and around the lake at the center of his small Iowa hometown, he sees two young boys along the road, hiking with knapsacks and toy rifles and canteens. An unsettling reminder of how young men in America play war games, the boys are spotted by Norman several more times during his circuits of the lake as the day slowly fades into dusk. Norman passes the boys for the last time on his 10th turn around the lake.

Young Soldier In the story "In the Field," an unnamed young soldier blames himself for Kiowa's death in the muddy field alongside the SONG TRA BONG River. The soldier had pulled out a picture of his girlfriend, Billie, from back home to show Kiowa. When the boy shone his flashlight on the picture, enemy fire erupted, hitting Kiowa and causing him to sink beneath the bubbling muck where the men were camped. Although this young soldier is never named, readers suspect that he is intended to be a younger version of the narrator Tim O'Brien since he introduces the story in the essay "Notes," which precedes it, by explaining that Norman Bowker "did not experience a failure of nerve that night. He did not freeze up or lose the Silver Star for valor. That part of the story is my own" (161).

FURTHER READING

Calloway, Catherine. "'How to Tell a True War Story': Metafiction in *The Things They Carried*," *Critique: Studies in Contemporary Fiction* 36 (1995): 249–257.

Coffey, Michael. "Tim O'Brien." *Publishers Weekly* 16 February 1990, 60–61.

Farrell, Susan. "Tim O'Brien and Gender: a Defense of *The Things They Carried*," *CEA Critic* 66, no. 1 (2003): 1–21.

Hellmann, John. *American Myth and the Legacy of Vietnam.* New York: Columbia University Press, 1986.

Herzog, Tobey C. *Vietnam War Stories: Innocence Lost.* New York: Routledge, 1992.

Kaplan, Stephen. "The Undying Certainty of the Narrator in Tim O'Brien's *The Things They Carried*," *Critique: Studies in Contemporary Fiction* 35, no. 1 (1993): 43–52.

Lewis, Lloyd. *The Tainted War: Culture and Identity in Vietnam War Narratives.* Westport, Conn.: Greenwood Press, 1985.

McDonough, Christopher Michael. "'Afraid to Admit We Are not Achilles': Facing Hector's Dilemma in Tim O'Brien's *The Things They Carried*," *Classical and Modern Literature* 20, no. 3 (2000): 23–32.

Naparsteck, Martin. "An Interview with Tim O'Brien," *Contemporary Literature* 32, no. 1 (1991): 1–11.

O'Gorman, Farrell. "*The Things They Carried* as Composite Novel," *WLA: War, Literature & the Arts* 10, no. 2 (1998): 289–309.

O'Brien, Tim. Transcript of President's Lecture. Brown University, Providence, R.I. 21 April 1999. Available online. URL: http://www.stg. brown.edu/projects/WritingVietnam/obrien.html. Accessed April 26, 2011.

Shay, Jonathan. *Achilles in Vietnam: Combat Trauma and the Undoing of Character.* New York: Simon & Schuster, 1995.

Smith, Lorrie. "'The Things Men Do': The Gendered Subtext in Tim O'Brien's *Esquire* Stories," *Critique: Studies in Contemporary Fiction* 36 (1994): 16–40.

Vernon, Alex. "Salvation, Storytelling, and Pilgrimage in Tim O'Brien's *The Things They Carried*," *Mosaic* 36, no. 4 (December 2003): 171–188.

Waugh, Patricia. *Metafiction: The Theory and Practice of Self-Conscious Fiction.* New York: Routledge, 1984.

"The Things They Carried" (1986)

First published in *Esquire* magazine in August 1986, "The Things They Carried" was later revised and included as the opening story in the 1990 collection, *The Things They Carried.* The story, which details the guilt felt by an American lieutenant in Vietnam over the accidental death of one of his soldiers, won a 1987 National Magazine Award for fiction and was included in *The Best American Short Stories of the Century,* a collection edited by John Updike.

SYNOPSIS

"The Things They Carried" tells two intertwining stories. The first involves a detailed account of the items that various soldiers in a small platoon in Vietnam carry with them into the field. The list begins with the actual physical objects the men carry—their helmets, ponchos, weaponry, canteens, toiletry items, etc. It then moves on to describe the more personal items carried by each man, including souvenirs, pictures and letters from home, good-luck charms, and similar items. Finally, the story details the intangibles carried by these men at war—their fear, their tough postures, their burdens of responsibility and guilt. Intermingled with the long lists of things that the men carry is the story of the death of Ted Lavender, an ordinary foot soldier who is shot in the head by a sniper after separating briefly from the other men to urinate. Lieutenant Jimmy Cross, who had been daydreaming about Martha, a girl he loves back home, rather than paying strict attention to his men, feels guilty for Lavender's death. After the dead soldier is taken away in a helicopter, the platoon burns down the nearby village of THAN KHE, and Jimmy Cross burns Martha's pictures and letters from home. The story ends with Cross resolving to be a better officer, to follow standard operating procedures (see SOP), and to enforce stricter discipline among his soldiers as they head out to search more villages.

COMMENTARY

The story "The Things They Carried" is about the weight of burdens that press on soldiers in the field and how they handle those burdens. O'Brien's genius in much of his fiction is his ability to take a large, metaphorical idea and render it in the most literal and simple of terms. In *Going After Cacciato*, for instance, he handles the theme of desertion, of fleeing the war, by having a character simply and literally walk away. Similarly, he takes all the messiness and dirtiness of the war, the metaphorical quagmire that involvement in Vietnam meant to the United States, and reduces it to the literal shitfield that Kiowa disappears into in the stories "Speaking of Courage" and "In the Field," which will appear in the novel version of *The Things They Carried*. In the story of Ted Lavender's death, O'Brien makes a similar move, compressing the psychological, emotional, political, and historical burdens carried by U.S. soldiers in Vietnam into the literal image of a soldier weighed down by more physical items than he can possibly carry.

The very specific, realistic lists of the items the men actually carry on patrol with them, whose weight is enumerated to the ounce, certainly work to create the impression of a literal heaviness. These lists affect the reader deeply because they add item to item, adding up to nearly unimaginable physical burdens that the men bear. But the heaviness felt by these soldiers is emphasized in other ways as well. Kiowa's description of Lavender's death, for instance, with his repeated insistence on the dead weight of the soldier's body—he says that the death was like "watching a rock fall, or a big sandbag or something . . . just boom, then down" (78)—adds to the overall feel of heaviness affecting these soldiers, as does the structure of the story itself. Ted Lavender's death is told about in increments, more details dribbled out each time it is returned to, again creating the illusion of weightiness through an accretion of detail and emphasizing the burden of guilt that Lieutenant Jimmy Cross feels for Lavender's loss. And it is the emotional burdens, such as Cross's guilt, that weigh most heavily on the men depicted in the story.

The weightiest of these emotions involve fear and shame. As O'Brien writes:

> The men carried all the emotional baggage of men who might die. Grief, terror, love, longing—these were intangibles, but the intangibles had their own mass and specific gravity, they had tangible weight. They carried shameful memories. They carried the common secret of cowardice barely restrained. (81)

The men in Jimmy Cross's platoon are weighed down by expectations of how soldiers at war will behave. They feel they must hide their fear even though it will inevitably erupt at certain times in incidents of crying, screaming, twitching, shooting off rifles uncontrollably, and making rash promises to God. But the one thing that keeps the soldiers marching, or HUMPING, despite their fear of death is the burden of a worse fear that each carries with him—the fear of being thought a coward by the other men. The story's narrator marvels at why the men endure, why they do not simply fall to the ground and refuse to move. Ironically, he concludes that it is not courage that keeps the men going: "Rather, they were too frightened to be cowards" (81). O'Brien dismantles traditional notions of bravery and cowardice here, showing how the two behaviors are more closely related than might initially be suspected.

Jimmy Cross's own emotional burden is complicated by the love he feels for Martha and the guilt he feels for Lavender's death. His love is described as heavy and complex. He understands that Martha has other boyfriends and that she does not return his feelings. But he imagines his own "dense, crushing love" (79) as burying the two of them alive under its weight. His constant speculation about whether or not Martha is a virgin suggests his longing for purity, for an innocence that he feels he no longer has since his war experiences. After all, as the commanding officer of this platoon, Cross must be the one that orders the burning of the village of THAN KHE in revenge for Lavender's death. Cross has seen and done bad things in the war, things that he believes Martha, who "belonged elsewhere" (81) could not possibly understand. To further complicate matters, he is daydreaming about Martha when Lavender is shot in the head. But readers should understand that Lavender's death was a random, unpredictable event that could not be prevented. It was much more likely that Lee Strunk would have been shot in the underground tunnel than it was for a sniper to attack Lavender so unexpectedly. While Cross's guilt may be unjustified—there was nothing he could have done to prevent Lavender's death—it can nevertheless be read as an attempt to attain control in a situation where he feels helpless. If Cross did something wrong to contribute to Lavender's death, there exists a possibility that he can change his behavior and prevent future deaths. Cross's blaming himself allows him to retain the illusion of control in the chaotic and often random world of war that he finds himself in.

The men in Cross's platoon try to shake off the heaviness of their lives through dreams of flight, particularly through fantasies of the airplanes that will take them home, away from the war. But like Cross, they also try as hard as they can to gain control over their circumstances. One way they do this is by posing as the tough soldiers they are expected to be: "Some carried themselves with a sort of wistful resignation, others with pride or stiff soldierly discipline or good humor or macho zeal. They were afraid of dying but they were even more afraid to show it" (80). Another way the men try to exert control is through the language they use and the jokes they tell. In an attempt to destroy the reality of death, they call it by other names, using a "hard vocabulary to contain the terrible softness"

(80) of death: *greased, offed, lit up, zapped while zipping*. They tell jokes about Lavender, feeling as if they are actors in movies, reciting lines from a script in which the emotional tone is that of "irony mixed with tragedy" (80). In this way, they are able to cope with the death they witness and make it through each day.

Jimmy Cross's final resolutions at the end of the story also have the air of a movie script about them. He determines that he will become the kind of strong, tough officer respected by his men whom he might have seen in war movies growing up. A new hardness even forms in his stomach as he banishes fantasies of Martha from his mind and plans to adopt his new pose. "He would be a man about it," O'Brien writes, emphasizing the cultural expectations of masculinity that Cross determines to take up at the end. He will dispense with love and anything smacking of weakness or femininity. But the futility of this new persona is suggested by the last lines in the story, in which Cross foresees the platoon saddling up, forming a column, and moving toward the villages west of Than Khe. No matter what pose Cross adopts, how desperately he wants to wrest control into his own hands, the suggestion is that the war will continue as it has been. The men will search villages without knowing what to look for, aimlessly kick over jars of rice, frisk young children and old men, and then move on to the next village, "where it would always be the same" (80).

Differences in Versions

The original *Esquire* magazine short story version of "The Things They Carried" is nearly identical to the version published four years later in the collection *The Things They Carried*. O'Brien made only a few, very minor changes to the story. In the revised version, Lieutenant Jimmy Cross is 24 rather than 22 years old. A few lines are also added concerning Jimmy's feelings for Martha after he burns the letters and pictures. In the revised version, O'Brien writes: "Virginity was no longer an issue. He hated her. Yes, he did. He hated her. Love, too, but it was a hard, hating kind of love" (24)—lines that do not appear in the original *Esquire* story. These lines emphasize even more Jimmy's resentment of Martha for being safe at home, for never asking about the war in her letters, and for being part of a different world, someone who he believes could not possibly understand his wartime experiences.

CHARACTERS

Bowker, Norman Norman Bowker is a member of the platoon who carries a diary with him in the field. Even though he is described by the story's narrator as "otherwise a very gentle person" (79), he also carries with him the thumb of a dead VIET CONG boy, cut off a corpse by Mitchell Sanders.

Cross, Jimmy Lieutenant Jimmy Cross is the 22-year-old commanding officer of the 17-man platoon depicted in the story. Obsessed with Martha, a girl back home, Jimmy looks at her pictures and rereads her letters at night in his foxhole, wondering if she is a virgin and what she means by the word *love*, with which she signs her letters. While Jimmy understands that Martha has other boyfriends, he cannot help himself from pretending that she loves him the way he loves her. When Ted Lavender is shot, Jimmy Cross feels the burden of guilt, believing that if he had been a better officer and more focused on his men rather than on Martha, Lavender might still be alive. Thus, he burns Martha's letters and pictures at the end of the story and resolves to dismiss love from his mind.

Dobbins, Henry Henry Dobbins, the largest man in the platoon, carries extra rations with him; he especially loves canned peaches in heavy syrup. Because of his size, he is a machine gunner who also carries the very heavy M-60, a weapon that weighs 23 pounds unloaded. But Dobbins's size also excuses him from tunnel duty, a dangerous mission that the other men fear.

Jensen, Dave Dave Jensen is a member of the platoon who practices field hygiene and thus carries with him a toothbrush, dental floss, soap, three pairs of socks, and a can of Dr. Scholl's foot powder. For luck, Jensen carries a rabbit's foot in the field as well.

Kiley, Rat Rat Kiley, the unit's medic, carries M&Ms, brandy, and comic books with him in the field, alongside his regular medical supplies which include a canvas satchel filled with morphine, plasma, malaria tablets, surgical tape, and similar items.

Kiowa Kiowa, who is a Native American from Oklahoma and a devout Baptist, carries with him in the field a New Testament, given to him by his father, a Sunday school teacher. But Kiowa also carries, "as a hedge against bad times" (77), his grandfather's old hunting hatchet and his grandmother's distrust of the white man. Kiowa, who witnesses Ted Lavender's death, cannot stop talking about how the dead man fell so heavily and finally—"no twitching or flopping. . . just boom, then down . . . not like the movies" (78). Watching Jimmy Cross cry for hours in his foxhole after Lavender's death, Kiowa wishes that he, too, could feel appropriate grief for the dead soldier, but he mostly feels happy that he himself is still alive.

Lavender, Ted Ted Lavender, who is afraid, carries tranquilizers and marijuana with him in the field. When he is shot in the head after parting from the men to urinate, Lavender's drugs become a source of jokes that the men tell to control their fear. Mitchell Sanders claims there is a moral to Lavender's death: "Stay away from drugs" because they are "mind-blowers" (80). It is Lavender's death that causes the men to seek revenge on the village of THAN KHE by burning it down and that causes Lieutenant Jimmy Cross to burn his pictures of Martha, his girlfriend from back home.

Martha Martha is a junior at MOUNT SEBASTIAN COLLEGE in New Jersey. A volleyball player and an English major who admires Virginia Woolf and Geoffrey Chaucer, Martha writes long letters to Jimmy Cross in Vietnam. She does not mention the war in her letters except to say, "Jimmy, take care of yourself" (76). Cross remembers Martha's gray eyes and her aloneness at college, and he longs to know her secrets. But Martha remains as mysterious to readers as she does to Jimmy Cross. We see Martha only through Cross's memories of her, which are shaped by his loneliness and guilt. At the end of the story, Cross burns Martha's letters and pictures, telling himself that she is from another world and that she belongs elsewhere. Jimmy Cross banishes all fantasies of Martha from his mind and resolves to be a better officer.

Sanders, Mitchell   Mitchell Sanders is the unit's radio-telephone operator. He carries the extremely heavy PRC-25 radio with him in the field, along with a pack of condoms and a pair of brass knuckles. Mitchell Sanders is also the soldier who cuts off the thumb of a dead VIET CONG boy and gives it to Norman Bowker to carry as a souvenir. Sanders talks often about the morality of the situations the men encounter, and he jokes about Ted Lavender's death, claiming that Lavender's drugs are "mindblowers" (80) after the tranquilized soldier is shot in the head.

Strunk, Lee   Lee Strunk is a member of the platoon who carries a slingshot with him in the field, which he describes as a "weapon of last resort" (78). Strunk is the unlucky man who draws the number 17 and is forced to go down into the Vietnamese tunnel to search it while the other members of the platoon nervously wait for his reappearance. While Strunk survives this very dangerous mission, Ted Lavender is randomly shot just as the men are laughing and joking about Strunk's safe return.

Tomcat in Love (1998)

Published by Random House's Broadway Books in 1998, *Tomcat in Love* is the story of Thomas H. Chippering, a pompous, flirtatious linguistics professor at the UNIVERSITY OF MINNESOTA who has recently been divorced from his wife, Lorna Sue, a woman he had long considered the girl of his dreams. The novel follows Chippering's comic and pathetic attempts to win Lorna Sue back and to gain revenge on the two men he blames for his ex-wife's defection: her new husband, who is a wealthy Florida businessman, and her brother, Herbie Zylstra, a former childhood friend of Chippering's who seems to have a too-close relationship with his sister. Along the way, the professor clumsily

attempts to seduce every pretty co-ed, waitress, and salesclerk he meets at the same time that he starts a new romantic relationship with a good-hearted married woman named Mrs. Robert Kooshoff. A wild, madcap, humorous novel, *Tomcat in Love* sets a marked departure in tone for O'Brien, all the while exploring his familiar themes of love, war, obsession, and the power of words to shape reality.

SYNOPSIS

Childhood
Told in the first person by Thomas Chippering himself, the novel begins in June 1952, when Thomas is a seven-year-old boy growing up in small-town OWAGO, MINNESOTA. He and his best friend, Herbie Zylstra, build an airplane by nailing two plywood boards together. When Thomas informs his father that he will need an engine for his new plane, Mr. Chippering seems to take the request seriously. After several months, however, he delivers to the boys a turtle instead of the long-coveted engine. At least partly because of the disappointment in not receiving the engine that had loomed so large in his imagination, Herbie moves on to a new project: He decides that the plywood boards are no longer an airplane but a cross, "Like in the Bible" (5), and that he will nail his younger sister, Lorna Sue, to it. While the boys are thwarted by Thomas's mother in their first attempt to hammer a nail through Lorna Sue's hand, Herbie actually performs the deed later in the front yard of the spooky old Zylstra home. When he seriously injures his seven-year-old sister, Herbie is sent away to a hospital-school run by Jesuits in the Twin Cities, and Thomas does not see him for nearly a year. Upon Herbie's return, he is different—more quiet and self-contained, a loner—and Thomas has found new friends.

The two boys do not have much contact again until Thomas's junior year in high school, when he begins to date Lorna Sue, a relationship of which Herbie and the entire Zylstra clan disapprove.

Marriage and Divorce
Despite her family's opposition, Thomas and Lorna Sue eventually marry, a marriage that lasts for two decades. When Lorna Sue meets a wealthy tycoon on a beach in Florida, and when Herbie exposes

a couple of secrets that Thomas has been keeping from his wife—fake checks written to a phony psychiatrist Thomas has been pretending to see to appease Lorna Sue, and a black ledger book containing detailed descriptions of his various flirtations with students and other women—Lorna Sue divorces Thomas, marries her tycoon, and moves to Florida. Devastated by the divorce, Chippering flies to TAMPA by himself on three successive weekends to spy on Lorna Sue and her new husband and to plot his revenge against the tycoon and against Herbie Zylstra, whom he largely blames for the breakup of his marriage. Chippering suspects that Herbie's lifelong closeness to his sister is the result of an incestuous love affair between the two. Punctuating his revenge plans is a trip back home to Owago that Chippering makes on his Easter break from the university eight months after his divorce is finalized. In Owago Chippering visits his old boyhood haunts and moons over Lorna Sue. Finding himself lying on the ground sobbing by a birdbath in the middle of his old backyard in the middle of one dark night, he is embarrassed to be discovered by the home's new owner, Mrs. Robert Kooshoff, a good-looking, middle-aged woman whose husband, a veterinarian, is serving a prison sentence for tax evasion. The two end up spending the spring break week together, marking the beginning of a tenuous new relationship.

Vietnam

Meanwhile, Chippering discloses to readers that he is a Vietnam War veteran. Drafted (*see* DRAFT) in 1968. Sent to the mountains of QUANG NGAI PROVINCE in January 1969, Chippering is assigned to be an awards clerk in the office of a battalion adjutant, where his primary task consists of writing citations for gallantry in action. His tour of duty is fairly uneventful until an incident occurs about a month before he is due to rotate back to the States. Ordered to join a group of six GREEN BERETS in manning a listening post in the mountains, Chippering is abandoned by the more experienced but secretive soldiers the first night they set up camp in the bush. Left to wander through the dense jungle and isolated countryside by himself for several days, he eventually stumbles upon

a villa that the small group of Greenies has been using as an operational headquarters. The six men allow Chippering to remain in the villa but assign him to constant KP duty so that he spends most of his time preparing food and cleaning up. When he meets a young Vietnamese girl named Thuy Ninh, one of a group of servants hired to tend the grounds of the villa, Chippering begins an intensely erotic relationship with her, which lasts until he witnesses her dancing naked one evening for the six other soldiers. Chippering leaves the villa that night and calls in an elaborate air strike, providing coordinates immediately adjacent to the large house, then walks away into the jungle, eventually winding up back at his original firebase. Before he leaves the country, Chippering writes himself a commendation, awarding himself the SILVER STAR for valor, and thus returns home a decorated veteran. Chippering's war experiences, however, do not stay in Vietnam but follow him back to Minnesota. The six Greenies, who survive the air strike although they are terrified by it, promise to hunt Chippering down and make him pay.

University Professor

Mixed in with flashbacks about his childhood, his Vietnam experiences, and his marriage to Lorna Sue, Chippering also relates his adventures back at the University of Minnesota after meeting Mrs. Robert Kooshoff, who has moved into his tiny apartment in the city in preparation for another trip to Tampa, which they plan to make together. Chief among his escapades is a dalliance with a pretty co-ed named Toni, a student in a course he is teaching that semester. Convinced that Toni is attracted to him, Chippering arranges for the two to have several private consultations about her honors thesis, both in his office and in the sitting room of her dormitory. When in one of these meetings Chippering quotes some lines from Shakespeare— "Then come kiss me, sweet and twenty/Youth's a stuff will not endure" (93)—Toni becomes angry and threatens to turn her professor in for sexual harassment unless he will write her thesis for her. Chippering spends the next two weeks hunkered down at his typewriter, writing the last six chapters of the thesis, all the while also teaching his regular course load, preparing for his trip to Tampa, and plotting his revenge against Herbie and the tycoon.

Tampa

Once in Florida, where it rains continually, Chippering works hard to stir up mischief. He places an anonymous call to Lorna Sue's new husband, leaving the message that his wife wants to be picked up at her brother's house. He then calls 911 to report a domestic dispute at the same location and takes a taxi to Herbie's house to watch the fireworks that unfold. Later, he places more phone calls, making a dinner and room reservation for Herbie and Lorna Sue at a local hotel, then seeing that the tycoon is informed of the plans. He also calls the police to leave an anonymous tip, suggesting that Herbie Zylstra is responsible for a series of recent church fires in the Tampa area. When confronted by Mrs. Robert Kooshoff about his meddling, Chippering nearly pushes her off their hotel room balcony, prompting her to pack her suitcase and leave. The Tampa trip goes even more disastrously when Chippering spends an evening by himself getting drunk in the hotel bar and is hog-tied and left all night by a waitress and female bartender annoyed by his sexist advances. Freed early the next morning by a janitor named Delbert, Chippering, always an inveterate talker, follows the man around, even scrubbing toilets in his place to persuade him to listen to his many tales of woe: the series of abandonments he has suffered at the hands of his Vietnam colleagues, his wife, and numerous girlfriends. On his final day in Tampa, Mrs. Robert Kooshoff unexpectedly appears back at the hotel with Herbie Zylstra and Chippering's black love ledger in tow. Herbie has told her the truth about Chippering's divorce and has shown her the evidence to back up his story. The plane ride home is a tense one.

Breakdown

Chippering's life continues to spiral downward after his return to Minnesota. Toni's roommate Megan has discovered the ghostwritten thesis and threatens to report them both unless Chippering will write her thesis as well. Most humiliating of all, Herbie and Lorna Sue's tycoon arrive one afternoon in the middle of Chippering's seminar, "Methodologies of Misogyny," and proceed to pull down his pants and

spank him with a plastic yardstick in front of all of Chippering's students, who seem to enjoy the show, even applauding at one point. Later that same day, Chippering is called into the university president's office, where Megan and Toni accuse him of sexual harassment and claim that he insisted on helping them with their theses, despite their protests. Fired from his job, Chippering returns to Mrs. Kooshoff's home in Owago, where he continues his plummet, hitting rock bottom after auditioning to host a local children's television show. He completely breaks down in the audition, which is telecast live, sobbing about his marriage and his ex-wife's incestuous relationship with her own brother, and eventually threatening to light a gasoline bomb while holding a young child on his lap. After this incident, Chippering is hospitalized for six days in a local mental institution. Upon his release, he spends six more days in bed at the home of Mrs. Robert Kooshoff, who barely tolerates his presence.

Conclusion

Although he quiets down after his hospital stay, Chippering continues to secretly plot his revenge, making and storing gasoline-filled bombs in the garage that he plans to use on the Fourth of July, when Herbie, Lorna Sue, and her new husband will be home visiting the Zylstra relatives. The various threads of his past come to a head that summer as Chippering spots Spider and others of his old Vietnam nemeses in the streets of Owago and as Mr. Robert Kooshoff, about to be released from prison and angry about his wife's betrayal, threatens to kill Chippering as well. On the afternoon of the Fourth, a neighbor spots Thomas wearing army fatigues, his face smeared with charcoal, and carrying binoculars, climbing up an apple tree adjacent to the Zylstra house as he performs reconnaissance for his planned revenge. But later that day, Chippering discovers that the firebombs are missing from Mrs. Kooshoff's garage. Indignant, he rushes to the Zylstra home and accuses Herbie of stealing them. For the first time since they were children, Thomas and Herbie have a serious talk, in which Herbie explains that Lorna Sue has been completely self-centered her whole life and that the best revenge Thomas could gain would be to simply forget her. Although he returns home to Mrs. Kooshoff's house somewhat mollified by this talk, Chippering is awakened later in the night when several of the firebombs go off in his yard and on the steps of the nearby ST. PAUL'S CATHOLIC CHURCH. Looking out the window, he sees the figure of Lorna Sue against the night sky. He quickly dresses and follows her back to the Zylstra house, with Mrs. Robert Kooshoff trailing closely behind. The novel's climactic scene take place in the Zylstra attic, with Lorna Sue threatening to launch another of the homemade bombs and demanding that Thomas admit he adores her. It is with great satisfaction that Thomas tells Lorna Sue to stop behaving like a seven-year-old, finally committing himself to his new love, Mrs. Kooshoff. The novel ends with Chippering and Mrs. Kooshoff moving to an undisclosed island in the Caribbean to start a new life together, where she spends her days making pottery and he earns a little money by braiding hair for tourists on the topless beaches of the nearby Club Med. Herbie occasionally visits the couple in their island retreat, and Thomas tries to control his tomcatting ways.

COMMENTARY

Tomcat in Love is in large part a satire that pokes fun at the excesses of academia. Thomas Chippering's pomposity as a linguistics professor, his lecherous flirtations with attractive, much younger students, and the arcane titles he develops for his seminar courses—"It's Your Thick Tongue," "Methodologies of Misogyny"—all work to deflate the pedantry and self-importance that sometimes attach themselves to the academic world. Tim O'Brien, himself about to become a university professor of creative writing at Texas State University, the holder of an endowed chair (though not the Rolvaag Chair in Modern American Lexicology which Chippering is said to occupy at the University of Minnesota), might well have been somewhat apprehensive about his impending move into academia when he wrote the book. While critics have generally been quite appreciative of O'Brien's works, his novels *Northern Lights* and *The Nuclear Age* were not particularly well received, and even his most-praised works, *Going After Cacciato* and *The Things They Carried*,

have come under fire from feminist critics for their depiction of women characters and gender relationships. Literary artists often have an uneasy relation with critics, and O'Brien in *Tomcat in Love* seems to enjoy skewering the vanity and pomposity of professors such as Chippering as well as the politically driven, humorless discourse of Chippering's feminist critics in the university, who are most often members of the Gender Studies Department. When Chippering reports in a footnote to his story that he "once paid dearly for using the term *cooze* [to describe the university president's wife] at a black-tie faculty party" (113), readers might be reminded that Rat Kiley uses the same word when describing Curt Lemon's sister in "How to Tell a True War Story" and that the narrator O'Brien repeats the word at the end of the story to depict a kindly, well-meaning woman listener. Surely O'Brien is having fun with some of his own feminist critics here. It is certainly understandable that after a string of serious, contemplative novels about war, loss, fear, courage, and the ability of the human imagination to overcome atrocity, O'Brien might want to switch gears, writing instead a more lighthearted, humorous book that is filled with wildly improbable situations and characters designed to make readers laugh (and wince).

But despite its humorous, satirical bent, *Tomcat in Love* is perhaps not so different from O'Brien's earlier novels as it might first appear. *Tomcat in Love* is, underneath the comic antics, a novel about the havoc that loss and abandonment wreak on the human heart. Thomas Chippering, while certainly a womanizing, misogynistic, pompous, self-important fool, also manages to remain a sympathetic character because he is so damaged and vulnerable and because he retains idealistic notions of love even as he himself, as well as those around him, betray those notions time and again. The novel opens with an epigraph consisting of the final lines from the poem "One Art" by ELIZABETH BISHOP, a meditation on the art of losing things:

—Even losing you (the joking voice, a gesture
I love) I shan't have lied. It's evident
The art of losing's not too hard to master
Though it may look like (*Write* it!) like disaster.

The poem opens by cataloguing small, trivial losses, gradually working its way up to more devastating ones. In these final lines, the speaker tries to convince herself that loss, even loss of a loved one, is not the tragedy that it really is. But readers, of course, see the ruse as the poet forces herself to write the word she is trying to repress—*disaster*. The epigraph works well as an introduction to the novel since *Tomcat in Love* illustrates the disaster of lost love. Thomas Chippering well understands the devastating nature of loss as he spends nearly the entirety of the novel mourning over his lost Lorna Sue. But Chippering has been no stranger to abandonment and loss his whole life, long before his divorce. As a seven-year-old, Thomas is forced to give up his imaginative dreams of flight when his father presents him with a turtle rather than the airplane engine he had expected. His friendship with Herbie Zylstra is destroyed when the boy is sent to the Jesuit hospital-school in the Twin Cities after attempting to nail Lorna Sue to a cross. And Thomas confesses to readers, "Back then, in 1952, [he] loved Herbie with the same volatile, high-octane passion that now fuels [his] hatred" (45). Thomas describes his father as "deserting" (230) him when he dies of heart failure in 1957, and he views his mother's death when he is a freshman in college as an "abandonment" (230). He is abandoned, as well, by the six Green Berets in Vietnam, who leave him to wander lost in the jungle for days, and later by his Vietnamese girlfriend, Thuy Ninh, who betrays him with the other soldiers.

Like previous O'Brien characters, including William Cowling in *The Nuclear Age* and John Wade in *In the Lake of the Woods,* Thomas Chippering is shaped by his experiences of loss and abandonment and his fear of losing love. His attempt to hold on to Lorna Sue has made him obsessive and led him into bizarre and inappropriate behavior, much like Cowling, who actually imprisons his wife, Bobbi, to prevent her departure, and Wade, who has possibly murdered his wife, Kathy, in order to possess her completely. Chippering, like these other characters, wants love to be permanent, not transitory. He laments the fact that he now feels Lorna Sue's absence as he had once felt "her thereness, her everness, her absolute and indestructible love,"

musing further that, "If a love dies, how can such love be love?" (15). For Chippering, the very definition of love involves an "unending alwaysness" (16), and he even tells Lorna Sue that he "had loved her before either of [them] had been born" (19). While Chippering may have been somewhat delusional in his belief in Lorna Sue's indestructible love for him, readers can sympathize with the underlying idealism of this sentiment. It would be nice if love were strong, permanent, and unbreakable, if husbands and wives always lived happily ever after as fairy tales teach us they should, if we each had a soul mate somewhere out there in the world waiting for us. But, as the novel clearly shows, the idealized forms of love valorized by Western culture often fail to match reality.

Chippering's desire to be loved fully and completely and permanently is at least partly an attempt to fill up what he perceives as an emptiness inside of himself. Just as John Wade enters politics because of his overwhelming need to be loved, Chippering admits to readers that he lives for the gratification of love:

> From childhood on, I had been consumed by an insatiable appetite for affection, hunger without limit, a bottomless hole inside me. I would (and will) do virtually anything to acquire love, virtually anything to keep it. I would (and will) lie for love, cheat for love, beg for love, steal for love, ghostwrite for love, seek revenge for love, swim oceans for love, perhaps even kill for love. (158)

Chippering's need to fill the "hole" inside of him echoes William Cowling's digging of an actual hole in his yard as a concrete representation of his fears—fears not only of losing Bobbi and his daughter, Melinda, but also of the impermanence of human beings living on the edge of extinction. Even more, Thomas Chippering believes that this desire to be loved, and the feelings of loss that arise when love is proven to be impermanent, are not simply failings of his own personality but part of the human condition, a view that O'Brien seems to endorse in these earlier novels as well. "Each of us," Chippering argues, "is propelled through life by a restless, inexhaustible need for affection" (158).

The professor accuses readers of sharing his obsessions, of being more like him than they might want to admit, when he invents the unnamed "you," whom he addresses repeatedly throughout the novel.

This reader, whom Chippering deliberately leaves nameless in order to emphasize the universality of her feelings, is like Chippering in that she suffers for love and is driven to extremes when she loses the object of that love. Chippering imagines that the woman's husband has left her for a younger woman, a redhead, whom he has moved with to FIJI. The "you" is devastated by this abandonment and eventually becomes so distraught that she even travels to the South Pacific island herself, desperate to regain her husband's affection. At the times in the novel when Chippering describes his most offensive, outrageous behavior, he often addresses this imaginary reader, cautioning her to remember her own situation, her own obsessions, and thus not to judge him too severely. This unnamed reader, Chippering points out, has a unique story, but also "represent[s] every brokenhearted lover on this planet, every stood-up date, every single mother, every bride left weeping at the altar, every widow, every orphan, every divorcée, every abandoned child, every slave sold down the river" (236). Chippering has deliberately chosen a female reader to address here, perhaps because he (as well as the author O'Brien) understands that women readers, put off by the misogyny the professor continually displays in the novel might be quick to condemn his behavior. The female "you," acting out her own obsessions around lost love, balances Chippering out and shows that love, obsession, and fear of loss are *human* emotions rather than simply the province of aging, lecherous men like the professor. Chippering reminds readers that "any sensitive human being" who has experienced the loss of love will behave erratically, telling readers to ask themselves this: "Is not all human bleakness, all genuine tragedy, ultimately the product of a broken heart?" (26). Although the "you" is a specific invented reader with a particular history, Chippering in his use of the second-person direct address seems to be speaking to *all* his readers in these asides, inviting them to empathize, if not with his

tomcatting behavior, at least with the broken heart that prompts some of his more outrageous antics.

A linguistics professor who is nearly as obsessed with language as he is with love, Chippering muses on the power of words throughout the novel, noting that words such as *engine, turtle,* and *Pontiac* are polluted for him now, because of memories that they invoke. After nearly pushing Mrs. Robert Kooshoff off the hotel balcony in Tampa, he thinks especially about the many meanings of the word *lost,* explaining:

> It could be said, for instance, that I was lost without Mrs. Robert Kooshoff. That I was at a loss. That I had lost her. That I had lost myself. It would be accurate, too, to say that I had been thrown for a loss, implying depression, distress, and exhaustion, or that I had lost a rare and magnificent opportunity for happiness, implying waste and forfeiture. Or that I was a lost soul. Or lost in space. Or lost in dreary, rainy Tampa—condemned, marooned, alone, helpless. (142)

Like Paul Berlin in *Going After Cacciato,* who, soon after his arrival in Vietnam, writes home to his father asking him to look up CHU LAI in the world atlas because he feels "a little lost" amid the confusing, tangled labyrinth of the military and the war, Thomas Chippering associates these feelings of being lost not only with his romantic relationships but also with his Vietnam experiences. When he remembers his six comrades abandoning him in the jungle during the listening post mission, Chippering again speculates about the word *lost* and its definitions: "A curious bit of relativism. *Lost* can be viewed as both a state of mind and a state of being, and the two conditions are not always in harmony. One can *feel* lost without *being* lost. One can *be* lost without *feeling* lost. Very tricky" (155). In this instance, Thomas Chippering is lost in both senses of the word. Not a good soldier, he feels lost on the mission; he literally becomes lost in the jungle when he is left alone to wander by himself for several days and nights through the dense foliage and unfamiliar terrain.

Chippering's meditations on loss and language evoke current thinking about language that is evident in postmodern literature and theory. Tim O'Brien, who uses postmodern techniques in many of his previous works, including metafictive (*see* METAFICTION) commentary on his own fiction, a blurring or mingling of disparate forms and genre, and a destabilizing of historical truth, illustrates the postmodern position that language must always mediate reality, that human beings never have access to reality itself, except through language. As Chippering speculates at one point in the novel, language may "contain history" the same way that "plywood contains flight" (18). For little boys building plywood airplanes, the only access to flight is through their imagination. For human beings who want to look back and understand history, the only access to the past is through the imagination as well, which is mediated and articulated by language. Language, then, according to postmodern theorists, always implies a loss, a loss of the "real." What is signified by language is not present. Or, as the critic Niall Lucy explains in his book *Postmodern Literary Theory*, "language must always 'lack' what it names" (23). Thomas Chippering, a sophisticated linguist and language theorist himself, understands this when he writes that "even back then," in his childhood, he grasped, "in a dark, preknowledge way," the "frailties and mutabilities" of language, "its potential for betrayal" (4).

As small boys, Herbie and Thomas read this "frailty" of language as a simple tendency toward lies and deception. "Your dad's a liar," Herbie informs Thomas after the boys are presented with the turtle, and Thomas is forced to agree, though he makes a halfhearted defense of his father: "Yeah, sort of . . . but not usually" (5). Herbie goes even further, accusing all fathers of being liars: "They just lie and lie. They can't even help it. That's what fathers are *for*. Nothing else. They lie" (5). Immediately after this exchange, Herbie picks up the plywood airplane, turns it on its side, and announces that it is a cross, to which he suggests nailing his younger sister, Lorna Sue. Herbie's resolve to nail Lorna Sue to the cross suggests a desire to challenge the ultimate father figure: God himself. Herbie, raised Catholic as is Thomas, perhaps wants to find out if God, too, is a liar, as he believes all fathers are, so he decides to replicate

God's sacrifice of Christ on the cross, his gift of mercy to sinful human beings, to find out if the central tenet of the Christian faith is a lie as well. While Herbie's only answer involves being sent to a hospital/reform school for a year, Thomas seems to internalize Herbie's belief that lies, perpetuated by language, constitute the essential component of human behavior. He reads Christianity itself as a religion inextricably intertwined with the deception, betrayal, and heartbreak that mark his own life, claiming that Judas betrayed Christ in the same way that the unnamed woman reader's husband "disclaimed and repudiated" her by taking up with a younger woman (26). He argues as well that Christ's question of God on the cross—"Why hast thou forsaken me?"—is "the abiding question of the ages" (236), suggesting that heartbreak and abandonment constitute the human condition.

Chippering thus adopts lying as his normal mode of behavior. He will lie to Lorna Sue in the Zylstra attic, claiming that her cat, Vanilla, bit him and that is why he dropped it out the window. Looking back at this event, Chippering writes, "A pattern was established on that Saturday morning" (77). Thomas's first significant lie, a lie told to "win love . . . to keep love" (77) sets up a future of lies and deceit, including awarding himself a spurious Silver Star for valor before he leaves Vietnam. Later, after Herbie shows her Chippering's black love ledger, Mrs. Robert Kooshoff will call her new boyfriend a "stinking liar," claiming that he does not even know "what truth *is*" (168). Chippering in an attempt to deflect the blame from himself raises Mrs. Kooshoff's complaint to a more abstract level, arguing for the postmodern notion that no one understands truth: not "the philosophers" nor Mrs. Kooshoff herself (168). Why should he be condemned for playing fast and loose with the truth when truth itself is such a slippery and unstable philosophical construct, when the very nature of religious belief as well as language itself implies loss and betrayal?

Chippering further justifies his behavior by presenting himself in his memoir as a performer, as he claims all human beings are. When he and Mrs. Kooshoff first discuss the reasons for his breakup with Lorna Sue, Chippering admits to the phony checks he wrote to a fictitious psychiatrist. But Mrs. Kooshoff, sensing that Chippering is only telling her part of the story, locks herself in the bathroom. Chippering lies flat on his belly, attempting to converse with his angry girlfriend through a tiny crack underneath the door. "My performance," Chippering tells readers, "was soulful. I pressed my heart to the door. I wept copiously" (81). He then goes on to justify himself, explaining that "the word *performance* . . . should in no way imply dissimulation on [his] part" (81). Chippering claims he was, in fact, "engaged in heart-felt truth telling . . . throwing an actor's light on the human spirit" (81). He then directly addresses the unnamed female reader, the "you" of the novel, reminding her of her own "linguistic performances" when her husband left her, and arguing that "virtually every human utterance represents a performance of sorts" (81). While as a boy Chippering saw language as deceitful, as a depository of lies, as a more sophisticated adult and professional university linguist, his arguments here suggest the notions of 20th-century language philosophers such as J. L. Austin, who argued that most language utterances, at their base, are performative—in other words that they actually *do* something rather than just *say* something. This theory is illustrated in the example Austin uses of the marriage ceremony, in which the official statement, "I now pronounce you man and wife," actually accomplishes the act of marriage. It should be no surprise then that when Chippering reaches his lowest point in the novel, when he loses control in the television studio and blurts out all his fears and grief live on the air, his physical and mental collapse—he spends six days in bed in the Owago Community Hospital and another six in Mrs. Robert Kooshoff's queen-size bed—is accompanied by a loss of language itself. One of the symptoms of Chippering's illness is that he becomes mute. As a contemporary linguist and postmodern theorist who sees language as "a performance," Chippering becomes unable to speak when he is unable to perform physically. But O'Brien seems to suggest that Chippering, in all his postmodern sophistication, is a sophist at heart, someone who uses argumentation to practice deception. The honesty of boys who proclaim

lies to be lies may be preferable to the nuanced, complicated arguments of adults and college professors like Chippering, who propounds sophisticated arguments but who perhaps deceives himself more than anyone else.

Chippering, of course, is not the only character in the novel who practices self-deception. Lorna Sue, long the object of his dreams and desires, turns out to be an egotistical monster who demands adoration from all the men around her. Her intimate relationship with her own brother, Herbie, while finally not sexually incestuous, is a manifestation of this narcissism. Like Roderick and Madeleine Usher in EDGAR ALLAN POE's famous short story "The Fall of the House of Usher," Herbie and Lorna Sue Zylstra live in an ancestral house described as a "mausoleum" (12) and reserve their strongest affections for each other, seeing their own family as separate and superior from those who surround them. "We're Zylstras," Lorna Sue explains primly to Thomas at one point. "We're not *most* families" (102). As a result of Herbie's nailing her to the cross as a child, Lorna Sue retains a permanent scar on her hand, which seems to her a stigmata, the mark of Christ's suffering. As Herbie explains to Chippering at the end of the novel, Lorna Sue had developed a Christ complex, which manifests in a love/hate relationship with the Catholic Church. A devout Catholic who refuses to use birth control during her marriage, who attends Sunday Mass faithfully every week, and who believes without question the doctrines of corporeal resurrection and the Immaculate Conception, Lorna Sue nevertheless, not Herbie or Thomas, turns out to have been the child responsible for setting St. Paul's Church in Owago on fire back in the 1950s. She also vandalized the church's statue of Christ, painting makeup on its face and constructing false breasts for it, in an attempt to remake Christ in her own image—to create a female Christ. As a grown-up, Lorna Sue is most likely the perpetrator as well of a rash of arson fires in churches around the Tampa area. While Lorna Sue is narcissistic and self-deceived enough to see herself as Christ-like and worthy of worship from those around her, she also seems to hate her religion for what it has done to her.

Thomas Chippering himself, despite being a lapsed Catholic, is still held under the sway of his religious upbringing. As we have seen, he reads the story of Christ's betrayal by Judas and His feelings of abandonment on the cross as indicative of the loss and treachery that mark not only Chippering's life but the human condition in general. Thus, in his memoir he interprets his final letting go of Lorna Sue and embracing of Mrs. Robert Kooshoff in religious terms—as a baptism. On the Fourth of July, when Herbie finally informs Chippering that Lorna Sue was the childhood arsonist, that she was "forever the maimed girl-goddess" demanding attention and love from all the men around her, and that Herbie himself was "forever her guardian and caretaker" (331), Chippering at first continues to insist that he was Lorna Sue's "prince" (318) and that she used to love him. But he also confesses that he "knew otherwise" (318) as he thinks over some of the low points in their marriage. The end of this encounter marks a real turning point in Chippering's view of Lorna Sue as well as in his poisoned relationship with Herbie, his former childhood best friend. Herbie does "an odd thing" before Chippering leaves: He takes Thomas's hand and presses it to his own cheek, indicating a renewal of their old affection. That night back at his childhood home Chippering again finds himself out in the backyard by the birdbath, the location where he had first met Mrs. Kooshoff, the new owner of the house. Feeling like a lost hiker who has finally returned to his home campfire, Chippering strips naked, dips his hands into the birdbath, and rinses away the charcoal he had rubbed over his face earlier in the day. This ritual cleansing or baptism works as a rebirth for the tired professor, who then stands up, "naked as a baby" and lets the night "bathe" him (319). Chippering has figuratively washed away the sins of his past here and will be able to denounce Lorna Sue later that night and commit to Mrs. Kooshoff in a very public and clear-cut way.

But Chippering does not get off the hook that easily. After his ritual cleansing, he is also made to undergo ritual punishment for his own crimes of misogyny and lechery. After begging Mrs. Kooshoff to marry him that Fourth of July night and after the two make love in what Chippering describes

as "A Fourth of July extravaganza! A lusty, withering, half-hour cannonade" (321), Chippering has a bloodcurdling dream in which an all-female Congress assembles to condemn him for his boorish and sexist behavior. The gathered horde of women in Chippering's dream includes the numerous students, salesclerks, waitresses, secretaries, prostitutes, and others that he had met and tried to seduce during the course of the novel. The angry women turn the tables on Chippering, stripping him naked, pawing him in private places, and generally "womanhandl[ing]" him in "the most unspeakable ways" (322). O'Brien here is playing again with notions of feminism and political correctness as Chippering dreams that the outspoken lesbian folk-rock duo the Indigo Girls perform while the events of the dream are taking place and that JANE FONDA, a feminist icon during the Vietnam War era, serves as the executioner who throws the switch on a makeshift electric chair that Chippering envisions himself strapped into. While readers understand that no baptism has been able to change Chippering completely—all the while that the mob of women is inflicting their punishment on the professor, he continues to notice such details as Toni's "beckoning brown thighs," Carla's tattoos, and Sissy's "moist little tongue" (323)—nevertheless the dream does seem to take its toll on him. The worst punishment, however, is not Chippering's own execution but Lorna Sue's burning of his black love ledger, the depository of the words that contain the history of his amorous adventures. For the linguistics professor, the burning of his words, his "life's work, his enduring gift to posterity" (323), is more real and painful than the burning of his own physical body.

Tomcat in Love embodies the paradoxes at the heart of human nature. The novel's title itself invokes a contradiction: A tomcat is not someone who is supposed to fall in love, but rather someone who plays the field, who has sex with many partners. Such contradictions abound in the novel. Words imply loss and betrayal, but Thomas Chippering revels in language and becomes a linguistics professor. Chippering is a coward at heart, but he behaves courageously once (when the Green Berets soldiers seek their revenge in a mock execution—ironically, this brave act guarantees that the Greenies will continue to haunt Chippering for the rest of his life). Chippering is a thorough misogynist, yet he loves women and everything about them. Lorna Sue is a devout Christian, but she burns churches. Herbie is the only character who fully recognizes Lorna Sue's monstrous egotism, yet he devotes his life to protecting her. Mrs. Robert Kooshoff is hurt repeatedly by Chippering, yet stands by him and agrees to marry him in the end. All of these contradictory behaviors point to the basic paradox at the heart of the novel: Love is absolutely essential to human beings, but it is also the one thing that cannot be counted on, the thing that leads people to act obsessively, often driving away the very love they hope to gain.

While the book ends hopefully—Mrs. Robert Kooshoff and Thomas Chippering start a new life for themselves on a Caribbean island—it leaves the basic paradox of love and loss unresolved. Thomas Chippering has undergone a baptism, has washed away his sins, only to begin sinning again. He keeps from Mrs. Kooshoff the fact that he earns money by braiding the hair of women tourists on the topless beaches of Club Med. He believes that his jolly young psychiatrist is attracted to him. His past haunts him, as he spots one of his old Vietnam nemeses, Death Chant, on the beach. Yet, despite the human tendency to slide into sin and deceit, even with the best intentions to reform, the novel suggests that redemption is still possible if one has faith, if one is willing to believe in the potential of true love even in the worst of circumstances. Chippering's memoir ends with his plea to the unnamed woman reader that she continue to believe that her husband loved her, despite the fact that he is in Fiji with another woman. He ends by urging the abandoned wife to take heart, to "embolden" herself and to "brave the belief" (342) that her husband knows his transgression and will return to her door someday and understand what the word *Fiji* has come to mean for her. Such belief is "a matter of faith" (342), according to Chippering, a matter of imagination.

CHARACTERS

Beth, Linda, Corinne, Ruthie, Pam Beth, Linda, Corinne, Ruthie, and Pam are junior high school girls in Owago whom Lorna Sue Zylstra accuses Thomas Chippering of kissing, along with Faith Graffenteen. She makes the discovery because Thomas had written the girls' names down on a list, a precursor to the famous black ledger book where he records all his romantic interludes—the book that gets him into so much trouble later in his marriage.

Beverly Beverly is a student sitting in the first row in Thomas Chippering's "Methodologies of Misogyny" class, whom he is just beginning to flirt with when Lorna Sue's tycoon and Herbie Zylstra arrive to administer a spanking with a plastic yardstick on the bare backside of the hapless professor. After his public humiliation, Chippering pathetically cries out to Lorna Sue, asking if she still loves him, and Beverly calmly proclaims, "Come on, man, be real . . . She hates you" (212).

Bonnie Prince Charming See GREEN BERETS.

Businesswoman on Plane On the plane ride home from TAMPA, FLORIDA, Mrs. Kooshoff loudly accuses Thomas Chippering of being "like some fickle, randy old alley cat," attracting the attention of a "buxom young businesswoman across the aisle" (174). Even as Mrs. Kooshoff chides him for his lecherous ways, Chippering is eyeing the businesswoman, with her "jade eyes" and "come-hither upper carriage" (174), whom he had noticed back at the boarding gate in Tampa. The woman cannot help but overhear as the argument escalates, with Mrs. Kooshoff reading from Chippering's ledger book about the 16 spankings that he has recorded there. Although she frowns at the professor and even emits audible groans as she listens in on Mrs. Kooshoff's accusations, the woman is completely misread by Chippering, who believes that she is preening to capture his attention. The scene ends with Mrs. Kooshoff moving across the aisle to sit with the businesswoman. The two are hunched over the ledger book, reading Chippering's romantic confessions together when he returns from the plane's bathroom, where he had fled.

Car Dealer One of Thomas Chippering's competitors when he auditions for the role of Captain

Nineteen on a local children's television program is an Owago Buick-Oldsmobile dealer, described by Chippering as a "an unctuous, beady-eyed sharpie" (260). Chippering fumes when during his audition the car dealer pronounces the word *nuclear* as "nu-cu-ler" and misuses the adjective *real*. In any event, the role is awarded to the car dealer after Chippering completely breaks down on camera during his own audition.

Carla   On Thomas Chippering's third trip to TAMPA, FLORIDA, to spy on Lorna Sue and Herbie, he meets a young salesgirl named Carla, who works in a hotel boutique specializing in women's undergarments. Carla kindly volunteers to model some of the merchandise for Thomas and soon discovers that the professor plans to purchase sexy lingerie in order to embarrass Lorna Sue's new husband by planting it in his car, a move designed to flame jealousy and distrust on Lorna Sue's part. Made aware of Chippering's plans for revenge, Carla reveals her own special interest in sadistic sexual objects, including handcuffs, leg irons, padlocks, etc. and urges her new friend to "plant some of this sick shit" (29) on the tycoon. Carla also confesses to Chippering her own sad tale of romance and revenge, the story of a motorcycle-riding boyfriend who loved his motorcycle more than he loved her. Chippering takes Carla out to dinner a few nights later, where the "punkish" (32) salesgirl confides in him several methods for revenge that she has devised, such as brushing arsenic on the flap of a self-addressed envelope and sending it to one's victim, who will die hours after mailing back the evidence. When Carla shows him the tattoos covering her body later that night, she declares "no touchies" (33) and then becomes infuriated when Chippering reaches out to pluck at a rose stenciled on her breast. But it is when Chippering remains confusedly silent after her suggestion that he wants to bite the rose, Carla grows even angrier. Clearly welcoming a biting, she flounces out of the room, snarling that guys like him should be "shot through the heart. Butchered like sheep" (34).

Carla's Boyfriend   The sadistic salesgirl Carla, who meets Thomas Chippering in an expensive

hotel boutique specializing in women's lingerie, confides in the professor that her former boyfriend loved his motorcycle more than he loved her. But Carla gained her revenge on the young man by tampering with his brakes. She tells Chippering that her ex-boyfriend is "history" (33).

Catchitt, Mrs.   Mrs. Catchitt was a neighbor of the Chipperings when Thomas was a boy growing up in the south-central Minnesota town of OWAGO. He recalls himself and Herbie Zylstra as young boys imagining that they are using their plywood airplane to bomb Mrs. Catchitt's garage. Thomas later explains that the woman lived on North Fourth Street, near ST. PAUL'S CATHOLIC CHURCH, the sanctuary of which was burned in an arson fire in 1957. When Thomas is a grown-up, returned to Owago after being fired from his job as a linguistics professor at the UNIVERSITY OF MINNESOTA, Mrs. Catchitt, now a very old woman, spots her former neighbor climbing an apple tree alongside the Zylstra house, dressed in army fatigues, his face smeared in charcoal, and carrying a pair of binoculars. Chippering, fairly mentally unhinged at this point, is scouting out his planned firebombing of the Zylstra house.

Chippering, Mr.   Thomas Chippering's father is a good-natured man who promises his son an engine for his plywood airplane when the boy is seven years old. Unable to provide his son a real engine, he instead brings him a turtle, named Toby, the first in a series of disappointments that will plague Thomas throughout his life. While Mr. Chippering does not play a very prominent role in the novel, his death from heart failure in 1957, when Thomas is only 12, does affect the boy deeply. Thomas reminisces about watching his father perform magic tricks for him and the Zylstra children back in 1952: "I see him now as he was then, athletic and graceful, utterly adult, standing near the birdbath in that silvery backyard. Sunlight surrounds him. He sparkles with the ferocity of here and now" (44). Later in the book, when Thomas has reached a low point in his sorrow over the end of his marriage to Lorna Sue, he reminds readers of earlier desertions, pointing particularly to his father's death: "He dropped dead in the gutter. He deserted me. At his funeral, I yelled, Why a goddamn *turtle?* No use. He was dead" (230). Thomas Chippering thus joins a list of O'Brien characters who are emotionally distraught by a father's death while they are still young: Paul and Harvey Perry of *Northern Lights* and John Wade of *In the Lake of the Woods.*

Chippering, Mrs. Readers do not find out much about Thomas Chippering's mother in the novel. Thomas does tell readers, though, that his mother "passed away" (230) during his freshman year at college. Thus, he explains, "loss and abandonment" were always his "most faithful companions" (230).

Chippering, Thomas H. The novel's narrator and protagonist, Thomas H. Chippering is a recently divorced professor of linguistics at the UNIVERSITY OF MINNESOTA who is in his mid-fifties when the novel begins. A self-important, pretentious, and somewhat ridiculous figure at six feet, six inches tall and weighing under 180 pounds, who describes himself as resembling "a clean-shaven version of our sixteenth president, gangly and benign" (27), Chippering is a shameless flirt who believes that every woman he meets is secretly in love with him. He also fancies himself a war hero, often reminding readers that he won the SILVER STAR for valor during his tour of duty in Vietnam, even though he also betrays the fact that he faked the paperwork in order to award himself the medal. Readers soon learn that his two-decades-long marriage to the former Lorna Sue Zylstra ended when she discovered several items that her husband kept hidden under their bedroom mattress—a series of phony checks written to an invented psychiatrist whom Chippering had been pretending to see in order to appease Lorna Sue's desire that he "get help" for his psychological problems, and a black ledger book containing detailed descriptions of his erotic fantasy life, mostly involving flirtations with female students and acquaintances. Since the divorce, Lorna Sue has remarried a wealthy businessman whom she met on the beach in Florida and moved to a new house in TAMPA. Chippering describes three successive trips he makes to Tampa to spy on Lorna Sue and her tycoon (a man

whose name Chippering cannot bring himself to pronounce) and to plot his revenge against Lorna Sue's brother, Herbie Zylstra, whom Chippering blames for the breakup of his marriage.

When, on an Easter trip to his small hometown of OWAGO, MINNESOTA, Chippering wanders into the backyard of his childhood home and falls down on the ground by a birdbath, sobbing uncontrollably about his loss of Lorna Sue, he is discovered by the new owner of the home, a woman named Mrs. Robert Kooshoff, whose husband is a veterinarian serving a prison sentence for tax fraud. The two enter into what will be a troubled romantic relationship, their growing affection always at the mercy of Thomas's sexual appetites for other women (though he claims not to actually *act* upon these appetites) and Mr. Robert Kooshoff's threats to do serious bodily damage to his rival. Thomas's ongoing obsession with the lost Lorna Sue, whom he describes as the love of his life, the girl of his dreams, also prevents him from fully committing to his new girlfriend. After a series of adventures in Tampa, Minneapolis, and Owago, in which Chippering repeatedly humiliates himself, getting publicly spanked in front of his students, fired from his job, and even spending time in a mental hospital briefly, he is finally able to let go of Lorna Sue. The novel ends with Chippering and Donna Kooshoff moving to an unnamed island in the Caribbean and starting a new life for themselves.

Constantine, Dr. Ralph Dr. Ralph Constantine is the name that Thomas Chippering invents for the phony psychiatrist he pretends to visit in order to appease Lorna Sue's demands that he seek help. The fraud is exposed when Herbie finds a series of uncashed checks written to the doctor stored under Thomas's mattress and reveals his discovery to Lorna Sue.

Death Chant See GREEN BERETS.

Delbert Delbert is an elderly African-American janitor who frees Thomas Chippering in the hotel bar in TAMPA, FLORIDA, after the professor has spent the night tied up by an angry waitress and a bartender, Peg and Patty. Delbert is amused by

Chippering's predicament and jokes that the professor "tied one on last night" (151), which leads to a verbal duel in which the two men exchange phrases that use the word *tie*. Chippering, verbose as always, insists that the janitor listen to his tales of woe and follows the old man around as he goes about his duties, even scrubbing toilets in Delbert's place to ensure that he retains his audience. That afternoon, after Chippering has talked himself out, Delbert escorts him to his hotel room and puts the "agitated and weepy" (164) professor to bed.

Dennis Dennis is junior high school boy in OWAGO, MINNESOTA, whom Thomas Chippering accuses Lorna Sue Zylstra of kissing when they are twelve years old. Thomas makes this accusation in response to Lorna Sue's discovery of a list in which Thomas had written down the names of all the girls he himself had kissed. Thomas also argues that Dennis does not love Lorna Sue.

Dern, Father Father Dern is the priest at ST. PAUL'S CATHOLIC CHURCH in OWAGO, MINNESOTA. When the church is vandalized and set on fire in 1957, he calls Herbie Zylstra and Thomas Chippering into his office to question the boys about their involvement. Thomas, indignant and eager to prove his innocence, begins to blurt out lies about his whereabouts the night of the arson, claiming he was taking a bath at two in the morning when the fire broke out. While the priest clearly believes that at least one of the boys is guilty, he nevertheless decides to protect them by breaking the blackened Mason jars he had found in the ruins rather than reporting these pieces of evidence to the police. At the end of the novel, readers discover it was actually Lorna Sue who set the church on fire and who disfigured a statue of Christ by painting it with rouge and lipstick and appending to it a pair of "distinctly feminine breasts" (39).

Dull-Faced Captain During his tour of duty in Vietnam, Thomas Chippering receives orders to join a group of six war-hardened GREEN BERETS as they man a listening post in the mountains of QUANG NGAI PROVINCE. Chippering reports to an officer he describes as a "young, dull-faced captain"

(59), who issues him supplies. The captain assures Chippering the assignment "Won't be too bad . . . Like Cub Scouts. Pretend it's a weenie roast" (59). The assignment turns out to be worse than Chippering could have imagined, as he is abandoned in the jungle by the six soldiers, then makes enemies for life out of them after he calls in an air strike on the old tea plantation where they have set up headquarters.

Evelyn Evelyn is the four-year-old daughter of Faith Graffenteen, the OWAGO girl whom Lorna Sue had angrily accused Thomas Chippering of kissing when they were 12. Chippering meets Evelyn when she comes under his charge at the day care center in Owago, where he takes a job after being fired from his university position. Believing that the traditional children's Dick and Jane readers, with their "'See Spot jump' nonsense," (242) are inane, Chippering, ever the linguist, instead teaches the children under his care to recite Lady Macbeth's famous "Out, damned spot" soliloquy from Shakespeare. Hearing her daughter recite profanity at the dinner table so angers Faith Graffenteen that she confronts Chippering, ordering him to stay away from her Evelyn. But Evelyn becomes attached to Chippering, eventually demanding that her new teacher try out for the role of Captain Nineteen on a local cable television show for children. Evelyn is the child that Chippering is holding on his lap when he breaks down on camera and threatens to light a homemade gasoline bomb.

Fleurette Fleurette is a French prostitute whom Thomas Chippering meets at the bar of the Ramada Inn where he has gone to drown his sorrows and to meet his new departmental secretary, Sissy Svingen, for a drink after work. When Sissy arrives, she is astonished to find the professor flanked by Fleurette and another prostitute from Russia, named Masha. But while Chippering wanders off and passes out for an hour, the three young women become friends. Later that evening, the foursome decide to drive to OWAGO, MINNESOTA, to the home of Mrs. Robert Kooshoff, who is less than delighted to be woken up at dawn by her new boyfriend and the three sleepy young women.

Fonda, Jane   On the night of July Fourth, Thomas Chippering has a dream in which all the women from his past make up an "all-female Congress" (321), convened to punish him for his misogyny over the years. At the end of the dream, a hooded executioner steps forward to throw the switch to an electric chair that Chippering has been strapped into. When the executioner begins to speak, Chippering is able to tell that it is none other than JANE FONDA, who bellows, "We're people, we're individuals!" (323). Incorrigible as ever, Chippering replies, "Well, for god's sake, of *course* you are, A to double-D, all shapes and sizes" (323). Furious that Chippering has perverted her statement in order to refer to women's physical attributes, she throws the lever that will pump electricity through Chippering's body as Lorna Sue begins to burn the professor's love ledger, an act that bothers him more than his impending execution. It is no accident that Jane Fonda, an Oscar-winning actress and outspoken feminist, appears in Chippering's dream. Fonda is a particularly controversial figure to Vietnam veterans. Strongly opposed to the war, she visited Hanoi in 1972, was photographed sitting on a North Vietnamese Army antiaircraft gun, and accused American prisoners of war, whom she visited in the notorious prison commonly called the Hanoi Hilton, of exaggerating claims of abuse at the hands of the North Vietnamese. She was later accused of treason and referred to as "Hanoi Jane" by her critics.

Goof   See GREEN BERETS.

Graffenteen, Faith   Faith Graffenteen is the name of a local OWAGO girl whom Lorna Sue Zylstra accuses Thomas Chippering of kissing when they are 12 years old. Faith had told Lorna Sue that Thomas "kissed her snot," but Thomas claims that Faith forced him into it. Faith will reenter the novel later as the mother of a toddler named Evelyn, who is one of Chippering's charges at the day care center where he obtains a job after being fired from his teaching position at the UNIVERSITY OF MINNESOTA. Faith objects when Chippering teaches the children portions of Lady Macbeth's "Out, damned spot" soliloquy, complaining about the use of profanity in a preschool class. As Faith leaves their meeting, she tells him she has not forgotten how he sucked on her nose when they were 12, and she warns him to stay away from her daughter.

Green Berets   Near the end of his tour of duty in Vietnam, Thomas Chippering is assigned to join six GREEN BERETS in manning a listening post in the mountains several kilometers away from the firebase where he is stationed. The men must hack their way through dense jungle for hours before setting up camp for the night. While the Greenies are silent, capable soldiers, used to spending time out in the bush, Chippering had been assigned a desk job previously. This, combined with his general lack of athleticism, leaves him exhausted and useless as the soldiers set up their perimeter that night. When Chippering wakes up at dawn the next morning, the six Green Berets have disappeared, leaving him alone in the jungle. After wandering by himself for several days in the dense wilderness, Chippering finally comes upon a villa in the jungle, an old tea plantation, which his six comrades have apparently been using as a headquarters for their mysterious operations. The soldiers do not seem surprised to see Chippering and assign him to do KP duty around the house while they spend time conducting secretive missions in the bush. Even the Greenies' names are classified according to Chippering, and he knows them only by their aliases—Spider, Goof, Wildfire, Death Chant, Tulip, and Bonnie Prince Charming.

Soon Chippering begins an intense love affair with a young Vietnamese woman named Thuy Ninh, who helps tend the grounds of the villa. But when he sees her dancing naked one night for his six comrades, he becomes infuriated and calls in an air strike on coordinates adjacent to the old plantation house. He then walks away into the jungle. Although no one dies in the air strike, the Greenies are terrified and very angry when they arrive at the firebase two nights later. They haul Chippering out of his bed, bind his hands, wrap a poncho around his head, and take him to the base perimeter, where they make a show of putting him before a firing squad. Surprising even himself, Chippering behaves with dignity throughout the ordeal, never showing fear. The Greenies end up taking him back to the base and buying him a beer, but they warn him that because he was brave they will have to gain their revenge later. They depart, telling him that now he must watch his back, "forever" (302). Sure enough, Chippering later spots Goof on the UNIVERSITY OF MINNESOTA campus as he is on his way to class, and Spider shows up in OWAGO, MINNESOTA, on the Fourth of July to put a piano wire around Chippering's neck and threaten to strangle him to death. Again, Thomas remains calm, and Spider ends up removing the wire but warning that he might be back again to try later: "Go on just like before, keep it a mystery," he explains to Chippering, "Maybe I'll be back someday, maybe I won't" (306). The continuing threat of the Greenies' revenge, combined with Mr. Robert Kooshoff's promises of retaliation, are two of the reasons that Chippering and Donna Kooshoff retire to the undisclosed Caribbean island at the end of the novel.

Hanson, Hans Hans Hanson, an OWAGO jeweler, played Captain Nineteen on an afternoon television show for children, which was broadcast over a local community access channel until his death in a car accident, which occurs when Thomas Chippering is working at a day care center in town. A four-year-old student of Chippering's named Evelyn, traumatized by the death of her beloved Captain Nineteen, insists that Chippering himself audition to replace Hanson in the role. The audition goes terribly wrong when Chippering loses control of himself on live television, blubbers about his ex-wife and her incestuous relationship with her brother, and threatens to blow himself and little Evelyn up with a homemade gasoline bomb, an incident that lands the former professor in a mental hospital.

Indigo Girls Thomas Chippering, in recounting to readers his dream on the night of July Fourth, in which he envisioned mobs of angry women exacting revenge against him for his lifelong misogyny, reports that the singing group the Indigo Girls performed amid the angry lectures and venomous speeches. The Indigo Girls are a real-life folk-rock duo, known for their political activism and for self-identification as lesbians.

Island Psychiatrist At the end of the novel, when Thomas Chippering and Mrs. Robert Kooshoff escape to their unnamed Caribbean island, Chippering makes good on his promise to Mrs. Kooshoff to see a psychiatrist to get help for his problems—his lying and womanizing. His compliance here contrasts sharply to the lies he told when his previous wife, Lorna Sue, made a similar request and Chippering invented a phony psychiatrist to whom he even wrote bogus checks. The island psychiatrist is never given a name in the novel, but she is described as "a jolly young lady of African descent and considerable insight" (341). While she speaks little English and Chippering has no command at all of the island patois, the two still communicate successfully, unbound by the strictures of precise language. When Chippering says the word *turtle* and sketches a picture of the creature in the dust, the psychiatrist exclaims, "Like you, mon! Big shell! Very slow! But live long forever!" (341).

Jessie Jessie is a young woman who works as a producer for the *Captain Nineteen* children's television show. When Thomas Chippering shows up to audition for a position as host of the show, Jessie introduces him to his competitors for the job: a local Buick-Oldsmobile dealer and a plumbing contractor. She also obliges Chippering by allowing him to squeeze into the too-small costume worn previously by Hans Hanson—the former Captain Nineteen—whom Jessie clearly respected. Yet, as he does with every young woman he meets, Chippering appraises Jessie in a purely physical way, describing her as "mouth-watering," as having "strawberry hair . . . eyes of cinnamon . . . and Virginia baked hams" (259). As usual, Chippering mistakenly believes that the young woman is flirting with him. He seems flabbergasted when she calls him sexist after he assumes she is a mere stagehand.

June June is the name of a woman whom Thomas Chippering meets when he is assigned to clerk's school in rural Kentucky after being drafted (*see* DRAFT) into the army. He writes, "My sole fond memory from this period is of a rubbery little Appalachian number by the name of June. Acrobatic tongue. Tooth decay. Illiterate in everything but love" (58).

Karen and Deborah Karen and Deborah are the names of two students whom Thomas Chippering meets in a campus bar where he goes to celebrate after finally completing Toni's honors thesis for her. The two young women accompany him home that night, where they play a "frisky game of Scrabble" (116) until Mrs. Robert Kooshoff appears near dawn, dressed in pink fuzzy slippers and black panties, and demands that the two girls leave the apartment.

Katrina, Caroline, Deb, and Tulsa Katrina, Caroline, Deb, and Tulsa are the names of four Victoria's Secret salesgirls in TAMPA, FLORIDA, who gleefully help Thomas Chippering pick out a "new wardrobe" for Lorna Sue, including "peekaboo bras, panties, negligées, camisoles, garters, chaps, teddies, [and] pigskin leggings" (166), which they pack up and send by courier to Lorna Sue's husband's downtown office with a note signed "Herbie." Later, Chippering will have a late lunch with the girls and collect the phone numbers of each before hurrying back to his hotel to call Mrs. Robert Kooshoff, who has left the hotel angry and frightened after nearly being pushed off the balcony by her new boyfriend, the lusty linguistics professor.

Kersten Kersten is the name of the businessman whom Lorna Sue marries after her divorce from Thomas Chippering. The man's name is mentioned only once in the novel since Chippering cannot bring himself to pronounce it. Readers are never sure if "Kersten" is actually a first name or a last name; we find out only that Lorna Sue shortens it, referring to her husband as "Kerr." Chippering speaks of the man most often as "the tycoon" as he tells readers of the various plots he hatches to gain his revenge on the man—phone calls and meetings intended to inflame the tycoon's jealousy over Lorna Sue's relationship with her brother, Herbie. The tycoon gains his own revenge on Chippering when he and Herbie administer a bare-bottomed

spanking to the linguistics professor in front of a full classroom of his students. After Chippering and Donna Kooshoff move to their Caribbean island, Herbie reports that Lorna Sue and her tycoon are doing well. While there is little passion in the marriage, Herbie explains that "the tycoon worships her and offers the everyday sacrifice of selfhood" (340) that Lorna Sue demands.

Kids in Perkins Park In an attempt to purchase firecrackers to serve as fuses for his homemade gasoline bombs, Thomas Chippering drifts from park to park in OWAGO, MINNESOTA, on the morning of July 3, trying to find a child willing to sell him the explosives. At one point in Perkins Park, a young boy on a teeter-totter stares at Chippering, "his eyes fluent with pity," and says quietly, "Firecrackers? . . . Shit, man. You're a grown-up aren't you?" (291). The next day, however, just before noon, Chippering is able to "score" (297) a pack of Joker's Wild firecrackers from a freckled-face 10-year-old boy in the same park. The child humiliates the professor as they make their black market deal, accusing him of crying on the *Captain Nineteen* show.

Kooshoff, Mr. Robert ("Doc") Mr. Robert Kooshoff is still married to his wife, Donna, when she begins her relationship with Thomas Chippering. Sentenced to five-to-seven years at Stillwater Prison for tax fraud, Robert Kooshoff was formerly a veterinarian nicknamed "Doc." His wife, who confesses to Chippering early on that she has been considering divorce, describes Doc Kooshoff as "ill-tempered and spiteful . . . a prototype bully . . . a cruel, cowardly, abusive rat" (182). She suspects he only took up the practice of veterinary medicine because he loved putting pets down. The pair had been college sweethearts at the University of South Dakota. Married for 16 years, they have been twice separated already. Much to Chippering's horror, he learns not long into his relationship with Mrs. Robert Kooshoff that the former veterinarian is extremely angry about his wife's new relationship, and further that he is to be paroled shortly. The professor receives a call from Kooshoff one night when the "good doctor" curses him out in a "particularly poetic" way (194) and threatens to kill

Chippering if he attempts to marry his wife. One of the reasons that Chippering and Mrs. Robert Kooshoff move to an undisclosed island at the end of the novel is to avoid her ex-husband's wrath.

Kooshoff, Mrs. Robert   Mrs. Robert Kooshoff is the current owner of Thomas Chippering's childhood home in OWAGO, MINNESOTA. Chippering meets her late one night when she discovers him blubbering about Lorna Sue in her backyard on the eight-month anniversary of his divorce. Lonely herself since her violent, veterinarian husband has been jailed for tax fraud, Mrs. Robert Kooshoff allows Chippering to stay with her over his Easter break. This new relationship proves quite fragile, however, due to Chippering's self-centeredness, his lies, his flirtations with other women, and above all, his continuing obsession with his ex-wife, Lorna Sue. Yet, Mrs. Kooshoff proves herself to be a remarkably resilient and forgiving woman, taking Chippering back time and again even though it takes weeks before he even learns her first name— Donna—or that she is actually of Irish, not Dutch, ancestry. By the end of the novel, as Chippering has slowly grown more dependent on Mrs. Kooshoff, he is finally able to choose her over Lorna Sue. Donna Kooshoff, it turns out, is an heiress whose father had been a two-term U.S. senator. She has enough money that she and Thomas can move to an unnamed island and start a new life for themselves.

Masha   Masha is a prostitute from Russia whom Thomas Chippering meets, along with her French friend Fleurette, in the hotel bar of a Ramada Inn near the UNIVERSITY OF MINNESOTA campus. Chippering had made a date with Sissy Svingen, his new departmental secretary, to meet after work in the hotel bar, but when Sissy is late, he passes the time with Masha and Fleurette, trying to drown his sorrows over having been publicly spanked and fired from his job earlier that same day. Much later in the evening, Masha suggests a midnight road trip to OWAGO, MINNESOTA. Chippering, the two prostitutes and Sissy in tow, arrives on the doorstop of Mrs. Robert Kooshoff's home near dawn. Needless to say, she is not pleased to see the professor at this

hour of the morning in the company of three sleepy and slightly tipsy young women.

Megan's Boyfriend, Jake, Ronny, Sid, Geoff, Billy Bob, Jumbo Tomilson   The trouble between UNIVERSITY OF MINNESOTA roommates Toni and Megan begins when Toni sleeps with Megan's boyfriend, a linebacker on the college football team. When Megan finds out, she threatens to expose the fact that Thomas Chippering wrote Toni's honors thesis for her. In his conversations with the two girls, Chippering soon discovers that they each had "dibs on" (188) certain members of the football team, including not only Megan's boyfriend but also a wide receiver named Jake and other players named Ronny, Sid, Geoff, Billy Bob, and Jumbo Tomilson. Each girl slept with several of the other's chosen favorites in an attempt to hurt her roommate. The fallout of this massive betrayal is that Chippering agrees to write Megan's thesis as well, on the promise that she will not expose him to the college administration as Toni's ghostwriter.

Oriel   Oriel is a salesgirl at Hanson's Fine Jewelry in OWAGO, MINNESOTA, where Thomas Chippering goes to buy Mrs. Robert Kooshoff an engagement ring. She calls Chippering a "skinflint" when he complains about the price of the ring, telling him that he should not be "such a miser" and that marriages, like diamonds, "go on and on and on" forever (233). Chippering, who believes the "saucy tart . . . the luscious little busybody" is flirting with him, mentally vows to revisit the shop with a dentist's drill somebody to teach the girl a lesson.

Peg and Patty   Peg is the name of a waitress who works at the cabana and restaurant of the hotel where Thomas Chippering and Mrs. Robert Kooshoff stay in TAMPA, FLORIDA. After Chippering nearly pushes Mrs. Kooshoff off the hotel balcony one day, she packs her suitcases and heads home for OWAGO, MINNESOTA. Later that evening, Chippering stops in at the hotel bar to console himself, where he regales Peg and a bartender named Patty with his sad stories of loss and abandonment. The two women eventually become impatient with

Chippering's self-centeredness as well as his clumsy sexual advances. Calling him a "pig" and a "lech" (148–49), they undress the tipsy linguistics professor, tie him up with their uniform bow ties and aprons, stuff a washcloth in his mouth, and leave him all night long.

Pillsbury, President Theodore Wilford   On the same day that he is spanked in front of his students by Lorna Sue's tycoon husband and Herbie Zylstra, Thomas Chippering is summoned to the office of the UNIVERSITY OF MINNESOTA president, Theodore Wilford Pillsbury. Expecting that he is finally going to win the Hubert H. Humphrey Prize for teaching excellence, Chippering confidently arrives at the office, only to shrink back in dismay when the door to the inner chambers of the president opens to reveal Megan Rooney and her roommate, Toni, seated alongside the president's desk. The two girls denounce him for sexual harassment, claiming that he forced them to accept unwanted help on their honors theses, and Chippering is forced to resign from his position as tenured professor.

Pillsbury, Mrs.   After he is fired from his job for sexual harassment, Thomas Chippering informs readers in a footnote that President Pillsbury "could hardly be counted upon to judge the case fairly" (219) since Chippering had called the president's wife a "dumb cooze" at a black-tie faculty party.

Pillsbury's Secretary   When Thomas Chippering is summoned to UNIVERSITY OF MINNESOTA President Pillsbury's office, he expects to be told that he is the winner of a prestigious teaching award. The president's secretary, described as a "pleasantly lanky" young woman, "flat as Nebraska, limber as the Platte" (216), hands Chippering a sheaf of paperwork and instructs him not to peek. Although she clearly understands the great trouble that Chippering is in, the secretary holds her tongue about the true reason for the meeting with the president. Chippering, as usual, misreads the woman's motives, believing that she is flirting with him. He describes her eyes as flashing with "risqué delight" and her posture as "just short of idolatrous" (216).

Plumbing Contractor   One of Thomas Chippering's competitors for the job of Captain Nineteen on a local children's television program is an OWAGO plumbing contractor whom Mrs. Robert Kooshoff thinks is "cute" because he looks like "a big panda bear" (262). Chippering becomes incensed when the plumber runs 37 seconds over his allotted audition time. When he complains to the producer, Jessie, whom he has already offended by mistaking her for a stagehand, the young woman angrily retorts: "Put a gag on and wait your turn like everybody else" (263).

Powell, Jerry and Ernest   As children, Thomas Chippering and his best friend, Herbie Zylstra, imagine using their plywood airplane to drop bombs on the homes of Jerry Powell and his cousin Ernest, two of the people whom the boys "feared or despised" (2). Later, when Thomas is 12 years old, Lorna Sue Zylstra will become angry at him for kissing a girl named Faith Graffenteen. In turn, Thomas will accuse Lorna Sue of kissing Jerry Powell.

Rebecca   Rebecca is one of Thomas Chippering's nurses during his six-day stay at the OWAGO, MINNESOTA, mental hospital after his breakdown on live television during his *Captain Nineteen* audition. Much to Chippering's disappointment, the nurses at the hospital prove to be "far inferior to their collective carnal reputation" (268). He estimates that Rebecca is at least 46 years old and adds that she is as "forbidding as a lunar landscape, hippy as the Iron Curtain" (268). While Chippering, as always, believes the woman is flirting with him—he writes that "the poor woman clearly entertained robust fantasies about me"—he attributes her brusqueness to "menopausal ill temper" (268) rather than to the fact that she is outraged by his sexual advances.

Rooney, Megan   After Thomas Chippering returns to work from his trip to TAMPA, FLORIDA, with Mrs. Robert Kooshoff, he is paid a visit in his office by Toni, the student who had coerced him into writing her honor's thesis. Toni announces that her roommate, Megan Rooney, has read Toni's diary, discovered the plagiarism, and is threatening to turn both Chippering and his student in to the college administration. It turns out that Toni had slept with Megan's boyfriend, as well as her "backup" boyfriend, infuriating her roommate, who paid Toni back by sleeping with all the young men on the college football team that Toni had claimed for herself. Soon after Toni's departure, Chippering arrives at Megan's dorm to confront her about her threat. Megan, a tiny girl with chestnut hair and gray eyes whom Chippering, of course, is immediately attracted to, turns out to be just as foul-mouthed as Toni, asking Chippering where her "slut roommate" is (187). But the two soon work out a deal. Megan promises to remain silent about the ghost-written thesis on the condition that Chippering agree to write her honor's thesis as well. Although the professor keeps his bargain, the two girls nevertheless end up turning him in to the college president, who fires Chippering from his appointment.

Salesclerk at Ben Franklin Store   When Thomas Chippering cannot get a rag fuse to ignite his homemade gasoline bombs, he goes to a Ben Franklin store on Main Street in OWAGO, MINNESOTA, and tells the salesclerk that he would like to buy two packs of firecrackers. The girl replies that fireworks are illegal but tells Chippering that if he waits until the Fourth of July, he should be able to buy them from any kid in town. On July 3 Chippering revisits the store on a whim, to ask again about the availability of firecrackers. The same salesgirl, impatient this time, sends him out to the town's playgrounds to find children willing to sell what he wants.

Sandra   Sandra is the name given to the new lover who runs off to FIJI with the husband of an unnamed female reader addressed only as "you" throughout the novel. Said to be a "tall willowy redhead half his age" (22), Sandra was apparently a friend of the woman reader. The woman introduced Sandra to her husband, not suspecting the betrayed that would soon befall her.

Sarah, Signe, Rhonda   Sarah, Signe, and Rhonda are the names of the "several droll, well-sculpted enrollees" in Thomas Chippering's seminar on "The Homographs of Erotic Slang" (24) with whom he tries to comfort himself after his divorce from Lorna Sue.

Schultz, Dr. Harold   Dr. Harold Schultz is the in-house psychiatrist at the mental hospital in OWAGO, MINNESOTA, where Thomas Chippering spends six days after his public breakdown on live television while auditioning to host a local children's program. Because one of Chippering's symptoms is a self-imposed muteness, Dr. Schultz himself refuses to speak as well, communicating with the ex-professor only by writing words on a yellow legal pad and passing them to his patient, who replies in kind. Chippering's sessions with the doctor consist mostly of long silences, punctuated by these brief, written exchanges; they eventually turn into a battle of wills to see who will speak first. The doctor loses when he breaks his silence to tell Chippering he has serious problems and that he is an "asshole" (271). On the fateful Fourth of July when Chippering plans to gain his revenge on the Zylstras, long after his release from the mental hospital, he experiences a blank time of about an hour after completing his homemade bombs. He is later informed that during this period he had left a garbled message on Dr. Schultz's answering machine.

Sebastian   Sebastian is the name of a python snake that Herbie and Lorna Sue Zylstra keep as a pet when they are children. The snake must be fed live rats, which Herbie dangles over Sebastian's cage, chanting "dinner, dinner" (72). One particularly lively rat wriggles out of Herbie's grasp, out the window, and onto a narrow ledge below the sash. Herbie decides to lower the family cat out the window by a rope to catch the rat. When he drops the cat as well, he himself climbs out the window, catches the cat—named Vanilla—by the scruff of the neck and passes it up to the waiting Thomas Chippering. When Herbie throws the rat up as well, Thomas accidentally drops Vanilla out the window, killing the family pet, a mistake that Lorna Sue never seems to forgive.

Spider   See GREEN BERETS.

Svingen, Sissy Sissy Svingen is a new secretary who begins work in Thomas Chippering's department offices the day he is fired from his job. The professor describes the secretary in the following terms: "Twenty-three years of age. Twenty-two-inch waist. Flared nostrils, sandy brown hair, bowling pin hips, hearing aid, bulging black sweater, a lamentable dusting of dandruff at the shoulders" (199). Despite what might be considered an unflattering description, Chippering is attracted to the young woman and invites her to meet him after work in the bar of the local Ramada Inn. At first hesitant, Sissy finally relents. When she arrives at the bar, Chippering has already been drinking with two prostitutes—a French woman named Fleurette and a Russian named Masha. The three women end up getting along well, having time to chat when Chippering falls asleep in a hotel chapel for an hour. The drunken group eventually decides to make a midnight road trip to OWAGO, MINNESOTA, where Chippering is confident that they "would be welcomed with hugs and a hearty breakfast in the home of Mrs. Robert Kooshoff" (229). Of course, Mrs. Kooshoff's reaction when they arrive an hour before dawn is anything but welcoming, and Chippering hurries the three girls on their way.

Swanson, Laurel Laurel Swanson is a librarian who works at the Owago County Library and helps Thomas Chippering locate a book on explosives on July 3, the day before he plans to exact his revenge on the Zylstras with homemade gasoline bombs. As with every young woman he meets, Chippering assesses Laurel's physical attributes, describing her as having "Viking-blue eyes, slim haunches, [a] boarding-ramp pelvis, elfin ears, a bust of telescopic grandeur, all professionally fitted on six sleek feet of high-grade Swedish soapstone" (289). Believing that the young woman is attracted to him, Chippering invites her to lunch. Laurel later calls to break the date but offers to come to his home that evening instead. Not understanding that she is an evangelical Christian intent on converting him to the Church of Jehovah, Chippering agrees and invites her over to Mrs. Robert Kooshoff's house. Although Mrs. Kooshoff is understandably angry when Laurel arrives on her doorstep that night,

the two women drink Jim Beam together long after Chippering has gone to bed, gossiping freely about the professor's shortcomings.

Thuy Ninh Thuy Ninh is a young Vietnamese woman in her late teens who enters into an intensely erotic relationship with Thomas Chippering when he is stationed at the old tea plantation in the jungle with the six GREEN BERET soldiers. The girl is one of an army of Vietnamese women who appear out of the jungle twice a week to tend the elaborate grounds of the villa. Chippering fancies that he is in love with Thuy Ninh and that she returns his affection, until one evening when he spies the girl naked, her body painted in blue and green, dancing seductively for the six Greenies. Chippering writes he instantly "understood the source of her expertise in the art of love. She was slick with treason" (162). In revenge for the perceived betrayal, Chippering calmly walks onto the verandah and calls in an air strike on coordinates immediately adjacent to the tea plantation. His motive, he tells readers, "was not to kill, merely to terrify" (163). Chippering then walks away into the jungle, never to see Thuy Ninh again.

Toby Toby is the name of the turtle that Mr. Chippering brings his son, Thomas, and his friend Herbie Zylstra instead of the real engine they had requested for their plywood airplane when the boys are seven and eight years old. Herbie, perhaps even more keenly disappointed than Thomas himself, tells Mr. Chippering that every turtle on earth is named Toby, and that "it's still just a stupid old turtle" (3). From that day forward, the word *turtle*—the "twin syllables," the "quick *t*'s on [his] tongue" (3)—will remind Thomas of childhood disappointment.

Toni Toni (short for Antonia) is a young student of Thomas Chippering's at the UNIVERSITY OF MINNESOTA, enrolled in a "pet course" of his called "It's Your Thick Tongue," which focuses on pronunciation, grammar, and vocabulary (87). When Toni asks for help with her honors thesis, Chippering begins meeting her in his faculty office as well as in the sitting room of her dormitory. After several such private "tutoring" sessions, he quotes Shakespeare lines to her, suggesting that he wants a more intimate relationship. In response, Toni becomes mock-furious and threatens to report him for sexual harassment unless he agrees to actually write her entire thesis for her. Professor Chippering will spend the next several weeks researching and typing the thesis—a close textual study of Western matrimonial vows—for the girl, who proves to be a harsh taskmistress, often sending Chippering back to the library or demanding that he rewrite sections that are "wooden" or "too dense" (95). Toni is "radiant," however, when her thesis is accepted with highest honors, her committee members remarking that she is "a gifted if somewhat verbose student," and that the thesis marks "an astonishing scholarly debut" (119). When Toni's roommate, Megan Rooney, finds out about the scheme, she demands that Chippering write her thesis as well. Eventually, the linguistics professor will lose his job when the two girls expose him to the university president, claiming that he forced his help upon them and sexually harassed them to boot.

Tulip   See GREEN BERETS.

Tycoon   See KERSTEN.

Unnamed Female Reader   Throughout the novel, Thomas Chippering frequently addresses his comments to an unnamed "you"—a female reader whose husband has left her and moved to FIJI with another woman, a redhead named Sandra. Whenever Chippering needs to defend his behavior, he will address this "you," demanding her sympathy by reminding her of her own crazy, uncontrollable behavior when her husband left her. Apparently, this woman, in a fit of jealousy, even traveled to Fiji to confront her ex-husband and his new love, much as Chippering travels repeatedly to TAMPA, FLORIDA, to spy on Lorna Sue. It is difficult to discern whether this "you" is intended to be a real person from his past or simply an imaginary reader whom Thomas has invented. It is even possible that this woman is intended to be Lorna Sue herself, since late in the novel Chippering tantalizes readers by writing: "I spotted your ex-husband

at one point. Or was he I? In which case, who would you be?" (294). Yet, at the end of the novel Thomas is living in the Caribbean—on an island "southeast of Tampa, somewhere north of Venezuela" (336)—with a blonde named Donna, not in Fiji (which is located in the South Pacific, not too far from Australia) with a redhead named Sandra, so this clue is somewhat confusing. It is also possible that readers are intended to view these particular remarks as the interjections of the narrator Tim O'Brien, who after all, has invented the narrator Thomas Chippering. Perhaps, then, O'Brien is stepping into his own novel on a metafictive level (*see* METAFICTION), addressing either a real or fictional woman from his own past. In any case, the repeated references to this unnamed woman remind readers that Thomas Chippering's is not such an unusual or isolated case—that all of us are capable of doing strange, embarrassing things for love. As Chippering points out, "Unique as you are—and do not for a moment think otherwise—you also represent every brokenhearted lover on this planet" (236).

Unnamed Female Reader's Husband   The husband of the unnamed female reader, whom Thomas Chippering frequently addresses in the second-person "you" throughout the novel, is said to have run off to FIJI with a new lover. Chippering claims that this reader learned that her husband spent Tuesday afternoons in room 622 of a Hilton hotel along a busy freeway with "a tall, willowy redhead half his age" (22) by discovering a book of matches in his pocket. The husband deserts his wife for this redhead, named Sandra, after 20 years of marriage, breaking the unnamed woman's heart after having vowed to love her forever.

Vanilla   Vanilla is the name of the cat owned by the Zylstra family when Herbie and Lorna Sue are children. One day Thomas Chippering is in the Zylstra attic with his friends, watching Herbie attempt to feed a rat to their pet python. When the rat manages to wriggle away and escape out the open attic window, Herbie decides to tie Vanilla to a rope and lower it to the ledge below to catch the rat. Vanilla, of course, is merely terrified by this game and ends up landing on the ledge as well after nearly being hanged. Herbie is then forced to climb outside the window and retrieve the cat by the scruff of its neck. He hands it up to Thomas, then captures the rat, which he tosses up at the window as well. Thomas, as he tries to catch the rat, loses his grip on Vanilla. The family pet plunges to its death out the open window. When Lorna Sue shouts "Killer" at Thomas, he lies that the cat bit him, thus setting into motion the decades of deceit and disappointment that will mark the Chipperings' marriage.

Wick, Miss Askold   Miss Askold Wick runs the day care center in OWAGO, MINNESOTA, where Thomas Chippering works after being fired from his university teaching position. Miss Wick works hard to keep a tight rein on Chippering, who gets into childish arguments with his charges, teaches them to recite speeches that include profanity, and often behaves in an inappropriate manner. She works out a compromise between her wayward teacher and Faith Grafenteen when Faith objects to Chippering's teaching her four-year-old daughter, Evelyn, to recite Lady Macbeth's "Out, damned spot" soliloquy, convincing Chippering at last "to locate less formidable texts for [his] students" (251).

Wildfire   See GREEN BERETS.

Zylstra, Earleen   Earleen Zylstra, described as "a wizened old lady in a wheelchair," is Lorna Sue Zylstra's paternal grandmother. A foul-mouthed and feisty old woman who has detested Thomas Chippering ever since his marriage to Lorna Sue, Earleen delightedly calls Mrs. Robert Kooshoff a floozy when she and Chippering go to visit the Zylstras over the Easter break that Chippering spends in OWAGO, MINNESOTA. Later, Earleen will accompany her daughter-in-law, Velva, on a visit to Chippering in the mental hospital, where he has been briefly confined after publicly breaking down on a local television show. "Seen you on the teleconfusion," she tells him, "too bad you didn't just blow yourself sky-high, save everybody a lot of trouble" (272).

Zylstra, Herbie   Herbie Zylstra is a childhood friend of Thomas H. Chippering and the older brother of Lorna Sue Zylstra. A hyperactive child with a strong imagination from a strange, reclusive, religiously minded family, Herbie attempts to nail his younger sister to a cross when he is eight years old and she is seven. Following this incident, in which he severely injures Lorna Sue's hand, Herbie is sent to a hospital-school run by Jesuits in the Twin Cities of Minnesota. Thomas does not see his childhood friend for nearly a year while he is hospitalized. Upon his return, Herbie is not the same child: He has become "a loner . . . silent and self-absorbed" (9). Thomas in the interim has made new friends, and he and Herbie go their separate ways through the rest of their childhood, until Thomas begins dating Lorna Sue in the middle of his junior year in high school. Herbie seems to disapprove of the relationship, and thus begins what will turn into an enmity between the former boyhood friends that lasts the next several decades, throughout Thomas's marriage to Lorna Sue and their divorce 20 years later. Thomas believes that Herbie is incestuously in love with his own sister, and thus that he played a key role in the divorce. Obsessed with gaining revenge on Herbie and winning Lorna Sue back, Thomas spies on the brother and sister at their new homes in TAMPA, FLORIDA, and tries to implicate Herbie in a series of church bombings in the Tampa area. Finally fed up with Thomas's mischief making, Herbie and Lorna Sue's new husband publicly administer a humiliating spanking to the linguistics professor in front of his students at the UNIVERSITY OF MINNESOTA. Eventually, Thomas will learn that Lorna Sue is the unbalanced arsonist and that Herbie, consumed with guilt over harming his sister when they were children, has been keeping careful watch over her throughout the years. By the end of the novel, Thomas and Herbie have reignited their fragile friendship, Herbie even coming to visit Thomas and Mrs. Robert Kooshoff on the unnamed island where they retreat to start a new life.

Zylstra, Lorna Sue   Lorna Sue Zylstra is the woman whom Thomas H. Chippering considers the love of his life through most of the novel. Readers first meet Lorna Sue when she is a very pretty child of seven, with black hair and "summer-brown skin" (5). The younger sister of the hyperactive Herbie Zylstra, Lorna Sue calmly allows her brother to try to nail her to a plywood cross in September 1952. The resulting scar on her hand is a stigmata that stays with her through the rest of her life. Lorna Sue begins dating Thomas Chippering when they are both 16 years old and juniors in high school, even though her family, including Herbie, does not approve of the relationship. She is the first girl whom Thomas Chippering makes love to, an act that takes place on the hood of his father's Pontiac in the middle of a Minnesota cornfield, and which Thomas talks Lorna Sue into by buying her an expensive watch. The childhood sweethearts eventually marry but get divorced two decades later after Herbie shows Lorna Sue a black ledger book that Thomas had concealed under their bedroom mattress. The book contains detailed records of all the women Thomas had flirted with over the years. Herbie also reveals to Lorna Sue a series of phony checks Thomas had made out to a nonexistent psychiatrist. He had only been pretending to "get help" for his psychological problems as Lorna Sue had demanded.

Not too long after the divorce, Lorna Sue marries a wealthy businessman and moves to TAMPA, FLORIDA. Still desperately in love with his ex-wife, Thomas flies to Tampa several times to spy on Lorna Sue, her new husband, and her older brother, Herbie, who lives nearby. In the early parts of the novel, readers place most of the blame for the failed relationship on Thomas Chippering, who comes off as a pompous, self-important womanizer, unable to let go of the past and deluded about the future. By the end of the novel, however, readers realize that Lorna Sue has her own share of psychological problems as well. It turns out she is the one who burned ST. PAUL'S CATHOLIC CHURCH as a child, even though Herbie and Thomas were questioned in the crime. Her childhood experience of being nailed to a cross has turned Lorna Sue into an extremely selfish woman who demands worshipful adoration from the men around her. Thomas finally learns that Herbie's close relationship with his sister is not born of incestuous desire as he has

long suspected but of a need to take care of Lorna Sue and to protect her when she threatens to harm herself or others.

Zylstra, Ned Ned Zylstra is the father of Herbie and Lorna Sue. Small-town gossip suggests that Ned had studied with the Jesuits, planning to become a priest himself before dropping out of seminary "in circumstances tainted by scandal" (38), possibly involving a secret marriage. Ned, like the entire Zylstra clan, loathes Thomas Chippering, at least partly because of the professor's arrogant condescension toward the family as well as his refusal to spend any time at their home, even during holidays, when he was married to Lorna Sue. When Chippering and Mrs. Robert Kooshoff go to visit the Zylstras during the Easter break they spend together, Ned, now in his mid-seventies, with a "bloated face . . . dyed hair, [and] pasty white skin" (65) is foul-mouthed and angry. He tells Chippering to stay away from Lorna Sue and calls Mrs. Robert Kooshoff a floozy.

Zylstra, Velva Velva Zylstra is the wife of Ned and mother of Herbie and Lorna Sue. It is whispered in town that the woman may have been a nun at one point, and the Zylstra house, filled with "religious relics" and "anonymous old nuns and priests who came and went like fugitives in the night" (38) suggests that there might be some truth to the rumors. When Thomas Chippering goes to visit the Zylstras with Mrs. Robert Kooshoff when he is back home during his Easter break, Velva is sitting on the sofa, watching television with her relatives and munching on candied popcorn. Like her husband, she is in her mid-seventies and sickly-looking, bloated and pale. Velva will appear again later in the novel when she and her ancient mother-in-law Earleen visit Chippering in the mental hospital in OWAGO, MINNESOTA, where he is confined for six days after breaking down on live television while auditioning to host a children's program. Velva has come to the hospital to warn Chippering to stay away from Lorna Sue when she comes home for the Fourth of July holiday. Rather than feeling admonished by this news, Chippering is pleased to learn that Lorna Sue will be home for the summer and begins plotting his revenge for the Fourth of July.

FURTHER READING

Heberle, Mark A. *A Trauma Artist: Tim O'Brien and the Fiction of Vietnam.* Iowa City: University of Iowa Press, 2001.

Herzog, Tobey C. "Tim O'Brien Interview," *South Carolina Review* 31, no. 1 (1998): 78–109.

Lucy, Niall. *Postmodern Literary Theory.* London: Wiley-Blackwell, 1997.

Weber, Bruce. "Wrestling with War and Love; Raw Pain, Relived Tim O'Brien's Way," Interview, *New York Times,* 2 September 1998, E1.

"Too Skinny" (2001)

First published in the *New Yorker* in September 2001, "Too Skinny" is a story about an overweight mop-and-broom factory owner named Marv Bertel. When Marv loses an enormous amount of weight and begins to date his attractive executive assistant, he invents an incredible lie about himself to keep the girl's interest. The story was later revised and included as chapter 19 of the 2002 novel, *July, July.*

SYNOPSIS

Marv Bertel, 41 years old, has been a fat man his whole life, the constant butt of jokes. But in March 1988, he begins dieting. By mid-October of that same year, he is down to 220 pounds, and to celebrate he files for divorce from his wife. Settling into his new life as a thin man, Marv continues to run his mop-and-broom factory, but he also begins going to bars at night, where he tells lies about himself to attractive younger women. Sometimes claiming to be a plastic surgeon, a former priest, or a rodeo cowboy, Marv basks in the attention of the adoring young women, but he never makes sexual advances toward any of them, until one night when he invites his beautiful and shrewd young executive assistant, Sandra DiLeona, out to dinner. Unable to stop himself, Marv blurts out to Sandra that he is in reality the famous, reclusive author Thomas

Pierce. Marv sleeps with Sandra that night, and the two begin a relationship that after a few months leads to their engagement. During these months, however, Marv is terrified that his lie will be discovered. He is no longer able to sleep or eat, and he begins to lose even more weight. Sandra, while at times suspicious of Marv's claim about his secret identity, nevertheless tells her friends and family that she is dating the famous writer Thomas Pierce. Eventually, after finding a fuzzy picture of Pierce on the Internet, Sandra finally forces Marv to admit the truth to her. Rather than canceling their marriage plans, though, the scheming young woman demands that Marv keep up the Pierce pretense so that she will not be humiliated in front of her friends and relatives. Sandra also demands that Marv give her a cash stipend, separate bedrooms, and a half interest in the factory. Marv complies with Sandra's wishes, but he also begins to eat again, soon gaining back nearly all the weight he had lost. To pass the time behind his locked office door at the mop and broom factory, Marv begins to write down memories of his skinny days. As he enlarges some details, invents others, and struggles with motives and meaning, he actually becomes the writer that he had only pretended to be earlier.

COMMENTARY

"Too Skinny," like numerous other O'Brien works, is a story about pretending and fiction making, and about how fiction can sometimes be more powerful than truth. Marv Bertel is a man stuck not only in a body he is ashamed of but in a job he does not enjoy. Although Marv owns the mop-and-broom factory, O'Brien writes that he "had never found the business challenging, or even mildly interesting," and the grossly obese man spends his time sluggishly "sitting at a big rosewood desk for hour upon profitable hour, more or less motionless, more or less dead" (92). Once Marv begins dieting, however, his imagination fires up. He begins daydreaming and "infinite new futures" appear to him (92). Like many O'Brien characters, including Paul Berlin in *Going After Cacciato* and Timmy in "The Lives of the Dead," Marv's fantasies begin to shape his real life. His daydreams inspire him to lose even more weight, and even his personality begins to change as he shifts from the reserved, quiet-spoken man he had always been to someone who tells jokes in elevators, passes along gossip to his young executive assistant, and flirts with the women he meets in local bars. He even begins to make up stories about his life—that he is a major league baseball coach, a plastic surgeon, a former priest, a rodeo cowboy. Marv, who had longed to be a writer during his college years, enjoys "the artifice, the make-believe, the amazing power of a big bold lie" (93). He feels strong and powerful as he shapes himself through his fictions into anything he wants to be, and as he sees the respect "that spilled out like paint in the eyes of fetching young women half his age" (93).

Marv's love of pretense, the power he feels when he makes up stories, should prepare readers for the enormous lie he tells his executive assistant, Sandra DiLeona, the night he invites her out to dinner: that he is the very famous, reclusive novelist Thomas Pierce. Although this story seems to pop into his head unbidden, Marv has already mastered the art of storytelling, and it should be no surprise that the identity he chooses to assume for himself is one of a celebrated fiction writer. O'Brien is also having fun with a few insider jokes here. Thomas Pierce is clearly meant to be a fictional version of the real-life writer THOMAS PYNCHON, also much admired in the literary community for his large, difficult books that contain intricate wordplay and dense symbolism, and also almost obsessively reclusive. O'Brien makes fun of literary fans as well when Marv asks Sandra if she has read his books and the young woman replies: "Of course not. Nobody does—that's not the point. You're famous. Everybody knows *about* you" (94). So, one of the ways that Sandra is so easily duped is because she, too, is living a fiction. She does not care about Pierce's literary output, about the books that he writes; she is only concerned with his fame and how it might reflect on her.

The line between fact and fiction becomes even murkier in the story when O'Brien writes that "Marv fell in love, or imagined he did" (95) with Sandra. This line invites readers to question if there is a difference between falling in love and imagining that one is falling in love. How can love

be tested, how can it be measured? Is there any way to determine if love is "real" or "imagined"? Isn't love, after all, a matter of the emotions, of the dreams and of the imagination, rather than an actual physical state of being? Thus, although Marv begins to worry horribly about his lie, about being discovered, to the extent that he can no longer sleep or eat, he is so afraid of losing Sandra "or the idea of her" (96) that he continues the pretense. Sandra is not a real person for Marv any more than Thomas Pierce is the real Marv. She is for him a symbol, "a living emblem of all those lovely young women who eight or nine months ago would not have given him the time of day" (96). Although Marv decries the young woman's "galling cynicism" (96) when she begins to ask questions about why Marv never seems to write and why his mail never deals with literary matters, the story itself is quite cynical about human relationships, suggesting that people do not really know one another, but respond mostly to fantasies about their loved ones they have built inside their heads and hearts.

Even more, the story marvels at the human willingness to believe these fantasies, no matter how outlandish they may become. Even when Sandra discovers the old picture of Thomas Pierce on the Web and sees that there is no resemblance to Marv Bertel, she is lured into belief again when he tells her a ludicrous story about working with a coauthor: "The fact is . . . two of us write those books. I'm shy, he's not. What you saw was the other guy's picture" (97). When he is once more able to fool Sandra, Marv realizes that "there is no outer limit to mankind's credulity" (97). And the bigger the lie, the better: "The human creature," O'Brien writes, "prefers an elusive miracle to an everyday lie" (97). Humans want so deeply to believe in the fictions that they create about themselves and others that accept all kinds of absurd stories: "The indelibility of love. A god with white whiskers and a hearty laugh" (97). Here readers see the real cynicism at the base of Marv Bertel's fictions. He diminishes even the most cherished "truths" that humans believe in—the power of love, the existence of God—to lies, to pretenses that accord with his own big lie about being Thomas Pierce.

Strangely, though, the pretenses in the story, the fictions or lies that are told, begin to shape reality, to become the new reality. As Marv continues to lose weight, as tufts of his hair fall out and his teeth loosen in his jaw, he begins to feel that he is actually living inside of a Thomas Pierce novel: "Each hour of his life, it now seemed, had the nap and weave of one of Thomas Pierce's most grotesque fictions, freakish and scary, ruled by entropy, a madhouse of make-believe looping back upon itself in infinite ellipses" (98). Fact and fiction comingle nearly inextricably when Sandra finally forces Marv to confess the lie, but to stick to it nevertheless so that she will not be embarrassed in front of the friends and family she has already told about Marv's secret identity. In this way Marv is able to secure "the glossy veneer of the wife he'd always wanted," (98) and Sandra is able to attach to herself the aura of fame that accompanies Pierce. Yes, their marriage is a sham, but is it really? Both seem to have gotten what they have fantasized about. Even more, the story ends with Marv having gained back almost all of the weight he had lost, locking himself into his office at the mop-and-broom factory to write down "memories of his encounter with skinniness" (99). He begins to have fun with sentences, to change a few names, to invent some things and enlarge upon others, and to chuckle to himself over questions of motive and meaning. Marv has finally turned into the writer he had always imagined becoming. The pretense has trumped reality, and Marv, locked in his office, works hard to finally "dissolve the fiction of his own fucked-up life" (99) through the new stories that he will tell about himself.

Differences in Versions

While the gist of the story version and the novel version of "Too Skinny" is the same—the characters and the key plot elements remain unchanged—nevertheless, O'Brien made numerous changes to the story's language when he revised it for inclusion in *July, July*. Some of these alterations involve fairly small changes in minor details, mostly intended to make Marv's weight loss and the lies he tells seem more realistic. For instance, in the story version it takes Marv only two weeks to move from

220 pounds to his new goal of 199. In the novel's version this is changed to a more believable three weeks. By January 1, 1989, in the story version, Marv is said to weigh 174 pounds and stand six feet, three inches tall. In the novel this is altered to a slightly more realistic 178 pounds and a height of six feet, two inches. Further, in the original story version it takes Marv only five additional days after the first of the year to get down to an even 170 pounds, while this new weight loss takes a more realistic 18 days in the novel. Other minor changes involve Marv telling young women in bars that he is a third base coach for the Chicago White Sox baseball team, not the Colorado Rockies as in the original story. This change makes Marv less likely to be caught in a lie since a young woman from Denver might conceivably know who the third base coach for the Rockies is. Also, O'Brien changes his description of Sandra DiLeona's eyes. While in the original story she is said to have "shrewd blue eyes" (93), in the novel she has "wily brown eyes" (*July* 253). In addition, the original story version has Sandra finding the picture of Thomas Pierce on the Web, while she actually has to go to the library to look up the picture in the revised version. O'Brien might have made this change because the original story could prompt readers to wonder why Sandra had not bothered to look up Pierce on the Web earlier. Going to the library takes more of a determined effort on her part.

Other changes involve the omission of several sentences in the novel's version that appear in the original short story. For example, when the narrator describes the lies Marv tells to the "fetching young women half his age" (93) in bars, the *New Yorker* story includes the following sentences: "He loved the artifice, the make-believe, the amazing power of a big bold lie. Also, he liked acting. Fantasy made him good at it. He underplayed his roles, reluctantly allowing pertinent misinformation to be pried piecemeal from tight, modest lips" (93). These sentences are removed from the revised version, possibly because they make Marv seem almost too calculating, contradicting, perhaps, the notion presented elsewhere in the story that Marv's lie-telling is more compulsion than cold-blooded calculation. Other sentences that are removed in the novel include a line about Marv becoming a shadow of his former self (96) and a line about the hurt he feels when he hears Sandra's suspicions about Thomas Pierce being "completely genuine" (96). There are other brief omitted lines and phrases as well, generally suggesting O'Brien's desire to tighten up the story and not to instruct readers too directly about how they should react to Marv and his lies. Finally, the novel version adds a few lines that do not appear in the original *New Yorker* story. Most important is Marv's insistence to Sandra when he overhears her hinting on the phone to a relative about Marv's secret identity that he cannot accept lies: "One thing I can't tolerate, not ever, is duplicity" (*July* 263). This phrase highlights even more fully than in the story version Marv's hypocrisy. He is transferring the guilt he feels about the enormous fraud that he himself has been perpetrating into anger at Sandra, whose crime of duplicity pales in comparison to his own.

CHARACTERS

Bertel, Marv   A 41-year-old grossly overweight owner of a mop-and-broom factory on the outskirts of Denver, Marv Bertel is trapped in a boring career and a loveless marriage. But when he begins dieting in March 1988, his entire life changes. When he gets down to 220 pounds, he divorces his wife, moves into a furnished apartment, and begins spending his evenings in trendy bars, telling lies about himself to attractive younger woman and basking in the attention he receives. However, Marv gets in over his head when he tells his beautiful and calculating young executive assistant, Sandra DiLeona, that he is, in reality, a famous, reclusive writer. Terrified of having his ruse discovered as he and Sandra begin to date, Marv's health begins to deteriorate. He is unable to eat or sleep, he loses even more weight, his hair begins to fall out, and several teeth become loose. When Sandra inevitably discovers the truth, she has already told several friends and family members about her fiancé's supposed secret identity. She demands that Marv marry her anyway and keep up the farce of the famous writer as well as provide her with a generous cash settlement and a half interest in the factory. Marv agrees and the couple goes through with

the wedding, but he begins to eat again, gains back a great deal of weight, and starts to write about his life secretly behind his locked office door.

Bertel, Mrs.   After Marv Bertel loses his first 41 pounds, his wife tells him that she is "incredibly, incredibly proud" of him (92). This is the first time that Marv remembers his wife offering him praise of any sort, and a few months later, he files for divorce.

DiLeona, Sandra   A 26-year-old MBA who works as Marv Bertel's executive assistant at the mop-and-broom factory, Sandra DiLeona is described as "a tall, slim, masterfully assembled blonde" with a "cover-girl complexion" and "pouty lips" (93). Yet, Sandra is also a shrewd and calculating young woman, "chilly by disposition, nothing if not canny" (93). Although initially skeptical when Marv "confesses" his secret identity as the reclusive writer Thomas Pierce to her, Sandra nevertheless accepts Marv's story, delighting in her closeness to such a famous man and such an acclaimed literary genius. When she finally discovers incontrovertible proof of Marv's lie—an old, fuzzy picture of Pierce on the Internet—Sandra has already bragged to several of her friends and family members about Marv being the famous writer. The calculating young woman insists that her fiancé marry her anyway, that he keep up the charade about Pierce, and also that he provide her with cash and a half interest in the mop-and-broom factory.

Niece of Sandra DiLeona   At the wedding of Marv Bertel and Sandra DiLeona, one of Sandra's nieces, "who came equipped with a suggestive smile and large bared breasts" (99), flirts shamelessly with Marv, believing that he is, in reality, the famous, reclusive writer Thomas Pierce. The niece's behavior, however, does not go unnoticed by the bride. During the toasts, Sandra taps Marv on the nose with her wedding ring and says, "If you put the scam on that bitch-niece of mine ever again . . . you're just a dirt-poor ex" (99).

Pierce, Thomas   Thomas Pierce is a well-known and highly respected writer but also so camera- and people-shy that no one knows what he looks like. Pictures of him do not appear on the jackets of his books; he never grants interviews; and he lives a hermitlike existence. This is how Marv Bertel can get away for so long with the lie that he is really Pierce. The figure of Thomas Pierce is based most likely on THOMAS PYNCHON, the famously reclusive contemporary American novelist.

"Underground Tests" (1985)

The story "Underground Tests," which depicts a group of five former college friends being trained as revolutionaries in Cuba, was originally published in *Esquire* magazine in November 1985. The story in slightly expanded form appears as well in O'Brien's 1985 novel, *The Nuclear Age.*

SYNOPSIS

Set in late 1968 and early 1969, "Underground Tests" is narrated by a young Vietnam War DRAFT dodger named William, who, along with four friends—Ollie, Tina, Ned Rafferty, and Sarah Strouch—finds himself in a Cuban training camp for political revolutionaries. While the first six days at the luxurious Cuban resort are spent leisurely, the five friends are woken up early on the seventh morning. For the next several weeks, they are drilled mercilessly all day in exhausting physical and mental exercises under the tutelage of two ruthless Vietnam veterans named Ebenezer Keezer and Nethro. Evenings are spent in education and indoctrination sessions where the five would-be revolutionaries learn terror tactics and study political ideology. The final exam for the training camp comes in December. The friends are expected to crawl across a beach under real rifle fire, make their way through several barbed wire barricades, and blow up a wooden tower. William, however, a poor soldier who had earlier defecated in his pants during a training exercise, fails the test miserably. Deciding that nothing is worth dying for, he gives up on the assigned mission and simply lies still on the beach. His girlfriend, Sarah, obviously disappointed with him,

nevertheless assures William that he can still be useful in the revolutionary movement by staying out of direct confrontations and playing the role of a courier instead. For the next two years, William works as a "network delivery boy" (259) while his friends become fugitives, Sarah's picture even appearing on page 12 of an issue of *Newsweek* magazine in March 1969.

COMMENTARY

The title of the story, "Underground Tests," suggests that this will be a tale of secret nuclear weapons tests, perhaps. But the underground here actually refers to the clandestine nature of the revolutionary movement that William is reluctantly part of, and it is William himself who is being tested. Will he prove suitable material to participate in the radical operations of this shady group or not? Readers see William's lack of commitment from the beginning of the story when Sarah Strouch, his girlfriend, yet a woman who William is "also a little afraid of" (252), admonishes him for having no passion for the movement, for lacking a "backbone" (254). "Love and war," Sarah chides him. "Sooner or later you have to choose sides" (254). William is unable to commit to either love or war—his relationship with Sarah seems nearly as nebulous as his feelings about being in Cuba. But William's real problem is that this revolutionary group so closely resembles the side it is fighting against. The tactics used to train the would-be revolutionaries are the tactics of military basic training, and the radical leaders are akin to drill sergeants. As William complains to Sarah at one point, "I can't tell the good guys from the bad guys, they're all gunslingers" (256). And after all, William evaded the Vietnam War draft in order to avoid the very violence and mayhem that he finds himself squarely in the middle of in Cuba: "Here, I realized, was everything I'd run from" (256). O'Brien satirizes stereotypical notions of flower children, love, and peace that are often associated with the 1960s counterculture. Ebenezer Keezer, Nethro, and even Sarah Strouch herself are serious revolutionaries, who consider themselves soldiers at war and who are willing to risk their lives and the lives of innocent people for their ideological beliefs.

In the evening political education seminars, Ebenezer Keezer points out some of the ironies inherent in America's involvement in Vietnam and in the revolutionary movement to stop the war. When he talks about *The Federalist Papers* and the American Revolution, he points out that America itself is a country "born in disobedience, even terrorism and that the faces that decorate our currency had once appeared on English wanted posters" (256). The original Founding Fathers, Keezer suggests, had more in common with the VIET CONG guerrillas that America is fighting against than with the current military-industrial establishment that marks America as one of the world's superpowers. Further, Keezer admonishes his trainees that they will use tactics borrowed not only from America's original guerrilla fighters but also from "Uncle Charlie" (256). The revolutionaries will make themselves into "ghost soldiers . . . like in the Nam" (256)—they will fashion themselves after the very enemy that America is fighting overseas. But William is no more a good revolutionary than other of O'Brien's characters are good soldiers. Like Paul Berlin in *Going After Cacciato*, William is overwhelmed by fear and even defecates on himself during a training session. He is unable to complete the final exam either, scared to move and convinced that nothing is worth dying for. William's mental and near-physical paralysis in these episodes might remind readers of the young Tim O'Brien in "On the Rainy River," who also seems to fail what might be considered a final exam. He is frozen with indecision at the end of the story, unable to jump from Elroy Berdahl's boat and swim the few remaining feet to Canada, and the story closes with the lines, "I was a coward. I went to the war" (*TTTC* 61). Whether soldiers or revolutionaries who violently oppose the war, O'Brien's characters are often torn by moral indecision, unable to act decisively or to be as brave as they would like to be.

The line between sanity and madness is another major theme in the story, just as it is in the novel *The Nuclear Age*, in which the story will be included. The "final exam" that William and the other trainees undergo seems like something out of a nightmare: Amplified voices in the night sing snatches of popular songs and imitate Groucho Marx and Looney Tunes characters as machine gun bullets rip through the air and flares light up the Caribbean sky, the lunacy and terror rivaling that depicted in the Francis Ford Coppola film *Apocalypse Now*. William reflects on the seeming insanity of the movement he has become involved with: "If you're sane, you see madness. If you see madness, you freak. If you freak, you're mad" (256). He finds himself in a no-win situation, a sort of catch-22. If William is sane enough to notice the madness around him, to be frightened by it, and to react accordingly, the others will consider him mad. And Sarah, at least, has no patience with William's doubts or his fears, accusing him of believing the whole war was invented just to ruin his day. She self-righteously calls his way of thinking "contemptible" (256) and argues angrily that they are there in Cuba to "stop the goddamn *killing*" (256).

But O'Brien also asks readers to question the pureness of the ideology that Sarah and the others so fiercely cling to. Sarah, for instance, while claiming to hate the war and everything it stands for, is also motivated by her own personal desire to feel wanted and the fact that she is not loved or needed by William as fully as she would like to be. "I want to be *wanted*," she tells William early on, "By you, by Interpol. Those handsome dudes on the FBI—doesn't matter, just wanted. I need that" (254). The end of the story reinforces this selfish motivation. When Sarah calls William to tell him that she is "famous," that her picture appears on page 12 of *Newsweek* magazine, she adds, "They want me" (259). O'Brien not only shatters stereotypes of a peaceful, nonviolent antiwar movement, showing how the radicals closely resemble the very side they are fighting against, he also satirizes the supposed noble motives of the protest movement as well, depicting how complex and tangled individual decisions to fight or not to fight, to act or remain passive, really are.

Differences in Versions
The novel version of the story is expanded quite a bit from the original *Esquire* version. The chapter in the novel titled "Underground Tests," for instance, opens in KEY WEST, FLORIDA, immediately after

the election of RICHARD NIXON as president. The friends are in mourning over the election, depressed by the political news. The novel then depicts Ollie Winkler arriving with a sleek boat captained by an unnamed Cuban who will ferry the friends to the island country for revolutionary training. Following this opening, the novel aligns more closely with the original story, although it does add some scenes and incidents. Ebenezer Keezer, when speaking about his experiences in Vietnam, adds a tale about shooting water buffalo that does not appear in the original *Esquire* version of the story. In the novel as well, Keezer is presented as slightly more cruel than in the story. For instance, he forces Tina to lift up her shirt, and he pokes at her obese belly, taunting her and calling her a pig. In addition, in order to mesh the story more smoothly with the rest of the novel, the revised version adds a few episodes in which William thinks back to his childhood, to hiding under the Ping-Pong table in his basement when he was 12 years old, and to his father's protecting him. Ned Rafferty, as well, attempts to protect William at one point in the revised version, demanding that Ebenezer Keezer and Nethro leave William alone after he defecates in his pants during the training exercise. This change reflects the budding friendship that will grow between Ned and William later in the novel.

CHARACTERS

Keezer, Ebenezer Ebenezer Keezer is a tough drill sergeant by day, an African-American Vietnam veteran who speaks in ghetto slang and toys mercilessly with the new recruits to the revolutionary movement. By night, however, Keezer dons a crisp suit and teaches the five friends lessons in political ideology with the careful enunciation and low-key air of a college professor. His mission is to take these young people and train them as committed, knowledgeable, and capable revolutionary saboteurs.

Nethro Nethro is the name of Ebenezer Keezer's sidekick in the Cuban training camp. More serious and less talkative than Keezer, Nethro nevertheless aids fully in the rigorous physical and mental training that the five former college friends undergo.

Ollie Ollie is one of the five friends who winds up in a terrorist-training camp in Cuba, studying to be a revolutionary. He, along with Tina, Ned, and Sarah, successfully completes the rigorous course and graduates to become a full-fledged provocateur and member of an unnamed radical underground political movement.

Rafferty, Ned Ned Rafferty, a former college football linebacker, teaches William how to play tennis during the leisurely first six days the group of radical friends spends in Cuba. Later, when the grueling revolutionary training starts, Ned will succeed in passing the course while William fails. Ned, like Sarah, Ollie, and Tina, will graduate to commit terrorist activities back in the United States in an attempt to subvert the war in Vietnam.

Strouch, Sarah Sarah Strouch is William's girlfriend in the story. A former college cheerleader, Sarah feels entirely at home in Cuba, telling William that this is the life she was made to lead. Although she hates the war in Vietnam, she also loves it because it allows her to become a revolutionary and commit herself fully to the cause. Sarah berates William for his own lack of commitment to violent antiwar protest, calling him "wishy-washy" and a "jellyfish" who lacks a spine (254). Despite her frequently expressed contempt for William, Sarah nevertheless reassures him after he fails the training camp's final exam that he can continue to work for the movement as a courier. The story ends with Sarah calling William on the phone after she participates in a night raid at a Selective Service office in downtown Miami. She triumphantly announces that she is now a wanted woman—her picture even appears in *Newsweek* magazine.

Tina Tina, sometimes called "Fat Tina" in the story, is one of the five friends who travel to Cuba to participate in a training camp for political radicals. Despite her physical limitations, Tina completes the training session successfully, a feat her friend William, the story's narrator, cannot accomplish.

William William, the story's narrator, is a Vietnam War DRAFT dodger who goes to Cuba with four friends to participate in an underground revolutionary training camp. William, however, unlike his friends, does not seem cut out for the life of a radical terrorist. To him the Cuban training camp resembles the worst aspects of the military service he had hoped to avoid. When William fails the camp's final exam, proving himself to be scared and incapable under fire, he is allowed to serve as a courier for the radical group while his friends commit clandestine acts of sabotage.

"The Vietnam in Me" (1994)

"The Vietnam in Me" is an essay Tim O'Brien published in the *New York Times Magazine* on October 2, 1994. The essay describes a return trip that O'Brien made to QUANG NGAI PROVINCE in Vietnam in February 1994, with his then-girlfriend, a HARVARD graduate student named KATE PHILLIPS. The essay alternates descriptions of the trip to Vietnam with images of a depressed O'Brien back in Cambridge, Massachusetts, in June and July 1994, near-suicidal after Kate has left him for another man.

SYNOPSIS

O'Brien's return visit to Vietnam is marked by the astonishing generosity and forgiveness of the villagers who greet him, especially in the little hamlet of Nuoc Man, near the former American base called LANDING ZONE GATOR, where he was stationed in the early months of 1969. The first American G.I. to return to the area, O'Brien is greeted by middle-aged women who smilingly introduce themselves by nicknames they were given by American soldiers 25 years earlier. "Dear God," O'Brien comments. "We should have bombed these people with love" (50). He explains as best he can to Kate that his time in Vietnam was marked not only by terror but also by love. The enforced intimacy with the death that constantly surrounded him created a new intimacy with life as well—an appreciation of what it means to be alive.

Yet, the trip is also marked for O'Brien by memories of loss and guilt. A few days later on a visit to

the village called My Lai 4 on American maps and THUAN YEN by local inhabitants, O'Brien meets several survivors of the MY LAI MASSACRE who tell him horrifying stories of playing dead under piles of bodies and of American soldiers shooting their guns again and again. O'Brien speculates on the American tendency to erase evil from our national mythology—he thinks about the blank faces of students when he visits high schools and colleges and mentions what happened in My Lai. O'Brien writes that after speaking with the My Lai villagers he gets the "guilt chills" (53), remembering how during his months in Quang Ngai he despised everything about the place. He understands the "black, fierce, hurting anger" (53) that arises when soldiers lose friends to enemy bombs or rifle fire, and he understands how the events of My Lai could happen. Nevertheless, O'Brien also argues that the men of ALPHA COMPANY, his own unit, never crossed the moral threshold that the soldiers of CHARLIE COMPANY did on March 16, 1968. O'Brien is angry at a military judicial system that declares everyone innocent, and he expresses outrage at the "almost cartoonish narcissism" (55) of an American policy that insists on searching for every American soldier killed or missing in the country while ignoring the tens of thousands of dead Vietnamese.

O'Brien's visit to Vietnam culminates with his small entourage—including himself, Kate, a *New York Times* photographer, and a Vietnamese interpreter—as they are led by a former captain from the 48th VIETCONG BATTALION named Mr. Tan in a search of two specific places O'Brien remembers from the war: a beautiful fishing village on an "impossibly white" (56) beach along the SOUTH CHINA SEA and a flooded rice paddy where Alpha Company took 13 casualties. Mr. Tan tells O'Brien that the American soldiers were never the main objective of the VIET CONG. Instead, the Viet Cong focused their efforts on ARVN (Army of the Republic of Vietnam) soldiers, understanding that if they could undermine the South Vietnamese the Americans would no longer have any reason to be in the country. Before Mr. Tan leads O'Brien into the beautiful fishing village by the lagoon, he makes sure to introduce O'Brien to a man who lived underground with his family for five years during the war as well as to a wreck of an old man, "both legs . . . gone from the upper-upper thigh" (56), as if to say, "Here is your paradise. Here is your pretty little fishing village by the sea" (56). When O'Brien finally finds the second location he is seeking, the paddy where so many of his friends died—and which seems to be the inspiration for the "shit field" in *The Things They Carried*—he notices the golden light shining on the field of rice, and he hopes that Kate remembers this when she leaves Vietnam.

Intermingled with these scenes from Vietnam in February 1994 are scenes that take place in the early morning hours in Cambridge in summer of that same year. O'Brien describes waking up at 4:00 in the morning on June 5, staring at a bottle of sleeping pills that are not working and contemplating suicide—"Not whether, but how" (50). Kate is living with another man, about seven blocks away, and O'Brien is deeply depressed. He confesses that he has been undergoing treatment for depression for many years. He acknowledges his own neediness, his desperation for love, connecting his willingness to go to war in the first place to his fear of being rejected by those he loved. While he fills his days by working out, writing, calling friends, visiting doctors, doing laundry, and other activities that make his days bearable, O'Brien writes, "The nights are not all right" (53). He is living on "war time," which, he informs readers, "is the time we're all on at one point or another: when fathers die, when husbands ask for divorce, when women you love are fast asleep beside men you wish were you" (55).

The article ends back in Vietnam, with Kate and O'Brien in Ho Chi Minh City, a place they both hate. Government speakers outside their hotel room blare loud American music most of the day, and O'Brien wonders what became of HO CHI MINH, what became of the revolution, what will become of him and Kate. The song "We Gotta Get Out of This Place" by the Animals becomes a fitting final statement for the essay, summing up both O'Brien's experiences in Vietnam and the psychological turmoil he finds himself back in Cambridge.

COMMENTARY

Many of the sentiments O'Brien expresses in this essay work their way into his published fiction as

well. When he explains to Kate how his intimacy with death in Vietnam brought about a new intimacy with life, readers might be reminded of the passage in "How to Tell a True War Story" from *The Things They Carried* in which the narrator writes that "proximity to death brings with it a corresponding proximity to life," that after a firefight, "there is always the immense pleasure of aliveness" (81). The narrator continues to probe this newly alive feeling, linking it to a new sense of the possibility of goodness in the world:

> You feel an intense, out-of-the-skin awareness of your living self—your truest self, the human being you want to be and then become by the force of wanting it. In the midst of evil you want to be a good man. You want decency. You want justice and courtesy and human concord, things you never knew you wanted. There is a kind of largeness to it, a kind of godliness. Though it's odd, you're never more alive than when you're almost dead. (81)

In ordinary life, one loses the sense of constant danger and fear of wartime, but one also loses this sense of largeness that the narrator describes in this passage, a sense that the stakes are extremely high. As O'Brien explains to Kate, his complex memories of Vietnam involve more than terror, they are partly about love. At war, he explains, "You love the miracle of your own enduring capacity for love" (51).

But the essay is marked much more by its sense of sorrow and loss than by the love or the new intimacy with life that O'Brien describes briefly. The pain he expresses in "The Vietnam in Me" appears throughout the novel that O'Brien was finishing up at the same time that he was writing the essay—*In the Lake of the Woods*—which was also published in 1994. *Lake,* like the essay, explores the circumstances and aftereffects of the My Lai Massacre alongside an unraveling love affair that leaves its protagonist in a precarious mental state. As is often the case in O'Brien's work, the line separating fact and fiction is permeable and elastic. Both O'Brien, as he presents himself in the essay, and John Wade in *Lake* are Vietnam veterans who have led outwardly successful lives for many years following their return from the war. Yet, despite this ability to function in the world, both men have arrived at a point where they must face the trauma of the past and its effect on the present. While O'Brien presents himself in the essay as suicidal rather than potentially homicidal like John Wade in the novel, nevertheless both men are tormented by feelings of guilt, and each fears losing love above all else. O'Brien's assertion in the essay that he went to war in the first place because he feared losing love might also remind readers of the story "On the Rainy River" from *The Things They Carried,* in which a fictional version of O'Brien, serving as narrator, explains to readers that he did not flee to Canada as he had considered doing at one point. Even though the young narrator believed the war was morally wrong, he was unable to defy the traditions and expectations he had been raised with. He was afraid of what people would say about him should he flee the DRAFT, and he could not bring himself to leave behind everything he knew and loved.

The "guilt chills" (53) that O'Brien describes in the essay arise at least partly from the hatred he felt for Quang Ngai Province. Although the My Lai Massacre was not yet public knowledge in spring of 1969 when he was stationed in Quang Ngai, O'Brien's unit patrolled the same area in PINKVILLE where LIEUTENANT WILLIAM CALLEY and members of Charlie Company had murdered hundreds of villagers a year earlier. O'Brien's views on the My Lai Massacre, as expressed in the essay, make their way into *In the Lake of the Woods* as well. In the essay, O'Brien argues that our collective amnesia concerning the My Lai Massacre is an example of the American tendency to erase evil from our national mythology. In the novel, O'Brien not only forces readers to acknowledge the tragedy of the My Lai Massacre by including scenes set in the village of Thuan Yen on March 16, 1968, he also fights the perception that the massacre was simply an anomaly in American history. He links My Lai to earlier atrocities in America's past, including those committed by both British soldiers and patriots during the Revolutionary War as well as the devastation visited upon Native Americans at Sandy Creek and upon the U.S. Cavalry at LITTLE BIGHORN. In one of his final footnotes, the novel's narrator, a self-described "biographer" or "historian" obsessed with John Wade, writes, "it's odd how the mind

erases horror" (298). While the narrator is referring specifically to John Wade's ability to repress the secret of his involvement in the My Lai Massacre, his statement also indicts the larger American tendency to overlook the ugly, unpleasant details of history, our tendency to romanticize American values. As O'Brien writes in the essay, "We salute ourselves and take pride in America the White Knight, America the Lone Ranger, America's sleek laser-guided weaponry beating up on Saddam and his legion of devils" (52).

The essay and the novel parallel each other as well in their ambiguous endings. Readers of "The Vietnam in Me" are left with a final picture of O'Brien and Kate together in Ho Chi Minh City, as she snaps pictures to "show her children someday" (57). Yet, from the scenes set in Cambridge later that year, we are also aware that Kate's relationship with O'Brien has ended and that she will most likely have a future apart from his own—her children will not be his children. O'Brien's decision to conclude the essay at this earlier point, however, before the breakup, suggests a certain ambiguity about the relationship. He seems to be trying to hold onto the past, to a moment that will not last, suggesting that he has not entirely given up on the relationship yet. The marriage between John and Kathy Wade in *In the Lake of the Woods* ends on a similarly ambiguous note. Kathy has disappeared, but does this mean that John has murdered her or that she has left him? The narrator at the very end of the novel raises the possibility of a happy ending—that the couple planned their mutual disappearance together and that the relationship will last despite the overwhelming odds against it. It is just such a slim hope of a happy ending, of a miracle, that O'Brien seems to be holding out for in the essay.

"The Way It Mostly Was" (1976)

Originally published in *Shenandoah* magazine in the winter of 1976, "The Way It Mostly Was" tells the story of an unnamed blond captain who watches a platoon of soldiers under his command march up a hill on a red clay road in Vietnam on their way to battle. As he watches the men, the captain thinks about war and mission and pride and fear, and he feels great love for his soldiers, even Spec Four Paul Berlin, the last man in the column of 59. The story was later rewritten and included as a chapter, also titled "The Way It Mostly Was," in O'Brien's 1978 novel, *Going After Cacciato*.

SYNOPSIS

The story opens with a description of a red clay road in Vietnam that winds straight up a steep hillside. While the road provides a magnificent view and would have been a good road for hiking or strolling, it makes a difficult march for the 58 soldiers and one native scout who plod up it, weighted down by the military paraphernalia they carry. It is July 13, and the soldiers, including Oscar Johnson, Eddie Lazzutti, Stink Harris, and others, are marching to a distant battle in the hills. A blond-headed captain stands alone at the summit of the hill, watching his men climb. Later, his lieutenants come to him to confer. They must consider whether it is better to use the road, which may be land-mined, to gain speed or to move through the rough country off the road, a safer but much slower mode of travel. The captain decides to stick to the road, and having made up his mind, does not rethink his decision. As he watches the soldiers march, the unnamed captain, recipient of a SILVER STAR for valor, contemplates men and mission. He is a practical man who understands that mission must come first; otherwise lives would be lost foolishly. Yet, he is also a man who believes in the pride of overcoming fear and testing one's self in battle, and who sees the men as individuals and cares deeply for them.

The point of view in the story switches periodically to that of the very last soldier in the column, Spec Four Paul Berlin, whose thoughts and motives contrast strongly with those of the captain. Berlin has no sense of mission. He feels that the road will never end and that the hill has no summit. Berlin, in fact, tries to focus on the pure physicality of his body as he toils up the hill. He knows that he will not perform well in battle, and he makes up his

mind to simply stop marching at some point—to fall down and lie still and get left behind. While he never actually does this, lacking even the simple will power to stop his legs from moving, he toys with the idea as he plods forward, feeling no love for his fellow soldiers and no desire to be brave. Ironically, the story ends with the captain watching Paul Berlin as he brings up the rear of the column. The captain feels great love and respect for this soldier, whose name he does not know, admiring his persistence and discipline as he plods along.

COMMENTARY

A Hemingwayesque tale with its flat descriptions of landscape, simple diction, and repeated phrases ("the day was too hot even for birds"), "The Way It Mostly Was" is a story about contrasts and contradictions. As O'Brien will later write in "How to Tell a True War Story," one way to identify a true war story is by its contradictory nature: Almost everything is true; almost nothing is true. In this short piece, readers see this maxim borne out through a series of competing perspectives that O'Brien develops. First, the description of the landscape itself is clearly a matter of perspective. The narrator recognizes from the beginning the rich scenic beauty of the mountain road, but this beauty is lost on a group of men weighted down by the responsibility of war and the dangerous battle that they are heading for. Like Stephen Crane in his well-known short story "The Open Boat," who comments that viewed from a balcony the small, fragile lifeboat that holds the fate of four weary and scared shipwreck survivors would no doubt be viewed as "weirdly picturesque," O'Brien understands that reality is not simply "out there," unchanging and factual. Rather, the outside world works *with* the perceiver of that world to make up reality—reality must always be seen and interpreted, and therefore it changes according to the circumstances and position of the perceiver. This is an important point in a story about the Vietnam War and the natural landscape. In many American accounts of the war, the land itself is presented as an enemy: mysterious, dangerous, and forbidding. In the novel *Going After Cacciato*, for instance, the North Vietnamese major Li Van Hgoc, trapped in the underground tunnel system himself, tells the American soldiers, "The soldier is but the representative of the land. The land is your true enemy" (GAC 86). But in this story O'Brien recognizes that positing the landscape itself as evil or threatening is part of an imperialist vision, similar perhaps to the European view of the Congo in Joseph Conrad's *The Heart of Darkness,* in which evil seemed to reside in the African rivers and jungles themselves. The natural environment of Vietnam, the story admonishes readers, is not inherently good or bad. "The mountains were not ugly" (36), the captain thinks to himself. Americans perceive the landscape as threatening because of their mission within it.

The story contrasts as well the differing perspectives of officers and enlisted men, again a common theme in American literature of the Vietnam War. However, while much Vietnam War literature presents officers as lazy, incompetent, or self-centered, "The Way It Mostly Was" works differently. The unnamed blond captain is "not stupid" (41). In fact, he is a thoughtful, brave man who has not only won the Silver Star but who deserved it, and who resembles in many ways Captain Johansen, the officer O'Brien so admired in his 1973 memoir, *If I Die in a Combat Zone, Box Me Up and Ship Me Home.* The captain in "The Way It Mostly Was" understands mission. While he knows that something is wrong with this war, and while he would rather have "fought his battles in France or at Hastings or at Austerlitz" (41), he nevertheless understands that he must value mission, "otherwise every life lost is lost dumbly" (37). Yet, he still loves his men as individuals, and he ultimately views war as a way for a man to test his character and individual will in the face of death. War offers a man "the chance to go through the [deathbed] emotion more than once, to think the final thoughts many, many times, as many times as there were battles" (42). If war were not a part of human nature, he speculates, men would have invented it for the opportunity to face death bravely and to "savor its lessons" (42).

Spec Four Paul Berlin contrasts sharply with the captain. While the officer believes that soldiers are "spirited and brave and wise human beings who know the important things about life and death" (40), Paul Berlin feels himself to be a mere machine. To him the march is "as automatic and mechanical as his rifle," his "muscles and fluids and gelatinous tissues . . . molded in a marvelous system of biological engineering" (39). The mechanistic language here is no accident as Berlin seems to have no free will. He is powerless to stop marching, even when he decides to do so. As the narrator explains, "It did not occur to him that he could no more stop marching than could a bumblebee stop bumbling, or a fox stop foxing" (39). Berlin marches up the road "with no exercise of will, no desire and no determination" (44). He has become a mere marching machine, "his muscles contracting and relaxing, his legs swinging alternately forward and back, lungs drawing and expelling, moving, climbing, but without thought and without the force of purpose" (44). When Berlin is unable to stop marching in fact, he is described as both a force of nature and a feat of engineering. He is like "a boulder in an avalanche, like a locomotive out of control" (44), but he is *not* like an individual asserting his will against death as the captain imagines.

The most ironic moment in the story comes near the end, when the captain focuses his attention on Paul Berlin as the young soldier toils up the hill, the last man in the long column. The captain feels "great respect and love for Spec Four Paul Berlin" and admires his "oxen persistence . . . thinking that the boy represented so much good—fortitude, discipline, loyalty, self control, vitality and toughness" (44–45). Further, "in admiration of Spec Four Paul Berlin's climb," the captain speculates that "The greatest gift of God . . . is freedom of will" (45). The captain completely misreads Paul Berlin, who, as we have seen, feels more like a machine than a man, completely lacking in will. The contrasting perspectives are driven home when Paul Berlin does not even notice the captain's hand raised in greeting but plods dumbly on, "dull of mind, blunt of spirit, numb of history" (45). War is an entirely different experience for the officer educated at West Point, schooled in the writings of THUCYDIDES and VON CLAUSEWITZ and concerned about pride and courage, than it is for the weary foot soldier, drafted (*see* DRAFT) into the army, forced to comply with orders, and merely trying to survive, unaware of the larger history, politics, or purpose of the war that he finds himself a part of. The story succeeds by capturing the contrasting experiences and perspectives of these two soldiers without portraying either one unsympathetically.

Differences in Versions

In the novel's version of "The Way It Mostly Was," O'Brien makes several surface changes. The number of men marching up the hill is reduced from 58 to 38, perhaps to better reflect the high number of casualties taken by the platoon previously in the novel. The unnamed, blond captain in the story transforms into Lieutenant Sidney Martin in the novel's version, and also becomes somewhat less sympathetic than the earlier officer, at least partly because of the role he plays elsewhere in the novel, but also because of specific changes in the later version. O'Brien tones down some of the language used in the original story about the blond officer loving his men and viewing them as "spirited and brave and wise human beings" (40). Sidney Martin, in the revised version, comes off as slightly colder and more no-nonsense than the earlier incarnation of the officer. He hopes that his men will come to understand that it is necessary to "make hard sacrifices" (GAC 163) during war, and it is explicitly stated in the novel that Martin does not coddle the men or seek their friendship, character traits not mentioned about the unnamed captain in the original story. Martin is also a bit more ambivalent as he watches Paul Berlin, the last man in the column, marching up the mountain. In the revised version, Martin looks at Berlin with "both sadness and pride" (165), and he understands that the young man may not yet be a good soldier. The earlier version of the officer had simply viewed Berlin "as a soldier," believing that "to call a man Soldier . . . was to call him good" (40). Nevertheless, Sidney Martin in the novel version still admires Paul Berlin, and he still thinks that freedom of will is "the greatest gift of God" (168). The two versions end on the same note, therefore, as they both contrast the dull, mechanical thoughts of the plodding Paul Berlin with the lofty speculations of the officer watching him.

CHARACTERS

Berlin, Paul Paul Berlin is the last man in the long column of 58 soldiers and one native scout who are climbing up a steep mountain road as they head toward a battle in Vietnam. The story's perspective shifts between that of the captain of the platoon, who contemplates the ideals of courage and will, and the views of Paul Berlin, who feels himself to be merely a marching machine, lacking in free will and without purpose. At one point in the story, Berlin, knowing that he will not fight well in the upcoming battle, decides to simply stop marching, to let his knees give in, to roll onto the ground, and to remain behind. But his brain cannot communicate this decision to his legs, which keep moving despite his desire to stop. Ironically, the captain admires and respects Paul Berlin's will power as he watches this last soldier plod up the hill, having no idea what Berlin is really thinking and feeling. When this story is rewritten as part of *Going After Cacciato*, Paul Berlin comes off as less mulish and unthinking than he does in the original version of the story. In the longer novel, readers witness Berlin's impressive powers of imagination as he concocts the fantastical tale of following Cacciato across LAOS, Burma, Turkey, Iran, and all the way to PARIS.

Berlin's Father Although Paul Berlin's father does not actually appear in the story, the young soldier as he marches on and on recalls that his father "had once told him that a soldier learns both how powerful he is and how impotent" (44). As he climbs the road, Berlin feels physically powerful but mentally impotent as he cannot force himself to stop marching, despite his decision to simply fall down on the ground. Berlin's father figures more prominently in the novel *Going After Cacciato*, where he is a house builder and a WORLD WAR II veteran.

Blond-Headed Captain Most of the story is told from the point of the view of an unnamed captain with blond hair who watches intently as a platoon of 58 men and one native scout under his command climb slowly and steadily up a mountain road leading to a battle. The captain is a good officer who works patiently through his lieutenants, honoring the military chain of command, and whose men respect him. An educated soldier who has read THUCYDIDES and VON CLAUSEWITZ on the theory of war, the captain considers war "a means to an ends, with a potential for both good and bad" (37). He has won the SILVER STAR for valor, but he is neither war-hungry nor afraid of battle, and he sees his soldiers as human beings, even though he understands that an effective military must value mission over men. While the captain knows that something is wrong with the Vietnam war, that the soldiers lack a sense of purpose, he also knows that "in war purpose is never paramount" (41). Although the captain remains unnamed in the story, he is a character very similar to Captain Johansen in O'Brien's 1973 memoir, *If I Die in a Combat Zone, Box Me Up and Ship Me Home*, a character modeled after one of O'Brien's real-life commanding officers in Vietnam, Captain BEN ANDERSON. When the story is rewritten for inclusion in *Going After Cacciato*, the unnamed captain is transformed into Lieutenant Sidney Martin.

Chassler, Rudy   Rudy Chassler, also a minor character in the later novel *Going After Cacciato*, is mentioned briefly in the story when Paul Berlin, marching behind him, notices the "shiny sweat like polish" on his back and on the back of Eddie Lazzutti.

Harris, Stink   Stink Harris, one of the men in the platoon of 58, smokes a cigarette as he climbs the red clay mountain road. At one point in the story, he will remove a belt of machine gun ammunition from around him and throw it into the weeds along the side of the road so that he can move more quickly. Stink Harris appears in *Going After Cacciato* as the scout of Third Squad, who disappears in PIRAEUS, GREECE after jumping ship.

Johnson, Oscar   Oscar Johnson, the black buck sergeant who talks the men of Third Squad into fragging (*see* FRAG) Lieutenant Sidney Martin in the novel *Going After Cacciato* appears briefly in the original 1976 version of the story "The Way It Mostly Was." As the long column of soldiers climb

the red clay road, Johnson is said to have a radio pressed against his ear and to be whistling with the music. He is also said to be from DETROIT, although his fellow soldiers in *Cacciato* will question this, since Oscar Johnson's mail gets sent to BANGOR, MAINE.

Lazzutti, Eddie   Eddie Lazzutti, one of the members of Third Squad who chases after the deserting Cacciato in the novel *Going After Cacciato*, is said to be smoking as he climbs the mountain road in "The Way It Mostly Was." Later, Paul Berlin will see "the shiny sweat like polish" (43) on Eddie's back as he climbs.

Lieutenants   The blond-headed captain in the story is said to be a good leader who works through his lieutenants "according to the old rules of command" (37). The lieutenants come to confer with the captain at one point, looking through binoculars and surveying the mountains where the battle will be fought. The lieutenants, like the captain himself, practice field discipline by wearing their shirts (unlike the enlisted men), and they seem to respect their commanding officer.

Native Scout   One native scout, who is a boy of 13, accompanies the platoon of 58 soldiers who march straight up the red clay road into the mountains on their way to a battle. At one point in the story, Spec Four Paul Berlin sees the native scout, who is said to weigh only 80 pounds, use his rifle like a walking stick, its muzzle pointed down.

"What Went Wrong" (2002)

"What Went Wrong" was first published in *Esquire* magazine in August 2002 before appearing in slightly revised form as chapter 22 of the novel *July, July*. The story focuses on the Vietnam War veteran David Todd, once a promising baseball player, who has lost a leg in the war. His marriage to his college sweetheart, Marla Dempsey, slowly turns sour as David is haunted by the ghosts of his wartime past.

SYNOPSIS

The story serves as a follow-up to a story called "July '69," which O'Brien had published in *Esquire* in July 2000. While the earlier story details David Todd's experiences in Vietnam as the sole survivor of an American platoon that undergoes a surprise VIET CONG attack, "What Went Wrong" follows David after he returns from the war. The injured soldier arrives at the HUBERT H. HUMPHREY VA HOSPITAL outside Minneapolis on the last day of July 1969, his left leg having been amputated in Japan. After a difficult several months, the young veteran is released from the hospital on Christmas Day 1969 and marries his college sweetheart, Marla Dempsey, that New Year's Eve. David worries that Marla, who had had a brief affair with a married high school teacher her junior year in college while she was also dating David, has married him out of pity rather than love. Marla, however, insists that she is simply a private person, not the type of the blushing bride, but that she will try her best to make the marriage work. The young couple rent a cheap two-bedroom house in St. Paul the first few years of their marriage. Marla takes a job as a paralegal in downtown Minneapolis, and David opens his own furniture-making company. While the two are companionable, they are also "uncomfortable in the marriage" (127) and unsure about their future together.

Nevertheless, in 1973 they buy a house in a Minneapolis suburb and attend Twins games together at Met Stadium, a place where David, a former ballplayer himself, seems to feel most at home. By 1975, however, David's Vietnam memories, his nightmares, and his strange night babble in a voice not quite his own begin to scare Marla. David also reveals to his wife that he knew about her college affair with the high school teacher. Despite their increasing differences, the marriage lasts until 1979, when Marla meets a young stockbroker. On Christmas Day of that year, she leaves David for the younger man, officially divorcing David in April 1980. Marla moves to Chicago, marries the stockbroker, gets pregnant, suffers a miscarriage, and finally goes through a painful second divorce. In 1987 she moves back to the Twin Cities, where

she and David become friends once again. At college reunions, the two are inseparable, and their friends often wonder what went wrong with the marriage, since from the outside David and Marla seem so perfectly suited to each other.

COMMENTARY

The most interesting issue raised in "What Went Wrong" is the question of fate versus free will. Readers are left to decide whether the breakup of David Todd's marriage to Marla Dempsey is the result of fate, a destiny that was inescapable, or whether David's own fears and expectations for the future worked to shape that very future to bring about the scenario he most dreaded. Key to answering this question is the issue of how readers are intended to view Johnny Ever, the seemingly supernatural voice that David periodically hears inside his head, beginning when he is first injured in Vietnam. O'Brien writes:

> And for almost five days, sometimes unconscious, sometimes luminous, he'd waited for a miracle, listening to the river and the jungle gibberish and a low, cocky, smart-ass Texas drawl that seemed to come from deep in the Milky Way. "I could go on and on," the man had whispered at one point. "I do, in fact. Name's Ever." During David's ordeal at the river, and then in Japan, and now in the hospital, the guy kept babbling about this and that and all things between, the curvature of the earth, the reasoning behind pi, why Marla Dempsey did not truly love him and never would. (125)

David, at least initially, believes that the voice of Ever comes from outside himself. Further, he believes that Ever is an omniscient being. Not only has he always existed, but he has secret knowledge of the future and the past. Readers of the earlier short story, "July '69," in fact, discover that David believes he owes his life to Ever—that his rescue after four days spent lying alongside the SONG TRA KY RIVER in Vietnam, the sole surviving member of his platoon, was the result of a bargain he made with the supernatural entity. David agrees to accept a depressing future in exchange for Ever sending in the medi-vac helicopter to rescue him. To David,

Johnny Ever is a truth-teller, an all-knowing being who refuses to let the wounded soldier fool himself or give in to daydreams about a happy future.

Yet, at times in the story David himself doubts Ever. When he builds the black-walnut nightstand for Marla one Christmas, David is able to tell himself that he is "happily married," that the "prophecies were bullshit, nothing but smoke, and Johnny Ever was one more blowhard with a microphone" (127). Readers learn as well that the voice that seems to belong to Ever emits from David himself, often when he is sleeping. Marla tape-records his "late-hour babble" (127) one night and plays the cassette back for David, arguing that the voice is both David and not David at the same time. David's reaction to this accusation seems to conjure up Johnny Ever. He responds to Marla in Ever's voice and idiom: "Chop off a leg, baby. Watch sixteen guys die. Smell the rot. See if you don't cuss in your sleep" (127). When the pain of his war memories becomes too unbearable for him, David seems to channel Ever, as if it is easier for him to project his darkest and violent feelings, his rage, onto an outside entity rather than accept these feelings as part of his own psyche.

The idea that Ever is the product of David's own damaged mind is certainly the theory of the female VA psychiatrist who vigorously assures David that "Johnny Ever was no angel, no devil, no ghost, no middleman; that, in fact, the man at the microphone was none other than David himself" (128). David sees the logic of this argument; it gibes with something deep inside that he had somehow known all along. When he accepts the psychiatrist's diagnosis, he is able to sleep better and his dreams quiet down. Yet, when unbearable pain rises again after Marla divorces him in 1980, Johnny Ever returns to make nasty remarks about the psychiatrist, whom David has begun to date. Ever allows David to express his rage and to vent his anger at Marla instead against the psychiatrist, whom Ever claims is "in for a shock when she finds out what I got waitin' on *her* down the pike" (128). But even in this instance, David seems to recognize Ever as part of himself: "David didn't speak. He had learned to tune out this chatter, to recognize its origins in his own heart and to let it go at that" (128).

Marla, who does not know about the persona of Johnny Ever even though she recognizes that David sometimes speaks in a dangerous voice that seems to be both him and not him at the same time, nevertheless feels that David has sabotaged their future together. After David reveals that he knows about her college affair, Marla replies that she has tried hard in the marriage, but she feels as if David never expected things to turn out well between them: "Sometimes, though, it felt like you'd already decided everything. Who I was. What I wanted. Almost like you needed to drive me away." She adds, "people get what they imagine" (128). And even more, David accepts this accusation as well, just as he believed the psychiatrist earlier. After his divorce, he muses to himself that "he'd believed in his own vision of things," and in the end, "to a greater or lesser degree, the belief had birthed the facts" (128). This passage suggests that David had been so convinced that his future was destined to be terrible that he had, in fact, shaped it to be that way. The human imagination in all of O'Brien's works is a strong and powerful force. When David recognizes that in his marriage he had experienced a "failure of nerve, which was also a failure of imagination, the inability to divine a happy ending" (128), readers may hear echoes of Paul Berlin after he returns to the war in *Going After Cacciato*. Berlin in very similar language muses that his inability to leave the war was a failure of the imagination, a failure to imagine a happy ending to his story. The best that David Todd can do, damaged as he is by his wartime experiences, is imagine and create for himself a future that while not truly happy at least involves an accommodation. While Marla might not turn out to be the "girl of his dreams" as he had originally hoped and wished for before his injury, she can at least be his friend, and upon occasion they can pretend that they are indeed the happy couple that their friends imagine they could be.

Differences in Versions

Several of the differences between the original version of "What Went Wrong" and the version that appears in *July, July* involve O'Brien's removal of background information that was needed in the stand-alone story but that was supplied elsewhere in the novel and thus might have seemed redundant if retained. For instance, the details about David first meeting Marla at DARTON HALL COLLEGE, which appear on the first and second pages of the story, are removed in the revised version. Some background information about Johnny Ever is removed as well when the story is incorporated into the novel. These are details which readers of *July, July* would already have learned about in chapter 2 of the novel, "July '69." The majority of other revisions that O'Brien made include the addition of short phrases and sentences. For example, in the novel's version, when Marla insists she is not marrying David out of pity, as she does in the story as well, she says a bit more about the war in general, about how it has wrecked the lives of so many people. Later in the novel's version, O'Brien says a little more about the spiritual emptiness that plagues Marla than he does in the story, adding that "She felt sealed off from things: from pain, from joy, from her own emotions. No big ups. No miserable downs" (*July* 289), sentences that do not appear in the *Esquire* story. In the novel Marla also makes additional comments about the "team costumes" at the baseball games she attends with David. Johnny Ever is occasionally a bit more expansive in his speech in the novel as well, adding a line, for instance, about David's former platoon mates in the afterlife, who have eons of time on their hands: "Just harps and halos and virgin-ass angels" (*July* 288).

Perhaps the most significant changes from the story to the novel version of "What Went Wrong," however, occur when David reveals to Marla what he knows about her college affair with the married high school teacher. In the original story version, David asks Marla about the teacher's antique Cadillac, a piece of information that Marla is surprised that David knows about. In the novel version, though, David knows about the pigtails of Anderson's wife and about the brand-new baby stroller in front of their house. While David might have seen Marla sitting in Anderson's Cadillac in the parking lot of her college dorm the day he dumped her, it is unlikely that he could possibly have knowledge of Anderson's wife and family life, unless he had followed Marla the day she rings the teacher's doorbell. These additions suggest that

David's intimate knowledge of Marla's past might come from the supernatural figure Johnny Ever. Elsewhere in the novel, this godlike persona, in the guise of Fred Engelmann and other minor characters, truly does seem to have omniscient knowledge about the characters. In the story version, readers are most likely to view Ever as the VA psychiatrist does—as simply a damaged part of David's own psyche. The novel, though, more strongly hints that Ever actually is some kind of angel or middleman to god—a supernatural figure who has access to knowledge unavailable to ordinary mortals.

CHARACTERS

Anderson, Jim Jim Anderson is the name of the married high school teacher who has a brief affair with Marla Dempsey when she is a junior at DARTON HALL COLLEGE. A "poisonously handsome specimen" (126) who owns an antique red Cadillac, Anderson ends the affair unceremoniously in a parking lot of Marla's dorm four weeks into the relationship, quoting condescending pieties about "guilt and insomnia and issues of honor" (126).

Anderson, Mrs. After Marla Dempsey is dumped by Jim Anderson, the married high school teacher with whom she had a brief affair her junior year in college, she jogs three miles to the teacher's house and rings the doorbell. She is greeted by Mrs. Anderson, described as an "emaciated, brittle-looking creature, thirty-five or so, her reddish-brown hair arranged in a pair of pigtails secured by rubber bands" (126). The woman seems to know exactly who Marla is, and after seeing Mrs. Anderson's "sad, unsurprised, washed-out face" (126), the young college student flees the house, believing "that she would never be forgiven" (126).

Dempsey, Marla Marla Dempsey is the DARTON HALL COLLEGE sweetheart of the injured soldier David Todd. She agrees to marry David even though she understands that she does not quite love him. Marla, readers discover, had been in love only once before, with a married high school teacher whom she had an affair with over three blissful weeks her junior year of college.

Since that time, Marla has had trouble making herself feel anything deeply. She experiences an inner numbness that she tries to explain to her husband: ". . . there's something inside me that's just totally alone, totally private. Like a rainy day that goes on and on" (126). Nevertheless, she tries her best to make the marriage work, even though she is frightened by the nightmarish babbling coming from David in the night as he remains haunted by his war memories. Marla, however, eventually leaves David for a younger man, a stockbroker who rides a motorcycle. She moves to Chicago, marries the stockbroker, becomes pregnant, has a miscarriage, and eventually suffers through a painful second divorce. When she moves back to the Twin Cities in 1987, she and David become friends again.

Ever, Johnny Johnny Ever is the name David Todd assigns to a voice that he first hears coming over Hector Ortiz's transistor radio as he lies injured in Vietnam. Ever seems to David to be a godlike, omniscient figure who has lived forever and who has knowledge of the future. David believes that Johnny Ever has predicted that his marriage to Marla will falter and that David's own future will be disastrous. When he is told by a VA psychiatrist that Ever is a figment of his imagination, a self-destructive part of himself, the theory makes sense to David, but he is still unable to erase the voice from his mind. In a scene in which David confronts Marla about her earlier college affair with a married teacher, he seems to channel the voice of Johnny Ever, which frightens his wife. While David never fully escapes the voice of Ever in the story, he learns to live with it, "to tune out this chatter, to recognize its origins in his own heart and to let it go at that" (128).

Ortiz, Hector Hector Ortiz was a fellow soldier in David Todd's platoon in Vietnam. While he is only mentioned briefly in "What Went Wrong," as the owner of a transistor radio that broadcasts "insane blather" (124) as David lies injured on the banks of the SONG TRA KY River, in the earlier story "July '69," readers discover that Ortiz was killed in the surprise VIET CONG attack of July 1969, shot through the face.

Paladino, Doc During the first month of his marriage, David Todd cannot shake the voices and faces of his dead comrades in Vietnam from his mind. He particularly remembers watching a medic named Doc Paladino "get sucked away into the tall, dry grass along the Song Tra Ky" River (126).

Stockbroker Marla Dempsey eventually leaves David Todd for a younger man, a stockbroker who rides a Harley Davidson motorcycle. She ruins all future Christmases for David by calling her lover to come pick her up early in the morning on Christmas Day 1979. Although Marla moves to Chicago and marries the stockbroker, this marriage, too, will end in divorce.

Todd, David David Todd, an American soldier during the Vietnam War, is the sole survivor of a VIET CONG attack that occurred in July 1969. He watched sixteen members of his platoon get killed, and he himself suffered serious injuries. "What Went Wrong" opens when David returns to Minneapolis from a hospital in Japan, where his left leg had been amputated. Despite his misgivings about the love his college sweetheart, Marla Dempsey, feels for him, David nevertheless marries her on New Year's Eve 1969. But Marla's secret college affair and David's traumatic wartime experiences plague the couple, eventually tearing their marriage apart. David believes that an omniscient, godlike figure named Johnny Ever speaks to him and has predicted the demise of his marriage. Despite being told by a VA psychiatrist that Johnny Ever is simply an aspect of David himself, a diagnosis that makes sense to the wounded veteran, David cannot shake the belief that his marriage to Marla is doomed to fail. His wife does eventually divorce him in order to marry a stockbroker who drives a Harley Davidson. But when Marla's second marriage falls apart, David is waiting in the wings, and the two become close friends again.

VA Psychiatrist During the late 1970s, David goes to see a VA psychiatrist twice a month in an attempt to tame the demons of his past. The psychiatrist, a woman of his own age whom he often smokes marijuana with, assures the veteran that the voice of Johnny Ever is not that of a supernatural being but rather is part of David himself. This advice makes sense to David, who is able to sleep better and control his nightmares somewhat during this period. Nevertheless, the psychiatrist does not make Johnny Ever vanish entirely, and when David begins dating her for a brief period after his divorce from Marla, Ever reappears to viciously mock the psychiatrist, telling David that he "can do better" and that the "the broad's in for a shock when she finds out what I got waitin' on *her* down the pike" (128).

"Where Have You Gone, Charming Billy?" (1975)

"Where Have You Gone, Charming Billy?" was first published in *Redbook* magazine in May 1975. The story details the young soldier Paul Berlin's first real day at war in Vietnam, where he witnesses the death of a fellow soldier, Billy Boy Watkins, from a heart attack. The story, with only minor modifications, was later published in 1978 as "Night March," a chapter in O'Brien's National Book Award–winning novel *Going After Cacciato*.

SYNOPSIS

The story opens with a platoon of 26 soldiers walking silently and single-file on a dark, moonlit night through the countryside in Vietnam. Private First Class Paul Berlin marches at the rear of the column. When the men take a brief break alongside a rice paddy, Berlin begins to remember the horrifying events that took place earlier that day, when he watched a fellow soldier, Billy Boy Watkins, die of a heart attack on the field of battle, scared senseless after stepping on a mine that blew off his foot. Adding to the surreal horror of the afternoon is the fact that Billy Boy's body falls from the sky into the muck of the rice paddy below when the DUSTOFF helicopter makes an abrupt turn. The men are forced to probe the mucky water with their rifle butts to retrieve Billy Boy. Try as hard as he might to pretend the death did not take place, images

from the day keep returning to Berlin as he gets up to continue the march. When the platoon takes its next rest break, Paul Berlin, overwrought by his own fear and the memory of Billy Boy's death, begins to giggle uncontrollably, despite being told repeatedly by a fellow soldier, nicknamed Buffalo, that he must remain silent. Berlin does eventually quiet down, his emotion having been spent. He imagines returning home and telling his father about Billy Boy's death, trying to comfort himself by reducing the death in his own mind to a funny war story, simply a good joke to share later.

COMMENTARY

"Where Have You Gone, Charming Billy?" is a story about the fear experienced by soldiers in war and how they handle that fear. The story illustrates what might be a young soldier's worst nightmare: literally being "scared stiff," or frightened to death on the field of battle. Private First Class Paul Berlin witnesses Billy Boy's death, an incident that will eventually in *Going After Cacciato* come to be called the "ultimate war story" on his very first real day of fighting, signifying that fear, especially fear of fear itself, is *the* overwhelming experience for Paul Berlin in Vietnam. Because this death happens on Berlin's very first day, it marks the rest of his time in country, serving as a marker for how fear and shame work together in the young soldier's life. The story of Billy Boy is doubly terrible because the young soldier's fear does not seem to end even after he is dead. When the body tumbles from the helicopter, Paul Berlin imagines Billy Boy still afraid, "as if trying to escape Graves Registration, where he would be tagged and sent home" (132). On the night march, Paul Berlin speculates that what he fears the most is "the fear of being so terribly afraid again" (128). He does not want to be like Billy Boy Watkins. Dying of fright suggests an ignominious, shameful sort of death for young men who have been raised on heroic stories of WORLD WAR II bravery. At one point in the story, Berlin imagines himself looking into his father's "stern eyes" and insisting that he "*wasn't* afraid" (128). Berlin's father here represents the older generation of veterans, those who fought in a strongly supported and less morally ambiguous war. Berlin is not only afraid, but he is also ashamed that he has not lived up to romanticized versions of World War II glory, images etched into the brains of young men growing up in the 1950s and early 1960s through cultural artifacts such as John Wayne movies.

Paul Berlin muses about fear during the long night march, wishing that he had paid more attention to the training he had undergone, but recognizing that bravery is not something that can be taught: "He could not remember what they'd said about how to stop being afraid; they hadn't given any lessons in courage—not that he could remember—and they hadn't mentioned how Billy Boy Watkins would die of a heart attack" (128). But after his first day, through actually experiencing what it is like to be at war, Berlin begins to understand that "fear came in many degrees and types and peculiar categories" (128). While he is still afraid during the night, he understands as well that his fear is not as bad as it had been earlier that afternoon, and he desperately hopes that with experience his fear will dissipate, that in the morning, when the platoon reaches the sea, "it would be better. The hot afternoon would be over, he would bathe in the sea and he would forget how frightened he had been on his first day in the war. The second day would not be so bad. He would learn" (127). As in many O'Brien works, such as when Norman Bowker wades into the lake at the end of "Speaking of Courage" from *The Things They Carried*, and when Thomas H. Chippering dips his hand into the backyard birdbath and washes his face in *Tomcat in Love*, soldiers long for some kind of cleansing ritual, a baptism that will wash away the sin and dirt of war. The sea, in Paul Berlin's imaginings, will offer just such a cleansing experience, rinsing away the terrible fear he felt on his first day at the war.

But lacking the ability to purify himself by washing his sins away, Berlin handles his fear and shame as best he can: by pretending. He pretends that he is a boy again, camping with his father along the DES MOINES RIVER, and he pretends as well that he did not watch Billy Boy Watkins die of a heart attack earlier that afternoon. One aspect of pretending is storytelling. As he mulls over the death, Berlin imaginatively reshapes the experience into a story that he will tell his father when the

war is over. And in the story Billy Boy's death can become less significant: "[H]e would tell his father the story of Billy Boy Watkins. But he would never let on how frightened he had been. 'Not so bad,' he would say instead, making his father feel proud" (128). Described at various times in nearly mindless, animalistic terms, as being like a "sheep in a dream" (81) or like "an insect, an ant escaping a giant's footsteps" (128), Paul Berlin is able to tame his feelings of insignificance through storytelling. In stories he can shape himself as better and braver and more in control than he actually was. Storytelling as a way to combat fear and gain control over chaotic events will take center stage in the novel that this story will later be incorporated into. In *Going After Cacciato*, Paul Berlin will spend a long night in an observation post by the sea, inventing an elaborate, highly detailed story of escaping the war by following a deserting soldier who believes he can walk all the way to PARIS.

The other way that Paul Berlin attempts to tame his fear in "Charming Billy" is through dark humor. Laughing at one's fear can diminish it, as O'Brien points out in his later novel *The Things They Carried*, when he describes how the soldiers of ALPHA COMPANY pretend death "was not the terrible thing it was" by using language that is "both hard and wistful," that transforms "bodies into piles of waste" (*TTTC* 238). Narrator O'Brien adds:

> I learned that words make a difference. It's easier to cope with a kicked bucket than a corpse; if it isn't human, it doesn't matter much if it's dead. And so a VC nurse, fried by napalm, was a crispy critter. A Vietnamese baby, which lay nearby, was a roasted peanut. 'Just a crunchie munchie,' Rat Kiley said as he stepped over the body. (*TTTC* 238–239)

The song that Berlin sings to himself, "Charming Billy," from which the title of the story derives, is just such an attempt to soften the death he has witnessed that afternoon. With its lyric, "Where have you gone, Billy Boy, Billy Boy, oh where have you gone charming Billy," the song mocks the death, making it something humorous rather than tragic. Berlin recognizes the absurdity of Billy's Boy death as well when he imagines a telegram sent home to the dead man's family: "SORRY TO INFORM YOU THAT YOUR SON BILLY BOY WAS YESTERDAY SCARED TO DEATH IN ACTION IN THE REPUBLIC OF VIETNAM . . ." (130). The fact that Paul Berlin cannot stop his fit of giggles, despite the danger that the noise of his laughing puts the entire platoon in, suggests the close link between fear and laughter. The story ends with Berlin again imagining telling the story of Billy Boy's death to his father, the traumatic incident becoming merely "a funny war story . . . a good joke" (132). Nevertheless, despite his best attempts at pretending and humor, and even though he is able to smell salt water and hear the sea at the end of the story, Paul Berlin still cannot stop being afraid. Billy Boy's death has traumatized him deeply.

Differences in Versions

While the story "Where Have You Gone, Charming Billy?" remained largely intact when it was rewritten as part of *Going After Cacciato*, O'Brien did make some changes. Some of these are minor and are designed to incorporate the story more smoothly into the novel. The perfumy smell of the Vietnamese graveyard the soldiers march through in the night, for instance, reminds Paul Berlin in the novel version of the perfume bottles on his mother's dresser where she hid her alcohol. And it is Eddie Lazzutti, the singing member of the platoon in *Cacciato* who first thinks of the Billy Boy song, while Paul Berlin conjures up the song on his own in the story version. Similarly, the soldier described simply as "the leader" (81) of the platoon in the story, who kneels down and signals a rest break outside a rice paddy, becomes in the novel Lieutenant Sidney Martin, the strict disciplinarian who will be fragged (*see* FRAG) by his own platoon. The soldier who offers Berlin a stick of gum and tries to hush his giggles at the end transforms from Buff into Cacciato, the childlike soldier who simply walks away from the war. This section, when Berlin laughs uncontrollably, is also expanded quite a bit and ends with Cacciato's observation that Paul Berlin will do "fine" at the war because he has "a terrific sense of humor" (GAC 218), clearly a misreading by the simpleminded soldier of Berlin's deep-seated fear.

Other changes are more significant. In the novel version of the story, O'Brien does not immediately inform readers that Billy Boy has died of a heart attack. Initially, Billy Boy is said simply to have died of fright on the field of battle, the heart attack mentioned only later. This alteration seems to emphasize Berlin's own fear even more strongly. At first, readers know of no actual, physical cause for Billy Boy's death. The novel also expands the actual description of Billy Boy stepping on the mine, detailing how Billy tries to lace the boot with his blown-away foot still in it back onto his leg and enlarging the role played by the medic, Doc Peret, an important character in the later novel. The novel version, while adding the details mentioned above, interestingly omits the scene in which Billy Boy's body falls out of the helicopter, although the story "In the Field" from *The Things They Carried* will include scenes of soldiers searching a muck-filled rice paddy for the body of Kiowa, similar to the way the three soldiers prod the swampy paddy with their rifles as they look for Billy Boy Watkins's body in the story version of "Charming Billy."

Finally, O'Brien also rewrites the novel version of the story to emphasize more clearly Paul Berlin's insistence in his imagined telling of his war experiences to his father that he did not join the other members of the platoon: "It was pretty bad at first," Berlin muses in the novel, "but I learned a lot and I got used to it. I never joined them—not them—but I learned their names and I got along, I got used to it" (210). This is different from the story version, in which Berlin anticipates the coming morning, when he will "begin to make friends with some of the other soldiers. He would learn their names and laugh at their jokes" (128). The reason for this change is that in the novel version O'Brien wants to emphasize Paul Berlin's guilt over the fragging death of Sidney Martin, a conspiracy Berlin clearly joined. However, if Berlin can pretend he held himself apart, that he never joined the others in the platoon, he can hold onto an idealized image of himself as innocent, as different from the others.

CHARACTERS

Berlin, Paul Private First Class Paul Berlin is a new soldier who just finished his first day at the war in Vietnam. The story opens with him marching at the rear of a single-file column of 32 men through a dark night after a day of strenuous fighting. As he marches, and as the platoon takes two rest breaks, Berlin cannot stop thinking about the horrific events he witnessed that afternoon—especially the death of fellow soldier Billy Boy Watkins from a heart attack in the midst of battle. Berlin meditates as well on his own fear, and he tries to comfort himself by imagining telling the story of the day's battle to his father after he returns home. In the imagined version of the story, Berlin pretends he was not nearly as frightened as he actually was. On the second rest break taken by the platoon, Berlin is so overwrought by emotion that he erupts into helpless laughter, which he cannot control despite the danger the noise brings to the group. Even though the group of soldiers is marching toward the SOUTH CHINA SEA, where they will be relatively safe, Paul Berlin is still afraid at the end of the story. Berlin will later become the main character in the novel *Going After Cacciato*, which incorporates the story "Where Have You Gone, Charming Billy?" as a chapter called "Night March."

Berlin's Father   As he marches through the dark night in the countryside of Vietnam, Paul Berlin tries to control his fear by imagining that he is simply camping out along the DES MOINES RIVER with his father. He also imagines telling the story of Billy Boy Watkins's death to his father after he returns home, reducing in the telling the overwhelming fear that he actually experienced during the day's events. At one point during a rest break, Berlin, on the verge of sleep, imagines screaming "I wasn't afraid" as he looks into his father's "stern eyes" (128). Berlin's father in the story is both a comforting figure whom Berlin remembers opening closet doors to dispel his childhood fears of boogiemen, and at the same time a figure whose stern eyes seem to represent the disappointment that Berlin fears from those back home when he does not behave like the heroic soldiers of stories and movies.

Berlin's Mother   When Paul Berlin's platoon wades into a dank rice paddy during their long night march, he imagines telling his mother about

the paddy smells after he returns home: "mud and algae and cattle manure and chlorophyll, decay, breeding mosquitoes and leeches as big as mice, the fecund warmth of the paddy waters . . ." (127–128). But Berlin consciously thinks that he will not tell his mother how frightened he had been that afternoon when Billy Boy Watkins died. One way that Berlin tries to control his fear is by imagining how his experiences will be shaped into war stories when he returns home, stories in which he will be able to make himself appear braver than he actually was.

Buffalo   A soldier named Toby, whose nickname is Buffalo, or sometimes simply Buff, prods Paul Berlin awake after the first break the platoon takes on their long night march following Berlin's first day of fighting in Vietnam. Buff warns the green young soldier not to sleep on duty: "You got a lot to learn, buddy. I'd shoot you if I thought you was sleepin'" (127). But on the second rest break, Buff is friendlier, offering Berlin a stick of chewing gum and marveling at the death of Billy Boy Watkins earlier that day. When Berlin begins laughing uncontrollably, however, Buff gets nervous about the noise, hissing at Berlin to be quiet. He actually rolls over onto the young soldier, smothering the laughter with his body when Berlin is unable to control himself. In the version of the story that appears in the novel *Going After Cacciato*, the gum-chewing soldier is transformed into Cacciato, and Buff is a big, strong, and patient soldier whose face gets shot off after a gun battle outside a Vietnamese village. He is found dead, facedown in his helmet, "hunched up like a praying Arab in Mecca" (GAC 281).

Peret, Doc   Doc Peret appears only briefly in the story "Where Have You Gone, Charming Billy?" He is the medic who treats Billy Boy Watkins after he steps on a mine and blows off his foot, shooting the injured soldier with morphine. Afterward, Doc Peret explains to the men that Billy Boy died not from his injury but from a heart attack: "He was scared he was gonna die—so scared he had himself a heart attack—and that's what really killed him. I seen it before" (132). Doc Peret will play a much larger role when the story is rewritten as part of the novel *Going After Cacciato,* where he serves Berlin's platoon in ALPHA COMPANY not only as a medic, but as something of a resident philosopher as well.

Watkins, Billy Boy   Billy Boy Watkins is a soldier whose death Paul Berlin witnesses on his very first day at the war. The men had been drinking Coca-Cola from red aluminum cans, relaxing right before they started the day's march, when Billy Boy steps on a mine that blows off his foot. Scared, Billy Boy begins to cry and to say that he is going to die, despite Doc Peret's assurance that his fears are "Nonsense" (130). Billy Boy ends up dying of a heart attack rather than the explosion, having scared himself to death. The death is especially horrific for Paul Berlin, who is also terribly afraid and who struggles to control his fear throughout the story, Billy Boy serving as a warning for what could happen to him.

"Winnipeg" (2000)

"Winnipeg" tells the story of Billy McMann, a 1969 college graduate who moves to Canada to evade the DRAFT after having been stood up at the airport by his college girlfriend, who had promised to accompany him. Billy nurses a grudge about the betrayal for years, through his marriage, the birth of his daughter, a successful career, and the death of his wife. The story was first published in the *New Yorker* magazine in August 2000 before being revised and included as chapter 9 of O'Brien's 2002 novel, *July, July.*

SYNOPSIS

Billy McMann flies to WINNIPEG, CANADA, on July 7, 1969, only 17 days after his graduation from DARTON HALL COLLEGE and nine days after receiving his draft notice requiring him to serve in the Vietnam War. Although Billy had planned to leave the country with his college girlfriend, Dorothy Stier, the young woman stands Billy up, never meeting him at the airport as planned. In Winnipeg Billy is lonely and angry. When he calls Dorothy on

the phone, she explains that she simply could not bring herself to run away with Billy. She is from a wealthy Republican background and the idea of leaving her country is repugnant to her. Billy eventually settles into life in Winnipeg, taking a job in the local library, marrying a pretty librarian from Calgary in 1976, and having a baby daughter with her. Yet, during his marriage and even after his wife's death in a hit-and-run accident in 1985, Billy remains obsessed by Dorothy's betrayal, hanging up on her when she calls to offer her sympathy.

During this time, Billy has become an increasingly successful businessman, eventually owning four hardware stores, a lumberyard, and a roofing company. When a young woman named Alexandra Wenz comes to work for him, it seems as if Billy will have a new chance at romance. However, Alexandra soon confesses she was the driver of the car that killed Billy's librarian wife. Alexandra was only 17 years old when the accident happened, and she tells Billy that his wife had intentionally jumped in front of her car. Although Billy and Alexandra date for several months, soon the weight of their secret knowledge about each other's pasts breaks the relationship up. When Billy's mother dies in 1992, he travels back to the Twin Cities for her funeral. While there, he arranges to meet his former girlfriend, Dorothy, at a hotel coffee shop. After 23 years, Billy still bears a grudge, and the meeting is superficial and unsuccessful, the well-dressed and elegant Dorothy refusing to allow Billy to ruffle her. The story ends with Billy suggesting to his daughter, Susie, that the two take a road trip to see something of the United States.

COMMENTARY

"Winnipeg" is a story about obsessions and how they can take over and destroy lives. Yet, Billy McMann's 23-year obsession with the betrayal of Dorothy Stier, his former college girlfriend, seems out of proportion to her crime, especially considering that in Canada Billy got married, had a daughter, and became a successful businessman. Thus, it seems logical to suppose that Dorothy's betrayal represents to Billy a larger betrayal, that it is not the loss of Dorothy that so obsesses him but the loss of everything that Dorothy represents.

A self-proclaimed Republican from a wealthy and privileged background who never questions the morality of the war and who is unwilling to cause herself inconvenience, Dorothy seems to represent for Billy what he calls the "caveman politics" (73) that sent him to war in the first place.

Elsewhere in his work, O'Brien has often written scathingly about the small-town ignorance and provincialism that sent him to serve in Vietnam. In "On the Rainy River" from *The Things They Carried,* for instance, O'Brien imagines himself "screaming" at the people from WORTHINGTON, MINNESOTA:

> . . . telling them how much I detested their blind, thoughtless, automatic acquiescence to it all, their simpleminded patriotism, their prideful ignorance, their love-it-or-leave-it platitudes, how they were sending me off to fight in a war they didn't understand and didn't want to understand. I held them responsible. By God, yes, I *did.* All of them—I held them personally and individually responsible—the polyestered Kiwanis boys, the merchants and farmers, the pious churchgoers, the chatty housewives, the PTA and the Lions club and the Veterans of Foreign Wars and the fine upstanding gentry out at the country club. (*TTTC* 45)

Like the people O'Brien decries in "On the Rainy River," Dorothy infuriates Billy by acquiescing to a political view that does not question the morality of the war. He understands that Dorothy values her own comfort over making tough moral choices: "She loved cashmere. She loved her father's country club" (73). In many ways, then, Dorothy Stier in "Winnipeg" becomes the focal point of all Billy's anger at his country, at what he perceives to be his country's betrayal and abandonment of him.

The story of the silver bracelet that Billy gives Dorothy for Valentine's Day points up Billy's true anger. While Dorothy hugs Billy and cries after receiving the gift, he never sees the bracelet again after that night. Billy realizes that such falseness is Dorothy's way: "With Dorothy, you had to pay attention to the things that were never said, the silences, the erasures and elisions" (73). This incident can be read as a parallel for the way that Bil-

ly's own country has treated him. While pretending to care for its young men, the country heedlessly drafts Billy, forcing him into an untenable position. When Billy moves to Canada, he feels that he has gone missing in a way, just like the bracelet, that his whole previous life has been erased. Although Billy never consciously makes this connection, his obsession with Dorothy's silence about the bracelet seems to signify and represent to him her silence about his own erasure, and even more, the silence of America about all the lives that were destroyed by the war. When Billy asks Dorothy about the bracelet on the phone, Dorothy does not even know what bracelet he is talking about. Her total ignorance about the things that are important to him signals to Billy that there is no hope for their relationship. He tells her to forget the bracelet and then adds, "It's over, I suppose. Whatever we had" (73). It is immediately after this that Billy also realizes Dorothy has worked to erase his memory by beginning to date a man named Ron, a former friend of Billy's.

Billy is unable to leave the past behind, even through his nine-year marriage and his success as a businessman. Perhaps he holds onto the past so fiercely because Dorothy and others seem so very willing to erase the past, to forget about Billy and get on with their lives. Even when Billy is given the chance at happiness through a relationship with Alexandra Wenz, he is unable to take it. The past weighs too heavily on both of them—not only Billy's obsession with Dorothy but also Alexandra's guilty secret that she was the driver of the car that killed Billy's librarian wife. Further, both Alexandra and Billy share the secret knowledge that Billy's wife was a suicide who jumped in front of the car intentionally. Even as the two agree to part, Alexandra explaining that Billy's obsession with Dorothy makes it seem as if someone died, as if he is "still hugging the corpse" (76), Billy understands that he is giving up what may be his last chance at happiness. He realizes that "on top of everything, he had now lost the rest of his life" (76).

But it takes an actual trip back to visit the places and people of his past before Billy can begin to let go. When his mother dies in 1992, Billy and his 15-year-old daughter, Susie, travel back to Minnesota for the funeral, and he arranges to meet Dorothy Stier in a hotel coffee shop in St. Paul. Dorothy looks just as Billy had imagined: well taken care of, expensively dressed. Her life has clearly been one of comfort and privilege. She has not experienced the kind of pain that Billy has undergone. When he requests that Dorothy not tell her husband, Ron, about their meeting, Dorothy agrees, her eyes "brown and shrewd" (76). It is at this point that it occurs to Billy "he was fortunate not to have married this woman" (76). Dorothy agrees to the small betrayal of her husband readily, suggesting that she is not a woman to be trusted. Later in the conversation, Billy believes Dorothy is lying when she laughs at the possibility that she has had any extramarital affairs. Perhaps what Billy realizes at this meeting is that the problem in their relationship lay with Dorothy, not with him. It is not that Billy was inadequate or that she loved Ron better than she loved Billy. The problem is that Dorothy is a shrewd and selfish woman willing to lie and manipulate to get what she wants. After this realization, Billy can no longer "locate the old bitterness" (77), and he is unable to say the hurtful things to Dorothy he had planned to say. The meeting ends on a superficial note, Dorothy breezily inviting Billy to come to dinner if he is ever in town again, as if he is simply any old friend she has not seen in a while.

Back in his hotel room, Billy contemplates all the years he has wasted. Yet, he also seems ready to make a change at last. He admits to his daughter that Dorothy did not try to seduce him, saying caustically, "She wanted a tennis partner" (77). Dorothy wanted someone to play with, to spar with, perhaps, but Billy sees clearly that she has not been pining for him or regretting the past the way that he has. When he suggests to Susie that the two of them take a road trip across the United States together, readers understand that Billy has begun to come to terms with his past. The meeting with Dorothy has not only dissipated his anger at his old girlfriend, it has also allowed him to begin to forgive the country that he feels betrayed him so many years ago. When Billy suggests to Susie that the two of them possibly see Dallas on the road trip, he seems ready to begin to start his life

over again. Alexandra Wenz had suggested that she might "head for Dallas" (76) after she and Billy had parted ways several months previously.

Differences in Versions

Quite a number of changes were made in the story when O'Brien revised it for inclusion in *July, July*. Some of these are small changes. For instance, in the novel Billy McMann's flight to Canada is moved from July 7, 1969, to July 1, 1969; Dorothy Stier lives in St. Paul rather than Minneapolis; Billy calls Dorothy a second time two weeks after his arrival in Winnipeg rather than waiting three weeks as he does in the story; and Alexandra Wenz's mother is obsessed with her becoming a majorette rather than a cheerleader. Some seemingly small changes, however, can lead to readers making meaningful inferences. For example, Billy marries the Calgary librarian in 1976 in the story, and his daughter Susie is eight years old when her mother dies in 1985. In the novel version, though, Billy marries the librarian in 1975, and Susie is 10 when her mother dies in 1985. While this may seem like a minor alteration, the change in date suggests that Billy perhaps married the librarian out of a sense of obligation because she was pregnant, a possibility that makes sense when readers consider how obsessed Billy still was with Dorothy Stier.

In other spots, O'Brien has removed entire paragraphs and at times inserted new incidents that do not appear in the original story. In general, these changes have two important effects: They tend to make Billy's transition to life in Canada seem more difficult in the novel version, and they define the character of Dorothy Stier more fully. For example, in the novel O'Brien has Billy while away several idle weeks in Canada, worrying that he might be going mad and having difficulty prying himself out of bed in the morning. He waits, in fact, until he is down to his last $100 before he gets a job. In addition, O'Brien adds several paragraphs detailing a trip Billy makes back over the U.S.-Canada border in order to attain "landed immigrant status" (*July* 116). This incident emphasizes Billy's terror at being caught and also the finality of his leaving his country behind—he weeps while signing the paperwork at the Canadian immigration office. As for the changes to Dorothy, O'Brien removes a paragraph from the original story in which Dorothy is said to have jumped naked on a bed in her college dorm room, wearing only the silver bracelet Billy had bought her for Valentine's Day. Perhaps O'Brien chose to cut this scene because it seems out of character for the reserved and stately Dorothy. But he further emphasizes Dorothy's rather trite patriotism in the novel when she claims as her reason for not catching the plane to Winnipeg not only that she is a Republican, but that she is an "American" (*July* 113). O'Brien adds as well a long paragraph to the novel in which Dorothy tries to justify violence and conventional views of masculinity by asking Billy if he would defend her if a VIET CONG guerrilla tried to rape her. Billy points up the absurdity of this argument when he replies that, yes, "if a VC rapist showed up at Darton Hall, flew in from Hanoi, in that case he'd hustle right over and dispatch the little pervert" (*July* 116).

The other major changes in the story occur at the end. In the novel version, Billy seems less bitter after the meeting with Dorothy in the coffee shop. When he goes up to his motel room in the novel, he thinks about the "all the squandered years" (*July* 126) rather than "all the fucking years" (77) as he does in the original story. Also, when Billy proposes to Susie a road trip in the United States in the novel version, he does not specifically suggest they visit Dallas, but rather modifies this to Texas. Perhaps O'Brien thought that the original story version made it too obvious, too certain, that Billy planned to look up Alexandra Wenz, who had talked about moving to Dallas. The novel version makes the ending subtler, more open-ended. O'Brien also removed the very last line of the original story when he revised it for inclusion in the novel. The novel ends with Billy's reason for wanting to take the road trip: "Because I lived here once" (*July* 127). The original story version had somewhat diluted this line by having Susie add after her father's statement, "Well, I guess that's a reason" (77). The revision makes for a stronger ending, as it emphasizes Billy's connections to the United States more fully, the possibility that he might have come to terms with the past.

CHARACTERS

Librarian After Billy McMann has been in Canada for seven years, he marries a pretty librarian from Calgary. Billy's wife is never given a name in the story, perhaps to show how little she really seems to have meant in Billy's life. Although the couple has a daughter together, Billy remains obsessed with Dorothy Stier during the marriage and does not seem too devastated by his wife's death in a hit-and-run accident in 1985.

McMann, Billy When the story begins, Billy McMann is a 22-year-old college graduate who decides to flee to Canada rather than honor his DRAFT notice. He is stood up at the airport by his college girlfriend, Dorothy Stier, who had promised to accompany him to WINNIPEG, CANADA, where the two planned to marry and start a family. Billy's anger with Dorothy turns into an obsession that shapes the next 20 years or more of his life. Even though he marries a pretty librarian from Calgary, he cannot forget about Dorothy, and it is this obsession that perhaps leads to the librarian's death. Readers discover that she jumped in front of the car that killed her in a hit-and-run accident. When at the end of the story Billy suggests to his daughter, Susie, that the two take a road trip in the United States, it is possible that his reunion with Dorothy at a hotel coffee shop has exorcized his demons, and that he is ready to confront his past, to forgive not only Dorothy but also his country for the wrongs he perceives it did him.

McMann, Mr. and Mrs. When he arrives in WINNIPEG, CANADA, on July 7, 1969, Billy calls home to explain to his parents that he has fled the DRAFT. His mother is angry on the phone, telling Billy that he is entitled to ruin his life, if that is what he wishes. Billy's father is more understanding, promising to send money and to talk to Billy's mother.

Ron Ron is the name of the man whom Dorothy Stier marries after she stands Billy McMann up at the airport, having initially planned to run away to WINNIPEG, CANADA, with him. While readers do not find out much about Ron, he is apparently a wealthy and successful businessman who used to be a friend of Billy's. In the coffee shop at the end of the story, Dorothy describes her marriage to Ron as a "total dream" (77), but she also seems to be lying when she tells Billy she has not had any affairs.

Stier, Dorothy   Dorothy Stier is the college girlfriend who makes plans to fly to WINNIPEG, CANADA, with Billy McMann, but who then stands him up at the airport. Dorothy explains on the phone that in the cab on the way to catch the flight the reality of her situation became clear and she could not bring herself to run away with Billy. Such a choice, she pleads, would have been "too dreamy, too romantic" (73) for her—she is a very practical woman. Described as having "smart brown eyes," a "year-round tan," and a "well-bred, well-schooled sorority-girl smile" (73), Dorothy comes from a privileged Republican background and is used to getting her own way. She begins dating a former friend of Billy's named Ron only a few weeks after Billy's departure. She ends up marrying Ron, having two boys with him, and living the life of a wealthy housewife. When she meets Billy in a hotel coffee shop 23 years after they had last seen each other, Dorothy is nonplussed, coolly speaking about Ron's work, her terrific sons, and the merits of vacation homes.

Susie   Susie is the name of Billy McMann's daughter, who is only eight years old when her mother, a librarian from Calgary, is killed in a hit-and-run accident in 1985. Seven years after her mother's death, Susie accompanies her father to the United States for her grandmother's funeral.

Although Susie is not present at the coffee shop meeting that Billy plans with Dorothy Stier, he has clearly spoken with his daughter about his former girlfriend. When Billy returns to their hotel room, Susie asks her father whether Dorothy tried to seduce him when the two met. At the end of the story, when Billy suggests a road trip through his former country, Susie insists that her father is a Canadian.

Wenz, Alexandra   Alexandra Wenz is a young woman with red hair and green eyes whom Billy McMann hires to handle the accounts for his hardware stores in WINNIPEG, CANADA, in 1991. The two begin to date, but Alexandra soon confesses that she was the driver of the car that killed Billy's wife in a hit-and-run accident back in 1985. She also tells Billy that his wife intentionally jumped in front of the car. While the couple date for several months, the relationship eventually breaks up. Not only is Alexandra unable to cope with Billy's obsession over his former college girlfriend, Dorothy Stier, but the weight of their shared knowledge about how Billy's wife died puts too much strain on them.

Wenz, Mrs.   During the months that Alexandra Wenz dates Billy McMann, she tells him stories about her mother, who was obsessed with wanting her daughter to become a cheerleader. "That's all my poor, nutso mom ever talked about," Alexandra explains to Billy, "all that cheerleader crap, like it was life goal or something . . ." (76). Billy, in exchange, tells Alexandra stories about Dorothy Stier and his own obsessions.

PART III

Related People, Places, and Topics

Achilles In his memoir, *If I Die in a Combat Zone,* Tim O'Brien remembers that his friend ERIK HANSEN had argued during army basic training that soldiers go to war and fight because they are "afraid to admit" (38) that they are not brave like Achilles, a Greek hero from HOMER's *Iliad* who fought in the Trojan War. Some recent scholarship, spurred by Jonathan Shay's influential 1994 study, *Achilles in Vietnam,* which notes connections between the kind of war trauma presented in classical Greek literature and that experienced by Vietnam War veterans, explores O'Brien's own debt to the classical literature of Homer. The critic Christopher McDonough, for instance, has published an article comparing O'Brien's narrator in *The Things They Carried* to the tragedy of HECTOR in *The Iliad* as both face dilemmas of courage and cowardice. The title of the article, "'Afraid to Admit We Are Not Achilles': Facing Hector's Dilemma in Tim O'Brien's *The Things They Carried,*" refers specifically to Erik Hansen's remarks in *If I Die.*

Adjemian, Kathy O'Brien Kathy O'Brien Adjemian is Tim O'Brien's younger sister. The two were close growing up, and like her older brother, Kathy also attended MACALESTER COLLEGE. She is mentioned briefly in *If I Die in a Combat Zone, Box Me Up and Ship Me Home,* when O'Brien writes about receiving mail from home during a bad time in Vietnam.

AIT AIT is the military acronym for Advanced Infantry Training. Tim O'Brien underwent this training in FORT LEWIS, WASHINGTON, in late 1968, after completing his army basic training and being selected to become a foot soldier in the war. In his memoir, *If I Die in a Combat Zone,* O'Brien describes the differences between basic training and AIT in this way: "On the outside, AIT looks like basic training. Lots of push-ups, lots of shoe-shining and firing ranges and midnight marches. But AIT is not basic training. The difference is the certainty of going to war: pending doom that comes in with each day's light and lingers all the day long" (51). Paul Berlin in the novel *Going*

After Cacciato contemplates his own experiences with AIT as he sits in his observation post (OP) one night. He remembers that the war did not seem real to him the summer he was drafted (*see* DRAFT): "He let himself be herded through basic training, then AIT, and all the while there was no sense of reality—another daydream, a weird pretending" (227).

AK-47 The AK-47 is an automatic assault rifle developed in the Soviet Union and used heavily by the VIET CONG during the American war in Vietnam. The weapon is mentioned in O'Brien's novel *Going After Cacciato* when the men hear a shot soon after Frenchie Tucker has been sent down a Vietnamese tunnel to search it. Trying to reassure themselves that Frenchie is all right, Stink Harris claims that the shot "didn't sound like an AK, anyway. 'No crack,' he said, 'That wasn't no AK'" (90). But Lieutenant Sidney Martin sends another member of the squad, Bernie Lynn, down the tunnel anyway to retrieve Frenchie. Bernie is shot and killed as well.

Alpha Company Alpha Company was the unit at LANDING ZONE GATOR to which Tim O'Brien was assigned during his service in the Vietnam War, as he reports in his memoir, *If I Die in a Combat Zone.* He will later fictionalize Alpha Company in the story collection *The Things They Carried.* Some of the soldiers in the fictional version of the company include Rat Kiley, Mitchell Sanders, Curt Lemon, Kiowa, Norman Bowker, and Lieutenant Jimmy Cross.

Americal Division The Americal Division of the U.S. Army, also known as the 23rd Infantry Division, was formed during WORLD WAR II, right after the attack on Pearl Harbor. It was then reactivated to serve in the Panama Canal Zone during the mid-fifties and again in Vietnam beginning in 1967. Tim O'Brien was assigned to the Americal Division during his service as an infantryman in Vietnam, and most of O'Brien's soldier characters in his Vietnam War novels are members of the Americal Division as well, including Paul Berlin in

Going After Cacciato, who had never heard of the Americal before being assigned there, most likely the men of ALPHA COMPANY in *The Things They Carried*, John Wade in *In the Lake of the Woods*, and Thomas H. Chippering in *Tomcat in Love*. The Americal Division was the single largest American unit in Vietnam.

Anderson, Captain Ben   Captain Ben Anderson was one of O'Brien's commanding officers during his service in Vietnam. O'Brien very much admired the courageous captain, who served as the model for Captain Johansen in his memoir, *If I Die in a Combat Zone, Box Me Up and Ship Me Home*.

Andros   The *Andros* is the name of the old, repainted passenger freighter that carries the men of Third Squad from IZMIR, TURKEY, to ATHENS, GREECE, in the novel *Going After Cacciato*. This is the ship that Stink Harris jumps overboard from when the men arrive in Greece and find the port city of PIRAEUS crawling with police and customs officials.

Angle Inlet   Angle Inlet is a small town located on the Northwest Angle in Minnesota, a part of the United States that can be reached only by driving through Canada or by taking a boat across the LAKE OF THE WOODS. It is the northernmost town in the contiguous 48 states. The town of Angle Inlet plays an important role in the novel *In the Lake of the Woods*. At six miles away from the cottage the Wades rent after the election defeat, it is the nearest place where they can buy gas and supplies. The Wades are seen in the town of Angle Inlet, drinking coffee at Arndahl's Mini-Mart and arguing the day before Kathy's disappearance.

Ankara, Turkey   Ankara is the capital of Turkey. It appears in the novel *Going After Cacciato* following the men of Third Squad's daring escape from a TEHRAN prison. As Paul Berlin drives the getaway car through the night, he crosses from Iran into Turkey. He pulls over in the broad plains above the city of Ankara and gets out of the car to rub his stiff legs. When Berlin returns to the car, Doc Peret is awake and comments that they are in "Nomad land" (248) now. It takes the men an hour to circle the city and to pick up the road to IZMIR.

Annamese Cordillera   The Annamese Cordillera is a range of mountains stretching 700 miles along the border of Vietnam and LAOS and into northern Cambodia. In the novel *Going After Cacciato*, the men of Third Squad find a map left behind by the AWOL (absent without leave) soldier Cacciato that plots his path through the mountain range: "In the left-hand corner a red dotted line ran through paddyland and up through the first small mountains of the Annamese Cordillera. The line ended there, apparently to be continued on a second map" (9).

AO   AO is the military acronym for Area of Operations. Tim O'Brien uses this and other acronyms frequently in his work, often without explaining to readers what the acronym stands for, perhaps in an attempt to at least partially mimic the confusion he and other new recruits experienced when they first found themselves at the war in Vietnam. In his memoir, *If I Die in a Combat Zone*, O'Brien uses the AO acronym in this way as seen in the following passage:

> I asked the Kid how many Alpha men had been killed lately, and the Kid shrugged and said a couple. So I asked how many had been wounded, and without looking up, he said a few. I asked how bad the AO was, how soon you could land a rear job, if the platoon leader were gung-ho, if Kid had ever been wounded, and the Kid just grinned and gave flippant, smiling, say-nothing answers. He said it was best not to worry. (78)

Appel, J. W. and G. W. Beebe   J. W. Appel and G. W. Beebe are psychiatrists who are quoted in one of the evidence chapters in the novel *In the Lake of the Woods*. In their work they argue that "there is no such thing as 'getting used to combat'" and that "psychiatric casualties are as inevitable as gunshots and shrapnel wounds in warfare" (27). This quote helps explain the mental suffering that John Wade experienced during his time in Vietnam.

Apollo 11 The *Apollo 11* space mission sent the first manned rocket to land on the Moon. In the novel *July, July*, the Vietnam War soldier David Todd listens over a small transistor radio to the progress of the *Apollo 11* rocket as he lies badly wounded alongside the Song Tra Ky river, all of the other members of his platoon killed in an ambush. The news of the Moon landing on July 20, 1969, seems nothing short of miraculous to David, and it sparks his desire to keep on living.

AR-15 The AR-15 is a semi-automatic assault rifle, similar to the M-16. In the novel *Going After Cacciato*, Paul Berlin is asked by a major at his promotion hearing about the muzzle velocity of a standard AR-15. Berlin correctly responds that it is 2,000 feet a second.

Aristotle A student of PLATO, Aristotle was a Greek philosopher who lived in the fourth century B.C.E. and who made significant intellectual contributions in the fields of science, logic, and poetry, as well as Western philosophy. In Tim O'Brien's 1973 memoir, *If I Die in a Combat Zone, Box Me Up and Ship Me Home*, he writes that he read enough Aristotle as a teenager growing up in WORTHINGTON, MINNESOTA, to make him prefer Plato.

Armour Meats In the story "On the Rainy River" from *The Things They Carried*, a young Tim O'Brien describes working at an Armour meat-packing plan in his hometown of WORTHINGTON, MINNESOTA, in the summer of 1968 after receiving his DRAFT notice. Although there was a real meat-packing plant in Worthington at that time, the real-life O'Brien never actually worked there.

Arndahl's Mini-Mart Arndahl's Mini-Mart is a convenience store with a sandwich counter located in the small town of ANGLE INLET in the novel *In the Lake of the Woods*. The day before Kathy Wade disappears, she and John drink coffee at Arndahl's Mini-Mart, where they are witnessed arguing by the waitress Myra Shaw.

Arrowhead The setting for the small town of SAWMILL LANDING in O'Brien's novel *Northern Lights*, the Arrowhead is a rugged region of approximately 10,000 square miles located in the northeast corner of Minnesota. Named for its pointed shape, the area encompasses lakes, mountains, and forest, and is mostly rural and sparsely populated. This is the wild landscape where the Harvey brothers will become lost in a blizzard while trying to ski home from the annual ski races at the not-too-distant town of GRAND MARAIS.

ARVN ARVN is a military acronym standing for Army of the Republic of Vietnam. These were the South Vietnamese allies of the American military during the Vietnam War. Ordinary American soldiers did not have much respect for the skills of ARVN soldiers, however, as Tim O'Brien demonstrates in the story "Sweetheart of the Song Tra Bong" from *The Things They Carried*, when medic Rat Kiley says, "As soldiers, the ARVNs were useless" (91).

Athens, Greece Athens, the ancient and largest city in Greece as well as its capital, makes an appearance in the novel *Going After Cacciato* when Paul Berlin imagines the men of Third Squad traveling aboard an old freighter called the ANDROS from IZMIR, TURKEY, to Greece. Although the port at the city of PIRAEUS is crawling with police officers and custom officials when the men first arrive, causing Stink Harris to dive overboard and not be seen again, Berlin imagines that the American soldiers walk through the crowd unmolested, arriving in Athens without further incident. Cacciato had told Berlin on the morning he left the war, "Make it to Athens and the rest is easy" (273). The city, representing the cradle of Western civilization, is the gateway to PARIS for the men of Third Squad. Berlin's imagined journey to Paris does indeed become easy after the men arrive in Athens.

Auden, Wystan Hugh W. H. Auden was a British-born poet who lived and wrote in the first half of the 20th century. Known early in his career for his left-wing politics and for exploring moral and ethical choices in his poetry, he moved to the United States in 1939 and eventually became an American citizen. In his memoir, *If I Die in a Combat Zone*,

O'Brien writes about a girl back home who sends him a poem by Auden when O'Brien is undergoing basic training in FORT LEWIS, WASHINGTON. He memorizes the poem, pretending to himself that the girl, not Auden, wrote the poem, and that it was written especially for him. In her letters to O'Brien, the unnamed girl claims that O'Brien "created her out of the mind" (34). This experience is possibly the basis for the relationship between Lieutenant Jimmy Cross and Martha in the story "The Things They Carried." Like O'Brien's relationship with the Auden-loving girl in the memoir, Cross's love affair with Martha seems largely a product of his own imagination and wishful thinking.

Austerlitz   The Battle of Austerlitz, in which he defeated a combined Russian and Austrian army in 1805, was one of Napoleon's greatest victories. Lieutenant Sidney Martin in the novel *Going After Cacciato* wishes that, instead of fighting in Vietnam, he could have been involved in more decisive battles—that he had fought at HASTINGS or Austerlitz. Despite longing for a clearer purpose, the lieutenant nevertheless understands that "battles are always fought among human beings, not purposes" (166).

Austin, Minnesota   Austin is the small town in southern Minnesota where Tim O'Brien was born. His family moved from Austin to WORTHINGTON in 1954, when O'Brien was seven years old.

Austin, Texas   Tim O'Brien moved to Austin, Texas, in 1999, when he accepted the Mitte Chair in Creative Writing at TEXAS STATE UNIVERSITY, located in San Marcos, a neighboring town.

Autry, Gene   Gene Autry, known as the "singing cowboy," was a 1930s movie star who also sang on radio programs in the 1940s and had his own television show in the 1950s. In the story "The Ghost Soldiers" from *The Things They Carried*, narrator Tim O'Brien refers to Gene Autry when he describes getting shot the first time: "For a long time I lay there all alone, listening to the battle, thinking *I've been shot, I've been shot*: all those Gene Autry movies I'd seen as a kid. In fact, I almost

smiled, except when I started to think I might die" (189).

AWOL   AWOL is a military acronym for "Absent Without Leave." It is used to refer to a soldier who has left his or her post without official permission. In *Going After Cacciato* the simpleminded soldier Cacciato is said to be AWOL after he disappears from his unit in the middle of the miserable rainy season. When Doc Peret and Paul Berlin inform Lieutenant Corson that Cacciato has left for PARIS, the seasoned lieutenant replies, "In other words, fuckin AWOL" (5).

AWOL bag   The U.S. Army supplied soldiers with small, hand-carried bags large enough to pack the few items needed when going on weekend leave—a change of clothes, shaving gear, and the like. These bags came to be called AWOL bags in military slang. In the novel *Going After Cacciato* Sergeant Oscar Johnson claims that the deserting soldier Cacciato actually packed his supplies into an AWOL bag, even though the other men have trouble believing this:

> "No, man, I saw it."
> "You say you saw it."
> "I saw it. Black vinyl, white stitching. I speak truth, I saw it."
> Quiet beaten by rain. Shifting sounds in the night, men rolling.
> Then Eddie's voice, disbelieving: "Nobody. Not even the C. Nobody uses them bags to go AWOL. It's not done."
> "Tell it to Cacciato."
> "It's not *done*." (24)

Later, in his invented story about the chase after Cacciato, Paul Berlin imagines that the members of Third Squad actually find Cacciato's abandoned AWOL bag on a train called the DELHI EXPRESS.

"Backflash"   "Backflash" is the title of a poem that William Cowling's wife, Bobbi, slips to him after he has imprisoned her and their daughter, Melinda, in the master bedroom of their home in the novel *The Nuclear Age*. The poem reads:

Here, underground, the flashes
are back, filaments of history
that light the tunnels
beneath the mind
and undermine the softer lights
of love and reason.
Remember this
as though in backflash:

A bomb.
A Village burning.
We destroyed this house
to save it.

In this poem Bobbi comments on a famous statement supposedly made by an American major about the village of Ben Tre during the Vietnam War: "It became necessary to destroy the village in order to save it." William Cowling in his attempt to save his marriage by preventing Bobbi's departure is, in effect, destroying his marriage.

Badlands   Badlands are a type of arid terrain where wind and water have eroded canyons, gullies, and ravines into the landscape. In the United States, badlands can be found in Montana, Wyoming, North and South Dakota, and Nebraska; these landscapes are often associated with western outlaws who sometimes used the areas as hideouts. Badlands figure into Tim O'Brien's novel *Northern Lights* when the young, half-Indian girl Addie teases Paul Perry about taking her to the badlands of South Dakota on vacation. When Addie asserts that "the badlands are actually quite spectacular. God's gift," Paul complains that they sound "terrible" (86). Addie replies that they can stay in a nice motel and play stud poker, adding that they can also "have a big shoot-out at high noon" (86). Paul in the novel is torn between Addie and the wildness she represents and the comforting domesticity associated with his wife, Grace.

Baez, Joan   Joan Baez is an American folk singer and political activist who was popular in the 1960s. She is mentioned briefly in the short story "Quantum Jumps" when William, the story's narrator, begins to sing as he digs an enormous hole in his yard that he will turn into a bomb shelter. "Many moons ago," William thinks to himself, "when we were out to sanitize the world, I could carry a tune like nobody's business, I could do Baez and Dylan and Seeger, and it wasn't soupy, it was music to march to, it meant something" (38). The references to folk singers in this passage were removed when the story was revised for inclusion in *The Nuclear Age*.

"The Balance of Power"   "The Balance of Power" is a poem written by William Cowling's wife, Bobbi, in the novel *The Nuclear Age*. The poem suggests that William may be losing his own mental balance at the same time that worldwide political relations grow increasingly strained. The term *balance of power* comes from international law and refers to a state of equilibrium among nations, when no single nation is powerful enough to enforce its will on others but is an old doctrine of international relations.

Bangor, Maine   Bangor, Maine, is the city where the tough-talking sergeant Oscar Johnson sends his mail in the novel *Going After Cacciato*. Although he claims to be from DETROIT, Oscar cannot name any current sports players from the city, and the other men in Third Squad are suspicious of his claims, often calling Oscar "the nigga from Ba-Haba" or "the Down-east Brother, the dude with lobster on his breath" (142). The mystery of Oscar's origins is never solved in the novel.

Bao Dai   Bao Dai was the emperor of Annam, the upper two-thirds of Vietnam, from 1926 until 1945, when the country was under French colonial rule. When Vietnam became an independent country in 1945, Bao Dai abdicated. He was brought back by the French in 1949 to serve as head of state, and the Bao Dai government was supported by the United States as well, even though Bao Dai himself lived largely in France during this period. In 1955 Bao Dai abdicated again, leaving NGO DINH DIEM as president of South Vietnam after a fraudulent referendum. In the story "On the Rainy River" from *The Things They Carried*, the Tim O'Brien character bemoans the small-town ignorance that sent him to war. He writes that the pious and patriotic people of WORTHINGTON, MINNESOTA, "didn't know Bao Dai from the man in the moon. They didn't know history" (45).

Jane Fonda as Barbarella, July 1967 *(AP Photo)*

Barbarella   *Barbarella* was an erotic science fiction film released in 1968, starring JANE FONDA in the title role. Tim O'Brien, in his 1973 memoir, *If I Die in a Combat Zone,* writes that during Advanced Infantry Training (AIT), the camp movie house showed *Barbarella* for three weeks straight. *Barbarella* plays a part as well in the story "The Ghost Soldiers" from *The Things They Carried.* Azar and the Tim O'Brien character go to see the movie to pass time on the night that they plot to torment the medic Bobby Jorgenson. While O'Brien thinks *Barbarella* is "a lousy movie" (206), Azar is crazy about Jane Fonda.

Barker, Bob   Bob Barker is the longtime host of the CBS television game show *The Price Is Right.* He appears briefly in the novel *The Nuclear Age* when William Cowling turns on the television on October 1, 1969, his birthday, in the KEY WEST, FLORIDA, headquarters of the radical activist group the COMMITTEE. Cowling notes the huge disparity between watching a contestant in a clown suit on the game show laughing with Bob Barker and the crate of machine guns stored in the attic of the house. It is as if two different Americas exist at the same time.

Batangan Peninsula   The Batangan Peninsula juts out into the SOUTH CHINA SEA off QUANG NGAI PROVINCE in Vietnam, approximately 100 miles south along the coast from the city of DA NANG. This is the area where Tim O'Brien was stationed for part of his year-long tour of duty during the Vietnam War, and it serves as the setting for many of his Vietnam stories and novels. The villages of My Lai, where the infamous massacre occurred, are located on the interior of the Batangan Peninsula. The area around these villages was known in military slang of the time as "PINKVILLE," a dangerous, heavily mined, and hostile region marked in pink on military maps to signify a "built-up area" (*If I Die* 115).

Battle of Little Bighorn   In the novel *The Nuclear Age,* FORT DERRY, MONTANA, William Cowling's tiny hometown, celebrates an annual festival called CUSTER DAYS in which they recreate the Battle of Little Bighorn, where GENERAL GEORGE ARMSTRONG CUSTER and the U.S. 7th Cavalry were defeated by Lakota and Cheyenne Indians. The annual recreation reinforces in the frightened young boy the idea that violent endings are inevitable and unavoidable. The Battle of Little Bighorn plays a role in the novel *In the Lake of the Woods* as well. O'Brien quotes from books that explore the massacre of Custer and the 7th Cavalry in an attempt to shed some light on what may have happened in the Vietnamese village of My Lai in 1968. The narrator/investigator of the novel also refers to the Battle of Little Bighorn in a long footnote, in which he explores the nature of mystery itself: "The thing about Custer is this," the narrator writes, "no survivors. Hence, eternal doubt, which both frustrates and fascinates" (266).

Beardslee, Frank   Frank Beardslee was an American soldier in CHARLIE COMPANY who was present at the MY LAI MASSACRE. He testified, at the court-martial of CAPTAIN ERNEST MEDINA, that Medina had fired two shots over a prisoner's head to extract information. Beardslee is quoted in one of the evidence chapters of O'Brien's novel *In the Lake of the Woods* as testifying at LIEUTENANT WILLIAM CAL-

LEY's court-martial that American troops did not receive any hostile fire from villagers the day of the massacre.

de Beauvais, Vincent   Vincent de Beauvais was a Dominican monk and the author of the most important encyclopedia used in the Middle Ages. He is mentioned briefly in the novel *Tomcat in Love* when Thomas H. Chippering writes that de Beauvais "describes the female of our species as 'the confusion of man, an insatiable beast, a continuous anxiety, an incessant warfare, a daily ruin, a house of tempest, a hindrance to devotion'" (217). Chippering is prompted to remember this description when two of his students, Megan and Toni, who have coerced the professor into writing their honors theses for them, turn him in to the university president for sexual harassment.

Benson's Funeral Home   In the story "The Lives of the Dead" from *The Things They Carried,* Tim O'Brien recalls asking his father, when he was a child, to take him to Benson's Funeral Home in WORTHINGTON, MINNESOTA, to see the body of Linda, his nine-year-old classmate who had died of a brain tumor. When the young O'Brien sees the body, he feels like some mistake must have been made: "The girl lying in the white casket wasn't Linda. There was a resemblance, maybe, but where Linda had always been very slender and fragile-looking, almost skinny, the body in that casket was fat and swollen. For a second I wondered if somebody had made a terrible blunder" (241).

Bierce, Ambrose   Ambrose Bierce was a late 19th-, early 20th-century American journalist and fiction writer who mysteriously disappeared in Mexico in 1914 after traveling to the country to observe the Mexican Revolution. A quote from Bierce's final letter home is cited in one of the evidence chapters of O'Brien's novel *In the Lake of the Woods*. In the letter Bierce writes, "Naturally, it is possible—even probable—that I shall not return. These be 'strange countries,' in which things happen; that is why I am going" (290). The mystery surrounding Bierce is comparable to that surrounding the disappearance of John and Kathy Wade in the novel. No one can be sure whether the writer

or whether the Wades planned their own disappearances or were murdered.

Bikini Atoll   The Bikini Atoll, part of the Marshall Islands in the Pacific Ocean, consists of 23 coral islands surrounding a large lagoon. The site was used for testing nuclear weapons between 1946 and 1958 (and also lent its name to the popular bikini swimsuit, introduced just a few days after the first nuclear test). Because William Cowling in O'Brien's novel *The Nuclear Age* is so obsessed with nuclear war, the atoll looms large in his imagination. In the first chapter of the novel, Cowling discusses the seriousness of the nuclear threat, even urging his readers to "take a trip to Bikini" (8) to discover the menace for themselves: "Bring your friends," he adds, "eat a picnic lunch, a quick swim, a nature hike, and then, when night comes, build a bonfire and sit on the beach and just *listen*" (8). Later in the novel, when Cowling is on a plane to flee the DRAFT, he thinks about Bikini again, imagining that he can see from his window LOS ALAMOS, where the bomb was invented, all the way "across the ocean to Bikini" (150).

Bishop, Elizabeth   Elizabeth Bishop was a Pulitzer Prize–winning American poet who served as the United States poet laureate from 1949 to 1950. The final lines of Bishop's poem "One Art" serve as the epigraph to O'Brien's novel *Tomcat in Love*. The lines comment on the nature of loss, as the speaker attempts to convince herself that losing the things one loves is not the disaster it appears to be:

> —Even losing you (the joking voice, a gesture
> I love) I shan't have lied. It's evident
> The art of losing's not too hard to master
> Though it may look like (*Write* it!) like disaster.

Black Jack gum   An aniseed-flavored chewing gum made by the Cadbury Adams company, Black Jack was first produced in the 1880s and was the first chewing gum to be sold in sticks. The gum continued to be produced and sold into the 1970s. Black Jack is Cacciato's favorite brand of chewing gum in Tim O'Brien's novel *Going After Cacciato*. The night after Billy Boy Watkins's death, which occurs on Paul Berlin's first day of combat,

Cacciato offers him a stick of Black Jack gum. Paul Berlin has never tried Black Jack before. After Cacciato goes AWOL, Berlin and the other men of Third Squad find abandoned Black Jack wrappers that help lead them along Cacciato's trail.

Bogart, Humphrey Humphrey Bogart was an American actor who starred in classic Hollywood films such as *Casablanca, To Have and Have Not,* and *Key Largo.* In his memoir, *If I Die in a Combat Zone,* O'Brien lists Bogart in the role of Rick, the proprietor of the Café d'Americain in *Casablanca,* as one of the favorite heroes of his youth. Bogie, like O'Brien's other heroes, was "removed from other men, able to climb above and gaze down at other men" (143). O'Brien remembers Bogart, as Rick "in his office, looking down at roulette wheels and travelers" (143). O'Brien also admired Bogart's character for his courage and self-sacrifice in sending his true love, Ilsa, played by Ingrid Bergman, away at the end of the film.

Bonn, Germany In *Going After Cacciato,* Paul Berlin imagines the men of Third Squad pursuing the AWOL soldier Cacciato through Southeast Asia and the Middle East, then into Western Europe. He imagines a train ride through the heartland of Germany and the men crossing the RHINE at dawn. There is a 20-minute wait in the city of Bonn, Germany, before the train begins rolling south toward LUXEMBOURG. Berlin feels more at home as his imagination works westward: "Things were familiar. Lightheaded and eager, he couldn't get over how easy it was. He felt he was riding on ice" (278).

Bonnie and Clyde *Bonnie and Clyde* is a 1967 American film starring Warren Beatty and Faye Dunaway as the infamous outlaws Clyde Barrow and Bonnie Parker. The film makes an appearance in O'Brien's novel *The Things They Carried* when Lieutenant Jimmy Cross remembers watching the movie with Martha back at MOUNT SEBASTIAN COLLEGE in New Jersey before he became a soldier. Cross touches Martha's knee under her tweed skirt during the movie, but the look she gives him makes him pull his hand back. Later, reflecting on the incident, Cross wishes he had "done something brave" (5). He thinks that he "should've carried her up the stairs to her room and tied her to the bed and touched that left knee all night long" (5). This strangely tender yet violent fantasy marks Cross's mixed feelings of love for Martha and yet anger that she never mentions the war when she writes and that she does not seem to fully return his affection.

Book of Revelation The Book of Revelation is the last chapter of the New Testament of the Christian Bible. An example of apocalyptic literature, rich with dream visions and symbolic imagery, the book purports to reveal hidden aspects of God's will—especially what will happen to Christians and non-Christians upon the return of the Messiah. Tim O'Brien uses a passage from Revelation as the epigraph to his 1975 novel *Northern Lights:*

> . . . and lo, there was a great earthquake;
> and the sun became black as sackcloth of hair,
> and the moon became as blood. And the stars
> of heaven fell unto the earth even as a fig tree
> casteth her untimely figs, when she is shaken of
> a mighty wind. And the heaven departed as a
> scroll
> when it is rolled together; and every mountain
> and island were moved out of their places . . .
> For the day of his wrath is come.
> And who shall be able to stand?

Apocalypse is a theme running throughout the novel, as Pehr Perry, a Lutheran minister and the father of Paul and Harvey, preaches apocalypse in his sermons and requests that his younger son build a bomb shelter in the yard of their Minnesota farmhouse during the CUBAN MISSILE CRISIS of 1962. Impending apocalypse is a major thread as well in O'Brien's novel *The Nuclear Age,* in which William Cowling lives his whole life in fear of nuclear destruction.

BOQ BOQ is a military acronym that stands for Bachelor Officers Quarters. In the novel *Going After Cacciato,* Lieutenant Corson remarks to Major Li Van Hgoc, after the men of Third Squad have fallen into an underground tunnel complex, that the VIET CONG officer has a "nifty setup" underground, "a real sweet BOQ" (92).

Borden, Lizzie Lizzie Borden was a young woman arrested and tried for killing her father and stepmother with a hatchet in Fall River, Massachusetts, in 1892. Although she was acquitted of the crime, the murder remains shrouded in mystery even today. The narrator of Tim O'Brien's novel *In the Lake of the Woods* mentions Lizzie Borden in a long footnote, where he argues that "eternal doubt . . . both frustrates and fascinates" (266). According to the narrator, if we knew definitively that Lizzie Borden took the ax and killed her parents, we would lose interest in the story. The narrator claims that the same sort of mystery surrounds the figure of John Wade: "Everything . . . is conjecture" (266), he argues, despite his best attempts to piece together what happened to Kathy Wade.

The Bottle Top The Bottle Top is the name of a bar where John and Kathy Wade used to go dancing during their college days in the novel *In the Lake of the Woods*. It is at The Bottle Top that they invent the game called "Dare You," in which one of them dares the other to perform slightly dangerous and reckless acts, such as Kathy daring John to remove her panty hose under the table or John daring Kathy to steal a bottle of Scotch from behind the bar. Kathy especially remembers the way John looked at her one New Year's Eve back in college when they'd gone dancing at The Bottle Top: "no tricks at all. Just young and in love" (173).

Bouncing Betty The term *Bouncing Betty* was originally used in WORLD WAR II by allied forces to describe the German S-mine, an explosive device that detonates upon impact (usually from a soldier stepping on it or from a tripwire rigged to it) and explodes waist high. The mines were also used by the Viet Cong during the Vietnam War. In the chapter called "Step Lightly" from his memoir, *If I Die in a Combat Zone*, O'Brien describes the various mines that threatened U.S. soldiers in Vietnam. The chapter begins with the sentence, "The Bouncing Betty is feared most" (123).

von Braun, Wernher Wernher von Braun was an influential rocket scientist who first helped develop German rockets used in WORLD WAR

II before coming to the United States, where he helped develop the intermediate range ballistic missile program and later worked at NASA on the *Saturn V* launch vehicle. Von Braun is mentioned briefly in O'Brien's novel *The Nuclear Age*, when William Cowling speculates about what has become of the heroes and villains of the COLD WAR. "Von Braun," he writes, "went quietly in his sleep" (127).

Brezhnev, Leonid Leonid Brezhnev was the leader of the Soviet Union from 1964 to 1982. As such, he plays an important role in William Cowling's COLD WAR fears in the novel *The Nuclear Age*. In the first chapter of the book, Cowling muses about the current year—1995—and how much times have changed from the 1960s. "Where's Mama Cass?" he asks, "What happened to Brezhnev and Lester Maddox? Where's that old gang of mine . . . ?" (8).

Brigadoon *Brigadoon* is a musical about a Scottish town that mysteriously appears for only one day every hundred years. The stage musical was made into a film starring Gene Kelly in 1954, then remade again as a television movie in 1966. In "How to Tell a True War Story" from *The Things They Carried*, Mitchell Sanders mentions *Brigadoon* when telling Tim O'Brien the story of a listening patrol of six men that is sent into the mountains. In the night, the men hear a symphony of inexplicable sounds, from chamber music to an opera, a glee club, and even a barbershop quartet. But when morning comes, Sanders reports, "things finally get quiet. Like you never even *heard* quiet before. . . . Like *Brigadoon*—pure vapor, you know? Everything's all sucked up inside the fog" (75).

Bronze Star The Bronze Star is a U.S. military decoration that is awarded for bravery or merit. It is the fourth-highest combat award given by the U.S. Armed Forces. In the novel *Going After Cacciato*, Cacciato is said to have won the Bronze Star "for shooting out a dink's front teeth" (8). Paul Berlin uses this incident to argue that the men should not consider Cacciato a coward, despite his desertion.

Bull of Karelia The Bull of Karelia is a figure from Finnish mythology that plays a role in

O'Brien's 1975 novel, *Northern Lights*. Said to be the hero of Pehr Peri, a stern Finnish immigrant and Lutheran preacher, and the grandfather of Paul and Harvey Perry, the bull is described as "a moose with antlers gone and head down in the dead of winter" (71). The bull seems to represent the ability to endure in a cold, harsh environment and is a fitting figure for Peri, whose sermons offer a bleak view of life, warning about apocalypse, denying the promise of salvation, and advising a stoic endurance as the only way to meet the future. Harvey Perry is also associated with bull mythology in the novel, having been nicknamed "Harvey the Bull" by his father and displaying the masculine qualities of courage and silent suffering most admired by his forebears.

Bundy, McGeorge   McGeorge Bundy served as U.S. National Security Advisor from 1961 to 1966, when he played a key role in escalating U.S. involvement in the Vietnam War. In the novel *The Nuclear Age*, William Cowling's father, angry about the war and the possibility of his son being drafted (*see* DRAFT), complains that he would like to murder the "whole jackass crew" at the Pentagon, along with all the diplomats who can't resolve the conflict. "I'd strangle the whole crew," he claims, "I *would*. My own two hands. March in and murder the sons of bitches, all those whiz-kid bastards. You think I'm not serious? Westmoreland, I'd nail him first, and then Bundy and Ho Chi Minh" (143).

C-4 explosives   C-4 explosives, used frequently by soldiers during the Vietnam War, are malleable, plastic explosive material that can be molded into various shapes. They are quite stable and can be set off only with a detonator, not by shaking or dropping, or burning. In the novel *The Nuclear Age*, William Cowling describes first meeting fellow PEVERSON STATE COLLEGE student Ollie Winkler in the school cafeteria. Ollie talks at length about C-4 explosives when the two young men meet, and Cowling will discover later that he is a detonation expert.

CA   CA is military shorthand for Combat Assault. O'Brien often uses the term as a verb in his work, as in the statement from *If I Die in a Combat Zone* that the soldiers of ALPHA COMPANY were "CA'd into

Pinkville" (103). In his memoir he describes the particular terror of the helicopter Combat Assault in the following way:

> The worst part of the Combat Assault, the thing you think about on the way down, is how perfectly exposed you are. Nowhere to hide. A fragile machine. No foxholes, no rocks, no gullies. The CA is the army's most potent offensive tactic of the war, a cousin to Hitler's blitzkrieg. The words are "agile," "hostile," and "mobile." One moment the world is serene, in another moment the war is there. It is like the cloudburst, like lightning, like the dropping of the bomb on a sleeping Hiroshima, like the Nazis' rush through Belgium and Poland and France. (110)

CACK   O'Brien writes in his memoir, *If I Die in a Combat Zone*, that CACK is an acronym for "corrosive-action-car-killer," which he describes as "nothing more than a grenade, its safety pin extracted and spoon held in place by a rubber band" (126). The explosive device is then placed in the gas tank of motorized vehicles. The gasoline eventually corrodes the rubber band, releasing the spoon of the grenade, and blowing up the vehicle. Although he says these devices were rarely encountered by infantry soldiers in Vietnam, they were sometimes used against rear echelon personnel.

Calley, Lieutenant William   Lieutenant William Calley was the only man convicted in the MY LAI MASSACRE court-martials. Found guilty of the premeditated murder of 22 Vietnamese civilians, Calley was sentenced to life in prison. However, he ended up serving only about three years under house arrest before his sentence was commuted. Calley is one of the real-life historical figures who appears as a character in the novel *In the Lake of the Woods*. As he interacts with the fictional John Wade during his time in Vietnam, the novel includes several actual quotes from Calley's court-martial. In his memoir, *If I Die in a Combat Zone*, O'Brien writes about his own unit patrolling the villages of My Lai a little more than a year after the massacre took place: "Pinkville and the villages called My Lai were well known to Alpha Company. Even before the headlines and before the names Calley and Medina took their place in history, Pinkville was a feared and special place on the earth" (116). Calley is mentioned as well in the novel *The Nuclear Age,* when William Cowling reports the important political news of 1971. He writes, "in Georgia, Lieutenant William Calley went on trial for murder" (239). Cowling will report as well that Calley was actually convicted of premeditated murder on March 29, 1971.

Cao Dai   Cao Dai is a monotheistic religion established in South Vietnam in 1926 that attempts to reconcile religious teachings of many different faiths. In the novel *Going After Cacciato,* Sarkin Aung Wan uses the Vietnamese phrase *Cao Dai* to refer to the evening prayers that a group of monks are undertaking in MANDALAY, Burma. When Paul Berlin spots Cacciato among the monks, he attempts to tackle the AWOL soldier but becomes crushed in the crowd. When he sits up afterward, Sarkin calls him, perhaps sarcastically, "a brave hero" for "disturbing Cao Dai," for "touching the untouchables" (122).

Carew, Rod   Rod Carew was a popular Major League Baseball player from 1967 to 1985 who won several batting titles and stole home 17 times in his career. In the novel *July, July,* David Todd listens to a transistor radio in July 1969, while lying alongside the SONG TRA KY River in Vietnam, alone and severely wounded. One of the pieces of news he hears is that Rod Carew had just stolen home for the seventh time in his career. David Todd in the novel "steals home" in a way as well. He is saved from almost certain death after he makes a bargain with the mysterious radio deejay Johnny Ever to keep on living, despite grim news about his future.

Carlson, Richard   Richard Carlson was the actor who played HERB PHILBRICK in the 1950s syndicated television show *I LED THREE LIVES.* William Cowling's father in *The Nuclear Age* is reminded of the show when he hands his son an envelope stuffed full of money as William prepares to go underground to evade the DRAFT. Mr. Cowling remembers particularly how much Carlson sweated in the role. William tells his father, "I'll go easy on the sweat" (144) in a moment of touching comradery.

Caro, Robert A.   Robert A. Caro is a biographer best known for his series of books about the U.S. president LYNDON JOHNSON, called *The Years of Lyndon Johnson.* Caro is one of the experts quoted in the evidence chapters of the novel *In the Lake of the Woods.* His comments about Johnson attest to the politician's great need for affection and his rage at a 1941 election defeat. An overwhelming need to be loved as well as uncontrollable rage at an election loss are qualities shared by O'Brien's protagonist John Wade.

Carter, Jimmy   Jimmy Carter, 39th president of the United States, is mentioned briefly in the novel *The Nuclear Age* when William Cowling reports that on January 21, 1977, President Carter issued a blanket pardon to DRAFT dodgers of the Vietnam War. This pardon comes after Cowling has already turned himself in to the local authorities in FORT DERRY, MONTANA, for evading the draft.

Cass, Mama   Cass Elliott, born Ellen Naomi Cohen, became known as Mama Cass when she was a member of the singing group the Mamas and the Papas in the late 1960s. Mama Cass is mentioned briefly in *Going After Cacciato* as Eddie Lazzutti's favorite folk singer. "'Man alive,'" Eddie says, "'if I could ever sing like that . . . A new town every night, pussy on my tail and bucks in my pocket'" (141). Mama Cass is mentioned as well in the novel *The Nuclear Age,* when William Cowling muses in the opening chapter about what has become of the 1960s. "Times change," he writes, "take a good hard look. Where's Mama Cass? What happened to Brezhnev and Lester Maddox?" (8).

Centennial Beach   As Norman Bowker drives around and around the lake in his small, Iowa hometown in the story "Speaking of Courage," the big Chevy is said to curve past Centennial Beach and the A&W root beer stand, where he will eventually stop to order food. The lake that Norman drives around is modeled after LAKE OKABENA in O'Brien's hometown of WORTHINGTON, MINNESOTA. The various parks that Norman drives through, including Centennial Beach, are real places located on Lake Okabena.

Centerville Junior College   Paul Berlin in the novel *Going After Cacciato* enrolls briefly in Centerville Junior College, where he earns 28 credits. Although he does well and enjoys his classes in English and history and even considers entering the University of Iowa to work toward a B.A. in education, he begins to feel restless in his second year at Centerville and drops out. It is after he quits college that Berlin is drafted (*see* DRAFT) to fight in the Vietnam War.

Chandni Chowk   One of the oldest and most popular street markets in DELHI, India, Chandni Chowk makes an appearance in O'Brien's novel *Going After Cacciato* when Paul Berlin imagines himself wandering through the stalls of the bazaar, snapping pictures of things he might want to remember while Sarkin Aung Wan is sleeping back at the HOTEL PHOENIX. Berlin imagines showing his mother and father a slide show of his travels once he is back home in FORT DODGE, IOWA. The name of the market in the novel, however, is misspelled as Chandi Chowk.

Charlie   Charlie was military slang used by American soldiers during the Vietnam War primarily to refer to enemy VIET CONG soldiers. The term *Charlie* derived from the military phonetic code for VC—"Victor Charlie." Because "Charlie" was the phonetic equivalent used for the letter C, there were also Charlie Companies during the war.

Charlie Company   Charlie Company of the 1st Battalion, 10th Infantry of the U.S. Army was the unit involved in the MY LAI MASSACRE in March of 1968. In the novel *In the Lake of the Woods*, John Wade is a member of Charlie Company during his service in Vietnam. As such, he witnesses the massacre firsthand, although he later covers up his involvement, altering records to make it appear as if he had belonged to a different unit.

Château-Thierry, France   Château-Thierry is a small city about 50 miles northeast of PARIS, France. In the novel *Going After Cacciato*, Paul Berlin imagines the men of Third Squad passing through Château-Thierry and into the suburbs of Paris aboard a train from LUXEMBOURG as they complete the final stage of their journey in pursuit of the AWOL soldier Cacciato.

Chautauqua Park   Chautauqua Park is one of the parks bordering the lake at the center of Norman Bowker's small midwestern hometown in the story "Speaking of Courage" from *The Things They Carried*. One July 4th late afternoon, after Norman's return from Vietnam, he drives aimlessly around and around the lake, in a circuit that runs from SLATER PARK to SUNSET PARK to Chautauqua Park. Like the other parks O'Brien mentions in the story, Chautauqua is a real park in his hometown of WORTHINGTON, MINNESOTA.

Chekhov, Anton   Anton Chekhov was a late 19th-century Russian playwright and short story writer who is quoted in one of the evidence chapters in O'Brien's novel *In the Lake of the Woods*, where he comments on the secret life lived by one of his characters: "He had two lives: one, open, seen and known by all who cared to know . . . and another life running its course in secret" (192). This quote can be read as a commentary on the politician John Wade in O'Brien's novel, who also lives a double life, hiding his involvement in the MY LAI MASSACRE from the world at large and even from himself.

Chic's Tavern   O'Brien in his 1973 memoir remembers spending the summer of 1968 drinking coffee and arguing about the war at a local café. The nights, he says, he would often spend at Chic's Tavern, "drinking beer with the kids from the farms" (17). Chic's might be the model for FRANZ'S GLEN, a tavern frequented by the Perry brothers in SAWMILL LANDING, Minnesota, in the 1975 novel *Northern Lights*.

Chieu Hoi   The Chieu Hoi program, which translates as "Open Arms," was begun by the South Vietnamese during the Vietnam War to encourage VIET CONG soldiers to defect to the South. In the novel *Going After Cacciato*, Lieutenant Corson tells the VIET CONG major Li Van Hgoc that he is free to join the Americans as they make their way out of the underground tunnel system. Corson mentions the Chieu Hoi program, but the Viet Cong major is terrified by the war and refuses to leave his safe underground prison. The Chieu Hoi program is mentioned again later in the novel, when the men of Third Squad are speaking to Captain Fahyi Rhallon in a bar in TEHRAN. When Rhallon inquires about SAPPERS, Stink Harris replies that they are "sleazy sons of bitches" (202). He tells a story of two converted sappers up at CHU LAI, "Chieu Hoi types," who gave a demonstration of how sappers operate, oiling up their bodies and slipping under barbed wire fences.

Chinook   The Chinook is a large, twin-rotored transport helicopter. It was used extensively during the Vietnam War. In the novel *Going After Cacciato,* Jim Pederson is killed by friendly fire from the door gunner of a Chinook that transports the men of ALPHA COMPANY into a COMBAT ASSAULT (CA) near the village of HOI AN.

Chittagong, Bangladesh   The second-largest city in Bangladesh, Chittagong appears in the novel *Going After Cacciato* when, in Paul Berlin's imagined pursuit story, the men of Third Squad travel through the city on the DELHI EXPRESS as they make their way from MANDALAY to DELHI. The older lieutenant, Corson, wakes up on the train and asks where they are. When he is told that the train is almost to Chittagong, he asks, "What's a Chittagong" (134), then proceeds to tell a story about getting busted down a rank after getting drunk in a bar in SEOUL, SOUTH KOREA with a SEABEE named Jack Daniels.

Cholon   Cholon is the name of the Chinese district in Ho Chi Minh City, formerly known as SAIGON. In the novel *Going After Cacciato,* the young refugee named Sarkin Aung Wan is said to be from Cholon originally. Her father had owned a restaurant there, but had been shot by the VIET CONG after being led out of a hospital where Sarkin's mother was giving birth to twin babies. When Sarkin's mother dies of grief two years later, and the city of Cholon turns into a combat zone, the family disperses. Sarkin Aung Wan, along with two elderly aunts and a yoked pair of water buffalo, head west looking for refuge.

Chu Lai Combat Center   During the Vietnam War years, there was a large U.S. military base located at Chu Lai, just south of Da Nang, in Vietnam. The base served as headquarters for the army's AMERICAL DIVISION, which Tim O'Brien was assigned to. In his memoir he describes the Combat Center at Chu Lai, where he spent his first week in Vietnam, as a "resortlike place, tucked in alongside the South China Sea, complete with sand and native girls and a miniature golf course and floor shows with every variety of grinding female pelvis" (70). The Combat Center at Chu Lai figures prominently in O'Brien's fiction as well. In his first published short story, "Claudia Mae's Wedding Day," a soldier named Robert proposes to his girlfriend, Claudia Mae, in a letter that he writes while sitting in a foxhole just south of Chu Lai. In addition, Private First Class Paul Berlin in *Going After Cacciato* is said to arrive at the Chu Lai Combat Center on June 3, 1968. In August, when Berlin's platoon returns to Chu Lai for a week's stand-down, Paul Berlin hikes to a nearby military unit, where he and Oscar Johnson, Eddie Lazzutti, and Doc Peret place phone calls home over a complicated satellite radio system. The men of ALPHA COMPANY in *The Things They Carried* are also based at Chu Lai, as stories such as "The Dentist," situated at camp rather than out in the bush, make clear. The story "Sweetheart of the Song Tra Bong" takes place in a small medical detachment in the mountains west of Chu Lai, where Rat Kiley was assigned before he joined Alpha Company.

CID   CID is a military acronym that stands for Criminal Investigation Division. In the story "Sweetheart of the Song Tra Bong" from *The Things They Carried,* Rat Kiley tells his fellow soldiers in ALPHA COMPANY the story of how Mary Anne Bell is flown to Vietnam, becomes obsessed with the war, and eventually goes missing in the jungle. After Mary Anne's disappearance, Rat explains, "there was an inquiry, of course . . . and for a time the Tra Bong compound went crazy with MP and CID types" (115). However, Mary Anne is never found, although rumors of her being spotted in the jungle wearing her culottes and a necklace of human tongues continue to swirl around.

Cisco Kid   The Cisco Kid was the main character in a series of popular western books and movies, as well as a television show that ran from 1950 to 1956. Cisco and his sidekick, PANCHO, though desperadoes on the run from the law themselves, travel the West helping the poor and downtrodden. In the story "The Ghost Soldiers" from *The Things They Carried,* the Tim O'Brien narrator mentions the Cisco Kid briefly when he describes preparing to gain his revenge on the medic Bobby Jorgensen by scaring him half to death. He says that in the darkness of the Vietnamese night he felt as if he were in a movie: "There's a camera on you, so you begin acting, you're somebody else. You think of all the films you've seen, Audie Murphy and Gary Cooper and the Cisco Kid, all those heroes, and you can't help falling back on them as models of proper comportment" (207).

von Clausewitz, Carl   Carl von Clausewitz was a Prussian general and military theorist who served in the Napoleonic Wars and wrote an influential book on military history and strategy called *On War.* In the novel *Going After Cacciato,* Lieutenant Sidney Martin, who trained at West Point, is said to have read the work of von Clausewitz. Despite his excellent education, Sidney Martin is not successful as a lieutenant in Vietnam. His men hate him for his by-the-books command style, especially for making them search Vietnamese tunnels before blowing them up. The men of Third Squad eventually murder the lieutenant with a fragmentation grenade.

Claymore mines   One of the explosive devices used frequently in the Vietnam War was the M18 Claymore antipersonnel mine, which fires spherical metal shrapnel out to distances of 100 meters. Frequently used on ambushes during the Vietnam War, the Claymore is described by O'Brien in several of his works. In *If I Die in a Combat Zone,* his 1973 war memoir, O'Brien recalls going out on night ambush and being given a Claymore by his lieutenant, Mad Mark. He carefully inserts the blasting cap into the mine and places the metal legs of the explosive into the earth before creeping back to his hiding spot with the firing device in his hand.

Ollie Winkler in the novel *The Nuclear Age* talks extensively about various explosive devices, including Claymore mines and their killing radius the first time he meets William Cowling. In addition, in the novel *Going After Cacciato* Oscar Johnson is sent out at one point to negotiate with the AWOL soldier Cacciato. When Johnson returns, he is questioned by his lieutenant about the weapons Cacciato carried, specifically whether he had any grenades or Claymore mines with him.

Cleveland Heights Senior High   In the story "Sweetheart of the Song Tra Bong" from *The Things They Carried,* the medic Mark Fossie flies his high school girlfriend to Vietnam. When Mary Anne Bell first arrives in country, she is described as a tall, "big-boned blonde . . . seventeen years old, fresh out of Cleveland Heights Senior High" (93).

Code of Conduct   The U.S. military Code of Conduct, an ethical guide to how a soldier should behave during combat and as a prisoner of war, was established by President EISENHOWER in 1955 following the KOREAN WAR. Tim O'Brien refers to the Code of Conduct in his novel *Going After Cacciato* when the narrator writes that the "routinization of the war" helped to make it tolerable (44). The men of Third Squad in the novel are said to be governed by "informal SOPs" (44) that tell them when to joke and when not to, when to rest and when to march, when to send out ambushes and when to fake them. These informal operating procedures, O'Brien writes, "were more important than the Code of Conduct" (44).

cold war   The cold war refers to the state of tense political conflict and competition that existed between the United States and the Soviet Union from the end of WORLD WAR II until the dissolution of the Soviet state in 1991. Marked by a nuclear arms race and specific moments of heightened tension such as the 1962 CUBAN MISSILE CRISIS, the cold war had a direct effect on U.S. involvement in Vietnam as well, since the U.S. goal in that country was to contain the spread of communism. The cold war plays a key role in O'Brien's novel *The Nuclear Age,* in which the protagonist

William Cowling lives his life terrified of imminent nuclear annihilation. In the story "On the Rainy River" from *The Things They Carried*, the young Tim O'Brien narrator speculates about the facts surrounding the Vietnam War, specifically wondering, "What about SEATO and the Cold War? What about dominoes?" (40).

Combat Assault   See CA.

Combat Infantryman Badge   The Combat Infantryman Badge is a decoration awarded to U.S. soldiers who fought in active ground combat during their military service. In the original version of the short story "Speaking of Courage," published in the *Massachusetts Review* in the summer of 1976, Paul Berlin, back home in his small midwestern hometown after fighting in the Vietnam War, imagines talking with his father about the medals he won as he drives around and around a lake at the town's center. Berlin imagines telling his father that his most precious medal—except for the one he did not win, the SILVER STAR—was the Combat Infantryman Badge, which "meant he had seen the war as a real soldier, on the ground" (247). When the story was revised for inclusion in the collection *The Things They Carried*, Paul Berlin was changed to Norman Bowker and the reference to the Combat Infantryman Badge was deleted.

the Committee   The Committee is the name of the radical organization initially formed by William Cowling and Ollie Winkler in the novel *The Nuclear Age*. Later, the group will expand to include members Tina Roebuck, Sarah Strouch, and Ned Rafferty.

CONELRAD   CONELRAD is an acronym standing for Control of Electromagnetic Radiation, a system of emergency broadcast and missile defense used during the COLD WAR. In the novel *The Nuclear Age*, William Cowling recounts his fear of nuclear destruction dating back all the way to his childhood. He specifically remembers listening to "all that CONELRAD stuff on the radio" (9) back in 1958, along with other ominous signs that danger was imminent.

Cong Giao   *Cong Giao* is a Vietnamese phrase used by Jim Pederson in the novel *Going After Cacciato* that means Vietnamese Catholic. Although Pederson is not himself Catholic, he enthusiastically repeats the phrase whenever he sees a villager wearing a crucifix or carrying rosary beads, since "he considered it his duty to reinforce Christianity in any of its forms" (143).

Connell, Evan S.   Evan S. Connell is the author of a book called *Son of the Morning Star: Custer and the Little Bighorn*. Tim O'Brien quotes from Connell's book in one of the evidence chapters of his novel *In the Lake of the Woods*, providing a glimpse into an earlier massacre in an attempt to give readers some understanding of what happened at the Vietnamese village of My Lai in March of 1968.

Coolidge, Calvin   William, the narrator of the short story "Quantum Jumps," refers to Calvin Coolidge, the 30th president of the United States, briefly when he thinks about his days as a 1960s campus radical: "We were not the lunatic fringe," he comforts himself. "We were the true-blue center. Middle class, middle-of-the-road, middle-Americans—the last of the diehard Conservatives, as patriotic as Nathan Hale, as conventional as Calvin Coolidge" (39). O'Brien removed the references to both Hale and Coolidge when he revised the story for inclusion in his novel *The Nuclear Age*.

Cooper, Gary   Gary Cooper was a U.S. movie star, famous especially for his roles in westerns and war films beginning in the late 1920s and lasting through the 1950s. Cooper is one of the figures that Tim O'Brien imagines in the crowd of people lining the shore of the RAINY RIVER and urging him to go to war in the novel *The Things They Carried*. One of the reasons that O'Brien finds it impossible to flee the DRAFT at the end of the story "On the Rainy River" is because he grew up watching films and television shows with actors such as Cooper playing heroic masculine characters who would always choose to fight for their country. These dramas never depicted the complex morality involved in going to an unjust war. In the story "The Ghost Soldiers," also from *The Things They Carried*,

O'Brien again mentions Gary Cooper when he writes about what it feels like to be on watch out in the "boonies": "You wonder if you're dreaming. It's like you're in a movie. There's a camera on you, so you begin acting, you're somebody else. You think of all the films you've seen, Audie Murphy and Gary Cooper and the Cisco Kid, all those heroes, and you can't help falling back on them as models of proper comportment" (207).

Costain, Thomas   Thomas Costain was a 20th-century Canadian author of historical fiction. He appears in Tim O'Brien's memoir, *If I Die in a Combat Zone*, when an army chaplain, whom O'Brien goes to see during basic training in order to express his moral reservations about the war, tells the young soldier that a simple reliance on faith is the answer to his ethical problems: "When you get down to it, faith is an ancient Christian principle. I think it originated with Christ himself. Anyway, it was certainly faith that moved the crusaders way back when. Faith kept them going, God knows. Anyone who's read Norah Lofts and Thomas Costain knows that" (58). Readers are intended to notice the confusing vagueness of the chaplain's language here, his blindness to using the Crusades as a lesson in ethical behavior, and his utter unhelpfulness to the morally torn O'Brien.

Crater, Judge Joseph Force   Joseph Force Crater was a New York City judge who disappeared on the night of August 6, 1930, on his way to see a Broadway show. Judge Crater's disappearance has remained a mystery ever since, with no one knowing for sure whether he was murdered, ran off with a woman, or staged his disappearance to avoid corruption charges. The Crater incident is cited by the narrator of O'Brien's novel *In the Lake of the Woods* in a long footnote that explores the nature of unsolved mysteries. The novel's narrator argues that human beings love enigma, despite our competing desire for certainty. Judge Crater would soon be forgotten if we knew what happened to him, but as an unsolved riddle, he holds our attention. The narrator claims the same status for John Wade, whose fate remains similarly open to conjecture.

C rations   C rations were individual, prepackaged meals eaten by American soldiers in Vietnam when out on patrol or in the field and away from regular mess halls. Although the term was officially discarded in 1958 when WORLD WAR II C rations were phased out and replaced with the "Meal, Combat, Individual ration," soldiers continued to use the older, more familiar term throughout the war. The meals weighed a little more than a pound and a half and consisted of a canned meat, a canned fruit or dessert, and a tin of crackers or bread with a fruit or cheese spread. Accessory packs contained salt and pepper, chewing gum, coffee powder, cigarettes, and toilet paper. Soldiers are depicted quite frequently eating C rations in O'Brien's Vietnam War books, and C rations are said to be one of the items that the men carry with them in the field in the novel *The Things They Carried*.

Crazy Horse   Crazy Horse was a warrior and leader of the Oglala Lakota Indian tribe in the late 19th century who fought in the BATTLE OF LITTLE BIGHORN. In the novel *The Nuclear Age*, William Cowling watches each year as the residents of FORT DERRY, MONTANA, recreate the battle during their annual CUSTER DAYS celebration. William's beloved father plays the role of GENERAL GEORGE ARMSTRONG CUSTER each year, and is ritually scalped by Crazy Horse again and again.

Crippled Children's School   In his memoir, *If I Die in a Combat Zone*, O'Brien remembers driving around LAKE OKABENA in his hometown of WORTHINGTON, MINNESOTA, the summer he received his DRAFT notice. As he circles the lake, he passes several parks that dot the shore, the Crippled Children's School, and "a long string of split-level houses, painted every color" (20). This memory serves as the basis for O'Brien's later story "Speaking of Courage" in which a character—Paul Berlin in the original story version, Norman Bowker in the version that appeared in *The Things They Carried*— drives aimlessly around his small hometown lake after returning from the Vietnam War.

Crito   The *Crito*, written by the Greek philosopher PLATO, is a dialogue between SOCRATES and a wealthy Athenian named Crito. When Crito urges Socrates to flee prison, where he is awaiting a death sentence for corrupting the youth of ATH-ENS, Socrates refuses, arguing that he owes a debt to the state. Because he was educated and raised in the state, and because he previously acquiesced to the laws of the state, it would be unjust for him to oppose the laws now that they have worked against him. In several instances in his work, O'Brien thinks of Plato's *Crito* as it relates to the situation of those drafted (*see* DRAFT) into the Vietnam War. As he internally debates fleeing the draft in his memoir, *If I Die in a Combat Zone*, O'Brien refers specifically to Socrates' reasoning in the *Crito:*

> More, I owed the prairie something. For twenty-one years I'd lived under its laws, accepted its education, eaten its food, wasted and guzzled its water, slept well at night, driven across its highways, dirtied and breathed its air, wallowed in its luxuries. I'd played on its Little League teams. I remembered Plato's *Crito*, when Socrates, facing certain death—execution, not war—had the chance to escape. But he reminded himself that he had seventy years in which he could have left the country, if he were not satisfied or felt the agreements he'd made with it were unfair. (18–19)

Socrates' reasoning appears in O'Brien's fictional works as well. The young Tim O'Brien in the story "On the Rainy River," for instance, thinks about what he owes his small hometown as he considers swimming across the river to Canada, and Paul Berlin, near the end of the novel *Going After Cacciato*, debates fleeing the war with the imagined refugee, Sarkin Aung Wan. Berlin argues that he has obligations to his family, friends, and country. "Obligation," he adds, "is more than a claim imposed on us; it is a personal sense of indebtedness. It is a feeling, an acknowledgment, that through many prior acts of consent we have agreed to perform certain future acts" (319). Berlin, echoing the *Crito* in this passage, chooses to stay at the war rather than flee.

Crossan, John Dominic John Dominic Crossan is the author of a book called *The Historical Jesus*,

which Tim O'Brien quotes from in one of the evidence chapters in his novel *In the Lake of the Woods*. The quote from Crossan echoes the novel's theme about the inaccessibility of absolute truth: "If you cannot believe in something produced by reconstruction," Crossan writes about the life of Jesus, "you may have nothing left to believe in" (294).

Cuban missile crisis In October 1962, U.S. spy planes confirmed that Cuba, with the support of the Soviet Union, had begun building offensive missile bases throughout the country. President KENNEDY, in a test of his resolve, ordered a naval blockade of Cuba. Even though the crisis was resolved by the end of the month when the Soviets agreed to dismantle the missiles in exchange for a noninvasion promise on the part of the United States, most historians agree that the October showdown was the moment when the COLD WAR came closest to descending into actual nuclear war. This historical moment figures into several of O'Brien's works. In the novel *Northern Lights*, the Lutheran minister Pehr Perry, the father of Paul and Harvey, asks his younger son to build a bomb shelter in the yard of the family home during the 1962 missile crisis. Although the old man dies shortly afterward, Harvey dutifully carries out his wishes, constructing the shelter as his father had requested. The Cuban missile crisis will play an even more important role in the later novel, *The Nuclear Age*, in which William Cowling lives his whole life terrified of the potential for nuclear destruction. Having grown up during the cold war, and witnessed the real fear evident in the American psyche during October 1962, William believes he has good reason to expect imminent atomic annihilation. He is amazed that other people can so easily repress the very real threat of such annihilation from their day-to-day lives. Like Harvey Perry, William Cowling also builds a bomb shelter in his yard.

Custer, General George Armstrong General George Armstrong Custer was a U.S. Army officer who fought in the Civil War, but who is best remembered for his disastrous defeat by the Lakota Sioux and Cheyenne Indian tribes at the BATTLE OF LITTLE BIGHORN. In the novel *The Nuclear*

General George Custer (Courtesy of the Library of
Congress)

Custer Days In the novel *The Nuclear Age*,
the small town of FORT DERRY, MONTANA, where
William Cowling grows up, celebrates an annual
festival called Custer Days, commemorating the
BATTLE OF LITTLE BIGHORN and the defeat of GEN-
ERAL GEORGE ARMSTRONG CUSTER. Every year,
William's father plays the role of Custer. William,
a boy already obsessed with death and destruction,
watches his father pretend to die in the role over
and over again, each time longing for "the miracle
of a happy ending" (11), but knowing the tragic
outcome in advance.

Age, the small town of FORT DERRY, MONTANA,
reenacts the battle each year during their CUSTER
DAYS celebration when William Cowling's father
takes on the role of the defeated general. Custer is
an important figure as well in the novel *In the Lake
of the Woods*. In several of the evidence chapters
of the book, O'Brien cites quotes from earlier massacres in an attempt to shed light on what happened in the village of THUAN YEN on March 16,
1968, during the infamous MY LAI MASSACRE. In
the quotes attributed to Custer, the general pleads,
"John! John! Oh, John!" (143; 199). According to
EVAN S. CONNELL, author of *Son of the Morning
Star*, John was the name regularly used by whites
when addressing Indians.

Daley, Richard Richard Daley was a longtime
powerful political boss of the Democratic Party in
Chicago, serving as the city's mayor from 1955 until
his death in 1976. He shocked many, especially the
political left, with his handling of the protesters
at the 1968 Democratic National Convention, in
which police violently clubbed men, women, and
children. Daley functions as a touchstone figure for
the 1960s in O'Brien's novel *The Nuclear Age*. In the
opening chapter, William Cowling, writing in 1995,
wonders what happened to the political figures of
the '60s, including Daley. Later in the book, writing
about his junior year of college in October 1966,
Cowling says that Richard Daley, at that time, "ruled
a peaceful city" (73). He mentions Daley again when
it is 1977 and President CARTER issues a blanket
pardon to DRAFT dodgers. "Richard Daley was dead"
(262) by that point, Cowling informs readers.

Damascus Lutheran Church In the novel
Northern Lights, Paul Perry's father and grandfather
both served as ministers of the Damascus Lutheran
Church in the tiny Minnesota town of SAWMILL
LANDING. Paul's grandfather, Pehr Peri, a former
lumberjack and itinerant preacher, hanged himself
from the church rafters in 1919, leaving his ministry in the hands of his son, Pehr Perry, Paul's
father.

Da Nang, Vietnam A major port city along the
south central coast of Vietnam, Da Nang was home
to a large U.S. Air Force base during the Vietnam
War. In the novel *The Nuclear Age*, William Cowling, keenly aware of world political events, notes

that, in 1964, "the Marines were digging in" (66) in Da Nang.

Danube River   In the novel *Going After Cacciato,* Paul Berlin imagines that the men of Third Squad cross the Danube River in Germany in a battered Volkswagen van they have taken from a disaffected American college drop-out. After having made it to ATHENS, then to ZAGREB, CROATIA, the journey through Austria and Germany as they make their way closer to PARIS is a smooth and easy one in Paul Berlin's imagination.

Darton Hall College   Darton Hall is a fictional liberal-arts college located in the St. Paul-Minneapolis area in Minnesota that serves as the alma mater for a wide assortment of characters in the novel *July, July.* The book is set in July 2000 as the 1969 graduating class of Darton Hall College gathers for their 30th reunion, one year late. Interspersed with scenes that actually take place during the reunion weekend are memories from the various characters' pasts. While the college is fictional, it is most likely modeled on O'Brien's own alma mater—MACALESTER COLLEGE, a small, liberal-arts school in St. Paul, Minnesota.

Darvon   Darvon is the brand name of a narcotic analgesic called propoxyphene, which is used for mild to moderate pain relief. In the novel *Going After Cacciato,* during the bad time along the SONG TRA BONG River in late July, Doc Peret is said to begin popping Darvon and smoking too much as he, like the rest of the men in ALPHA COMPANY, becomes increasingly restless and edgy, waiting to see action.

David, Lester   Lester David is the author of a book called *The Lonely Lady of San Clemente,* a biography of PAT NIXON. O'Brien quotes from this book in one of the evidence chapters of his novel *In the Lake of the Woods.* David argued that Pat Nixon hated the role of politician's wife, and O'Brien uses this information to shed light on Kathy Wade, who also despised politics.

Delhi   Delhi, the second-most populous city in India, is a stop on the road to PARIS for the mem-

bers of Third Squad as they pursue an AWOL fellow soldier in the novel *Going After Cacciato.* The men arrive in Delhi after taking a train called the DELHI EXPRESS from MANDALAY, Burma. It is in Delhi where the men stay at the HOTEL PHOENIX and Lieutenant Corson falls in love with the proprietor, an Americanized Indian woman named Hamijolli Chand.

Delhi Express   The Delhi Express is the train that the men of Third Squad take from MANDALAY to CHITTAGONG in Paul Berlin's imagined pursuit story in the novel *Going After Cacciato.* As Berlin imagines "the cramped, second class coaches" filled with "kids staring with hollow eyes, babies bawling, dogs and chickens," and women who "crouched before small fires in the aisles" (137), a shameful war memory begins to creep in and superimpose itself on his invented story. The memory involves Lieutenant Sidney Martin ordering the men to frisk a group of villagers, mostly children, women, and old men, in one of the villages along the SONG TRA BONG River.

Dellinger, Dave   Dave Dellinger was a pacifist and radical social activist who was part of the Chicago Seven, arrested for disrupting the 1968 Democratic National Convention. He is mentioned briefly in the novel *The Nuclear Age* when William Cowling writes that, in 1969, "Hoffman and Rubin and Dellinger were raising hell in public places" (210).

Des Moines River   In his watchtower in Vietnam during one long, late November night in 1968, Paul Berlin from the novel *Going After Cacciato* reminisces about camping with his father along the Des Moines River when he was home on leave in May 1968, following basic training and (AIT) (Advanced Infantry Training). Berlin's father tells him that his time in Vietnam will be "all right," that his son will "see some terrible stuff, sure," but that he should also "try to look for the good things. Try to learn" (227). Berlin's imagined story about the pursuit of Cacciato all the way to PARIS is his attempt to follow his father's advice. The story is rich in detail as Berlin constructs a fantasy that allows him to observe both the good and bad of the war.

Detroit Oscar Johnson in the novel *Going After Cacciato* claims to be from Detroit. He says that the cold, rainy weather the men of ALPHA COMPANY experience at the beginning of the book reminds him of Detroit in the month of May: "'Lootin' weather,' he liked to say. 'The dark an' gloom, just right for rape an' lootin'" (2). Despite his claims, however, Oscar cannot name any recent sports figures from Detroit, and his mail goes to BANGOR, MAINE, leading the other members of Third Squad to suspect that Oscar's tough ghetto stance is self-invented. They tease the sergeant by calling him "the nigga from Ba-Haba" (142).

Dewey, Thomas E. Thomas E. Dewey was a two-time Republican candidate for president, in 1944 and 1948, who is quoted in O'Brien's novel *In the Lake of the Woods* as one of the real-life experts in the evidence chapters. Dewey writes about how shocking election losses can be for candidates, after all that they have gone through while campaigning. His comments are relevant to John Wade, who seems to be in a state of shock after his own election loss, which perhaps explains his strange reaction when his wife, Kathy, goes missing.

Diem Diem River In his memoir, *If I Die in a Combat Zone,* O'Brien describes participating in a CA (combat assault) near the villages of My Lai. As the unit moves north, they cross the Diem Diem River, where they take continuous sniper fire. The men are forced to cross over one at a time while the rest of the troops spray out protective fire.

Diem, Ngo Dinh Ngo Dinh Diem, a Catholic trained at a Jesuit seminary in New Jersey, was installed as the first president of South Vietnam by the United States. He served in this capacity from 1955 to 1963, when he was deposed and assassinated in a bloody coup, tacitly supported by the KENNEDY administration, his relationship with the United States having deteriorated as his persecution of Buddhists in the south grew increasingly more ruthless. Diem figures into Tim O'Brien's work because of the important political role he played in the early stages of American involvement in Vietnam. In his memoir O'Brien

recalls arguing with an army chaplain during basic training about whether South Vietnam under the Communist HO CHI MINH would be any worse off than it was under Diem. Several of O'Brien's fictional characters, including William Cowling in *The Nuclear Age* and the young Tim O'Brien in "On the Rainy River," recognize Diem's tyranny and ask similar questions. The narrator of "On the Rainy River" complains as well about the ignorance of small town WORTHINGTON, MINNESOTA. The people who sent him to war, he writes, "didn't know history. They didn't know the first thing about Diem's tyranny, or the nature of Vietnamese nationalism, or the long colonialism of the French" (45).

Dillon, Matt Matt Dillon was the fictional U.S. marshal of Dodge City, Kansas, in the long-running television series *Gunsmoke*. The character is mentioned in the novel *Going After Cacciato* when Jolly Chand, the proprietor of the HOTEL PHOENIX in DELHI, India, waxes nostalgic about American television: "television is one of those unique products of the American genius," she opines, "a means of keeping a complex country intact. Just as America begins to explode every which way . . . along comes the TV to bring it all together. Rich and poor, black and white—they share the same heroes, Matt Dillon and Paladin" (149). Jolly Chand comments here on the western mythology that inspired many young men with heroic visions of war to fight in Vietnam.

dink Dink is a racist term that was used by American soldiers to describe Vietnamese people. Michael Herr, in his well-known journalistic account of the war, *Dispatches,* suggests that the term might have originated from the phrase *rinky-dink* used to describe the enemy, but this derivation is uncertain. O'Brien, in his memoir, *If I Die in a Combat Zone,* describes learning the word *dink* along with many other G.I. slang words when he first arrived in Vietnam. He writes that he quickly learned "that no one in Alpha Company gave a damn about the causes or purposes of their war: It is about 'dinks and slopes,' and the idea is simply to kill them or avoid them" (80).

The Divine Comedy   *The Divine Comedy* is an epic poem written by the Italian poet Dante Alighieri in the early 14th century. It tells of Dante's journey through the three realms of the Christian afterlife: Hell, Purgatory, and Paradise. Tim O'Brien uses lines from *The Divine Comedy* (in their original Italian) as the epigraph to his 1973 memoir, *If I Die in a Combat Zone, Box Me Up and Ship Me Home.* The epigraph reads:

> Lo maggior don che Dio per sua larghezza / fesse creando . . . / . . . fu de la volanta la libertate

Loosely translated, the lines read: "The greatest gift that the bountiful God made, in all creation, was free will." The epigraph suggests that O'Brien, despite being drafted (*see* DRAFT) into the war, and despite undergoing hellish experiences while in Vietnam, does not see himself as an automaton, forced into battle. He depicts himself as a thinking man, who acts on his own free will and makes his own choices about whether to serve in what he believes is an unjust war or whether to flee the draft. O'Brien examines the moral and philosophical repercussions of these choices in the memoir as well as in several of his later stories and novels, including *Going After Cacciato* and "On the Rainy River" from *The Things They Carried.*

Doines, Rennard   Rennard Doines was one of the soldiers in 1st Platoon of CHARLIE COMPANY, which was under the command of LIEUTENANT WILLIAM CALLEY during the MY LAI MASSACRE. At Calley's court-martial, Doines testified that he left 10 or 15 Vietnamese prisoners with Calley that day. When he returned to the location where he had left them, the prisoners were all dead. O'Brien, in one of the evidence chapters in his novel *In the Lake of the Woods,* quotes from Doine's court-martial testimony, in which he describes a group of women and little kids "lying on the ground, bleeding from all over" (144).

domino theory   The domino theory, largely credited as being the foreign policy that motivated U.S. involvement in Vietnam, held that if one country in a region of the world were to fall to communism, the surrounding countries would fall as well, like a chain of dominoes. In the story "On the Rainy River" from *The Things They Carried,* the young Tim O'Brien speculates about the mysterious causes of the Vietnam War, wondering specifically, "What about SEATO and the Cold War? What about dominoes?" (40). He acknowledges that America was divided on these and numerous other issues, thus arguing that the American war in Vietnam was wrong because "Certain blood was being shed for uncertain reasons" (40).

Donut Dollies   The Donut Dollies in Vietnam were a group of 627 young, college-educated women recruited to serve in the American Red Cross Supplemental Recreation Overseas Program. They spent a one-year tour of duty in Vietnam, serving Kool-aid, coffee, and donuts to American G.I.s, listening to soldiers' stories, writing letters for them, and playing games. Their mission was to "add a touch of home" to the soldiers in the war. In the novel *Going After Cacciato,* Paul Berlin marvels at the logistically complex support structures set up for American soldiers when he first arrives at the CHU LAI COMBAT CENTER in Vietnam. Twelve Red Cross Donut Dollies are stationed there, along with a plethora of other military support personnel.

Dostoyevsky, Fyodor   Tim O'Brien quotes from the great 19th-century novelist Fyodor Dostoyevsky in one of the evidence chapters in his novel *In the Lake of the Woods.* In the excerpt included in the novel, Dostoyevsky asserts that all men have secrets that they are afraid to tell even themselves. "Man is bound to lie about himself" (145), the writer concludes.

draft   Military conscription, commonly known as "the draft" was in place in the United States at various times in its history, including during the Civil War, during World War I, and from 1940, before the U.S. entry into WORLD WAR II, up through 1972, when draft calls for the Vietnam War ended. From the years 1964 to 1972, slightly more than 2 million young men were inducted into military service. Deferments were available for medical conditions, for fathers with dependent children, and for full-time college students, although exempt status for students was revoked in the later years of the Vietnam War draft. Draft call-ups were conducted by local draft boards until complaints about fairness prompted the institution of a national draft lottery in 1969. The Vietnam War draft was commonly perceived to pull more heavily on young men from minority groups and lower social classes, largely because wealthier, better educated young men went to college in large numbers and could also afford to pay private doctors to write medical excuses that might exempt them from service or hire lawyers who might counsel them on ways to avoid the draft. Many young men volunteered for duty in the navy, air force, Coast Guard, or National Guard during this period to avoid being inducted into the army. Others practiced outright draft resistance—fleeing the country, usually to Canada or Sweden, or else living underground lives in the United States. Tim O'Brien received his draft notice in the summer of 1968, entered the service in August of that year, and was released from active duty on March 30, 1970. In his memoir, *If I Die in a Combat Zone*, O'Brien writes that he actively considered resisting the draft by fleeing to Canada during his AIT (advanced infantry training) at FORT LEWIS, WASHINGTON, although he finally could not bring himself to do so. O'Brien's fiction often depicts characters who consider resisting the draft or even deserting the army. The young Tim O'Brien in the story "On the Rainy River" considers escaping to Canada, but instead goes to the war, while William Cowling in *The Nuclear Age* flees the draft to live underground in KEY WEST, FLORIDA, and Billy McMann in *July, July* departs for Canada after he is drafted. Paul Berlin in *Going After Cacciato* meditates on whether to desert or stay in the army during a long night spent on an observation tower.

Dumas, Alexandre Alexandre Dumas, a 19th-century French writer and author of *The Three Musketeers*, is cited in one of the evidence chapters in O'Brien's novel *In the Lake of the Woods*. The quote included in the novel is from Dumas's memoir, in which he writes about taking a gun upstairs in his childhood home after his father's death, planning "to kill God, who killed Father"

(197). This memory echoes John Wade's own rage and anger following the death of his father when he was only 14 years old.

Dunn, J. P. J. P. Dunn, Jr. is the author of a book called *Massacres of the Mountains* that describes the massacre of approximately 300 Cheyenne Indians, half of them women and children, that took place at SAND CREEK in 1864. O'Brien quotes a passage from this book in one of the evidence chapters of his novel *In the Lake of the Woods* in an attempt to show that the U.S. military committed atrocities comparable to those at My Lai in the past.

dustoff Dustoff was military slang used during the Vietnam War for a helicopter-assisted medical evacuation. When soldiers in O'Brien's Vietnam War novels are killed or wounded, the commanding officer will radio back to headquarters for a dustoff.

Dylan, Bob O'Brien refers briefly to the well-known American singer/songwriter Bob Dylan in his story "Quantum Jumps," first published in *Ploughshares* magazine in 1983. As he is obsessively digging a bomb shelter in his yard, William, the story's narrator, begins to sing and to think about his past as a 1960s radical: "Many moons ago, when we were out to sanitize the world, I could carry a tune like nobody's business, I could do Baez and Dylan and Seeger, and it wasn't soupy, it was music to march to, it meant something" (38). The references to JOAN BAEZ, Bob Dylan, and PETE SEEGER were removed when O'Brien revised the story for inclusion in his novel *The Nuclear Age*.

dysentery Dysentery is an infection of the intestines that causes stomach cramps and severe diarrhea with blood in the feces. The older lieutenant, Corson, suffers from dysentery in O'Brien's 1978 novel, *Going After Cacciato*. The illness often leaves him too weak to properly command his men, allowing for Sergeant Oscar Johnson to step in and serve as the shadow commander of the unit.

E-8 E-8 is a military paygrade for enlisted men. In the army, an E-8 carries the rank of either master sergeant or first sergeant. In the novel *Going*

After Cacciato, Paul Berlin, upon first arriving at LANDING ZONE GATOR, where he joins his assigned unit, encounters an E-8 who takes him aside and conspiratorially offers him a rear job, a "nice comfy painting job" with "no paddy humpin', no dinks" (41). When Berlin smiles back at the sergeant, the man replies, "Well, then . . . I fear you come to the wrong . . . fuckin . . . place" (41).

Eden Prairie   Eden Prairie is a fictional suburb of the Twin Cities in Minnesota where former DARTON HALL COLLEGE classmates Jan Huebner and Amy Robinson both live within a few blocks of each other in the novel *July, July*. Both women were idealistic political activists in college, who now live as middle-class, divorced suburbanites.

Eiffel Tower   In the novel *Going After Cacciato*, Paul Berlin imagines that he and refugee Sarkin Aung Wan climb the famous Eiffel Tower shortly after their arrival in PARIS, France. He further imagines that, at midnight, a tour guide looks out over the city and says, "Paris is not a place. It is a state of mind" (298). Berlin smiles at this, but O'Brien writes that, "secretly he hoped it was more than that" (298).

Einstein, Albert   The work of the famed 20th-century physicist Albert Einstein is often credited as involving theoretical breakthroughs that led to the later development of the atomic bomb. Thus, Einstein is an important figure to William Cowling, narrator of the novel *The Nuclear Age*, who is obsessed with the possibility of nuclear annihilation. Einstein is mentioned briefly in the book when Sarah Strouch accuses William of selling out his antiwar ideals. She sarcastically refers to Einstein as the "sweetest old geezer who ever lived" (273). When William tries to defend the famous scientist by saying that at least Einstein warned people of the danger of the bomb, Sarah replies, "That's how sweet he was! Invents the end of the world, then sounds the alarm. Isn't that how relativity works? (273).

Eisenhower Avenue   In the novel *Going After Cacciato*, Paul Berlin imagines that the men of Third Squad travel down a broad street called Eisenhower Avenue as they escape the SAVAK in TEHRAN, speeding through the outskirts of the city in a getaway car supplied by Cacciato himself. The men are ambushed by the secret police as Eisenhower Avenue empties into a huge traffic circle—a dozen tanks and armored personnel carriers had been hiding in the center of the traffic circle's rotary. The description of this ambush is quite similar to the description in the chapter "Landing Zone Bravo" of a CA (combat assault) helicopter landing in a hot zone just before Jim Pederson's death. Berlin's war memories are seeping into his imagined story, no matter how hard he tries to repress them.

Eisenhower, Dwight D.   Dwight D. Eisenhower, both a WORLD WAR II general and the 34th president of the United States, plays a role in O'Brien's novel *Going After Cacciato*. Not long after the men of Third Squad arrive in PARIS, Paul Berlin imagines that they receive the news of Eisenhower's death, which depresses the lieutenant, Corson, a great admirer of the president. Berlin imagines seeing two pictures of Eisenhower in the French newspaper—one of him as a cadet at West Point, the other showing him "riding into Paris, the famous grin, his jeep swamped by happy Frenchmen" (301). Eisenhower is a figure who suggests the popularity and moral imperative associated with World War II as opposed to the Vietnam War. Paul Berlin has trouble feeling much sorrow about Eisenhower's death but supposes his father "would feel the right things" (302). Interestingly, Eisenhower died on March 28, 1969, which coincides with the time that Berlin imagines the men of Third Squad making it to Paris. Yet, the question remains: If Berlin's whole journey to Paris is an adventure he dreams up in late November 1968 while serving watch on the observation tower above the SOUTH CHINA SEA, how could he have known about Eisenhower's death the following spring? This is a question that has disturbed some critics of the novel.

Ellis, Richard   Richard Ellis is the author of an essay called "Young Children: Disenfranchised Grievers," which is quoted in one of the evidence chapters in O'Brien's novel *In the Lake of* the Woods. In the quote Ellis argues that young children often repress anger over the death of a parent because they believe they have been deliberately abandoned. He adds that children whose grief remains unresolved will experience negative consequences in adulthood. This quote can be understood as possibly explaining some of John Wade's psychological damage in O'Brien's novel. He has never fully resolved the grief he felt as a 14-year-old when his father hanged himself in the family garage.

Emerson College   O'Brien taught briefly as a writer-in-residence at Emerson College in Boston in the late 1970s. He was teaching at Emerson when he was named the winner of the 1979 National Book Award for his novel *Going After Cacciato*.

48th Vietcong Battalion   The 48th Vietcong Battalion was an enemy unit with a fearsome and elusive reputation among American soldiers in Vietnam. It was the unit that CHARLIE COMPANY had been sent to root out in spring of 1968, when the MY LAI MASSACRE occurred. O'Brien's own unit in Vietnam was sent to perform a series of combat assaults (*see* CA) against the storied battalion in late April and May 1969, which he describes in his memoir, *If I Die in a Combat Zone*. ALPHA COMPANY receives its orders from Colonel Daud, who draws the soldiers around him and tells them:

> The Forty-eighth Battalion is a helluva fighting unit. They're tough. Some of you have tangled with them before. They're smart. That's what makes them tough. They'll hit you when you're sleeping. You look down to tie your boot laces, and they'll hit you. You fall asleep on guard— they'll massacre you. You walk along the trails, where they plant the mines because Americans are lazy and don't like to walk in the rice paddies, and they'll blow you all back to the world. Dead. (106–107)

Alpha Company does indeed suffer heavy losses during their engagements with the 48th Battalion. The unit makes several appearances as well in

O'Brien's fiction. In *Going After Cacciato*, Li Van Hgoc, the officer imprisoned in the underground tunnel system, is a member of the 48th Vietcong Battalion, and John Wade, from *In the Lake of the Woods*, pursues the unit around the villages of My Lai with his fellow soldiers.

Fall, Bernard   Bernard Fall was a mid-20th century academic as well as a Vietnam War correspondent and historian. A European-born Jew, he fought in the French Resistance during WORLD WAR II before moving to the United States for graduate studies. Tim O'Brien mentions reading Fall's work in his memoir, *If I Die in a Combat Zone*. When he tells an army chaplain that he read arguments against the war put forth by Bernard Fall, the chaplain blows up at him, spluttering: "I've read Bernard Fall. He's a *professor*. A lousy *teacher*" (59). The chaplain then lectures the young soldier about the dangers of communism.

Fermi, Enrico   Enrico Fermi was a Nobel Prize–winning Italian-born physicist who worked on the later stages of the Manhattan Project to develop an atomic bomb. He is mentioned briefly in the novel *The Nuclear Age* when Sarah Strouch accuses William Cowling of betraying his antiwar ideals after discovering uranium in the remote mountains of Montana. When William replies that he is "sweet," Sarah answers that OPPENHEIMER was sweet, that EINSTEIN was sweet, and that "Fermi was a pussycat" (273).

Fiji   Fiji is a country made up of an archipelago of islands located in the South Pacific that plays an important role in the novel *Tomcat in Love*. Professor Thomas H. Chippering, the novel's narrator, often addresses an unnamed "you" in the book, an imagined female reader whose husband has left her to live in Fiji with another woman. This imaginary reader is devastated by her husband's abandonment, eventually becoming so distraught that she travels to the South Pacific herself, desperate to regain her husband's affection. Chippering often addresses this imaginary reader when he describes his most offensive, outrageous behavior, cautioning her to remember her own situation, her own obsessions, and thus not to judge him too severely.

"Fission"   "Fission" is a short poem written by William Cowling's wife, Bobbi, in the novel *The Nuclear Age.* The poem reads as follows:

> Protons, neutrons.
> Break the bonds.
> Break the heart.
> Fuse is lit.
> Time to split.

William correctly interprets this poem as Bobbi's announcement that she will be leaving him and the marriage shortly.

FNG   FNG was common military slang used during the Vietnam War. The acronym stands for "Fucking New Guy," and was often used by more experienced soldiers to denigrate new arrivals, or those just out of training. In his memoir, *If I Die in a Combat Zone,* Tim O'Brien describes being pulled out of sleep on his third night at LANDING ZONE GATOR by the sounds of an attack on the base camp. Two American soldiers and eight VIET CONG fighters are killed that night. The next day, a soldier named Wolf tells O'Brien that the night-time skirmish was only a minor event:

> Wolf said, "Look, FNG, I don't want to scare you—nobody's trying to scare you—but that stuff last night wasn't *shit!* Last night was a lark. Wait'll you see some really *bad* shit. That was a picnic last night. I almost slept through it." I wondered what an FNG was. No one told me until I asked. (77)

FO   FO is a military acronym that stands for Forward Observer, a military position that involves working with front-line troops, often behind enemy lines, to gather intelligence and adjust levels of gunfire. In the novel *Going After Cacciato,* when Paul Berlin first joins ALPHA COMPANY on June 11, 1968, he encounters three squads that are manned by 12, 10, and eight soldiers. He notes that First Platoon had "no fire-teams, no SOPs (standard operating procedures)

for tactical maneuvers or covering fire. There was no FO. There was no platoon sergeant" (42).

Fonda, Jane   Jane Fonda, an American actress who appeared in popular 1960s films such as BAR-BARELLA and *Cat Ballou,* also made a name for herself as an anti–Vietnam War activist. When she visited Hanoi in 1972 and was photographed sitting on a North Vietnamese anti-aircraft gun, she was nicknamed "Hanoi Jane" and earned the hatred of many American service personnel. Jane Fonda is mentioned often in O'Brien's work. In *The Nuclear Age,* William Cowling reports that, in 1964, "Jane Fonda was a starlet" and that Vietnam, by daylight at least, "was still a fairy tale" (66). By October 1966, he writes that "in Hollywood, Jane Fonda began setting an agenda" (74). By 1968, "Jane Fonda was making choices" (112), while in 1969, "Jane Fonda was on the stump" (210). In the story "On the Rainy River" from *The Things They Carried,* one of the many people that the young Tim O'Brien character sees on the banks of the RAINY RIVER, when he is deciding whether or not to flee the DRAFT is "Jane Fonda dressed up as Barbarella" (58). And in the later story from the same collection, "The Ghost Soldiers," Azar and O'Brien see the film *Barbarella* the same night they torment the young medic Bobby Jorgenson. "Sweet Janie boosts a man's morale," Azar says, then he shows O'Brien with his hand "which part of his morale got boosted" (206). Jane Fonda appears as well in the novel *Tomcat in Love,* as the hooded executioner in Thomas Chippering's nightmare of feminists wreaking revenge on him.

Ford, Gerald   Gerald Ford, 38th president of the United States, had served as Republican Minority Leader in the U.S. House of Representatives during most of the Vietnam War years. William Cowling, in the novel *The Nuclear Age,* mentions Ford briefly when he writes about the fallout from the MORA-TORIUM TO END THE WAR IN VIETNAM: "In the nation's capital Barry Goldwater and Gerald Ford harmonized on the grand old themes" (224).

Fort Derry, Montana   Fort Derry, Montana, located 58 miles from Yellowstone National Park and 80 miles from Helena, the state capital, is the hometown of William Cowling and his family in the novel *The Nuclear Age*. Described as "a typical small town, with the usual gas stations and parks and public schools" (9–10) and a population of just over a thousand, Fort Derry represents millions of other small towns across America in the 1950s. While seemingly idyllic places in which to grow up, these small towns nevertheless experience the fears of the COLD WAR and the specter of nuclear annihilation. "We were not high on the Russian hit list," Cowling writes, "But how could you be sure? Fort Derry, it *sounded* like a target" (11).

Fort Dodge, Iowa   Fort Dodge is an actual small city of 25,000 residents in central Iowa, located along the DES MOINES RIVER. It is also the hometown of Paul Berlin in the novel *Going After Cacciato*. Berlin's father works as a home builder in Fort Dodge, while his mother is an alcoholic housewife who tries to hide the evidence of her drinking from her husband and son.

Fort Lewis, Washington   Fort Lewis, Washington, was the location where Tim O'Brien underwent his army basic training, beginning in mid-August, 1968. He also undertook AIT (advanced infantry training) in the same camp. As he writes in his memoir, it was during advanced training that he seriously contemplated fleeing the military for Canada.

frag   Frag is military slang meaning to murder an officer, usually by fragmentation grenade. While exact numbers are hard to pinpoint, most military historians agree that fragging occurred more frequently in the latter years of the U.S. war in Vietnam than in previous armed conflicts. According to historians, more than 200 suspected fragging cases were investigated in 1969, with more than 300 cases being investigated in both 1970 and 1971. O'Brien acknowledges the reality of fragging in several of his works. In his memoir, *If I Die in a Combat Zone*, he discusses learning soon after his arrival in Vietnam that the term *frag* referred to a hand grenade (80). Later, in his 1978 novel, *Going After Cacciato*, O'Brien focuses the action

around the fragging death of Lieutenant Sidney Martin by the men of ALPHA COMPANY. Several critics argue that guilt over his complicity in this death is what motivates the American soldier Paul Berlin to invent his fanciful story of the pursuit of Cacciato as he tries to repress his painful memories of the war, especially Martin's death, during his long night on his watchtower by the sea.

Franz's Glen   Franz's Glen is the name of a drinking and dancing establishment in the small town of SAWMILL LANDING, Minnesota, in O'Brien's 1975 novel, *Northern Lights*. When Harvey Perry arrives home from Vietnam, his brother, Paul, takes him out to Franz's Glen for a drink. It is there that Harvey meets Addie, a young, part-Indian woman who is dancing with a crowd of kids her own age. When Harvey begins to date Addie, Paul Perry has to control his jealousy since he, too, is attracted to the girl.

Fraser, Arvonne   Arvonne Fraser, herself a political activist who ran for the office of Minnesota lieutenant governor, was the wife of Donald Fraser, a longtime Minneapolis mayor and U.S. congressman. Ms. Fraser is quoted in one of the evidence chapters in O'Brien's novel *In the Lake of the Woods* as asserting that many political wives are unhappy in Washington: "They have no life of their own and wonder, who am I? Am I just somebody's wife? Or is there something more?" (263). Arvonne Fraser's questions here might very well be the same questions Kathy Wade asked herself, since she, too, was dissatisfied with playing the role of the politician's wife.

Fred's Café   In his memoir, *If I Die in a Combat Zone*, O'Brien recalls spending the summer of 1968 drinking coffee at Fred's Café in WORTHINGTON, MINNESOTA. He and his friends and acquaintances would discuss politics and the war, "mapping out arguments on Fred's napkins" (17). Fred's is perhaps the model for the fictional GOBBLER CAFÉ in the story "On the Rainy River." The young Tim O'Brien imagines that, if he were to flee the DRAFT, the conversation at the Gobbler would turn to him, that the townspeople would begin to speculate about "the young O'Brien kid, how the damned sissy had taken off for Canada" (*TTTC* 15).

Freistadt, Austria While stationed in Vietnam, Tim O'Brien dreamt about traveling to Freistadt, Austria. In his memoir, *If I Die in a Combat Zone*, he writes that he considered renting a cottage in Freistadt after the war, a town just across the Czechoslovakian border: "Freistadt would be the ideal place. The mountains were formidable, the air was clean, the town had a dry moat around it, the beer was the best in the world, the girls were not communists, and they had blue eyes and blond hair and big bosoms" (94).

Freud, Sigmund The great Austrian psychoanalyst Sigmund Freud is quoted in one of the evidence chapters in O'Brien's novel *In the Lake of the Woods* as asserting that the art of biography is closely related to fiction: "Whoever undertakes to write a biography binds himself to lying, to concealment, to flummery. . . . Truth is not accessible" (291). This claim is also the position taken up by the novel's investigator/narrator figure who has spent many years tracking down evidence about John and Kathy Wade, only to conclude that the truth of what happened to them is finally not accessible. Their fate must remain shrouded in mystery.

Friar Tuck In legends about Robin Hood, Friar Tuck is said to be a member of the outlaw's band of merry men. Usually depicted as a rotund, balding, jovial figure, fond of eating and drinking, in many of the tales Friar Tuck is also portrayed as a skilled swordsman and capable fighter. The slightly chubby, prematurely balding soldier Cacciato is compared to Friar Tuck several times in the novel *Going After Cacciato*. When the soldier first disappears, a member of his platoon, Stink Harris, says that Cacciato is "Dumber than marbles . . . Dumber than Friar Tuck" (10). This comment might be what motivates Paul Berlin, in his made-up story about the pursuit of Cacciato, to imagine at one point that the deserting soldier is dressed as a monk. Berlin imagines spotting Cacciato on the streets of MANDALAY wearing a long brown robe

that "gave him the look of Friar Tuck, the same round-faced piety" (120).

Fromm, Erich Erich Fromm (1900–80) was a German-born psychologist and political philosopher who theorized about human character and its effect on social and political structures. Fromm decried authoritarian moral systems, believing that individuals could use reason and the creative capacity of love to alter society. During the COLD WAR period, he advocated democratic socialism, critiquing both Western-style capitalism and Soviet communism. In his memoir, *If I Die in a Combat Zone*, O'Brien lists Erich Fromm as one of the authors he read as a teenager in WORTHINGTON, MINNESOTA.

Frost, Robert A beloved American poet who lived from 1874 to 1963 and who read his poem "The Gift Outright" at JOHN F. KENNEDY's inauguration, Robert Frost was a New Englander who wrote about nature and the rural life, but also about the frightening, spiritually-bereft modern world. Frost figures into O'Brien's work several times. In his 1973 memoir, O'Brien remembers his friend from basic training, ERIK HANSEN, saying that "Frost, by just about any standard, is the finest of a good bunch of American poets" (37). In the short story "Quantum Jumps," originally published in *Ploughshares* magazine in 1983, O'Brien refers to Frost again when he has his narrator, William Cowling, disparage poets, whom he feels traffic in metaphor when their attention should be turned to the real world. Cowling quotes lines from "Fire and Ice," a short, ironic Frost poem in which the narrator muses about how the world will end.

The Fugitive *The Fugitive* was a television series that ran from 1963 to 1967 and depicted the story of Dr. Richard Kimble, falsely accused of his wife's murder, convicted, and sentenced to death. Kimble escapes and travels the country searching for a one-armed man who he believes is his wife's true killer. The television series is mentioned in the novel *Going After Cacciato* when the Indian hotel owner Jolly Chand, who had studied at Johns Hopkins University and loves all things American, is delighted to hear from the soldiers of Third Squad about the final episode of *The Fugitive* in which Kimble had finally tracked down the one-armed man. In addition, in *The Nuclear Age* William Cowling and his parents discuss the television show as the couple drives their son to the bus depot to help him evade the DRAFT. They agree that *The Fugitive* is "the greatest TV program in history" (144). William's mother jokingly says that she will look for her son in the next episode.

Fulda, Germany   Fulda is the German city in the novel *Going After Cacciato* where the Volkswagen van that the men of Third Squad have taken from a disaffected American college girl breaks down. Paul Berlin imagines that the men abandon the van in Fulda, then march two miles to the railroad depot, where they board the next train west. This is the train that will take the American soldiers the rest of the way to PARIS.

Gare du Nord   The Gare du Nord is a well-known PARIS train station and the busiest train station in all of Europe. In the novel *Going After Cacciato*, Paul Berlin imagines the men of Third Squad arriving in Paris at the Gare du Nord aboard the TRAIN ROUGE from LUXEMBOURG. As passengers begin to crowd the aisles of the newly arrived train, the American soldiers shake hands, clap shoulders, and hug one another, unable to believe that they have really made it all the way to Paris.

Gaulle, Charles de   Charles de Gaulle led the Free French forces during WORLD WAR II and later became the president of France. In the novel *Going After Cacciato*, Paul Berlin imagines that he and Sarkin Aung Wan have a drink in a small stand-up bar after agreeing to rent an apartment in INVALIDES, an area of France dedicated to military monuments and museums. The bar is hung with pictures of de Gaulle, "hatless, sitting behind a microphone" (301), which alternate with photographs of students clashing with riot police. These images in Berlin's invented story suggest the conflict he is experiencing internally, as he is torn between his military duty and his desire to rebel against his government by fleeing from the service.

Geneva Accords   The Geneva Accords were a set of treaties signed by France and Vietnam and several other countries in 1954 that brought an official end to the French war in Indochina. The accords granted independence to Vietnam, but also divided the country into northern and southern zones to facilitate an end to military hostilities. This division was supposed to be temporary, and the country to be reunified in 1956 following free, democratic elections. But the elections were never held. O'Brien refers to the Geneva Accords in several of his works. For instance, in *The Nuclear Age* William Cowling wonders about the Vietnam War: "Was it a correct war. Was it a civil war? Was Ho Chi Minh a nationalist or a Communist, or both, and to what degree, and what about the Geneva Accords . . .?" (84). The young Tim O'Brien in the story "On the Rainy River" from *The Things They Carried* asks nearly identical questions as he contemplates fleeing the DRAFT: "Was Ho Chi Minh a Communist stooge, or a nationalist savior, or both, or neither? What about the Geneva Accords?" (40).

Geneva Conventions on the Laws of War   The Geneva Conventions on the Laws of War, negotiated in 1949 following the end of WORLD WAR II, lay out rules for protecting civilians in war zones, for the treatment of prisoners of war, and for the care of the sick and wounded. O'Brien in one of the evidence chapters in his novel *In the Lake of the Woods* quotes a passage from the Geneva Conventions that underscores the unjust treatment of Vietnamese civilians during the MY LAI MASSACRE: "Persons taking no active part in the hostilities . . . shall in all circumstances be treated humanely" (139).

George, Alexander and Juliette   Alexander and Juliette George are the authors of a biography about the former U.S. president WOODROW WILSON. A quote from their book, in which they discuss the teasing that the future president endured from his father when he was a boy, appears in one of the evidence chapters in O'Brien's novel *In the Lake of the Woods*. John Wade in O'Brien's novel also experienced frequent, mean-spirited teasing from his father when he was young.

Giessen, Germany   Giessen is one of the towns in the German heartland that the men of Third Squad ride through on the train that takes them on the last leg of their journey to PARIS in the novel *Going After Cacciato*. As the train passes through the various German towns, Paul Berlin rushes for a window to see the streetlights and church steeples and "neon-lighted ads for Coke and Bromo-Seltzer" (277). To Berlin, these are the signs of civilization.

Gobbler Café   In the story "On the Rainy River" from *The Things They Carried*, the Tim O'Brien character talks about the moral split he experienced after receiving his DRAFT notice: Should he flee to Canada or allow himself to be sent to Vietnam? He writes that he feared losing the respect of his parents and community if he fled the draft: "My hometown was a conservative little spot on the prairie," he writes, "a place where tradition counted, and it was easy to imagine people sitting around a table down at the old Gobbler Café on Main Street, coffee cups poised, the conversation slowly zeroing in on the young O'Brien kid, how the damned sissy had taken off for Canada" (45).

Goldwater, Barry   Barry Goldwater was a long-time U.S. senator from Arizona who ran unsuccessfully for president of the United States in 1964. He appears briefly in the novel *The Nuclear Age* when William Cowling writes about the large antiwar demonstration known as the MORATORIUM TO END THE WAR IN VIETNAM. Cowling reports that RONALD REAGAN decried the protests in Sacramento while "in the nation's capital Barry Goldwater and Gerald Ford harmonized on the grand old themes" (224).

Gonzales, Leonard   Leonard Gonzales was one of the soldiers in CHARLIE COMPANY who was present during the MY LAI MASSACRE. He is quoted in one of the evidence chapters in O'Brien's novel *In the Lake of the Woods* as having witnessed a soldier named Roshevitz fire into a crowd of nude village women, killing them all with a canister from his M-79.

Goodell, Charles   Charles Goodell served as a U.S. senator from New York appointed in 1968 to fill the vacancy left by ROBERT KENNEDY's assas-

sination. He advocated that the United States withdraw completely from Vietnam. Goodell is mentioned briefly in the novel *The Nuclear Age* when William Cowling tells readers that in 1969, "Senator Charles Goodell was legislating in behalf of final withdrawal" (223).

gook   Gook is derogatory military slang for Southeast Asians. While it most likely originated among U.S. Marines serving in the Philippine-American War between 1899 and 1902, the term came into widespread use during the Vietnam War, where it was often used to refer to Vietnamese people, whether enemies or not. O'Brien's characters in his Vietnam War novels use the term frequently, such as when Doc Peret in *Going After Cacciato* suggests that the VIET CONG are using a "gook version" (103) of psychological operations to torment the American soldiers.

Grand Marais, Minnesota   Grand Marais, Minnesota, is the town in the novel *Northern Lights* where the Perry brothers, along with Paul's wife, Grace, and Harvey's girlfriend, Addie, go to participate in the winter ski races. It is at Grand Marais that Addie leaves Harvey for a younger, more accomplished skier, much as Brett Ashley in ERNEST HEMINGWAY's THE SUN ALSO RISES starts an affair with a young bullfighter. Harvey and Paul Perry make plans to ski home to SAWMILL LANDING from Grand Marais but get lost in a blizzard and wander in the wilderness without food or shelter for many days.

Grant Park   Grant Park is a large public park in Chicago where the worst of the police brutality took place against anti–Vietnam War protesters during the 1968 Democratic National Convention. In the novel *The Nuclear Age*, the narrator William Cowling spends the summer of 1968 back home in FORT DERRY, MONTANA, watching dramatic political events unfold. He writes, "There was violence in Grant Park" (119), and he speaks as well about the assassination of ROBERT KENNEDY.

Gray, J. Glenn   J. Glenn Gray is the author of a book called *The Warriors: Reflections on Men in*

Battle, originally published in 1959. Gray is one of the experts quoted in the evidence chapters in O'Brien's novel *In the Lake of the Woods.* The three quotes attributed to Gray in these chapters posit a moral line over which soldiers must not step in war. Gray argues that soldiers must ultimately obey their "own notions of right and good" (142) rather than following immoral orders from a superior.

Graz, Austria   In the novel *Going After Cacciato,* the men of Third Squad drive through Graz, the second-largest city in Austria, in a Volkswagen van stolen from an American college drop-out as they make their way to PARIS in Paul Berlin's invented pursuit story of an AWOL soldier.

Green Berets   The Green Berets, officially known as the U.S. Army Special Forces, were a group established in 1952 whose main mission was unconventional warfare: Small units were trained in the use of guerrilla tactics in order to harass and disrupt enemy operations. President KENNEDY, keen on counterinsurgency measures, encouraged the Special Forces to wear the green berets to which their training entitled them. Members of the Special Forces began serving as advisers in Vietnam as early as the 1950s. Their numbers greatly increased when Kennedy sent 400 Green Berets to help train the South Vietnamese in methods of counterinsurgency. Tim O'Brien in several of his works writes about Green Beret soldiers, often noting their reputation for violence, for being able to endure harsh conditions, and for disappearing on mysterious, covert missions. Mad Mark, the platoon leader he writes about in his memoir, *If I Die in a Combat Zone,* is said to be a Green Beret. Mary Anne Bell, from the story "Sweetheart of the Song Tra Bong," goes out on night ambush with a group of six Green Beret soldiers who live on the perimeter of a small medical detachment outside of CHU LAI. In addition, the six soldiers that Thomas H. Chippering is ordered to accompany to a listening post in the remote jungle in *Tomcat in Love* are members of the Special Forces as well. Chippering snidely writes, "I was later to learn that these six filthy gentlemen referred to themselves as 'Greenies,' an abbreviation of 'Green Berets,' itself

an abbreviation for a rare condition of mental and spiritual gangrene" (58).

Gromyko, Andrei   Andrei Gromyko was a Soviet diplomat who served as the country's minister for foreign affairs during the Vietnam War years. In the novel *The Nuclear Age,* William Cowling tells readers that he liked to imagine how the world should be. In his mind at night, he often "carried on internal dialogues with important world personages," setting up, for instance, meetings between "LBJ and Andrei Gromyko and Ho Chi Minh" in which he, Cowling, "would preside as an instrument of moderation and compromise, a peacemaker" (69).

grunts   The term *grunts* is military slang for ordinary infantrymen. In *The Things They Carried,* O'Brien writes that American foot soldiers assigned to combat duty "were called legs or grunts" (3).

Grzesik, Ronald   Ronald Grzesik was a team leader for the First Platoon of CHARLIE COMPANY during the MY LAI MASSACRE. In testimony at WILLIAM CALLEY's court-martial, Grzesik claimed he followed orders to round up Vietnamese civilians in the village, but that he refused to fire on them. Grzesik is quoted twice in the evidence chapters of O'Brien's novel *In the Lake of the Woods.* In the first quote, from an account of Calley's court-martial, Grzesik says, "Look, I don't remember. It was three years ago" (137). In the second quote, also from the court-martial, Grzesik describes seeing 35 to 50 dead bodies in a ditch in the village.

Guide Story Book   Paul Berlin in *Going After Cacciato* remembers that he and his father went camping in the Wisconsin woods as members of the INDIAN GUIDES organization when he was a child. He recalls wearing headbands and feathers and a father who adopted the name Big Fox telling stories out of the *Guide Story Book* around the campfire at night.

Guide Survival Guide   In the novel *Going After Cacciato,* Paul Berlin remembers a book called the *Guide Survival Guide* used by the INDIAN GUIDES organization that he and his father belonged to when he was a child. One of the group's activities on a camping trip in the Wisconsin woods involved a father going into the forest and leaving tracks for his son to follow, aided by the *Guide Survival Guide*. But Berlin, as Little Bear, was no more adept at following his father's tracks than he will be later as a soldier in the Vietnam War. He gets lost in the woods and winds up crying under a giant spruce tree until one of his friends, Little Elk, finds him.

Gulf of Tonkin   The Gulf of Tonkin, located on the western coast of Vietnam, is part of the SOUTH CHINA SEA. In 1964 an incident in which American destroyers sank a North Vietnamese torpedo boat in the gulf based on questionable instrument readings and surveillance information led to the Gulf of Tonkin Resolution, granting President LYNDON JOHNSON the power to defend against so-called communist aggression and leading to the escalation of the conflict in Vietnam. In the novel *The Nuclear Age*, William Cowling, who gauges the years of his life by major political events taking place, writes, "Autumn 1964, and there was a war on, and people were dying. There were jets over the Gulf of Tonkin" (66). In the story "On the Rainy River" from *The Things They Carried*, O'Brien speculates about the mysterious facts underlying the beginnings of the war: "Who started it, and when, and why? What really happened to the USS *Maddox* on that dark night in the Gulf of Tonkin?" (40).

Guthke, Karl S.   Karl S. Guthke is the author of a book called *B. Traven: The Life Behind the Legends*, about a mysterious 20th-century American novelist known only by a pseudonym. A quote from Guthke, which speculates about TRAVEN's desire for anonymity, is included in one of the evidence chapters in O'Brien's novel *In the Lake of the Woods*.

Haeberle, Ronald   Ronald Haeberle was a U.S. Army photographer present during the MY LAI MASSACRE who took the famous and disturbing photographs first published in the *Cleveland Plain Dealer* in November 1969. Haeberle's statement at LIEUTENANT WILLIAM CALLEY's court-martial that he could not "specifically recall" (137) whether he

had reported what he witnessed that day is quoted in one of the evidence chapters of O'Brien's novel *In the Lake of the Woods*. In a later chapter, Haeberle's 12 photographs of victims at THUAN YEN, are entered into the record of evidence.

Hale, Nathan   Nathan Hale was an American spy during the Revolutionary War. Before he was hanged by the British, Hale famously said, "I only regret that I have but one life to give for my country." In O'Brien's short story "Quantum Jumps," William, the story's narrator, thinks back about his life as a campus radical in the 1960s: "We were not the lunatic fringe," he tells himself. "We were the true-blue center. Middle class, middle-of-the-road, middle-Americans—the last of the diehard Conservatives, as patriotic as Nathan Hale . . ." (39). O'Brien removed this reference to Hale when he revised the story for inclusion in his novel *The Nuclear Age*.

Hall, Charles   Charles Hall was an assistant gunner in CHARLIE COMPANY who was present during the MY LAI MASSACRE. At the court-martial of LIEUTENANT WILLIAM CALLEY, Hall testified that he had seen numerous dead bodies in the village of My Lai on March 16, 1968. He is quoted in one of the evidence chapters in O'Brien's novel *In the Lake of the Woods* as saying the bodies "were in piles and scattered. They were very old people, very young people, and mothers. Blood was coming from everywhere. Everything was all blood" (140).

Hansen, Erik   Erik Hansen is a lifelong friend of Tim O'Brien's, whom he first met during basic training at FORT LEWIS, WASHINGTON. Hansen appears as an important character in O'Brien's memoir, *If I Die in a Combat Zone, Box Me Up and Ship Me Home*, although he is identified only by his first name in the book. O'Brien also dedicated his 1978 novel *Going After Cacciato* to Hansen.

The Hardy Boys   The Hardy Boys was a popular series of books about teenage detectives Frank and Joe Hardy. First published in 1927, the series lasted until 2005, undergoing many changes and incarnations during its nearly 80-year existence. O'Brien mentions being an avid reader of Hardy boys mysteries in his 1973 memoir, *If I Die in a Combat Zone.*

Harlem Globetrotters   In the novel *Going After Cacciato,* Eddie Lazzutti loves the pickup basketball games that the men of Third Squad play throughout the month of July. He even compares the hastily composed teams to the Harlem Globetrotters, the famous African American exhibition basketball team: "Harlem Globetrotters, Eddie kept saying. He got a bang out of it—Harlem Globetrotters bring their traveling show to Bic Kinh Mi, Suc Ran, My Khe 3, Pinkville. Goodwill ambassadors to the world, Eddie said" (102).

Harriman, Averell   Averell Harriman was a Democratic politician and U.S. diplomat who served as the chief negotiator for the United States during the Paris peace talks on ending the Vietnam War. Harriman is mentioned briefly in the novel *The Nuclear Age.* In the summer of 1968, when William Cowling is home in Fort Derry, Montana, after graduating from college, he watches news about the peace talks on television. He sees the "flags and limousines at the Hotel Majestic (*see* Majestic Hotel)" (121) as well as Averell Harriman shaking hands with Vietnamese ambassador Xuan Thuy. Cowling wishes for a breakthrough in the talks, to spare himself from having to make the decision whether to go to war or join Sarah Strouch's radical activist group.

Harvard University   O'Brien attended graduate school in government at Harvard University from 1970, shortly after his return from the Vietnam War, until he withdrew from the program in early 1976, having completed all requirements toward the Ph.D. except for writing his dissertation. Already the author of an acclaimed war memoir, a first novel, and several short stories by this time, O'Brien left Harvard to devote himself full time to his writing career.

Hastings   The Battle of Hastings took place in 1066 during the Norman conquest of England. William, duke of Normandy, won a decisive victory and was crowned king of England on Christmas

Day. In the novel *Going After Cacciato,* Lieutenant Sidney Martin watches his men march up into the mountains and muses about the nature of war. He understands that the Vietnam War lacks a common purpose, and he wishes that he could have fought his battles instead at Hastings or Austerlitz. Later in the novel, Doc Peret, talking to Captain Fahyi Rhallon in Tehran about whether or not all wars are alike, asserts that "troops at Hastings or the Bulge had the same problem" (197) that troops in Vietnam did—difficulty in figuring out what was happing and what they were fighting for.

Havana, Cuba   Havana, the capital of Cuba, is the city where William Cowling and his group of college activist friends first arrive after leaving their headquarters in Key West, Florida, to undergo paramilitary training in the novel *The Nuclear Age.* After eating lunch in Havana, they will be taken on a four-hour bus ride along a coastal highway to a compound just outside the city of Sagua la Grande.

Hawthorne, Nathaniel   The 19th-century American novelist and short story writer Nathaniel Hawthorne, best known for his novel *The Scarlet Letter,* is quoted in one of the evidence chapters in O'Brien's novel *In the Lake of the Woods.* In the quote, which comes from the story "Wakefield," about a man who leaves his wife and home to live unnoticed in a nearby street for many years, Hawthorne writes that his protagonist "had happened to dissever himself from the world—to vanish—to give up his place and privilege with living men, without being admitted among the dead" (294). The same status could be ascribed to John Wade, the protagonist of O'Brien's novel. Readers are never quite sure what becomes of him; he has vanished, but we cannot be completely certain whether he is dead or alive.

HE   HE is a military acronym that stands for High Explosive. In the novel *Going After Cacciato,* Lieutenant Sidney Martin calls in an air strike on the village of Hoi An after the death of Jim Pederson. Martin requests that several rounds of white phosphorus be dropped on the village, followed by "a dozen HE" (78).

Hector   In Greek mythology Hector, the son of King Priam of Troy, is killed by the Greek warrior ACHILLES during the Trojan War. O'Brien in his memoir, *If I Die in a Combat Zone*, compares the loss of Captain Jorgensen, the commander of ALPHA COMPANY when he first arrives in Vietnam, to the Trojans losing Hector. Both men gave the soldiers under them "some amount of reason to fight" in wars that were "silly and stupid" (145). Yet, O'Brien also acknowledges that while it is easy for a soldier to make such comparisons about others, it is more difficult to think of one's self in such terms, as "the eternal Hector, dying gallantly" (146). In fact, he adds, "It is impossible. That's the problem. Knowing yourself, you can't make it real for yourself. It's sad when you learn you're not much of a hero" (146). Recent critics have begun to pay increasing attention to the classical underpinnings of O'Brien's work, including his use of characters from Greek mythology such as Hector. Christopher McDonough, for instance, compares O'Brien's narrator in *The Things They Carried* to the tragedy of Hector in *The Iliad* as both men face dilemmas of courage and cowardice "posed by the warrior mentality" (23).

Hemingway, Ernest   An American modernist writer and member of the Lost Generation of expatriates living in PARIS following World War I, Ernest Hemingway is best known for his novels *THE SUN ALSO RISES*, *A Farewell to Arms*, *For Whom the Bell Tolls*, and *The Old Man and the Sea*. Having served in the Italian ambulance corps during the war where he suffered severe injuries in an explosion, Hemingway became nearly as famous for his macho heroics and out-sized personality as for his fiction. But Hemingway's influence on later 20th-century literature is immense. His short, crisp sentences and simple, stripped-down vocabulary, along with his descriptions of nature, seem to have particularly influenced Tim O'Brien, whose own writing style bears traces of Hemingway's throughout. In his memoir, *If I Die in a Combat Zone*, O'Brien refers to Hemingway several times, speculating at one point that "the men in war novels and stories and reportage seem to come off the typewriter as men resigned to bullets and brawn.

Hemingway's soldiers especially. They are cynics" (93). Later in the book, when O'Brien ponders the issue of courage, he points out that some people say Hemingway "was obsessed by the need to show bravery in battle" (140). Yet, O'Brien adds, after reading Hemingway's war stories and war journalism, he has come to the conclusion "that he was simply *concerned* about bravery, hence about cowardice, and that seems a virtue, a sublime and profound concern that few men have" (140). O'Brien speaks as well about his early love for the character FREDERIC HENRY from *A Farewell to Arms*:

> Before the war, my favorite heroes had been make-believe men. . . . Especially Frederic Henry. Henry was able to leave war, being good and brave enough at it, for real love, and although he missed the men of war, he did not miss the fear and killing. And Henry, like all my heroes, was not obsessed by courage; he knew it was only one part of virtue, that love and justice were other parts. (142)

Hemingway's influence on O'Brien is perhaps best seen, however, in *Northern Lights*, O'Brien's first novel, which very self-consciously models itself after portions of Hemingway's *The Sun Also Rises*. The two novels share several themes and situations, including a wounded war veteran who attempts to heal himself through nature; an attractive, free-spirited woman who blithely abandons a previous lover to make a conquest of a handsome young athlete; and an emphasis on the mythology surrounding bulls and fertility.

Hennepin Avenue   Hennepin Avenue is a real street in Minneapolis, one of the main downtown thoroughfares. In the novel *July, July*, as well as the story "Little People," Jan Huebner, a 1969 graduate of DARTON HALL COLLEGE, performs guerrilla street theater on Hennepin Avenue the summer after she graduates. It is on Hennepin that she meets the large-headed, diminutive man named Andrew Henry Wilton, who persuades her to pose nude for erotic photos.

Henning, Doug   Doug Henning was a Canadian-born magician and escape artist who gained worldwide fame in the 1970s and '80s. Henning's book on the great illusionist HARRY HOUDINI is quoted in one of the evidence chapters in O'Brien's novel *In the Lake of the Woods*. In the excerpt Henning explains Houdini's fascination with a trick called "Palengenisia," in which a man is dismembered, then restored. This trick, Henning argues, illustrates the motif of death and resurrection that recurred in all of Houdini's performances.

Henry, Frederic   One of the "make-believe men" (*If I Die* 142) that O'Brien lists as being among his favorite heroes before the war, Frederic Henry is the main character in ERNEST HEMINGWAY's novel *A Farewell to Arms*. An ambulance driver serving in the Italian Army during World War I, Frederic Henry eventually flees the war to live in Switzerland with his pregnant girlfriend, a nurse named Catherine Barkley. O'Brien writes that he admires Henry because he was "good and brave enough" to leave the war "for real love," as well as for his understanding that courage is only one part of virtue, "that love and justice were other parts" (*If I Die* 142).

Herborn, Germany   Herborn is one of the small towns in the German heartland that the men of Third Squad speed through on the train that takes them on the last stage of their journey to PARIS in the novel *Going After Cacciato*. These German towns possess all the indicators of civilization that Berlin has so missed during his time in Vietnam: lighted streets, church steeples, and neon ads.

Herman, Judith   Judith Herman is a well-known psychiatrist and researcher who has written about the effects of trauma and incest. Herman is one of the experts quoted several times in the evidence chapters of *In the Lake of the Woods*. Her book *Trauma and Recovery* acknowledges the "capacity for evil in human nature" (26).

Hersbruck, Germany   In the summer of 1967, when Tim O'Brien was studying in PRAGUE, CZECHOSLOVAKIA, as part of the Student Project for Amity among Nations (SPAN) program, he traveled to Hersbruck, Germany, where he had a

motorcycle accident that put him in the hospital for a week.

Hiroshima   Hiroshima, Japan, the site where the United States dropped the first nuclear weapon in history, on August 6, 1945, looms large in the imagination of William Cowling in the novel *The Nuclear Age*. In the book's opening chapter, Cowling implores readers to "ask the wall shadows at Hiroshima" (7) whether or not nuclear apocalypse is a fantasy as he insists that he is not crazy, that the threat of nuclear destruction is very real.

Ho Chi Minh   Ho Chi Minh was the president of the Democratic Republic of Vietnam, the official name for North Vietnam, from 1945 until his death in 1969. A Vietnamese nationalist and Communist revolutionary, Ho was involved in defeating the French prior to the American war in Vietnam. He was a beloved figure in the North, referred to as "Uncle Ho," but reviled as a ruthless dictator by anticommunists in the United States and in South Vietnam. Because of his importance during the Vietnam War years, Ho Chi Minh is an important figure in much of O'Brien's work. He is first mentioned in the 1973 memoir, *If I Die in a Combat Zone*, when O'Brien argues about the morality of the war with an army chaplain. "You think Ho Chi Minh is gonna bring *heaven* to South Vietnam?" (59) the angry chaplain asks, and the young soldier replies that there is not much evidence to suggest the South would be worse off under Ho than under DIEM or KHANH, American-supported leaders. In the chapter, "The Things They Didn't Know" from *Going After Cacciato*, Paul Berlin wonders about a young Vietnamese girl and her desires for the future. He imagines LYNDON JOHNSON and Ho Chi Minh rubbing magic lanterns at the end of the war, and contemplates what the girl would ask for: "Justice? What sort? Reparations? What kind?" (265). Ho is mentioned in the novel as well during Paul Berlin's interview for promotion to SPEC 4 when he is asked what effect the death of Ho Chi Minh would have on the population of North Vietnam. Berlin smiles because he knows the expected answer. He replies, "Reduce it by one, sir" (269).

Ho Chi Minh *(Courtesy of the Library of Congress)*

William Cowling in *The Nuclear Age,* an anti-war radical during the Vietnam years, thinks often of Ho Chi Minh. In his college dorm room, he imagines arranging informal summit conferences between LBJ and Ho. Cowling also recognizes the complications of the war and wonders whether Ho Chi Minh is a nationalist or a Communist or both, whether he is a tyrant or a benevolent figure—questions that the young Tim O'Brien in the story "On the Rainy River" ponders as well.

Hoffman, Abbie   Abbie Hoffman was a 1960s radical who cofounded, with JERRY RUBIN, the Youth International Party, or Yippies. He was one of the Chicago Eight, arrested in 1968 for disrupting the Democratic National Convention. In the novel *The Nuclear Age,* Hoffman is an important figure to William Cowling. Early in the novel, Cowling informs readers that he, too, was a radical activist

and "could've been another . . . Hoffman" had he wanted to (8). As Cowling recounts the years of the '60s, he mentions Hoffman again several times, first to report that, in 1964, "Abbie Hoffman was a nobody" (66), but that, by 1967, he "was now a somebody" (112). By 1969 Cowling reports, Hoffman and other radicals "were raising hell in public places" (210). Abbie Hoffman is also one of the figures that the young Tim O'Brien imagines waving to him from the banks of the RAINY RIVER in *The Things They Carried.*

Hoffman, Julius   Judge Julius Hoffman became famous as the presiding justice in the trial of the Chicago Eight, who were arrested for inciting a riot at the Democratic National Convention in 1968. His scornful attitude and the harsh sentences he handed down to the defendants earned him the hatred of many war protestors. Hoffman appears briefly in the novel *The Nuclear Age,* when William Cowling writes that, in 1969, "Judge Julius Hoffman presided over a discomposed courtroom" (223).

Hoi An   Hoi An is the name of the small Vietnamese village near the spot where Jim Pederson is killed by friendly fire in the novel *Going After Cacciato.* To gain revenge for Pederson's death, Lieutenant Sidney Martin calls in an air strike on the village. As white phosphorous burns the huts, Paul Berlin thinks to himself: "Kill it" (78). At the end of chapter 11, which describes this incident, the village is described as a "hole." The burning of the village and the "hole" that it becomes will later be incorporated into Paul Berlin's imagined story of the pursuit of Cacciato when he pretends that the men of Third Squad fall into a deep hole in the road on the way to PARIS.

Homer   Homer, the legendary Greek poet who is traditionally considered the author of *The Iliad* and *The Odyssey,* is one of the figures that the young Tim O'Brien believes he sees among the throng of people cheering and waving to him from the banks of the RAINY RIVER in *The Things They Carried.* O'Brien reports that a "blind poet scribbling notes" (58) is in the crowd. Homer's legendary blindness as well as O'Brien's interest in Greek philosophy and mythology suggest that this figure is meant to be the Greek epic poet.

Homewood Estates   Homewood Estates is the name of the retirement community in TUCSON, ARIZONA, that Karen Burns directs in the novel *July, July*. Karen, along with a small group of elderly residents, is left in the desert to die of a thirst by a drug smuggler named Darrell Jettie, who had recently been hired as the bus driver for the community.

hootch   Hootch is military slang for a hut or simple living quarters. During the Vietnam War, the term was used to describe both military lodgings and simple Vietnamese dwellings. In the novel *Going After Cacciato*, a staff sergeant leads Paul Berlin to "a hootch containing eighty bunks and eighty lockers" (36) on his very first day in Vietnam.

Hopkin, Mary   Mary Hopkin was a folk singer popular in the late 1960s. She is best remembered for her hit single, "Those Were the Days." In the story "The Ghost Soldiers" from *The Things They Carried*, Tim O'Brien and Azar listen to Mary Hopkin on the tape deck in O'Brien's HOOTCH after setting up the ropes and ammo cans designed to scare the medic Bobby Jorgensen. As O'Brien listens to that "high elegant voice" (210), he imagines that when the war is over, he will go to London and ask Mary Hopkin to marry him. Azar brings an end to O'Brien's reverie, however, by switching off the tape and commenting, "Shit, man . . . Don't you got *music?*" (210).

Hotel Minneapolis   The Hotel Minneapolis is the place where the men of Third Squad stay in MANDALAY, Burma, during their pursuit of an AWOL soldier in the novel *Going After Cacciato*. Described as a "teetering, three-story clapboard building, leaning leeward" (113), the hotel is run by a woman with a mustache who is wearing leather sandals and a "greasy brown robe" (113). "Number One cheap-cheap hotel" (113), she tells the American soldiers when she lets them in.

Hotel Phoenix   In *Going After Cacciato*, the men of Third Squad stay at the Hotel Phoenix in DELHI, India, a city where they continue their pursuit of the AWOL soldier, Cacciato. The hotel is run by an Indian woman named Homijolli Chand, who had studied hostelry at Johns Hopkins University and loves everything about America. The sick lieutenant, Corson, falls in love with Jolly Chand and has to be physically carried away from the hotel by his men after they see a newspaper picture of Cacciato at the TAPIER STATION, preparing to board a train headed for KABUL.

Houdini, Harry   The world-famous Harry Houdini was the best-known magician and escape artist of all time. As such, he is referred to several times in O'Brien's novel *In the Lake of the Woods*, a book in which the politician John Wade is himself an amateur magician, fascinated by the art of illusion. In the evidence chapters of the novel, O'Brien quotes from Houdini's biographers, including BERNARD C. MEYER and DOUG HENNING.

Hubert H. Humphrey VA Hospital   David Todd in the novel *July, July* is sent to the United States to recover at the Hubert H. Humphrey VA Hospital, just outside of Minneapolis, after being severely wounded in Vietnam and having his right leg amputated in Japan. David spends several months in the hospital, arriving there on July 31, 1969, and being released on Christmas Day of the same year.

Huck Finn   Huck Finn, the mischievous, lovable hero of Mark Twain's classic, *Adventures of Huckleberry Finn*, is one of the figures that the young Tim O'Brien reports seeing in the crowd of people cheering and waving to him from the banks of the RAINY RIVER in *The Things They Carried*. The vision or hallucination O'Brien experiences at the end of the story mixes people he knew from his hometown of WORTHINGTON, MINNESOTA, with famous political and cultural figures, and even fictional characters. It makes sense that O'Brien includes Huck Finn in this list since the boy famously "lit out for the territories," at the end of Twain's novel, fleeing west to escape the strictures of civilized society.

O'Brien himself in the story is torn about whether to flee or honor his DRAFT notice.

hump   In *The Things They Carried*, O'Brien discusses the various meanings of the word *hump* as used in G.I. lingo:

> To carry something was to hump it, as when Lieutenant Jimmy Cross humped his love for Martha up the hills and through the swamps. In its intransitive form, to hump meant to walk, or to march, but it implied burdens far beyond the intransitive. (3–4)

I Corps   During the Vietnam War, South Vietnam was divided by the U.S. military into four tactical zones: I Corps, II Corps, III Corps, and IV Corps. I Corps, the area of operations where Tim O'Brien was stationed during his year-long tour of duty, was the northernmost of the four zones. It covered 10,000 square miles and extended from the demilitarized zone in the North, which separated North and South Vietnam, to just below QUANG NGAI PROVINCE in the South. Most of O'Brien's soldier characters in his Vietnam War novels are stationed in the I Corps area as well, including Paul Berlin in *Going After Cacciato*, who "had never heard of I Corps" (36) before arriving in Vietnam.

I Led Three Lives   *I Led Three Lives* was an American television series that ran in the mid-fifties. It depicted the life of an advertising executive who infiltrated the U.S. Communist Party and served as an FBI informant. The series is mentioned briefly in *The Nuclear Age* when William Cowling's father hands him an envelope full of money as his son prepares to go underground to escape the DRAFT. "You know what this reminds me of," Mr. Cowling asks. "That TV show—*I Led Three Lives*" (144).

ICBM   ICBM is an acronym for Intercontinental Ballistic Missile, a long-range nuclear (especially) weapon delivered by rocket. In the novel *The Nuclear Age*, William Cowling, as a child growing up in the 1950s, was terrified of the prospect of nuclear war and used to dream about "radioactive gleamings and ICBMs whining in the dark" (9).

Ikaria, Greece   Ikaria is one of the Greek islands located in the Aegean Sea. Paul Berlin in the novel *Going After Cacciato* imagines the men of Third Squad cruising past the island on the freighter ANDROS as they make their way from IZMIR, TURKEY, to ATHENS, GREECE.

Île de la Cité   Île de la Cité is a natural island in the Seine River in the heart of PARIS where the Cathedral of NOTRE DAME is located. In the novel *Going After Cacciato*, Paul Berlin imagines enjoying the cool quiet of PLACE DAUPHIN, a public square on the island, with Sarkin Aung Wan, the Chinese-Vietnamese refugee he invents to accompany the men of Third Squad in their pursuit of the AWOL American soldier.

illum   Illum is military slang for an illumination flare, fired either by mortar or artillery. The term is used by O'Brien in his novel *Going After Cacciato* when Lieutenant Corson radios back to headquarters that he is in pursuit of the enemy after the unit first starts following the deserting soldier, Cacciato. The radio-voice on the other end offers to send in all kinds of firepower to help in the pursuit, at one point saying, "So here's what I'm gonna do. I'm gonna give you a dozen nice illum, how's that? Can you beat it? Find a place in town that beats it and we give you a dozen more, no charge" (13). The lieutenant ends up cutting the call short, calling the man on the other end of the radio a "monster" (13).

Indian Guides   The Indian Guides were a YMCA-sponsored organization founded in 1926 that supported father-son bonding through the adoption of perceived Native American values, including a love for the outdoors. Over the years, the YMCA added auxiliary groups, such as Indian Maidens, which focused on mother-daughter relationships, Indian Princesses, which encouraged father-daughter bonding, and Indian Braves, a mother-son group. In recent years, after Native American activists accused the group of perpetuating racist stereotypes, the program has dropped the Native American trappings in favor of a more generalized focus on respect for the natural world. Tim

O'Brien in his novel *Going After Cacciato* depicts Paul Berlin and his father as members of the Indian Guides. During his long night on the OP (observation post), Berlin remembers camping in the Wisconsin woods with his father and other members of the group, the pair adopting the names Big Bear and Little Bear. Berlin recalls that he was not a very successful Indian Guide—that he had trouble paddling his canoe and that he got lost in the Wisconsin woods. Big Bear and Little Bear ended up breaking camp early and stopping for hamburgers and root beer on the drive home, and talking about baseball, "white man talk" (41).

Instant NCOs   In his memoir, *If I Die in a Combat Zone, Box Me Up and Ship Me Home*, Tim O'Brien writes that, during his first month in Vietnam, he learned that noncommissioned officers "who go through a crash two-month program to earn their stripes are called 'Instant NCOs'" (80). O'Brien's platoon contains many such officers, who often serve as squad leaders. To mark their "instant" status, the soldiers nickname these noncommissioned officers with monikers such as "Ready Whip," "Nestle's Quick," and "Shake and Bake" (80–81).

Irawaddy River   The city of MANDALAY in Burma is located along the banks of the Irawaddy River. Paul Berlin in the novel *Going After Cacciato* imagines that he and the refugee Sarkin Aung Wan follow the Irawaddy through the city as they explore the streets of Mandalay, eventually coming upon a traveling zoo, "where the girl made faces at the peafowl and geese and apes and pythons" (116).

Izmir, Turkey   The third-largest city in Turkey, Izmir is a port city located on the Aegean Sea. It makes an appearance in the novel *Going After Cacciato* when Paul Berlin imagines the men of Third Squad driving into Turkey after a daring escape from the prison in TEHRAN, where they had been threatened with execution. After circling the city of ANKARA, the men pick up the road to Izmir just before dawn. After having breakfast in SALIHLI, they drive on to Izmir, where they see the "white stone and white plaster" (249) of the city build-

ings. In Izmir the men book a three-day passage to ATHENS.

Janssen, David   David Janssen played the role of Richard Kimble in the 1950s television series THE FUGITIVE, a show that is well liked by characters both in *Going After Cacciato* and in *The Nuclear Age*. In *Cacciato*, the Indian hotel owner Jolly Chand asks the American soldiers how the show ended, while in *The Nuclear Age* William Cowling and his parents discuss Janssen and *The Fugitive* on their drive to the bus depot, where William will depart from Montana to flee the DRAFT. The Cowlings agree that the show is the greatest television program in history.

Jeffers, Robinson   Robinson Jeffers was an American modernist poet famous as well as an outdoorsman and an early icon in the environmental movement. In his memoir, *If I Die in a Combat Zone*, Tim O'Brien recalls receiving a letter from his boot-camp friend ERIK HANSEN, who reports that he has lately discovered the poetry of Jeffers, which he describes as "harsh yet beautiful" (104).

Jig's Confectionary   Jig's Confectionary is a soda fountain where William Cowling sometimes spends evenings alone playing pinball and drinking cherry phosphates after pretending to his parents that he is going on a date in the novel *The Nuclear Age*. When William returns home to FORT DERRY, MONTANA, in the summer of 1967, he really does date Sarah Strouch, whom he had grown close to in college. The two spend nights at the drive-in theater, drink root beers at the A&W, and play pinball together at Jig's Confectionary.

John Ransom's Andersonville Diary   John Ransom was a 20-year-old Union soldier held as a prisoner of war in Georgia at the notorious Andersonville Prison during the Civil War. Tim O'Brien's book *The Things They Carried* opens with an epigraph from Ransom's prison diary that asserts the "truthfulness" of what is to come as well as claiming that the book is "a statement of actual things by one who experienced them to the fullest." Here O'Brien is setting up the tension between fact and fiction that will be one of the book's main themes.

Johnson, Lyndon Baines Lyndon Baines Johnson was the 36th president of the United States. He had served as JOHN F. KENNEDY's vice president and came into office when Kennedy was assassinated in November 1963. Johnson was elected in his own right by a large margin in 1964. Despite overseeing key legislation such as the Voting Rights Act and instituting domestic reforms through his Great Society program, Johnson's accomplishments were overshadowed by his escalation of U.S. involvement in the Vietnam War. Due largely to antiwar protest, he declined to run for reelection in 1968. Because of Johnson's key role in sending U.S. troops to Vietnam and in the political arena of the 1960s, he is an important figure in

the work of Tim O'Brien. In O'Brien's memoir, *If I Die in a Combat Zone,* he writes that when EUGENE McCARTHY became an antiwar candidate in the 1968 Democratic primary, "Lyndon Johnson was almost forgotten, no longer forbidding or feared" (16). Later, when O'Brien has a long conversation in Czechoslovakia with a young lieutenant in the North Vietnamese Army named Li, O'Brien asks him if he thinks LBJ is an evil man. Li replies in the negative, stating that he believes Johnson is simply "misguided and wrong," but he adds that "most North Vietnamese were not so lenient" (95). Johnson is an important figure as well to William Cowling in the 1985 novel, *The Nuclear Age.* During his college years, Cowling, terrified of nuclear war, imagines holding long conversations between LBJ and other world leaders, in which he would serve as a moderator, a "peacemaker" (69). Cowling's

President Lyndon B. Johnson greets troops in Vietnam, 1966 *(Courtesy of the National Archives)*

friends who arrange his flight to KEY WEST, FLOR-IDA, when he dodges the DRAFT, play a joke on the young man by assigning him the pseudonym of "L.B. Johnson" on his plane tickets. Johnson is also one of the figures from Western history that the young Tim O'Brien sees on the opposite shore of the RAINY RIVER when he contemplates fleeing to Canada in *The Things They Carried*. The former president figures as well in the novel *In the Lake of the Woods*. Quotes about LBJ's ravenous desire for affection and his reputation as a notorious liar, from ROBERT CARO's biography, are included in some of the evidence sections.

Johnson, Van   Van Johnson was an American movie star of the 1940s who gained fame for playing the freckle-faced, boy-next-door type who is also a successful soldier or sailor. Johnson is mentioned briefly in the original story version of "The Ghost Soldiers," when the first-person narrator, an injured soldier named Herbie, describes what it is like to be out on ambush at night: "Unreal, unreal. As if molting, you seem to slip outside yourself. It's like you're in a movie. There's a camera on you, so you begin acting, following the script: 'Oh Cisco!' You think of all the films you've seen, Audie Murphy and Gary Cooper and Van Johnson and Roy Rogers, all of them, and certain lines of dialogue come back to you—"I been plugged! . . ." (96). When the story was revised for inclusion in *The Things They Carried*, the references to Van Johnson and Roy Rogers were removed.

Jordan, Robert   Robert Jordan, the hero of ERNEST HEMINGWAY's 1940 novel, *For Whom the Bell Tolls*, is an American university professor who becomes an anti-Fascist guerrilla fighter during the Spanish civil war. In his memoir, *If I Die in a Combat Zone*, O'Brien compares Robert Jordan's courage in the novel, his "resolution to confront his own certain death" (144), to the courage displayed by his commanding officer during his early days in Vietnam—Captain Jorgensen. O'Brien says that both men, the fictional Jordan and the real-life Jorgensen, served as models that he could never match. "In Jordan's place," he writes, "I would have climbed back on my horse, bad leg and all, and

galloped away till I bled to death in the saddle" (144–45).

Josephson, Matthew and Hannah   Matthew and Hannah Josephson are the authors of a book called *Al Smith: Hero of the Cities*, which is cited in O'Brien's novel *In the Lake of the Woods* in one of the evidence chapters. The quote asserts that Smith's loss of the 1928 U.S. presidential race rankled in him for a long time because Smith, like everyone else, desired to be loved. John Wade shares these qualities with politician AL SMITH: Both view an election defeat as a mandate on their value as human beings, reading defeat as a personal rejection.

Kabul, Afghanistan   Kabul is the capital of Afghanistan and a city that the men of Third Squad travel through on a train bound for TEHRAN in the novel *Going After Cacciato*. When they spot a picture of the AWOL American soldier at a train station in a DELHI newspaper, the men realize Cacciato is heading for Afghanistan. Paul Berlin imagines a newer, faster train than the DELHI EXPRESS, which had brought them to India, climbing up into the high, cold country of the mountains as they travel "through Punjam and Peshawar and Kabul, and beyond Kabul" (176).

Kaplan, Justin   Justin Kaplan is a Harvard-trained editor and writer who published biographies of Mark Twain and Walt Whitman, among other figures. His essay "The Naked Self and Other Problems," which explains how an "unfinished person" (265) might try to transform himself by taking on a new name, is quoted in one of the evidence chapters in O'Brien's novel *In the Lake of the Woods*. O'Brien includes the quote from Kaplan because it potentially sheds light into John Wade's multiple self-transformations, first into Little Merlin or Little HOUDINI, then into Sorcerer, and finally into the lieutenant governor of Minnesota.

Karen, Robert   Robert Karen is the author of an essay called "Shame" that appeared in the February 1992 issue of the *Atlantic*. This essay is quoted twice in the evidence chapters of O'Brien's novel *In the Lake of the Woods*. In the quotes Karen discusses how shame can be instilled in a person at an early age because of a contemptuous parental voice. He goes on to argue that this sense of overwhelming shame often remains repressed, but that it can distort the personality nevertheless. Karen's arguments are relevant to O'Brien's novel in that John Wade possibly developed an unbearable level of shame due to his father's merciless teasing of him when he was a young boy, thus warping his personality in later life.

Kennedy, John F. The critic John Hellmann in his influential book *American Myth and the Legacy of Vietnam*, argues that the source of the idealism propelling American soldiers in the early stages of the Vietnam War derives largely from President John F. Kennedy and his metaphor of the New Frontier. Hellmann argues that frontier mythology—stories of courageous, solitary cowboy/sheriffs/gunslingers leaving corrupt cities for the West, where they could live virtuous lives according to individual moral codes outside the purview of established authority—have long shaped the American character. Although the western American frontier was officially closed in 1890 by the superintendent of the Census, Americans, according to Hellmann, could regain a sense of themselves as explorer/adventurers and virtuous fighters for the right with Kennedy's evoking of a New Frontier (whether through space travel or in Indochina). But Vietnam had a special pull on young Americans of this generation because it offered a vision of redemption from the sins of America's frontier heritage—the Indian massacres of the 18th and 19th centuries. In the new frontier of Vietnam, idealistic young Americans believed they could protect rather than destroy their "darker" brothers. President Kennedy is an important figure in the work of Tim O'Brien, who describes the slain president as a "hero" (47) in his memoir, *If I Die in a Combat Zone*. William Cowling, the narrator of the novel *The Nuclear Age*, worries about the possibility of atomic destruction, especially in the face of the standoff between Kennedy and Soviet leader NIKITA KHRUSHCHEV during the COLD WAR years.

Kennedy, Robert Robert F. Kennedy, who served as U.S. attorney general under his brother,

President JOHN F. KENNEDY, and who was a U.S. senator from 1965 until 1968, entered the 1968 race for president after the candidate EUGENE MCCARTHY made a strong showing in the New Hampshire primary against President LYNDON JOHNSON. Kennedy, however, was assassinated following the California primary in June 1968. Because of his political profile in the late 1960s and because his entry into the race split the antiwar vote between himself and Eugene McCarthy, Kennedy plays a pivotal role in much of Tim O'Brien's work. In his 1973 memoir, O'Brien recalls the political situation of the summer of 1968, when he was drafted (*see* DRAFT) into the Vietnam War. Robert Kennedy, he writes, "was dead but not quite forgotten" (16). William Cowling, in *The Nuclear Age*, often cites political events that marked his college years. He remembers that in 1966 Robert Kennedy "waffled" about the war, and that SIRHAN SIRHAN, Kennedy's assassin, "came into possession of a .22 caliber Iver Johnson revolver" (73). William also remembers watching Robert Kennedy being shot in 1968 as if in slow motion, on a "fine bright expansive day in June when the theater of things becomes a kitchen, and there's a chef and there's a terrorist, so it happens" (120). Kennedy was shot to death in a kitchen passageway of the Ambassador Hotel in Los Angeles. Kennedy plays a role as well in the original short story version of "The Nuclear Age," published in the *Atlantic* magazine in June 1979. William, still obsessed with his old girlfriend, Bobbi, nevertheless feels resentment that many years ago she had switched loyalties from Eugene McCarthy to Robert Kennedy, thus betraying William's political principles.

Kent State University On May 4, 1970, Ohio National Guardsmen opened fire on Vietnam War protestors at Kent State University in Ohio, killing four students and wounding nine others. William Cowling refers briefly to the massacre in the novel *The Nuclear Age* when he watches the "aftershocks" (229) of the Kent State shootings on the *Today* show at the Royalton Hotel in New York. This is during the period that Cowling is working as a courier for the radical political organization, THE COMMITTEE.

Kenya In the short story "Keeping Watch by Night," the U.S. soldier Jim Pederson had served as a Christian missionary in Kenya before being sent to fight in the Vietnam War. Doc Peret says that Pederson has a "moral stance" (65), in that he considers the ethics of his behavior more fully than most of the other soldiers.

Key West, Florida Key West, a city at the southern tip of the Florida Keys and famous as a haunt of ERNEST HEMINGWAY in the 1930s, is the location where the radical political group the COMMITTEE sets up its headquarters after the members graduate from college in Montana in the novel *The Nuclear Age*. William Cowling, at first ambivalent about his commitment to the group's radical politics, nevertheless joins Sarah Strouch and his other friends in Key West, partly in an attempt to avoid being drafted (*see* DRAFT) into the Vietnam War.

Khanh, Nguyen Nguyen Khanh was a South Vietnamese general who participated in the 1963 coup against South Vietnamese President NGO DINH DIEM. Diem was assassinated, and a military junta led by General Duong Van Minh was installed. In 1964, just three months after the overthrow of Diem, Khanh himself came to power in another coup, this time a bloodless one. Khan retained control of the country for about a year, his own government being overthrown in another military coup in 1965. Tim O'Brien refers to Khanh in his memoir when he is speaking to an army chaplain at basic training about the morality of the war. O'Brien tells the chaplain that there is little evidence suggesting that the Communists would do a worse job ruling South Vietnam than Diem or Khanh. In *Going After Cacciato*, Paul Berlin speculates along similar lines. O'Brien writes, "[H]e did not know where truth lay; he didn't know if communist tyranny would prove worse in the long run than the tyrannies of Ky or Thieu or Khanh—he simply didn't know" (264).

Khios, Greece Khios is a Greek island in the Aegean Sea that makes a brief appearance in the novel *Going After Cacciato*. Paul Berlin imagines the men of Third Squad cruising past the island on the second day of their journey aboard the ANDROS, an old passenger freighter that takes the men from IZMIR, TURKEY, to ATHENS, GREECE.

Khrushchev, Nikita Nikita Khrushchev served as first secretary of the Communist Party and leader of the Soviet Union from 1953 until 1964, during the height of the COLD WAR. In the novel *The Nuclear Age*, he is an important political figure to William Cowling, who grows up during the cold war and is obsessively afraid of nuclear destruction. One day, speaking with his therapist while a high school student, William explains that his fear is not irrational or unfounded: "It's not mental," he argues, "Kennedy and Khrushchev—I didn't make those guys up out of thin air" (48). Later, as Cowling explains to readers the world political situation in 1964, he writes that "Khrushchev was on the skids" (66).

King, Coretta Scott The wife of the slain civil rights leader Martin Luther King, Jr., Coretta Scott King makes a brief appearance in the novel *The Nuclear Age* when William Cowling reports watching news footage of the massive antiwar protest that took place on October 15, 1969, and was called the MORATORIUM TO END THE WAR IN VIETNAM. The news broadcast concludes with a collage that includes "the American flag at half-staff in Central Park, a graveyard vigil in Minneapolis, Eugene McCarthy reciting Yeats" and "Coretta King reciting Martin Luther King" (224).

Kissinger, Henry Henry Kissinger served as both National Security Advisor and U.S. secretary of state in the administration of President RICHARD M. NIXON. Generally hated by antiwar activists for engineering secret bombings in Cambodia as well as other activities, Kissinger nevertheless was the chief U.S. negotiator for the PARIS PEACE ACCORDS of 1973. As an important political figure during the late 1960s and early '70s, Kissinger is a man whom William Cowling in the novel *The Nuclear Age* is intensely interested in. Cowling writes that in 1969, "Kissinger was calling trick shots" (210), referring, quite likely, to the Cambodian bombing campaign.

klick Klick is military shorthand for kilometer, or a distance of 1,000 meters. The term entered into widespread use among American soldiers during the Vietnam War, and it is a term used frequently by O'Brien in his Vietnam novels.

Korean War Often called the "Forgotten War," because it receives less media and historical attention than WORLD WAR II or the Vietnam War, the Korean War was fought from 1950 until 1953 between North Korea and South Korea, with the U.S. intervening on the side of the South Koreans. In his memoir, *If I Die in a Combat Zone*, O'Brien recounts learning about both World War II and the Korean War when he was growing up in WORTHINGTON, MINNESOTA. He writes that the Korean War was "a gray war fought by the town's Lutherans and Baptists" (13). It was a war O'Brien learned about when "the town hero came home, riding in a convertible, sitting straight-backed and quiet, an ex-POW" (13). The grizzled, DYSENTERY-ridden Lieutenant Corson in *Going After Cacciato* is a veteran of both World War II and the Korean War.

Krupp, Alfred Alfred Krupp was a German industrialist during WORLD WAR II who was convicted of crimes against humanity for using Jewish slave labor in his factories. Krupp was later pardoned for his crimes. In O'Brien's short story "The Nuclear Age," Krupp is mentioned briefly when Sarah Strouch obliquely accuses William of selling out his ideals when he buys a mountain rich in uranium deposits from a local farmer. Sarah asserts that she and William and other college friends had "conned that poor old fairy" out of his land, but William replies that they "did it sweetly" (60). In response Sarah comments, "Krupp was sweet. Szilard was sweeter. Einstein was the sweetest old geezer who ever lived" (60). This passage was changed slightly, and Krupp's name was removed when O'Brien revised the story for inclusion in the novel version of *The Nuclear Age*.

Ky, Nguyen Cao Nguyen Cao Ky served as prime minister of South Vietnam from the years 1965 to 1967, after which he became vice president of the country. In the novel *Going After Cacciato*, Paul Berlin thinks about all the things he does not know about the war. He wonders specifically about the ideologies and political leaders fighting in Vietnam, asking himself "if communist tyranny would prove worse in the long run than the tyrannies of Ky or Thieu or Khanh," but he must acknowledge finally that "he simply didn't know" (264). In the novel *The Nuclear Age*, Ky is mentioned briefly as well when William Cowling, the book's narrator, speculates about the Vietnam War in a similar way: "Was Ho Chi Minh a tyrant, and if so, was his tyranny preferable to that of Diem and Ky and Thieu?" (130).

Lac Son In the novel *In the Lake of the Woods*, John Wade and the members of CHARLIE COMPANY stumble into a minefield near a village in PINKVILLE called Lac Son on February 25, 1968. One soldier says, "I'm killed" (103) right before he dies. This is one of the events contributing to the anger and frustration in members of the unit that will explode in the villages of My Lai the following month.

Laches The *Laches* is a Socratic dialogue written by the Greek philosopher PLATO that attempts to define the virtue of courage. In his memoir, *If I Die in a Combat Zone*, O'Brien includes a long excerpt from the *Laches* in which SOCRATES prods Laches to define courage as "wise endurance" (137). O'Brien then questions whether his own endurance of his life as a soldier has been a wise or a foolish one. He goes on to ask whether his "apparent courage in enduring" is merely "a well-disguised cowardice" (139). This question will be translated again and again into O'Brien's fictional work as he repeatedly examines characters torn between their country's demand that they go to war and their conviction that the war is unjust.

Lake Country Lake Country, or "World's Greatest Lake Country" is the nickname given by Doc Peret in the novel *Going After Cacciato* for a heavily bombed, mountainous region of Vietnam where the men of Third Squad see action toward the end of August 1968. This is the place where the men plan the fragging (*see* FRAG) death of Lieutenant

Sidney Martin. The nickname derives from the numerous bomb craters in the area, which are filled with filthy water. The simpleminded soldier Cacciato, not fully understanding that Doc's nickname for the area is a joke, actually attempts to fish in one of the craters.

Lake of the Woods   Lake of the Woods is a real-life lake situated on the border of Ontario, Canada, and northwestern Minnesota that provides the title of Tim O'Brien's fifth novel, *In the Lake of the Woods*. In the novel the politician John Wade has retreated to a small fishing cabin on the shores of the Lake of the Woods with his wife, Kathy, to recover from his recent defeat in the election for U.S. senator. When Kathy goes missing a few days after their arrival, the novel speculates about what might have happened to her.

Lake Okabena   Lake Okabena is a large lake situated near the center of WORTHINGTON, MINNESOTA, Tim O'Brien's hometown. He writes in his memoir, *If I Die in a Combat Zone*, about walking down to the lake at night, looking at the houses where the pretty girls lived, and pondering philosophical questions about the nature and existence of God. Lake Okabena is the model for the lake that Norman Bowker drives around repeatedly one Fourth of July in his small midwestern hometown in the story "Speaking of Courage" from *The Things They Carried*.

Lake Peri   In the novel *Northern Lights*, Harvey Perry, after his return home from Vietnam, leads his older brother, Paul, deep into the woods surrounding their home town of SAWMILL LANDING, Minnesota, in search of a small lake where he used to go fishing with his father when he was a boy. When the brothers at last find the remote body of water, Harvey tells Paul that he and his father had named it Lake Peri, using the old spelling of their family name. The brothers swim in the icy-cold water, then rest on the bank to eat lunch. Afterward, they dive into the water again, where Paul nearly drowns in the swift-moving stream that feeds into the lake before Harvey rescues him. The experience reminds Paul of his troubled relationship

with his father when he was a boy—uncomfortable with the masculine expectations of hunting and fishing and being at ease in the harsh Minnesota wilderness, Paul did not accompany Harvey and the senior Perry on these boyhood fishing trips.

LaMartina, Salvatore   Salvatore LaMartina, a U.S. soldier present at the MY LAI MASSACRE, testified during the court-martial of LIEUTENANT WILLIAM CALLEY that his orders were to "kill anything that breathed." This quote is included in one of the evidence chapters in O'Brien's novel *In the Lake of the Woods* (207).

Laos   Laos is a country in Southeast Asia immediately to the west of Vietnam. Parts of the country were invaded by the North Vietnamese Army during the Vietnam War and used as a staging ground for assaults against the South. In Tim O'Brien's novel *Going After Cacciato*, Laos marks the point of no return for the men of Third Squad as they pursue deserting soldier, Cacciato. In Berlin's imagined story, the men come to the Laotian border and debate whether or not to turn back: Does continuing after Cacciato amount to duty or desertion? Harold Murphy argues for turning back, but the men cross the river separating the two countries anyway, proceeding into Laos.

Landing Zone Bravo   Landing Zone Bravo is the title of chapter 20 in the novel *Going After Cacciato*, which describes the men of ALPHA COMPANY being choppered into a combat assault (*see* CA) near the village of HOI AN. Landing Zone Bravo is the name of the clearing where the CHINOOK helicopter hovers briefly above the ground. Jim Pederson, afraid of flying, has to be thrown off the aircraft and is shot by friendly fire as he wades through a rice paddy.

Landing Zone Gator   After spending a week at the CHU LAI COMBAT CENTER when he first arrived in Vietnam, Tim O'Brien was sent to Landing Zone Gator, headquarters for the 5th Battalion, 46th Infantry. Paul Berlin in *Going After Cacciato* is also transported to LZ Gator, where he joins a rifle company after spending a week at the Combat Center. The men of ALPHA COMPANY in *The Things They*

Carried are stationed at LZ Gator as well. The base is specifically mentioned in the story "Enemies," which depicts Lee Strunk and Dave Jensen getting into a fistfight while out on patrol near the landing zone.

Landing Zone Minuteman In the spring of 1969, O'Brien's unit in Vietnam moved from LANDING ZONE GATOR to a base on a hill in the middle of the hot, dusty BATANGAN PENINSULA, called Landing Zone Minuteman. In his memoir, *If I Die in a Combat Zone*, O'Brien recalls writing letters and playing chess during the day and going out on nighttime patrols and ambushes while he is stationed at LZ Minuteman. He also describes an accidental mortar attack that artillery gunners based at LZ Minuteman launched upon a small squalid village along a lagoon near the firebase, believing that they were firing upon uninhabited target areas. The men of ALPHA COMPANY had set up camp near the lagoon to provide security for the village, but they were helpless to do much the night the village was mistakenly mortared. Thirteen villagers ended up dead in the accidental firing and 33 more were wounded. O'Brien ends the chapter describing the attack with these words: "Certain blood for uncertain reasons. No lagoon monster ever terrorized like this" (168).

LaRue, Lash Lash LaRue was a movie star famed for the roles he played in westerns during the 1940s and 1950s. Born Alfred LaRue in New Orleans, he received the nickname "Lash" because of the trademark bullwhip that his cowboy film persona used to capture bad guys. In the novel *Going After Cacciato*, Stink Harris refers to Lash LaRue after the men of Third Squad panic and shoot the water buffalo belonging to Sarkin Aung Wan and her ancient Vietnamese aunts. Stink compares his own reaction speed during this incident to the well-known cowboy: "Lash LaRue . . . Lash L. LaRue . . . Like lighting, man! Zip, zap! . . . Greased lightning . . . Hands like bullwhips" (51).

Lawrence, Seymour Seymour Lawrence was O'Brien's longtime editor and publisher at Delacorte Press and later at Houghton Mifflin until his

death in 1994. Well known as an independent-minded book publisher and literary talent scout, Lawrence had overseen the publication of Katherine Anne Porter's *Ship of Fools* (1962) and Kurt Vonnegut's *Slaughterhouse-Five* (1969) when, in 1972, he decided to take a chance on a philosophical Vietnam War memoir by a then-unknown former infantry soldier. The book, of course, became *If I Die in a Combat Zone, Box Me Up and Ship Me Home.*

Lawrence, T. E. Lieutenant Colonel Thomas Edward Lawrence, better known as T. E. Lawrence, was a British military officer famed for his role in the Arab revolt against the Ottoman Empire, beginning in 1916. At the outbreak of World War I, Lawrence was a scholar who had traveled widely in the Mideast. After volunteering for military service, he fought with the Arabs in a guerrilla-style war against the Turks and later campaigned for Arab independence from Britain. Lawrence is best remembered in the popular imagination through the 1962 film *Lawrence of Arabia*, which chronicled his life. Tim O'Brien discusses Lawrence in his memoir, *If I Die in a Combat Zone*, where he recalls that ERIK HANSEN, his close friend at FORT LEWIS, was reading a copy of Lawrence's book, *The Mint*, an account of his service in the British Royal Air Force, during the early days of basic training. Erik gives O'Brien the book to read, and it affects the young recruit greatly. He writes, "With *The Mint* I became a soldier, knew I was a soldier. I succumbed. Without a backward glance at privacy, I gave in to soldiering" (34).

Le Loi Le Loi was a famous Vietnamese general who won Vietnam's independence from China in 1428. He was declared emperor after the victory and went on to rebuild Vietnam's roads and canals, to redistribute land, and to reform the country's economy and laws. Today, he is revered as a national hero in Vietnam. Le Loi is mentioned briefly in the story "The Man I Killed" from *The Things I Carried*, when O'Brien imagines that the dainty young dead man he possibly killed with a hand grenade had grown up hearing heroic stories about Vietnamese who protect their country against foreign invaders, including the TRUNG SISTERS, general TRAN HUNG DAO, and Le Loi. O'Brien writes, "He would have been taught that to defend the land was a man's highest duty and highest privilege" (125).

"Leaves"   "Leaves" is the title of a poem that Bobbi Haymore Cowling writes for her husband, William, in the novel *The Nuclear Age* after he imagines that he witnesses the sky opening up in nuclear war during a peaceful summer Sunday afternoon. William tells Bobbi that all he wants in the world is for her to stay with him always. "I won't let you leave me" (285), he adds. The poem reads:

> What do the leaves mean?
> Autumn comes to fire
> on hillside flesh,
> but you ask:
> What do the leaves mean?
> The oak, the maple, and the grass.
> Winter comes and leaves
> and each night you touch me
> to test the season.
> Here, I say, and you ask:
> What do the leaves mean?

legs   Legs is a nickname used in Vietnam for American foot soldiers. In *The Things They Carried,* O'Brien writes that ordinary infantryman assigned to combat duty "were called legs or GRUNTS" (3).

"The Legend of Sleepy Hollow"   "The Legend of Sleepy Hollow" is a short story published by the American writer Washington Irving in 1820. The story tells the tale of schoolmaster Ichabod Crane who is pursued by the ghostly headless horseman through the woods of lower New York. O'Brien mentions the story in his memoir, *If I Die in a Combat Zone,* in a chapter called "Ambush," in which he describes the terror of night patrols: "The pace was slow, and the march brought back thoughts of basic training. I thought of the song about the Viet Cong: 'Vietnam, Vietnam, every night while you're sleepin' Charlie Cong comes a-creepin' all around.' I thought of the *Legend of Sleepy Hollow,*

of imminent violence and guileless, gentle Ichabod Crane" (88).

LeMay, Curtis   Curtis LeMay was a general in the U.S. Air Force, who served as Air Force chief of staff beginning in 1961. A notorious hawk, LeMay argued in favor of bombing Cuban missile sites during the crisis of 1962 and urged a harsher bombing campaign against the North during the Vietnam War. In the novel *The Nuclear Age,* Curtis LeMay is mentioned briefly when William Cowling muses about what had become of all the polarizing figures of the 1960s: "What became of Brezhnev and Nixon and Curtis LeMay? No more heroes, no more public enemies" (127).

"Lemon Tree"   "Lemon Tree" is a folk song written in the 1960s that was made famous by the singing group Peter, Paul, and Mary. In the story "How to Tell a True War Story" from *The Things They Carried,* the narrator Tim O'Brien distinctly remembers fellow soldier Dave Jensen singing "Lemon Tree" as he throws body parts of a fellow soldier down from a tree in Vietnam. Curt Lemon had blown himself up by stepping on an explosive round, and pieces of him are left dangling from the tree.

Les Halles   Les Halles was a large, open-air market in central PARIS that was torn down and rebuilt underground in 1971. In the novel *Going After Cacciato,* Paul Berlin imagines spotting the AWOL American soldier Cacciato in Les Halles, "among the oranges and turbot and baby pigs dangling from their hocks, among bins of celery and pushcarts piled high with spring turnips" (314). Berlin follows Cacciato as he moves through the market, eventually tracking him to a part of the city that Berlin has never seen, an area with tenement apartments "running in bleak rows like barracks, one to the next," with "no beauty . . . no elegance or charm" (314–315).

Les Invalides   The Invalides is a group of buildings in PARIS, France, containing museums and monuments honoring the country's military past. In the novel *Going After Cacciato,* Paul Berlin imagines that he and Sarkin Aung Wan rent a sixth-floor apartment in a building that is near the top of a steep hill behind Invalides. Even in his invented story, Berlin seems unable to entirely escape the pull of his military duty.

Limburg, Germany Limburg is a small town in the German heartland that the men of Third Squad pass through on the train on the final leg of their journey to PARIS in the novel *Going After Cacciato*. Paul Berlin imagines that Limburg, like the towns of GIESSEN and HERBORN, represents the comforts of Western civilization that he has missed in Vietnam. As the train speeds through the German heartland, Berlin feels that "the end was coming . . . Already he anticipated the textures of things familiar: decency, cleanliness, high literacy and low mortality, the pursuit of learning in heated schools, science, art, industry bearing fruit through smokestacks" (277).

Lincoln, Abraham In the story "On the Rainy River" from *The Things They Carried*, one of the people that Tim O'Brien imagines seeing on the bank of the RAINY RIVER calling and waving to him is Abraham Lincoln, 16th president of the United States.

Linz, Austria Linz is the third-largest city in Austria. The men of Third Squad in the novel *Going After Cacciato* drive through the city on their way from ZAGREB, CROATIA, to their final destination of PARIS. They have stolen a battered Volkswagen van from an American college drop-out, a girl who assumed they were military deserters. These incidents take place in Paul Berlin's imagination, as he spends the night on an observation post (*see* OP), spinning out details of what might have happened if the American soldiers had continued to pursue the AWOL Cacciato all the way to Paris.

Lofts, Norah Norah Lofts was a 20th-century British novelist who wrote best-selling historical fiction as well as murder mysteries. Her work often took an interest in the condition of the poorer classes in Britain and espoused social reforms. Tim O'Brien mentions Norah Lofts in his 1973 memoir,

If I Die in a Combat Zone, when he writes about going to visit an army chaplain to express his moral reservations about the war in Vietnam. The chaplain, who does not take O'Brien's philosophizing seriously, tells the young soldier that he must have faith and that "any who's read Norah Lofts . . . knows that" faith is what has kept people going throughout history (58).

London Blitz The London Blitz was a period of intense bombing of the city of London by the Nazis, beginning in September 1940 and lasting through May 1941. In the short story "Claudia Mae's Wedding Day," Claudia Mae's father and his friend, Mr. Stein, listen to a phonograph record of the famous journalist EDWARD R. MURROW's reporting during the London Blitz. The two men are obsessed with World War I and WORLD WAR II and fail to understand the experiences of Robert, Claudia Mae's fiancée and a Vietnam War veteran. Claudia Mae's father assumes that Robert used drugs during the war and that he fits the stereotype of the crazy veteran.

Lone Ranger The Lone Ranger was a western hero from U.S. radio and television programs running from the 1930s through the 1950s. A masked Texas ranger who travels with his Indian sidekick, Tonto, fighting injustice, the Lone Ranger is a figure important in Tim O'Brien's childhood mythology. In the story "On the Rainy River" from *The Things They Carried*, he writes that he thought of himself as having secret reserves of courage in his youth: "Tim O'Brien: a secret hero. The Lone Ranger" (39). Later in the story, O'Brien imagines that one of the figures he sees waving to him from the opposite bank of the RAINY RIVER is himself as a "seven-year-boy in a white cowboy hat and a Lone Ranger mask and a pair of holstered six-shooters" (57). In *The Nuclear Age*, William Cowling writes that he, too, imagined himself as an isolated but heroic figure in his younger days: "I zipped myself into a nice cozy cocoon, a private world, and that's where I lived. Like a hermit: William Cowling, the Lone Ranger" (35).

Long Binh Long Binh was the site of a U.S. Army base during the Vietnam War where Tim

O'Brien's friend from basic training, ERIK HANSEN, was stationed. In a letter that O'Brien includes in his memoir, *If I Die in a Combat Zone*, Erik writes, "But here I am in Long Binh, this sprawling, tarred, barbed-wired sanctuary for well-bred brass and well-connected lifers" (170). In comparing his situation to O'Brien's experience as an actual foot soldier, Erik asserts that Long Binh is not really part of Vietnam, not "with all the cement and Pepsi-Cola and RCA television sets" (171).

Loon Point Loon Point is the name of an actual family vacation resort near Grand Rapids, Minnesota. The resort also appears in several fictional works by Tim O'Brien. In the novel *In the Lake of the Woods*, Kathy Wade has an affair with a dentist named Harmon at Loon Point. Similarly, in the novel *July, July* Ellie Abbott carries out an affair with former college classmate Harmon Osterberg, also a dentist, at the Loon Point Resort. In this novel, however, Harmon drowns while swimming at the resort, and Ellie must deal with her guilt and shame over the death. Previous to either novel, O'Brien published a short story called "Loon Point" in *Esquire* magazine in 1993. This story is the basis for incidents that occur in both novels.

Los Alamos Los Alamos is a national scientific laboratory located in northern New Mexico. It was founded during WORLD WAR II as a development site for the Manhattan Project, the U.S. secret effort to develop nuclear weaponry. Because of this, the laboratory plays an important role in the imagination of William Cowling, the nuclear-obsessed protagonist of O'Brien's novel *The Nuclear Age*. In the opening chapter of the novel, Cowling insists to readers that the threat of nuclear annihilation is very real: "Ask the rattlesnakes and butterflies on that dusty plateau at Los Alamos" (7) he urges readers. Later in the novel, as he takes a plane to Miami to flee the DRAFT, Cowling imagines that he looks out of the window and sees all the way from Los Alamos to the BIKINI ATOLL in the Pacific Ocean.

LP LP is a military acronym that stands for Listening Point. In the story "How to Tell a True War Story" from *The Things They Carried*, Mitchell Sanders describes a group of six U.S. soldiers who are sent up into the mountains to man a listening post and who begin to hear crazy, unnatural noises. Sanders claims that the moral of his story is that nobody listens, as he explains to fellow soldier Tim O'Brien: "Nobody hears nothin'. Like that fatass colonel. The politicians, all the civilian types. Your girlfriend. My girlfriend. Everybody's sweet little virgin girlfriend. What they need is to go out on LP. The vapors, man. Trees and rocks—you got to *listen* to your enemy" (76).

Luxembourg In his imagined pursuit story of Cacciato, Paul Berlin in the novel *Going After Cacciato* imagines his small squad of soldiers taking a train through Germany, across the RHINE RIVER, and into the hilly, rolling country of Luxembourg as they approach their final destination. In Luxembourg, on April 1, 1969, the men board the TRAIN ROUGE for PARIS.

Luxembourg Gardens The Luxembourg Gardens, the largest public park in PARIS, is one of the places that Paul Berlin imagines he and the beautiful Vietnamese refugee Sarkin Aung Wan visit at the end of their journey in the novel *Going After Cacciato*. Berlin pretends that the couple has picnics in the Luxembourg Gardens after arriving in Paris.

LZ LZ is a military acronym standing for Landing Zone, a clearing often used for supply helicopters. Some landing zones, such as the ones O'Brien writes about in his work, including LANDING ZONE BRAVO, LANDING ZONE GATOR, and LANDING ZONE MINUTEMAN, are larger and function as base camps.

M-16 The M-16 rifle by 1969 had become the primary weapon used by U.S. infantry soldiers in Vietnam. This is the rifle that O'Brien most frequently describes his characters using in his Vietnam narratives. In *Going After Cacciato*, Paul Berlin and the other soldiers in his small squad carry M-16s, and it is an M-16 that Oscar Johnson has all the squad members touch in PARIS the night they actually capture Cacciato in a hotel room.

The radical war protester Sarah Strouch in *The Nuclear Age* brings a stolen crate of M-16 rifles to the Florida house where she and her comrades live. Later, William Cowling and Ned Rafferty will throw the guns into the Atlantic Ocean. The M-16 rifle figures as well into the long lists of the items the men of ALPHA COMPANY carry with them in *The Things They Carried*. O'Brien writes, "As PFCs or SPEC 4s, most of them were common grunts and carried the standard M-16 gas-operated assault rifle. The weapon weighed 7.5 pounds unloaded, 8.2 pounds with its full 20-round magazine" (5).

M-60   The M-60 is a large, belt-fed machine gun used by the U.S. military since 1957. Because of its size, the gun is usually operated by a team of two or three soldiers. In the novel *Going After Cacciato*, a member of ALPHA COMPANY nicknamed Water Buffalo, or Buff for short, was the M-60 operator. After Buff's death—he is found on his knees in a ditch, facedown in his helmet—the men reminiscence about Buff's skill with the big gun:

"He knew that M-60 like . . . like, he really knew it. Take it apart in twenty seconds, remember that? Twenty fuckin seconds."
"Sure."
"Zip, pow. Just like that. Take it apart so fast you'd shit. I mean, he really knew that gun."
"I guess Murphy gets it now." (283)

The M-60 is mentioned in the short story "The Things They Carried," as well, as one of the three standard weapons the men carry with them. The other two are the M-16 assault rifle and the M-79 grenade launcher.

M-79   The M-79 was a shoulder-fired grenade launcher first used during the Vietnam War. In *The Things They Carried*, O'Brien writes that, "Among the grunts, some carried the M-79 grenade launcher, 5.9 pounds unloaded, a reasonably light weapon except for the ammunition, which was heavy" (6).

Macalester College   Tim O'Brien entered Macalester College in St. Paul, Minnesota, in 1964 and graduated in 1968 with a major in political

science. While at Macalester, a small, private liberal arts college, he served as both junior class and senior class president and was active on the debate team. He spent the summer of 1967, between his junior and senior years, studying in PRAGUE, CZECHOSLOVAKIA, as part of the Student Project for Amity among Nations (SPAN) program.

Mackenzie, Lieutenant Frederick   Lieutenant Frederick Mackenzie was a British soldier who fought at the battles of Lexington and Concord during the American Revolutionary War. He is quoted in one of the evidence chapters in O'Brien's novel *In the Lake of the Woods* as admitting that British troops "were so enraged at suffering from an unseen enemy that they forced open many of the houses . . . and put to death all those found in them" (259). This behavior is eerily similar to that of American troops in Vietnam during the MY LAI MASSACRE.

MACV   MACV is a military acronym standing for Military Assistance Command, Vietnam. Created in 1962, the MACV was the unified command structure for all U.S. military operations in Vietnam. In O'Brien's novel *Going After Cacciato*, Paul Berlin is assigned by MACV Computer Services in Cam Ranh Bay to the AMERICAL DIVISION, the single largest U.S. unit in Vietnam.

Maddox, Lester   Lester Maddox was the segregationist governor of Georgia from 1967 to 1971. He is mentioned in O'Brien's novel *The Nuclear Age* several times, as an important figure from the '60s era, when William Cowling's political views were being formed. In the novel's opening chapter, Cowling wonders what happened to all the old 1960s political figures, including the Soviet leader LEONID BREZHNEV and Lester Maddox. Later, Cowling describes staying in a Kansas City motel room in 1969 while working as a radical operative and watching Lester Maddox sing "God Bless America" on late-night television.

Madigan, Elvira   In his memoir, *If I Die in a Combat Zone*, O'Brien writes that on his first night with ALPHA COMPANY in Vietnam, he "watched Elvira

Madigan and her friend romp through all the colors, get hungry, get desperate, and stupidly—so stupidly that you could only pity their need for common sense—end their lives" (74). The reference is to a late 19th-century Danish circus performer who was shot to death by her married lover in a suicide pact after the pair ran away together and became destitute. The pair packed a final picnic, then the lover, a former cavalry officer, shot both Elvira and himself. The story of Elvira Madigan was made into a Swedish film in 1967, and it is this film that O'Brien watches his first night with Alpha Company. He writes that the film disgusted him because Elvira's lover was too proud to take a menial job to earn money, which is what led to the pair's death.

Majestic Hotel   The PARIS PEACE ACCORDS, which ended direct U.S. military involvement in Vietnam, were signed at the Majestic Hotel in PARIS on January 27, 1973. In the novel *Going After Cacciato,* Paul Berlin imagines a scene that mimics the peace talks. He and Sarkin Aung Wan face off at the Majestic Hotel from opposite sides of "a large circular table topped with green baize and rimmed with chrome" (316). Like diplomats, each in turn gets up to speak, offering a justification for whether Berlin should flee the war or stay and fight. In addition, in the novel *The Nuclear Age* William Cowling, home from college during the summer of 1968 after his graduation, watches dramatic political events unfold on television with his parents, including scenes of the Paris peace talks: "There were flags and limousines at the Hotel Majestic. Averill Harriman was shaking hands with Xuan Thuy" (121).

The Man Who Never Was   *The Man Who Never Was* is a 1956 WORLD WAR II film about the real-life plan by British intelligence agents to deceive the Axis powers into thinking that Sardinia and Greece were the true targets of the Allied invasion of Italy. The British agents put a corpse into the sea with a briefcase attached to him containing papers that identify Sardinia and Greece as the Allied objectives. The body is found by Spanish intelligence agents who pass on the information to the

Nazis. In the story "The Lives of the Dead" from *The Things They Carried,* the movie that nine-year-old Timmy and Linda are taken to see by Mr. and Mrs. O'Brien is *The Man Who Never Was.* O'Brien carefully chose this movie for its relevance to the theme of the book as a whole—he further blurs the line between fact and fiction by showing that made-up or imagined stories can be as "true" and as effective as "real" stories.

Mandalay   Mandalay is the second-largest city in Burma (also known as Myanmar). Located along the IRAWADDY RIVER, the city has a population of 1 million residents. In the novel *Going After Cacciato,* the members of Third Squad, in Paul Berlin's imagined pursuit story, emerge onto the streets of Mandalay after Sarkin Aung Wan leads them through the complex underground tunnel system inhabited by the North Vietnamese prisoner Li Van Hgoc. It is in Mandalay that the American soldiers spot Cacciato dressed as a monk in the midst of a large throng gathering in a park for evening prayers.

MARS   MARS is a military acronym for Military Affiliate Radio System. In the novel *Going After Cacciato,* Paul Berlin, along with Oscar Johnson, Eddie Lazzutti, and Doc Peret hike from CHU LAI, where they are on stand-down in late August 1968, to a nearby military detachment where they place phone calls home over the MARS radio-telephone hookup. While the others are able to get through and talk to relatives back home, Berlin's family phone in FORT DODGE, IOWA, just rings and rings. Oscar tries to comfort Berlin by telling him "The world don' stop" (159) just because he is in Vietnam.

Marsilius   Marsilius of Padua was an Italian scholar and political theorist born in the late 13th century. He argued, radically for the time, that the Roman Empire should be separate from the papacy. Marsilius is mentioned briefly in O'Brien's novel *Going After Cacciato* when Doc Peret begins talking about "Peace and domestic tranquillity" early in the squad's pursuit of the AWOL soldier, Cacciato, a line that he attributes to the ancient Italian scholar.

"Martian Travel"   "Martian Travel" is the name of a poem that TWA stewardess Bobbi Haymore pins to the pocket of passenger William Cowling's coat before he leaves a plane in Miami in the novel *The Nuclear Age*. William will later discover that Bobbi has given poems to other male passengers previously, but he nevertheless remains obsessed with her and ends up marrying her many years later. All that readers find out about the content of the poem is that, in William's words, "it had to do with flight and fantasy and pale green skin" and that "it was hard to follow" (152).

Masjid-i-Sulaiman   Masjid-i-Sulaiman, the Persian name for the Temple of Solomon, is mentioned in the novel *Going After Cacciato* when Paul Berlin imagines, as part of his invented pursuit story of Cacciato, that the men of Third Squad meet an Americanized Indian woman in DELHI named Jolly Chand. Educated in the United States, Jolly Chand describes her time studying at Johns Hopkins University as "the loveliest period of her entire life" (148). Berlin imagines that "America rang in her head like the golden bells of Masjid-i-Sulaiman" (148).

Mason, Patience H. C.   Patience H. C. Mason is the author of a book called *Recovering from the War: A Woman's Guide to Helping Your Vietnam Vet, Your Family, and Yourself*, published in 1990. She is one of the experts who is quoted several times in the evidence chapters in the novel *In the Lake of the Woods*. Her comments reflect on the difficulties that Kathy Wade has dealing with John's traumatic war experiences and the psychological damage he has undergone when he returns home. Mason writes about married veterans who wake up in the night with their hands around their wife's throat and how frightening this is to both the vet and the wife, who wonders, "Is he crazy? Does he hate me?" (146). John Wade in the novel, like the veterans Mason describes, has trouble sleeping and will often shout out threats in the night.

Master's Masters, The   In the novel *Going After Cacciato*, *The Master's Masters* is said to be a classical radio program broadcast out of DA NANG and narrated by Master Sergeant Jake Eames. Eddie Lazzutti, who claims to hate classical music, nevertheless listens to the program at six o'clock every Saturday evening. When the program ends, Eddie is usually quiet for a while, but then he often begins to sing. Paul Berlin remembers that when Eddie sang "the night could sometimes be fine" (141).

Maxim's   Maxim's is a famous restaurant in PARIS that first opened in 1893 and catered to rich celebrities throughout most of the 20th century. The restaurant is mentioned in the novel *Going After Cacciato* when Doc Peret and Paul Berlin are discussing Cacciato's desertion and his attempted journey to Paris. Berlin delights in the notion that Cacciato might make it all the way to Paris and imagines the childlike young soldier eating at the famous restaurant:

> "By God! Lunch at Maxim's!"
> "What?"
> "A cafeteria deluxe. My old man ate there once . . . truffles heaped on chipped beef and toast." (18)

McCarthy, Eugene   Eugene McCarthy was a candidate for the Democratic nomination for president in 1968 who ran on an anti–Vietnam War platform. McCarthy's early success as a candidate prompted LYNDON BAINES JOHNSON to decline to run for reelection and drove ROBERT F. KENNEDY to join the race. After Kennedy was assassinated following the California Democratic primary, McCarthy continued to do well as a candidate, but he was eventually defeated in the primaries by Johnson's vice president, Humbert Humphrey. O'Brien, keenly interested in political philosophy his whole life, refers to McCarthy in many of his works. In his memoir, *If I Die in a Combat Zone*, O'Brien mentions that the candidate brought "quiet thought" (16) to issues of war and peace and that he along with other college students tried to help McCarthy's campaign. O'Brien adds that although he was not a pacifist in college he was a "confirmed liberal" (22) and would have voted for Eugene McCarthy. Similarly, in the story "On the Rainy River" from *The Things They Carried*, the Tim O'Brien narrator

Eugene McCarthy *(Courtesy of the Library of Congress)*

recalls ringing doorbells for Gene McCarthy as a college student. McCarthy is an important historical figure as well in the novel *The Nuclear Age*. William Cowling, digging a bomb shelter in his Montana yard in 1995, wonders what has become of Eugene McCarthy and the heroes of his past. But he also remembers that his radical friends had grown tired of McCarthy's clean-cut image and tactics after the shooting of Kennedy. Ollie Winkler, for instance, tells William that "the McCarthy business had gone bust after California. Clean-cut candidate, clean-cut defeat" (146). McCarthy's loss in the primaries, Ollie says, made him want to "crack a few skulls" (146), and indeed, the radical political group William had been part of in college will grow increasingly violent as the years pass.

McGovern, George George McGovern was a Democratic U.S. senator who unsuccessfully ran for president against RICHARD NIXON in 1972, largely on an anti–Vietnam War platform. He is

mentioned in the novel *The Nuclear Age*, when William Cowling writes that he and former 1960s activists pat themselves on the back now because they "marched a few miles" and "voted for McGovern" (131). Later in the novel, Cowling writes that the autumn of 1969 was a time when "George McGovern took a fresh look at his options" (223).

McKinley, William William McKinley, 25th president of the United States, makes a brief appearance in Tim O'Brien's memoir, *If I Die in a Combat Zone*, when an army chaplain discussing the young soldier's moral reservations about the war tells him that McKinley had agonized over the Spanish-American War. When O'Brien insists that the Vietnam War was "conceived in man's intellect" (59) rather than mandated by God, the chaplain responds by using the example of McKinley: "The Spanish-American War," he claims, wasn't some cold-blooded human decision. President McKinley waited and waited. He prayed to the Lord, asking for guidance, and the Lord finally told him to go to war" (59). All that O'Brien can find to say to this unhelpful argument is, "We read different books" (59).

McNamara, Robert Robert McNamara was the U.S. secretary of defense from 1961 until 1968. He is mentioned in O'Brien's novel *The Nuclear Age* when William Cowling, who periodically reviews political events taking place in the world, writes that in October 1966 "Robert McNamara entertained misgivings" about the war (74). Later, he adds that in November 1967 Robert McNamara "was having second thoughts" (112). In a book written many years after the war had ended, McNamara claimed that he became reluctant to engage more troops as the war progressed and that he grew increasingly skeptical about U.S. involvement in Vietnam.

Meadlo, Mrs. Myrtle Mrs. Myrtle Meadlo was the mother of the American soldier Paul Meadlo, who publicly admitted firing his rifle into a crowd of Vietnamese civilians during the MY LAI MASSACRE in a CBS television news interview. Mrs. Meadlo is quoted in one of the evidence chapters in O'Brien's novel *In the Lake of the Woods* as saying that she raised her son "to be a good boy," but that the army "made a murderer out of him" (136–37).

Meaux, France   Meaux is a small city located on the northeast outskirts of the Parisian metropolitan area. In the novel *Going After Cacciato*, Paul Berlin imagines the men of Third Squad speeding through Meaux on the TRAIN ROUGE, bound for PARIS.

Medina, Captain Ernest   Captain Ernest Medina was the commanding officer of CHARLIE COMPANY during the MY LAI MASSACRE. Court-martialed in 1971, Captain Medina was found not guilty although LIEUTENANT WILLIAM CALLEY, at his own court-martial, claimed he was simply following the orders of his superior officer. O'Brien mentions Captain Medina in his 1973 memoir, *If I Die in a Combat Zone*, writing that the area of PINKVILLE, where O'Brien's unit patrolled was well known to the men as a notorious VIET CONG hotspot even before "the headlines and before the names Calley and Medina took their place in history" (116).

Merricks, Chip   Chip Merricks was an African-American soldier from Orlando, Florida, who was a good friend of Tim O'Brien's during his stint in Vietnam and who served—at least partially—as the model for Curt Lemon in *The Things They Carried*. Merricks died on May 9, 1969, a few days after O'Brien himself was injured in combat.

metafiction   Metafiction, a technique often associated with postmodern writers, is best understood as fiction that comments on or draws attention to its own status as fiction in order to explore the relationship between fiction and the real world. Clearly, Tim O'Brien uses the techniques of metafiction in several of his works. Paul Berlin, during his long night on the watchtower in *Going After Cacciato*, muses about storytelling and the power of his own imagination to control his fear, just as the larger novel meditates on the ability of narrative to imagine new endings, a way out of the tangled web of war. *The Things They Carried* takes its exploration of the relationship between fiction and reality even further. The book is narrated by a fictional char-

acter who shares a name with the real-life author, Tim O'Brien. It mixes autobiographical facts with made-up events, and it is even dedicated to its characters. More important, though, the O'Brien narrator comments throughout the book on the art of storytelling, drawing attention to the invented nature of the characters and events he describes. By using these metafictive techniques, O'Brien invites readers to question the nature of truth itself. He argues that "story-truth," which communicates the emotional weight of an event, can sometimes be more true than "happening-truth," which, at best, can only reconstruct events after the fact and as perceived by fallible human beings. *In the Lake of the Woods* is a metafictional novel as well; it draws attention to the artificiality of historical narration as its biographer/historian, introduced to readers only in footnotes to the main text, supplies numerous hypotheses for what might have happened to Kathy Wade, refusing to settle on a definitive answer to the essential mystery at its core. Despite the human desire for truth, for firm knowledge of why human beings behave the way they do, the book suggests that all we really have are stories—we tell stories to understand and make sense of the world around us, to shape and give meaning to the "real" world we live in.

Metz, France   Metz is a city in northeast France. In the novel *Going After Cacciato*, Paul Berlin imagines that the men of Third Squad take the TRAIN ROUGE from LUXEMBOURG into France. They turn straight west at Metz before continuing through the French countryside and into PARIS.

Meyer, Bernard C.   Bernard C. Meyer is the author of the book *Houdini: A Mind in Chains* and one of the experts quoted in the evidence chapters in O'Brien's novel *In the Lake of the Woods*. Meyer speaks of the pleasure for spectators in watching HOUDINI's tricks, noting that watchers enjoyed "yielding passively to an omnipotent and mysterious force," of having their reason "overthrown" and their judgment "scuttled" (94–95).

Military Payment Certificates   Military Payment Certificates were alternate banknotes used during the Vietnam War, since an influx of U.S. dollars had tended to destabilize local economies where American soldiers were based. In the novel *The Things They Carried,* Military Payment Certificates are said to be one of the items that the men carry with them in the field.

Miracle Mets   The Miracle Mets is the nickname given to the 1969 Major League Baseball team the New York Mets, who started the season as underdogs but went on to win the World Series. In O'Brien's novel *July, July,* the injured U.S. soldier David Todd listens to news of the Mets' victories over a transistor radio as he lies badly wounded and alone along the banks of the SONG TRA KY River in Vietnam. Todd hears or imagines he hears a radio deejay named Master Sergeant Johnny Ever talk to him about the "raggedy ass Mets . . . [a] bunch of has-beens and never-will-bes" (31) who have been surprising everyone with their recent wins, even Johnny Ever himself. The Miracle Mets, along with the amazing APOLLO 11 Moon landing, which he also hears news of over the radio, inspire David Todd to fight for his life.

M&Ms   M&M's are small, round, chocolate candies with a hard shell produced by the Mars Company. They figure into the work of Tim O'Brien in his novel *Going After Cacciato* when the AWOL soldier, Cacciato, leaves a trail of M&Ms for the men of Third Squad to follow as they pursue him though Vietnam and into LAOS. Paul Berlin most likely incorporates M&Ms into his imagined story of the chase after Cacciato because the candies were part of his traumatic war experiences. When Bernie Lynn is mortally wounded in the VIET CONG tunnels after being sent down to retrieve Frenchie Tucker, Doc Peret places two of the candies on Bernie's tongue and tells him to swallow, pretending that the chocolates are medicine. The men of Third Squad understand the significance of the M&Ms— Doc uses them only as palliative care in hopeless cases—and they move away from the dying man.

Moeller, Lorna Lue   Lorna Lue Moeller is the name of a real-life ten-year-old girl who died of a brain tumor on September 11, 1956, in WORTHING-

TON, MINNESOTA. Lorna Lue is the model for the fictional Linda, who appears in "The Lives of the Dead," the final story in the collection *The Things They Carried.* According to personal records housed at the Harry Ransom Humanities Research Center at the University of Texas at Austin, O'Brien's parents really did take him and Lorna Lue to see a movie together in Worthington. And just as in the story, Lorna Lue wore stocking caps to school to hide scars from her surgery.

Moeller, Marvis   Marvis Moeller was the mother of LORNA LUE MOELLER, the real-life model of nine-year-old Linda in the story "The Lives of the Dead." Marvis Moeller wrote a long letter to Tim O'Brien, dated March 22, 1991, in which she thanked him for his fictional portrait of her daughter and reminisced about Lorna Lue and Tim as children. The letter is currently housed, along with other personal records of O'Brien's, at the Harry Ransom Humanities Research Center at the University of Texas at Austin.

"The Mole in His Hole"   "The Mole in His Hole" is a poem written by William Cowling's wife, Bobbi, in the novel *The Nuclear Age,* as William becomes increasingly obsessed with digging a bomb shelter in the yard of his Montana home. The poem reads:

> Down, shy of light, down
> to that quilted bedrock
> where we sleep as reptiles
> dreaming starry skies and ash
> and silver nuggets that hold
> no currency in life misspent.
> Down, a digger, blind and bold,
> through folds of earth
> layered like the centuries,
> down
> to that brightest treasure.
> Fool's gold.

Bobbi suggests that William is blind like the mole, that while trying to protect his family by digging a bomb shelter, he is really pursuing fool's gold. She implies that her husband is so afraid of life that he neglects to live it.

Montparnasse   Montparnasse is a neighborhood in PARIS located on the Left Bank of the Seine River. In the novel *Going After Cacciato*, Paul Berlin imagines eating fried potatoes and drinking wine in the cheap sidewalk restaurants along Montparnasse Boulevard with the beautiful refugee, Sarkin Aung Wan. Afterward, he imagines that they go out dancing with Eddie Lazzutti and some of the other men of Third Squad.

Moore, Marianne   An American modernist poet, Marianne Moore is one of the writers admired by Tim O'Brien's friend at basic training in FORT LEWIS, WASHINGTON—ERIK HANSEN—whom he writes about in his memoir, *If I Die in a Combat Zone*. O'Brien remembers that Erik rated ROBERT FROST the finest of American poets, but that he considered Marianne Moore second on that list.

Moratorium to End the War in Vietnam   The Moratorium to End the War in Vietnam was a large-scale, nationwide demonstration that was held on October 15, 1969, protesting the Vietnam War. In the novel *The Nuclear Age*, William Cowling watches news footage of the moratorium in a motel room in Kansas City during the time that he is working as a courier for the radical organization the COMMITTEE. He describes the large numbers of protesters that turned our for the moratorium in detail, writing, "In Boston, 100,000 people swarmed across the Common. New York City, 250,000; New Haven, 40,000; Des Moines, 10,000 plus tractors . . ." (223). Cowling goes on to describe the news footage more fully.

MOS   MOS is a military acronym for Military Occupational Specialty. In his memoir, *If I Die in a Combat Zone*, Tim O'Brien writes that a lieutenant sitting next to him on the bus from FORT LEWIS to SEATTLE asks him his MOS. O'Brien replies that he has been assigned to the infantry.

Mount Ranier   Located approximately 50 miles southeast of SEATTLE, Washington, Mount Ranier is the tallest peak in the Cascade Mountains. In his memoir, *If I Die in a Combat Zone*, O'Brien writes about seeing the towering Mt. Ranier reaching to the sky, "white and cold" (32), 60 miles dis-

tant from FORT LEWIS, where he underwent basic training. The mountain, O'Brien writes, "stood for freedom" (32).

Mount Sebastian College   Mount Sebastian College in New Jersey is the institution attended by Lieutenant Jimmy Cross's would-be girlfriend, Martha, in the opening story of *The Things They Carried*. Martha writes Jimmy letters when he is stationed in Vietnam, talking about her studies. She is an English major who respects Chaucer and has "a great affection for Virginia Woolf" (1).

MP   MP is a military acronym that stands for Military Police. After Mary Anne Bell goes missing in the jungle in the story "Sweetheart of the Song Tra Bong," Rat tells the other men of ALPHA COMPANY that the medical compound near the village of TRA BONG "went crazy with MP and CID types" (115) who investigate her disappearance. But nothing ever comes of the search; Mary Anne is never found, although rumors of her being glimpsed in the jungle circulate among the men.

Murphy, Audie   The most-decorated American veteran of WORLD WAR II, Audie Murphy later became an actor who starred in Hollywood war movies and westerns. Many young men fighting in the Vietnam War, Tim O'Brien included, grew up watching heroes like Audie Murphy perform in such films. In his memoir, *If I Die in a Combat Zone*, O'Brien describes thinking about Audie Murphy and other heroes during his army basic training, as he wonders whether or not he will go to war. Later, in the story "The Ghost Soldiers" from *The Things They Carried*, the Tim O'Brien narrator, as he stages the ropes and sandbags that will be used to frighten the green young medic Bobby Jorgenson, writes about feeling as if he himself were in a movie. He thinks about all the movie heroes of his youth, including Audie Murphy, and he writes that he "can't help falling back on them as models of proper comportment" (*TTTC* 207).

Murrow, Edward R.   In the short story "Claudia Mae's Wedding Day," Claudia Mae's father and his friend, Mr. Stein, while waiting for the rain to stop and the wedding between Claudia Mae and a Vietnam veteran named Robert to begin, put on a record of famous WORLD WAR II broadcast journalist Edward R. Murrow describing the LONDON BLITZ. "Wow. That was a war" (149), comments Claudia Mae's father, himself a World War II veteran. The story depicts how people back home have difficulty understanding the experiences of the U.S. soldier in Vietnam. The women in the story naively associate medals with gallantry, and the men wax nostalgic for earlier wars.

My Khe   In his memoir, *If I Die in a Combat Zone*, Tim O'Brien describes ALPHA COMPANY making a combat assault (*see* CA) in the area of Vietnam known as PINKVILLE, outside a village called My Khe. Although the landing zone is cold, the American soldiers spot Vietnamese running out of the village, and they charge after them, "like storm troopers through My Khe" (111). The day ends with two dead enemy soldiers and one dead American. Later, in May, the men of Alpha Company will be choppered back into the villages that make up My Khe. O'Brien himself is injured by a hand grenade when the men walk into an ambush, but a big soldier named Clauson takes the brunt of the attack. The men return to the My Khe–My Lai area in July under the command of Captain Smith. Several soldiers are killed and injured when a group of Armored Personnel Carriers retreats over them, an incident that O'Brien blames largely on the ignorance of their commanding officer. The villages of the My Khe area are also mentioned in the novel *Going After Cacciato*. During the hot July of 1968, when the men of Third Squad are patrolling in the muddy villages along the SONG TRA BONG River they begin to play pickup basketball games. At a village called My Khe 2, Paul Berlin's team wins a game by the lopsided score of 110 to 38. My Khe figures into the novel *The Things They Carried* as well. When O'Brien invents a life story for the dainty young man he supposedly kills with a hand grenade while on ambush, he imagines that the soldier had been born in 1946 "in the village of My Khe near the central coastline of Quang Ngai Province" (125). In the story "Ambush," O'Brien describes the ambush in which the young man is

killed as taking place outside the village of My Khe. Finally, in the story "Ghost Soldiers" from the same collection, Norman Bowker informs O'Brien, who is back at headquarters after suffering an injury, about the death of Morty Phillips, who dies of a "VC virus" (195) after swimming in a stream outside of My Khe.

My Lai Massacre   On the morning of March 16, 1968, CHARLIE COMPANY of the 1st Battalion, 10th Infantry of the U.S. Army attacked a small cluster of villages, identified as "My Lai 4" on American maps, in the QUANG NGAI PROVINCE in Vietnam, an area known to be a VIET CONG stronghold. Having suffered heavy casualties in the weeks previous to the attack, the unit expected robust enemy return fire, but there was none. Nevertheless, the Americans went into the village, shooting weapons and throwing grenades. American soldiers that day ended up massacring between 400 and 500 unarmed Vietnamese civilians, mostly women, children, and the elderly. Civilians were tortured and raped and groups of unarmed people were lined up and shot, their bodies falling backward into drainage ditches. News of the massacre was kept hidden for more than a year, until a soldier named Ronald Ridenhour wrote a long, anguished letter to President RICHARD NIXON and several other politicians, detailing what he had heard about the atrocity. The story began to appear in American newspapers in November 1969, and *Life* magazine published full-color photographs shot by an army photographer in December 1969. Although 26 soldiers were originally charged with criminal offenses, only one, LIEUTENANT WILLIAM J. CALLEY, was convicted. Calley ended up serving approximately three years under house arrest for his crimes. The My Lai Massacre is important in Tim O'Brien's work, largely because he served in the same area where the killings occurred, about a year later. His memoir, *If I Die in a Combat Zone*, includes a chapter titled "My Lai in May," which details action that his unit saw around the villages. O'Brien describes the area as "a feared and special place on the earth" (116). The O'Brien work in which My Lai figures most prominently, however, is the novel *In the Lake of the Woods*. The novel details the story of John Wade, the lieutenant governor of Minnesota, who is running for a seat in the U.S. Senate when his secret past at My Lai is exposed in the media, destroying his political career. O'Brien includes in the novel scenes depicting the actual massacre, although he uses the original Vietnamese name for the village—THUAN YEN—rather than the Americanized name My Lai.

91st Evac Hospital   The 91st Evac Hospital is where narrator Tim O'Brien is sent to recover after being shot for the second time in the story "The Ghost Soldiers" from *The Things They Carried.* Because he is shot in his posterior, O'Brien has to lie on his stomach for a month in the hospital and endure the nurses making jokes about "diaper rash" (191). It is in the hospital that O'Brien's anger against incompetent medic Bobby Jorgenson begins to blossom.

Nash, Jay Robert   Jay Robert Nash is the author of a book called *Among the Missing,* from which O'Brien quotes in one of the evidence chapters in his novel *In the Lake of the Woods.* In the quote Nash claims that the Bureau of Missing Persons in New York handles more than 30,000 cases a year. O'Brien includes this figure in order to demonstrate that mysteries, such as the one that surrounds the disappearance of John and Kathy Wade in the novel, might be more common than we think.

Naxos   Naxos is a Greek island in the Aegean Sea, which makes a brief appearance in the novel *Going After Cacciato* when Paul Berlin imagines the men of Third Squad steaming around its lower tip aboard the freighter ANDROS as they make their way from IZMIR, TURKEY, to ATHENS. Naxos has mythic importance in the story of Theseus and Ariadne, a Greek tale that O'Brien plays with in the novel. It is the island where Theseus, in many versions of the myth, is said to have abandoned Ariadne, despite his promise to take her to Athens with him and marry her.

NCO   NCO is a military acronym for Non-Commissioned Officer. In the U.S. Army all ranks of sergeant are noncommissioned officers, who are

often quite experienced in the field and serve as a link between enlisted personnel and commissioned officers. Characters in O'Brien's books have many interactions with NCOs. In his memoir, *If I Die in a Combat Zone,* O'Brien describes "INSTANT NCOs"—men who have gone through a crash two-month training period to earn their stripes. Oscar Johnson is an NCO in *Going After Cacciato,* as is the "huge black man" (38) Paul Berlin encounters who yells "Boomo" randomly during a training drill his first few days in Vietnam.

Nixon, Pat   The wife of President RICHARD NIXON, Pat Nixon is described in one of the evidence chapters in O'Brien's novel *In the Lake of the Woods* as hating her role as the president's wife. According to her biographer, "Politics was anathema to Pat . . . she made this luminously clear to persons she knew and trusted" (263). O'Brien includes this passage in his novel because it helps explain Kathy Wade's attitude about her role as political wife. Kathy, like Pat Nixon, hated politics, yet played the role of supportive wife to her ambitious husband.

Nixon, Richard   The 37th president of the United States, Richard Nixon was elected to office in 1968, greatly disappointing those active in the antiwar movement. O'Brien depicts this frustration in *The Nuclear Age,* when William Cowling and his group of radical friends are so depressed by Nixon's election that they end up going to Cuba to participate in military-style revolutionary training. While O'Brien declares himself a political liberal rather than a radical like the antiwar protesters he depicts in *The Nuclear Age,* he nevertheless looked forward to Nixon's likely defeat in 1968 as well. Musing on the political landscape in the summer before the election in his memoir, *If I Die in a Combat Zone,* O'Brien writes that at that time, "Richard Nixon looked like a loser" (16). Nixon appears as a figure as well in the novel *In the Lake of the Woods.* He is referred to three times in the evidence sections of the book: First in a quote from his memoir in which he declares that his mother "was a saint" (29); again in another quote from the memoir that addresses the emotional exhaustion that comes immediately after a crisis situation (100); and finally in a quote from a biography of PAT NIXON that discusses Nixon's deep depression after his resignation from office (264).

Noah   The biblical ark-builder Noah is mentioned twice in the original story version of "Quantum Jumps," first published in *Ploughshares* magazine in 1983. At the opening of the story, as the narrator William is digging a deep bomb shelter in his yard, he tells himself to "keep at it," to "find the rhythm" and to "think about Custer and Kissinger. Think about Noah" (12). William imagines his work as being utterly necessary if he is to save himself and his family from nuclear apocalypse, as Noah saved his family and two of each animal in the world during the biblical flood. Later, after his daughter, Melinda, calls him "nutto," William tells himself that there is nothing crazy about trying to survive: "Nutto? . . . Was Noah nutto? Custer?" (15). These two references to Noah were removed when O'Brien revised the story for inclusion in the novel *The Nuclear Age*.

Nogales, Mexico   Nogales is a Mexican city in the state of Sonora that borders on Arizona. In the novel *July, July,* a man named Darrell Jettie, who works as a bus driver for HOMEWOOD ESTATES, a retirement community in TUCSON, proposes a trip to Nogales for a few of the community's elderly residents. Karen Burns, the director of Homewood Estates, who is secretly attracted to Darrell Jettie, agrees to the trip. But Jettie never takes Karen and the four old people to Nogales as promised, instead driving right through the city and into the Mexican countryside, where he has set up a drug smuggling operation. Back in Arizona, Jettie leaves Karen and her elderly charges in a remote desert location to die of thirst and exposure.

Notre Dame   In the novel *Going After Cacciato,* Paul Berlin imagines the men of Third Squad chasing the AWOL American soldier, Cacciato, all the way to PARIS. The last leg of the invented pursuit story takes place aboard the TRAIN ROUGE, which speeds from LUXEMBOURG to Paris. When the men finally arrive in the city, Berlin imagines that it

is raining and foggy. However, he also pretends that he can glimpse the twin towers of the famous Notre Dame Cathedral for a brief instant through the thunderheads from the train window. He imagines that one of the cathedral's gargoyles flies off the church roof in the wild weather: "He sees a gargoyle's wild eyes. The gargoyle is torn from its mount, wings flapping, and it flies—it does. Bat wings, screeching, caught up in the acceleration, picked up and flying" (291).

Nuoc Mau   In his memoir, *If I Die in a Combat Zone,* O'Brien describes being assigned to ALPHA COMPANY, a unit headquartered at LANDING ZONE GATOR in the BATANGAN PENINSULA in Vietnam. The base is situated atop a hill. At the foot of the hill lies a small village called Nuoc Mau (spelled "Nouc Mau" later in the book), which O'Brien describes as "filled with pleasant, smiling people, places to have your laundry done, a whorehouse" (73). Later, O'Brien argues with Major Callicles, one of his commanding officers at LZ Gator, about the MY LAI MASSACRE, which Callicles claims was justified because the "so-called civilians" there were "killers" (196). O'Brien replies that using such a philosophy the men "might as well go down into Nouc Mau, the little village down by the gate, and just kill them all (196–97). The major explodes: "Bullshit! Nouc Mau sure as hell isn't My Lai 4" (197).

Nuoc Ti   Nuoc Ti is the name of a Vietnamese hamlet in *Going After Cacciato* where the men of ALPHA COMPANY are on patrol on July 13, 1968. The American soldiers' usual pickup basketball game is rained out at Nuoc Ti, and the men become fidgety and nervous as they wait throughout the afternoon for the rain to stop. This day marks the beginning of what Paul Berlin will refer to as a bad time at the war. Through the rest of July and the beginning of August, the men grow increasingly restless and edgy, and fights begin to break out as they wait for something bad to happen. When Rudy Chassler steps on a mine on August 13, it comes as a relief for all the men.

Nuremberg Principles   The Nuremberg Principles were developed by the International Law

Commission after the Nuremberg trials of prominent Nazis who argued in their defense that they were just following orders. The Nuremberg Principles state that a person is responsible for a war crime he or she commits even if ordered to do so by a superior, provided that a moral choice was possible. Tim O'Brien quotes from the Nuremberg Principles in one of the evidence chapters of his novel In the Lake of the Woods when he writes, "The fact that a person acted pursuant to order of his Government or of a superior does not relieve him from responsibility under international law" (98). These principles are directly relevant to the MY LAI MASSACRE, an atrocity in which American troops murdered nearly 500 unarmed Vietnamese villagers. The defense used by LIEUTENANT WILLIAM CALLEY and other soldiers was that they were following the orders of their superior officers.

Nürnberg, Germany Nürnberg (more commonly spelled Nuremberg in English) is a German town that the men of Third Squad drive through in a Volkswagen van on their way from ZAGREB, CROATIA, to PARIS. In Paul Berlin's imagined pursuit story, the American soldiers pass through Nürnberg at midnight, just before the van, stolen from an American college drop-out, breaks down.

NVA NVA is an acronym for the North Vietnamese Army, the official military of Communist North Vietnam. The term NVA was used during the war years to distinguish Communist soldiers in the North from Communist guerrilla fighters in the South, called the VIET CONG. Tim O'Brien's soldier characters generally engage with Viet Cong soldiers rather than soldiers from the NVA.

O'Brien, Ann Weller Ann Weller O'Brien was Tim O'Brien's first wife. The couple was married in 1973, when Ann Weller was working as an editorial assistant at Little, Brown Publishing Company. Their divorce was finalized in 1995, after they had been separated for many years.

O'Brien, Ava Tim O'Brien's mother, Ava Schultz O'Brien, was a former Navy WAVE (see

WAVES) and elementary school teacher. Originally from Minnesota, she moved back to her home state after meeting and marrying Bill O'Brien while both were in the service and stationed in Norfolk, Virginia.

O'Brien, Greg Greg O'Brien is Tim O'Brien's younger brother. As a boy growing up in WORTHINGTON, MINNESOTA, Greg was an excellent baseball player and golfer. He is mentioned briefly in If I Die in a Combat Zone when O'Brien speculates about the purpose of his book. "It would be fine," he writes, if his book were a plea for peace, if it were written "to persuade [his] younger brother and perhaps some others to say no to wrong wars" (23). But O'Brien must admit that his book does not really serve this purpose.

O'Brien, Meredith Baker Meredith Baker O'Brien is Tim O'Brien's second wife. An actress and drama teacher whom O'Brien met in the mid-1990s, Meredith lives with her husband in AUSTIN, TEXAS, and is the mother of the couples' two children, TIMMY and TAD O'BRIEN.

O'Brien, Tad Tad O'Brien is the younger son of Tim O'Brien and his second wife, MEREDITH BAKER O'BRIEN, born when the writer was nearly sixty years old. He is two years younger than his brother TIMMY.

O'Brien, Timmy The oldest son of Tim O'Brien and his second wife, MEREDITH BAKER O'BRIEN, Timmy O'Brien was born on June 20, 2003. In the fall of 2004, O'Brien published a moving piece in Life magazine called "A Letter to My Son," which briefly explores his experience of late-in-life fatherhood.

O'Brien, William T. (Bill) Tim O'Brien's father, William T. O'Brien, was born in Brooklyn, New York, served in the U.S. Navy during WORLD WAR II, and worked as an insurance salesman in Minnesota while O'Brien was growing up. A charming alcoholic who left the family for several stays in rehabilitation hospitals during the early 1960s, Bill O'Brien had an extremely close but troubled relationship with his oldest son. The young O'Brien loved his father deeply, played golf and baseball with him, but also felt that he could not please the older man, who tended, when drunk, to tease his son mercilessly. Difficult father/son relationships would later become a theme in several of O'Brien's works: *Northern Lights*, in which Paul Perry is raised by a stern, demanding Lutheran minister who appears to favor his younger brother, Harvey, over him; *In the Lake of the Woods*, in which John Wade's alcoholic father hangs himself in the family garage when John is only 14 years old; and *Tomcat in Love*, in which Thomas H. Chippering's father fails to honor his promise to procure an airplane engine for his young son, providing him with a turtle instead, thus leading to Chippering's lifelong preoccupation with the disappointments inherent in language.

OCS OCS is a military acronym for Officer Candidate School. In his memoir, *If I Die in a Combat Zone*, O'Brien recalls riding the bus from his advanced infantry training (*see* AIT) at FORT LEWIS, WASHINGTON, into SEATTLE on a weekend pass. On the bus ride, he sits next to a lieutenant who had also been drafted (*see* DRAFT) but who signed up for Officer Candidate School in order to delay being sent to Vietnam.

Oliver, Gene Gene Oliver was one of the U.S. soldiers present during the MY LAI MASSACRE. In one of the evidence chapters in the novel *In the Lake of the Woods*, Oliver is quoted as testifying at LIEUTENANT WILLIAM CALLEY's court-martial that most of the Vietnamese he had seen in the village of My Lai were dead and that bodies were "all over" (139).

Olson, Gregory T. Gregory T. Olson was one of the U.S. soldiers present during the MY LAI MASSACRE. His testimony to the PEERS COMMISSION is quoted in O'Brien's novel *In the Lake of the Woods*. Olson tells investigators that "the attitude of all the men, the majority, I would say, was a revengeful attitude" (256).

Olson, Johnny Johnny Olson was a U.S. television announcer, famous especially for introducing contestants on *The Price Is Right*. He appears briefly in the novel *The Nuclear Age* when William Cowling on his birthday in 1969 turns on the television in KEY WEST, FLORIDA, where he lives with his radical friends. He imagines that "Johnny Olsen's [sic] deep baritone" calls, "William—*come* on down!" (216). William further imagines that he is offered, behind three closed doors, three different futures: going to Rio de Janeiro with Sarah Strouch, a trip to the Moon, and, behind door number three, marrying a blond stewardess. At this point in his life, William is confused and unsure what his future holds.

OP OP is a military acronym for Observation Post. Paul Berlin in the novel *Going After Cacciato* spends all night in late November 1968 standing watch on an observation post above the SOUTH CHINA SEA. O'Brien uses the acronym when he describes Berlin thinking, at 3:00 in the morning: "This was the dangerous time. He'd heard stories of how OPs were attacked: always during the darkest hours, whole squads blown away, men found days later without heads or arms" (124).

Operation Rolling Thunder Operation Rolling Thunder was the name given to a U.S. bombing campaign against North Vietnam that began in March 1965 and lasted until November 1968. William Cowling in the novel *The Nuclear Age* reports that, by his junior year of college in October 1966, "Operation Rolling Thunder closed in on Hanoi. The dead were hopelessly dead" (73).

Operation Russell Beach In his memoir, *If I Die in a Combat Zone*, Tim O'Brien reports that ALPHA COMPANY had taken part in a massive operation known as Russell Beach in January 1969, about a month or so before he arrived in Vietnam. Operation Russell Beach was a joint venture of the army, marines, navy, and air force intended to root out VIET CONG opposition in the area of the BATANGAN PENINSULA known as PINKVILLE. O'Brien informs readers, however, that "despite publicity and War College strategy, the operation did not produce the anticipated results" (116).

Oppenheimer, J. Robert   The American theoretical physicist J. Robert Oppenheimer served as director of the Manhattan Project at LOS ALAMOS National Laboratory and is remembered as the father of the atomic bomb. As such, he is an important figure to William Cowling, the narrator of the novel *The Nuclear Age*, who is obsessed by the specter of nuclear annihilation. Oppenheimer is mentioned briefly in the novel when Sarah Strouch accuses William of giving up his old antiwar ideals after discovering uranium on a Montana mountainside. When Cowling protests that he is sweet, Sarah counters, "Nixon was sweet. Oppenheimer was sweeter. Einstein—sweetest old geezer who ever lived" (273).

Ord, General Edward O.   General Edward O. Ord was a Union Army officer during the Civil War who later fought in the Indian Wars. He is quoted in one of the evidence chapters in Tim O'Brien's *In the Lake of the Woods* as ordering the destruction of as many members of the Apache tribe as possible: "I have encouraged the troops to capture and root out the Apache by every means, and to hunt them as they would wild animals. This they have done with unrelenting vigor. Since my last report over two hundred have been killed" (260). In this particular evidence chapter, O'Brien cites previous massacres involving the U.S. military in an attempt to gain some understanding of what happened in the Vietnamese village of My Lai in 1968.

Oswald, Lee Harvey   Conspiracy theories and uncertainty continue to swirl around the figure of Lee Harvey Oswald, assassin of President JOHN F. KENNEDY. Whether Oswald acted on his own in killing the president, or whether he was merely a puppet in some larger conspiracy involving the Soviet Union, Cuba, or even the CIA remains open to conjecture in many peoples' minds, despite the conclusions of three different government investigations that Oswald was the sole assassin. The unnamed investigator/narrator of Tim O'Brien's novel *In the Lake of the Woods* refers to Lee Harvey Oswald in a long footnote in which he speculates about the nature of mystery itself. If it were proved definitively that Oswald acted alone, the narrator claims, "nothing more would beckon, nothing would tantalize" (266). Human beings love mystery and enigma, he argues, and that is the reason that he himself has remained so fascinated by the disappearance of John and Kathy Wade. There are no definite answers to the mystery of what happened in that cabin at the LAKE OF THE WOODS.

Ovissil, Afghanistan   Ovissil is a small town where the men of Third Squad in the novel *Going After Cacciato* stop briefly on their train ride through Afghanistan and into Iran in Paul Berlin's invented story of the pursuit of Cacciato. The mayor of the cold, isolated mountain town invites the men to spend the night in his warm stone house, and the mayor's wife serves them mutton stew and biscuits and cups of milk. Berlin imagines the mayor telling the American soldiers that he speaks only of history, not of the future, because "history is the stronger science" (179).

Owago, Minnesota   Owago, Minnesota, is the small town where Thomas H. Chippering and Herbie and Lorna Sue Zylstra grow up in the novel *Tomcat in Love*. Chippering returns to Owago after being fired from his teaching job at the UNIVERSITY OF MINNESOTA. He moves in with Mrs. Robert Kooshoff, the new owner of his boyhood home.

Owago Community Day Care Center   After Thomas H. Chippering is fired from his position as a linguistics professor at the UNIVERSITY OF MINNESOTA in the novel *Tomcat in Love*, he returns to his small hometown of OWAGO, MINNESOTA, where he briefly finds work teaching preschoolers at the Owago Community Day Care Center.

P-38   The P-38 was a can opener used by U.S. military personnel to open C RATIONS beginning in WORLD WAR II. In the novel *Going After Cacciato*, Paul Berlin sits near a ditch with Cacciato, who is eating a can of peaches after a soldier named Buff has been shot in the face. Buff, short for Water Buffalo, had been found on his knees, facedown in his helmet. As Berlin lies with his eyes closed, trying not to think about the recent death, he hears Cacciato next to him opening a can of boned chicken.

Berlin smells a briny odor and hears the click of the P-38. He thinks to himself that one cannot fake sadness, and he acknowledges that he actually feels relief it was Buff who was shot and not him.

Paladin   Paladin is the name of a gentleman gunfighter who lived in San Francisco in the television series *Have Gun—Will Travel*, which ran from 1957 through 1963. In the novel *Going After Cacciato*, the Indian hotel owner Jolly Chand comments that television is something that brings Americans of all classes and races together—they share the same heroes, she says, including MATT DILLON from *Gunsmoke* and Paladin. In *The Things They Carried*, Paladin is mentioned as well. When Mitchell Sanders cuts the thumb off a dead VIET CONG boy and hands it to Norman Bowker to carry as a souvenir, he says there is a moral to the scene: "It's like with that old TV show—Paladin. Have gun, will travel" (13). Critics of Vietnam War literature such as John Hellmann have argued that the Vietnam generation was raised on western frontier mythology that encouraged them to think of war in heroic terms, at least before actually experiencing it for themselves. References to the television and movie westerns American soldiers grew up watching are a commonplace in the literature.

Palegenisia   In one of the evidence chapters in the novel *In the Lake of the Woods*, O'Brien quotes from a book written by the magician DOUG HENNING about HARRY HOUDINI. Henning writes about a famous illusion called Palegenisia, in which a man is seemingly dismembered, then later appears intact. Henning claims that this trick illustrates the theme of death and resurrection, a motif that appeared in all of Houdini's illusions. The Palegenisia illusion is important to O'Brien's novel in a number of ways. First, John Wade can be said to have attempted just such an illusion when he rewrote his service history while in Vietnam. He kills off the former John Wade, who had participated in the MY LAI MASSACRE, and invents a new identity. Second, the novel's reference to this trick may be read as possible evidence that Kathy Wade is not dead at all—that she and John and planned their disappearances together and will later "resur-

rect" themselves under new identities, perhaps in VERONA, ITALY.

Pancho   Pancho is the sidekick of the Mexican outlaw the CISCO KID in a 1950s television series as well as a popular succession of western movies in the 1940s. In the original story version of "The Ghost Soldiers," published in *Esquire* magazine in March 1981, an injured soldier named Herbie clowns around with the medic Teddy Thatcher after Herbie gets shot the first time. As Herbie is loaded onto a medical chopper, Teddy says, "Adios amigo" in his fake Mexican accent. Herbie moans, "Oh, Cisco," and Teddy wraps his arms around the injured man, kisses his neck, and replies, "Oh, Pancho" (90). When the story was revised for inclusion in *The Things They Carried*, these characters were changed to the narrator Tim O'Brien and medic Rat Kiley. The "Oh, Cisco . . . Oh, Pancho" exchange was removed as well.

Paris   The city of Paris figures prominently in O'Brien's 1978 novel, *Going After Cacciato*. Paris is Cacciato's intended destination when he walks away from his unit in Vietnam, and Paul Berlin imagines the men of Third Squad actually following Cacciato all the way to the French city. Paris has several symbolic ramifications. First, as the "City of Light," Paris suggests to the men the heart of the civilized world, a center of culture and learning far away from the jungles of Vietnam. Paris becomes, as well, a symbol of peace—of the possibility for peace—through its connection to the end of several previous wars. It is the location where ERNEST HEMINGWAY and the writers of the Lost Generation went to heal after their involvement in World War I. It is the city that the Allies triumphantly liberated from German control in August 1944 during WORLD WAR II, the so-called good war. Paris is also the location where talks intended to negotiate a peaceful resolution to the Vietnam War were held between the United States, the government of South Vietnam, and the North Vietnamese, beginning in 1968. The PARIS PEACE ACCORDS, signed in 1973, ended direct U.S. military involvement in Vietnam. In chapter 44 of *Cacciato*, "The End of the Road to Paris," Paul

Berlin imagines himself and the Vietnamese refugee Sarkin Aung Wan at the MAJESTIC HOTEL in Paris, debating his return to the war as if they are diplomats debating the Peace Accords. Finally, Paris evokes as well a continuing preoccupation in American literature with the West as a place of spiritual and physical renewal, with the romance of the frontier. The soldiers in *Cacciato* head west to escape the war just as HUCK FINN "lit out" for the western territories to escape oppressive American institutions.

Paris Peace Accords   The Paris Peace Accords, signed in January 1973, brought an end to direct U.S. military involvement in Vietnam. The agreement brought to a close peace talks that had begun taking place secretly in PARIS as early as March 1968. The novel *Going After Cacciato* refers to these talks when O'Brien writes, "In Quang Ngai they did not speak of politics. It wasn't taboo or bad luck, it just wasn't talked about. Even when the Peace Talks bogged down in endless bickering over the shape and size of the bargaining table, the men in Alpha Company took it as another bad joke—silly and sad—and there was no serious discussion about it, no sustained outrage" (269). Later in the novel, Paul Berlin will imagine debating the Vietnamese refugee Sarkin Aung Wan in a scene that is meant to be reminiscent of the Paris peace talks. Each will appear as a diplomat at the MAJESTIC HOTEL in Paris, seated at a large round table. Sarkin will rise to speak first, giving reasons why Berlin should leave the war. Paul Berlin then supplies a rebuttal, arguing that he has a duty to stay and fight.

Parrish, Robert   Robert Parrish was a semiprofessional magician and mentalist who was the author of the best-selling 1944 guide *The Magician's Handbook*. An authority on magic who is quoted several times in the evidence chapters of O'Brien's novel *In the Lake of the Woods*, Parrish admonishes his readers never to reveal their secrets, arguing that the fascination of magic lies in a trick retaining its mystery: "It is a paradox, a riddle, a half-fulfillment of an ancient desire, a puzzle, a torment, a cheat and a truth" (96). Parrish's words here could

be said to describe the novel itself. O'Brien, as magician/author, retains the secret of his mystery novel, never revealing the so-called truth to readers. For O'Brien, the inability to get at truth might be a more accurate depiction of the real world than the tidy answers provided in conventional mystery novels.

Passau, Germany   In the novel *Going After Cacciato,* the men of Third Squad drive through the town of Passau, Germany, on their way to PARIS in Paul Berlin's imagined pursuit story of an AWOL American soldier. The American soldiers are driving in a battered Volkswagen van that they had stolen outside of ZAGREB, CROATIA, from an American college girl who dropped out of school to protest the Vietnam War.

Patton, George S.   George S. Patton was an outspoken general in WORLD WAR II who commanded U.S. troops during the Battle of the Bulge. In the novel *Going After Cacciato,* O'Brien writes in chapter 39, "The Things They Didn't Know," that Vietnam War soldiers did not have the experience of victory or a sense of necessary sacrifice. He continues, "No sense of order or momentum. No front, no rear, no trenches laid out in neat parallels. No Patton rushing for the Rhine, no beachheads to storm and win and hold for the duration" (270). As often happens in Vietnam War literature, O'Brien expresses here a longing for a war with more clear lines of battle, stronger support on the home front, and a clearer moral imperative.

Pearson's Texaco station   Pearson's Texaco station is the only gas station in the small town of ANGLE INLET in the novel *In the Lake of the Woods.* It is owned by the part-time deputy sheriff Vinnie Pearson, who suspects John Wade murdered his wife. County Sheriff Art Lux will set up a makeshift headquarters for the search team in the work bay at Pearson's Texaco station after Kathy Wade disappears.

Peers Commission Report   In November 1969 General William Peers was ordered to conduct a thorough investigation into the MY LAI MASSACRE and the cover-up that followed. The Peers Commission Report, which was highly critical of the behavior of officers in the chain of command during the incident, was released in March 1970. O'Brien quotes frequently from the Peers Commission Report in the evidence chapters of his novel *In the Lake of the Woods*. The report is also said to be one of the books appearing in "Exhibit Eight: John Wade's Box of Tricks, Partial List" (262).

Pendleton, Richard   Richard Pendleton was a rifleman in CHARLIE COMPANY during the MY LAI MASSACRE. He is quoted twice in the evidence chapters in O'Brien's novel *In the Lake of the Woods*, first as testifying at LIEUTENANT WILLIAM CALLEY's court-martial that he had seen "a large mound of dead Vietnamese" (139) in a ditch in the village, and later, that "People were talking about killing everything that moved" (256).

Peter the Hermit   Peter the Hermit was a 12th-century French priest who organized and led a pauper's crusade to the Holy Land. He is a figure referred to by the army chaplain who dismisses Tim O'Brien's moral concerns about the war in his memoir, *If I Die in a Combat Zone*. The chaplain tells the young O'Brien that faith is the answer to his ethical questions and despairs that young people do not read Peter the Hermit any longer.

Pevee Weekly   The *Pevee Weekly* is the college newspaper at PEVERSON STATE COLLEGE in the novel *The Nuclear Age*. William Cowling tells readers that he and Ollie Winkler recruited members for their radical organization, the COMMITTEE, by taking out an ad in the *Pevee Weekly* calling for volunteers.

Peverson State College   Peverson State is the college attended by William Cowling, Sarah Strouch, Ollie Winkler, Tina Roebuck, and Ned Rafferty in the novel *The Nuclear Age*. It is at Peverson State College that this group of young students first becomes radicalized and begins to protest the war in Vietnam.

PF   See RUFF-AND-PUFF.

PFC   PFC is a military acronym for Private First Class, a military rank for enlisted men that is just above Private and below Corporal or Specialist. In Tim O'Brien's novel *Going After Cacciato*, Paul Berlin is a PFC when he first joins the 1st Platoon of ALPHA COMPANY on June 11, 1968. Later in the novel, he will be promoted to the rank of Specialist 4.

Philbrick, Herb   Herb Philbrick was a real-life Boston advertising executive and FBI informant whose life became the basis for the 1950s television series, *I LED THREE LIVES*. In the novel *The Nuclear Age*, William Cowling's father reminisces about the show as he hands his son an envelope full of money to help him go underground and evade the DRAFT:

> "You know what this reminds me of" he said. "That TV show—*I Led Three Lives.* Herb Philbrick, remember? That trench coat of his. Always pulling up the collar and ducking into phone booths, sweating to beat holy hell. Remember that?" (144)

Phillips, Catherine Hale (Kate)   Kate Phillips was the HARVARD graduate school girlfriend of Tim O'Brien who accompanied him on his return visit to Vietnam in February 1994. O'Brien writes about the trip and about his devastating breakup with Kate in the piece "The Vietnam in Me," published in the *New York Times Magazine* in October 1994.

Phoenix Program   The Phoenix Program was a secret CIA operation in Vietnam during the years 1967 to 1972 designed to identify and neutralize key members of the VIET CONG insurgency. In O'Brien's novel *July, July*, Dorothy Stier's neighbor, the mysterious Fred Engelmann, a formal Marine colonel in Vietnam who somehow knows Dorothy's most intimate secrets, is said to have been "affiliated in some cryptic way with the Phoenix program, which as he sketchily described it, had to do with terminal solutions" (197).

Pinkville   Pinkville was American military slang used during the Vietnam War for a dangerous area that stretched along the northern coast of South

Vietnam. O'Brien in his memoir, *If I Die in a Combat Zone,* reports that the area got its name "from the fact that military maps color it a shimmering shade of elephant pink, signifying what the map legends call a 'built-up area'" (115–16). Pinkville was a notorious VIET CONG stronghold and the region in which the villages of My Lai were located, where an American massacre of Vietnamese villagers took place in March 1968. In his memoir, *If I Die in a Combat Zone,* O'Brien recalls that the men of ALPHA COMPANY were transported to Pinkville initially in January 1969, about a month before O'Brien actually reached Vietnam, to carry out a series of combat assaults (*see* CA) against the 48th VIETCONG BATTALION. Several men were injured or killed by stepping on mines, and O'Brien writes that "Alpha Company was boiling with hate when it was pulled out of Pinkville" (116). O'Brien himself sees action in Pinkville when the unit is ordered back to the area in May and again in July. Pinkville appears as well in much of O'Brien's fiction concerning the war. Third Squad in *Going After Cacciato* patrols the area of Pinkville in the summer of 1968, playing pickup basketball games after destroying the dusty villages along their route, and the men of Alpha Company in *The Things They Carried* also see action in the Pinkville area, particularly along the SONG TRA BONG River. Pinkville plays an important role in the novel *In the Lake of the Woods* as well. John Wade patrolled the location as a member of Charlie Company, the unit that committed the My Lai massacre.

Piraeus, Greece   Piraeus is a port city just outside of ATHENS in Greece. In the novel *Going After Cacciato,* Paul Berlin imagines that the men of Third Squad arrive at the passenger terminal in Piraeus after a three-day trip aboard a freighter from IZMIR, TURKEY. However, Berlin is unable to invent for the soldiers a smooth arrival at the cradle of Western civilization—in his imagined story, the port is overrun with police and customs officials. While Oscar Johnson and Doc Peret seem almost resigned that their journey has come to an end, Stink Harris becomes angry and fidgety. He eventually strips and jumps off the ship in an attempt to elude the officers. Stink disappears in the waves, not to be

seen again. Following Stink's disappearance, Paul Berlin imagines that the men simply walk through the crowds on the wharves with their eyes down, unbothered by the hordes of police and customs agents.

piss-tube   A piss-tube was military slang used during the Vietnam War to describe vertical tubes for urinating that were buried two-thirds of their length into the ground. When Paul Berlin in *Going After Cacciato* first arrives at the CHU LAI COMBAT CENTER in Vietnam, a staff sergeant tells him not to leave his HOOTCH "unless it's to use the piss-tube" (37). Bewildered, Paul Berlin merely nods in response, "fearful to ask what a piss-tube was" (37).

Place Dauphin   The Place Dauphin is a public square located on the ÎLE DE LA CITÉ, an island in the Seine River right in the center of PARIS. In the novel *Going After Cacciato,* Paul Berlin imagines himself and Sarkin Aung Wan enjoying the cool quiet of the Place Dauphin once the men of Third Squad actually arrive in the city. He imagines pigeons and old-fashioned lampposts and chestnut trees dotting the square, signs of civilized living unavailable to him in Vietnam.

Plato   Plato was a philosopher and writer of the Greek classical period. He was the student of SOCRATES and the teacher of ARISTOTLE. In his memoir, *If I Die in a Combat Zone,* O'Brien writes that when he realized he could not hit a baseball and was too small for football, he began to read seriously. Plato is one of the authors he mentions who meant a great deal to him. He opens chapter 22 of the memoir, "Courage is a Certain Kind of Preserving," with a lengthy quote from Plato's *The Republic.* In several of his fictional works, as well, O'Brien contemplates Plato's notion that courage consists of "wise endurance."

Pliney's Pond   Pliney's Pond is an algae-ridden body of water located in the forest not far from the Perry house in the novel *Northern Lights.* The pond plays an important role in Paul Perry's life. His father had taught him to swim in the pond, forcing Paul into the dirty water against his will. At various points in the novel, Paul goes to the pond to observe the decaying plant life and to think things over. The mayor of SAWMILL LANDING, Jud Harmor, believes that Paul is depressed and says that he expects to find the young man "floatin' face down" (91) in the pond one day. At the end of the novel, however, Paul walks into the pond in a near-Baptism ritual. Upon his emergence, he sees the beautiful northern lights and is able to recommit himself to his wife Grace and the life they share.

Poe, Edgar Allan   In the novel *The Nuclear Age*, William Cowling tells a therapist named Charles Adamson that he feels worthless. Cowling explains to the doctor that "a disturbed guy" like Edgar Allan Poe, the famous 19th-century American writer, was able to benefit from his strangeness: "All those weird visions running through his head, fruitcake stuff. But I'll tell you something, he didn't go crying to some stupid counselor. He *used* his nuttiness. He *made* something out of it" (45). Later, in a chapter set in the present time—1995—Cowling imagines that the hole in his yard orders him to dig deeper. He again refers to Poe when he makes light of and attempts to justify his own mental instability: "Obsession? Edgar Allan Poe was obsessed" (62).

Pont du Carrousel   The Pont du Carrousel is a bridge in PARIS that crosses the Seine River in front of the Louvre. In the novel *Going After Cacciato*, Paul Berlin imagines walking with Sarkin Aung Wan along the Seine, then pausing on the Pont du Carrousel to watch the canal boats before crossing over to the Right Bank for a long lunch.

Pound, Ezra   An American expatriate poet who lived in PARIS during the 1920s, Ezra Pound was well known for encouraging and supporting younger writers, including ERNEST HEMINGWAY, T. S. Eliot, and ROBERT FROST. Although he became a fascist during WORLD WAR II, supporting Benito Mussolini in Italy and later was harshly imprisoned in a U.S. Army detention camp, he nevertheless had a profound influence on American and British literature of the 20th century. Tim O'Brien in his memoir, *If I Die in a Combat Zone*, writes about

how his friend from basic training, ERIK HANSEN, admired and respected the work of Ezra Pound, whom he believed had written "the truest of poems" (37). O'Brien tells readers that Erik recited a portion of Pound's famous poem "Hugh Selwyn Mauberly," with its lines claiming that soldiers during World War I were "quick to arm," at least partially from "fear of censure" (*If I Die* 37). Hansen then argues that Pound is right—that soldiers like himself are afraid of appearing weak, of not being seen as brave, or as real men. This is an idea that O'Brien will explore throughout his fiction—the notion that men go to war, fight and die, because they are ashamed not to.

POW   POW is an acronym for prisoner of war. When the men of Third Squad encounter the VIET CONG major Li Van Hgoc in the underground tunnel system in *Going After Cacciato*, the gracious major is forced to inform the Americans that they cannot leave because, as he puts it, "according to the rules, I fear you gentlemen are now my prisoners. You see the problem? Prisoners of war" (92). Lieutenant Corson sighs and replies, "Now I'm beginning to see the stopper. I think I see it. POWs, you say?" (92). When the little major refuses to bend the rules, the American soldiers overpower him and tie him up. But they soon learn that Li Van Hgoc does not know the way out of the tunnel system any more than they do—he is a prisoner of the maze as well.

Prague, Czechoslovakia   Following his junior year at MACALESTER COLLEGE, Tim O'Brien spent the summer of 1967 studying in Prague, Czechoslovakia, as part of the Student Project for Amity among Nations (SPAN) program. O'Brien reminisces about his summer in Prague in his memoir, *If I Die in a Combat Zone*, where he writes about meeting a young Czech student who introduces O'Brien to his North Vietnamese roommate in the program. One evening O'Brien has a three-hour chat with the man, named Li, about the morality of the war in Vietnam. When O'Brien asks Li if the North Vietnamese were sending troops to the South in order to establish a Communist regime, the student tells O'Brien that it is "historically and politically incorrect" (95) to speak of a divided Vietnam. When he asks whether Li believes that President JOHNSON is an evil man like Hitler, Li replies that, while most Vietnamese would not be so lenient, he himself feels that Johnson is mostly misguided and wrong. At the end of the talk, Li shakes hands with O'Brien and informs him that he is a lieutenant in the North Vietnamese Army.

PRC-77   The PRC-77 is a portable radio transceiver used in combat. In *The Things They Carried*, O'Brien lists the transceiver as one of the items that American soldiers carried in the field with them during the Vietnam War: "Taking turns, they carried the big PRC-77 scrambler radio, which weighed 30 pounds with its battery" (14).

Psara, Greece   Psara is the Greek island in the Aegean Sea where Paul Berlin imagines the men of Third Squad docking for the first night during their shipboard journey from IZMIR, TURKEY, to ATHENS, GREECE, in the novel *Going After Cacciato*.

Psy-Ops   Psy-Ops is military shorthand for Psychological Operations, techniques used to influence the emotions, attitudes, and behavior of enemies during warfare. The term appears twice in the novel *Going After Cacciato*, first when Paul Berlin imagines the men of Third Squad questioning the former VIET CONG major Li Van Hgoc in the underground tunnels. One of the questions Berlin would like to ask the major involves "the time of silence along the Song Tra Bong" (85). Berlin wonders if this was really a Psy-Ops operation conducted by the VIET CONG. Later, in chapter 16, "Pickup Games"—a war memory chapter—the men of the 1st Platoon, ALPHA COMPANY, are rained out of their afternoon basketball games on July 13, 1968. A soldier named Buff smells something odd, and the men become increasingly nervous and irritable as they wait out the rain. When Doc Peret mumbles, "Psy-Ops . . . That's what it is, the gook version of Psy-Ops. Slope Psych" (103), Oscar Johnson tells him to be quiet.

PT   PT is a military acronym for Physical Training. In the novel *Going After Cacciato*, Paul Berlin

on his observation tower at approximately 2:15 A.M. bends down and does "PT by the numbers, counting softly, loosening up his arms and neck and legs" (80). He then walks twice around the tower's small platform before lighting a cigarette and returning to his invented story of pursuing Cacciato.

punji pits   Punji pits were an inexpensive, homemade weapon used by the VIET CONG during the Vietnam War. They consisted of deep holes dug along trails and paths frequented by the American military. The pits were lined with sharpened wooden sticks, the tips of which were often smeared with human feces to heighten the risk of infection. The holes were then camouflaged by grass or bushes so that they would remain hidden. Tim O'Brien in the chapter "Nights" from his 1973 memoir, *If I Die in a Combat Zone*, discusses walking carefully through the rice paddies at night, looking out for mines, snipers, ambushes, and punji pits.

Pusan   Pusan, the second-largest city in South Korea, was the site of a well-known battle during the KOREAN WAR in which a United Nations coalition of troops defended a perimeter in Southeast Korea against the North Korean Army. In the short story "Going After Cacciato," Lieutenant Corson moans that he is a sick man and that "it wasn't this way on Pusan, I'll tell you that" (52). The lieutenant is a Korean War veteran who feels out of place in Vietnam. The reference to Pusan was removed when the story was revised as part of the novel *Going After Cacciato*.

PX   PX is a military acronym for Post Exchange, a type of retail store found on U.S. Army bases. When Paul Berlin in the novel *Going After Cacciato* first arrives at the CHU LAI COMBAT CENTER in Vietnam, he is stunned by the size and complexity of the base, which contains, in addition to the military units it houses, two hospitals, a legal services center, a PX, a stockade, a USO, a mini golf course, and a swimming beach, among many other support services for the military personnel assigned there.

Pyle, Ernie   A Pulitzer Prize–winning war correspondent who was killed in combat during WORLD WAR II, Ernie Pyle was one of the war writers Tim O'Brien grew up admiring. In his memoir, *If I Die in a Combat Zone*, O'Brien writes that he wonders how "writers such as Hemingway and Pyle could write so accurately and movingly about war without also writing about the rightness of their wars" (93).

Pynchon, Thomas   Thomas Pynchon is a well-known contemporary American writer famous for his postmodern style and long, difficult, but funny novels. O'Brien quotes from Pynchon's novel *The Crying of Lot 49* in one of the evidence sections in the novel *In the Lake of the Woods*. The passage is about a princess locked in a tower who must realize that what keeps her there is "magic, anonymous and malignant, visited on her from outside and for no reason at all" (26). Pynchon is alluded to as well in the novel *July, July* when Marv Bertel, the owner of a mop and broom factory, pretends to be the reclusive writer Thomas Pierce in order to impress his attractive young assistant. Pierce is probably modeled on the real-life writer Thomas Pynchon, also a famous recluse.

Quang Ngai Province   Quang Ngai Province is located in the central coastal region of Vietnam, along the shores of the SOUTH CHINA SEA. Known as a VIET CONG stronghold during the war, it is the area where Tim O'Brien was posted during his year-long tour of duty in Vietnam. It is also the area where the MY LAI MASSACRE occurred, in March 1968, about a year before O'Brien served in the region. Speaking of Quang Ngai in his memoir, O'Brien recalls how the landscape itself seemed mysterious and threatening to him: "[T]he land seemed to fold into itself. There were creases in the dusk: reflections, mysteries, ghosts. The land moved. Hedges and boulders and chunks of earth—they *moved*. Things shimmied and fluttered" (28). Quang Ngai serves as the setting as well for a number of Tim O'Brien's fictional works. It is the area where Paul Berlin and the members of Third Squad are stationed in the novel *Going After Cacciato* and also the location of ALPHA COMPANY

in *The Things They Carried*. John Wade from *In the Lake of the Woods* served in Quang Ngai Province and participated in the My Lai Massacre. In addition, Thomas Chippering from *Tomcat in Love* and David Todd from *July, July* are both Vietnam War veterans who served in the Quang Ngai area.

Rainy River   The Rainy River stretches for 85 miles along the U.S.-Canadian border, separating northern Minnesota from Ontario. The river takes on mythological status in O'Brien's story "On the Rainy River" from *The Things They Carried*. Torn about being drafted (*see* DRAFT) into the war, the young O'Brien flees to a small, nearly deserted fishing resort along the river to consider his options. When the lodge's owner, Elroy Berdahl, takes him within a few feet of the Canadian side of the river in his fishing boat, O'Brien cannot bring himself to cross to the other side. He imagines that he sees a large group of people on the far bank of the river waving at him and cheering. They include members of his family, people he knows from his small hometown of WORTHINGTON, MINNESOTA, famous political figures, and even characters from literature he has read. The weight of all these people pushing him toward war is more than O'Brien can bear, and he eventually allows himself to be shipped to Vietnam. Because the Rainy River in the story represents the dividing line between two very different lives, it is analogous to the River Styx in Greek mythology, which served as the boundary line between Earth and the Underworld. Elroy Berdahl is like Charon, the mythical ferryman who rows souls across to the other side.

Reagan, Ronald   Ronald Reagan, 40th president of the United States, was serving as governor of California in the late 1960s while the most heated of the anti–Vietnam War protests took place across the country. Reagan is mentioned in the novel *The Nuclear Age* when William Cowling writes about the MORATORIUM TO END THE WAR IN VIETNAM, an enormous, nationwide demonstration that took place on October 15, 1969: "In Sacramento, Ronald Reagan talked about the perfidious nature of the day's events, which gave 'comfort and aid to the enemy'" (224).

Reed, John   John Reed was an early 20th-century journalist and activist best remembered for his account of the 1917 Russian revolution, *Ten Days That Shook the World*. Reed is mentioned briefly in O'Brien's novel *The Nuclear Age* when William Cowling speculates about human psychology: "I'd learned to distrust the easy explanations of human behavior; it's all too ambiguous; the inner forces ricochet like pinballs. John Reed: a Harvard cheerleader. How do you draw conclusions?" (106).

Regensburg, Germany   Regensburg is a German city that the men of Third Squad drive through on their way from ZAGREB, CROATIA, to PARIS in the novel *Going After Cacciato*. Paul Berlin imagines that the men have stolen a Volkswagen van from an American college drop-out, a girl who assumed the soldiers were deserters from the war.

"Relativity"   "Relativity" is a poem written by William Cowling's wife, Bobbi, in the novel *The Nuclear Age*. It reads:

Relations are strained
in the nuclear family.
It is upon us, the hour
of evacuation,
the splitting of blood
infinitives.
The clock says fission
fusion
critical mass.

The term *critical mass* in the poem is from physics and refers to the smallest amount of nuclear material needed to set off an explosion. Bobbi here makes the point that the Cowlings' marriage has reached critical mass and is on the verge of falling apart.

REMF   REMF is military slang used by American soldiers during the Vietnam War. The acronym stands for "rear echelon mother fucker" and was often used as a derogatory term to describe soldiers assigned to less dangerous positions away from the front lines. REMF is part of the lingo that Tim O'Brien describes having to learn during his first month in Vietnam in his memoir, *If I Die in a Combat Zone*.

Resor, Stanley   Stanley Resor, winner of both the SILVER STAR and BRONZE STAR for his service during WORLD WAR II, was appointed secretary of the army by President LYNDON JOHNSON in 1965. Paul Berlin, during his promotion interview in the novel *Going After Cacciato*, correctly names Resor as the secretary of the army.

re-up   Re-up is military shorthand for reenlisting in military service. When Paul Berlin in the novel *Going After Cacciato* first arrives at the CHU LAI COMBAT CENTER in Vietnam, a "bored master sergeant deliver[s] a re-up speech" to him (36), right after a Vietnamese barber cuts his hair.

RF   See RUFF-AND-PUFF.

Rhine River   The Rhine, originating in Switzerland and flowing through Germany, France, LUXEMBOURG, and into the Netherlands, is one of the longest rivers in Europe. In the novel *Going After Cacciato*, Paul Berlin imagines the men of Third Squad crossing the Rhine at dawn on a train that takes them through the German heartland and ever closer to PARIS. This stage of Berlin's imagined pursuit of Cacciato is easy, as he pictures the men traveling through more familiar countryside.

Rickover, Admiral Hyman George   Hyman George Rickover was a long-serving admiral in the U.S. Navy who is credited with development of the nuclear submarine. He appears briefly in O'Brien's novel *The Nuclear Age* when William Cowling speculates about what has happened to the heroes and villains he grew up with in the 1950s and '60s. "As if to beat the clock," he writes, "the fathers of our age have all passed away—Rickover was buried at sea, von Braun went quietly in his sleep" (127).

Ro Son Shei   Ro Son Shei is a small Vietnamese village in the novel *Going After Cacciato* where the men of Third Squad beat Second Squad in a pickup basketball game by a score of 83 to 50. A few Vietnamese women and children watch the game from the sidelines.

The Road to Hong Kong *The Road to Hong Kong* was a 1962 film starring Bob Hope and Bing Crosby. It was the last in the "Road" series of comic films with Hope and Crosby and Dorothy Lamour that had started in 1940 with *The Road to Singapore*. *The Road to Hong Kong* is mentioned in *Going After Cacciato* when the men of Third Squad are about to pass through CHITTAGONG, BANGLADESH, on the DELHI EXPRESS. Lieutenant Corson says he has never been to Chittagong, then asks Berlin if he has seen *The Road to Hong Kong*, asserting, "Lordy, they made movies then. Real movies," but adding, "Who the hell'd ever pay to see *Road to Chittagong?*" (135). This scene reinforces the idea that Vietnam is not the lieutenant's war, that he is too old and sick to understand the new way of fighting in Vietnam, a lament he makes frequently in the novel.

Robinson, Edward Arlington E. A. Robinson was an American poet who won the Pulitzer Prize three times during the 1920s. He is one of the poets admired by ERIK HANSEN, Tim O'Brien's friend at basic training in FORT LEWIS, WASHINGTON, whom he writes about in his memoir, *If I Die in a Combat Zone*. Erik considered Robinson second in rank only to the American modernist poets ROBERT FROST and MARIANNE MOORE.

Roschevitz, Gary Gary Roschevitz was a U.S. soldier and member of CHARLIE COMPANY who participated in the MY LAI MASSACRE. According to testimony from another soldier, LEONARD GONZALEZ, given during LIEUTENANT WILLIAM CALLEY's court-martial, Roschevitz fired an M-79 grenade launcher into a crowd of naked and unarmed Vietnamese woman, killing all of them. This piece of testimony is cited in one of the evidence chapters in O'Brien's novel *In the Lake of the Woods*.

Rocket Pocket In the story "The Dentist" from *The Things They Carried*, the Tim O'Brien narrator reports that the men of ALPHA COMPANY in February 1969 were "working in an area of operations called the Rocket Pocket, which got its name from the fact that the enemy sometimes used the place to launch rocket attacks on the airfield at Chu

Lai" (87). Other Vietnam War reference materials describe the Rocket Pocket as covering an area five miles southwest of CHU LAI.

Rodin Museum In the novel *Going After Cacciato*, Paul Berlin imagines behaving like a tourist when he and the men of Third Squad first arrive in PARIS. One of the city landmarks he imagines visiting with Sarkin Aung Wan is the Rodin Museum, which displays the works of the French sculptor Auguste Rodin.

Rogers, Roy Roy Rogers was a singer and actor who starred in more than 100 western movies as well as a long-running 1950s television show. He is mentioned briefly in the original *Esquire* magazine version of O'Brien's story "The Ghost Soldiers." The young narrator, Herbie, asserts that being on ambush at night is an unreal experience, like being in a movie: "There's a camera on you, so you begin acting, following the script . . . You think of all the films you've seen, Audie Murphy and Gary Cooper and Van Johnson and Roy Rogers, all of them . . ." (96). When the story was revised for inclusion in the collection *The Things They Carried*, the references to Van Johnson and Roy Rogers were removed.

Ross, Martin In his memoir, *If I Die in a Combat Zone*, O'Brien describes Martin Ross as a "gung-ho marine who wrote with . . . fervor about his Korean War days, about his preference for the front lines over the rear areas" (180). O'Brien, safely stationed in a rear desk job at this point, understands Martin's distaste for the monotony of the rear, but still considers it "a major triumph of heroism to give up monotony for its horrible opposite" (180).

RTO RTO is a military acronym for Radio Telephone Operator, a soldier responsible for carrying a unit's radio in the field. In his memoir, *If I Die in a Combat Zone*, Tim O'Brien recalls being an RTO during his first months at the war and carrying the radio for Captain Johansen, an officer he admired greatly. Mitchell Sanders is identified as his unit's RTO in the novel *The Things They Carried*.

Rubin, Jerry Jerry Rubin was a radical activist in the 1960s who led Vietnam War protests and who cofounded, along with ABBIE HOFFMAN, the Youth International Party or Yippies. Rubin was arrested for disturbing the Democratic National Convention in Chicago in 1968. In the opening chapter of the novel *The Nuclear Age*, William Cowling tells readers that he, too, was a 1960s radical: "I was a mover in the deep underground," he writes. "I could've been another Rubin or Hoffman; I could've been a superstar" (8). Later in the novel, when Cowling recounts logging thousands of miles on airplanes working as a courier for a radical antiwar group, he recalls that 1969 was the year that Rubin and others "were raising hell in public places" (210).

Ruff-and-Puff Ruff-and-Puff was derogatory U.S. military slang for RF/PF, an acronym that stood for regional and popular forces—South Vietnamese military units that protected home villages and district areas. American soldiers in Vietnam did not have much respect for their South Vietnamese allies. O'Brien makes this point clear in the story "Sweetheart of the Song Tra Bong" when Rat Kiley explains that the security for his former medical unit outside of CHU LAI was provided by "a mixed unit of RFs, PFs, and ARVN infantry. Which is to say virtually no security at all. As soldiers, the ARVNs were useless; the Ruff-and-Puffs were outright dangerous" (91).

Rusk, Dean Dean Rusk was the U.S. secretary of state from 1961 to 1969. In the novel *The Nuclear Age*, William Cowling, a keen observer of political events, writes that in October 1966 Dean Rusk assured the country "that rectitude would soon prevail, a matter of attrition" (73). Yet, Cowling also notes that the dead in Vietnam remained dead, and that for them, "there was no rectitude" (73). By November 1967, Cowling writes that "Dean Rusk was having bad dreams" (112) since the American troop presence in Vietnam had approached 500,000.

Sagua la Grande, Cuba Sagua la Grande is a small city located on the northern coast of Cuba.

In the novel *The Nuclear Age*, William Cowling and his radical college friends undergo paramilitary training at a beachside compound located a few miles west of Sagua la Grande.

Saigon, Vietnam Saigon is the largest city in Vietnam and was the capital of the South during the Vietnam War years. After the Communist takeover in 1975, Saigon was renamed HO CHI MINH City. In the novel *The Nuclear Age*, William Cowling refers to Saigon when he relates the political happenings of 1964. He writes, "in Saigon the generals played their flamboyant games of hopscotch" (66), referring to the military maneuvering that marked the start of the war.

Saint George One of the people that the young Tim O'Brien imagines waving to him and cheering from the riverbank in the story "On the Rainy River" from *The Things They Carried* is St. George, a Roman Catholic saint and Christian martyr who was said to have slain a dragon in the most famous legend about him.

Salihli, Turkey Salihli is a large town in Turkey near the Aegean Sea. In the novel *Going After Cacciato*, Paul Berlin imagines that the men of Third Squad stop for gas and breakfast in Salihli as they make their way across Turkey to the port city of IZMIR.

Salle des Fêtes The Salle des Fêtes is the old conference room in the MAJESTIC HOTEL in PARIS where Paul Berlin imagines debating Sarkin Aung Wan about whether or not he should flee the war in the novel *Going After Cacciato*.

San Diego State University In the novel *Going After Cacciato*, Paul Berlin imagines that the men of Third Squad catch a ride north of ZAGREB, CROATIA, and through the Austrian frontier with a girl from California, a drop-out from San Diego State University who drives a battered old Volkswagen bus. The girl assumes the soldiers are deserters and tells them that she understands their dilemma since she's a drop-out herself, unable to hack "all the bullshit" (275) at San Diego State University after spending two years there. Oscar Johnson stares at the girl after this comment and asks, "You say it's same-same? Nam and fucking San Diego State?" (275). The men end up ordering the girl out along the shoulder of the highway and driving off in her van.

Sand Creek Massacre   The Sand Creek Massacre refers to an incident in which the Colorado Territory militia of the U.S. Army attacked a village of Cheyenne and Arapahoe Indians in present-day Oklahoma in 1864, killing dozens of men, women, and children and badly mutilating the bodies. O'Brien references this earlier massacre in one of the evidence chapters of his novel *In the Lake of the Woods*, to show readers that atrocities similar to those at My Lai have occurred in the past.

Sand, George   George Sand was the pen name of the 19th-century French author Aurore-Lucile Dupin. She is quoted in one of the evidence chapters in O'Brien's novel *In the Lake of the Woods* as saying that "Vice never sees its own ugliness—if it did, it would be frightened by its own image" (256). This quote is relevant to the novel in that the men from CHARLIE COMPANY who participated in the MY LAI MASSACRE did not see themselves as bad or evil men, even though they committed unspeakable atrocities on March 16, 1968.

sappers   In the context of the Vietnam War, sappers were members of the North Vietnamese Army or of the VIET CONG who were trained in the use of explosive devices. They often performed sabotage missions on U.S. firebases by slipping through barbed wire to detonate explosives. In the novel *Going After Cacciato*, the men of Third Squad are imagined by Paul Berlin to crawl like sappers, on their hands and knees and on their bellies, as they make their way out of the underground tunnel complex. Later in the novel, when speaking with Captain Fahyi Rhallon in TEHRAN, Stink Harris will tell a story about two VIET CONG defectors who demonstrated how sappers operate, by greasing up their bodies so they can slip under wires.

Sassoon, Siegfried   Siegfried Sassoon was a British poet and fiction writer who served in World War I and whose work often offered scathing indictments of the war. He was also the author of a three-volume fictionalized autobiography that was influential on the work of Americans such as Philip Caputo who wrote memoirs about their experiences in the Vietnam War. Tim O'Brien's 1978 novel *Going After Cacciato* begins with an epigraph from Sassoon: "Soldiers are dreamers." This line comes from the poem "Dreamers," in which Sassoon depicts soldiers in horrendous circumstances longing for the simple pleasures they left behind at home:

> Soldiers are citizens of death's gray land,
>   Drawing no dividend from time's to-morrows.
> In the great hour of destiny they stand,
>   Each with his feuds, and jealousies, and sorrows.
> Soldiers are sworn to action; they must win
>   Some flaming, fatal climax with their lives.
> Soldiers are dreamers; when the guns begin
>   They think of firelit homes, clean beds, and
>   wives.
>
> I see them in foul dug-outs, gnawed by rats,
>   And in the ruined trenches, lashed with rain,
> Dreaming of things they did with balls and bats,
>   And mocked by hopeless longing to regain
> Bank-holidays, and picture shows, and spats,
>   And going to the office in the train.

Paul Berlin in O'Brien's novel is a dreamer who spends a long night on guard duty in a watch tower above the SOUTH CHINA SEA, imagining that his platoon had followed a deserting soldier all the way to PARIS.

Savak   The Savak was the internal security and intelligence agency in Iran from 1957 to 1979. An institution feared and hated by the people of Iran because of its notorious use of torture, the Savak was closed down after the overthrow of the shah during the Iranian Revolution. In the novel *Going After Cacciato*, Paul Berlin imagines the men of Third Squad being captured and imprisoned by the Savak during their stay in TEHRAN. At first they are treated kindly by a captain named Fahyi Rhallon, a member of His Majesty's Royal Fusiliers who is on temporary duty with the Savak. But after being released and rearrested, they are threatened with execution by a much sterner Savak agent.

Sawmill Landing   Sawmill Landing is the fictional small northern Minnesota town where Paul Perry lives with his wife, Grace, in the 1975 novel *Northern Lights.* His father had been the minister of the DAMASCUS LUTHERAN CHURCH in town, and Paul works as an agent for the U.S. Department of Agriculture. The novel describes the early settlement of Sawmill Landing, pointing out that the first people to arrive in the area were the Sioux, then the Chippewa. French fur trappers came next, followed by Swedish farmers who tried to plant corn in a land meant for spruce trees. Finally, Germans, who opened taverns and shops, arrived in the town. Paul Perry's own grandfather immigrated to the United States from Finland when he was 16 years old. After a year in Baltimore, he traveled west to northern Minnesota, where he worked in lumber camps for five years before settling down in Sawmill Landing. At the time of the novel, in the late 1960s, Sawmill Landing is described as a dying town, with "rusting machinery, uncut weeds, unpainted buildings, unstopped forest" (72).

Schelling, Thomas   Thomas Schelling is an American economist and foreign affairs specialist who published influential books about the arms race. He is mentioned briefly in the original story version of "Quantum Jumps," first published in *Ploughshares* magazine in 1983. As he is digging the giant hole for a bomb shelter in his yard, William, the story's narrator, thinks about the "cold-blooded jargon" of Schelling and REAGAN and "those crew-cut grad students in applied physics" (31), and he wonders why everyone is not out digging with him. The reference to Schelling was omitted when O'Brien revised the story for inclusion in *The Nuclear Age.*

SDS   SDS is the acronym for Students for a Democratic Society, a leftist student political organization active during the 1960s. The group is mentioned briefly in the novel *The Nuclear Age,*

in which William Cowling and his college friends start their own radical antiwar group called the COMMITTEE. Speculating that former 1960s radicals might one day get together for a reunion at the Chicago Hilton, Cowling imagines "the SDS bunch dressed to kill in their pea coats and Shriner's hats" (131).

Seabees   The Construction Battalions of the U.S. Navy were called the Seabees because of their military acronym—CBs. In Vietnam the Seabees not only built military support facilities but also worked on schools, hospitals, roads, and other community-oriented projects. Paul Berlin in the novel *Going After Cacciato* notes that among the thousands of support personnel at the CHU LAI COMBAT CENTER, where he is initially stationed, is a detachment of Seabees. Later in the novel, Lieutenant Corson will tell a story about being busted in rank after spending the night drinking with a large Seabee named Jack Daniels in SEOUL, KOREA.

The Second Book of Esdras   The Second Book of Esdras is an apocryphal book found in many versions of the Christian Bible. Tim O'Brien uses a quote from it—chapter 16, verses 23–29, which predicts the end of the world—as the epigraph to his novel *The Nuclear Age.*

Seeger, Pete   The American folk singer Pete Seeger is mentioned briefly in O'Brien's short story "Quantum Jumps." As the story's narrator, William, digs a hole in his yard intended to be a bomb shelter, he begins to sing and to think about the past: "Many moons ago, when we were out to sanitize the world, I could carry a tune like nobody's business, I could do Baez and Dylan and Seeger, and it wasn't soupy, it was music to march to, it meant something" (38). However, the references to JOAN BAEZ, BOB DYLAN, and Seeger were removed when O'Brien revised the story to appear as part of his novel *The Nuclear Age.*

Seoul, Korea   Seoul, Korea, is the city where Lieutenant Corson in the novel *Going After Cacciato* gets drunk with a SEABEE named Jack Daniels during his stint in the KOREAN WAR. When the large man starts a brawl, both men get arrested. Corson is later reduced in rank.

SEATO SEATO, which stands for Southeast Asia Treaty Organization, refers to a group of nations that organized for collective national defense and to block the spread of Communism in 1954. The organization, modeled after NATO (North Atlantic Treaty Organization) lasted until 1977. Tim O'Brien mentions SEATO in several of his works. In *The Nuclear Age*, William Cowling, speculating about the morality of the Vietnam War, wonders about the organization, among other things related to the war: "Was Ho Chi Minh a nationalist or a Communist, or both, and to what degree, and what about the Geneva Accords, and what about SEATO, and what is worth killing for, if anything, and what is worth dying for, and who decides" (84). The young Tim O'Brien in the story "On the Rainy River" from *The Things They Carried* asks nearly identical questions as he debates whether to flee to Canada or honor his DRAFT notice: "What about the Geneva Accords? What about SEATO and the cold war? What about dominoes?" (40).

Seattle In his memoir, *If I Die in a Combat Zone*, Tim O'Brien recalls taking a bus into Seattle one weekend while he is undergoing advanced infantry training (*see* AIT) at FORT LEWIS, WASHINGTON. He has made plans to desert the military by fleeing to Canada. After finding a cheap hotel to spend the night in, O'Brien describes going to a sorority house at the University of Washington to ask for a date. The girls living there make excuses not to go out with him, however. Suffering from a bad headache that lasts most of the weekend, O'Brien ends up burning the letters of explanation he had written to his family and taking the bus back to the fort, unable to follow through on his desertion plans.

Sergeant York Sergeant Alvin York, the most-decorated American soldier of World War I, was the subject of a popular 1941 film titled *Sergeant York*, in which GARY COOPER played the lead role. In his 1973 memoir, *If I Die in a Combat Zone*, O'Brien mentions Sergeant York as one of the past

war heroes—including SOCRATES, JOHN F. KENNEDY, and AUDIE MURPHY—whose lives he contemplates while he undergoes basic training at FORT LEWIS, WASHINGTON.

Shan Plateau Paul Berlin in *Going After Cacciato* in his complicated, imagined story about the pursuit of the AWOL soldier imagines exploring the city of MANDALAY, Burma, with the refugee Sarkin Aung Wan. He muses that "violet evenings were the best time" in the city because "he liked watching night flow down from the Shan Plateau, the purply shades growing on one another" (119). The Shan Plateau is a real place in eastern Burma. It is a highland area where many precious stones are mined.

Shane A 1953 classic western movie starring Alan Ladd as a mysterious gunslinger who protects a homesteading family from a ruthless cattle rancher *Shane* helped shape the young Tim O'Brien's views of courage and heroism. In his memoir, *If I Die in a Combat Zone*, O'Brien writes that Alan Ladd's Shane was one of the heroes of his youth, a "hard and realistic" (143) character, like the other make-believe men O'Brien admired. He specifically remembers Shane as being "removed from other men . . . loving the boy, detesting violence, looking down and saying good-bye aboard that stocky horse" (143).

Sherman, General William Tecumseh William Tecumseh Sherman was a general in the Union Army during the Civil War who practiced a scorched earth policy during his march through Georgia. He later went west to serve as a U.S. commander in the Indian Wars. He is quoted in O'Brien's novel *In the Lake of the Woods* as saying that, "We must act with vindictive earnestness against the Sioux, even to their extermination, men, women, and children" (257). Sherman's attitude here is comparable to the beliefs of several of the U.S. soldiers involved in the MY LAI MASSACRE.

shining Shining is the name of a game that the Perry brothers and their friends play growing up in the remote northern Minnesota town of SAW-

MILL LANDING in O'Brien's 1975 novel, *Northern Lights*. The game is played by driving a car into the dark town junkyard at night, waiting for a certain period of time, then quickly turning on the car headlights in order to catch an animal—perhaps a rat or a starving moose or even a bear—foraging in the trash. One night Paul and his wife, Grace, along with Paul's brother, Harvey, and his girlfriend, Addie, play the game together and catch a rat, blinded in the car's headlights. The brothers exit the car, and Harvey urges Paul to smash the rat with a piece of board. Paul reluctantly raises the board over his head and brings it smashing down, but the rat escapes, running under an old mattress. This incident not only illustrates the rivalry between the Perry brothers but emphasizes Harvey's traditional masculine qualities as opposed to Paul's ambivalence about hunting, violence, and war.

short The term *short* was military slang used during the Vietnam War for a soldier who was a short-timer, one who had only a few months, weeks, or days left of his year-long tour of duty. In his memoir, *If I Die in a Combat Zone*, O'Brien writes that this is one of the mysterious terms he had to learn during his first few weeks assigned to ALPHA COMPANY. In the novel *Going After Cacciato*, Paul Berlin, sitting in a latrine and reading the graffiti on the wall during his first days at the war, takes out a pencil and carefully writes, "I'm so short, I can't see the forest for the trees" (42).

Silver Star The Silver Star is a military decoration awarded by the U.S. Armed Forces. It is the third-highest combat award for valor. In the novel *Going After Cacciato*, Paul Berlin, high in his watch tower above the SOUTH CHINA SEA, thinks about how he "almost won the Silver Star for valor" (81) by volunteering to retrieve a soldier named Frenchie Tucker who is shot while searching a Vietnamese tunnel. Berlin, though, is afraid, and a member of the platoon named Bernie Lynn goes down the tunnel instead. Bernie, like Frenchie, is killed in the tunnel, shot through the throat. Norman Bowker in the novel *The Things They Carried* fantasizes about winning the Silver Star as well. He

imagines telling his father the story of his friend Kiowa's death—how the man sank into the mud and filth of a water-logged field one dark night. Norman was unable to hold onto Kiowa's boot, and thus never won the medal for bravery. The award figures as well in the 1998 novel *Tomcat in Love*. Thomas H. Chippering writes a false commendation near the end of his service in Vietnam, awarding himself the Silver Star for valor.

Singh In In *Going After Cacciato*, Paul Berlin imagines himself and the men of Third Squad questioning Li Van Hgoc, the former major in the 48th VIETCONG BATTALION whom they meet in the complex underground tunnel system the men fall into while on their journey. One of the questions Berlin imagines asking the major is whether or not he witnessed the battle at Singh In in the mountains. Berlin seems to be referring here to the battle that the men march to in chapter 25 of the novel, "The Way It Mostly Was," when Lieutenant Sidney Martin muses about war as he watches the line of 38 soldiers and one native scout wind their way up into the mountains.

Sirhan Sirhan Sirhan Sirhan was the man convicted of assassinating ROBERT KENNEDY in 1968. He is mentioned several times in the novel *The Nuclear Age*, first when William Cowling is reporting on the political state of the country in October 1966, his junior year in college. He writes, "In Los Angeles, Sirhan Sirhan came into possession of a .22-caliber Iver Johnson revolver" (73), and he even imagines watching the transaction. He later writes that in November 1967, during his senior year in college, "Sirhan Sirhan was taking target practice" (112). When the assassination actually occurs, in June 1968, William reports:

> There was violence in Grant Park. There was Sirhan Sirhan, who shot Robert Kennedy, and there was Robert Kennedy, who died. I saw it in slow motion, as we all did, but I also imagined it, and still do, how it can happen and will happen, a twitch of the index finger, a madman, a zealot, an aberration in human history, Kennedy's wide-open eyes . . . (119)

William watches footage of the assassination on television like millions of Americans, but he becomes nearly obsessed with the death since it marks for him how suddenly and unexpectedly death can come, which is how he also imagines the world itself will end.

Slater Park Slater Park is one of the many parks along the shores of LAKE OKABENA in Tim O'Brien's hometown of WORTHINGTON, MINNESOTA. In his memoir O'Brien recalls driving around the lake and seeing kids playing in Slater Park. The carefree children serve as a contrast to O'Brien himself, who is scheduled to report for military duty the very next day. Norman Bowker in the story "Speaking of Courage" from *The Things They Carried* also drives past Slater Park as he circles the lake in his hometown; Bowker is a recently returned Vietnam War veteran adrift in the midst of the places where he used to belong.

slope American soldiers in Vietnam often used the racist term *slope* to refer to a person of Vietnamese origin. The term originated from the supposed "slant" of the eyes of Asian peoples. Tim O'Brien's characters frequently use this and other derogatory terms, such as DINK and GOOK to refer to the Vietnamese. In his 1973 memoir, *If I Die in a Combat Zone*, O'Brien writes that he quickly learned how the men of ALPHA COMPANY viewed the Vietnamese: "no one . . . gave a damn about the causes or purposes of their war: It is about 'dinks and slopes,' and the idea is simply to kill them or avoid them" (80).

Smith, Al In the novel *In the Lake of the Woods*, O'Brien quotes from a book about the politician Al Smith, who served as governor of New York for four terms, but was defeated for the U.S. presidency by Herbert Hoover. The authors of the book, MATTHEW AND HANNAH JOSEPHSON, write about how Al Smith was rankled for a long time by his election defeat because, "Like everyone else, he wanted to be loved" (101). This quote helps explain why John Wade in the novel reacts so strongly to his own election defeat—he, too, has a nearly insatiable desire to be loved.

Socrates Socrates was a Greek philosopher who examined ethical questions concerning virtue, courage, obligation, and other matters. Because none of Socrates' own writings exist today, he is known only through the work of his students, chief among them PLATO, who wrote accounts of philosophical dialogues that Socrates held with other Greek thinkers. Tim O'Brien, who read Plato's Socratic dialogues as a teenager growing up in WORTHINGTON, MINNESOTA, was influenced especially by the CRITO, in which Socrates refuses to escape from an Athenian prison where he is awaiting execution. In his memoir, *If I Die in a Combat Zone*, O'Brien recalls, as well, undergoing army basic training and imagining Socrates as a brave Athenian soldier marching alongside him. He wonders if Plato neglected to record Socrates' weeping over his eventual fate.

Song My In his 1973 memoir, *If I Die in a Combat Zone*, Tim O'Brien describes Song My as a village in Vietnam—the parent village of My Lai and MY KHE, the hamlets where the notorious 1968 American massacre of Vietnamese civilians took place, and the chief inhabited area in the vicinity known in GI slang as PINKVILLE.

Song Tra Bong The Song Tra Bong is a river located in the QUANG NGAI PROVINCE of Vietnam. The river plays an important role in several of O'Brien's Vietnam War novels. In *Going After Cacciato*, the men of Third Squad march through villages along the banks of the Song Tra Bong from early July through mid-August. Rudy Chassler, Frenchie Tucker, Bernie Lynn, and Jim Pederson all die during this period. The novel *The Things They Carried* includes a story called "Sweetheart of the Song Tra Bong," about a soldier who brings his high school girlfriend over to a small medical attachment on a hill west of CHU LAI that overlooks the Song Tra Bong. An American soldier named Kiowa in the novel dies in a mud-filled field alongside the Song Tra Bong, a spot that narrator Tim O'Brien will later visit with his young daughter, Kathleen. And in the story "Ghost Soldiers," the Tim O'Brien character is shot for a second time along the Song Tra Bong and nearly dies of shock because the scared, green medic Bobby Jorgenson takes so long to get him.

Song Tra Khuc The Song Tra Khuc is a river in the QUANG NGAI PROVINCE in Vietnam. It is mentioned briefly in O'Brien's novel *In the Lake of the Woods,* when CHARLIE COMPANY, John Wade's unit in the war, is said to head south toward the river the morning after the MY LAI MASSACRE.

Song Tra Ky In O'Brien's novel *July, July,* David Todd is severely wounded in both feet alongside the Song Tra Ky River when he is serving as a raw young first lieutenant during the Vietnam War. All of the other members of his platoon have been shot and killed, and David finds several bodies floating in the river when he eventually drags himself to the swift-moving stream and plunges his wounded feet into the cold water.

SOP SOP is a military acronym for Standard Operating Procedure. In the novel *Going After Cacciato,* O'Brien writes that the men of the 1st Platoon of ALPHA COMPANY were organized around two sorts of SOPs, formal and informal: "Formally, it was SOP to search tunnels before blowing them. Informally, it was SOP to blow the tunnels and move on, without a search, without risking life" (43–44). When Lieutenant Sidney Martin, a West Point-trained young officer, forces the men to follow the formal SOPs and search tunnels, the men hate him for it and eventually plan his fragging (*see* FRAG) death.

Sophocles Sophocles was a Greek playwright who lived in the fifth century B.C.E. and who is best known as the author of *Antigone* as well as a cycle of plays about the Greek legendary figure, King Oedipus. O'Brien quotes from Sophocles' play *Oedipus at Colonus* in one of the evidence chapters of his novel *In the Lake of the Woods:* "We couldn't see the man—he was gone—nowhere! . . . his departure was a marvel" (295). This line from the play could be read as a comment on John Wade, the protagonist of O'Brien's novel, who also disappears without a trace, his departure shrouded in mystery.

South China Sea The South China Sea is part of the Pacific Ocean and is located along the eastern coast of China and Vietnam. One of the largest bodies of water in the world, the South China Sea extends south to Singapore and north to the Strait of Taiwan. It figures in the work of Tim O'Brien because the CHU LAI COMBAT CENTER, where he was stationed for part of his time in country, lies alongside the sea. Paul Berlin's watchtower in the novel *Going After Cacciato* rises up along the very edge of the South China Sea, and Berlin occasionally imagines "using it as a means of escape—stocking Oscar's raft with plenty of rations and foul-weather gear and drinking water, then shoving out through the first heavy breakers, then hoisting up a poncho as a sail, then lying back and letting the currents carry him away—to Samoa, maybe, or to some hidden isle in the South Pacific, or to Hawaii, or maybe all the way home" (46). Such dreams of escaping the war also fuel Berlin's long, elaborate fantasy of chasing the deserting soldier Cacciato all the way from Vietnam to PARIS.

Soviet SS-4 SS-4s were nuclear missiles constructed by the Soviet Union during the COLD WAR period. In the novel *The Nuclear Age,* William Cowling as a young boy growing up during the 1950s in FORT DERRY, MONTANA, imagines that he hears a Soviet SS-4 whiz right over his house one night. William sees bright flashes and believes that the world is ending; he runs to the fallout shelter in his basement, where his father finds him, terrified and shouting.

"Space Walk" "Space Walk" is the title of the last poem that William Cowling's wife, Bobbi, writes for him in the novel *The Nuclear Age.* As William becomes increasingly obsessed with digging the bomb shelter in their yard, Bobbi suggests they separate, commenting that she needs her space. "What does space mean?" (297) William asks. Later, she writes her husband the poem called "Space Walk," the text of which is not included in the novel.

Spartacus Spartacus was a slave who led an uprising against the Roman Republic in the first century B.C.E. In the novel *July, July*, the U.S. soldier David Todd, lying badly wounded along the banks of the SONG TRA KY River in Vietnam, hears or imagines he hears a deejay named Johnny Ever speaking to him over a small transistor radio. Ever calls himself a "very hip, ten-thousand-year-lifer" (31) who is not easily surprised. But Ever says that Spartacus did surprise him.

Spec 4 Spec 4 is military shorthand for the rank of Specialist of the lowest order in the U.S. Army. This is a rank for enlisted men that comes immediately above Private First Class. In the novel *Going After Cacciato*, Paul Berlin is promoted to the rank of Spec 4 in September 1968 after answering a series of questions before the battalion promotion board. The key question, which wins Berlin his promotion, comes when a major asks the following: "What effect would the death of Ho Chi Minh have on the population of North Vietnam?" (269). Berlin's reply—"Reduce it by one, sir"—is exactly the answer that the major is looking for.

St. Germain The Boulevard St. Germain is a major PARIS street on the Left Bank of the Seine. In the novel *Going After Cacciato*, Paul Berlin imagines that the men of Third Squad take rooms in a small brick hotel off St. Germain, a block away from the Italian embassy. In Berlin's imagined story, the hotel's rooms "were dimly lighted, the walls papered in brown and gold, the beds made of brass" (293).

St. Paul's Catholic Church In the novel *Tomcat in Love*, St. Paul's Catholic Church in OWAGO, MINNESOTA, the small town where Thomas H. Chippering grows up, is set on fire in 1957. While Thomas is suspected of the crime, readers later discover that is was actually Lorna Sue Zylstra who set the fire. She also disfigured a statue of Christ outside the church, painting it with rouge and lipstick and appending to it a pair of "distinctly feminine breasts" (39).

St. Vith St. Vith is a city in Belgium that the United States briefly defended against German assault during the Battle of the Bulge in 1944.

Although the United States ended up retreating from the city, leaving it open for German recapture, the defense of St. Vith altered the German plan of attack. In the work of Tim O'Brien, mention of St. Vith is often associated with nostalgia for "the good war"—WORLD WAR II—which seemed to many Americans more morally justified than the war in Vietnam. In his memoir, *If I Die in a Combat Zone*, O'Brien tells a fellow soldier named Barney that the name of a Vietnamese village is St. Vith, drawing attention to the disjunction between the Vietnam War and World War II. While the names of seemingly heroic World War II battles echo in the minds of the soldiers, the names of Vietnamese villages all run together, becoming indistinguishable from one another. St. Vith is mentioned again later in the memoir when O'Brien speaks to his battalion commander at FORT LEWIS about his objections to the war. The commander, an old veteran, does not listen to O'Brien but instead reminisces about past wars, claiming that the Americans saw some real "street fighting" at St. Vith (62). O'Brien again depicts nostalgia for the earlier war when in *Going After Cacciato* the narrator describes by-the-books Lieutenant Sidney Martin as he watches his men march. While Martin believes in mission, he also knows that something is "wrong with this war," and the narrator explains that Martin "would rather have fought at St. Vith" (165).

Stalin, Joseph Joseph Stalin led the Soviet Union as general secretary of the Communist Party from 1922 until 1953. A ruthless dictator who murdered millions in party purges, Stalin is mentioned briefly in O'Brien's novel *The Nuclear Age*. William Cowling, looking back at his college years, speculates that peoples' political lives could not be separated from "the matrix of life in general" (80). Stalin, he muses, was the son of a poor cobbler. What turned him into the man he became?

starlight scope The starlight scope is a night vision device first introduced during the Vietnam War. It allowed riflemen to aim their weapons at night, giving them a range of 1,000–3,000 feet. Tim O'Brien mentions the starlight scope in his memoir, *If I Die in a Combat Zone*, when he writes about a fellow soldier named Barney who carries the scope and shows it to his friend Chip. O'Brien describes the scope as "maybe two feet long, shaped like a blunt telescope, [and] painted black" (29). The scope utilized natural night light, such as that emitted by the moon, stars, or campfires, and intensified it, turning items seen through the eyepiece into an eerie green color. Looking through the starlight scope seemed to O'Brien to magnify the spookiness of the landscape at night. In the story "The Things They Carried," one of the items carried by Ted Lavender before he is killed is a starlight scope, "which weighed 6.3 pounds with its aluminum carrying case" (TTTC 9–10). In addition, Paul Berlin in the novel *Going After Cacciato* looks through a starlight scope when he spends his long night on the observation tower above the SOUTH CHINA SEA. As he watches QUANG NGAI PROVINCE in the night, Berlin is reminded of how "he had witnessed the ultimate war story" (207) on his very first day of battle. Other Vietnam War writers have also probed the strange visionary effects of the starlight scope, perhaps most memorably the poet Yusef Komunyakaa in his poem, "Starlight Scope Myopia."

Stars and Stripes   *Stars and Stripes* is a daily newspaper published for U.S. military personnel. In the novel *Going After Cacciato*, Paul Berlin is amazed by the enormously complex support structures set up for soldiers at the CHU LAI COMBAT CENTER when he first arrives in Vietnam. Along with two hospitals, a PX, a USO club, a mini golf course, chapels, dentist offices, and even a swimming beach, is a *Stars and Stripes* detachment.

State Theater   In the story "The Lives of the Dead" from *The Things They Carried,* Tim O'Brien describes going on a date with a nine-year-old girl named Linda, who will later die of a brain tumor. O'Brien's parents take the children to the State Theater in WORTHINGTON, MINNESOTA, to see the movie THE MAN WHO NEVER WAS.

Street of False Confessions   Paul Berlin in the novel *Going After Cacciato* imagines shopping for new clothes and a pair of hiking boots with Sarkin

Aung Wan on the Street of False Confessions in MANDALAY, Burma.

Street of Sweet Pines   In his invented pursuit story of Cacciato in the novel *Going After Cacciato,* Paul Berlin imagines himself and the part-Vietnamese refugee Sarkin Aung Wan walking through the city of MANDALAY, Burma, behaving like civilians. On the Street of Sweet Pines, Sarkin throws bread to the pigeons.

strontium 90   Strontium 90 is a by-product of nuclear fission and is present in nuclear waste. It can get into human bones and cause cancer. In the novel *The Nuclear Age,* William Cowling ascribes his fear of nuclear annihilation to growing up during the COLD WAR. One of the rumors he hears in 1958 is that strontium 90 is present in the milk he and other children drink.

Strouch Funeral Home   The Strouch Funeral Home is owned by the parents of the radical activist Sarah Strouch in the novel *The Nuclear Age.* In the summer of 1967, Sarah takes William Cowling, the novel's narrator, on a tour of the funeral home, where her family also lives.

Summer, Donna   Donna Summer was a popular U.S. disco singer in the 1970s and early '80s, best known for her song "Love to Love You, Baby." She is mentioned briefly in the short story "Quantum Jumps" when William, the story's narrator, muses about a possible reunion of 1960s political radicals: "[W]e'll dance to Donna Summer," he tells himself, "we'll parade through Lincoln Park singing our lungs out. . . ." (40). This reference to Summer was removed, however, when O'Brien revised the story for inclusion in the novel *The Nuclear Age.*

The Sun Also Rises   ERNEST HEMINGWAY published *The Sun Also Rises,* his tale of a wounded World War I veteran who travels through PARIS and Spain, drinking heavily and attending bull fights with a group of disillusioned, expatriate friends in 1926. The novel was immensely popular and influential. O'Brien's own first novel, *Northern*

Lights, is heavily influenced by *The Sun Also Rises.* Like Jake Barnes, Harvey Perry has been injured in a war and falls in love with a free-spirited woman who abandons him for a younger man who is an honored athlete. Both novels, as well, toy with the possibility that spiritual wounds may be healed in the natural world, and both rely heavily on images of bulls and their association with fertility rites.

Sunset Park   Sunset Park is one of the many parks strung out around the shores of LAKE OKABENA in WORTHINGTON, MINNESOTA, Tim O'Brien's hometown. In his memoir, *If I Die in a Combat Zone,* O'Brien remembers driving around the lake the summer he is drafted (*see* DRAFT) and passing Sunset Park, "with its picnic table and little beach and a brown wood shelter and some families swimming" (19–20). The normalcy of the life going on in the park runs counter to the turmoil within O'Brien as he thinks about going off to war. Sunset Park appears as well in the story "Speaking of Courage" from *The Things They Carried.* As Norman Bowker drives around and around the lake in the center of his own small midwestern hometown, he passes the park several times.

Sweetheart Mountains   The Sweetheart Mountains are a fictional location in Montana where William Cowling builds a home with his wife, Bobbi, in the novel *The Nuclear Age.* The mountains, said to be just outside the small town of FORT DERRY, are also the location where Cowling and his radical college friends had discovered uranium in early 1980, a find that makes them all wealthy.

Szilard, Leo   Leo Szilard was a Hungarian-born physicist who made a key contribution to the Manhattan Project through his concept of the nuclear chain reaction. Szilard is mentioned briefly in the novel *The Nuclear Age* when Sarah Strouch mocks William Cowling for betraying his antiwar ideals after he and his group of friends discover uranium in the SWEETHEART MOUNTAINS of Montana. When Cowling claims that he is "sweet," Sarah replies that OPPENHEIMER and EINSTEIN were sweet as well, and that "Szilard was a sweetie," too (273).

Tacoma Library   While undergoing advanced infantry training (*see* AIT) at FORT LEWIS, WASHINGTON, Tim O'Brien goes to the library at Tacoma to research army desertion—where deserters go, what organizations exist to help them, costs of bus travel and air flights, etc. He seriously considers deserting the military himself but at the last minute is unable to make himself go. O'Brien writes about these experiences in his 1973 memoir, *If I Die in a Combat Zone, Box Me Up and Ship Me Home.*

Tampa, Florida   Tampa, a city located on the west coast of Florida, plays an important role in the novel *Tomcat in Love.* It is the city where Lorna Sue Zylstra, the former wife of the linguistics professor Thomas H. Chippering, lives with her new husband. Chippering makes several covert trips to Tampa from his home in Minnesota to spy on Lorna Sue and her tycoon. Eventually, he and his new girlfriend, Mrs. Robert Kooshoff, travel to Tampa together, but the trip is disastrous. While Chippering is able to stir up trouble between Lorna Sue and her new husband as he hopes, he also drives Mrs. Kooshoff away, flirts shamelessly with a waitress in a hotel bar, and ends up spending an entire night hog-tied in the bar by the waitress and her bartender friend, who are annoyed by Chippering's sexual advances.

Tan Mau   Tan Mau is the name of a small village along the muddy SONG TRA BONG River in the novel *Going After Cacciato,* where the men of Third Squad beat Rudy Chassler's team in a pickup basketball game by a score of 56 to 16.

Tapier Station   Tapier Station is the name of the train station in DELHI, India, where the men of Third Squad believe they see Cacciato in a newspaper photo in the novel *Going After Cacciato.* The AWOL American soldier is depicted in front of a train headed for KABUL. Although Paul Berlin realizes that finding the picture is an unbelievable coincidence, he includes this detail in his invented story anyway, justifying it to himself by thinking, ". . . so what? If not this way, some other way—a bold leap of the mind—just close the eyes and make it happen" (173).

Tehran, Iran In Paul Berlin's invented pursuit story in the novel *Going After Cacciato*, the men of Third Squad are detained in Tehran, Iran, shortly after witnessing the beheading of a young Iranian army deserter. At first treated kindly by a sympathetic captain in His Majesty's Royal Fusiliers named Fahyi Rhallon, the men are briefly released, only to be rearrested and treated cruelly by a colonel in the Iranian secret police who threatens to execute the American soldiers. Paul Berlin can conjure up only a fantastical ending to this disturbing part of his story—in a scene reminiscent of many a chase scene in an American movie, Berlin imagines the men escape their Tehran prison in a getaway car left for them by Cacciato.

Teller, Edward Edward Teller was a theoretical physicist who worked on the Manhattan Project and is known as "the father of the hydrogen bomb." He is mentioned briefly in O'Brien's short story "Quantum Jumps," which was originally published in *Ploughshares* magazine in 1983. The story's narrator, William, obsessed with the possibility of nuclear war, thinks to himself that the "fathers" of his age, "as if to bow out before they were tarred and feathered . . . have all passed away" (36). "Einstein's brains were pickled in formaldehyde," he adds, "Teller made his final appearance on *Issues and Answers;* von Braun went quietly in his sleep; Rickover was buried at sea" (36). The same lines appear as well in the story "The Nuclear Age," published in the *Atlantic* magazine in June of 1979. The references to EINSTEIN and Teller in this passage were removed when the two stories were revised for inclusion in the novel *The Nuclear Age,* although the mentions of VON BRAUN and RICK-OVER were retained.

Texas State University O'Brien accepted a position as the Mitte Professor of Creative Writing at Texas State University in San Marcos, Texas, beginning in 1999, a post he has held for more than a decade.

Than Khe In *The Things They Carried,* Ted Lavender is shot in the head outside the village of Than Khe in mid-April 1969. The men of ALPHA COMPANY burn the village and destroy the village well in revenge for Lavender's death.

Thap Ro In the novel *Going After Cacciato,* the men of Third Squad begin playing pickup basketball games in a tiny hamlet called Thap Ro along the SONG TRA BONG River on July 8, 1968. A door gunner on a resupply chopper had tossed a Spalding Wear-Ever basketball out the door to Paul Berlin. Eddie Lazzutti then ripped the bottom out of a Vietnamese woman's wicker grain basket and attached it to a tree with a wire. The men continue the games throughout the month of July and into August. On August 13, Rudy Chassler steps on a mine, bringing the pickup games to an end.

Thieu, Nguyen Van General Nguyen Van Thieu served as head of state in South Vietnam under the government of Nguyen Cao Ky from 1965 to 1967, then as president of South Vietnam from 1967 to 1975, immigrating to Taiwan just before the fall of SAIGON. Tim O'Brien speculates in several of his works about the corrupt government the United States supported in South Vietnam, wondering if the South would be any worse off under communism than it was under the rule of a series of dictators and military generals. In his memoir, *If I Die in a Combat Zone,* O'Brien tells an army chaplain at basic training that "there is no good evidence that all this horror [the war itself] is worth preventing a change from Thieu to Ho Chi Minh" (60). In the novel *Going After Cacciato,* Paul Berlin speculates that Communist tyranny might not prove worse "than the tyrannies of Ky or Thieu or Khanh" (264)—military generals who took over South Vietnam in various coups. William Cowling, protagonist of *The Nuclear Age,* muses along similar lines: "Was Ho Chi Minh a tyrant, and if so, was his tyranny preferable to that of Diem and Ky and Thieu?" (130). He also mentions that in the period of the war known as "Vietnamization," when the United States tried to get the South Vietnamese to take a larger responsibility for the war, President Nguyen Van Thieu "proposed that the United States equip his nation with a modest nuclear capability" (222–23).

President Lyndon B. Johnson's visit to Cam Ranh Bay, South Vietnam; (Front row l-r: President Lyndon B. Johnson, Gen. William Westmoreland, Lt. Gen. Nguyen Van Thieu, Prime Minister Nguyen Cao Ky) *(Photo by Yoichi R. Okamoto/LBJ Library)*

Thin Mau   Paul Berlin in the novel *Going After Cacciato* wonders what the Vietnamese villagers he encounters think about him. He wishes he could explain to them that he does not want to harm anyone, and he wishes he could tell them that many of the things he witnesses make him sad and angry. One of these incidents occurred outside a village called Thin Mau, when Oscar Johnson and Rudy Chassler "shot down ten dogs for the sport of it," an act that Berlin thought was "mean-spirited and self-defeating and wrong" (263).

Thuan Yen   Thuan Yen is the original Vietnamese name for one of the villages in the cluster of small hamlets identified as "My Lai 4" on American maps. In his novel *In the Lake of the Woods*, when he describes scenes from the notorious MY LAI MASSACRE, O'Brien uses the place name Thuan Yen rather than the more familiar My Lai.

Thucydides   Thucydides was a Greek historian who lived in the fifth century B.C.E. and wrote *History of the Peloponnesian War*. In the novel *Going After Cacciato*, Lieutenant Sidney Martin, trained at West Point, is said to have been schooled in common sense and military strategy. He has read Thucydides and other theoreticians of war, and he considers war a means to an end, "with a potential for both good and bad" (163). Despite the lieutenant's book learning, however, his insistence on following formal SOPs (standard operating procedures), such as searching tunnels before blowing them, makes his men hate him and eventually murder him with a fragmentation grenade.

Tillich, Paul   Paul Tillich was an early 20th-century German-American theologian and philosopher who applied existential theory to questions about God and Christianity. Tim O'Brien in his memoir, *If I Die in a Combat Zone,* recalls reading Tillich as a teenager in WORTHINGTON, MINNESOTA. He reports walking around his small hometown at night, thinking about Tillich's philosophy, particularly his statements that "God is both transcendent and imminent" and that "God is Being-Itself" (*If I Die* 15). Reading Tillich provoked O'Brien to ponder large theological questions concerning the existence of God and the nature of God.

The Tip Top Lodge The Tip Top Lodge is the name of the nearly deserted fishing resort where the young Tim O'Brien flees after receiving his DRAFT notice in the story "On the Rainy River" from *The Things They Carried.* The lodge is owned by a crafty old man named Elroy Berdahl, who offers O'Brien the opportunity to flee to Canada. But O'Brien cannot make himself leave the country and ends up going to the war instead.

toe popper *Toe popper* was a slang term used by American soldiers in Vietnam to describe the M-14 antipersonnel mine, a small explosive device that did not usually prove fatal but that often destroyed the foot of a victim who stepped on it. As O'Brien writes in his memoir, *If I Die in a Combat Zone,* the toe popper "will take a hunk out of your foot" (125). He goes on to describe two fellow soldiers who were injured in this way—a man named Smitty who lost a set of toes, and another unnamed soldier who lost his left heel.

Tra Bong In the story "Sweetheart of the Song Tra Bong" from *The Things They Carried,* Rat Kiley is said to have been assigned to a small medical detachment in the mountains west of CHU LAI when he first arrived in Vietnam. The medical unit sits on a hill above a small Vietnamese village called Tra Bong. Later in the story, Mary Anne Bell, Mark Fossie's high school sweetheart, whom he flies into Vietnam, will insist on visiting the village of Tra Bong, despite repeated warnings that the idea is "way too dangerous" and "the VC owned the place" (96). Mary Anne and Mark will stroll through the village "like a pair of tourists" (96), Mary Anne not appearing nervous at all.

track *Track* is the slang term given by American GIs to the M113 armored personnel carrier, the most widely used armored vehicle during the Vietnam War. O'Brien uses the term in his 1973 memoir to describe the tanklike vehicles that crush a number of U.S. soldiers during a retreat.

Tracy, Mike Mike Tracy is the real-life model for the character Nick Veenhof in the story "The Lives of the Dead" from *The Things They Carried.* In a letter that MARVIS MOELLER wrote to Tim O'Brien in March of 1991, she describes Mike Tracy as a fourth grade bully who bothered the other children of WORTHINGTON, MINNESOTA, for years.

Train Rouge The Train Rouge is the train that carries the men of Third Squad from LUXEMBOURG to their final destination of PARIS in the novel *Going After Cacciato.* Paul Berlin imagines the final leg of the men's pursuit of Cacciato occurring on April 1, 1969, as the men take the short four-hour train ride into Paris through the small towns of Luxembourg and the villages of the French countryside. The men arrive in Paris aboard the speeding train in the midst of rain and fog. "If you can imagine it," Berlin tells himself, "it's always real. Even peace, even Paris—sure, *it's real*" (291).

Tran Hung Dao Tran Hung Dao was a skillful Vietnamese general whose armies, largely made up of poor peasant conscripts, turned away two Mongol invasions in the 13th century. He is revered as a national hero in modern-day Vietnam. In the story "The Man I Killed" from *The Things They Carried,* O'Brien imagines that the dainty young man with a star-shaped hole where his eye should have been, whom he killed with a hand grenade, was a quiet scholarly boy who grew up hearing heroic stories of great Vietnamese warriors, such as Tran Hung Dao, who defended their countries against invading armies. O'Brien imagines further that, secretly, the stories frightened the young man, who "was not a fighter" (125).

Traven, B. B. Traven was the pen name of a 20th-century American novelist whose real identity remains a mystery even today. Traven's best-known work was *The Treasure of the Sierra Madre,* made into a film by John Huston in 1948. In one of the evidence chapters of his novel *In the Lake of the Woods,* O'Brien cites a book about Traven that speculates about the author's longing to vanish without a trace, to disappear "without a name, or with a fictitious name, so that his true identity would be lost forever" (265). This quote possibly lends evidence to the theory that John and Kathy Wade planned their disappearances together, desiring to lose their own identities and start over with new names and selves.

Tri Binh   In his first book, *If I Die in a Combat Zone,* O'Brien reminisces about his first month at war. He writes that "it was not a bad war" until ALPHA COMPANY "sent a night patrol into a village called Tri Binh 4" (83). After platoon leader Mad Mark had been gone about an hour, the men back at the base camp receive a radio call that they had come upon about 10 VIET CONG soldiers in the middle of the village and opened fire. Back at camp later that night, Mark unwraps a bundle of cloth to show a souvenir of the battle: a human ear, cut from the head of one of the dead Viet Cong. Later in the book, a gung-ho officer named Major Callicles, drunk after spending the evening in the officer's club, orders the young O'Brien to accompany him and a Vietnamese scout on a surprise night raid to the same village. Callicles apparently falls asleep while waiting to spring an ambush after rigging up a CLAYMORE mine next to a village trail. The raid is a bust, but Callicles is unabashed, strutting around his office the next morning and bragging that "All it takes is guts" (204). In the story "The Ghost Soldiers" from *The Things They Carried,* Tri Binh is mentioned again (without a number attached this time). The Tim O'Brien narrator informs readers that he was shot twice while in the war. The first time was "out by Tri Binh" (189), where the shot knocks O'Brien against a pagoda wall and into medic Rat Kiley's lap. Kiley ties on a compress and returns frequently from the fighting to check on O'Brien. This is very different from the behavior of the green young medic Bobby Jorgensen who is initially afraid to treat O'Brien the second time he is shot.

Trinh Son 2   In the novel *Going After Cacciato,* the men of ALPHA COMPANY have a difficult July when they are on patrol in the muddy villages along the SONG TRA BONG River. It's a bad time during the war—the men are restless, scared, and edgy. On August 12 Lieutenant Sidney Martin announces that the soldiers will be entering a village called Trinh Son 2 the next day, where they will search tunnels before blowing them. The next day, Rudy Chassler steps on a mine as the men walk up a clay path leading into the village.

Trung Sisters   Trung Trac and Trung Nhi were Vietnamese sisters who lived in the first century A.D. They famously led a rebellion against the Chinese occupying their country in A.D. 39, leading an army of mostly women soldiers. Although the rebellion was defeated by the much larger Chinese Army in A.D. 43 and the sisters committed suicide, they are nevertheless revered as heroines in modern-day Vietnam. In the story "The Man I Killed" from *The Things They Carried,* O'Brien imagines that the dainty young dead man he killed with a hand grenade would have grown up hearing heroic stories about the Trung Sisters and other Vietnamese who died defending their lands against invading armies.

T'Souvas, William   William T'Souvas was the father of the U.S. soldier and MY LAI MASSACRE participant Robert T'Souvas, one of the real-life figures fictionalized in O'Brien's novel *In the Lake of the Woods.* Robert T'Souvas ended up a homeless alcoholic who was shot to death under a bridge in Boston by a female drinking companion in 1988. O'Brien includes an account of the death that appeared in the *Boston Herald* in an evidence chapter in the novel. William T'Souvas is quoted in the newspaper story as saying that his son "had problems with Vietnam over and over. He didn't talk about it much" (261).

Tucson, Arizona   In the novel *July, July,* one of the DARTON HALL COLLEGE graduates of 1969, Karen Burns, a former roommate of Jan Huebner and Amy Robinson, will go on to direct a retirement community called HOMEWOOD ESTATES in

Tucson, Arizona, in the 1990s. Karen is murdered when a drug-smuggling bus driver who works for Homewood Estates strands her in the remote Arizona desert, along with four elderly retirees.

Turkey Capital of the World   In his memoir, *If I Die in a Combat Zone*, O'Brien comments that his hometown of WORTHINGTON, MINNESOTA, called itself the Turkey Capital of the World. He remembers that the town would hold a parade every September to celebrate Turkey Day, which climaxed when "the farmers herded a billion strutting, stinking, beady-eyed birds down the center of town" (14). O'Brien and his friends stood on the curb and "blasted the animals" (14) with their peashooters. In his 1998 novel, *Tomcat in Love*, O'Brien playfully gives Thomas Chippering's small hometown of OWAGO, MINNESOTA, the nickname "Rock Cornish Game Hen Capital of the World," clearly poking fun at his own hometown of Worthington.

University of Minnesota   In the novel *In the Lake of the Woods*, Kathy Wade worked as the director of admissions at the University of Minnesota before going missing at the lake. Thomas H. Chippering in the novel *Tomcat in Love* also works at the University of Minnesota as a linguistics professor who occupies the Rolvaag Chair in Modern American Lexicology, until he is fired for helping young female students by writing their theses.

USO   USO stands for United Service Organizations, a private, nonprofit corporation that provides recreational and entertainment services for U.S. military personnel. During the Vietnam War, USOs were sometimes located in combat zones, a situation perhaps most memorably depicted in the Francis Ford Coppola film *Apocalypse Now*. In the novel *Going After Cacciato*, Paul Berlin notes that the CHU LAI COMBAT CENTER, where he is stationed when he first arrives in Vietnam, has a USO club, along with hospitals, a PX, a mini golf course, and swimming beaches—all in all, a bewildering array of support services.

USS *Maddox*   The USS *Maddox* was the U.S. destroyer involved in the GULF OF TONKIN incident.

The ship fired upon three North Vietnamese patrol boats on the night of August 2, 1964, but a supposed attack by the North Vietnamese two nights later, on August 4, seems not to have actually happened. Radar readings signaling an attack have been ascribed to weather conditions and overeager sailors. In the story "On the Rainy River" from *The Things They Carried*, Tim O'Brien writes that the "very facts" underlying the war "were shrouded in uncertainty" (40), and he specifically questions, "What really happened to the USS *Maddox* on that dark night in the Gulf of Tonkin?" (40).

VC   VC is an abbreviation of VIET CONG. The acronym was commonly used by American soldiers to describe the enemy they were fighting during the Vietnam War. *See* VIET CONG for more information.

Vere, Captain   Captain Vere is one of the main characters in Herman Melville's novella *Billy Budd*. After the innocent and childlike Billy accidentally kills Master-at-Arms John Claggart, Vere reluctantly decides that Billy must be hanged in order for justice to be served. In Tim O'Brien's memoir, *If I Die in a Combat Zone*, he lists Captain Vere as one of his "favorite heroes" (142) before the war. The young O'Brien had admired Vere's courage in making the wrenchingly difficult decision to send Billy to the gallows, as well as the captain's tormented seeking of justice.

Verona, Italy   Verona is a city in northern Italy, the setting for Shakespeare's play *Romeo and Juliet*. In O'Brien's novel *In the Lake of the Woods*, John and Kathy Wade dream about escaping to Verona after John's crushing election defeat. In the opening chapter, the couple lies on the porch, dreaming about Verona and the 38 babies they will drive around on a bus. These early dreams of Verona might lend credence to the theory that the Wades planned Kathy's disappearance together, that they staged their deaths in order to assume new identities and escape the past.

Versailles   One of the places that the American soldier Paul Berlin in the novel *Going After Cacciato* imagines visiting when he finally arrives in PARIS is the Palace of Versailles. In his made-up story, he pretends that he and Sarkin Aung Wan take a bus to Versailles, located in the Paris suburbs.

Victory at Sea   *Victory at Sea* was a 1950s television documentary about naval warfare during WORLD WAR II. The music from the documentary was later made into a record album. The short story "Claudia Mae's Wedding Day" ends with Claudia Mae's father, a World War II veteran himself, retreating back into his house after his daughter's wedding ceremony and putting his *Victory at Sea* record on the stereo. The story highlights the difficulty that people back home have in understanding the Vietnam War and the experiences of U.S. soldiers who fought in it. Claudia Mae's new husband, Robert, is a Vietnam veteran. When he returns home, Claudia Mae and other women in the story are mostly interested in his medals, which they believe make him look dashing. The men in the story, including Claudia Mae's father, are suspicious of Vietnam veterans, whom they view as drug users who are psychologically "messed-up" (143).

Viet Cong   *Viet Cong* is a shortened, Americanized version of a longer Vietnamese term that means "Vietnamese Communist." The Viet Cong, officially known as the National Liberation Front, were guerrilla soldiers located in South Vietnam who supported the Communist government in the North. These are the soldiers that U.S. troops engaged with most often during the war. But they were also elusive, well-trained guerrilla fighters whose tactics involved the use of sniper fire, rigged explosive devises, and night ambushes rather than set battles. In the work of Tim O'Brien, Viet Cong soldiers (referred to as "VC" or "CHARLIE" in military slang) are presented as almost ghostlike figures with magical abilities to frighten and to elude detection.

VUES OF VIETNAM   *VUES OF VIETNAM* is the title that the simpleminded soldier Cacciato hand-letters on the front cover of the photo album that he takes to Vietnam with him in the novel *Going After Cacciato*. Inside are pictures of Cacciato's family and home carefully labeled. The album also includes photos taken in Vietnam—Cacciato posing with weapons and other soldiers and, most gruesome, squatting beside the corpse of a dead VIET CONG boy, holding up the head by the hair and smiling.

Viet Cong soldier crouching in a bunker with an SKS rifle, 1968 *(Courtesy of the National Archives)*

Wallace, George   The longtime segregationist governor of Alabama and unsuccessful candidate for U.S. president, George Wallace, left paralyzed by a 1972 assassination attempt, was a touchstone for the political battles dividing Americans in the late 1960s. He is mentioned briefly in the novel *The Nuclear Age* when William Cowling imagines thousands of 1960s political figures and activists getting together for a reunion in the Chicago Hilton. Among them would be "Wallace in his wheelchair" (131).

Washington, George George Washington is mentioned briefly in O'Brien's novel *The Nuclear Age* when William Cowling speculates about what makes men take certain paths in life, what determines their political impulses. He writes, "It occurred to me . . . that our political lives could not be separated from the matrix of life in general. Joseph Stalin: the son of a poor cobbler in Tiflis. George Washington: a young neurotic who could not bring himself to tell a modest lie. Why does one man vote Republican, another Socialist, another not at all?" (80). O'Brien's interest in such questions is evidenced as well by his decision to study political science at MACALESTER COLLEGE and, later, government at HARVARD UNIVERSITY.

Washington Post O'Brien worked as an intern reporter at the *Washington Post* during the summers of 1971 and 1972, while he was a graduate student in government at HARVARD UNIVERSITY. In addition, thinking he would like to work at the paper when he finished his degree, he took a leave of absence from Harvard during the 1973–74 academic year to work at the *Post* as a national affairs reporter.

WAVES WAVES is an acronym standing for "Women Accepted for Volunteer Emergency Service," a division of the U.S. Navy during WORLD WAR II that was made up entirely of women volunteers who held similar ranks and earned the same pay as their male counterparts. The group

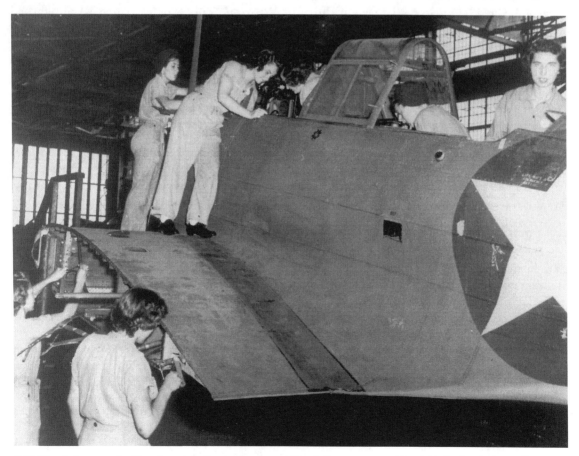

WAVES aviation metalsmiths at work in the Assembly and Repair Department at Naval Air Station Jacksonville, Florida, on 24 July 1943 *(Courtesy of U.S. Navy)*

was founded in August 1942, two months after a similar group had been established for the U.S. Army—the WAACs, or Women's Auxiliary Army Corps. Immediately popular among women, by the end of the war, the WAVES totaled 8,000 officers and 80,000 enlisted women. While most WAVES worked in administrative or secretarial jobs, thousands also worked in jobs that had not previously been open to women, including communications, intelligence, and science and technology. Tim O'Brien's mother, Ava Eleanor Schultz O'Brien, served in this group during World War II.

We Were There *We Were There* is a compilation of both British and American accounts of the Revolutionary War battles at Lexington and Concord, edited by Vincent J-R Kehoe. O'Brien cites this collection in one of the evidence chapters in his novel *In the Lake of the Woods*. The battle descriptions he quotes refer to great cruelty, including the putting to death of entire families by British troops and the scalping and mutilating of bodies by Americans. O'Brien includes these accounts in his novel in order to demonstrate that past wars have produced atrocities similar to those that occurred in the Vietnamese village of My Lai.

Weathermen The Weathermen (or Weather Underground as it was later called) was a radical leftist political organization formed in 1969 from a faction of the Students for a Democratic Society (*see* SDS). The group advocated revolution and was willing to use violence to achieve its ends. They instituted a bombing campaign in the early 1970s, targeting mostly banks and government buildings. The radical organization called the COMMITTEE in O'Brien's novel *The Nuclear Age* may be modeled after the Weathermen. The group is specifically mentioned in the novel when William Cowling explains to readers the major political events of 1969: "In Chicago, Judge Julius Hoffman presided over a discomposed courtroom, and in the streets, within shouting distance, the Weathermen went hand to hand with riot cops" (223).

Westmoreland, General William General William Westmoreland was the U.S. military commander in Vietnam from 1964 to 1968. He is referred to in the novel *The Nuclear Age* when William Cowling writes that by October 1966, during his junior year at college, "General Westmoreland called for fresh manpower" (73) in Vietnam, continuing to escalate the war. In November 1967 Cowling notes that Westmoreland had declared "we have reached an important point when the end begins to come into view" (112). Later, as William prepares for the plane flight he will take to flee the DRAFT, Mr. Cowling tells his son that he believes all the politicians and generals involved in the Vietnam War are "Goddamned idiots," adding, "Westmoreland, I'd nail him first" (143).

Wharton, Edith Edith Wharton, a late 19th- and early 20th-century American novelist, was the first woman to win the Pulitzer Prize. She is quoted is one of the evidence chapters in O'Brien's novel *In the Lake of the Woods* as claiming that human beings do not know themselves very well: "We live in our own souls as in an unmapped region, a few acres of which we have cleared for our habitation" (190).

White Bear Lake In the novel *July, July*, Spook Spinelli, one of the members of the 1969 graduating class of DARTON HALL COLLEGE, is said to currently live in "an expensive brick house at 1202 Pine Hills Drive in White Bear Lake, Minnesota, a suburb of the Twin Cities" (89). Spook also lives in a more modest home at 540 Spring Street, also in White Bear Lake. The reason for the two houses is that Spook is married to two different men, both of whom know about the other and "more or less" (89) accept their strange living arrangement.

White, Lieutenant Mark Lieutenant Mark White, who killed himself in a rented hotel room soon after returning from the Vietnam War, was the real-life model for the character Mad Mark in O'Brien's memoir, *If I Die in a Combat Zone, Box Me Up and Ship Me Home.*

Whitefish Lake In the story "On the Rainy River" from *The Things They Carried*, the Tim

O'Brien narrator (a character in the story not to be confused with the real-life, autobiographical Tim O'Brien), imagines himself as a young man at the TIP TOP LODGE deciding whether or not to flee the DRAFT. As he looks back, he imagines his younger self choosing to go to Canada and writing a letter of explanation home to his parents in which he describes the country up north which reminds him of the family vacations they used to take at a place called Whitefish Lake. Of course, this is only an imagined memory, since in the story (as in real-life), Tim O'Brien went to the Vietnam War rather than fleeing the draft.

Widmark, Richard   Richard Widmark was an American actor best known for playing film villains. Particularly memorable was his role as Tommy Udo in the 1947 film *Kiss of Death*, which earned him an Academy Award nomination. In the novel *Going After Cacciato*, Stink Harris refers to Richard Widmark shortly after the men of Third Squad witness a disturbing public execution in TEHRAN. Stink speculates that the young boy who was beheaded may have deserved his punishment: "'A murderer maybe,' said Stink Harris. 'I wouldn't doubt it. The kid's eyes, I mean—just like Richard Widmark's eyes. That real shiny look'" (188). Later, the American soldiers will discover that the boy had actually been an Iranian army deserter.

Widmer, Fred   Fred Widmer was one of the U.S. soldiers in the First Platoon of CHARLIE COMPANY who participated in the MY LAI MASSACRE. He is quoted in one of the evidence chapters in O'Brien's novel *In the Lake of the Woods* as wondering, 20 years later, how he could have done such things: "Why? Why did I do that? That is not me. Something happened to me" (262).

Williams, Esther   Esther Williams was a competitive swimmer who became a movie star in the 1940s and 50s, starring in a series of musicals that featured elaborate sequences of synchronized swimming. She is mentioned briefly in O'Brien's novel *July, July* when the injured U.S. soldier David Todd listens to a transistor radio while lying alone in a field alongside a river in Vietnam, all the other members of his platoon having been shot and killed. Todd hears, or possibly imagines he hears, a deejay broadcasting over the radio who identifies himself as Master Sergeant Johnny Ever. Ever claims to be thousands of years old and also asserts that very little has surprised him in his life. Two exceptions he mentions are the Roman slave SPARTACUS and Esther Williams.

Willie Peter   *Willie Peter* is military slang for white phosphorus, an incendiary material used in Vietnam that cannot be extinguished by water. The nickname derives from the chemical's acronym: WP. O'Brien mentions Willie Peter frequently in his Vietnam War novels. For instance, Lieutenant Sidney Martin in *Going After Cacciato* orders an air strike of white phosphorus on the village of HOI AN after Jim Pederson's death. In *The Nuclear Age*, Ollie Winkler talks about white phosphorus and C-4 explosives at length the first time he meets William Cowling, in their college cafeteria.

Wilson, Colonel William V.   Colonel William V. Wilson was a U.S. army Investigator who oversaw the initial investigation into the MY LAI MASSACRE, which took place in April through June 1969. Wilson's book, *American Heritage*, published in 1990, is quoted several times in the evidence chapters of O'Brien's novel *In the Lake of the Woods*. Wilson writes that he is "struck by how little of these events" (137) he can or even wishes to remember. His well-known line—"I had prayed to God that this thing was fiction" (255) is quoted in the novel as well.

Wilson, Woodrow   Woodrow Wilson, the 28th president of the United States, asked Congress to declare war in 1917, despite having run on the campaign slogan of having kept the United States out of World War I. Wilson is quoted several times as one of the experts in the evidence chapters of the novel *In the Lake of the Woods*. In these quotes Wilson speaks about his desperate desire to be loved and about his lack of close friends, traits associated with John Wade in the novel.

Winnipeg, Canada   Winnipeg, the capital city of Manitoba, Canada, is the place where Billy

McMann flees to escape being drafted (*see* DRAFT) into the Vietnam War in the novel *July, July*. His college girlfriend, Dorothy Stier, was supposed to catch the flight to Winnipeg with Billy, but she backs out at the last minute and never shows up at the airport, leaving Billy to start a new life all by himself.

Wolff's Drugstore   Wolff's Drugstore is a fictional shop in the small town of SAWMILL LANDING, Minnesota, where Paul and Grace Harvey live in the novel *Northern Lights*. On Friday nights Paul and Grace will occasionally drive into town from their farmhouse to have ice cream at Wolff's Drugstore and to window shop along Main Street. The store is owned and operated by a German immigrant named Herb Wolff, who periodically runs for mayor of Sawmill Landing, and who had served on the DRAFT board that sent Paul's brother, Harvey, to the Vietnam War.

Wood, Roy   Roy Wood was one of the U.S. soldiers involved in the MY LAI MASSACRE who testified during the court-martial of LIEUTENANT WILLIAM CALLEY about killings of unarmed women and children. A brief excerpt from his testimony is included in one of the evidence chapters in O'Brien's novel *In the Lake of the Woods*.

World War II   Tim O'Brien's parents were both veterans of World War II. His father, WILLIAM T. O'BRIEN, served in the navy and his mother, AVA SCHULTZ O'BRIEN, was a member of the WAVES (Women Accepted for Volunteer Emergency Service). In his memoir, *If I Die in a Combat Zone, Box Me Up and Ship Me Home*, O'Brien recalls playing war games as a child growing up in WORTHINGTON, MINNESOTA, where the boys would pretend to be their fathers "taking on the Japs and Krauts along the shores of Lake Okabena" (12). He also remembers listening to veterans in town talking about the war in front of the courthouse. In much American literature about the Vietnam War, O'Brien's work included, World War II serves as the model of a "good war"—a war with a much clearer moral purpose and one more fully supported at home than the Vietnam War. Thus, characters in these books

often long to have fought the war of their fathers rather than their own war. The veterans O'Brien listens to do not talk about causes or reasons: "the war was right, they muttered, and it had to be fought" (*If I Die* 13). Young Americans sent to Vietnam often grew up watching John Wayne and AUDIE MURPHY movies, which tended to present a sanitized and romanticized view of war, and many expected a similar heroic experience when they went off to fight. One of the hallmarks of Vietnam War literature, however, is a sense of disillusionment. These narratives usually tell antiheroic stories that assert the moral ambiguity of America's involvement in Vietnam and deflate notions of patriotism or glory sometimes associated with war.

Worthington *Daily Globe*   The Worthington *Daily Globe* was the local newspaper in Tim O'Brien's small Minnesota hometown. As a high school student, O'Brien wrote occasional articles for the *Daily Globe*. The paper's editor, who had been a friend and mentor of O'Brien's in high school, thought so highly of the young man that he wrote to him in the summer of 1967, a year before O'Brien was scheduled to graduate from MACALESTER COLLEGE, to offer him a full-time position as a reporter for the newspaper upon his graduation. In his memoir, *If I Die in a Combat Zone*, O'Brien recalls that on August 13, 1968, the day he departed WORTHINGTON on a bus that was to take him to basic training, a photographer from the *Daily Globe* took his picture "standing by a rail fence with four other draftees" (21).

Worthington, Minnesota   Tim O'Brien moved with his family from AUSTIN, MINNESOTA, to Worthington when he was 7 years old. A town that called itself the "TURKEY CAPITAL OF THE WORLD," Worthington is located in the southwest corner of the state, near the Iowa border. In his memoir, *If I Die in a Combat Zone*, O'Brien describes Worthington as having been built on what was originally Indian land, land taken from the Sioux and Cherokee. Norwegian and Swedish and German settlers hoping to farm the land came next, but O'Brien writes that the town eventually became a place for working class people. "It is a place for wage earners today," he writes in his memoir, "not very spirited people, not very thoughtful people" (13). According to O'Brien, Worthington, while he was growing up in the fifties and early sixties, was a typical, small, patriotic, midwestern town. He played Little League baseball there in the summers and listened to speeches and watched fireworks on the Fourth of July. Although O'Brien tells of attending Democratic Party meetings in high school, he eventually decided that there was not much difference between the people at those meetings and the Republican supporters of RICHARD NIXON and Henry Cabot Lodge: "The essential thing about the prairie, I learned, was that one part of it is like any other part" (*If I Die* 15). O'Brien left Worthington when he went to MACALESTER COLLEGE in 1964. In his memoir he writes that the town did not miss him very much when he was gone. Worthington appears as the hometown of the fictional version of Tim O'Brien in the story "On the Rainy River" from *The Things They Carried*. The fictional town of SAWMILL LANDING in *Northern Lights* seems to have been at last partly modeled on Worthington, as does FORT DODGE, IOWA, Paul Berlin's hometown in *Going After Cacciato*, FORT DERRY, MONTANA, in *The Nuclear Age*, and OWAGO, MINNESOTA in *Tomcat in Love*.

Xa   In *Going After Cacciato*, Li Van Hgoc, the VIET CONG major trapped in the underground tunnel system, tells the men of Third Squad about an ancient Vietnamese ideograph—the word *Xa*—which means, according to the refugee Sarkin Aung Wan, "community, and soil, and home" (86). The major explains that *Xa* has other meanings as well, but that "at heart it means that a man's spirit is in the land, where his ancestors rest and where the rice grows. The land," he adds, "is your enemy" (86).

Xa Hoi   The VIET CONG major Li Van Hgoc explains to Berlin and his fellow soldiers in *Going After Cacciato* that the Vietnamese Communist Party, Xa Hoi, has its vision in the word XA, meaning

"the land." Thus, the major concludes that the land itself is the true enemy of the American soldiers.

Xuan Thuy   Xuan Thuy was the chief negotiator for North Vietnam during the PARIS peace talks that began in 1968 and lasted sporadically until an agreement was signed in 1973. He makes a brief appearance in O'Brien's novel *The Nuclear Age* when William Cowling watches news footage of the talks on television with his parents during the summer of 1968, after he has graduated from college. The news shows the American ambassador AVERELL HARRIMAN shaking hands with Xuan Thuy.

Yeats, William Butler   William Butler Yeats was an early 20th-century Irish poet and playwright. A pair of lines from his poem "The Snare's Nest by My Window" serve as the epigraph to O'Brien's novel *July, July*:

> We had fed the heart on fantasies,
> The heart's grown brutal from the fare.

In the poem the lines refer to the Irish civil war of 1922–23 and the violent results of the fiery rhetoric of revolution. The quotation is relevant to O'Brien's novel in that it possibly speaks to the fantasies of the idealistic young graduates of DARTON HALL COLLEGE in 1969, intent on changing the world. But instead, the world has changed them. The hearts of these romantic young people have suffered and grown coarse as they have aged, made compromises with their beliefs, and largely abandoned their youthful idealism.

Zagreb, Croatia   Zagreb is the capital of Croatia as well as its largest city. In the novel *Going After Cacciato*, Paul Berlin imagines the men of Third Squad taking a bus from ATHENS to Zagreb in their pursuit of the AWOL soldier, Cacciato. After spending a night in Zagreb, the American soldiers hitch a ride north with a girl from California in a battered Volkswagen bus.

PART IV

Appendixes

CHRONOLOGY

1914

February 28: O'Brien's father, William T. O'Brien, born in Brooklyn, New York, to William Timothy O'Brien and Mary Frances Kinsley O'Brien.

1916

March 23: O'Brien's mother, Ava Eleanor Schultz, born in Beaver Township, Minnesota, to Paul C. Schultz and Myrtle Leona Hungerford Schultz.

1942

January 13: Bill O'Brien enters into the Naval Reserve in New York.

1943

October 7: Ava Schultz joins the Navy WAVES (Women Accepted for Volunteer Emergency Service)

1944

October 6: William T. O'Brien and Ava Eleanor Schultz marry at the Naval Operating Base in Norfolk, Virginia.

1945

September 25: Bill O'Brien leaves active service in the U.S. Navy.

1945

October 6: Ava O'Brien discharged from the WAVES.

1946

October 1: William Timothy O'Brien (Tim O'Brien) born at St. Olaf Hospital in Aus-

tin, Minnesota. Christened at the Methodist Church in Austin.

1954

O'Brien family (Bill and Ava along with their three children, Tim, Kathy, and Greg) move to Worthington, Minnesota.

1956

September 11: Lorna Lue Moeller, model for character Linda in "The Lives of the Dead," dies of a brain tumor in Worthington, Minnesota.

1960–1964

Tim O'Brien attends Worthington Senior High School. Member of the debate team and the National Honor Society. Works as a sports and features writer for the *Worthington Daily Globe.*

1964

Graduates with honors from high school; in top 10 percent of his graduating class.

1964–1968

Attends Macalester College in St. Paul, Minnesota. Active on the debate team. Serves as a volunteer for the Eugene McCarthy presidential campaign. Writes a column called "Soapbox" for the school paper. Serves as student body president both his junior and senior year.

1967

Summer: Travels to Czechoslovakia as part of the SPAN (Student Project for Amity Among

Nations) Program. Injured in a motorcycle accident in Hersbruck, Germany. Drafts large portion of a novel as part of his SPAN project.

1968
Graduates summa cum laude with a B.A. in political science from Macalester. Wins a Woodrow Wilson National Fellowship to attend graduate school.

1968
Summer: Receives draft notice.

1968
August 14: Inducted into the U.S. Army.

1968
Fall: Undergoes Basic Training at Fort Lewis, Washington. Assigned to serve as a combat infantryman. Begins Advanced Artillery Training, also at Fort Lewis.

1969
February: Arrives at the Chu Lai Combat Center in Vietnam. Assigned to the American Division, Alpha Company, 5th Battalion, 46th Infantry, 198th Infantry Brigade.

1969
Spring/Summer: Serves as a rifleman, radio-telephone operator, and squad leader in the "Pinkville" region of Quang Ngai Province.

1969
May 3: Injured in combat by a rifle shot. Receives the Purple Heart.

1969
Fall: Assigned to a rear job as a battalion clerk. Serves as editor of *The Professional,* a publication of the 5th Battalion, 46th Infantry.

1970
March 30: Honorably discharged from the service with the rank of sergeant (E-5) having entered as a private (E-1).

1970
July: Article "Step Lightly" published in *Playboy* magazine.

1970–1976
Attends Harvard University School of Government; works toward Ph.D. degree.

1971
June–September: Works as an intern at the *Washington Post* newspaper.

1972
June–September: Again serves as a summer intern at the *Washington Post.*

1973
October: First short story, "Claudia Mae's Wedding Day," published in *Redbook* magazine. Nominated for a National Magazine Award.

1973
If I Die in a Combat Zone, Box Me Up and Ship Me Home published by Delacorte Press.

1973
Marries Ann Weller, an editorial assistant at Little, Brown Publishing House.

1973–1974
Takes a leave of absence from Harvard to work as a national affairs reporter for the *Washington Post.*

1974
Short story, "A Man of Melancholy Disposition," published in *Ploughshares* magazine.

1975
Northern Lights published by Delacorte Press.

1975
May: Short story "Where Have You Gone, Charming Billy?" published in *Redbook.*

1975
August: Short story "Landing Zone Bravo" published in *Denver Quarterly.*

1976
Withdraws from graduate school to devote himself to writing full time.

1976
Short stories "Speaking of Courage," "The Way it Mostly Was," "Keeping Watch by Night," "Going After Cacciato," and "Centurion" published in various journals.

1976
Story "Night March" (first published as "Where Have You Gone, Charming Billy?) chosen as an O. Henry Prize winner.

1977
October/December: Short story "The Fisherman" published in Esquire. Short story "Calling Home" published in *Redbook*.

1978
Going After Cacciato published by Delacorte Press.

1978
Story "Speaking of Courage" selected as an O. Henry Prize winner.

1978–1979
Teaches as visiting writer-in-residence at Emerson College in Boston.

1979
Going After Cacciato wins the National Book Award.

1979
June: Story "The Nuclear Age" published in the *Atlantic*.

1981
March: Story "The Ghost Soldiers" published in *Esquire*.

1982
"The Ghost Soldiers" selected as an O. Henry Prize story.

1983
Story "Quantum Jumps" published in *Ploughshares* magazine.

1985
November: Story "Underground Tests" published in *Esquire*.

1985
The Nuclear Age published by Knopf.

1986
August: Short story version of "The Things They Carried" published in *Esquire*.

1987
"The Things They Carried" wins the National Magazine Award for fiction.

1987
October: Story "How to Tell a True War Story" published in *Esquire*.

1989
January/July: Stories "The Lives of the Dead" and "Sweetheart of the Song Tra Bong" published in *Esquire*.

1990
"Sweetheart of the Song Tra Bong" a finalist for the National Magazine Award for fiction.

1990
March/August: Story "Enemies and Friends" published in *Harper's*. Story "Field Trip" published in *McCall's*.

1990
The Things They Carried published by Houghton Mifflin. Chosen as one of the 10 best works of fiction for the year by the *New York Times*. Wins the *Chicago Tribune* Heartland Prize and the French *Prix du Meilleur Livre Ètranger*.

1991
The Things They Carried selected as a finalist for the Pulitzer Prize in fiction.

1992
January: Story "The People We Marry" published in the *Atlantic*.

1993
January: Story "Loon Point" published in *Esquire*.

1994
February: O'Brien returns to Vietnam with his then-girlfriend, Kate.

1994

October: Essay "The Vietnam in Me" published by the *New York Times Magazine.* Story "How Unhappy They Were" published by *Esquire.*

1994

In the Lake of the Woods published by Houghton Mifflin. Named by *Time* magazine one of the 10 best works of fiction of 1994. Wins an editor's choice award from the *New York Times.*

1995

In the Lake of the Woods awarded the James Fenimore Cooper Prize for best historical fiction.

1995

Divorce from Ann Weller O'Brien finalized (the couple had been separated for many years).

1996

February: Story "Faith" published in the *New Yorker.*

1996

March 5: Television movie version of *In the Lake of the Woods* premieres on the Fox Network.

1998

March: Story "Class of '68" published in *Esquire.*

1998

September: Story "The Streak" published in the *New Yorker.*

1998

November 8: "A Soldier's Sweetheart," a television movie based on "Sweetheart of the Song Tra Bong," premieres on Showtime.

1998

Tomcat in Love published by Random House

1999

Accepts Mitte Chair in Creative Writing at Texas State University in San Marcos; moves to Austin, Texas.

1999

March: Story "Nogales" published in the *New Yorker.*

2000

July/August: Story "July '69" published in *Esquire.* Story "Winnipeg" published in the *New Yorker.*

2001

September/October: Story "Too Skinny" published in the *New Yorker.* Story "Little People" published in *Esquire.*

2002

July/August: Story "Half Gone" published in the *New Yorker.* Story "What Went Wrong" published in *Esquire.*

2002

July, July published by Houghton Mifflin.

2003

"What Went Wrong" selected as an O. Henry Prize story.

2003–2005

Marries longtime girlfriend, Meredith Baxter.
June 20, 2003: Son Timmy is born. A second son, Tad, is born two years later, in late **June, 2005.**

2007

O'Brien appears in documentary film "Operation Homecoming: Writing the Wartime Experience."

2009

Essay "Telling Tails" published in the *Atlantic* fiction issue.

2010

Release of newly edited and revised version of *The Things They Carried* in celebration of the novel's 20th anniversary.

BIBLIOGRAPHY OF O'BRIEN'S WORKS

Books

If I Die in a Combat Zone, Box Me Up and Ship Me Home, New York: Delacorte Press, 1973.

Northern Lights. New York: Delacorte Press, 1975.

Going After Cacciato. New York: Delacorte Press, 1978.

The Nuclear Age. New York: Knopf, 1985.

The Things They Carried. New York: Houghton Mifflin, 1990.

In the Lake of the Woods. New York: Houghton Mifflin, 1994.

Tomcat in Love. New York: Random House/Broadway Books, 1998.

July, July. New York: Houghton Mifflin, 2002.

Short Fiction

"Claudia Mae's Wedding Day." *Redbook,* October 1973, 102–103.

"A Man of Melancholy Disposition." *Ploughshares,* 02/2.6 (1974), 46–60.

"Where Have You Gone, Charming Billy?" *Redbook,* May 1975, 81, 127–132.

"Landing Zone Bravo." *Denver Quarterly* 4 (August 1975), 72–77.

"Speaking of Courage." *Massachusetts Review,* 17 (Summer 1976), 243–253.

"The Way It Mostly Was." *Shenandoah* 27 (Winter 1976), 35–45.

"Keeping Watch by Night." *Redbook,* December 1976, 65–67.

"Going After Cacciato." *Ploughshares,* 03/1.9 (1976), 42–65.

"Centurion." *Literary Cavalcade,* 28, no. 7 (April 1976), 14.

"The Fisherman." *Esquire,* October 1977, 92, 130, 134.

"Calling Home." *Redbook,* December 1977, 75–76.

"The Nuclear Age." *Atlantic,* June 1979, 58–67.

"Civil Defense." *Esquire,* August 1980, 82–88.

"The Ghost Soldiers." *Esquire,* March 1981, 90–100.

"Quantum Jumps." *Ploughshares,* 09/4, no. 32 (1983): 11–44.

"Underground Tests." *Esquire,* November 1985, 252–254, 256, 258–259.

"The Things They Carried." *Esquire,* August 1986, 76–81.

"How to Tell a True War Story." *Esquire,* October 1987, 208–215.

"The Lives of the Dead." *Esquire,* January 1989, 134–142.

"Sweetheart of the Song Tra Bong." *Esquire,* July 1989, 94–105.

"Enemies and Friends." *Harper's,* March 1990, 30–31.

"Field Trip." *McCall's,* August 1990, 78–79.

"The People We Marry." *Atlantic,* January 1992, 90–98.

"Loon Point." *Esquire,* January 1993, 90–94.

"How Unhappy They Were." *Esquire,* October 1994, 136–138.

"Faith." *New Yorker,* 12 February 1996, 62–67.

"Class of '68." *Esquire,* March 1998, 160.

"The Streak." *New Yorker,* 28 September 1998, 88–91.

"Nogales." *New Yorker,* 8 March 1999, 69–73.

"July '69." *Esquire,* July 2000, 102–109.

"Winnipeg." *New Yorker,* 14 August 2000, 72–77.

"Too Skinny." *New Yorker,* 10 September 2001, 92–100.

"Little People." *Esquire,* October 2001, 98–108.

"Half Gone." *New Yorker,* 8 July 2002, 66–71.

"What Went Wrong." *Esquire,* August 2002, 124–128.

Selected Essays and Miscellaneous Works

"The Youth Vote." *New Republic,* 19 and 26 August 1972, 12–15.

"Medals! Medals! Everyone's Got Medals." *Los Angeles Times*, 18 March 1973, sec. 6, 1+.

"The Crumbling of Sand Castles." *Washington Post*, 18 November 1973, C1, C5.

"Prisoners of Peace." *Penthouse*, March 1974, 44–46; 61–64; 113–117.

"Revolt on the Turnpike: The Mounting Rage of Independent Truck Drivers." *Penthouse*, September 1974, 63–64; 132; 147–148; 156–160.

"The Vietnam Veteran." *Penthouse*, November 1974, 76–78; 128; 140–145.

"Author's Choice (*Obligations: Essays on Disobedience, War, and Citizenship*, by Michael Walzer)." *Book-of-the-Month Club News*, October 1978, 22–23.

"Darkness on the Edge of Town." *Feature*, January 1979, 42–49.

"Falling Star." Review of *Incandescence*, by Craig Nova. *Saturday Review*, 17 February 1979, 53–54.

"Tales His Father Told Him." Review of *The Duke of Deception: Memories of My Father*, by Geoffrey Wolff. *Saturday Review*, 29 September 1979, 46–48.

"The Ballad of Gary G." Review of *The Executioner's Song*, by Norman Mailer. *New York*, 15 October 1979, 67–68.

"Burning Love." Review of *Endless Love*, by Scott Spencer. *Saturday Review*, 27 October 1979, 41–42.

"The Violent Vet." *Esquire*, December 1979, 96–104.

"Honor Thy Commander." Review of *A Game Men Play*, by Vance Bourjaily. *Saturday Review*, 16 February 1980, 50.

"We've Adjusted Too Well." In *The Wounded Generation: America after Vietnam*, edited by A. D. Horne, 205–207. Englewood Cliffs, N.J.: Prentice Hall, 1981.

Review of *July's People* by Nadine Gordimer. *New York*, 22 June 1981, 64–65.

"The Magic Show." In *Writers on Writing*, edited by Robert Pack and Jay Parini, 175–83. Hanover, N.H.: Middlebury College Press, 1991.

"Ambush! (Significance of Ambush of British Troops on April 19, 1775)." *Boston Magazine*, April 1993, 62+.

"The Vietnam in Me." *New York Times Magazine*, 2 October 1994, 48–57.

"The Mystery of My Lai." In *Facing My Lai: Moving Beyond the Massacre*, edited by David Anderson, 171–178. Lawrence: University of Kansas Press, 1998.

The Putt at the End of the World. Co-written with Les Standiford, Ridley Pearson, Tami Hoag, Lee K. Abbott, Richard Bausch, Dave Barry, James W. Hall, and James Crumley. New York: Warner Books, 2000.

"The Whole Story." In *Novel History: Historians and Novelists Confront America's Past (and Each Other)*, edited by Mark C. Carnes, 344–345. New York: Simon & Schuster, 2001.

"Just Like a Woman: Author Tim O'Brien Is Inspired by Art from Mariko Mori." *Harper's Bazaar*, September 2002, 424–425.

"A Letter to My Son." *Life*, 15 October 2004, 15.

"The Best of Times." *Life*, 16 June 2006, 19.

"Telling Tails." *Atlantic*, Fiction 2009.

"Fenced In: The Novelist Revisits his Past to Come to Terms with his Rural Hometown," *Smithsonian* 40, no. 8 (November 2009): 14–16.

BIBLIOGRAPHY OF SECONDARY SOURCES

Books on O'Brien

Heberle, Mark A. *A Trauma Artist: Tim O'Brien and the Fiction of Vietnam.* Iowa City: University of Iowa Press, 2001.

Herzog, Tobey C. *Tim O'Brien.* New York: Twayne, 1997.

Kaplan, Stephen. *Understanding Tim O'Brien.* Columbia: University of South Carolina Press, 1995.

Smith, Patrick A. *Tim O'Brien: a Critical Companion.* Westport Conn.: Greenwood, 2005.

Tegmark, Mats. *In the Shoes of a Soldier: Communication in Tim O'Brien's Vietnam Narratives.* Uppsala, Sweden: Uppsala, 1998.

Books with Significant Portions on O'Brien

Bates, Milton J. *The Wars We Took to Vietnam: Cultural Conflict and Storytelling.* Berkeley: University of California Press, 1996.

Beidler, Philip D. *American Literature and the Experience of Vietnam.* Athens: University of Georgia Press, 1982.

————. *Re-Writing America: Vietnam Authors in Their Generation.* Athens: University of Georgia Press, 1991.

Donovan, Christopher. *Postmodern Counternarratives: Irony and Audience in the Novels of Paul Auster, Don DeLillo, Charles Johnson and Tim O'Brien.* London: Routledge, 2005.

Herzog, Tobey C. *Vietnam War Stories: Innocence Lost.* New York: Routledge, 1992.

————. *Writing Vietnam, Writing Life: Caputo, Heinemann, O'Brien, Butler.* Iowa City: University of Iowa Press, 2008.

Hofmann, Bettina. *Ahead of Survival: American Women Writers Narrate the Vietnam War.* Frankfurt, Germany: Peter Lang, 1996.

Jason, Philip K., ed. *Fourteen Landing Zones: Approaches to Vietnam War Literature.* Iowa City: University of Iowa Press, 1991.

Kinney, Katherine. *Friendly Fire: American Images of the Vietnam War.* Oxford: Oxford University Press, 2000.

Myers, Thomas. *Walking Point: American Narratives of Vietnam.* New York: Oxford University Press, 1988.

Neilson, Jim. *Warring Fictions: American Literary Culture and the Vietnam War Narrative.* Jackson: University Press of Mississippi, 1998.

Park, Jinim. *Narratives of the Vietnam War by Korean and American Writers.* New York: Peter Lang, 2007.

Ringnalda, Don. *Fighting and Writing the Vietnam War.* Jackson: University Press of Mississippi, 1994.

Searle, William J. Ed. *Search and Clear: Critical Responses to Selected Literature and Films of the Vietnam War.* Bowling Green, Ohio: Bowling Green State University Press, 1988.

Spanos, William V. *American Exceptionalism in the Age of Globalization: The Specter of Vietnam.* Albany: State University of New York Press, 2008.

Vernon, Alex. *Soldiers Once and Still: Ernest Hemingway, James Salter, and Tim O'Brien.* Iowa City: University of Iowa Press, 2004.

Wesley, Marilyn. *Violent Adventure: Contemporary Fiction by American Men.* Charlottesville: University of Virginia Press, 2003.

Articles in Books

Beidler, Philip. "Re-Writing America: Literature as Cultural Revision in the New Vietnam Fiction." In *America Rediscovered: Critical Essays on Literature and Film of the Vietnam War,* edited by Owen W. Gilman, and Lorrie Smith, 3–9. New York: Garland, 1990.

Bikos, Dimitri A. "Propaganda of Heroism: the Important Vietnam War Literature of Tim O'Brien." In *The Image of the Hero in Literature, Media and Society: Selected Papers 2004 Conference Society for the Interdisciplinary Study of Social Imagery, March 2004, Colorado Springs, Colorado*, edited by Will Wright, and Steven Kaplan, 243–246. Pueblo: Society for the Interdisciplinary Study of Social Imagery, Colorado State University-Pueblo, 2004.

Bonn, Maria S. "A Different World: The Vietnam Veteran Novel Comes Home." In *Fourteen Landing Zones: Approaches to Vietnam War Literature*, edited by Philip K. Jason, 1–14. Iowa City: University of Iowa Press, 1992.

Bowie, Thomas G. "Reconciling Vietnam: Tim O'Brien's Narrative Journey." In *The United States and Viet Nam from War to Peace*, edited by Richard M. Slabey, 184–197. Jefferson, N.C.: McFarland, 1996.

Calloway, Catherine. "Pluralities of Vision: *Going After Cacciato* and Tim O'Brien's Short Fiction." In *America Rediscovered: Critical Essays on Literature and Film of the Vietnam War*, edited by Owen W. Gilman Jr. and Lorrie Smith, 213–224. New York: Garland, 1990.

Christ, Tomás. "Uses of German Characters and Language in 20th-Century American Fiction: Some Examples from Stein, Hemingway, O'Brien, and DeLillo." In *The German Presence in the U.S.A.*, edited by Josef Raab, and Jan Wirrer, 397–416. Berlin, Germany: Lit, 2008.

Daley, Chris. "The 'Atrocious Privilege': Bearing Witness to War and Atrocity in O'Brien, Levi, and Remarque." In *Arms and the Self: War, the Military, and Autobiographical Writing*, edited by Alex Vernon, 182–201. Kent, Ohio: Kent State University Press, 2005.

Dunnaway, Jen. "Approaching a Truer Form of Truth: The Appropriation of the Oral Narrative Form in Vietnam War Literature." In *Soldier Talk: The Vietnam War in Oral Narrative*, edited by Paul Budra, and Michael Zeitlin, 26–51. Bloomington: Indiana University Press, 2004.

Franklin, Bruce. "Kicking the Denial Syndrome: Tim O'Brien's *In The Lake of the Woods*." In *Novel History: Historians and Novelists Confront America's Past (and Each Other)*, edited by Mark C. Carnes, 332–343. New York: Simon and Schuster, 2001.

Harrison, Brady. "Tim O'Brien." In *A Reader's Companion to the Short Story in English*, edited by Erin Fallon, et al. 309–316. Westport, Conn.: Greenwood Press, 2001.

Jarvis, Brian. "Skating on a Shit Field: Tim O'Brien and the Topography of Trauma." In *American Fiction of the 1990s: Reflections of History and Culture*, edited by Jay Prosser, 134–147. London: Routledge, 2008.

Juncker, Clara. "Not a Story to Pass On? Tim O'Brien's Vietnam." In *Transnational America: Contours of Modern U.S. Culture*, edited by Russell Duncan, and Clara Juncker, 111–124. Copenhagen, Denmark: Museum Tuscalanum, 2004.

Kaylor, Noel Harold. "Postmodernism in the American Short Story: Some General Observations and Some Specific Cases." In *The Postmodern Short Story: Forms and Issues*, edited by Farhat Iftekharrudin, 246–266. Westport, Conn.: Praeger, 2003.

Marín Madrazo, Pilar. "Tim O'Brien's Fabulation." In *Figures of Belatedness: Postmodernist Fiction in English*, edited by Javier Gascueña Gahete, and Paula Martín Salván, 153–167. Córdoba, Spain: Universidad de Córdoba, 2006.

McCay, Mary. "The Autobiography of Guilt: Tim O'Brien and Vietnam." In *Writing Lives: American Biography and Autobiography*, edited by Hans Bak, and Hans Krabbendam, 115–121. Amsterdam, Netherlands: VU University Press, 1998.

Myers, Thomas. "Tim O'Brien." In *American Novelists Since World War II: Fourth Series*, edited by James R. Giles, and Wanda H. Giles, 140–157. Detroit, Mich.: Thomson Gale, 1995.

Nelson, Marie. "Two Consciences: A Reading of Tim O'Brien's Vietnam Trilogy: *If I Die in a Combat Zone, Going After Cacciato*, and *Northern Lights*." In *Third Force Psychology and the Study of Literature*, edited by Bernard J. Paris, 262–279. Rutherford, N.J.: Farleigh Dickinson University Press, 1986.

Norris, Nanette. "Imagination and the Civilized Man: Paris in Tim O'Brien's *Going After Cacciato*." In *The Image of the City in Literature, Media, and Society*, edited by Will Wright, and Steven Kaplan, 111–115. Pueblo: Society for the Interdisciplinary Study of Social Imagery, University of Southern Colorado, 2003.

Rosso, Stefano. "Labyrinths and Tunnels: from the Jungle to Sewage." In *America Today: Highways and Labyrinths: Proceedings of the XV Biennial Conference, Siracusa, November 4–7, 1999*, edited by Gigliola Nocera, 133–146. Siracusa, Italy: Grafià 2003.

———. "Notes on the Point of View of the Enemy." In *Red Badges and Courage: Wars and Conflicts in American Culture*, edited by Biancamarie Pisapia, Ugo Rubeo, and Anna Scacchi, 192–199. Rome, Italy: Bulzone, 1998.

————. "Public and Private in the Narration of the Vietnam War (and Environs)." In *Public and Private in American History: State, Family, Subjectivity in the Twentieth Century*, edited by Raffaella Baritono, 123–146. Turin, Italy: Otto, 2003.

Salka, Agnieszka. "American Short-Story Cycles and the Changing Sense of Community." In *Discourses of Literature: Studies in Honour of Alina Szala*, edited by Leszek S. Kolek, 137–151. Lublin: Maria Curie-Sklodowska University Press, 1997.

————. "Re-Visioning the Democratic Imagination: Tim O'Brien's Vietnam Fiction." In *Polish-American Literary Confrontations*, edited by Joanna Durczak, and Jerzy Durczak, 113–129. Lublin: Maria Curie-Sklodowska University Press, 1995.

Schroeder, Eric James. "The Past and the Possible: Tim O'Brien's Dialectic of Memory and Imagination." In *Search and Clear: Critical Responses to Selected Literature and Films of the Vietnam War*, edited by William J. Searle, 116–134. Bowling Green, Ohio: Bowling Green State University Press, 1988.

Schwininger, Lee. "Ecofeminism, Nuclearism, and O'Brien's *The Nuclear Age*." In *The Nightmare Considered: Critical Essays on Nuclear War Literature*, edited by N. Anisfield, 177–185. Bowling Green, Ohio: Bowling Green State University Press, 1991.

Slabey, Robert. "*Going After Cacciato*: Tim O'Brien's 'Separate Peace.'" In *America Rediscovered: Critical Essays on Literature and Film of the Vietnam War*, edited by Owen Gilman, and Lorrie Smith, 205–212. New York: Garland, 1990.

Wiedemann, Barbara. "American War Novels: Strategies for Survival." In *War and Peace: Perspectives in the Nuclear Age*, edited by Ulrich Goebel, and Otto Nelson, 137–144. Lubbock: Texas Tech University Press, 1988.

Zins, Daniel. "Imagining the Real: The Fiction of Tim O'Brien." In *Twayne Companion to Contemporary Literature in English*, edited by Amanda Cockrell, and R. H. W. Dillard, 151–162. New York: Twayne/Thomson Gale, 2002.

Journal Articles

Bates, Milton J. "Tim O'Brien's Myth of Courage." *Modern Fiction Studies* 33 (1987): 263–279.

Blyn, Robin. "O'Brien's *The Things They Carried*," *Explicator* 61, no. 3 (2003): 189–191.

Bonn, Maria S. "Can Stories Save Us? Tim O'Brien and the Efficacy of the Text," *Critique* 36 (1994): 2–15.

Bulla, Elizabeth. "Tim O'Brien's *Sweetheart of the Song Tra Bong*: the Woman Warrior Tale Updated," *Overland Review* 31, nos. 1–2 (2003): 57–63.

Busby, Mark. "Tim O'Brien's *Going After Cacciato*: Finding the End of the Vision," *Conference of College Teachers of English Proceedings* 47 (September 1982): 63–69.

Calloway, Catherine. "'How to Tell a True War Story': Metafiction in *The Things They Carried*," *Critique: Studies in Contemporary Fiction* 36 (1995): 249–257.

Campbell, Christopher D. "Conversation across a Century: The War Stories of Ambrose Bierce and Tim O'Brien," *WLA: War, Literature, and the Arts* 10 (1998): 267–288.

Carpenter, Lucas. "'It Don't Mean Nothin'": Vietnam War Fiction and Postmodernism," *College Literature* 30, no. 2 (2003): 30–50.

Caulfield, Peter. "Vietnam Voices; or Uncle Ho Meets Country Joe (and the Fish)," *Writing on the Edge* 11, no. 2 (Spring–Summer 2000): 21–32.

Chen, Tina "'Unraveling the Deeper Meaning': Exile and the Embodied Poetics of Displacement in Tim O'Brien's *The Things They Carried*," *Contemporary Literature* 39 (1998): 77–97.

Ciocia, Stefania: "Conradian Echoes in Vietnam War Literature: Tim O'Brien's Rewriting of Heart of Darkness in 'Sweetheart of the Song Tra Bong,'" *Symbiosis*: 11, no. 1 (2007): 3–30.

Cordle, Daniel. "In Dreams, in Imagination: Suspense, Anxiety and the Cold War in Tim O'Brien's *The Nuclear Age*," *Critical Survey* 19, no. 2 (2007): 101–120.

Couser, G. Thomas. "*Going After Cacciato*: The Romance and the Real War," *Journal of Narrative Technique* 13 (1983): 1–10.

Dayley, Glenn. "Familiar Ghosts, New Voices: Tim O'Brien's *July, July*," *War, Literature, and the Arts* 15, nos. 1–2 (2003): 316–322.

Dunnaway, Jen. "'One More Redskin Bites the Dirt': Racial Melancholy in Vietnam War Representation," *Arizona Quarterly* 64, no. 1 (Spring 2008): 109–129.

Farrell, Susan. "Tim O'Brien and Gender: a Defense of *The Things They Carried*," *CEA Critic* 66, no. 1 (2003): 1–21.

Fertel, R. J. "Vietnam War Narratives and the Myth of the Hero," *WLA: War, Literature, and the Arts* 11, no. 1 (1999): 268–293.

FitzPatrick, Martin. "Indeterminate Ursula and 'Seeing How It Must Have Looked,' or, 'the Damned Lemming' and Subjunctive Narrative in Pynchon, Faulkner, O'Brien, and Morrison," *Narrative* 10, no. 3 (2002): 244–261.

Foertsch, Jacqueline. "Not Bombshells but Basketcases: Gendered Illness in Nuclear Texts," *Studies in the Novel* 31, no. 4 (1999): 471–488.

Froelich, Vera P. "O'Brien's *Going After Cacciato*." *Explicator* 53, no. 3 (Spring 1995): 181–183.

Goluboff, Benjamin. "Tim O'Brien's Quang Ngai," *ANQ: A Quarterly Journal of Short Articles, Notes, and Reviews* 17, no. 2 (2004): 53–58.

Griffith, James. "A Walk Through History: Tim O'Brien's *Going After Cacciato*," *WLA: War, Literature and the Arts* 3, no. 1 (1991): 1–34.

Hantke, Steffen. "Disorienting Encounters: Magical Realism and American Literature on the Vietnam War," *Journal of the Fantastic in the Arts* 12, no. 3 (2001): 268–286.

Haswell, Janis E. "The Craft of the Short Story in Retelling the Vietnam War: Tim O'Brien's *The Things They Carried*," *South Carolina Review*, 37, no. 1 (2004): 94–109.

Herzog, Toby. "*Going After Cacciato*: The Soldier-Author-Character Seeking Control," *Critique: Studies in Contemporary Fiction* 24 (1983): 88–96.

———. "Tim O'Brien's *True Lies*," *Modern Fiction Studies* 46, no. 4 (2000): 893–916.

Horner, Carl S. "Challenging the Law of Courage and Heroic Identification in Tim O'Brien's *If I Die in a Combat Zone* and *The Things They Carried*," *WLA: War, Literature & the Arts* 11, no. 1 (1999): 256–267.

Jakaitis, John M. "Two Versions of an Unfinished War: *Dispatches* and *Going After Cacciato*," *Cultural Critique* 3 (Spring 1986): 191–210.

Jarraway, David R. "'Excremental Assault' in Tim O'Brien: Trauma and Recovery in Vietnam War Literature," *Modern Fiction Studies* 44 (1998): 695–711.

Jones, Dale W. "The Vietnam of Michael Herr and Tim O'Brien: Tales of Disintegration and Integration," *Canadian Review of American Studies* 13 (1982): 309–320.

Kaplan, Stephen. "The Undying Certainty of the Narrator in Tim O'Brien's *The Things They Carried*," *Critique: Studies in Contemporary Fiction* 35, no. 1 (1993): 43–52.

Kaufmann, Michael. "The Solace of Bad Form: Tim O'Brien's Postmodernist Revisions of Vietnam in "Speaking of Courage," *Critique: Studies in Contemporary Fiction* 46, no. 4 (2005): 333–343.

King, Rosemary. "O'Brien's 'How to Tell a True War Story,'" *Explicator* 57, no. 3 (Spring 1999): 57–59.

Kinney, Katherine. "American Exceptionalism and Empire in Tim O'Brien's *Going After Cacciato*," *American Literary History* 7, no. 4 (1995): 633–653.

Liparulo, Steven P.: "'Incense and Ashes': the Postmodern Work of Refutation in Three Vietnam War Novels." *WLA War, Literature, and the Arts* 15, nos. 1–2 (2003): 71–94.

Loeb, Jeff. "Childhood's End: Self-recovery in the Autobiography of the Vietnam War," *American Studies* 37, no. 1 (1996): 95–116.

Lucas, Brad. "Traumatic Narrative, Narrative Genre, and the Exigencies of Memory," *Utah Foreign Language Review*, 9, no. 1 (April 1999): 30–38.

Lustig, T. J. "'Moments of Punctuation': Metonymy and Ellipsis in Tim O'Brien," *Yearbook of English Studies* 31 (2001): 74–92.

———. "'Which Way Home?': Tim O'Brien and the Question of Reference," *Textual Practice* 18, no. 3 (2004): 395–414.

Martin, Terry J., and Margaret Stiner. "*Sweetheart of the Song Tra Bong*: Tim O' Brien's (Feminist?) *Heart of Darkness*," *Short Story* 9, no. 2 (2001): 94–104.

McCarthy, Gerald. "Static Essentials: Voices of Vietnam War Literature," *Mid-American Review*, 4, no. 2 (Fall 1984): 96–100.

McDonough, Christopher Michael. "'Afraid to Admit We Are not Achilles': Facing Hector's Dilemma in Tim O'Brien's *The Things They Carried*," *Classical and Modern Literature* 20, no. 3 (2000): 23–32.

McWilliams, Dean. "Time in Tim O'Brien's *Going After Cacciato*," *Critique: Studies in Contemporary Fiction* 29, no. 4 (Summer 1988): 245–255.

Meas, Marth Minford. "Robert Flynn and Tim O'Brien: Driving the Vehicle of the Vietnam War as Writing Process," *Publications of the Mississippi Philological Association* (1995): 39–45.

Melley, Timothy. "Postmodern Amnesia: Trauma and Forgetting in Tim O'Brien's *In the Lake of the Woods*," *Contemporary Literature* 44, no. 1 (2003): 106–131.

Misra, Kalidas. "The American War Novel from World War II to Vietnam," *Indian Journal of American Studies* 14, no. 2 (July 1984): 73–80.

O'Gorman, Farrell. "*The Things They Carried* as Composite Novel," *WLA: War, Literature & the Arts* 10, no. 2 (1998): 289–309.

Ording, Dominic. "Portraits of the American Heartland at the Crossroads of the Counterculture," *The Yearbook of the Society for the Study of Midwestern Literature* 31 (2004): 104–114.

Palaima, Thomas. "Courage and Prowess Afoot in Homer and the Vietnam of Tim O'Brien," *Classical and Modern Literature: A Quarterly* 20, no. 3 (Spring 2000): 1–22.

Palm, Edward F. "Falling In and Out: Military Idiom as Metaphoric Motif in *Going After Cacciato*," *Notes on Contemporary Literature* 22 (1992): 8.

Pasternak, Donna. "Keeping the Dead Alive: Revising the Past in Tim O'Brien's War Stories," *Irish Journal of American Studies* 7 (1998): 41–54.

Piwinski, David J. "My Lai, Flies, and Beelzebub in Tim O'Brien's *In the Lake of the Woods*," *WLA: War, Literature, and the Arts* 12, no. 2 (2000): 196–202.

Poppleton-Pritchard, Rosalind. "World Beyond Measure: an Ecological Critique of Tim O'Brien's *The Things They Carried* and *In the Lake of the Woods*," *Critical Survey* 9, no. 2 (1997): 80–93.

Pratt, John Clark. "Tim O'Brien's Reimagination of Reality: An Exercise in Metafiction," *War, Literature, and the Arts* 8, no. 2 (Fall–Winter 1996): 115–132.

Raymond, Michael W. "Imagined Responses to Vietnam: Tim O'Brien's *Going After Cacciato*," *Critique: Studies in Contemporary Fiction* 24 (1983): 97–104.

Robinson, Daniel. "Getting it Right: The Short Fiction of Tim O'Brien," *Critique: Studies in Contemporary Fiction* 40, no. 3 (1999): 257–264.

Saltzman, Arthur M. "The Betrayal of the Imagination: Paul Brodeur's *The Stunt Man* and Tim O'Brien's *Going After Cacciato*," *Critique: Studies in Contemporary Fiction* 22, no. 1 (1980): 32–38.

Schramer, James. "Magical Realism in Tim O'Brien's Vietnam War Fiction," *Revista Canaria de Estudios Ingleses* 39 (1999): 135–146.

Scott, Grant F. "*Going After Cacciato* and the Problem of Teleology," *Siena Studies in Literature* 31 (1991): 30–36.

Seung, Ah Oh. "Women in Vietnam War Literature and the Discourse of Heteronormative Domesticity: Tim O'Brien and Erica Jong," *Feminist Studies in English Literature* 16. no. 1 (Summer 2008): 71–90.

Shim, Kyung Seok. "The Journey of Dream: Tim O'Brien's Metaphysical Exploration in *Going After Cacciato*." *Journal of English Language and Literature* 44, no. 4 (Winter 1998): 831–848.

Silbergleid, Robin. "Making Things Present: Tim O'Brien's Autobiographical Metafiction," *Contemporary Literature* 50, no. 1 (Spring 2009): 129–155.

Slay, Jack Jr. "A Rumor of War: Another Look at the Observation Post in Tim O'Brien's *Going After Cacciato*," *Critique* 41, no. 1 (1999): 79–85.

Smiley, Pamela. "The Role of the Ideal (Female) Reader in Tim O'Brien's *The Things They Carried: Why Should Real Women Play?*" *Massachusetts Review*, 43, no. 4 (2002): 602–613.

Smith, Lorrie. "'The Things Men Do': The Gendered Subtext in Tim O'Brien's *Esquire* Stories," *Critique: Studies in Contemporary Fiction* 36 (1994): 16–40.

Stephenson, Gregory. "Struggle and Flight: Tim O'Brien's *Going After Cacciato*," *Notes on Contemporary Literature* 14 (1984): 5–6.

Stocks, Claire. "Acts of Cultural identification: Tim O'Brien's *July, July*," *European Journal of American Culture* 25, no. 3 (2006): 173–188.

Taft-Kaufman, Jill. "'How to Tell a True War Story': the Dramaturgy and Staging of Narrative Theatre," *Theatre Topics* 10, no. 1 (2000): 17–38.

Taylor, Mark. "Tim O'Brien's War," *Centennial Review*, 39, no. 2 (1995): 213–230.

Timmerman, John H. "Tim O'Brien and the Art of the True War Story: 'Night March' and 'Speaking of Courage,'" *Twentieth Century Literature* 46, no. 1 (2000): 100–114.

Tran, Jonathan. "Emplotting Forgiveness: Narrative, Forgetting, and Memory," *Literature and Theology: An International Journal of Religion, Theory, and Culture* 23, no. 2 (June 2009): 220–233.

Tuttle, Jon. "How You Get That Story: Heisenberg's Uncertainty Principle and the Literature of the Vietnam War," *Journal of Popular Culture* 38, no. 6 (2005): 1,088–1,098.

Twister, Marquiss. "Westward Ho! (Chi Minh): Tim O'Brien and the Wounding of the American Cowboy Mythos," *Southwestern American Literature* 29, no. 2 (Spring 2004): 9–15.

Uchmanowicz, Pauline. "Vanishing Vietnam: Whiteness and the Technology of Memory," *Literature and Psychology* 41, no. 4 (1995): 30–50.

Uehling, Edward. "Truth Telling Medieval and Modern," *Cresset* 57, no. 7 (1994): 10–15.

Vannatta, Dennis. "Theme and Structure in Tim O'Brien's *Going After Cacciato*," *Modern Fiction Studies* 28 (1982): 242–246.

Vernon, Alex. "Salvation, Storytelling, and Pilgrimage in Tim O'Brien's *The Things They Carried*." *Mosaic* 36, no. 4 (December 2003): 171–188.

———. "Submission and Resistance to the Self as Soldier: Tim O'Brien's Vietnam War Memoir," *A/B Auto/Biography Studies* 17, no. 2 (Winter 2002): 161–179.

Volkmer, Jon. "Telling the 'Truth' about Vietnam: Episteme and the Narrative Structure in *The Green Berets* and *The Things They Carried*," *WLA: War Literature and the Arts* 11, no. 1 (1999): 240–255.

Wesley, Marilyn. "Truth and Fiction in Tim O'Brien's *If I Die in a Combat Zone* and *The Things They Carried*," *College Literature* 29, no. 2 (2002): 1–18.

Wharton, Lynn. "Hand, Head, and Artifice: The Fictive World of Tim O'Brien," *Interdisciplinary Literary Studies: A Journal of Criticism and Theory 3, no. 1 (Fall 2001): 131–135.

———. "Tim O'Brien and American National Identity: A Vietnam Veteran's Imagined Self in *The Things They Carried*," *49th Parallel: An Interdisciplinary Journal of North American Studies* 5 (Spring 2005): n. pag.

Wilhelm, Albert E. "Ballad Allusions in `Where Have You Gone, Charming Billy?'" *Studies in Short Fiction* 28 (1991): 218–222.

Worthington, Marjorie. "The Democratic Meta-Narrator in *In the Lake of the Woods*," *Explicator* 67, no. 2 (Winter 2009): 67–68.

Young, William. "Missing in Action: Vietnam and Sadism in Tim O'Brien's *In the Lake of the Woods*," *The Midwest Quarterly* 47, no. 2 (2006): 131–143.

Zins, Daniel L. "Imagining the Real: The Fiction of Tim O'Brien," *Hollins Critic* 23 (1986): 1–12.

Interviews/Profiles

Bourne, Daniel, and Debra Shostak. "A Conversation with Tim O'Brien," *Artful Dodge* 17 (1991): 74–90.

Bourne, Daniel. "This is True," *PEN America: A Journal for Writers and Readers* 4, no. 2 (2002): 208–211.

Bruckner, D. J. R. "A Storyteller for the War That Won't End," *New York Times*, 3 April 1990: C15+.

Caldwell, Gail. "Staying True to Vietnam," *Boston Globe*, 29 March 1990: 69+.

Calloway, Catherine. "History Has a Way of Dissolving: A Conversation With Tim O'Brien," *Tampa Review*, 20 (2000): 24–35.

Coffey, Michael. "Tim O'Brien," *Publishers Weekly*, 16 February 1990: 60–61.

D'Amore, Jonathan. "Every Question Leads to the Next': An Interview with Tim O'Brien," *Carolina Quarterly* 58, no. 2 (2007): 31–39.

Edelman, David Louis. "Tim O'Brien Interview: The Things He Carried," *Baltimore City Paper*, 19 October 1994. Available online. URL: http://www.davidlouisedelman.com.

Herzog, Tobey C. "Tim O'Brien Interview," *South Carolina Review*, 31, no. 1 (1998): 78–109.

Hicks, Patrick. "Tim O'Brien: The Progressive Interview," *Progressive* (July 2004): 37+.

———. "A Conversation with Tim O'Brien," *Indiana Review*, 27, no. 2 (2005): 85–95.

Kaplan, Stephen. "An Interview with Tim O'Brien," *Missouri Review*, 14 (1991): 93–108.

LeClair, Thomas. "Tim O'Brien." In *Anything Can Happen: Interviews with Contemporary American Novelists*, 262–278. Urbana: University of Illinois Press, 1983.

Lee, Don. "About Tim O'Brien," *Ploughshares*, 21, no. 4 (1995): 196

Leepson, Marc. "Tim O'Brien: The Thinking Man's Vet in the Nuclear Age," *Gallery*, August 1986: 27–30.

Lyons, Gene. "No More Bugles, No More Drums," *Entertainment Weekly*, 23 February 1990: 50–52.

Marsh, Steve. "The Stories He Carries: Author Tim O'Brien on Reality, War, and Reunions," *Minneapolis-St. Paul Magazine*, January 2003: 26.

McCaffery, Larry. "Interview with Tim O'Brien," *Chicago Review*, 33 (1982): 129–149.

McNerney, Brian C. "Responsibly Inventing History: an Interview with Tim O'Brien," *WLA: War, Literature, and the Arts* 6, no. 2 (1994): 1–26.

Mort, John. "The *Booklist* Interview: Tim O'Brien," *Booklist* 90 (1994): 1,990–1,991.

Naparsteck, Martin. "An Interview with Tim O'Brien," *Contemporary Literature* 32, no. 1 (1991): 1–11.

Schroeder, Eric James. "Two Interviews: Talks with Tim O'Brien and Robert Stone." *Modern Fiction Studies* 30 (1984): 135–164.

———. "Maybe So." In *Vietnam, We've All Been There: Interviews with American Writers*, 124–143. Westport, Conn.: Praeger, 1992.

Schumacher, Michael. "Writing Stories From Life," *Writer's Digest* 71 (1991): 34–39.

Slater, Judith. "An Interview with Tim O'Brien," *Short Story Review*, 4, no. 2 (Spring 1987): 4–5.

Tambakis, Anthony. "Tim O'Brien: An Interview." *Five Points* 4, no. 1 (1999): 94–114.

Weber, Bruce. "Wrestling with War and Love; Raw Pain, Relived Tim O'Brien's Way," *New York Times*, 2 September 1998: E1.

Wharton, Lynn. "Journeying from Life to Literature: An Interview with American Novelist Tim O'Brien," *Interdisciplinary Literary Studies: A Journal of Criticism and Theory* 1, no. 2 (Spring 2000); 229–247.

Bibliographies

Calloway, Catherine. "Tim O'Brien (1946-): A Primary and Secondary Checklist," *Bulletin of Bibliography* 50 (1993): 223–229.

Jason, Philip K. *The Vietnam War in Literature: An Annotated Bibliography of Criticism*. Pasadena, Calif.: Salem Press, 1992.

Newman, John. *Vietnam War Literature: An Annotated Bibliography of Imaginative Works about Americans Fighting in Vietnam*. Lanham, Md.: Scarecrow, 1996.

Wittman, Sandra M. *Writing about Vietnam: A Bibliography of the Literature of the Vietnam Conflict*. Boston: Hall, 1989.

INDEX

Boldface page numbers indicate major treatment of a topic. *Italic* page numbers denote photos or illustrations.

Pyle, Ernie **424**
Pynchon, Thomas 166, 328, 331, **424**

Q

Quang Ngai Province 7, 11, 60, **424**
   Charlie Company in 60
   in "Field Trip" 36–37
   in *Going After Cacciato* 52, 424
   in *In the Lake of the Woods* 123–124
   in *The Things They Carried* 272, 274, 296, 424
   in *Tomcat in Love* 305, 316, 424
   in "The Vietnam in Me" 334–336
"Quantum Jumps" 249–252
   Coolidge (Calvin) in 371
   Custer (General George Armstrong) in 414
   Frost (Robert) in 383
   Hale (Nathan) in 387
   imagination in 251, 252, 414
   Noah in 414
   Schelling (Thomas) in 429
   singers in 361, 378, 429, 435
   Teller (Edward) in 437

R

racism 104–105
Rainy River 6, **424**
   in "On the Rainy River" 239–240, 241, 242, 244, 273, 424
Random House 304
Ranier, Mount. *See* Mount Ranier
Ransom, John 276, 394–395
Reagan, Ronald **424**
reality
   in "The Ghost Soldiers" 45–47
   in *Going After Cacciato* 54, 58

   in *If I Die in a Combat Zone* 100
   in *In the Lake of the Woods* 127–128, 133
   in "July '69" 146
   in *The Nuclear Age* 218, 219, 223–224
   in "The People We Marry" 245, 246
   in *The Things They Carried* 277, 278, 279, 280, 295, 409
   in *Tomcat in Love* 308, 310
   in "Too Skinny" 327, 329, 330
   in "The Way It Mostly Was" 337
Recovering from the War (Mason) 407
Redbook 8, 9, 17, 25, 170, 345
Reed, John **425**
Regensburg (Germany) **425**
"Relativity" (poem in *The Nuclear Age*) **425**
religious faith
   in "Faith" 32
   in "Keeping Watch By Night" 170–172
   in *Tomcat in Love* 311–312
REMF (rear echelon mother fucker) **425**
Republic, The (Plato) 421
Resor, Stanley **425**
re-up **425**
Revelation. *See* Book of Revelation
Revolutionary War 125, 128, 336, 387, 405, 444
Rhine River 364, 404, **425**
Rickover, Admiral Hyman George **425**
Ridenhour, Ronald 135, 412
Road to Hong Kong, The (film) **426**
Robinson, Edward Arlington **426**
Rocket Pocket **426**
Rodin Museum (Paris) **426**
Rogers, Roy **426**
Romano, John 222–223
Romeo and Juliet (Shakespeare) 94

Roschevitz, Gary 140, 385, **426**
Ro Son Shei **425**
Ross, Martin **426**
Roth, Phillip 277
RTO (Radio Telephone Operator) 70, 115, **426**
Rubin, Jerry 391, **427**
Ruff-and-Puff (RF/PF) 263, **427**
Rumor of War, A (Caputo) 98
Rusk, Dean **427**

S

Sagua la Grande (Cuba) 216, 231, 388, **427**
Saigon (Vietnam) 369, **427**
Saint George 243, **427**
Salihli (Turkey) **427**
Salle des Fêtes (Paris) **427**
Sand, George 132, **428**
Sand Creek Massacre 378, **428**
San Diego State University 69, **427–428**
Sands of Iwo Jima, The (film) 98
sappers 100, 101, 106, 108, 369, **428**
Sassoon, Siegfried **428**
satellite technology 17–19
Savak 53, 63, 75, 76, **428–429**
Sawmill Landing (Minnesota) 200–202, 204, 205, 208–213, 359, **429**
Scarlet Letter, The (Hawthorne) 388
Schelling, Thomas **429**
Schmid, Charles 196
Schultz, Ava. *See* O'Brien, Ava
SDS **429**, 444
Seabees **429**
Sea of Tranquility 145, 146, 147, 157
SEATO 99, 371, 377, **430**
Seattle (Washington) 7, **430**
   in *If I Die in a Combat Zone* 107, 111, 113, 114, 115, 430
   in *The Nuclear Age* 216

Second Book of Esdras, The **429**
secrets
   in "Faith" 31–32, 36
   in "The Fisherman" 42
   in *Going After Cacciato* 62–63, 72
   in "How Unhappy They Were" 94
   in *In the Lake of the Woods* 11, 124, 128, 130–133, 154, 155, 247, 368, 377, 413, 419
   in *July, July* 152, 154–156, 189, 420
   in "The Magic Show" 191, 192
   in "On the Rainy River" 243
   in "The People We Marry" 245–246, 247
   in *The Things They Carried* 154, 282, 289, 403
   in *Tomcat in Love* 305, 306
   in "Too Skinny" 327, 329, 330
   in "The Way It Mostly Was" 336
   in "Winnipeg" 349, 350
Seeger, Pete 361, 378, **429**
Seoul (Korea) **429–430**
Sergeant York **430**
Shakespeare, William 94, 305
"Shame" (Karen) 396–397
Shane (film) 97, 104, **430**
Shan Plateau **430**
Shay, Jonathan 284, 357
Shenandoah 336
Sherman, General William Tecumseh **430**
shining **430–431**
short **431**
Silver Star **431**
   in *Going After Cacciato* 62, 431
   in *If I Die in a Combat Zone* 110
   in "Speaking of Courage" 253, 254, 256, 257, 290, 371